D0236581

Student Collection
Seven Day Loan

Return date

Books may be renewed online or telephone (01206 873187) unless they have been recalled.

University of Essex
Library Services
WITHDRAWN
FROM COLLECTION

University of Essex

143025171

NATIONAL HUMAN RIGHTS INSTITUTIONS IN THE ASIA-PACIFIC REGION

THE RAOUL WALLENBERG INSTITUTE
HUMAN RIGHTS LIBRARY
VOLUME 27

NATIONAL HUMAN RIGHTS INSTITUTIONS IN THE ASIA-PACIFIC REGION

BY

BRIAN BURDEKIN

ASSISTED BY JASON NAUM

THE RAOUL WALLENBERG INSTITUTE HUMAN RIGHTS LIBRARY
VOLUME 27

MARTINUS NIJHOFF PUBLISHERS
LEIDEN/BOSTON
2007

University of Essex
Library Services
WITHDRAWN
FROM COLLECTION

A C.I.P. record for this book is available from the Library of Congress.

JC 599. A77

1430 2517 1

Printed on acid-free paper.

ISSN: 1388-3208
ISBN-13: 978 90 04 15336 3
ISBN-10: 90 04 15336 5

© 2007 by Koninklijke Brill NV, Leiden, The Netherlands.
Koninklijke Brill NV incorporates the imprints Brill, Hotei Publishers, IDC Publishers, Martinus Nijhoff Publishers and VSP.

http://www.brill.nl

All rights reserved. No part of this publication may be reproduced, stored in a retrieval system, or transmitted in any form or by any means, electronic, mechanical, photocopying, microfilming, recording or otherwise, without written permission from the Publisher.

Authorization to photocopy items for internal or personal use is granted by Brill provided that the appropriate fees are paid directly to The Copyright Clearance Center, 222 Rosewood Drive, Suite 910, Danvers MA 01923, USA.
Fees are subject to change.

Printed and bound in The Netherlands.

PRINTED BY DRUKKERIJ WILCO B.V. - AMERSFOORT, THE NETHERLANDS

For my mother – who made it all possible

TABLE OF CONTENTS

TABLE OF CONTENTS

PREFACE

The purpose of this book is to provide a consolidated collection of materials to facilitate comparison of the various national human rights institutions (NHRIs) already established in the Asia-Pacific region, against a background of selected international materials and with the assistance of several comparative tables. The latter are not intended to be exhaustive, but are designed to assist in identifying and considering the strengths and weaknesses inherent in the legislative mandates of each national institution.

In terms of the normative standards which should determine the legislative mandates and operational aspects of NHRIs, these materials are based on the United Nations Principles relating to the status of National Institutions (the Paris Principles). These Principles, however, were minimum standards prepared by a disparate group of practitioners to prevent, or at least discourage, states from establishing "window dressing" institutions designed to placate domestic critics or impress international donors. (They were, given our objective of U.N. General Assembly endorsement, simply the best consensus we could construct in 1991.) In view of their acknowledged limitations I have considered it appropriate to regularly refer to other more recent, related guidelines which have also been prepared by practitioners and have the significant advantage of being more rigorous, more detailed, more simply written and, in several important respects, more relevant to the work of NHRIs in the Asia-Pacific region.

While the collection is primarily intended for teaching purposes, I hope it will also be useful to countries considering establishing a national human rights commission or, for those which have already done so, strengthening its mandate. For this reason I have included several sections outlining the relationship which should exist between NHRIs, the Executive, the Legislature, the Judiciary and other related institutions and a short section on the importance of the process which should precede their establishment.

There are many challenges confronting NHRIs – and numerous strategies for addressing them. This book does not attempt to enumerate or evaluate these. However, because it may be of some assistance to recently established NHRIs with limited resources, I have included a brief section on conducting national inquiries – a strategy which has proved particularly effective in promoting and protecting human rights and in enhancing an institution's accessibility in a cost-effective manner. The challenges I have addressed – protecting economic, social and cultural rights and operating in situations involving armed conflict – are among those practitioners in the region currently consider the most complex and difficult.

PREFACE

In the last 20 years I have had the privilege of establishing a national human rights commission in my own country and working in nearly 60 other countries to establish or strengthen NHRIs. While this book is focused on the Asia-Pacific region, the suggestions I offer also reflect experiences – good and bad – in our efforts to establish effective NHRIs in various countries in Africa, Latin America and Central and Eastern Europe.

Brian Burdekin
December 2005

GLOSSARY OF ABBREVIATIONS

ACJ	Advisory Council of Jurists
APF	Asia-Pacific Forum of National Human Rights Institutions
ASEAN	Association of Southeast Asian Nations
CAT	The Convention Against Torture, and Other Cruel, Inhuman or Degrading Treatment or Punishment
CAT – OPT	Optional Protocol to the Convention against Torture and Other Cruel, Inhuman or Degrading Treatment or Punishment
CEDAW	The Convention on the Elimination of All Forms of Discrimination Against Women
CEDAW – OPT	Optional Protocol to the Convention on the Elimination of All Forms of Discrimination Against Women
CERD	The Convention on the Elimination of All Forms of Racial Discrimination
CHR	The United Nations Commission on Human Rights
CMW	International Convention on the Protection of the Rights of All Migrant Workers and Members of Their Families
CRC	The Convention on the Rights of the Child
CRC – OPT – AC	Optional Protocol to the Convention on the Rights of the Child on the involvement of children in armed conflict
CRC – OPT – SC	Optional Protocol to the Convention on the Rights of the Child on the sale of children, child prostitution and child pornography
DCAF	Geneva Centre for the Democratic Control of Armed Forces
DPKO	Department of Peacekeeping Operations
DPP	Director of Public Prosecutions
ECOSOC	The United Nations Economic and Social Council
HREOC	The Human Rights and Equal Opportunity Commission of Australia
HRRT	Human Rights Review Tribunal
ICC	International Criminal Court
ICCPR	The International Covenant on Civil and Political Rights
ICCPR – OPT	The First Optional Protocol to the International Covenant on Civil and Political Rights
ICCPR – OPT2	The Second Optional Protocol to the International Covenant on Civil and Political Rights
ICESCR	The International Covenant on Economic, Social and Cultural Rights
IDP	Internally Displaced People
IFI	International Financial Institution
MP	Member of Parliament
NGO	Non Government Organisation
NHRAP	National Human Rights Action Plan
NHRC	National Human Rights Commission

GLOSSARY OF ABBREVIATIONS

NHRI	National Human Rights Institution
OECD	Organisation for Economic Cooperation and Development
OHCHR	Office of the U.N. High Commissioner for Human Rights
RWI	Raoul Wallenberg Institute for Human Rights and Humanitarian Law
TBs	The United Nations Treaty Bodies
UDHR	Universal Declaration of Human Rights
U.N.	United Nations
UNDP	United Nations Development Programme
UNGA	United Nations General Assembly
UNHCHR	United Nations High Commissioner for Human Rights
UNHCR	United Nations High Commissioner for Refugees
UNICEF	United Nations Children's Fund
UNOG	United Nations Office in Geneva
UNV	United Nations Volunteers

CHAPTER 1: INTRODUCTION AND OVERVIEW

1.1. THE EVOLVING INTERNATIONAL ORDER

In the last few decades the international order has changed dramatically – and many of the changes have important implications for human rights and for those institutions generally expected or specifically designed to protect them.

Almost all of the authoritarian regimes in Latin America, many in Africa and several in south east Asia have been replaced by democratically elected governments and the end of the cold war unleashed a wave of democratisation in central and eastern Europe which is still breaking on the shores of central Asia.

However, the assumption that democratically elected legislatures, an independent judiciary and executive governments subject to the periodic discipline of the ballot box would guarantee respect for human rights has been replaced by a recognition that this "division of powers", while fundamentally important, has frequently failed to protect human rights – even when these were constitutionally entrenched. The recognition that governments courting political popularity have frequently been prepared to sacrifice respect for the human rights of unpopular or marginalised minorities in their quest to retain power has been one impetus in the movement to create independent national human rights institutions (NHRIs).

The sterile rhetorical confrontations of the cold war era regarding the relative importance of civil and political rights and economic, social and cultural rights have gradually given way to a more mature recognition that all rights are equally important; that poverty is one of the most prevalent and insidious human rights violations; that corruption is a major threat to human rights; and that the right to life implies the right to a safe and clean environment.

There has been a growing recognition – by the United Nations, international financial institutions (IFIs) and most wealthy donor governments – that human rights are an integral element of "good governance" and that good governance is essential for sustainable development. There has also been increasing recognition that systemic discrimination and widespread violations of human rights, including the rights of ethnic, religious or linguistic minorities, invariably lead to political turmoil and conflict – with serious implications for national stability and, in some cases, regional security. In recognition of these realities, development assistance has, since the end of the cold war, increasingly been conditioned, by both multilateral and bilateral donors, on respect for human rights and reforms designed to enhance good governance – with significant effects in many (but not all) new, emerging or restored democracies. NHRIs which protect the rights of minorities have now been recognised as an important element in contributing to national stability and security.

International law, including international human rights law, has increasingly been recognised and applied in national courts as well as international tribunals and accountability for gross violations of human rights has increasingly been demanded of those responsible – including military leaders and civilian dictators in Africa, Latin America, Europe and Asia. Ad hoc tribunals, established to deal with horrific human rights violations in Rwanda, Sierra Leone and the former Yugoslavia, while cumbersome and relatively ineffective, have laid the groundwork for the world's first international criminal court (ICC) – and the contention of leaders who grossly abused the rights of those within their jurisdiction that they could shelter behind the "doctrine" of state sovereignty has been roundly rejected in theory – if not always reflected in reality.

The influence of civil society in all its dimensions, but particularly in the impact of non government organisations (NGOs), has invigorated and transformed the human rights debate and the impact of the communications revolution, accelerated by access to the internet, has made the current generation of activists and human rights defenders the most well informed and potentially the most influential in the history of our planet.

The impact of globalisation on the world's major legal systems has been to raise the level of scrutiny from a human rights perspective – and to expose the inadequacies of traditional systems which are, at best, reactive and often inaccessible. There has been a growing awareness of international human rights jurisprudence and a greater recognition that remedies must be made more accessible if human rights are to be protected. This has been accompanied by the development of alternative investigation and dispute resolution mechanisms with a proactive mandate – such as national human rights commissions.

However, the increasing influence of multinational and transnational corporations has not been matched by any adequate formulae for ensuring an appropriate degree of "corporate social responsibility". The fact that the world's largest corporations now enjoy more real power than many of the world's poorest states has enormous implications for the enjoyment of economic and social rights in particular.

INTRODUCTION AND OVERVIEW

Privatisation of previously state-controlled public utilities has increased dramatically – but this has frequently not been accompanied by states regulating or licensing the delivery of services in accordance with their international human rights treaty obligations. The trend to privatisation is now so pervasive it extends from public health services to prisons. Indeed, over 200 million people, many in some of the world's poorest countries, now have even their water supplied by private corporations – at a time when water is becoming an increasingly scarce and expensive commodity. This trend looks set to continue.

The importance of ideology as a driving political force has dramatically diminished – but in the world's most populous country, China, the autocratic structures originally associated with it remain intact. There is currently, and for the immediate future, only one super power – but the United States' attitude to international human rights law has recently been to disparage its importance and denigrate those institutions designed to maintain and develop it.

Most recently, the attacks of "9/11" and the subsequently declared "war against terror" have substantially shifted the focus of the human rights debate and multiplied the challenges for all those concerned to achieve an appropriate balance between protecting the right to life of every individual and other hard won and highly valued rights and freedoms embodied in internationally accepted human rights treaties (including the right to a fair trial and the right not to be tortured or treated in a cruel, inhuman or degrading manner).

The tremendous diversity and size of the Asia-Pacific region – encompassing China, India and Indonesia, three of the world's four most populous countries, as well as the mini states and micro states of the Pacific – means the impact of this changing global balance of forces affects different countries in our region in very different ways. States such as Indonesia and the Philippines have done away with autocrats and dictators, while oppressive military or authoritarian regimes remain in control in countries such as Burma and North Korea. The region itself is now, economically, the fastest growing in the world – but huge disparities in the distribution of wealth, widespread poverty, endemic corruption, gender-based discrimination, religious extremism and resurgent nationalism still present tremendous challenges in the fight for human rights.

A corollary of the region's complexity and diversity is that generalisations are dangerous – particularly when they rely uncritically on the assimilation of Oceania and the Asian continent. However, the recent political instability and continuing corruption characterising many Pacific

Island states – from Fiji to the Solomon Islands – present challenges for governance, human rights and development comparable to those in their much larger Asian neighbours.

While several of these subjects are generally regarded as the primary concern of economists, sociologists and political scientists they have had, and will continue to have, a major impact on human rights and human rights law at both the national and international level. Together they present a series of complex and interconnected opportunities and challenges which are reflected, in various ways and to differing degrees, in the challenges confronting national institutions specifically designed to promote and protect human rights.

1.2. THE UNITED NATIONS AND NATIONAL HUMAN RIGHTS INSTITUTIONS IN THE ASIA-PACIFIC REGION: AN OVERVIEW

> "Building strong human rights institutions at the country level is what in the long run will ensure that human rights are protected and advanced in a sustained manner. The emplacement or enhancement of a national protection system in each country, reflecting international human rights norms, should therefore be a principal objective of the Organization. These activities are especially important in countries emerging from conflict."
>
> *(Kofi Annan "Strengthening of the United Nations: an agenda for further change". Report of the Secretary-General, 9 Sept. 2002)*

In the last four decades most countries have signed, ratified or acceded to the major human rights treaties negotiated over the past sixty years under the auspices of the United Nations. When it comes to honouring their commitments to implement the rights embodied in those instruments, however, most States have conspicuously failed in important respects. Many States, in all regions, have also failed to honour their obligations to cooperate with the international monitoring mechanisms established pursuant to these treaties.

With the exception of the Asia-Pacific, the major geographic regions have established regional machinery – courts, commissions and related institutions – to monitor human rights protection at the regional level. The diversity, complexity and sheer size of the Asia-Pacific region make similar institutions in this region unlikely or, in the event that they are established, make it likely they will be relatively weak and ineffective.

Against this background of international and regional institutional challenges, in the late 1980s, at a time when many Asian governments were brutally repressing dissent, several heads of national human rights commissions began discussions on strategies to strengthen existing national institutions in this region and to encourage the creation of new ones.

Our discussions were based on the conviction, born of experience in our own countries, that effective implementation and monitoring of international human rights standards must primarily be accomplished at the national level. The reality is that no matter how sophisticated they are, international and regional mechanisms are, and will remain, inaccessible to the overwhelming majority of the world's population – two thirds of whom live in Asia. This is particularly true for the most vulnerable and disadvantaged groups in the poorest countries – those whose human rights are most frequently violated and who are therefore most in need of protection.[1]

However, very few countries – in the Asia-Pacific region or elsewhere – established NHRIs until the 1990s. The exceptions were the New Zealand Human Rights Commission established in 1978, the Australian Human Rights Commission established in 1981[2] and the Philippines Human Rights Commission established in 1987.

1.2.1. The United Nations

Almost since its founding the United Nations had considered, albeit sporadically, the subject of NHRIs; indeed the first recorded discussion took place in the Economic and Social Council (ECOSOC) in 1946 when ECOSOC invited Member States ". . . to consider the desirability of establishing information groups or local human rights committees within their respective countries to collaborate with them in furthering the work of the Commission on Human Rights".[3] However, apart from diplomatic debates and occasional resolutions,[4] there was little significant progress for the next 30 years. This was in spite of the growing number of important international human rights treaties and the fact that many diplomats and

---

[1] It is currently estimated that nearly 700 million people in Asia live on less than $1 a day; this is nearly two thirds of the world's poorest people. See "In Larger Freedom; Towards Development, Security and Human Rights for All". UN.Doc A/59/2005 at p.11 – Progress on the Millennium Development goals.

[2] The Australian Human Rights Commission, originally established with part-time Commissioners, was replaced in 1986 by the Human Rights and Equal Opportunity Commission, an institution with full-time Commissioners and an expanded mandate.

[3] ECOSOC Resolution 2/9 of 21 June 1946.

[4] ECOSOC did adopt a resolution in 1960 that acknowledged the importance of NHRIs in a more proactive way – including in monitoring the implementation of international standards (ECOSOC Resolution 772B(XXX) of 25 July 1960.

human rights advocates recognised the need for national monitoring mechanisms to complement the international mechanisms being established to monitor these treaties.

In 1978 the Commission on Human Rights (CHR) convened a seminar in Geneva which produced guidelines that were subsequently endorsed by the Commission and by the General Assembly.[5] These guidelines still identified national human rights institutions in a very general way, including all government agencies and public organisations concerned with human rights – rather than focusing on independent institutions with a specific legislative mandate to promote and protect human rights. They did, however, represent an advance in the conceptual debate by addressing more specifically the types of promotional and advisory activities national institutions should carry out and the institutional modalities involved.

But the reality was that United Nations activity had still produced very little in the way of practical results. Indeed, only a very small number of independent NHRIs had been established in any region before 1990,[6] when the Commission on Human Rights decided to hold a meeting on the subject of National Human Rights Institutions.[7] This conference, convened in Paris in 1991, prepared a set of "Principles Relating to the Status of National Institutions" – now commonly referred to as the "Paris Principles".

Following the preparation of these Principles and their adoption by the Commission on Human Rights in 1992[8] and the United Nations General Assembly in 1993[9] twelve countries in the Asia-Pacific region had, by mid 2005, established NHRIs considered to be in compliance with these

---

[5] A/Res/33/46 of 14 December 1978.

[6] While it is difficult to be certain about Africa, the total number in all other regions by the end of 1990 was only eight. (Three in the Asia-Pacific region – Australia, New Zealand and the Philippines; three in the Americas – Canada, Mexico and Guatemala; and two in Europe – France and Denmark.) Three African countries had allegedly established NHRIs – Togo (1987), Benin (1989) and Morocco (1990). However, the Togolese institution was effectively abolished after a brief period (when its reports embarrassed the government) and replaced with an institution which was not genuinely independent. Neither the institution in Benin nor the institution in Morocco originally complied with the most rudimentary standards for NHRIs.

[7] CHR Res.1990/73 of 7 March 1990.

[8] Resolution 1992/54.

[9] GA Resolution 48/134 of 20 December 1993.

international standards.[10] Those established since 1993 are in: Fiji, India, Indonesia, Malaysia, Mongolia, Nepal, South Korea, Sri Lanka and Thailand.

These institutions are, however, still young – and in most cases they are still evolving.

The "Paris Principles" prescribe several criteria essential for NHRIs to be effective. These include: a clearly defined, broad-based human rights mandate – incorporated in legislation or, preferably, constitutionally entrenched; independence from government; membership that broadly reflects the composition of society; appropriate cooperation with civil society, including NGOs; and adequate resources. The Principles do not, however, address in any detail several issues which are essential for a national institution to be effective. These include the necessity for it to be readily accessible[11] – and this and several related issues are dealt with in subsequent sections.

The Principles also envisage that NHRIs will perform a wide variety of functions in promoting and protecting human rights. These include: research; public education; promoting the ratification of international human rights treaties; ensuring that national legislation, policies, programmes and practices are consistent with international norms; contributing to reports to United Nations treaty bodies and investigating complaints concerning violations of human rights.

With respect to investigating individual complaints concerning violations of human rights, the Principles envisage that NHRIs may have "quasi-judicial" powers[12] – to compel the production of evidence and the attendance of witnesses – in order to work effectively.

While some NHRIs have "quasi-judicial" powers in relation to obtaining evidence, they are clearly not judicial bodies and they do not purport to make enforceable decisions. Generally they operate by way of recommendations; proceed far less formally than courts; frequently resolve complaints by mediation or conciliation; and do not charge fees. They generally have the power to refer appropriate matters to other state agencies, for example the Ombudsman or Director of Public Prosecutions (DPP), where these are more appropriate.

---

[10] See below, the section on the Asia-Pacific Forum of NHRIs and its role in assessing compliance with the Paris Principles.

[11] The key factors in ensuring accessibility are dealt with in Chapter III.

[12] See Chapter II for the background to the terminology actually used in the Paris Principles.

Some NHRIs do have the power to make "orders", "determinations" or "findings" and, if these are not respected by relevant parties, seek to have them enforced by the courts. In a number of countries NHRIs are also empowered to intervene in court proceedings, with the leave of the court, to present arguments on relevant human rights issues.

In several States, institutions which do not yet meet the standards laid down in the "Paris Principles" have been established (Iran, Jordan, the Maldives, Palestine, Qatar and Timor-Leste). In others, (e.g. Bangladesh, Japan, Pakistan and Papua New Guinea) governments have prepared legislation for a NHRI but have not yet effectively established one. In one country, Afghanistan, the status of the institution is under review by the Asia Pacific Forum (APF) and it may well soon become the thirteenth NHRI in this region recognised as complying with the Paris Principles.

In several countries (Afghanistan, Thailand, Fiji and the Philippines) the NHRI is constitutionally entrenched. In most, however, it has simply been established by an Act of Parliament.[13]

While independence enshrined in an adequate constitutional or legislative mandate is essential, the effectiveness of NHRIs ultimately depends on the integrity, ability and commitment of those appointed to lead them. Several NHRIs were originally established by governments with dubious motivations – to alleviate international pressure for reform or otherwise impress potential donors; however most have now evolved into credible protagonists for human rights.

NHRIs take a variety of forms. In the Asia-Pacific region they are all specifically mandated to promote and protect human rights and all can investigate individual complaints. However several, such as the recently established "Provedor" in Timor-Leste, have broader mandates which include combating corruption[14] and monitoring propriety in public

---

[13] Afghanistan's Independent Human Rights Commission was entrenched in their new, 2004 Constitution – so if it becomes a member of the APF, four NHRIs in the region which comply with the Paris Principles will be constitutionally entrenched.

[14] Most countries which have established NHRIs – in the Asia Pacific and all other regions – have been strongly advised not to combine anti-corruption responsibilities with a human rights mandate; almost all have heeded that advice. The problem, in the author's experience, is that fighting corruption effectively requires coercive powers which go well beyond those envisaged in the Paris Principles and generally conferred on NHRIs. In addition, corruption is so pervasive and corrosive of "good governance" that it justifies (except perhaps in the smallest countries) the establishment of a separate institution dedicated to that issue alone. Nor, as is commonly believed, is corruption primarily a problem in developing countries – as

administration. All, except East Timor, have a collegiate membership – as required by the Paris Principles – and with the exception of East Timor, all institutions in this region are designated as "Commissions" and their members are generally referred to as "Commissioners".

In some NHRIs the Commissioners are full-time appointees, in some they are part-time or voluntary and in others (such as the South Korean Human Rights Commission) some Commissioners are full time and some are part time. In one country, Fiji, the Ombudsman is an ex officio member of the Human Rights Commission; in others, such as India, the heads of several other related institutions are ex-officio members of the Commission.

While the NHRIs established in the Asia-Pacific region generally meet the formal requirements prescribed in the "Paris Principles" – in terms of the range of their functions and the membership of the institution – some are inadequately resourced. In several cases (e.g. Fiji, Indonesia, Mongolia, Nepal and Sri Lanka) these institutions have received substantial support in their formative years from international donors. But some NHRIs have not. Adequate financial support from their own governments is essential for all NHRIs if they are to achieve effectiveness and credibility in the longer term.

NHRIs in this region have repeatedly demonstrated a willingness to assist and learn from each other. They have established their own regional

---

demonstrated recently in the 2005 Volker reports on the U.N. Oil-for-Food Programme. See for example "Kickbacks aren't just for the poor nations: Iraq – UN Oil-for-Food scandal exposes illicit practices even in rich countries".

"Many prominent companies that were cited in the independent inquiry into the flawed United Nations program for Iraq had headquarters in wealthy Western countries that had toughened laws against bribery, eliminating tax deductions for kickbacks . . . But many experts doubt that this scandal, with almost 2400 companies paying $1.8 billion in kickbacks through oil surcharges or "after-sales service fees" on humanitarian goods will lead to many prosecutions".

Article by D. Carvajal, International Herald Tribune, 4 November 2005 at page 3. (The Western countries referred to in the article included the United States, France, Germany, Finland, Sweden and Switzerland.) The Australian Wheat Board has also since been implicated in this scandal.

Almost all of the companies involved in paying these kickbacks came from countries which have recently signed the first international Convention against Corruption! This Convention was formally adopted by the U.N. General Assembly in October 2003. It has so far been signed by 118 countries and ratified by 15. It will come into force when 30 countries have ratified it. (See the Report of the U.N. Secretary-General on the Work of the Organisation; General Assembly, Official Records, Sixtieth Session, Supplement No. 1 (A/60/1), 2005. Para. 117 at pp. 24–25).

organisation, the Asia Pacific Forum of National Human Rights Institutions (APF), to facilitate these efforts and, together with support from United Nations Agencies and various bilateral and multilateral donors, this is likely to ensure they will play an increasingly important role in promoting and protecting human rights.

All the institutions in the Asia-Pacific region have made significant contributions to promoting and protecting human rights in their respective countries; but all still confront substantial challenges. Many of these relate to political, economic and social factors which are largely beyond their control as independent statutory bodies. There is, however, a growing recognition that human rights, good governance,[15] democratisation, the rule of law and sustainable development are closely inter-related – and that institutions such as NHRIs can only function effectively to the extent that other essential elements of a democratic society – a representative and accountable parliament, an executive which is ultimately subject to the authority of elected representatives and an independent, impartial judiciary – are fulfilling their legitimate roles.

---

[15] "Good governance" can be broadly defined as "the responsible use of political authority to manage a nation's affairs" (C. J. Dias and D. Gillies, *Human Rights, Democracy and Development* (the International Centre for Human Rights and Democratic Development, Montreal, 1993)).
The concept of governance was first used by the World Bank in the late 1980s (Sub-Saharan Africa: from crisis to sustainable growth, Washington, World Bank, 1989).

This report, written as a response to Africa's severe economic crisis, which had been significantly deepened during the "lost decade" of the 1980's, analysed why structural adjustment programmes had failed to create economic growth. The report's authors identified the economic crisis as a "crisis of governance" - governance meaning "the manner in which power is exercised in the management of a country's economic and social resources for development" (p.60). "Bad governance", according to the authors, meant state officials serving their own interests without being held accountable, the reliance on personal networks for survival rather than on holding the state accountable, personalised politics and patronage, illegitimate leadership, and excessive control of information and of associations. The narrow focus on management was thus broadened and supplemented with concepts such as accountability and transparency. In the publications that followed, governance was further elaborated on and made more universally applicable.

See generally the collection of essays in: H. Sano and G. Alfredsson (eds.), *Human Rights and Good Governance, Building Bridges*, (Kluwer Law International, Hague, 2002).

To the extent that the legislature and the judiciary are impeded in their respective "monitoring" roles by a dominant executive which obstructs or inhibits scrutiny and accountability the task of any national human rights institution is correspondingly more difficult.

1.3. THE 1993 WORLD CONFERENCE ON HUMAN RIGHTS:

> "The World Conference on Human Rights reaffirms the important and constructive role played by national institutions for the promotion and protection of human rights, in particular in their advisory capacity to the competent authorities, their role in remedying human rights violations, in the dissemination of human rights information, and education in human rights . . .
>
> The World Conference on Human Rights encourages the establishment and strengthening of national institutions, having regard to the "Principles relating to the status of national institutions" and recognising that it is the right of each State to choose the framework which is best suited to its particular needs at the national level."[16]

The World Conference on Human Rights convened in Vienna in 1993 against a background of several decades of sterile debates in international fora concerning the relative importance of civil and political rights on the one hand and economic, social and cultural rights on the other. The leading protagonists for the primacy of the former were several wealthy developed countries, led by the United States, and for the latter, socialist countries led by the former Soviet Union.

The end of the Cold War and the quickening pace of globalisation produced a political climate in which the World Conference was able to unanimously agree that human rights were indivisible and interdependent. World leaders also agreed that human rights were universal: an important step for human rights defenders in the Asia-Pacific region in particular, who had continuously confronted opposition from several prominent Asian leaders who maintained that the "universality" of human rights was subordinate to an ill-defined doctrine of "Asian values".

The goals of the World Conference, as prescribed by the U.N. General Assembly in its decision, were ambitious. The two objectives of most interest to human rights practitioners were to: "examine the ways and means to improve the implementation of existing human rights standards" and to

[16] The Vienna Declaration and Programme of Action – adopted by the World Conference on Human Rights, Vienna, 25 June 1993 (A/CONF.157/24; part 1 paragraph 36).

"formulate concrete proposals for improving the effectiveness of the United Nations' activities and mechanisms in the field of human rights".[17] Given that the raison d'etre for NHRIs is to ensure implementation of international human rights norms and, inter alia, assist the international treaty bodies and other U.N. mechanisms (such as Special Rapporteurs) in their monitoring role, the Paris Principles were transmitted to the Preparatory Committee for the World Conference. Various preparatory meetings which were held in 1991-93, including several involving NHRIs, were used to mobilise support – to ensure that the World Conference accorded appropriate attention to the necessity for establishing effective NHRIs.[18]

It was against this background that leaders of national human rights institutions met in Vienna, simultaneously with the World Conference. We prepared submissions to the Conference consistent with the Paris Principles and these submissions were accompanied by an intensive lobbying campaign – conducted by several of the most senior NHRI representatives and directed at key government delegates. After protracted negotiations the conference plenary finally agreed to a formula which emphasised the importance of independent NHRIs and the Paris Principles – but with a specific caveat concerning "the right of each State" to establish an institution "best suited to its particular needs".

The World Conference also called on all States to strengthen their national human rights institutions – an appeal unfortunately subsequently ignored by many governments in both developed and developing countries –

---

[17] UNGA Res. 45/155 of 18 December 1990.

[18] However, there was strong resistance from a number of governments involved in the Preparatory Committee, with several vigorously opposing any specific reference to the Paris Principles. Hundreds of hours were spent in late 1992 and throughout 1993 in lobbying governments and organising meetings of NHRIs to influence the Preparatory Committee and the World Conference itself. Two of these conferences in particular made substantial contributions to ensuring that NHRIs would be an important focus in Vienna. The first was a "Workshop on National Institutions", organised by the Commonwealth Secretariat from 30 Sept. to 2 Oct. 1992 in Ottawa. The conclusions of this conference were based on the paper prepared by the author for the 1991 meeting in Paris (Infra, footnote 32). The second conference, jointly organised by the U.N. Centre for Human Rights and the Federal Human Rights Commissioner of Australia, took place in Sydney in April 1993. Again, documents from this conference, emphasising the importance of establishing genuinely independent and effective NHRIs, were forwarded to the Preparatory Committee and played a significant part in preparations for the World Conference. See Doc. A/CONF.157/PC/92/Add.2, Add.3 and Add.5 (1993).

and to develop national human rights plans[19] as an additional strategy to ensure that each State's voluntarily undertaken international human rights treaty commitments were actually implemented. In the Asia-Pacific region some progress has been made on establishing national plans – but establishing NHRIs has, to date, proved significantly more effective in protecting human rights.[20]

However, the World Conference did play a fundamentally important role in shifting the U.N.'s focus to concentrate more specifically on mechanisms and strategies to promote and protect human rights at the national level. This shift, together with the creation of the post of U.N. High Commissioner for Human Rights and the decision by the first High Commissioner to make NHRIs a significant area of emphasis, prepared the ground for a dramatic expansion of NHRI activity throughout the 1990s. The World Conference was also significant as the first major United Nations conference at which NHRIs were allocated time to speak in their own right.[21]

1.4. THE PROCESS OF ESTABLISHMENT:

- "The process of establishing an NHRI should be seen, in itself, as critical to the success of the project.
- The establishment of an NHRI should be seen as a national project of highest priority.
- The process should also:
    - be consultative, inclusive and transparent;
    - be led and supported at the highest level of government; and
    - involve and mobilize all relevant elements of the State and civil society."

("National Human Rights Institutions – Best Practice" Commonwealth Secretariat, 2001)

---

[19] This proposal was an initiative of the Australian government of the time.

[20] Several other world conferences have also emphasised the important role which NHRIs can and should play in protecting human rights e.g. the Fourth World Conference on Women in Beijing in 1995 – see the report in A/CONF.177/20 (October 17, 1995) and the World Conference Against Racism in Durban in 2001.

[21] It is important to note, however, that the relevant United Nations regulations – the ECOSOC Rules of Procedure – have never been amended to permit the participation of NHRIs in United Nations meetings. Their participation in the various World Conferences in 1993, 1995 and 2001 was based on ad hoc decisions by each Conference.

The Paris Principles omit any specific reference to the process of establishing an NHRI, although the provisions relating to its membership imply the necessity for consultation with civil society – at some point. However, the process preceding the establishment of an NHRI is particularly important in ensuring its legitimacy and success.

Whether the original initiative comes from civil society or government there should be an extended period of consultations involving human rights advocates, NGOs, lawyers, educators, academics, and community leaders – as well as relevant bureaucrats and politicians. The consultations should be public and should address all significant issues, including not only the mandate powers and functions of the institution but also the desirable composition and characteristics of its membership and the manner in which its members are to be chosen.

At the political level it is important, wherever possible, to achieve bi-partisan political agreement from government and opposition parties. Inevitably there will be differing views among MPs concerning details of the legislation, but it is essential for the institution's survival and success that there is broad consensus on the need for its establishment and the essential elements of its charter.

There are many reasons for such an inclusive approach. It is important the community has a sense of "ownership" – and realistic expectations about what the institution can be expected to achieve – particularly in its formative phase. Public discussions concerning the mandate, powers and functions to be accorded to the commission can also be important in allaying unjustified fears concerning the powers the institution will exercise; this is particularly the case with institutions exercising quasi-judicial powers in pursuing their investigative function.

In some countries this process has taken over a decade (e.g. Fiji, Mongolia and Thailand); in others it has been completed in two to three years (e.g. Malaysia and Nepal). In several countries the formation of a steering committee, including key stakeholders, has been important in facilitating an effective consultative process. However, there is no general rule that can be applied – except that experience clearly indicates that inadequate consultation will usually mean that the institution is established with an inadequate legislative mandate, an unrepresentative membership and insufficient resources.

Experience has also underlined the danger that unless the community is consulted in advance there is a real likelihood that the institution, when established, will be seen by the general public as representing a collection of "special interest" groups rather than as an advocate for human rights for everyone on a non-discriminatory basis. Without the confidence of the wider community NHRIs cannot perform many of their functions effectively.

CHAPTER 2: MANDATES POWERS AND FUNCTIONS

2.1. MANDATES:

- "A national institution shall be vested with competence to promote and protect human rights.
- A national institution shall be given as broad a mandate as possible, which shall be clearly set forth in a constitutional or legislative text, specifying its composition and its sphere of competence."

(Paris Principles, Articles 1 and 2)

There was general agreement among practitioners meeting in Paris in 1991 that national human rights institutions should be given a mandate both to promote and to protect human rights. As we have seen, this agreement was reflected in subsequent United Nations resolutions and in the reaffirmation by the 1993 World Conference that all human rights are equally important – indeed are "universal, indivisible, interdependent, and interrelated".[22]

There was also general agreement in Paris that NHRIs should be accorded a broad mandate. Behind this formulation lay a well-founded concern that a number of governments were preparing to establish a "Children's Commission" or similar body – to deflect international pressure – but would not create any mechanism to protect women's rights, minorities, indigenous peoples, people with disabilities and other vulnerable groups. We were also concerned that many countries, including several in the Asia-Pacific region, had constitutionally entrenched a certain selection of human rights – with important omissions.[23]

---

[22] Vienna Declaration and Programme of Action, U.N. Doc A/CONF.157/23 (12 July 1993).

[23] These concerns were also reflected subsequently in Amnesty International's 2001 "Recommendations on National Human Rights Institutions", which provide that:

> "NHRIs should enjoy the broadest possible mandate to address human rights concerns as set out in international human rights law and standards. The mandate should not be defined solely in terms of those rights that are specifically provided for in the country's constitution – particularly as some constitutions do not contain key rights such as the right to life. Rather NHRIs should take as their frame of reference the definitions of human rights as set out in international human rights instruments and standards, whether or not the state has ratified the relevant treaties. The mandate

While we secured agreement on both these important principles, and while governments subsequently endorsed them, we have been less successful in ensuring their incorporation in the legislative mandates of NHRIs in the region – as demonstrated in Tables A, B and C set out below.

The third important element stipulated in Article 2 of the Paris Principles was that a national institution's mandate must be clearly defined. There are many reasons for this. (Several are addressed in more detail in subsequent sections concerning the relationship between NHRIs, the courts and other institutions). It is essential that Commissioners and staff understand the full potential – and limitations – of their charter. It is also important that members of the public can be clearly informed of the institution's capacity to assist them. These issues concern not only the range of rights included in the institution's mandate, but also whether its charter extends to the private as well as the public sector.[24]

Stipulating that the mandate must be prescribed ". . . in a constitutional or legislative text" was an attempt to avoid the possibility that some governments would establish a national institution by presidential decree (a concern subsequently borne out by events in Indonesia)[25] – an unsatisfactory strategy for many reasons, including the institution's vulnerability to being abolished by a subsequent decree if its activities offended the Executive.[26]

---

should include the power to protect and promote economic, social and cultural rights, as well as civil and political rights."

These recommendations, which were prepared in consultation with the author during his term as Special Advisor on National Institutions to the United Nations High Commissioner for Human Rights, are set out in full in Appendix II.

[24] While the various international human rights treaties impose legal obligations primarily on States, the Universal Declaration of Human Rights (UDHR) clearly envisages that protecting and promoting human rights is the responsibility of everyone in society (Article 29(1)) This is stipulated in more detail in the ICCPR and ICESCR.

[25] The Indonesian Human Rights Commission, KomnasHAM, was first established in 1993, by Presidential decree. This has since been replaced by legislation (see Table A).

[26] This has not been as much of a problem in the Asia – Pacific region as it has in others – particularly Africa. For a brief summary of the existing African NHRIs see B. Burdekin, "National Human Rights Institutions in Africa", in C. Heyns (ed.), *Human Rights Law in Africa Volume 1* (Martinus Nijhoff Publishers, Leiden/Boston, 2004) pp. 850–852. For a more comprehensive analysis of the strengths and weaknesses of NHRIs in other regions see: B. Lindsnaes, L. Lindholdt and K. Yigen (eds.), *National Human Rights Institutions: Articles and Working Papers* (Danish Centre for Human Rights; 1st revised edition, December 2001).

2.1.1. The Importance of International Instruments

Most, but not all, of the NHRIs in the Asia-Pacific region have a mandate which incorporates by specific reference some or all of the major international human rights instruments. This is important for a number of reasons.

First, it serves as a convenient point of reference by which the degree of domestic implementation of internationally recognised human rights may be assessed – both domestically and internationally.

Second, it facilitates the development of experience and jurisprudence in applying international standards which, though framed by reference to national conditions, will frequently be applicable or relevant in other jurisdictions.

Third, it has become increasingly clear that the international machinery[27] for the protection of human rights, both Charter based (such as the Commission on Human Rights (CHR) and mechanisms created under its mandate), and the treaty based Committees[28] (in their function of receiving individual complaints and in consideration of reports) are limited in the number of cases they can handle. This is not to denigrate the importance of these bodies or the need to provide them with adequate resources and pursue means of making their operation more effective. (In the case of the Commission on Human Rights it has fallen into disrepute and may soon be replaced or modified – if current proposals for United Nations reform are successful.)[29]

---

[27] For a succinct summary of the United Nations human rights machinery and its evolution see "Intergovernmental Enforcement of Human Rights Norms: The United Nations System", in H. J. Steiner and P. Alston, *International Human Rights in Context: Law, Politics, Morals* (Oxford University Press, Oxford, 2000) pp. 592–694.

[28] The major U.N. treaty-based bodies are: (the treaties to which they relate are in brackets)
The Committee on the Elimination of Racial Discrimination (CERD)
The Human Rights Committee (ICCPR)
The Committee on Economic, Social and Cultural Rights (CESCR)
The Committee on the Elimination of Discrimination Against Women (CEDAW)
The Committee Against Torture (CAT)
The Committee on the Rights of the Child (CRC)

[29] The reform of CHR is by no means certain. The U.N. Secretary General has proposed that CHR be replaced by a smaller, standing Human Rights Council, as a principal organ of the United Nations or subsidiary body of the General Assembly. See "In Larger Freedom; Towards Development, Security and Human Rights for

However, with growing international acceptance of these mechanisms, or reformed versions of them (in the case of CHR) and in particular of the treaty based provisions for individual complaints, there is a need to recognise the danger of overloading the machinery which should form the peak of the international system for protection and promotion of human rights by placing excessive reliance on it to perform tasks which, in the first instance, should be more appropriately and effectively addressed at the national level. This reality has recently been specifically addressed in the Optional Protocol to the Convention Against Torture, which makes specific provision for the designation of national institutions to actively implement this important international treaty.[30]

Fourth, as far as the international system is concerned, national machinery has important prevention and early intervention functions – either in preventing human rights violations from occurring, or in achieving resolution of cases and redress for violations of rights – before the international level is reached.

Fifth, where an individual complaint is not resolved at the national level and comes before a body such as the Human Rights Committee, the Committee on the Elimination of Racial Discrimination or the Committee Against Torture (where the nation concerned has taken the requisite steps to make those procedures available), prior consideration of the matter based on the same international standards by a national body is likely to be of considerable assistance to the international Committee concerned.

Sixth, with respect to the reporting systems instituted under United Nations instruments, a national institution dealing directly with the international human rights instruments may be of great assistance – not only to the monitoring body in gaining accurate and authoritative information, but also to the Government concerned in compiling information to fulfil its reporting obligations. Given the proliferation of reporting requirements, the

---

All". UN.Doc A/59/2005 at p. 61. However, there is likely to be considerable opposition to these reforms from some U.N. Member States.

[30] Article 17 of the Optional Protocol (Part IV: National Preventive Mechanisms) See Appendix VIII for the full text of Part IV of the Optional Protocol. Note that Article 17 does not stipulate that the NHRI (if one exists) must be the organisation chosen by the State. However, Article 18 (4) makes specific reference to the Paris Principles and since almost all NHRIs in the Asia-Pacific have mandates which require them to prevent torture, those that have such a mandate (see Tables A, B and C) should be an obvious choice.

extent of overlap between requirements under different treaties,[31] and the difficulties experienced by many governments in collecting information to fulfil their obligations, the model of an integrated national commission, dealing with all or many of the international human rights instruments to which the State is party, has particular advantages. In some cases, depending on the extent of the national commission's jurisdiction, the annual report of such a body could effectively serve as the basis for substantial parts of the State's report under the relevant instruments.[32]

One particularly important advantage of national institutions having a mandate based on international human rights instruments is that it addresses the problem of many human rights violations falling through gaps in domestic legal categories. It is clear, for example, that common law systems, although containing important human rights elements, by themselves offer very inadequate protection of human rights. Indeed, the much vaunted common law, inherited by many countries, including a number in the Asia-Pacific region, was primarily concerned with property, commerce and the individual rights of those in society able to fend for themselves. In terms of protecting the rights of the most vulnerable and disadvantaged – children, indigenous peoples, the homeless, the poor and those with disabilities – it was generally an abysmal failure.

It is also important to understand in this context that "the rule of law", important as it is, is not necessarily synonymous with the protection and promotion of human rights. Indeed, from a human rights perspective, the law is sometimes part of the problem – not part of the solution – and NHRIs have a clear responsibility to identify and attempt to have amended national laws which conflict with internationally accepted human rights norms.[33]

---

[31] There have, however, been significant reforms proposed and agreed to by the Treaty Bodies in recent years.

[32] This extract is adapted from a paper prepared for the 1991 Paris meeting of national institutions: B. Burdekin, "Human Rights Commissions", reprinted in K. Hossain et al. (eds), *Human Rights Commissions and Ombudsman Offices* (Kluwer Law International, Great Britain, 2001) pp. 801–834. Significant sections of the Paris Principles are based on the twenty recommendations proposed by the author at the conclusion of this paper – including the section on "quasi-judicial powers" (*infra*, footnote 37).

[33] From a practitioner's perspective, many of the most useful international human rights instruments do not have the status of treaties or conventions – i.e. they cannot be ratified by governments, nor do they impose binding legal obligations as a matter of international law. There is a large number and wide variety of these instruments – "Principles", "Declarations", "Standard Minimum Rules" etc. Governments in the

CHAPTER 2

2.2. POWERS AND FUNCTIONS:

The Paris Principles are less definitive on the critical issue of the powers which should be conferred on a national institution to enable it to effectively carry out its functions.

While a more detailed description is set out below, national institutions' functions can broadly, but not precisely, be divided into six categories:

- Research and advice
- Education and promotion

Asia-Pacific region have generally been reluctant to give NHRIs mandates which include rights embodied in these subsidiary instruments – (see Tables A and B in Chapter II). In reality, however, NHRIs frequently refer to these instruments – several of which are set out in the following extract from Amnesty International's "Recommendations on national human rights institutions".

"The mandate should include the power to monitor government fulfillment of international and regional human rights treaties and human rights obligations under domestic law. This should include the power to monitor and report – independently on its own behalf, not on behalf of its government – on compliance with and implementation of relevant and necessary international human rights standards, essential to the promotion and protection of human rights, including the Universal Declaration of Human Rights, the International Covenant on Civil and Political Rights (ICCPR), the International Covenant on Economic, Social and Cultural Rights (ICESCR), the UN Declaration and Convention against Torture, the Convention of the Rights of the Child, the Convention and Elimination of All Forms of Discrimination against Women, the Convention on the Elimination of All Forms of Racial Discrimination, as well as the Declaration on the Right and Responsibility of Individuals, Groups and Organs of Society to Promote and Protect Universally Recognized Human Rights and Fundamental Freedoms, the UN Code of Conduct for Law Enforcement Officials, the UN Body of Principles for the Protection of All Persons under Any Form of Detention or Imprisonment, the UN Rules for the Protection of Juveniles Deprived of their Liberty, the Basic Principles on the Use of Force and Firearms by Law Enforcement Officials and the UN Principles on the Effective Prevention and Investigation of Extra-legal, Arbitrary or Summary Executions. They should also assess compliance with standards relating to the administration of justice, such as the Basic Principles on the Role of Lawyers, the Basic Principles on the Independence of the Judiciary, the Guidelines on the Role of Prosecutors, and the Declaration of Basic Principles of Justice for Victims of Crime and Abuse of Power."

Extract from Amnesty International's "Recommendations on national human rights institutions", 3.4 "Participation in international human rights law fora" – see Appendix II for the full text.

- Monitoring
- Investigating, conciliating and providing remedies
- Cooperating with other national and international organizations and
- Interacting with the Judiciary

One important issue at stake in the negotiations in 1991 was the importance that should be accorded to conferring on NHRIs the power to effectively investigate complaints concerning human rights violations – considered by many human rights advocates to be essential for any national human rights institution. It is a function conferred on human rights commissions established in common-law countries – in every region. NHRIs in the Asia-Pacific region all exercise this function (as indicated in Table A). However, their powers and the types of complaints they can investigate vary significantly (as indicated in Table B and the associated Notes).

Those negotiating the Paris Principles included representatives from a wide variety of human rights commissions, institutes, centres and ombudsmen in Europe, Africa, Latin America and Asia.[34] Those representing national institutions with a broad human rights mandate in Latin American and Asian countries generally exercised powers to investigate individual complaints concerning human rights violations; however, we were in a minority.[35] Those representing European and African institutions generally did not – and the largest number of institutions attending were from Europe. There was a corresponding division of opinion concerning the necessity to include in the Principles a specific reference to adequate powers to receive complaints from individuals and to effectively conduct investigations.[36]

---

[34] The Conference appointed a Drafting Committee to prepare a text for approval by all participants. The Drafting Committee comprised representatives from the National Human Rights Commissions of France, Mexico, The Philippines and Australia. The author, who was a member of the Committee in his capacity as Federal Human Rights Commissioner of Australia, had previously held discussions with the President of the Philippines Human Rights Commission and the head of the New Zealand Commission concerning the issues under consideration.

[35] Only five countries from the entire Asia-Pacific region were represented (Australia, New Zealand, Japan, the Philippines and Thailand) of which only three (Australia, New Zealand and the Philippines) then had NHRIs.

[36] The position taken by those of us who advocated the necessity for NHRIs to have the power to conduct effective investigations was subsequently strongly endorsed at a conference of NHRIs and NGOs for the Asia-Pacific region in Sri Lanka in 1999. At this meeting – which was co-sponsored by the Asia Pacific Forum of National

The matter was finally resolved by incorporating, at the conclusion of the Principles, a section entitled "Additional principles concerning the status of commissions with quasi-jurisdictional competence".[37]

While the Paris Principles are not explicit concerning the relationship between the powers and functions of NHRIs, it is essential, for national institutions to be credible and effective, that the powers conferred on them are commensurate with the functions for which their mandates make them responsible. It is equally important that these powers are clearly set out in the enabling legislation – to ensure the institution can function effectively and unnecessary disputes and litigation can be avoided.

Based on the provisions of Article 3 of the Paris Principles and taking account of the ways in which NHRIs in the Asia-Pacific region have exercised their investigatory and related powers the functions of NHRIs in this region can be summarised as follows:

- Providing advice to the Government, Parliament and other relevant entities on any issues related to legislation or administrative practices, or proposed legislation, or policies or programmes within their jurisdiction.
- Establishing advisory committees from civil society to assist the institution in the performance of its functions.
- Educating the public concerning human rights – including by preparing and disseminating information both through formal educational institutions and more widely to the general public.

Human Rights Institutions (APF), Office of the High Commissioner for Human Rights (OHCHR) and the Asia Pacific NGO Human Rights Facilitating Team – participants unanimously agreed that:

" … it was vital that national institutions should have their own independent investigations capacity"

See the Kandy Program of Action: Cooperation Between National Institutions and Non-Governmental Organisations, Asia Pacific Forum of National Human Rights Institutions, Workshop on National Institutions and Non-Governmental Organisations: Working in Partnership, Kandy, Sri Lanka 26–28 July 1999. Hereafter referred to as the Kandy Declaration.

[37] The negotiating group was working in French. The agreement we reached related to "commissions with quasi-**judicial** powers". This was subsequently mistranslated into English as "quasi-**jurisdictional** competence" and the mistake was perpetuated in the final text (which was not cleared with participants before publication).

- Preparing and delivering information and educational materials and programmes to particular "target groups" – such as the police, prison officials, the military, the judiciary and others.
- Monitoring compliance by Government, government agencies and private sector entities with international human rights treaty obligations.
- Promoting the ratification of human rights treaties and advising on the development of new international human rights instruments.
- Contributing to Government reports to international Treaty Bodies and following up and disseminating reports by the Treaty Bodies.
- Cooperating as appropriate with the United Nations, relevant international agencies, other NHRIs and relevant national and international NGOs.
- Inspecting custodial facilities and places of detention.
- Receiving and investigating complaints of human rights violations, conciliating[38] such complaints where appropriate, or providing other remedies.
- Compelling the attendance of witnesses and production of documents when necessary to conduct effective enquiries or investigations and taking evidence on oath or affirmation.
- Conducting national or local public enquiries into systemic violations of human rights.
- Doing anything incidental or conducive to the performance of the preceding functions which is consistent with their mandate to protect and promote human rights.[39]

---

[38] "Conciliation" is a term which now has several general as well as specific meanings – depending on the context. In relation to the work of NHRIs it involves bringing together the parties to a complaint (generally referred to as the complainant and the respondent) in a confidential process which provides both parties with an opportunity to discuss and consider the issues involved and reach an agreement. It is not necessary for the parties to have legal representatives – but they may do so in cases where this is appropriate and would assist in achieving "equality" between them for the purposes of the process. Throughout the conciliation the NHRI (usually the staff, but in complex cases Commissioners may be involved) functions as an independent mediator.

[39] This "incidentals power" is specifically incorporated in the founding legislation of the majority of NHRIs in the Asia-Pacific region. These include: Australia, India, Malaysia, Nepal, Sri Lanka, Thailand and the Republic of Korea (see Table A). The precise legislative formulations are slightly different in each case.

In addition to the powers prescribed in their legislative mandates (see Tables A and B and accompanying notes)[40] NHRIs' Commissioners generally have power to delegate their functions. In some cases this is addressed in their enabling law but frequently it is a matter governed by more general canons of administrative law which apply to NHRIs.

NHRIs also exercise discretionary powers – which are particularly important to ensure their effective functioning. At one level these powers are exercised with respect to determining their overall priorities; but they are also particularly important in enabling NHRIs, in certain circumstances, to determine whether or not they will investigate particular complaints which may technically be within their jurisdiction.

[40] NHRIs in the Asia-Pacific region have developed and will continue to develop numerous techniques and strategies to discharge the disparate and extremely challenging range of functions conferred by their respective mandates. Their annual reports and other publications provide a rich source of information on their different approaches. This book does not attempt to analyse or categorise these – since a great deal of this information is now available on various websites – including that of the Asia Pacific Forum of National Human Rights Institutions. <www.asiapacificforum.net.>

NOTE TO THE FOLLOWING TABLES

The purpose of Tables A–H, which are included in Chapters 2–4, is to provide an overview of the mandates, powers, functions and composition of the 12 NHRIs in the Asia-Pacific region which currently meet the criteria prescribed in the Paris Principles.

In relation to several of the most important features of these NHRIs, however, a more detailed analysis is provided in the Notes appended to the Tables. These areas have been selected on the basis that experience has underlined their particular importance in ensuring the effectiveness of these institutions. The purpose is also to identify priority areas for the attention of countries in the process of establishing NHRIs or which may be considering amending the legislative mandates of institutions already established.

LEGISLATIVE MANDATES OF NATIONAL HUMAN RIGHTS INSTITUTIONS IN THE ASIA PACIFIC REGION[***]

Table A[i]

	Australia	Fiji	India	Indonesia	Malaysia	Mongolia	Nepal	New Zeeland	Philippines	Republic of Korea	Sri Lanka	Thailand
LEGAL MANDATE[ii]	HREOC Act 1986	HRC Act 1999	PHR Act 1993	Leg. No. 39 1999	HRC Act 1999	NHRC Act 2000	HRC Act 1997	HR ACT 1993	Exec. Order No. 163 1987	NHRC Act 2001	HRC Act No. 21 1996	NHRC Act 1999
Established in the National Constitution		◆							◆			◆
Power to receive and investigate complaints[iii]	◆	◆	◆	◆	◆	◆	◆	◆[iv]	◆	◆	◆	◆
Power to conduct investigations on their own initiative (*Suo Motu*)	◆	◆	◆	◆	◆	◆	◆	◆	◆[v]	◆	◆	◆
Power to subpoena information and examine witnesses	◆	◆	◆	◆	◆	◆	◆			◆	◆	◆
Power to enter and inspect premises *only detention facilities **must be announced or requested	◆		◆[vi]	◆**	◆*	◆	◆	◆	◆*	◆	◆*	◆**

	Australia	Fiji	India	Indonesia	Malaysia	Mongolia	Nepal	New Zeeland	Philippines	Republic of Korea	Sri Lanka	Thailand
Power to resolve complaints by conciliation and/or mediation	◆	◆	[vii]	◆		◆	◆[viii]	◆	◆[ix]	◆	◆	◆
Mandate to educate and conduct research with regard to human rights	◆	◆	◆	◆	◆	◆	◆	◆	◆	◆	◆	◆
Power to advise/make recommendations to Government and/or Parliament on laws, regulations, policies or programs/international treaties	◆	◆	◆	◆	◆	◆	◆	◆	◆	◆	◆	◆
Power to provide* or recommend** compensation and/or seek it through a court or specialist tribunal***	◆**	◆ ***	◆**			◆[x]	◆**	◆ ***	◆**	◆*	◆*	◆[xi]
Power to intervene or assist in Court proceedings related to human rights (with permission of the Court)	◆	◆	◆	◆		◆	◆	◆		◆	◆	

[***] It should be noted that some NHRIs (including those in Australia, India, Sri Lanka, Thailand, Malaysia, Nepal and the Republic of Korea) have an "incidentals" clause – i.e. a section of their legislation which follows the enumeration of their specific powers and functions with a provision to the effect that the Commission can "do anything incidental or conducive to the performance of any of the preceding functions". (Section 11(1)(p) of the Australian HREOC Act; see also Section 12(j) of the Indian PHR Act, which states: "such other functions as it may consider necessary for the protection of human rights"). Several institutions have made extensive use of this power. Other institutions (e.g. Malaysia) may be using this power in areas we are unaware of.

[i] This table represents the 12 Full Members of the Asia-Pacific Forum (APF) – as at 1 August 2005. As of this date the APF also has 3 "Associate Members" (i.e. National Human Rights Institutions that are not, or have not yet been found to be, established in accordance with the Paris Principles). These are: the Afghanistan Independent Human Rights Commission, the Palestinian Independent Commission for Citizens' Rights, and the Jordan National Centre for Human Rights. For further details *see* Chapter 6.

[ii] *See* appendix A for the full titles of the relevant legislation (Note: this applies to laws and does not extend to subordinate legislation).

[iii] If not otherwise stipulated, this includes complaints related to allegations of violations of those human rights included in the mandate (see Table B).

[iv] The Commission can only accept complaints involving unlawful discrimination and "gather information" in its attempts to conciliate complaints alleging unfair discrimination. (Part III, in particular section 76 of the Act).

[v] Only in cases involving violations of civil and political rights (but *see also* the notes elaborating Table B).

[vi] The Commission may enter any place and seize documents related to matters of inquiry (Section 13(3) of the Indian PHR Act). However, when related to detention and detention facilities, inspection can only take place after advance notice to the State Government (Section 12(c) of the Indian PHR Act).

[vii] See endnote *** and Sec. 12(f) of the Indian PHR Act.

[viii] As Table A indicates, we are aware that the Commission resolves complaints by conciliation and/or mediation. However, there is no specific provision in the HRC Act of Nepal that expressly empowers the Commission to do so (*see also* endnote ***).

[ix] As Table A indicates, we are aware that the Commission resolves complaints by conciliation and/or mediation. However, there is no specific provision in Executive Order 163 that expressly empowers the Commission to do so.

[x] Although the NHR Act does not explicitly state that it can provide compensation, Section 19.2 empowers Commissioners to write or deliver demands which could theoretically include a recommendation/demand for payment of compensation (*see also* the notes to Table H):

> "19.2. Commissioners shall write and deliver demands to relevant organisations in order to restore human rights and freedoms and eliminate the violations if he/she [sic] has considered that business entity, organisation or official has violated human rights and freedoms."

[xi] Although there are no provisions in the NHRC Act that expressly state that the Commission can provide/recommend compensation, Section 28 of the Act empowers the Commission to prepare and submit a report (to a person or agency involved a human rights violation) that may propose remedial measures which could include the payment of compensation.

DEFINITIONS OF "HUMAN RIGHTS" IN NHRI ESTABLISHING LEGISLATION* — *TABLE B***

	Australia	Fiji	India	Indonesia	Malaysia	Mongolia	Nepal	New Zeeland	Pilippines	Republic of Korea	Sri Lanka	Thailand
1. All international human rights standards and norms												
2 All international covenants and conventions								◆				
3. International human rights treaties ratified by the State + some of the rights incorporated in the national constitution + customary international law										◆		
4. All international human rights standards incorporated in treaties and conventions + rights incorporated in the constitution.		◆										
5. International human rights treaties ratified by the State + rights incorporated in national laws and the constitution						◆					◆	
6. International human rights treaties ratified by the State + some of the rights incorporated in the national constitution							◆					◆
7. Selected international human rights treaties (ICCPR and ICESCR) to the extent that they are enforceable in the courts + some of the rights incorporated in the national constitution			◆									
8. Selected international human rights instruments and rights included in specific national laws	◆											
9. Only those rights incorporated in the national constitution or specific national laws				◆	◆							
10. Only civil and political rights									◆			

* See Table C for the Treaties and Optional Protocols thereto to which each State is a Party.

** For further analysis on the definition of "human rights" found in the establishing legislation of NHRIs see the following section, "Elaboration of Table B".

CHAPTER 2

NHRI Mandates - Elaboration of Table B:

This section provides a brief description of the provisions of each Commission's mandate that deal with the interpretation of the term "human rights" or those rights that are applicable according to the relevant statute(s).

The issue of complaints and complaint handling is also briefly addressed, focusing on the relationship between a Commission's human rights mandate, i.e. the human rights definition found in the Acts, and the rights with respect to which the Commission can accept complaints alleging violations. Some national statutes have a broad definition of human rights but the NHRIs are only empowered to accept complaints alleging abuse of a smaller, select group of rights (e.g. only civil and political rights or certain rights found in the Act itself or in specific sections of the national constitution).

AUSTRALIA

Interpretation of the term Human Rights:

> ***"human rights"*** means the rights and freedoms recognised in the Covenant, declared by the Declarations or recognised or declared by any relevant international instrument (Part I, 3).

This formula now includes:

1. *International Covenant on Civil and Political Rights*
2. *Convention on the Rights of the Child*
3. *Declaration on the Rights of the Child*
4. *Declaration on the Rights of Disabled Persons*
5. *Declaration on the Rights of Mentally Retarded Persons*
6. *Declaration on the Elimination of All Forms of Intolerance and of Discrimination Based on Religion or Belief*
7. *ILO Convention No. 111, Concerning Discrimination in Respect of Employment and Occupation.*

Complaints:

Under Section 11(1)(aa) the Commission can receive complaints alleging unlawful discrimination:

11(1) *The functions of the Commission are:*

(a) such functions as are conferred on the Commission by the *Age Discrimination Act 2004*, the *Racial Discrimination Act 1975*, the *Sex Discrimination Act 1984,* the *Disability Discrimination Act 1992* or any other enactment;

(aa) to inquire into, and attempt to conciliate, complaints of unlawful discrimination;

(ab) to deal with complaints lodged under Part IIC ["Referral of discriminatory awards and determinations of other bodies"]

Under the HREOC Act the Commission is also empowered to inquire into a breach of human rights as they are defined in the Act (the process, however, is significantly different from complaints received under the Racial Discrimination Act, Sex Discrimination Act, and the Disability Discrimination Act).

FIJI

Interpretation of the term Human Rights:

Section 2 of HRC Act states:

"**Bill of Rights**" means the Bill of Rights contained in Chapter 4 of the Constitution;

. . .

"**human rights**" means the rights embodied in the United Nations Covenants and Conventions on Human Rights and includes the rights and freedoms set out in the Bill of Rights;

Section 43 of the Fiji Constitution further stipulates, in terms of applicable human rights:

Section 43 Interpretation

(1) The specification in this Chapter of rights and freedoms is not to be construed as denying or limiting other rights and freedoms recognised or conferred by common law, customary law or legislation to the extent that they are not inconsistent with this Chapter.

Complaints:

Same scope as the mandate – with the exception of the power to proceed to the court if conciliation is unsuccessful; these cases are limited to complaints involving unfair discrimination or a violation of the Bill of Rights in the Constitution.[41]

INDIA

Interpretation of the term Human Rights:

The Act defines "human rights" to include only the right to life, liberty, equality and dignity of the individual contained in the Constitution, the ICCPR and the ICESCR, and enforceable by the courts. It stipulates in Section 2 (d) and (f):

> (d) "**human rights**" means the rights relating to life, liberty, equality and dignity of the individual guaranteed by the Constitution or embodied in the International Covenants and enforceable by courts in India.
>
> . . .
>
> (f) "**International Covenants**" means the International Covenant on Civil and Political Rights and the International Covenant on Economic, Social and Cultural Rights adopted.

Complaints:

Same scope as the mandate – with the exception of complaints involving alleged abuse by the armed forces. The Commission may not investigate these cases. It may request a report from the Government and make recommendations (Note, however, that the Indian Commission has "interpreted" this provision proactively).

MALAYSIA

Interpretation of the term Human Rights:

> "**human rights**" refers to fundamental liberties as enshrined in Part II of the Federal Constitution. (Section 2).

(Part II of the Constitution contains the following basic rights: the right to life and liberty of the person; freedom from slavery and forced labour; equality; freedom of movement; freedom of speech, assembly and association; freedom of religion; and rights related to property and education.)

---

[41] See Sections 34(3) and 36(1) of the HRC Act, Fiji.

Complaints:

Same scope as the mandate

12. (1) The Commission may, on its own motion or on a complaint made to it by an aggrieved person or group of persons or a person acting on behalf of an aggrieved person or a group of persons, inquire into allegation of the infringement of the human rights of such person or group of persons.

MONGOLIA

Interpretation of the term Human Rights:

The Act does not expressly define "human rights", however, Section 3.1. of the Act states that the Commission is charged with promoting, protecting and implementing those human rights found in the Constitution, national laws and in international treaties Mongolia is a party to. Specifically the Act provides:

Article 2. Legislation on the Commission

2.1. Legislation on the Commission shall consist of the Constitution of Mongolia, this Law and other legislative acts enacted in conformity with them.

2.2. If an international treaty to which Mongolia is a State Party (the international treaties of Mongolia) provides otherwise than this Law, the provisions of that international treaty shall prevail.

Article 3. The Commission and its Operational Principles

3.1. The Commission is an institution mandated with the promotion and protection of human rights and charged with monitoring over the implementation of the provisions on human rights and freedoms, provided in the Constitution of Mongolia, laws and international treaties of Mongolia.

Complaints:

Same scope as the mandate

Article 9. Right to Lodge Complaints

9.1. Citizens of Mongolia, either individually or in a group, shall have the right to lodge complaints to the Commission in accordance with this Law, in case of violations of human rights and freedoms, guaranteed in the

Constitution of Mongolia, laws and international treaties of Mongolia, by business entities, organisations, officials or individual persons.

9.2. Unless otherwise provided in laws and international treaties of Mongolia, foreign citizens and/or stateless persons who are residing in the territory of Mongolia, shall exercise the same right to lodge complaints to the Commission on equal footing as the citizens of Mongolia.

INDONESIA

Interpretation of the term Human Rights:

The act does not specifically define human rights (see definition below) but rather it defines *human rights violations* as a violation of the human rights "*guaranteed by the provisions set forth in this Act*" and lists a number of "basic" rights and "human rights and freedoms" in Chapters 2 and 3 of the Act. (emphasis added).

Article 1(6)

Human rights violations mean all actions by individuals or groups of individuals, including the state apparatus, both intentional and unintentional, that unlawfully diminish, oppress, limit and/or revoke the human rights of an individual or group of individuals *guaranteed by the provisions set forth in this Act*, and who do not or may not obtain fair and total legal restitution under the prevailing legal mechanism. (emphasis added).

Human rights mean a set of rights bestowed by God Almighty in the essence and being of humans as creations of God which must be respected, held in the highest esteem and protected by the state, law, Government, and all people in order to protect human dignity and worth.

The "Notes to the Act" state that they are a "Supplement to the State Gazette of the Republic of Indonesia No. 3886", and when referring to the term "human rights", the Notes state that the human rights provisions in the Act were determined using other treaties and conventions as guidelines – and not as authoritative sources:

In this Act, provisions concerning human rights are determined using as guidelines the United Nations Declaration of Human Rights, the United Nations Convention concerning the Eradication of All Forms of Discrimination Against Women, the United Nations Convention of Children's Rights, and several other international instruments governing human rights. This Act is also adjusted to fit the legal requirements of society and the need to develop national law based on Pancasila and the 1945 Constitution.

Complaints:

The Commission may receive complaints alleging violation of human rights – which as defined above relate only to those human rights "*guaranteed by the provisions set forth in this Act*". (emphasis added).

Article 90 (1) stipulates that:

> All people and groups of people who have strong grounds that their human rights have been violated may submit an oral or written complaint to the National Commission on Human Rights.

NEW ZEALAND

Interpretation of the term Human Rights:

The Act does not define the term "human rights". However, the long title of the Act states that its aim is to "provide better protection of human rights in New Zealand in general accordance with United Nations Covenants or Conventions on Human Rights".

Complaints:

The Commission can only accept complaints involving unlawful discrimination and "gather information" in its attempts to conciliate complaints alleging unfair discrimination. See Part III, in particular Section 76.

This is a much more limited mandate than the reference in the long title of the act would suggest.

NEPAL

Interpretation of the term Human Rights:

Section 2(f) Definitions states:

> **"Human Rights"** means the rights relating to life, liberty, equality and dignity of the individual guaranteed by the Constitution and other prevailing laws and the rights embodied in the international treaties relating to human rights to which Nepal is a party.

Complaints:

Same scope as the mandate – with the exception of matters under the jurisdiction of the Military Act (Section 10. (a) of the HR ACT dealing with "Matters Not Subject to Jurisdiction of the Commission").

Section 9. Functions and Duties of the Commission:

(2) In order to perform the duty referred to in sub-section (1), the Commission may carry out the following functions:

(a) To conduct inquiries into and investigations on the following matters, upon a petition or complaint presented to the commission by a victim himself / herself or any person or any person on his / her behalf or upon the information received from any source, or on its own initiative:-

(1) Violation of human rights and abetment thereof,

(2) Carelessness or negligence in the prevention of violations of the human rights by any person, organization or authority concerned

PHILIPPINES

The Executive Order does not define "human rights". However it limits the scope of the Commission's investigations to complaints involving civil and political rights.[42] Although it states that the Commission has the power to investigate complaints involving all forms of human rights violations involving civil and political rights, no further information is provided to qualify civil and political rights:

Section 3

The Commission on Human Rights shall have the following powers and functions:

---

[42] It should be noted, however, that the current Commission interprets Section 2 of Article II of the Philippines 1987 Constitution (which deals with Principles and State Policies) as the basis for intervening in matters concerning economic, social and cultural rights – as well as civil and political right that are expressly stated to fall under the Commission's mandate according to Executive Order 163. Section 2 of Article II states:

"The Philippines renounces war as an instrument of national policy, *adopts the generally accepted principles of international law as part of the law of the land* and adheres to the policy of peace, equality, justice, freedom, cooperation, and amity with all nations." (emphasis added)

Investigate, on its own or on complaint by any party, all forms of human rights violations involving civil and political rights;

Complaints:

Same scope as the mandate – see the Section excerpted above.

REPUBLIC OF KOREA

Interpretation of the term Human Rights:

Article 2 (Definitions)

The definitions of terms used in this Act shall be as follows:

1. The term "human rights" means any of human dignity, worth, liberties and rights which are guaranteed by the Constitution and Acts of the Republic of Korea or recognized by international human rights treaties entered into and ratified by the Republic of Korea and international customary law;

Complaints:

The Commission can only investigate complaints alleging violations of 13 out of the 30 Articles found in Chapter II of the Constitution (entitled "The Rights and Duties of Citizens"). In addition to these 13 Articles (Articles 10 to 22) the Commission can investigate alleged violations involving discrimination – as defined by the Act.

Note that although the Act does not expressly say only citizens can lodge complaints, complaints appear to be limited to violations of rights which only pertain to citizens – so although one could theoretically be a non-citizen and lodge a complaint involving an alleged violation of a citizen's rights it appears that non-citizens could not file a complaint on their own behalf.

Article 30 (Matters Subject to Investigation of Commission)

(1) In any case falling under the following subparagraphs, the person whose human rights are violated (hereinafter referred to as a "victim") or any other person or organization, that comes to know the violation of human rights, may file a petition to the Commission:

1. In case such human rights as guaranteed in Articles 10 through 22 of the Constitution are violated by the performance of duties (excluding the legislation of the National Assembly and the trial of a court or the Constitutional Court) of state organs, local governments or detention or protective facilities; or

2. In case there exists a discriminatory act of any violation of the right of equality by a juristic person, organization or private individual.

SRI LANKA

Interpretation of the term Human Rights:

The Act defines "human rights" as those rights contained in the two major international covenants, the ICCPR and the ICESCR – which Sri Lanka has ratified. However, it states that the Commission can only investigate allegations/complaints regarding the violation of those fundamental rights in the Constitution. *See* Part I Section 9(a).

Fundamental rights are defined as those rights declared and recognized by the constitution.[43]

Section 33 states:

> "**fundamental right**" means a fundamental right declared and recognized by the Constitution;
>
> "**human right**" means a right declared and recognized by the International Covenant on Civil and Political Rights and the International Covenant on Economic Social and Cultural Rights;

Section 9 states the functions of the Commission shall be:

> (a) to inquire into, and investigate, complaints regarding procedures, with a view to ensuring compliance with the provisions of the Constitution relating to fundamental rights and to promoting respect for and observance of, fundamental rights;
>
> (b) to inquire into and investigate complaints regarding infringements or imminent infringements of fundamental rights, and to provide for resolution thereof by conciliation and mediation in accordance with the provisions hereinafter provided

Complaints:

The Commission can only investigate allegations/complaints regarding the violation of fundamental rights in the Constitution. However, its mandate with respect to education and promotion is defined more broadly to include

---

[43] It is interesting to note that the Constitution of Sri Lanka does not contain a specific provision on the right to life. The Supreme Court has derived protection of the right to life by interpreting other provisions in the Constitution (U.N. Doc. CCPR/CO/79/LKA (2003)).

"human rights" as defined in the Act as excerpted above. (Section 9(f) of the Act stipulates that the Commission shall have the power "to promote awareness of, and provide education in relation to, human rights".)

THAILAND

Interpretation of the term Human Rights:

Section 3 in this Act stipulates:

> "**human rights**" means human dignity, right[sic], liberty and equality of people which are guaranteed or protected under the Constitution of the Kingdom of Thailand or under Thai laws or under treaties which Thailand has obligations to comply;

Complaints:

Same scope as the mandate:

> Section 18. The Office of the National Human Rights Commission has the responsibility in the general affairs of the Commission and shall have the powers and duties as follows:
>
> (1) to be responsible for the administrative works of the Commission;
> to receive petition of human rights violation and submit it to the Commission and to investigate or examine matters which are petitioned as entrusted by the Commission;

TABLE OF RATIFICATIONS

Table C

TREATY	Australia	Fiji	India	Indonesia	Malaysia	Mongolia	Nepal	New Zeeland	Philippines	Republic of Korea	Sri Lanka	Thailand
CERD	◆	◆	◆	◆		◆	◆	◆	◆	◆	◆	◆
CCPR	◆		◆	◆		◆	◆	◆	◆	◆	◆	◆
CCPR – OPT	◆					◆	◆	◆	◆	◆	◆	
CCPR – OPT2	◆						◆	◆				
CESCR	◆		◆	◆		◆	◆	◆	◆	◆	◆	◆
CEDAW	◆	◆	◆	◆	◆	◆	◆	◆	◆	◆	◆	◆
CEDAW – OPT						◆		◆	◆		◆	◆
CAT	◆			◆		◆	◆	◆	◆	◆	◆	
CAT – OPT												
CRC	◆	◆	◆	◆	◆	◆	◆	◆	◆	◆	◆	◆
CRC – OPT – AC			◆			◆		◆	◆	◆	◆	◆
CRC – OPT – SC			◆			◆	◆		◆	◆		◆
CMW									◆		◆	

LIST OF ABBREVIATIONS

CERD: The Convention on the Elimination of All Forms of Racial Discrimination
CCPR: The International Covenant on Civil and Political Rights
CCPR – OPT: The Optional Protocol to the International Covenant on Civil and Political Rights
CCPR – OPT2: The Second Optional Protocol to the International Covenant on Civil and Political Rights
CESCR: The International Covenant on Economic, Social and Cultural Rights
CEDAW:. The Convention on the Elimination of All Forms of Discrimination against Women
CEDAW – OPT: Optional Protocol to the Convention on the Elimination of All Forms of Discrimination against Women
CAT: The Convention Against Torture, and Other Cruel, Inhuman or Degrading Treatment or Punishment
CAT – OPT: Optional Protocol to the Convention against Torture and Other Cruel, Inhuman or Degrading Treatment or Punishment
CRC: The Convention on The Rights of the Child
CRC – OPT – AC: Optional Protocol to the Convention on the Rights of the Child on the involvement of children in armed conflict
CRC – OPT – SC: Optional Protocol to the Convention on the Rights of the Child on the sale of children, child prostitution and child pornography
CMW: International Convention on the Protection of the Rights of All Migrant Workers and Members of Their Families

CHAPTER 3: OTHER ESSENTIAL CHARACTERISTICS

3.1. INDEPENDENCE:

The most critical factor in determining the effectiveness of an NHRI is its capacity to act independently in pursuing its mandate. However, achieving and sustaining independence involves a variety of factors – all of which are important, but some of which require a continuing and sometimes difficult balance with legitimate demands for accountability.

Ideally, a NHRI should be constitutionally entrenched, with a specific section in the national constitution briefly describing its role and prescribing its independence from the Executive. Details of its mandate, membership, powers and functions should then be embodied in an Act of Parliament. However, in the Asia-Pacific region only three of the 12 NHRIs established in accordance with the Paris Principles enjoy this status (the Human Rights Commissions in Fiji, the Philippines and Thailand).

In Afghanistan, Fiji and Thailand enabling legislation has been passed, following the NHRIs' incorporation in recently adopted constitutions. In the Philippines, however, there is, as yet, no specific legislation (see Table A).

The enabling Act of Parliament should clearly stipulate that the institution is independent and accord it sufficient status, powers and resources to enable it to function independently and effectively. Independence does not, however, entail a lack of accountability. Generally, NHRIs must be accountable through their reports to Parliament which, after they have been tabled, should be publicly available and accessible.

In some jurisdictions the NHRI will report to the legislature through the Executive – usually by transmitting its annual report and any reports on specific issues to the relevant minister. The enabling law should clearly require that this minister tables these reports in the Parliament – and that the government responds to any recommendations made. Similarly, the law should enable the institution to operate effectively by requiring government departments and agencies, as well as private sector entities and individuals, to cooperate with the NHRI in the exercise of its functions.

Sanctions for failure to comply with lawful requests, directions or determinations by NHRIs are also an important element in ensuring the institution can operate independently and effectively. Not all NHRIs, however, enjoy this advantage (see Table H below). If the institution itself is unable to impose sanctions it should be able to refer recalcitrant respondents to the appropriate authorities (usually the director or public prosecutions, the attorney-general or the courts) to impose appropriate penalties.

It is essential that the enabling legislation should empower the institution to adopt its own internal rules and regulations relating to management, personnel and financial administration (provided these are consistent with accepted public service standards) and, importantly, in relation to investigations and complaint handling (provided these are consistent with the rules of natural justice). In this context it is important to understand that the functional autonomy which NHRIs are entitled to enjoy must be practised within the parameters of widely accepted legal and public service norms. This does not mean, as is sometimes erroneously suggested, that NHRIs can enjoy only "limited" independence.[44] Independence and accountability are not mutually inconsistent concepts; on the contrary, both are fundamental to the effective functioning of a national human rights commission.

Finally, as already noted, independence depends not only on appropriate legal prescriptions, but also on several other factors which are addressed in the following sections of this Chapter. The most important of these is the integrity capacity and commitment of those who lead the institution.

3.2. ACCESSIBILITY:

The success of NHRIs is directly related to their accessibility. Indeed one of the primary reasons motivating their establishment was the realisation among human rights activists and a belated acknowledgement by governments that the courts, notwithstanding their fundamental role in protecting human rights, were almost completely inaccessible to many of those within their jurisdiction whose rights were frequently and sometimes systematically violated.

In order to ensure that they are accessible, national institutions must address a number of geographical, social, procedural and financial issues.

Geographical realities are generally the most difficult challenge, since most NHRIs have very limited financial and human resources. Strategies which have been developed by institutions in the Asia-Pacific region include: opening regional or provincial offices; appointing local

---

[44] In other respects, the United Nations Handbook on NHRIs contains a useful summary of the various factors affecting independence. See United Nations Handbook on National Human Rights Institutions (Professional Training Series No. 4) United Nations, New York and Geneva 1995 at pp. 10–12 ISBN 92-1-154115-8.

representatives to carry out certain specific functions;[45] negotiating cooperative arrangements with appropriate state or provincial agencies with similar or analogous mandates; and, in the case of the Mongolian and Sri Lankan Commissions, appointing United Nations funded volunteers as representatives or assistants in remote areas. All of these arrangements entail significant administrative challenges, but all have substantially enhanced these institutions' accessibility. In several countries the NHRI's enabling legislation makes specific provision for such "decentralisation", but in most cases these arrangements are not prescribed by law.

Many individuals who are most in need of assistance will also be difficult to reach through the more orthodox channels of communication. NHRIs therefore need to develop proactive strategies and innovative techniques to assist those who are the most vulnerable and disadvantaged. A wide variety of strategies have already been successfully developed by a number of NHRIs in this region; these range from national inquiries,[46] conducted by Commissioners moving around the country to take evidence from isolated communities, to strategies which enlist the advice and support of advocacy groups and carer NGOs.

One of the most important advantages enjoyed by national institutions is their capacity to conduct investigations and enquiries without complying with all the evidentiary requirements and rules of procedure incumbent on the courts. This capacity to expedite proceedings, as long as the rules of natural justice are complied with, is one of the major factors in ensuring the institutions' accessibility. Some institutions have also developed simple regulations, for example, for accepting complaints by phone or facsimile from people in remote areas and for providing assistance in lodging complaints to people who may be illiterate.

[45] In some countries these local representatives are not on the staff of the Commission but are volunteers who are provided with appropriate training and perform important functions on behalf of the Commission (for example the Barangay local representatives in the Philippines). In general they do not exercise formal powers delegated by the Commission and, indeed, NHRI Commissioners should not attempt to delegate their powers to anyone other than their own staff – with the exception of retired judges or other highly qualified and experienced individuals who are sometimes appointed by NHRIs to assist with their inquiry and investigation functions.

[46] See the summaries of national inquiries included as Appendices X–XII.

The institution's location should be close to major public transport routes and in an appropriate building.[47] Physical accessibility of Commission offices is also particularly important and special provision must be made for access by people with physical disabilities.

The necessity for the membership of NHRIs to be representative of the community is clearly related to the public's perception of the institution's accessibility. (This is addressed in more detail in subsequent sections and in Tables D and E). However, diversity among the staff is also essential and while selection based on merit is an indispensable prerequisite for effectiveness, ethnic, linguistic, religious and cultural considerations – as well as gender balance – need to be appropriately incorporated in staff selection criteria.

As far as possible NHRIs should make their library facilities and documentation centres available to NGOs and other members of the general public. While considerations of confidentiality and privacy obviously preclude unrestricted access to their databases, national institutions should also consider making some on-line research capacity available to those interested in human rights – especially in poorer countries where such facilities are still extremely limited.[48]

One of the most important factors in ensuring accessibility is "visibility" and national institutions must ensure that the public is aware of their existence, their location and their mandate. NHRIs must make publicly available simple brochures and information sheets explaining their responsibilities, requirements for lodging complaints etc. and, where necessary, provide this material in more than one language. NHRIs in the Asia-Pacific region have developed a wide range of strategies in this context – including radio, television and newspaper articles and advertisements, preparing material for the electronic and print media, participating in "talk shows" on radio and television, arranging "open days" in cities and towns across the country, and conducting pubic inquiries.

To ensure that their reports are accessible, national institutions may, in some cases, have to issue several versions. Reports of major national

---

[47] NHRIs do not have to have their own building – although this is preferable when resources permit – but neither their head office nor any regional offices should be co-located with the police, the military, security forces or any other institutions which may deter or intimidate potential complainants.

[48] Providing money, facilities and training to enable NHRIs to make their libraries and on-line facilities available to NGOs and other members of the public is a major component of projects to assist NHRIs conducted by the Swedish Raoul Wallenberg Institute – in the Asia-Pacific and other regions.

inquiries, for example, must be comprehensive and thoroughly documented if they are to be the catalyst for substantial reforms. However, many members of the general public may find an abridged version or a summary of the conclusions and recommendations more accessible and useful.

Finally, NHRIs should provide their services free of charge. The costs involved in litigation are a major factor in many vulnerable and disadvantaged groups' inability or unwillingness to use the courts to defend their rights and NHRIs can frequently provide appropriate remedies – including in cases where the human rights violations involved may not be unlawful. In several countries governments have attempted to get NHRIs to charge fees for handling complaints; so far, however, these inappropriate attempts to make institutions "cost-effective" have been successfully resisted.

3.3. ADEQUATE RESOURCES:

> "The national institution shall have an infrastructure which is suited to the smooth conduct of its activities, in particular adequate funding. The purpose of this funding should be to enable it to have its own staff and premises, in order to be independent of the Government and not be subject to financial control which might affect its independence."[49]

Ensuring the financial independence of NHRIs is essential, but always potentially problematic. In principle the institution should be granted its own "budget line" in the national appropriations process. In practice, however, most NHRIs are financed as part of a "portfolio budget" (together with the ministry of justice or its equivalent and, in some countries, other related commissions or tribunals). This invariably pits the institution against mainstream government departments or larger and more powerful agencies in the annual struggle for adequate resources.

This problem can be addressed in several ways – none of which are mutually exclusive. First, the enabling law should stipulate that the NHRI will receive "adequate funding" to enable it to carry out its mandate. Second, the institution's budget should be approved by the parliament, or by the parliament acting in concert with the executive (but not simply by the treasury, department of finance, or some other government ministry). Third, the institution's budget should be prepared by the Commission itself (not government officials). Fourth, the chairperson or his or her nominee should

[49] Principles relating to the status of national institutions, Article 3 (2).

have the right to address the parliament or its relevant committee, as well as any ministry involved, when the Commission's budget is being considered.

Inadequate resources can obviously have a major impact on an NHRI's accessibility and credibility. In a number of countries, including several in the Asia-Pacific region, governments have been firmly advised not to establish their NHRI until they were prepared to allocate sufficient funds to at least meet all of the institution's "core expenses" (including salaries, equipment, communication costs, rental, etc.) – and international assistance has been delayed until the government has agreed to do this.[50]

As noted earlier, the international community has financially assisted many of the recently established NHRIs in the Asia-Pacific region – with funding from both multi-lateral and bi-lateral donors. (The principal U.N. organisations involved have been the OHCHR, UNDP and, to a lesser extent, UNICEF, UNHCR and UNV. The principal bi-lateral donors have been OECD member countries, sometimes working through, or in close cooperation with, one of their major national human rights institutes or centres.)

While there have rarely been instances of donors attempting to exert undue influence in terms of the institutions' priorities and performance there is, nevertheless, a serious risk of over-reliance on donor support emerging in several countries. Governments which establish NHRIs should not anticipate financial assistance beyond the first five years of the institution's existence. Donors, for their part, should ensure that their efforts are effectively coordinated – and do not result in a multiplicity of projects imposing additional management burdens on emerging institutions.

Based on experience, one of the most important elements in ensuring an adequate budget is the institution's credibility in the community and its reputation for integrity and effectiveness in the conduct of its affairs. Those institutions which are held in high esteem by the public will generally find, at least in democracies, that various pressure groups in civil society will lobby on their behalf if governments are disinclined to provide them with adequate resources. Similarly, NHRIs which are not well regarded by the community they have been established to serve may soon find governments feel at liberty to reduce their budgets.

[50] In several cases involving the author, this also required the cooperation of bi-lateral donor governments – which needed to be persuaded that premature commitment of funds would prejudice the institution's credibility and quite possibly preclude the national government's commitment to an adequate budget for the institution.

3.4. THE MEMBERSHIP OF THE INSTITUTION:

No human rights commission can function independently, regardless of its legal mandate, without Commissioners of integrity, commitment and capacity.

Such individuals are unlikely to accept appointment unless the legislative mandate of the institution accords with the basic requirements outlined in the preceding sections and they are offered terms and conditions consistent with their responsibilities. In most countries, including those in the Asia-Pacific, this is achieved by equating the chairperson of the Commission with a senior judicial appointment and the other Commissioners with mid-level judges or very senior civil servants. The formulae adopted for appointment and the number of Commissioners appointed vary considerably (see Tables D and E) and while most are appointed on a full-time basis, several Commissions have only part-time members and some countries have opted for a combination of full-time and part-time Commissioners (e.g. Korea). A detailed breakdown is provided in Table F.

While experience has clearly demonstrated that full-time Commissioners can work more effectively, there are circumstances in which eminent, independently minded individuals whose appointment may enhance an institution's credibility and effectiveness, will only accept a part-time appointment. The criteria for appointment are therefore a critical issue and one which should be addressed in the enabling law. These criteria fall broadly into two categories – those relating to the necessity for the institution's membership to be "representative"[51] and those related to the necessity for the individuals to have appropriate "human rights credentials". Given the practical limitations on the number of Commissioners who can be appointed if the institution is to function effectively, these two categories are inevitably interconnected – at least implicitly. However, there must be some explicit formulation included in the legislation and the variety of criteria identified by different countries is illustrated in Table D.

[51] "The NHRI members and staff should as far as possible include representation of all sections of society, including women, ethnic minorities, and people with disabilities, who may be under-represented in other official bodies and would have particular relevant experience of the needs of those sectors of society. Non-nationals should not be deterred or specifically prohibited from taking up a post at the NHRI." Amnesty International's "Recommendations on National Human Rights Institutions"; op.cit. 2.4 "Representation of Society".

Ideally the appointment of Commissioners should be preceded by a process of consultation involving civil society[52] and, in several countries (e.g. Thailand), this occurs. This is not, however, the norm – in the Asia-Pacific or any other region. Whether or not there is such a process, the enabling legislation should set out a procedure for appointment involving not only the government but also representatives of other political parties and/or officers of the legislature or senior judicial appointees. (The variety of approaches adopted is illustrated by the legislative requirements in Fiji, India, Indonesia, Mongolia, Nepal and Korea (see Table D).

Commissioners are not judges and should not be appointed for life. However, it is essential to ensure the independence of the institution that they be given a substantial fixed-term appointment. Experienced practitioners generally agree that this should be five to seven years and this is the case with most NHRIs in this region. However, in three countries Malaysia (two years), Korea (three years) and Sri Lanka (three years) Commissioners' terms are substantially shorter – (see Table F).

In most countries, Commissioners may be reappointed following their initial term – but in several countries they may be reappointed only once. In some countries Commissioners cannot be reappointed at all (see Table F). There are legitimate arguments for allowing reappointment of some Commissioners – including, in particular, to preserve some continuity in the leadership of the institution. However, there are also cogent arguments in favour of prohibiting reappointments – including, in particular, to ensure the

---

[52] "The independent procedures of selection, appointment, removal and terms of tenure of NHRI members and staff should be clearly specified, laid down in its founding legislation, so as to afford the strongest possible guarantees of competence, impartiality and independence.

The selection, appointment, and removal procedures of the members of the NHRI should not be handled exclusively by the executive branch of government.

The method of selection and appointment of the members of the NHRI should be fair and transparent, so as to afford all necessary guarantees of independence. Broad representation is also important, and steps should be taken to guarantee this – for example – by allowing members of civil society to nominate possible candidates for membership of the NHRI.

The selection and appointment process should involve representatives of civil society, especially human rights defenders representing the interests of particularly vulnerable sections of society (and members of those groups also), and may also include NGOs, opposition leaders, trade unionists, social workers, journalists.

Civil society should participate in the selection and appointment process as far as possible."
Ibid. 2.3 "Selection procedures and consultation".

independence of Commissioners by precluding potential reappointment from influencing them in any way in the discharge of their duties.

In some countries, the chairperson of the Commission must be a retired superior court judge.[53] However, while this formula has proved successful in several NHRIs it has several significant drawbacks. First, it restricts the most senior appointments to a very small pool of highly qualified people who may not, necessarily, be "representative". Second, it relies on the availability of experienced judges – who may or may not be retired – and many of whom, in the final stages of their career, may be unwilling to make themselves available.

The founding laws should also clearly prescribe the grounds on which Commissioners may be dismissed. These should generally be strictly circumscribed and approximate the conditions and safeguards which attend the impeachment and removal of senior judges (see Table G). However, Commissioners and those to whom they may be able to delegate their powers should only enjoy immunity from criminal or civil proceedings for conduct, in good faith, in the course of their official functions.

It is also essential that NHRIs have the authority to select and appoint their own staff (a number of governments have initially insisted that they should select and appoint the Director General of staff). Where the institution has the option of seconding staff from other government agencies or departments the enabling law should stipulate that these appointments are accompanied by guarantees that the individuals involved will report only to the Commission during the term of their secondment and will not disclose information to anyone outside the institution unless expressly authorised.

[53] In India he or she must be the former Chief Justice of the Supreme Court.

NUMBER OF COMMISSION MEMBERS AND METHODS OF APPOINTMENT

Table D

NHRI	NUMBER	*METHOD*	PROVISION
AUSTRALIA	6 (President & 5 Commissioners)	The Governor-General appoints the President of HREOC, HR Commissioner, and Aboriginal and Torres Strait Islander Social Justice Commissioner. The 3 other Commissioners are appointed under their respective correlating legislation.[i]	HREOC Act: § 3, 8A-B, & 46B
FIJI	3 (Chairperson & 2 others)	The Constitutional Offices Commission appoints the Ombudsman (who is the chairperson) following consultations with the Prime Minister (PM). The President appoints the other 2 Members on the advice of the PM (following consultations with the Leader of Opposition and the Standing Committee of the House of Reps. responsible for human rights matters).	Const. of Fiji: § 42 & 163
INDIA	5 (Chairperson & 4 others)[ii]	The President appoints the Chairperson and other Members after obtaining recommendations from a committee consisting of the PM and Speaker of the House of the People – among others.[iii]	PHR ACT: § 3 & 4
INDONESIA	35 (Members)	The House of Representatives selects Members, based on recommendations by the Commission itself, which are validated by the National President.[iv]	Leg. No. 39: Art. 83
MALAYSIA	20 (Members or less)	The King (Yang di-Pertuan Agong) appoints Members on the recommendation of the PM, and from among those appointed Members the King designates one as the Chairman.	HRC Act: § 5
MONGOLIA	3 (Commissioners)	The State Great Hural (Parliament) appoints Members nominated by the Speaker of The State Great Hural, based on proposals by the President, the Parliamentary Standing Committee on Legal Affairs and the Supreme Court. The State Great Hural, based on a proposal by the Speaker of the State Great Hural, then appoints a Chief Commissioner from among the Commissioners.	NHRC Act: Art. 3 & 5
NEPAL	5 (Chairperson & 4 others)	The King appoints the Chairman and other Members upon the recommendation of the Recommendation Committee (consisting of the PM, Chief Justice and the Leader of the Opposition in the House of Reps.).	HR Act: § 1 & 4
NEW ZEALAND	8 (Commissioners)[v]	The Governor-General appoints the Commissioners (including the Chief Commissioner) on the recommendation of the Minister of Justice.	HR Act: § 8
PHILIPPINES	5 (Chairman & 4 others)	The President appoints the Chairman and other Members of the Commission.	Exec. Order No. 163: § 2
REP. OF KOREA	11 (President & 10 others)	The National Assembly nominates 4 Commissioners, the President another 4, and the Chief Justice of the Supreme Court nominates the remaining 3. The President appoints the President of the HRC from among the Commissioners.	NHRC Act: Art. 5 & 6
SRI LANKA	5 (Chairperson & 4 Members)	The President appoints the Members on the recommendation of the Constitutional Council.[vi]	HRC Act:§ 2
THAILAND	11 (President & 10 others)	The King appoints the Members who have been elected by the Senate from a list of nominees drawn up by the Selection Committee, which consists of the President of the Supreme Court, the President of the Supreme Administrative Court, the Prosecutor-General, the Chairman of the Law Council, Rectors/Representatives from institutions of higher education and representatives of private organisations in the field of human rights.	NHRC Act: § 5 & 8

[i] Although the "Interpretation" section of the HREOC Act (Part I Section 3(b)) defines "appointed members" as the President or the Human Rights Commissioner, Section 46B provides for an "Aboriginal and Torres Strait Islander Social Justice Commissioner, who is [also] to be appointed by the Governor-General". The remaining three Commissioners: *Disability Discrimination, Race Discrimination, and Sex Discrimination* are appointed under their correlating Acts. In fact the current situation in Australia is somewhat uncertain. The Government has not appointed substantive Commissioners to several of these areas and is committed to introducing legislation which would significantly alter the original structure and powers of the Commission.

[ii] It is also important to note that: "The Chairpersons of the National Commission for Minorities, the National Commission for the Scheduled Castes and Scheduled Tribes and the National Commission for Women shall be deemed to be Members of the Commission for [all of its functions except conducting inquiries]".

[iii] The Committee consists of: (a) The Prime Minister – Chairperson, (b) Speaker of the House of the People – Member, (c) Minister in-charge of the Ministry of Home Affairs in the Government of India — Member, (d) Leader of the Opposition in the House of the People – Member, (e) Leader of the Opposition in the Council of States – Member, and (f) Deputy Chairman of the Council of States – Member.

[iv] The Chair and the two Vice-Chairs are elected by and from among the Members.

[v] Section 8 of the HR Act 1993 expressly provides for the appointment of 3 full-time Commissioners ((a) a Chief Commissioner, (b) a Race Relations Commissioner, and (c) an Equal Employment Opportunities Commissioner.) and allows for the possibility of appointing 5 additional part-time Commissioners.

[vi] Section 2 (4) of the HRC Act also stipulates that the President shall nominate one of the appointed members to the position of Chairman. It does not, however, state who, if anyone, will appoint the President's nominee.

CRITERIA AND CONDITIONS FOR APPOINTMENT OF COMMISSIONERS[i]

Table E

	Australia	Fiji	India	Indonesia	Malaysia	Mongolia	Nepal	New Zeeland	Philippines	Republic of Korea	Sri Lanka	Thailand
Non-specific but "appropriate" qualifications[ii]	◆	◆										
Human Rights knowledge/experi ence			◆	◆		◆	◆	◆		◆	◆	◆
Legal knowledge/experi ence			◆	◆		◆	◆	◆	◆			
Diversity of personal characteristics[iii]		◆	[iv]		◆[v]					◆[vi]	◆[vii]	◆[viii]
Citizenship				◆		◆	◆		◆[ix]			◆[x]
Age requirement						◆[xi]	◆[xii]		◆[xiii]			◆[xiv]

[i] Note that this table does not take into consideration or represent criteria for appointment of Commissioners with a specific thematic portfolio, e.g. New Zealand's Race Relations Commissioner and Australia's Race Discrimination Commissioner, which may, as in the case of these two countries, prescribe specific additional or alternative criteria.

[ii] This refers to legislation that does not stipulate specific criteria as a prerequisite for appointment – but requires (as in the case of Australia's HREOC Act) that candidates must have "appropriate qualifications, knowledge or experience" – or some other similar, general formulation.

[iii] This category includes provisions that are aimed at securing a diverse and broadly representative group of members. All legislation that could be construed as attempting to achieve this representative composition was included.

[iv] See endnote ii of Table D.

[v] Section 5(3) of the HRC Act stipulates that "Members of the Commission shall be appointed from amongst prominent personalities including those from various *religious and racial backgrounds*" (emphasis added).

[vi] Article 5(5) of the NHRC Act stipulates that "Four or more of the commissioners shall be women".

[vii] Section 2(3) of the HRC Act stipulates that "In making recommendations . . . the Constitutional Council and the Prime Minister shall have regard to the necessity of the minorities being represented . . . [on] the Commission".

[viii] Section 6 of the NHRC Act stipulates that members shall be appointed "from the persons having apparent knowledge or experiences in the protection of rights and liberties of the people, having regard also to the participation of men and women and representatives from private organisations in the field of human rights".

[ix] Section 2(a) of Executive Order No. 163 requires candidate members to be "natural-born citizens" of the Philippines. Similar provisions can be found in the legislation of Indonesia, Mongolia and Nepal, however, with the omission of the phrase "natural-born". One could infer, with regard to the last three countries (and this omission), that naturalized citizens would also be eligible for membership.

[x] Section 6 of the NHRC Act requires, inter alia, that candidate members must be "of Thai nationality by birth".

[xi] Article 4.1. of the NHRC Act provides, inter alia, that member candidates must be at least 35 years of age.

[xii] Section 3(2)(b) of the HR Act states that in order to be eligible for appointment to the Commission individuals must be at least 40 years of age.

[xiii] Section 2 of Executive Order No. 163 provides, inter alia, that member candidates must be at least 35 years of age.

[xiv] Section 6 of the NHRC Act requires candidate members be at least 35 years of age.

TERMS OF OFFICE, AND "WORKING CAPACITY" OF COMMISSIONERS

Table F

	Australia	Fiji	India	Indonesia	Malaysia	Mongolia	Nepal	New Zeeland	Philippines	Republic of Korea	Sri Lanka	Thailand
Term of Office in Years	7	NR[i]	5	5	2	6[ii]	5	5	7	3	3	6
Possibility of reappointment (*only once)	◆	NR	◆	◆	◆	◆*	◆	◆		◆*	◆	
No possibility of reappointment		NR							◆			◆
Full-time[iii]		◆	◆	NR		◆	NR		◆			◆
Part-time				NR	◆[iv]		NR				◆[v]	
Mixed (allows for both full and part-time)	◆[vi]			NR			NR	◆[vii]		◆[viii]		

[i] **NR** indicates that there was "no reference" to this item in the establishing legislation and will be used to reflect this throughout the table in relation to other institutions as well.

[ii] Note that the Chief Commissioner is appointed for a term of three years; Commissioners are appointed for six.

[iii] The term "full-time" applies to those Commissions that require their Commissioners to work full-time, or to not engage in any other paid employment.

[iv] Although the HRC Act does not expressly provide for part-time Commissioners, it states in Section 10(d)(i) that a Commissioner may be terminated if he/she has "engaged in any paid office or employment *which conflicts with his duties as a member of the Commission*"(emphasis added). This formulation is similar to that described above in endnote iii, however with one important difference. It does not prohibit ***any*** form of paid employment outside the duties of the Commission - only those "which conflict with his duties" as a Commissioner. (In practice, all Commissioners appointed to date have been part-time).

[v] Support for interpreting the HRC act to permit part-time Commissioners can be found in Section 3(1)(ii) of the HRC Act (a formulation similar to Section 10(d)(i) of Malaysia's HRC Act – see endnote v.) which states a member may be terminated if they engage in "any paid employment outside the duties of his office, which in the opinion of the President . . . *conflicts with his duties as a member of the Commission* . . .".(emphasis added).

[vi] Section 8A and B of the HREOC Act state the following respectively: "The President is to be appointed . . . as a full-time member or a part-time member" and the "Human Rights Commissioner is to be appointed . . . as a full-time member". All of the other Commissioners are full-time appointees.

[vii] Section 18(1) of the HR Act states that the Chief Commissioner, the Race Relations Commissioner and the Equal Employment Opportunities Commissioner shall all be full-time members. It further states that there shall be "[n]o more than 5 other Commissioners, whose offices are each part-time ones".

[viii] Article 5(1) of the NHRC Act states "The Commission shall be comprised of eleven commissioners for human rights . . .including one president and three full-time Commissioners".

TERMINATION OF APPOINTMENT OF MEMBERS OF THE COMMISSION[i]

Table G

NHRI	METHOD	PROVISION
AUSTRALIA	The Governor-General may terminate the appointment of a member by reasons of misbehavior or physical or mental incapacity, including: if a member becomes bankrupt, engages in unapproved paid employment, or is absent from duty for a prescribed period of time.	HEROC Act: § 41
FIJI	The Constitutional Offices Commission may terminate the appointment of a member for inability to perform the functions of office (whether arising from infirmity of body or mind or any other cause) or for misbehavior.[ii]	Const. of Fiji: § 172
INDIA	The President, after a Supreme Court inquiry and subsequent recommendation, may order termination on a number of grounds including "proved misbehaviour or incapacity". The President may also dismiss a Commissioner, without a recommendation, on the following grounds: insolvency, engages in paid employment outside the duties of his/her office, is unfit to continue in office by reason of infirmity of mind or body, is of unsound mind and stands so declared by a competent court, or if a Commissioner is convicted and sentenced to imprisonment for an offence which in the opinion of the President involves moral turpitude.	PHR ACT: § 5
INDONESIA	The Plenary Council may put forward a resolution to terminate the appointment of a member, which must be communicated to the House of Representatives and ratified by the President.[iii]	Leg. No. 39: Art. 85
MALAYSIA	The King (Yang di-Pertuan Agong) may terminate an appointment if the member is deemed insolvent by the courts, declared physically or mentally incapable by medical personnel, or if a member is absent without leave for 3 consecutive meetings. With a recommendation by the PM the King can also terminate on other grounds including conduct that will bring the Commission into disrepute.	HRC Act: § 10
MONGOLIA	The State Great Hural (Parliament) may terminate the appointment of a Commissioner who has been judged and convicted of committing a crime by a court. If a Commissioner has been arrested for allegedly committing a criminal act the State Great Hural can, based on a proposal from a "competent authority", suspend (or restore) the powers of a Commissioner.	NHRC Act: Art. 8
NEPAL	The Human Rights Committee of the House of Representatives can terminate the appointment of a member, after adopting a resolution approved by the House of Representatives, on grounds of incompetence or misbehaviour, "[p]rovided that a Member accused of such charge shall be given a reasonable opportunity to defend himself in the Human Rights Committee of the House of Representatives".	HR Act: § 6

NHRI	METHOD	PROVISION
NEW ZEALAND	The Governor-General may terminate an appointment for "incapacity affecting performance of duty, neglect of duty, or misconduct" which has been proven to the "satisfaction of the Governor-General". Section 20G further states that a member may be terminated if found to be bankrupt.	HR Act: § 20G
PHILIPPINES	There are no provisions in Executive Order 163 that provide for the termination of members.	Exec. Order No. 163: §
REP. OF KOREA	Commissioners' appointments may be terminated[iv] if they are "sentenced to imprisonment without labor or a heavier punishment". Commissioners may also "retire" based on physical or mental grounds that inhibit them from performing their duties, if two-thirds or more of all the Commissioners pass a resolution to that effect.	NHRC Act: Art. 8
SRI LANKA	The President may terminate a Commissioner's appointment on several enumerated grounds including conviction of an offence involving moral turpitude, or missing three consecutive Commission meetings without the leave of the Commission. Parliament may also initiate a Presidential order of termination on grounds of proved misbehaviour or incapacity if the majority of Parliament supports such action.	HRC Act: § 3.1
THAILAND	Commissioners' appointment may be terminated based on several grounds including being addicted to drugs, bankrupt, or of unsound mind or suffering mental infirmity. Members of the House of Reps. or Senators may also initiate termination procedures by submitting a complaint[v] requesting the President of the Senate to pass a resolution of termination based on misconduct or immoral conduct that may seriously affect or damage the performance of the Commissioner's duties.	NHRC Act: § 11 and 12

[i] The primary intention of this table is to highlight who has the power to terminate the appointment of members, the relevant safeguards that exist, and the grounds on which termination may be based.

[ii] Section 172 provides a further safeguard in that if the Constitutional Offices Commission "considers that the question of removal from office ought to be investigated" it may appoint a tribunal "consisting of a chairperson and not less than 2 other members" who must look into the matter and provide a report to the Constitutional Offices Commission with a possible recommendation for termination.

[iii] Grounds for termination include: committing a "reprehensible act or other act which the Plenary Council deems to besmirch the dignity and reputation, and/or diminish the independence and credibility of the National Commission on Human Rights".

[iv] The Act does not state who or what entity is responsible for initiating or carrying out termination of members' appointment.

[v] In order to lodge a complaint of this nature "[m]embers of the House of Representatives or senators of not less than one-fourth of the total number of the existing members of each house" must be in favour of doing so.

3.5. COOPERATION WITH NON GOVERNMENT ORGANISATIONS (NGOS):

It is important for NHRIs to cooperate appropriately with other independent national agencies, other national human rights institutions and the United Nations – particularly the various Treaty Bodies which have been established to monitor governments' performance in implementing their international human rights treaty obligations. These subjects are dealt with in subsequent sections.

However, the Paris Principles particularly emphasise, in several sections,[54] the importance of national institutions establishing and maintaining close relations with non government organisations working in the field of human rights. NGOs frequently have extensive networks of contacts and particular expertise which make them an important source of information for national institutions. Many recently established NGOs are highly specialised and can make important contributions in assisting national institutions to discharge their responsibility to provide education and training, both for the general public and for groups such as police and prison officials where targeted programmes are essential.

Experience has demonstrated that in relation to particularly vulnerable groups, such as indigenous peoples, religious and ethnic minorities, people with disabilities and others, the cooperation of NGOs is particularly valuable in understanding and effectively addressing the most important issues. In some cases the relevant NGOs describe themselves as "human rights" organisations – but in many instances they simply see themselves as "carer" support groups or community-based organisations. Regardless of their titles

[54] The relevant sections of the Paris Principles are those dealing with:
"Composition and guarantees of independence and pluralism" – Section 1(a);
"Methods of operation" – Section (g)
"In view of the fundamental role played by non-governmental organisations in expanding the work of national institutions, develop relations with non-governmental organizations devoted to promoting and protecting human rights, to economic and social development, to combating racism, to protecting particularly vulnerable groups (especially children, migrant workers, refugees, physically and mentally disabled persons) or to specialised areas".
"Additional principles concerning the status of commissions with quasi-jurisdictional competence. (sic)"
"A national institution may be authorised to hear and consider complaints and petitions concerning individual situations. Cases may be brought before it by individuals, their representatives, third parties, non-governmental organisations . . . ".

it is essential to consult and coordinate with these organisations if NHRIs are to discharge their responsibilities effectively.

The legislative mandates of most NHRIs recognise, either explicitly or implicitly, the importance of NGOs and empower national institutions to work closely with them.

Several of the strategies developed by national institutions, such as national inquiries, rely heavily on the involvement of NGOs – both for the preparation of appropriate terms of reference for the inquiry and for ensuring that evidence presented comes from those in the community most directly affected. (These issues are addressed in more detail in the section below on national inquiries.) It is therefore important for those entrusted with the responsibility of leading national institutions to spend time maintaining contacts and developing relationships with relevant NGOs. NHRI Commissioners, many of whom themselves come from an NGO background, do this in various ways – both in formal consultations and regular informal contacts. Some NHRIs have also found it necessary to appoint a particular staff member as an NGO liaison officer.

Some NHRIs have established "Advisory Boards" comprising representatives from NGOs, professional groups and other members of civil society to assist them in establishing priorities and implementing programmes. While these bodies generally operate with a minimum of formalities, at least one NHRI has found it expedient to approve detailed regulations which govern not only the establishment of the board and its membership, but also its procedures, frequency of meetings, financing and relationship to the national human rights commission itself.[55]

While we attempted to incorporate essential elements in the Paris Principles, the most comprehensive and useful set of guidelines relating to the relationship between NHRIs and NGOs was formulated subsequently, in 1999, at the Asia-Pacific "Workshop on National Institutions and Non-Government Organisations Working in Partnership".[56] As a general principle:

> "The Workshop reaffirmed faith in the crucial importance of cooperation between national human rights institutions and NGOs and recognised they should work together on the basis of their common commitment to the

[55] The National Human Rights Commission of Mongolia (NHRCM), on 7 April 2004, approved "Regulation on the National Human Rights Commission's Ex-Officio Board". This Board, according to the regulations, must meet at least quarterly – see NHRCM's annual report, 2005, Appendix Three, p. 72.

[56] Op.cit., footnote 36.

> universality and indivisibility of human rights as expressed in the Universal Declaration of Human Rights, international human rights instruments and the Vienna Declaration. The Workshop also recognised that national human rights institutions and NGOs have different roles in the promotion and protection of human rights and that the independence and autonomy of civil society and NGOs and of national human rights institutions must be respected and upheld."

The Workshop also agreed on detailed guidelines relating to: mechanisms of co-operation; education; complaints and investigations; public inquiries; relations with legislatures; legislation; establishment of new national institutions; the Asia-Pacific Forum of National Human Rights Institutions; and international activity. Several of these guidelines are referred to in more detail in subsequent chapters.[57]

There should be no misapprehension on the part of governments establishing a national institution that this mechanism in any way minimises or derogates from the central role which a vigorous non-government sector has to play in protecting human rights. The roles of NHRIs and NGOs are entirely complementary.

---

[57] With respect to "Structures and mechanisms of co-operation" participants agreed the Workshop emphasised the need to:

"Recognise the importance of, and implement, better consultation processes between national human rights institutions and NGOs, which should be regular, transparent, inclusive and substantive; encourage NGOs to decide on what processes and mechanisms best suit their circumstances and relations with the national human rights institution in their country; encourage national institutions to establish focal points to facilitate relations with NGOs;

Hold joint training programs;

Consider temporary personnel attachments between national institutions and NGOs;

Cooperate where possible when making recommendations to governments or other national bodies;

Cooperate and seek advice from OHCHR in encouraging the development of national human rights action plans;

Hold workshops on specific issues of mutual interest, with a particular focus on ensuring a balanced approach to participation and organisation; and

Establish mechanisms for discussion between national institutions and NGOs with a view to maximising possibilities of using information technology to keep each other informed of their activities and issues arising from monitoring of human rights questions as well as relevant recommendations."

Op.cit., footnote 36, Section 2.1–2.7 of the Kandy Declaration.

CHAPTER 4: RELATIONS WITH THE EXECUTIVE, PARLIAMENT, THE JUDICIARY AND OTHER INSTITUTIONS

Independent monitoring mechanisms, including NHRIs, can only function effectively to the extent that other "institutions" on which they depend, or with which they must interact, are fulfiling their legitimate roles.

If the Parliament is dominated by the Executive, experience in many countries indicates that it is unlikely Parliament will seriously consider reports from NHRIs or other institutions which expose the government's shortcomings. Governments uninhibited by an effective parliamentary opposition have frequently demonstrated a blatant disregard for the human rights of their opponents and contempt for institutions attempting to protect them – even those with a legislative mandate.

The credibility and effectiveness of any NHRI is also closely related to the independence and effectiveness of the judiciary. There are many reasons for this – including because NHRIs must sometimes rely on the courts to enforce their findings and recommendations and to sanction any failure to cooperate with legitimate requests from Commissions in the conduct of their investigations and inquiries into alleged human rights violations. In countries where the courts are dysfunctional or the judges incompetent or corrupt there is usually an increased burden for NHRIs involving complaints concerning the administration of justice or failure to receive "equal protection of the law", as guaranteed by the ICCPR.

4.1. RELATIONS WITH THE EXECUTIVE:

As already indicated, the independence of a NHRI from the executive branch of government is an essential condition for its effective functioning and credibility.

However, national human rights institutions must develop and sustain the capacity to work with governments constructively – as well as, when necessary, criticising any government actions that are in breach of, or inconsistent with, the state's human rights treaty obligations. This essential balance between the institutions' "advisory" and "adversarial" functions is not always easy to maintain. Indeed, notwithstanding the explicit guarantees of the institutions' independence, incorporated in constitutional or legislative texts, governments have frequently demonstrated an unwillingness to respect the independence of NHRIs which criticise them. In a number of cases national institutions in the Asia-Pacific region have not only been criticised but in several instances (for example Thailand and Australia), Commissioners have been vilified by prime ministers and had their budgets and staffing levels substantially reduced following reports the government did not like.

Members and staff of national institutions, must, however, always remember that they are not elected and that they have an important responsibility to ensure that criticism, including of those who are elected, is accurate and that reports and any public statements are balanced and fair. Criticism should, whenever appropriate, be accompanied by acknowledging positive steps taken by governments to improve the human rights situation.

NHRIs must also give priority to proactive strategies which will assist government and government agencies in discharging their human rights obligations. There are many ways in which this can be done and strategies which have been developed by NHRIs in the Asia-Pacific region include, for example, working with government departments and agencies to develop general and specialised educational programmes and with both public and private sector organisations to develop and implement nondiscriminatory codes of conduct for management. It is, in other words, incumbent on NHRIs to prevent human rights violations, wherever possible – not simply respond to violations after they have occurred.

NHRIs should also provide appropriate assistance to governments in fulfilling their reporting obligations under the various international human rights treaties the state has ratified. Clearly, the nature of this cooperation will depend on governments' willingness to include in their reports accurate information on the human rights situation in the country. In the absence of such willingness, NHRIs must not compromise their independence and may consider sending alternative reports or commentaries to the Treaty Bodies.

Governments, for their part, should provide NHRIs not only with adequate resources (as already indicated), but also with all appropriate cooperation, and the Executive should issue instructions to all departments and agencies for which government is responsible (including the police and prison services) to do likewise.

Government cooperation should also extend to ensuring that the NHRI's reports are tabled in the parliament in a timely manner and that sufficient time is allocated for serious debate of the institution's recommendations. (Governments have frequently demonstrated their unwillingness to do this when they consider that the NHRI's reports provide "ammunition" for their political opponents to criticise the government).

Similarly, NHRIs can only function effectively if governments fulfil their responsibility to respond to criticisms offered and recommendations made. Given the nature of modern parliamentary democracies it is therefore important that while the government may often disagree with a NHRI's assessments it should respect and facilitate its role as an important independent agency.

Whether required by law or not, governments must also enable the institution to function effectively by appointing, and when necessary reappointing, Commissioners in a timely manner. (In several countries governments have "punished" NHRI's whose reports they found embarrassing by leaving vacant the positions of Commissioners whose terms have expired.)

Finally, the sensitivity of many human rights issues – such as the rights of refugees, asylum seekers and internally displaced people – means that there will always be elements of tension between NHRIs conscientiously implementing their mandates and governments. In some cases governments have sought to minimise and even discredit the importance of NHRI reports by alleging that the institution was interfering in "political" issues or that its work had become illegitimately "politicised". Clearly, national human rights institutions should not become involved in party politics – but all important human rights issues are legitimate subjects for political debate. Suggestions that NHRIs do not have the right to advance findings and recommendations on politically sensitive subjects in an appropriately forthright and impartial manner are therefore completely unjustified.

4.2. RELATIONS WITH THE PARLIAMENT:

The ballot box is still a relative novelty in many countries, including in the Asia-Pacific region, and, as already observed, NHRIs in most countries are still evolving – along with other "institutions" of democracy, including freely elected parliaments.

Experience has clearly demonstrated that national human rights institutions cannot assume that Members of Parliament (MPs) understand NHRIs' role as independent entities – even those who were present when the Parliament adopted the enabling legislation. It is therefore essential that NHRIs establish and develop contacts and appropriate working relationships with elected politicians and relevant Parliamentary Committees.[58]

---

[58] Several Parliaments in the region have had committees or sub-committees dedicated to dealing with human rights issues. More frequently, however, these have been dealt with by the Legal Affairs Committee or the Constitutional and Legal Committee – or by sub-committees of other Standing Committees – such as the

In democratic theory, the Legislature is supposed to perform dual functions – on the one hand passing laws appropriate to regulate the lives of those who elect the legislators and on the other, acting as an "institution of accountability" where governments and their ministers can be called to account for their actions. As indicated at the outset, it is the decline of the latter function and the increasing domination of the Legislature by the Executive in many countries that has been another important factor in motivating the creation of independent statutory authorities such as Anti-Corruption Commissions and NHRIs.

One fundamental element in the relationship between Parliament and NHRIs is that parliaments are elected by, and frequently represent the interests of majorities – whereas human rights institutions will frequently find that their investigations and reports are focused on disadvantaged minorities. This is not to suggest, of course, that most MPs are unconcerned about human rights issues; rather to underline the reality that in many cases their most pressing preoccupation is getting re-elected – rather than advancing the interests of groups which may be politically powerless or electorally relatively insignificant. When minorities have been the victim of discrimination by the majority, NHRIs may find their task particularly challenging.

Interacting effectively with Parliament is essential because legislators will determine the fate of many recommendations made by NHRIs in their reports. The annual report is an important vehicle for informing MPs but again, experience indicates that if this has not been preceded by other contacts, very few MPs will bother to read it – let alone debate its contents. Ensuring this does happen requires contact with MPs throughout the year and there are several ways to facilitate this. These include: arranging to give evidence to Parliamentary Committees whenever possible; inviting MPs to NHRI events; arranging workshops for MPs; private briefings by the Commissioners; and inviting MPs to give evidence at public inquiries conducted by the Commission.[59]

Foreign Affairs Committee. The recent trend, however, is for Parliaments to establish committees or sub-committees specifically designated to deal with human rights – e.g. the Standing Committee on Human Rights and Equal Opportunities established by the Fiji House of Representatives in 2004 (Fiji Human Rights Commission; 2004 Annual Report, p. 10). This is an encouraging development.

[59] A number of Australian legislators, both senators and members of the lower house, gave evidence at the National Inquiries on homeless children and the rights of the mentally ill (see Chapter 7 and Appendices X & XII). This was critical in securing necessary legislative and policy reforms and obtaining substantially

In some cases it may be appropriate to organise separate meetings with the various political parties represented in the Parliament. In this context it is entirely proper, and indeed desirable, for NHRIs to urge each political party to include a section on human rights in its party platform – and such a strategy has a great deal to recommend it.[60]

The most effective strategy for ensuring MPs do respond appropriately to NHRIs' reports has been the national inquiry. Annual reports can be comprehensive – but boring – in necessarily systematically chronicling all significant activities of the institution in the previous year. Reports focused on particular human rights issues, preceded by public hearings and media coverage, have proved far more likely to elicit the interest of MPs and put pressure on governments to respond appropriately.

When MPs understand that NHRIs can assist them in their day-to-day work – for example, by dealing with appropriate complaints from their constituents – they generally respond very positively. In the author's experience however, in most countries, the great majority of MPs do not realise this until it is explained to them – privately or in seminars or workshops.

---

increased funding for services for the homeless and those affected by mental illness following the release of these reports.

[60] The 1999 Conference of NHRIs and NGOs in the Asia-Pacific Region, already referred to above, concluded that in their relations with legislatures NHRIs and NGOs should:

"Cooperate in promoting constructive relations and joint meetings with legislatures and legislators aimed at promoting and protecting human rights;

Consider holding workshops aimed at strengthening the capacity of national institutions and NGO personnel to lobby legislatures effectively including through campaigns aimed at promoting specific action by legislatures on human rights issues;

Consider jointly participating in workshops aimed at better informing legislators about human rights and the role and functions of national institutions and NGOs;

Encourage legislatures to establish human rights committees; where appropriate, approach the Inter-Parliamentary Union to encourage the national parliament to give greater emphasis to human rights; and

Work jointly in order to bring the protection and promotion of human rights into political party platforms."

Op.cit., footnote 36, Section 6.1–6.5 of the Kandy Declaration.

4.3. RELATIONS WITH THE JUDICIARY:

The relationship between NHRIs and the courts is an extremely important one. While the adversarial nature of judicial proceedings is neither appropriate nor necessary in dealing effectively with many human rights cases, it is the courts which must ultimately ensure that human rights are protected.

One of the major advantages of NHRIs is the fact that they are a more cost-effective, and therefore a more accessible method of conflict resolution than the courts.[61] As already noted, they are able to investigate complaints without applying the formal and in some cases rigid rules of evidence and their ability to proceed informally means they are often less intimidating to complainants than the formalities associated with courts. Moreover, NHRIs' services are free and they frequently use conciliation or mediation in the process of conflict resolution.

Those who have suffered human rights violations should be able to exercise the option of approaching either an NHRI or the courts. In some cases the victim may seek a remedy from both – although this is unusual. In order to avoid conflict between the courts and national institutions the enabling legislation for NHRIs usually includes a specific provision stipulating that they may not investigate a matter which is already before a judicial body – or review cases which have already been decided by the courts.

However, "equal protection of the law" is a fundamentally important human right and NHRIs should not be precluded from commenting on

---

[61] Governments and judges are also beginning to recognise the fact that NHRIs, in addition to assisting victims of human rights violations, are taking a significant burden off the courts which, in many developing countries, are overstretched and under-resourced. The Indian Commission, for example, operating with less than 400 staff, in a country of one billion people, handled over 74,000 complaints in 2004–2005. This has increased from 496 complaints in 1993–94, the first year of the Commission's operation. (Presentation by the Registrar and Deputy Registrar of the Indian Commission – "National Human Rights Commission of India – Achievements and Shortcomings"; RWI-APF Training Programme for NHRIs of the Asia-Pacific region, Bangkok, Thailand, 21 November – 2 December 2005).

The Mongolian Commission, with a staff of only nine, operating in a country of 2.7 million people, has received over 560 complaints since its establishment in 2001. (Presentation by Commissioner Dashdorj Jadamba and Ms. Saruul Arslan, National Human Rights Commission of Mongolia; RWI-APF Training Programme, Bangkok, Thailand, 21 November – 2 December 2005).

matters relating to access to the courts on a non discriminatory basis.[62] Indeed in many countries, including in the Asia-Pacific region, equal protection of the law exists in theory but not in practice. Systemic problems, such as corruption or incompetence in the judiciary, are also matters on which NHRIs have a right to make recommendations – although this must be appropriately tempered if there is an independent body, such as a judicial commission, with a specific mandate to supervise the judiciary.

The jurisdiction of an NHRI may also, in important respects, go beyond matters on which the courts are able to adjudicate. This is because many violations of human rights are not, strictly speaking, "unlawful" – but they frequently involve discriminatory practices, omissions or neglect which may be in violation of international human rights norms and therefore, at least in the Asia-Pacific region, within the jurisdiction of most NHRIs.

Some investigations of human rights violations, including evidence which may be placed before the Commission in a public inquiry, will disclose criminal conduct. In such cases the institution has an obligation to refer appropriate information to the relevant authorities – usually the Director of Public Prosecutions or the police – to consider whether further investigation and prosecution in the courts is necessary.

The Paris Principles provide very little guidance in relation to NHRIs which exercise quasi-judicial powers in executing their mandate to investigate individual violations of human rights. However, a useful summary for NHRIs which do have this responsibility is included in the Commonwealth's "Best Practice" manual.[63] This may also provide a useful checklist for those currently engaged in preparing legislation to establish NHRIs in a number of countries in the Asia-Pacific region.

- NHRIs should play a role complementary to that of the courts.
- There should be an expressly established mechanism for the enforcement of appropriate NHRI decisions by the courts.
- Individuals should be able to access the court system directly to seek a remedy for a human rights violation and should not be required to first file a complaint with the NHRI.

---

[62] This right is guaranteed in the International Covenant on Civil and Political Rights in Article 14.

[63] National Human Rights Institutions – Best Practice: Commonwealth Secretariat, 2001, at p. 29.

- NHRIs should be more accessible and offer a more cost-effective and less formal means of conflict resolution than the courts.
- NHRI staff and members should try to establish a co-operative working relationship with the courts.
- NHRIs should not commence investigations into matters already pending before the courts unless required as part of the duty of NHRIs to investigate systemic issues relating to equal protection under the law and access to justice.
- Courts should permit NHRIs to provide assistance to individuals seeking to redress grievances through the courts.
- NHRIs should be accorded standing to bring complaints to court in their own right.
- Courts should accord NHRIs official status as a friend of the court.[64]
- Courts should grant to NHRIs the right to join as a party in relevant cases.
- The decisions of NHRIs should be subject to judicial review.

In practice, NHRIs are extremely selective about the cases in which they will seek leave to intervene in judicial proceedings. Among the principal reasons for this selectivity is the cost and time involved in court actions and the limited resources they have at their disposal. Most NHRIs in the Asia-Pacific region have developed internal guidelines for such interventions. These generally relate to the gravity of the violation(s) in issue and the national significance of the specific case.

---

[64] In a number of countries the courts have initially been cautious about granting leave to NHRIs to intervene as *amicus curiae* in cases concerning human rights. However, as the reputation of NHRIs has grown and their role has been better understood, courts have increasingly relied on NHRIs to assist them in interpreting international human rights treaties or constitutional provisions relating to human rights.

The Fiji Human Rights Commission has, for example, successfully intervened in a number of cases as *amicus curiae* – both on its own initiative and at the request of the court. E.g. in *Naushad Ali* v. *the State* (Criminal Appeal No HAA 0083 of 2001 L) the Commission intervened, at the request of the High Court, to assist the Court with submissions on whether corporal punishment in prison was consistent with the Bill of Rights provisions in the Fiji Constitution prohibiting freedom from torture and cruel or degrading treatment or punishment. (Section 25 of the Constitution) As a result, the Court held that corporal punishment in prisons and schools was unconstitutional.

When NHRIs do intervene in judicial proceedings they have frequently demonstrated their value in assisting the courts to interpret and appropriately apply international human rights instruments.[65] They have also frequently

---

[65] One of the most important examples of the role which NHRIs can and should play is the decision by the Australian High Court in *Minister of State for Immigration and Ethnic Affairs* v. *Teoh, 1995,* 183 CLR 273 (the Teoh Case).

Following the National Inquiry on Homeless Children (See below Chapter 7) and the ratification by Australia of the Convention of the Rights of the Child (CRC), the Australian Human Rights and Equal Opportunity Commission intervened in the Australian High Court, in 1994, to protect the rights of children whose mother had become dysfunctional due to drug abuse and whose father was the subject of a deportation order. The Teoh Case resulted in a landmark decision. It clearly established, for the first time, that decision makers in Australia had to give effect to the rights embodied in international human rights treaties in making administrative decisions – even if those treaties had not been incorporated into Australian law by an Act of Parliament.

The Teoh decision was particularly important – not only because Australia has failed to incorporate into domestic law many of its international treaty obligations – but also because Australia has no Bill of Rights to protect its citizens, and others within its jurisdiction – such as refugees and asylum-seekers – from arbitrary actions by government officials. See generally B. Burdekin, "The Impact of a Bill of Rights on Those Who Need it Most", in P. Alston (ed.), *Towards and Australian Bill of Rights* (Centre for International and Public Law, Canberra, 1994).

In the course of their judgement in the Teoh Case, Mason CJ and Deane J said:

"ratification by Australia of an international Convention is not to be dismissed as a merely platitudinous or ineffectual act, particularly when the instrument evidences internationally accepted standards to be applied by courts and administrative authorities in dealing with basic human rights affecting the family and children. Rather, ratification of a Convention is a positive statement by the executive government of this country to the world and to the Australian people that the executive government and its agencies will act in accordance with the Convention. That positive statement is an adequate foundation for a legitimate expectation, absent statutory or executive indications to the contrary, that administrative decision-makers will act in conformity with the Convention and treat the best interests of the children as "a primary consideration". It is not necessary that a person seeking to set up such a legitimate expectation should be aware of the Convention or should personally entertain the expectation; it is enough that the expectation is reasonable in the sense that there are adequate materials to support it."
The importance of this case was not confined to Australia. Other courts, including the Indian Supreme Court and superior courts in the UK and New Zealand, have subsequently followed the Teoh decision.

played a creative and proactive role in securing decisions which have wide-ranging implications for protecting human rights – going beyond the particular case in which they have intervened.[66] In addition to their value as legal precedents, these cases have an important educative value – not only for the judiciary but, because of the publicity they frequently receive, for the general public as well.

Finally, while some NHRIs exercise quasi-judicial powers it must be understood that in generic terms they are administrative bodies and are all ultimately subject to the supervision of the courts. However, the way in which they relate to the courts is complex and differs from jurisdiction to jurisdiction – both in relation to their access to the courts and their capacity to have courts enforce their findings or determinations and, in some cases, impose penalties for non compliance with their requests. Because of the importance of this relationship and the fact that it is frequently misunderstood, relevant information from the legislation in a number of countries is summarised in Tables A and H and the following notes on specific legislative provisions. These include a section on "The Power to Provide or Recommend Compensation for Human Rights Violations". While in most cases NHRIs in the Asia-Pacific region are only able to recommend compensation (see Table A) several Commissions have made quite significant awards in a number of cases – and the moral authority of the Commission has resulted in the amounts awarded actually being paid by most respondents.[67]

---

[66] One excellent recent example is the case of: *Charanjit Singh and the National Human Rights Commission* v *State and Ors.*, High Court of Delhi, 4 March 2005. In this case, involving a mentally ill prisoner who had been in gaol, on remand, for 20 years, the Indian Human Rights Commission intervened and, inter alia, secured his release. The Indian Commission, however, also drafted detailed guidelines which should be followed in cases involving mentally ill prisoners and the High Court, in its decision, directed that the Judicial Academy should conduct courses for all Judicial Officers to sensitise them on how to deal with persons affected by mental illness. The High Court also directed that a copy of their Order should be sent to all Sessions Judges, Additional Sessions Judges and Metropolitan Magistrates so that they could pass appropriate orders in accordance with the Guidelines prepared by the Indian Commission.

[67] The NHRI which has used this "power" most successfully is the National Human Rights Commission of India. In the year 2004–2005 the Commission recommended "interim relief" under Section 18(3) of its Act to a total amount of Rs 23,27,000 (approximately US$50,000). Since 1993 the Commission has recommended the equivalent of more than US$2.2million by way of "interim relief" in 632 cases.

RELATIONS WITH THE EXECUTIVE, PARLIAMENT, THE JUDICIARY AND OTHER INSTITUTIONS

(Presentation by the Registrar and Deputy Registrar of the Indian Commission; Bangkok Training Programme; November – December 2005; op.cit. footnote 61.)

SANCTIONS FOR NON-COMPLIANCE WITH COMMISSION REQUESTS/RECOMMENDATIONS OR FOR OBSTRUCTION OF THE COMMISSION

Table H

	Australia	Fiji	India	Indonesia	Malaysia	Mongolia	Nepal	New Zeeland	Philippines	Republic of Korea	Sri Lanka	Thailand
Sanctions (fines and/or imprisonment) for refusing to attend/ be sworn / give information or produce a document		◆	◆									◆
Sanctions (only fines) for refusing to attend/ be sworn / give information or produce a document	◆							◆		◆		
Power to recommend to or request the Courts[i] to impose sanctions for refusing to attend/ be sworn / give information, produce a document, or for acting in contempt of the Commission*				◆[ii]		◆[iii]					◆[iv]*	
Sanctions (fines and/or imprisonment) for obstructing the Commission, Commissioners /and Staff in the performance of the Commission duties	◆	◆								◆		
Sanctions for falsifying evidence and/or making false statements.		◆[v]	◆[vi]							◆[vii]		

[i] The NHRIs listed in this category have provisions in their Acts which explicitly state that they "may approach" or "may seek the assistance" of the court in relation to non-compliance with Commission requests/orders.

[ii] From the formulation of the Indonesian provision related to seeking the assistance of the Court with regard to non-compliance, one could infer that the Commission could not only seek penalties for non-compliance but also other Court ordered interventions aimed at enforcing the Commission's request:

> "Article 95
>
> Should a person called on fail to appear or refuse to give a statement, the National Commission on Human Rights may seek the assistance of the Head of Court [sic] to enforce its request, in accordance with prevailing law.".

[iii] Article 19.5 does not explicitly state what Commissioners can request the Court to do in instances of non-compliance. It simply states that Commissioners "may approach the Court, according to procedures established by law, with regard to the business entities, organisations or officials which have refused to undertake relevant measures as provided under his/her demands and/or recommendations".

[iv] Section 21 (1) of the HRC Act states: "Every offence of contempt committed against, or in disrespect of, the authority of the Commission shall be punishable by the Supreme Court as though it were an offence of contempt committed against, or in disrespect of, the authority of that Court, and the Supreme Court is hereby vested with jurisdiction to try every such offence.".

Section 21 (3)(d) of the HRC Act further provides, in relation to persons who do not comply with Commission requests, "such person shall be guilty of the offence of contempt against, or in disrespect of, the authority of the Commission". In such cases the Commission may transmit to the Supreme Court a Certificate signed by the Chairman of the Commission stating such determination, which may be used by the Supreme Court in "any proceedings for the punishment of an offence of contempt which the Supreme Court may think fit to take cognizance".

[v] May request the imposition of both fines and imprisonment.

[vi] Ibid.

[vii] May request the imposition of fines or imprisonment.

CHAPTER 4

The Relationship Between NHRIs and the Courts[68]

	Australia	Fiji	India	Indonesia	Malaysia	Mongolia	Nepal	New Zeeland	Philippines	Republic of Korea	Sri Lanka	Thailand
Power to intervene or assist in Court proceedings related to human rights (with permission of the Court)	◆	◆	◆	◆		◆	◆	◆		◆	◆	

The following selection of legislative provisions relating to the relationship between NHRIs and the courts does not purport to provide a comprehensive picture of this very important but sometimes complex and evolving relationship. It is merely intended to assist consideration of the various formulae that may be considered appropriate in establishing an NHRI or amending legislation prescribing its functions.

INDIA

Section 12(b) of the Protection of Human Rights Act empowers the Commission to "intervene in any proceeding involving any allegation of violation of human rights pending before a court with the approval of such court". Furthermore, Section 18(2), under the heading "Steps after inquiry", enables the Commission to "approach the Supreme Court or the High Court concerned for such directions, orders or writs as that Court may deem necessary". The Supreme Court has in several cases specifically remitted matters to the National Human Rights Commission. In one case the Supreme Court has even authorised the Human Rights Commission to function outside the provisions of its own enabling statute and subject to the directions of the court (Case No. 1/1997/NHRC).

SRI LANKA

Section 11(c) of the HRC Act states that the Commission may "intervene in any proceedings relating to the infringement or imminent infringement of the fundamental rights, pending before any court, with the permission of such court". The Act also prescribes collaboration between the Supreme Court

---

[68] If not otherwise specified, the Sections and Articles referred to in this part are provisions in the legislation establishing the NHRI in question.

and the Commission in Sections 10(e), 11(e) and 12(1). These provisions oblige the Commission to inquire into or report on matters referred to it by the Supreme Court.

Section 15(3)(b) also empowers the Commission to refer to the Courts, matters which were either appropriate for conciliation or mediation, but all the parties objected to it, or where attempts at conciliation or mediation have been unsuccessful.

NEW ZEALAND

Section 92H of the Human Rights Act 1993 gives the Commission the right to appear and be heard in proceedings relating to matters that are or have been before the Human Rights Review Tribunal (HRRT) provided the HRC considers this would facilitate the performance of its functions under Section 5(2)(a) to advocate for human rights and to promote and protect, by education and publicity, respect for, and observance of, human rights. This is a limited right, since the HRRT has the power to receive complaints only about unlawful discrimination.

Section 5(2)(j) also gives the Commission the right to apply to a court or tribunal to:

- Be appointed as intervener; or
- Be counsel assisting the court; or
- Take part in proceedings before the court or tribunal in another way permitted by its rules or regulations

if, in the Commission's opinion, taking part in the proceedings in that way will facilitate the performance of any of its functions under Section 5(2)(a).

Section 6 further gives the Commission the right to institute proceedings for a declaratory judgment or order from the High Court provided the Commission considers such proceedings would facilitate the performance of its functions under Section 5(2)(a).

Section 92B gives the Commission the right to institute proceedings in the HRRT about a complaint of a breach of the Human Rights Act (unlawful discrimination) provided:

a) The complainant has not brought such proceedings,
b) The complainant agrees to the Commission bringing the proceedings, and
c) The Commission considers the proceedings would facilitate the performance of its functions under Section 5(2)(a).

The proceedings are brought on behalf of the Commission by the Director of Human Rights Proceedings.

If an inquiry under Section 5(2)(h) [a general inquiry into an infringement of human rights] discloses what the Commission considers to be a breach of the Human Rights Act, Section 92E gives the Commission the right to institute proceedings in the HRRT provided the Commission considers such proceedings would facilitate the performance of its functions under Section 5(2)(a).

Finally, Section 97 gives the Commission the right to institute proceedings in the HRRT to seek a declaration that an act, omission, practice, requirement, or condition that would otherwise be unlawful [discrimination] is not unlawful because it is either:

a) A genuine occupational qualification or
b) A genuine justification

provided the Commission considers such proceedings would facilitate the performance of its functions under Section 5(2)(a).

NEPAL

Under Section 9(2)(d) the Commission may inquire into any issue under judicial consideration involving the violation of human rights, with the permission of the court.

AUSTRALIA

Section 46PV (1) empowers a "special-purpose Commissioner" to assist the Federal Court and Federal Magistrates Court as *amicus curiae* in the following proceedings:

> "a) proceedings in which the special-purpose Commissioner thinks that the orders sought, or likely to be sought, may affect to a significant extent the human rights of persons who are not parties to the proceedings;
> b) proceedings that, in the opinion of the special-purpose Commissioner, have significant implications for the administration of the relevant Act or Acts;
> c) proceedings that involve special circumstances that satisfy the special-purpose Commissioner that it would be in the public interest for the special-purpose Commissioner to assist the court concerned as *amicus curiae*."

Section 46PV (2) further states "[t]he function may only be exercised with the leave of the court concerned".

Under Section 46PP of the Act the HREOC can apply to the Courts to grant an interim injunction to maintain: (a) the status quo, as it existed immediately before the complaint was lodged; or (b) the rights of any complainant, respondent or affected person. The Commission cannot however, by this means obtain payment of damages, as indicated in Section 46PP(5) below:

> "5) The court concerned cannot, as a condition of granting the interim injunction, require a person to give an undertaking as to damages."

FIJI

The Commission can institute court proceedings, in relation to a complaint or investigation on the Commission's own initiative, against the person against whom a complaint is made or to whom the investigation relates.

Section 36(2) provides that the "Proceedings Commissioner may, under subsection (1), bring proceedings on behalf of a class of persons if the Commissioner considers that a person . . . has engaged in unfair discrimination which affects that class or has contravened the Bill of Rights in relation to that class".

The Commissioner involved with Court proceedings (the Proceedings Commissioner) may, with the leave of the Court, "appear and be heard in relation to any proceedings . . . in which human rights are an issue". (Section 37(1).)

Section 40(2) states that the Commission may request an interim court order "in the interests of justice . . . to preserve the position of the parties pending the result of the investigation and the final determination of any proceedings resulting from the investigation".

INDONESIA

In Article 89(3)(h) the Commission is authorised, with the approval of the Court, to: "provide input into particular cases currently undergoing judicial process if the case involves violation of human rights of public issue and court investigation, and the input of the National Commission on Human Rights shall be made known to the parties by the judge".

Through its mediation role the Commission can also recommend, under Article 89(4)(c), that the parties resolve their dispute through the courts.

MALAYSIA

Section 13(2) stipulates that the Commission shall have the power (related to an inquiry involving the infringement of human rights under section 12) "to refer the matter, where appropriate, to the relevant authority or person with the necessary recommendations".

It does not, however, expressly state anywhere in the Act that the Commission can make recommendations to the Courts or intervene in court matters related to human rights.

MONGOLIA

The Commission may, under Article 17.1.1, "submit claims to the Courts with regard to issues of violations of human rights and freedoms by business entities, organisations, officials or individual persons to participate in person or through a representative in judicial proceedings in accordance with procedure established by the law".

The Commission may also issue recommendations and demands with respect to the violation of human rights under Article 19. If these "recommendations" or "demands" are not followed by the relevant party the Commission, under Article 19(5), "may approach the Court, according to the procedure established by law, with regard to the business entities, organisations or officials which have refused to undertake relevant measures as provided under his/her demands and/or recommendations".

PHILIPPINES

There are no provisions in Executive Order 163 (1987) that specifically provide for intervention in court proceedings.

REPUBLIC OF KOREA

In relation to a trial "which significantly affects the protection and promotion of human rights" Article 28 empowers the Commission, either after being requested by the court or on its own initiative, to "present its opinions on *de jure* matters to the competent division of the court or the Constitutional Court". With respect to a trial involving a case investigated or handled by the Commission under the NHRC Act, the Commission may not only present its opinions on *de jure* matters but also on *de facto* ones.

THAILAND

According to Section 22 of the NHRC Act the Commission cannot propose remedial measures under the Act related to matters "being litigated in the Court or that upon which the Court has already given final order or judgement".

The Power to Provide or Recommend Compensation for Human Rights Violations[69]

	Australia	Fiji	India	Indonesia	Malaysia	Mongolia	Nepal	New Zeeland	Philippines	Republic of Korea	Sri Lanka	Thailand
Power to provide* or recommend** compensation and/or seek it through a court or specialist tribunal***	◆ **	◆ ***	◆ **			◆	◆ *	◆ ***	◆ **	◆ *	◆ *	◆

INDIA

Although the Act does not specifically state that the Commission can grant compensation to victims of human rights violations, it does, under Section 18, state that it can recommend "immediate interim relief", which in practice has frequently been equated with the payment of interim compensation. Section 18, titled "Steps after inquiry", empowers the Commission to:

> "1) where the inquiry discloses, [sic] the commission of violation of human rights or negligence in the prevention of violation of human rights by a public servant, it may recommend to the concerned Government or authority the initiation of proceedings for prosecution or such other action as the Commission may deem fit against the concerned person or persons;
> 2) approach the Supreme Court or the High Court concerned for such directions, orders or writs as that Court may deem necessary;
> 3) recommend to the concerned Government or authority for the grant of **such immediate interim relief** to the victim or the members of his family as the Commission may consider necessary;" (emphasis added).

In a recent development (June 2004) the Commission has even recommended the payment of interim compensation for violations by the armed forces. In doing so the Commission first invoked Section 18.3 and

---

69 If not otherwise specified, the Sections and Articles referred to in this part are provisions in the legislation establishing the NHRI in question.

then, based on a subsequent response from the Ministry of Home Affairs, which held that violations involving the armed forces were not subject to Section 18.3 and that these violation were dealt with under Section 19,[70] reevaluated the case and stated that Section 19 would in any case support a recommendation for compensation:

> "The Commission emphasized that the power under section 19(1)(b) of the Act is wide in its amplitude, and, would include without any doubt, the power, to recommend, including grant of 'interim relief' to the victims or the members of their family as the Commission may consider appropriate in the nature of 'immediate interim relief' envisaged under section 18(3) of the Act."[71]

SRI LANKA

Under Section 16(6) the Commission can make a decision to provide compensation to fulfill a settlement made exercising its conciliation powers.

> "16 (6) Where a matter is referred to for [sic] conciliation or mediation under this section and a settlement is arrived at, the Commission shall make such directions (**including direction as to the payment of compensation**) as may be necessary to give effect to such settlement." (emphasis added)

NEW ZEALAND

The Commission's role in relation to compensation is limited to the resolution of disputes about breaches [unlawful discrimination] of the Human Rights Act 1993. This dispute resolution service is free, private and confidential to those involved and does not require parties to have legal representation.

Resolution of a dispute may be achieved by:

- An apology

---

[70] Section 19(1) of the Protection of Human Rights Act, 1993, states:
"Procedure with respect to armed forces
(1) Notwithstanding anything contained in this Act, while dealing with complaints of violation of human rights by members of the armed forces, the Commission shall adopt the following procedure, namely :
(a) it may, either on its own motion or on receipt of a petition, seek a report from the Central Government; (b) after the receipt of the report, it may, either not proceed with the complaint or, as the case may be, make its recommendations to that Government"

[71] *Human Rights Violations by the Armed Forces; Commission can recommend interim compensation*, National Human Rights Commission, India, <nhrc.nic.in/disparchive.asp?fno=771>, visited on 18 August 2004.

- An assurance not to discriminate in the future
- Undertaking an education or training programme
- Provision of a reference
- Compensation
- Anything the parties agree will resolve the dispute.

If the dispute cannot be resolved, the complainant may issue proceedings before the Human Rights Review Tribunal. In limited circumstances, the Commission, through the Director of Human Rights Proceedings, is able to provide assistance to the complainant to bring such proceedings.

NEPAL

Section 13(2) empowers the Commission, with respect to complaints investigated under the Act, to provide victims of human right violations "**with necessary compensation**". (emphasis added.)

REPUBLIC OF KOREA

If both parties to a dispute/complaint willingly submit to the conciliation process provided for in the Act, and do not reach a compromise with respect to the issue in question, the Commission may decide to provide compensation for damage, which will have the same effect as a settlement at court if the parties concerned do not object within two weeks of being served with the decision.

> "Article 42 (Conciliation)
> (4) The decision in lieu of conciliation may include any of the following:
> 1. Stoppage of an act of violating human rights subject to the investigation;
> 2. **Restitution, compensation for damage o**r other necessary remedies; or
> 3. Measures necessary for the prevention of recurrence of the same or similar act of violating human rights (emphasis added).
>
> Article 43 (Effect of Conciliation)
> The conciliation under the provision of Article 42 (2) and the decision in lieu of conciliation in case of no objections under the provision of Article 42 (6) shall have the same effect as a settlement at court."

PHILIPPINES

Under Section 3(06) the Commission can "[r]ecommend to the Congress effective measures to promote human rights and to provide **for compensation to victims** of violations of human rights, or their families . . ." (emphasis added).

CHAPTER 4

AUSTRALIA

According to Section 29, upon the conclusion of an inquiry into a human rights violation, the Commission may make a report that includes recommending "**the payment of compensation** to, or in respect of, a person who has suffered loss or damage as a result of the act or practice" (emphasis added).

Even if the Commission terminates a complaint the respondent may still receive compensation. If a complaint to the Commission is terminated by the Commission, the courts, under Division 2 Section 46PO, may accept an application which they believe involves unlawful discrimination, and make a number of orders pertaining to the case, including "an order requiring a respondent to pay to an applicant damages by way of compensation for any loss or damage suffered because of the conduct of the respondent".

As already noted above there are other provisions in the legislation to which the Commission may resort if it considers a recommendation of compensation is appropriate. (Cf the "incidentals" power referred to in endnote *** of Table A).

FIJI

Under Court proceedings initiated by the Proceedings Commissioner (the Commissioner designated to handle court related matters), complainants may seek a number of different remedies, including damages, as a result of being subject to unfair discrimination or a contravention of the Bill of Rights.

Further elaboration is provided in Section 39(2), which states:
"Subject to subsection (3), the Commission must pay any damages recovered by the Proceedings Commissioner under this section to the complainant or the aggrieved person on whose behalf the proceedings were brought."

MONGOLIA

Section 19.2 empowers Commissioners to write or deliver demands which could theoretically include a recommendation/demand for payment of compensation:

> "19.2. Commissioners shall write and deliver demands to relevant organisations in order to restore human rights and freedoms and eliminate the violations if he/she has considered that business entity, organisation or official has violated human rights and freedoms."

THAILAND

There are no provisions in the NHRC Act that expressly state that the Commission can provide/recommend compensation. However, Section 28 of the Act empowers the Commission to prepare and submit a report (to a person or agency involved in a human rights violation) that may propose remedial measures which could include the payment of compensation. Section 28 states:

> "If the Commission is . . . of the opinion that there is a commission or omission of acts which violate human rights, the Commission shall prepare a report of the examination which shall specify details of the circumstances of human rights violation, reasons for such opinion and remedial measures for solving human rights violation which shall clearly set forth the legal duties and methods of performance of a person or agency, including the period for implementation of such measures."

4.4. RELATIONS WITH OTHER INSTITUTIONS:

Because NHRIs have a very broad mandate they will frequently come into contact with other institutions, particularly those responsible for "good governance and accountability". In federal systems, such as those in Australia and India, they may also have important relationships with state or provincial human rights, equal opportunity or non discrimination agencies. Obviously these relationships are important and the leadership of all NHRIs needs not only to establish and maintain appropriate contacts but also, in some cases, to develop protocols or in-house regulations to assist their staff in dealing with these bodies and avoid uncertainties or delays for members of the public seeking assistance.

In most countries the agency with which there will most frequently be contacts in this context is the Ombudsman – and it is common in countries in the Asia-Pacific region to have both an Ombudsman and a national human rights commission.

The institution of the Ombudsman has now been extended to many areas of both the public and private sectors (from banking to insurance and telecommunications to poker machines). However, we are here concerned primarily with the "classical Ombudsman", who has a mandate to ensure propriety and legality in public administration and investigate bureaucratic omission, malfeasance and neglect.

In a number of countries the jurisdictional boundary between the Ombudsman and NHRIs is becoming blurred. However this is not the case in the Asia-Pacific region where the traditional Ombudsman is still an institution: headed by a single individual; concerned with public administration[72] – not the private sector; and generally restricted to applying domestic law in determining the legality and fairness of administrative conduct.[73] NHRIs, by comparison, are multiple member institutions which

---

[72] The judiciary and the legislature are usually excluded from the Ombudsman's jurisdiction – but there are several countries where the Ombudsman does have jurisdiction to monitor the judiciary.

[73] Originally the Ombudsman was appointed by and accountable to the parliament. However in several countries the Ombudsman is appointed by the executive – sometimes on the recommendation of the parliament. For a comprehensive account of the evolution of various types of Ombudsman and human rights institutions, see L.C. Reif, "Building Democratic Institutions: The Role of National Human Rights Institutions in Good Governance and Human Rights Protection", 13 *Harvard Human Rights Journal* (Spring, 2000).

are generally concerned to promote and protect a wide range of human rights in both the public and private sectors and whose mandate incorporates both national law and international human rights law.

In a number of cases human rights violations in the public sector will fall within the jurisdiction of both the Ombudsman and the NHRI (for example, a case involving sex discrimination or sexual harassment in a government department). In practice, as long as an appropriate understanding is reached between the two institutions, this overlapping jurisdiction should not cause any difficulty. The most effective way to avoid confusion, given that there will always be some overlapping jurisdiction, is simply to accord both NHRIs and Ombudsmen the power to refer matters, where necessary, to more appropriate agencies where these exist.

CHAPTER 5: COOPERATION BETWEEN NHRIS, THE INTERNATIONAL TREATY BODIES, THE U.N. COMMISSION ON HUMAN RIGHTS AND OTHER CHARTER-BASED MECHANISMS

> "But the human rights treaty bodies, too, need to be much more effective and more responsive to violations of the rights that they are mandated to uphold. The treaty body system remains little known; is compromised by the failure of many States to report on time if at all, as well as the duplication of reporting requirements; and is weakened further by poor implementation of recommendations. Harmonized guidelines on reporting to all treaty bodies should be finalized and implemented so that these bodies can function as a unified system."[74]

5.1. THE INTERNATIONAL TREATY BODIES:

There is increasingly close cooperation between NHRIs and the international Treaty Bodies (TBs) established to monitor the most important international human rights treaties referred to in Chapter II. The experts on the various Treaty Bodies rely increasingly on reports from NHRIs[75] and generally welcome their active participation – both in providing the TBs with information on the human rights situation in their respective countries and in following up and monitoring the implementation of TB reports.

NHRIs in the Asia-Pacific region are also increasingly active in providing the public with information on the work of the TBs and, in the limited number of cases where this is possible, assisting individuals in submitting complaints to the relevant TBs.[76] However, the recent statement of the U.N. Secretary-General quoted above remains accurate – and NHRIs

---

[74] In larger freedom: towards development, security and human rights for all. Report of the U.N. Secretary-General, 21 March 2005. Op.cit., para. 147 at p. 38.

[75] The establishment of a Special Advisor on NHRIs by the U.N.'s First High Commissioner for Human Rights, in 1995, facilitated increased contacts during international meetings between NHRI representatives and experts from the TBs. By the year 2000, consultations between the TBs and NHRI representatives had become a regular practice for most of the Special Rapporteurs, Working Groups and independent experts established by the Commission. See e.g. Doc. A/56/244(2001), paras. 53–55.

[76] The reality is that, for many reasons, the number of individuals able to lodge a complaint with the TBs will continue to be a tiny fraction (much less than 1%) of those who lodge complaints with NHRIs.

need to be candid in warning potential complainants of the serious limitations and extended delays which still characterise the TB procedures.

We included interaction with the TBs as an important element in the Paris Principles because NHRIs are, in essence, implementing agents for the international human rights standards. While several of the TBs were slow to recognise this, others have not only welcomed interaction with NHRIs but have also adopted decisions designed to recognise their role, facilitate their participation and encourage their contributions.

Appendices III, IV and V set out the considered views (referred to as "General Comments" or "General Recommendations") of three of the TBs: The Committee on the Elimination of all Forms of Racial Discrimination; the Committee on Economic, Social and Cultural Rights and the Committee on the Rights of the Child.[77] It is interesting to note the evolution in the response of the TBs. The most recent comment, General Comment No. 2 by the Committee on the Rights of the Child, is by far the most detailed.

There is no prescribed or ideal format for the manner in which NHRIs provide information to the Treaty Bodies.[78] States Parties are themselves increasingly incorporating in their reports information on the activities of their NHRIs and in some cases are requesting NHRIs to contribute directly to the drafting process. However, it is essential that national human rights institutions do not allow their independence to be compromised in this process and, in order to ensure that the TBs receive an accurate account of their concerns, some NHRIs choose to submit their own reports to the TBs.[79] Where NHRIs have conducted national inquiries or major projects on issues

[77] These are not the only relevant General Comments or General Recommendations by the Treaty Bodies. For example, the Committee on the Elimination of all Forms of Racial Discrimination adopted a General Recommendation (No. 28) in 2002 on the "Follow-up on the World Conference Against Racism, Racial Discrimination, Xenophobia and Related Intolerance" – recommending that NHRIs should assist states in relation to their reporting obligations.

[78] It is important to remember that the treaties impose the reporting obligation on the States Parties themselves. Several governments have attempted to persuade their NHRIs to prepare the entire report. This is not appropriate, – nor should NHRIs be the principal presenter of the report to the TBs; they can, however, certainly assist in appropriate ways in both the preparation and presentation. Some TBs have expressed specific views on this subject; see, for example, para. 21 of the CRC's General Comment No. 2 – Appendix V.

[79] For a general consideration of this and related issues see "Performance and Legitimacy: National Human Rights Institutions", International Council on Human Rights Policy, Versoix, Switzerland, 2000.

within the mandates of the respective TBs, governments should ensure that this information is conveyed to the TBs in question; if they do not, NHRIs should themselves ensure that the TBs receive it.

Given the very limited accountability which the TBs are able to impose on States Parties,[80] NHRIs can play an important role in ensuring that the TBs' concluding observations and recommendations are made known to the general public and appropriately responded to by governments. This is another important area in which NHRIs increasingly work in consultation with NGOs. While some NGOs were initially skeptical of the role which NHRIs could play in this regard, they now generally accept that NHRIs have the responsibility and the resources to assist in ensuring that Treaty Body recommendations are followed up.[81]

5.2. SPECIAL PROCEDURES:

The Commission on Human Rights has established several types of "Special Procedures" to assist it in discharging its mandate. These include: Special Rapporteurs, Special Representatives, and Working Groups. In the last decade there has been a substantial increase in the number of these mechanisms and there are currently 43 "Procedures" in existence. The Special Rapporteurs, in particular, are working increasingly closely with NHRIs.[82] It is indicative of the increasing cooperation between national and

---

80 After their initial report, States Parties to the various Human Rights Treaties and Conventions are only required to report every four or five years (depending on the requirements stipulated in each Convention) – and the TBs have no "enforcement mechanisms".

81 "NHRIs should as far as possible attend and participate in international meetings and fora including the treaty monitoring bodies and UN political bodies concerned with human rights. When doing so, they should represent themselves as independent NHRIs, rather than representing their government."
Amnesty International's "Recommendations on national human rights institutions", extract from para 3.4, Participation in international human rights law fora. For the full text see Appendix II.

87 "Although the mandates given to special procedure mechanisms vary, they usually are to examine, monitor, advise, and publicly report on human rights situations in specific countries or territories, known as country mandates, or on major phenomena of human rights violations worldwide, known as thematic mandates. Various activities can be undertaken by special procedures, including

international mechanisms that several of the recently appointed Special Rapporteurs or Working Group members have been the chairpersons or executive directors of NHRIs (several experienced individuals from NHRIs also serve on various Treaty Bodies).

5.3. THE UNITED NATIONS COMMISSION ON HUMAN RIGHTS (CHR):

Since 1996 NHRIs have been permitted to address the Commission, in their own right – but only under the agenda item specifically related to NHRIs. Initially, from 1996–1997, NHRIs were only permitted to participate from the seat of their own national Government delegation. However, following submissions drawn up by the High Commissioner's Special Advisor and representations by the HC to the Chair of CHR, in 1998 NHRIs were allocated a separate section in the CHR conference room designated "National Institutions".[83] In recent years, as CHR proceedings have

---

conducting studies, providing advice on technical cooperation, responding to individual complaints, and engaging in general promotional activities.

In carrying out their mandates, special rapporteurs and other mandate-holders undertake country visits (sometimes referred to as fact-finding missions) and report back to the Commission on Human Rights. These missions take place at the request of the relevant special procedure or at the invitation of the country concerned. Many countries have extended standing invitations to all thematic special procedures of the Commission.

The activities which can be undertaken, along with the scope and length of the mandate of each special procedure, are set out in the Commission on Human Rights resolutions on the specific mandate. All special procedures are required to report on their activities to the annual session of the Commission on Human Rights, which takes place in March-April each year."

The countries which have Special Rapporteurs, Special Representatives or other experts assigned are: Belarus, Burundi, Cambodia, Cuba, Democratic People's Republic of Korea, Democratic Republic of the Congo, Haiti, Liberia, Myanmar, Palestinian territories occupied since 1967, Somalia, Sudan, and Uzbekistan.

The current working groups are the "Working Group on people of African descent"; the "Working Group on Arbitrary Detention"; and the "Working Group on Enforced or Involuntary Disappearances",

Reference <www.ohchr.org> website visited on 7 November 2005.

For a full list of the Special Rapporteurs handling Thematic mandates see Appendix IX.

[83] See Doc. E/CN.4/1998/47, paras. 6–9; and CHR Res. 1998/55 of 17 April 1998 (paras. 11–13). Also CHR Res. 1999/72 of 29 April 1999 (paras. 14–15) stipulating

deteriorated, there has been pressure to further reduce the very limited time originally allocated to NHRIs to address the CHR. In spite of the best efforts of several supportive governments this pressure has unfortunately been successful. However, (should the CHR continue in its present form) it is likely that from 2006 the range of agenda items in which NHRIs can participate will be broadened.[84]

that the practice of permitting NHRIs to address the Commission behind the nameplate "National Institutions" is continued.

[84] At its 61st Session, in 2005, the Commission on Human Rights decided to consider extending the participation of NHRIs in CHR deliberations (CHR Res.2005/74).

CHAPTER 6: REGIONAL COOPERATION

6.1. BACKGROUND:

The absence of a formal human rights mechanism in the Asia-Pacific region[85] was one of the factors motivating practitioners in their early

[85] There have been numerous initiatives (by academics, lawyers, MPs and NGOs) to establish human rights charters or instruments of various kinds in Asia or in the Asia-Pacific region. Several of these have involved proposals which detracted from, or were inconsistent with, the major international human rights instruments. Perhaps the most troubling of these is a "Draft Charter" prepared by Asian MPs – which involves very significant derogations from the standards embodied in the major international human rights treaties. (For this reason the initiative has been vigorously opposed by the author and others.)

For the past 12 years, since 1993, there have been discussions concerning a proposal to establish an "ASEAN Human Rights Mechanism" – but these are proceeding very slowly and, in their latest version, envisage as an initial step the creation of an "ASEAN Commission for the Promotion and Protection of the Rights of Women and Children". For a detailed account of the evolution of this initiative see V. Muntarbhorn, "Roadmap for an ASEAN Human Rights Mechanism", 1 *Thailand Human Rights Journal* (2003). (In the author's view there are significant dangers in proposing a regional body which would focus only on two specific groups – important as they are – for similar reasons to those which motivated our insistence on the need for NHRIs to have a broad mandate, in Paris in 1991.)

In 1998 over 200 NGOs from Asian countries formulated the "Asian Human Rights Charter" which reflected, inter alia, the growing recognition by NGOs of the importance of NHRIs. This Charter stipulated (in Section 15.4c) that:

"All states should establish human rights commissions and specialised institutions for the protection of rights, particularly of vulnerable members of society. They can provide easy, friendly and inexpensive access to justice for victims of human rights violations. These bodies supplement the role of the judiciary. They enjoy special advantages: they can help establish standards for the implementation of human rights norms; they can disseminate information about human rights; they can investigate allegations of violations of rights; they can promote conciliation and mediation; and they can seek to enforce human rights through administrative or judicial means. They can act proactively. (Asian Human Rights Commission and Asian Legal Resource Centre, *Our Common Humanity – Asian Human Rights Charter*. (Hong Kong, AHRC and ALRC, 1998, p. 27)

There have also been other proposals for sub-regional human rights charters or instruments in West Asia and South Asia. In the Pacific, the Pacific Islands' Forum recently received a report from a "Group of Eminent Persons" which supported the development of NHRIs in the Pacific. Further consideration is being given to a initiatives to strengthen existing national human rights institutions and to assist in establishing them in countries which did not have them. However, we recognised the necessity to have certain minimum standards – and the Paris Principles were an attempt to establish basic benchmarks which governments, including those in the Asia-Pacific region, could be expected to observe – if they wished their institutions to be considered "legitimate".

During the late '80s and early '90s there were significant contacts between the three NHRIs which did exist in the region – but these were on an exclusively bi-lateral basis. In 1989–90[86] the heads of NHRIs from Australia, New Zealand and the Philippines had discussed the formation of a regional organisation of NHRIs – but had decided that such an organisation could not be credible until at least five countries in the region had established such institutions – including, preferably, at least one of the most populous democracies, India or Indonesia.[87] In fact, the adoption of the Paris Principles in 1991, the lead-up to the World Conference in 1993 and several other factors contributed to the establishment of NHRIs in both India and Indonesia in 1993.

Following the World Conference, in early 1994, the Australian Human Rights and Equal Opportunity Commission (HREOC) developed a detailed proposal on the structure and objectives of an "Asia Pacific Conference" of NHRIs.[88] Throughout 1994 and 1995 there were further discussions – with

---

proposal to establish a regional commission – in view of the very small populations in a number of the Pacific Island states, where NHRIs may not be viable.

[86] The one occasion on which we were all able to get together was at the U.N. sponsored Asia-Pacific Workshop on Human Rights in Manila in May 1990. During this meeting we held a number of informal discussions over three days. The other meetings took place during bi-lateral visits to Australia of the Chairpersons of the Philippines and New Zealand Commissions.

[87] At this stage Indonesia was clearly an "emerging" democracy.

[88] "Objectives

The objectives of the Asia-Pacific Conference would be to examine human rights issues of mutual concern to the national commissions and to assist with the implementation of the Vienna Declaration and Program of Action in the Asia-Pacific region. The objectives could be achieved through the following types of activities:

providing mutual assistance – through training, community education programs, information campaigns, and other co-operative activities;

organising staff exchanges between national commissions;

providing a regular forum for discussion of human rights issues of concern to the region and matters affecting national institutions more generally;

the Indian Commission in particular – which was prepared to support the creation of a regional forum of NHRIs – provided that it functioned as a loose coalition and did not purport to act as a spokesperson for its members. The Indonesian Commission was also generally supportive of the idea. The discussions included consideration of a small secretariat and, given the limited resources available, HREOC tentatively agreed to provide this as an initial step.[89]

During this period, the United Nations, working through the Office of the High Commissioner for Human Rights, had established an "Asia-Pacific Human Rights Framework" which was formally adopted at a regional meeting in 1998 in Teheran. This "Framework" built on an earlier agreement, reached at a U.N. sponsored conference in Jakarta in 1993, that work on human rights in the Asia-Pacific region should be based on a "step-by-step" approach. Governments agreed that within this framework there should be four essential elements: national human rights action plans; national human rights education; national human rights institutions; and realisation of economic, social and cultural rights and the right to development. The most significant results so far have been achieved in the establishment and strengthening of NHRIs.

---

making proposals for the further deployment of regional co-operation, for example, the establishment of an inter-governmental body or a regional charter of human rights.

Structure

The Asia-Pacific Conference should have a small, established secretariat headed by a Secretary-General with 3-5 appropriately qualified officers drawn from countries with established national commissions."

These two sections are extracts from: "Human Rights: Regional Arrangements in the Asia-Pacific region: Non-Paper" (unpublished). This paper was used as the basis for discussions with NHRIs during 1994. While several governments in the region were aware of our discussions, the subject was a sensitive one – particularly in India and Indonesia – and the "non-paper" initially had a limited circulation.

[89] In fact, when the Asia-Pacific Forum was established, HREOC hosted the secretariat for over five years, from 1996 to early 2002, when the APF was established as a fully independent organisation. The burden of initially resourcing the secretariat was considerable – at a time when the Australian Commission's resources were being drastically reduced by a hostile government.

6.2. THE ASIA-PACIFIC FORUM OF NATIONAL HUMAN RIGHTS INSTITUTIONS:

The First Asia-Pacific regional workshop of national human rights institutions was held in Darwin, Australia in July 1996.[90] At this meeting, representatives of national human rights commissions from Australia, India, Indonesia and New Zealand agreed to the establishment of the Asia-Pacific Forum of National Human Rights Institutions (APF).[91] The Philippines Human Rights Commission had also been invited but was unable to attend.

Membership of the APF is open to all NHRIs in the region that comply with the normative standards prescribed in the Paris Principles. The Forum regularly receives applications from new NHRIs, which are required to supply detailed information concerning their legislative mandate and any other relevant matters required by the current APF membership.

The objectives of the Forum, as set out in its charter (the "*Larrakia Declaration*") are to:

- respond where possible with personnel and other support to requests from governments in the region for assistance in the establishment and development of national institutions;
- expand mutual support, co-operation and joint activity among member commissions through:
    - information exchanges
    - training and development for commission members and staff
    - development of joint positions on issues of common concern
    - sharing expertise
    - periodical regional meetings
    - specialist regional seminars on common themes and needs
- respond promptly and effectively to requests from other national institutions to investigate violations of the human rights of their nationals present in a country that has a national institution;
- welcome as participants in the Forum other independent national institutions which conform with the Paris Principles;

---

[90] The credit for finally establishing the Forum must go to my colleague and successor as Federal Human Rights Commissioner, Chris Sidoti, and his staff – particularly Kieren Fitzpatrick, the current director of the Forum.

[91] The meeting was also attended by observers from governments and non-government organisations throughout the region.

- encourage governments and human rights non government organisations to participate in Forum meetings as observers.

The APF is the most credible and effective regional organisation of NHRIs currently in existence and is undertaking a number of important initiatives to support both its full members and associate members – in line with the objectives in its charter. As of 1 August 2005 there were 12 Full Members: the NHRIs of Australia, Fiji, India, Indonesia, Malaysia, Mongolia, Nepal, New Zealand, Philippines, Republic of Korea, Sri Lanka, and Thailand. At this date there were also three Associate Members; the NHRIs of Afghanistan, Jordan and Palestine.[92] There were also pending applications to join the APF (as either associate members or candidate members) from NHRIs in Timor Leste and Qatar.

Among the most important reasons for the APF's credibility is the fact that its rules require NHRIs to comply with the minimum standards prescribed in the Paris Principles before they can be admitted to full membership. In addition, the Constitution contains specific provisions providing for the expulsion of NHRIs which have been admitted if they fail to continue to comply with the Paris Principles.[93] The APF Constitution also

---

[92] The APF Constitution "provides for three categories of membership: **Full Members** – are national human right institutions that fully comply with the Paris Principles. Full Members are the key decision-makers of the APF . . . **Candidate Members** – are institutions which currently do not completely comply with the Paris Principles but could do so within a reasonable period of time. Admission as a Candidate Member requires a commitment from the applicant institution that active steps will be taken to meet the Paris Principles. A Candidate Member can become a Full Member of the APF once it complies with the Paris Principles . . . **Associate Members** – are institutions which currently do not comply with the Paris Principles and are unlikely to do so within a reasonable period. Associate Member institutions must, however, possess a broad human rights mandate and only one institution will be admitted per Member State of the United Nations . . ." www.asiapacificforum.net/about/membership/categories.html, visited on 30 August 2005.

[93] The relevant provisions of the APF Constitution are:

"*11.4 Review of compliance by full members with the Paris Principles*

(a) Occasion for review

(1) The Forum councillors may, on their own motion and at any time, decide to review the compliance of a full member with the Paris Principles.

(2) A full member must notify the Forum if there has been any change to the constitutional and/or legislative base or administration of the institution which

stipulates that "candidate members" can be expelled from the Forum for failure to continue taking active steps to comply with the Paris Principles.[94]

One of the APF's most important initiatives has been to establish an Advisory Council of Jurists (ACJ) comprising one eminent lawyer nominated by each of the APF's full members. The ACJ prepares opinions and provides advice on the development of human rights-related law and practices. Its advices to date have included reports on: the death penalty; child pornography on the internet; trafficking in women and children; questions related to the rule of law and the impact of terrorism; and torture.
The range and frequency of the APF's activities to assist its members has increased each year and in 2005 included: regional workshops in several countries on economic, social and cultural rights, IDPs, and trafficking; training in investigation techniques and dealing with the media; assistance for member institutions in computerised complaints handling; and several needs assessment missions. The APF secretariat also arranged staff

---

materially impacts upon its compliance with, or ability to comply with, the Paris Principles.
(b) Review
(1) Following a decision to review under rule 11.4(a)(1) or receipt of a notification under rule 11.4(a)(2), the Forum councillors must meet to consider whether the institution complies with the Paris Principles.
(2) If the Forum councillors decide that the institution does not so comply, they may, by resolution, expel a member under rule 12.2."

[94] "*11.5 Review of commitment by candidate members to comply with the Paris Principles*
(a) Occasion for review
(1) The Forum councillors may, on their own motion and at any time, decide to review the commitment of a candidate member to take active steps to comply with the Paris Principles within a reasonable period.
(2) A candidate member must notify the Forum if there has been any change to the constitutional and/or legislative base or administration of the institution which materially impacts upon its commitment or ability to take those active steps to comply with the Paris Principles within a reasonable period.
(b) Review
(1) Following a decision to review under rule 11.5(a)(1) or receipt of a notification under rule 11.5(a)(2), the Forum councillors must meet to consider whether the institution is taking active steps to comply with the Paris Principles.
(2) If the Forum councillors decide that the institution is not taking those active steps, they may, by resolution, expel a member under rule 12.2."

exchanges between member institutions and co-sponsored[95] a comprehensive two-week regional training programme in human rights for staff from 14 Asia-Pacific NHRIs.

[95] This course, which is now an annual event, is co-sponsored with the Raoul Wallenberg Institute.

CHAPTER 7: CHALLENGES AND STRATEGIES

> "The roles of NHRIs will need to evolve as the nature of human rights challenges evolves. New problems will emerge and old challenges will require fresh approaches."[96]

> "I have become increasingly convinced of the necessity to focus on preventive strategies. This has convinced me of the importance of creating strong, independent national human rights institutions to provide accessible remedies, particularly for those who are most vulnerable and disadvantaged."[97]

The greatest challenge for NHRIs is to contribute to creating a culture of human rights – of tolerance, non-discrimination and respect for individual difference. This certainly requires a capacity to handle individual complaints of violations and provide redress where rights are violated. But beyond remedial action it necessitates strategies which are positive, proactive and preventive.

This challenge relates to all human rights – but in the Asia-Pacific region it is perhaps most problematic in the area of economic, social and cultural rights. Widespread poverty, inequality and disparate legal systems, which have all, in different ways, contributed to entrenching systemic discrimination, constitute major hurdles. Continuing conflicts in several countries in the region also present formidable problems.

7.1. ECONOMIC, SOCIAL AND CULTURAL RIGHTS:

> "National institutions have a potentially crucial role to play in promoting and ensuring the indivisibility and interdependence of all human rights. Unfortunately this role has too often not been accorded to the institution or has been neglected or given a low priority by it. It is therefore essential that full attention be given to economic, social and cultural rights in all of the relevant activities of these institutions."[98]

---

[96] National Human Rights Institutions: Best Practice. Commonwealth Secretariat, London 2001 p. 39.

[97] Mary Robinson, U.N. High Commissioner for Human Rights in the First Annual Dag Hammarskjöld lecture, "Human Rights: Challenges for the 21st Century", 1 October 1998.

[98] General Comment No. 10 of the Committee on Economic, Social and Cultural Rights. For the full text see Appendix III. The Committee formulates and adopts general comments to provide guidance on the interpretation and application of the provisions of the Covenant. These general comments, together with those adopted

Beyond exhorting governments to give NHRIs "as broad a mandate as possible" the Paris Principles make no specific reference to economic, social and cultural rights – and while most governments in the region have ratified the Convention on Economic, Social and Cultural Rights, not all those that have established NHRIs have opted to accord them jurisdiction in relation to these rights. (See Table B and associated notes and Table C.)

Nevertheless, several national institutions have done a great deal of significant work in promoting and protecting economic, social and cultural rights. They include both Commissions which have a mandate that specifically incorporates these rights, such as those in India and Mongolia, and Commissions that do not. The Indian Commission has, for example, conducted inquiries and other monitoring activities to combat child labour and, in a number of cases, has investigated violations of the rights to adequate nutrition, to health, to housing and to free education.

The Mongolian Commission recently took to the Mongolian Supreme Court a case involving the economic and social rights of many thousands of rural and nomadic citizens who had "migrated" to the outskirts of the capital, Ulaanbaatar, and several provincial capitals in search of employment and a better life for their families.[99] The city councils concerned attempted to charge these people substantial "resettlement fees" and refused to provide them with basic services. Following an extensive investigation,[100] the Commission succeeded in an application on their behalf to have the Supreme

---

by other United Nations Human Rights Treaty Bodies, are compiled in U.N. Doc. HRI/GEN/1/Rev.6.

[99] The Mongolian Constitution incorporates provisions on the right to freedom of movement and residence which reflect Article 12 of the ICCPR.

[100] "The investigation involved 18,665 individuals belonging to 4,754 households who were unable to pay the resettlement fees. 58.8% of these individuals were unemployed despite their fitness to work, 41.2% were children, elderly people and people with disabilities. The investigation showed that 60.8% or 2,891 households of the 4,754 households had income below the minimum living standards or no income at all.

Inability to pay the resettlement fees seriously impacted the exercise of their rights and freedoms. For instance, their children dropped out of school, thus being unable to exercise their right to education; similarly, their rights to health and medical care, free choice of employment, remuneration, material and financial assistance, and the right to own land were affected."

This extract is from a statement by Commissioner Dalaijamts of the Mongolian Human Rights Commission, delivered at the training course conducted by the Raoul Wallenberg Institute for NHRIs in the Asia-Pacific Region, in Bangkok in December 2004.

Court order the councils to rescind the resettlement fees and respect their rights to receive basic services.

One of the most effective strategies, first developed by the Australian Human Rights and Equal Opportunity Commission in the late 1980s, is the conduct of National Inquiries. Not only have these enabled NHRIs to promote and protect economic, social and cultural rights – even when these were not specifically included in their legislative mandate[101] – they have effectively and repeatedly demonstrated in practice the indivisibility and equal importance of all human rights.[102]

These inquiries clearly demonstrated that even in parliamentary democracies gross violations of the human rights of particularly vulnerable and disadvantaged groups can occur. They also demonstrated the important role that a NHRI can play in addressing systemic violations of human rights and identifying remedies – including in countries where the "justiciability" of economic, social and cultural rights is highly problematic.[103]

The deficiencies inherent in the Paris Principles were one of the major factors motivating an initiative by the Commonwealth to bring together in 2001 a group of seven practitioners[104] to prepare more comprehensive,

[101] In this context it should be noted that while some governments have not included these rights in the mandate of the NHRI they established, in 1993, in the U.N. General Assembly, governments emphasised the importance of strengthening NHRIs to ensure their capacity to "prevent and combat **all** violations of human rights". (emphasis added) UNGA Res. 48/134 (20 December 1993).

[102] Several summaries of inquiries dealing with the rights of homeless young people, indigenous peoples and other minorities, and people with psychiatric disabilities are included in Appendices X–XII.

[103] See Henry J. Steiner and Philip Alston, op. cit. at pp. 298–310.

[104] The members of this group and their capacities were:

Justice Emile Short:	Chairman, Commission on Human Rights and Administrative Justice, Ghana
Prof. Mohd. Hamdan Adnan:	Member, Human Rights Commission, Malaysia
Mr Chris Lawrence:	Commissioner, Human Rights Commission, New Zealand
Mrs Shirley Mabusela:	Deputy Chairperson, Human Rights Commission, South Africa
Mr Kieren Fitzpatrick:	Director, Asia Pacific Forum of National Human Rights Institutions
Mrs Lawrence Laurent:	Secretary/Treasurer, Caribbean Ombudsman Association, St Lucia

detailed, and useful guidelines for NHRIs – including, specifically, in respect to their responsibility to promote and protect economic, social and cultural rights.[105] These guidelines, which are now widely used in training members and staff of NHRIs in the Asia-Pacific region, stipulate:

- An NHRI should employ all available means to respond to inquiries related to the advancement of economic, social and cultural rights, whether or not its enabling statute or national constitution recognises economic, social and cultural rights as justiciable.
- An NHRI should advise the government on the development and implementation of economic policies to ensure that the economic, social and cultural rights of people are not adversely affected by economic policies, e.g. structural adjustment programmes and other aspects of economic management.
- An NHRI should work towards facilitating public awareness of government policies relating to economic, social and cultural rights and encourage the involvement of various sectors of society in the formulation, implementation and review of relevant policies.

Since we prepared these guidelines five years ago, various and very diverse factors have produced an increased awareness of the tremendous inequities inherent in the current global distribution of wealth and the gross violations of economic, social and cultural rights continuously inflicted on hundreds of millions of the world's poorest citizens. However, while there is recognition, there is far too little action – as the limited progress made to date towards achieving the Millennium Development Goals attests.[106] In 1993, in its report to the World Conference, the U.N. Committee on Economic, Social and Cultural rights concluded that:

> " . . . despite the rhetoric violations of civil and political rights continue to be treated as though they were far more serious and more patently

---

Mr Brian Burdekin:	Special Adviser on National Institutions to the United Nations, High Commissioner for Human Rights

[105] National Human Rights Institutions: Best Practice. Commonwealth Secretariat 2001, pp. 33–34.
[106] The Millennium Development Goals, together with certain specific targets, are included in Appendix VI.

> intolerable, than massive and direct denials of economic, social and cultural rights".[107]

While the rhetoric has changed, in reality that summation is still essentially accurate – and ensuring that states meet their obligations to recognise and implement these rights is one of the greatest challenges confronting NHRIs in the Asia-Pacific region.

This is not to denigrate or underestimate the progress that has been made at the international level in establishing a framework for progress and identifying definite goals to be achieved. Respected international experts have formulated several important sets of principles and guidelines which reflect the growing awareness and widespread (although not universal) acceptance that economic, social and cultural rights are not only universal but must be treated with the same importance as civil and political rights.[108]

Under the auspices of the United Nations:

> "In the economic and social spheres, the Millennium Development Goals now serve as a common policy framework for the entire United Nations

---

[107] U.N. Committee on Economic, Cultural and Social Rights, statement to the World Conference on Human Rights, U.N. Doc.E/1993/22, Annex. III para. 5.

[108] The most significant of these documents are: "The Limburg Principles on the Implementation of the International Covenant on Economic, Social and Cultural Rights", formulated in 1986 and "the Maastricht Guidelines on Violations of Economic, Social and Cultural Rights" formulated in 1997. The Maastricht Guidelines provide:

> "Like civil and political rights, economic, social and cultural rights impose three different types of obligations on States: the obligations to respect, protect and fulfil. Failure to perform any one of these three obligations constitutes a violation of such rights. **The obligation to respect requires States to refrain from interfering with the enjoyment of economic, social and cultural rights.** Thus, the right to housing is violated if the State engages in arbitrary forced evictions. **The obligation to protect requires States to prevent violations of such rights by third parties.** Thus, the failure to ensure that private employers comply with basic labour standards may amount to a violation of the right to work or the right to just and favourable conditions of work. **The obligation to fulfil requires States to take appropriate legislative, administrative, budgetary, judicial and other measures towards the full realization of such rights.** Thus, the failure of States to provide essential primary health care to those in need may amount to a violation." (Section II, The Meaning of Economic, Social and Cultural Rights, Article 6: "Obligation to respect, protect and fulfil") – emphasis added.

For the full text of the Maastricht Guidelines see Appendix VII.

> system, and indeed for the broader international development community."[109]

The difficulty is, however, as the U.N. Secretary General recently admitted:

> "As things stand now, different governance structures for the many parts of the system, overlapping mandates and mandates that reflect earlier rather than current priorities all combine to hobble our effectiveness".[110]

The reality is that equal access to education, the right of the sick to be appropriately treated, the right of the poor to equal protection of the law and everyone's right to adequate shelter are primarily national issues requiring national responses – and effective national advocacy in the absence of appropriate policies and allocation of resources. The reality also is that even in states where governments take their international human rights treaty obligations seriously, government officials in the departments of education, health, housing and social welfare generally have no idea that the international human rights treaties exist – let alone what they require by way of implementation. NHRIs therefore have a major role to play in educating civil servants – as well as the politicians to whom they report.

7.2. NHRIS IN CONFLICT SITUATIONS:

Virtually all human rights are imperiled by armed conflict. While the number of active international conflicts has recently decreased[111] there are still many internal conflicts – in which it is generally estimated that 90% of those injured are civilians, of which half are children. Nor is the cessation of hostilities any guarantee that the human rights situation will rapidly improve; approximately half of all countries that emerge from war relapse into violence within five years.[112]

When we were drafting the Paris Principles in 1991 – and indeed throughout 1990 when some of us were preparing papers for the meeting –

---

[109] "In Larger Freedom; Towards Development, Security and Human Rights for All". UN.Doc A/59/2005 at pp. 39–40 para. 155–156.

[110] *Ibid.*

[111] Since the early 1990's the number of such conflicts has dropped from some 50 to 30 (in 2004). See L. Harbom and P. Wallensteen, "Armed Conflict and its International Dimensions, 1946 – 2004", 42:5 *Journal of Peace Research* (2005) pp. 623–635.

[112] United Nations General Assembly, "In Larger Freedom; Towards Development, Security and Human Rights for All" Report of the Secretary General, Addendum: Peace Building Commission, UN doc. A/59/2005 at Add.2 (23 May 2005) p. 1.

we were not envisaging a significant role for NHRIs in situations of serious military conflict. Nevertheless, a number of Asia-Pacific NHRIs have subsequently had to function in such situations – including those in Indonesia, Fiji, Nepal and Sri Lanka. In several countries these conflicts have been nation-wide; in others, such as the Philippines and Thailand, they have been insurgencies confined to particular regions – but having significant human rights implications for the entire country.[113]

Two of the three institutions which are associate members of the Asia-Pacific Forum, those in Afghanistan and Palestine, are also currently attempting to promote and protect human rights in countries where armed conflicts (and the presence of external forces) present tremendous challenges. The recently established institutions in Timor-Leste and the Maldives are also attempting to establish themselves in the aftermath of conflict and repression (in the former, externally imposed and in the latter, the product of an internal struggle for democracy and human rights).

Given the absence of any guidance in the Paris Principles, the prevalence of conflicts in the region, and the fact that a number of NHRIs are in Commonwealth countries we attempted to set out some general guidelines in the Commonwealth "Best Practice" publication. These stipulate:

- NHRIs should continue to work in conflict situations to protect and promote human rights and the peace process.
- An NHRI should do whatever lies within its powers to assist particularly vulnerable groups.
- An NHRI should work with other organisations, such as the UNHCR, NGOs and other relief organisations, to address the needs of refugees and internally displaced persons.
- An NHRI should assist in the implementation of the U.N. Guidelines on Internally Displaced Persons.[114]

[113] Following the coup attempt in Fiji by George Speight, in May 2000, the Fiji Human Rights Commission played a critical role in several cases which established that the 1997 Constitution in Fiji had not in fact been abrogated by the coup. (See *Chandrika Prasad* v. *the Republic of Fiji and the Attorney-General (H. Ct)* Civil Jurisdiction Action No. HBC 0217.00L and *the Republic of Fiji* v. *Chandrika Prasad (CA)* Civil Appeal No. ABU 0078 of 2000 S).

[114] While the number of refugees (as defined by UNHCR) has decreased in recent years – to a global total of approximately 9.2 million in 2004 – the number of IDPs displaced by conflict or human rights violations has grown and is now estimated at 25 million. (Report of the U.N. Secretary-General on the Work of the Organisation. U.N. New York, 2005. Para. 151 at p.32)

The fact remains, however, that the most important role NHRIs can play is preventive – addressing systemic violations of human rights in advance – before they produce or contribute to community unrest, violence or ultimately conflict. Generally they will achieve this through a variety of educational programmes relating to tolerance and non-discrimination (in both institutional and non-institutional settings). In some cases, however, they will interact with the executive, the legislature or even the judiciary on matters of urgency and national significance.[115]

The Asia-Pacific Forum is working with its member institutions in Indonesia, India, Nepal, The Philippines, Sri Lanka and Thailand to develop strategies and programmes to assist internally displaced persons (IDPs). This is also an area in which we are using the experience of NHRIs in the Asia-Pacific region to inform NHRIs in other regions.[116]

In situations of continuing conflict and, in post-conflict environments, security and strategic concerns frequently dominate the agenda – sometimes to the exclusion of any significant emphasis on human rights or on

---

[115] One of the most important examples of an NHRI intervening in such a situation occurred in India, in the State of Gujarat, with community violence which began on 27 February 2002. In this case, in which 14 people were burned alive, the Indian Human Rights Commission, following its own inquiries, intervened in 2003 after a trial in which all the witnesses had turned "hostile", all the accused had been acquitted, and the State Government had behaved in an irresponsible manner. The Indian Commission filed a Special Leave Petition in the Indian Supreme Court seeking to have the judgement of the Trial Court set aside and a further investigation and re-trial conducted. In 2004 the Supreme Court set aside the judgement of the Trial Court and ordered a re-trial – outside the State of Gujarat, in the State of Maharashtra. The Commission, in the course of its intervention, made comprehensive recommendations concerning the situation and the protection of the human rights of those who had been affected. (Presentation by the Registrar and Deputy Registrar of the Indian Commission; Bangkok Training Programme; November – December 2005; op. cit. footnote 61).

What was at stake in this case (now commonly referred to as the "Best Bakery Case") was not only the administration of justice but the confidence of the community in the capacity and willingness of government to protect all citizens – whether from the Hindu majority or the Muslim or some other minority. (Further details of this case are available on the Indian Commission's website – <www.nhrc.nic.in.> and in the "Journal of the National Human Rights Commission of India", Vol. 3, 2004, at pp. 164–165).

[116] For example, most recently, in Georgia, Armenia and Azerbaijan where recently established NHRIs are attempting to assist large numbers of IDPs displaced by various conflicts.

institutions designed to protect them. Nevertheless NHRIs must attempt to function impartially and as effectively as possible.

The complexities of post-conflict "peacebuilding" have recently been the subject of substantially increased international attention[117] and the United Nations has decided that it is essential to reinforce its capacity by creating a "Peacebuilding Commission". However, this will essentially be an intergovernmental advisory body[118] " . . . to improve the coordination of all relevant actors[119] . . . ". According to the formal communiqué of the 2005 World Summit, the Commission will begin its work by 31 December 2005.[120]

Given that poverty, economic injustice and abuse of minorities are among the major causes of conflict, and given the role of NHRIs in addressing these issues, they have a significant role to play – both in the prevention of future conflicts and in contributing in an appropriate way to post-conflict peacebuilding.[121]

---

[117] Since 1948 the United Nations has been involved in 60 "Peacekeeping Operations". However, 45 of these have been instituted since the end of the Cold War.

[118] See the 2005 World Summit Outcome, Final document of the High-level Plenary Meeting of the General Assembly, U.N. Doc. A/60/L.1 of 15 September 2005, para. 97.

[119] "The main purpose of the Peacebuilding Commission is to bring together all relevant actors to marshal resources and to advise on and propose integrated strategies for post-conflict peacebuilding and recovery. The Commission should focus attention on the reconstruction and institution-building efforts necessary for recovery from conflict and support the development of integrated strategies in order to lay the foundation for sustainable development. In addition, it should provide recommendations and information to improve the coordination of all relevant actors within and outside the United Nations, develop best practices, help to ensure predictable financing for early recovery activities and extend the period of attention by the international community to post-conflict recovery. The Commission should act in all matters on the basis of consensus of its members."
Ibid., para. 98.

[120] *Ibid.,* para. 105.

[121] This is an area in which countries in the Asia-Pacific region which have experienced or are suffering conflicts based on ethnic, religious or other differences can learn valuable lessons from solutions adopted in other regions. For example, the National Human Rights Commissions established in South Africa and Uganda have played an important part in rebuilding societies of tolerance and non-discrimination, following regimes which perpetrated gross violations of human rights on their citizens. Nor are these examples confined to developing countries. The Human

7.3. NATIONAL INQUIRIES:

> "Following a two-year inquiry by the Human Rights Commissioner Brian Burdekin, the Burdekin Report, *Our Homeless Children*, was released in 1989. It revealed that between 20,000-25,000 Australian children, some as young as 12, were homeless. Its findings rightly shocked our nation. Most of these children had fled from adults who were abusing them physically, sexually and emotionally, and were now living on the streets, behind shopping centres, in the bush, under bridges and in clothing bins."
>
> *(Foreword by the Honourable Sir William Deane,*
> *former Governor General of Australia,*
> *to "Mean Streets; Kind Heart. The Father Chris Riley Story")*[122]

One of the greatest challenges confronting all NHRIs is implementing a broad mandate with very limited resources. Practitioners have therefore sought to identify strategies which enable them to perform several of their functions simultaneously and in the most cost-effective way. While national circumstances differ greatly, national institutions from countries as diverse as Australia and Mongolia are now using national inquiries to both promote and protect a wide range of human rights.[123]

Brief summaries of several of these inquiries are included in Appendices X-XII.[124] In one case a more extensive summary is reproduced to

---

Rights Commissions which the author assisted in establishing in Ireland and Northern Ireland following the Good Friday Peace Agreement also provide valuable precedents for societies wracked by divisions based on religion.

[122] Harper Collins Publishers, Australia 2003 by Sue Williams.

[123] The Mongolian Human Rights Commission is currently conducting a "National Inquiry on Torture and Other Cruel Inhuman or Degrading Treatment or Punishment" which will, I believe, serve as an important and instructive precedent for addressing this still prevalent abuse of human rights for NHRIs in all regions. This Inquiry is still underway but is expected to report in late 2005 or early 2006. The full Terms of Reference for the Inquiry can be found in the Commission's "Report on Human Rights and Freedoms in Mongolia – 2005", in Appendix 6 at pp 81–83.

[124] The full reports for two of these inquiries can be found in:
"Our Homeless Children: Report of the National Inquiry into Homeless Children by the Human Rights and Equal Opportunity Commission". Australian Government Publishing Service, Canberra 1989 ISBN No.: 0644 08597 5; and
"Human Rights and Mental Illness: Report of the National Inquiry into the Human Rights of People with Mental Illness by the Human Rights and Equal Opportunity Commission". Australian Government Publishing Service, Canberra 1993 ISBN No. Set: 0 644 32184 9; ISBN No. Vol. 2: 0 644 32186 5.

demonstrate the advantages of this technique for addressing and redressing human rights violations; they can be summarised as follows.[125]

First, through a national inquiry, a large number of individual complaints can be dealt with in a proactive and cost-effective way – including cases of individuals who for various reasons, including disability, isolation or ignorance of the human rights Commission's mandate or even its existence, would not have been able to approach the institution for assistance.

Second, the process of preparing terms of reference for the inquiry should be conducted in consultation with NGOs and others representing, or advocating on behalf of, affected individuals. This process has a dual benefit – in enhancing NGOs' understanding of the NHRI's role and in enabling the institution to better inform itself by consultations with those in the community directly involved in the relevant issues.

Third, conducting public hearings open to the media is an extremely cost-effective way of educating both the general public about the institution and its responsibilities and also informing particular groups within the community who have specific responsibilities for the issues being investigated and their human rights implications. These "groups" include politicians responsible for framing legislation and programmes and bureaucrats responsible for policy advice.

Fourth, a national inquiry can most effectively address systemic violations of human rights – based on the evidence from individual cases, but also embracing an examination of the laws, policies and programmes (or lack of them) which have given rise to the violations in question. It is important to understand that many of the most vulnerable and disadvantaged groups, who most need the assistance of NHRIs, have been victims of widespread, systematic and sometimes systemic discrimination.

Fifth, as the national inquiries concerning homeless young people, indigenous peoples and those affected by mental illness clearly demonstrate, information assembled on a national basis, through hearings, submissions and research, enables the institution to effectively discharge its advisory functions in respect of legislation and government policies and programmes.

Sixth, since such inquiries afford opportunities to politicians, bureaucrats and other independent agencies, to present their views in submissions or at

---

[125] For further details of several other national inquiries see B. Lindsnaes and L. Lindholt "National Human Rights Institutions: Standard-setting and Achievements" in National Human Rights Institutions: Articles and working papers, op.cit. at pp. 34–35.

hearings, this strategy enables the NHRI to strengthen its cooperation with other important "institutions".

Seventh, based on experience, the scope of the national inquiry illustrates and educates, better than any other strategy, the indivisibility and interdependence of civil and political rights and economic, social and cultural rights. This is important for achieving practical results – particularly in jurisdictions where civil and political rights are regarded as being justiciable – but economic, social and cultural rights are not.

Eighth, as the national inquiries on homeless children and the human rights of those affected by mental illness demonstrate (see Appendices X and XII) these inquiries are premised on the principles prescribed in relevant international human rights treaties and other instruments. This is an extremely effective way of actually "implementing" these standards – by using them as benchmarks against which national laws, policies and programmes can be assessed.[126]

---

[126] In the case of the National Inquiry on Human Rights and Mental Illness we first had to prepare international standards concerning the human rights of those affected. These standards, the "Principles for the Protection of Persons with Mental Illness and for the Improvement of Mental Health Care" were prepared by a working group of NHRIs, NGOs and several governments under the auspices of the United Nations and adopted in 1991 by the U.N. General Assembly. The author played an active role in drafting these Principles, which we then used as the basis for our National Inquiry on Human Rights and Mental Illness. As a result of this Inquiry the Federal Government adopted, for the first time, a national mental health policy. This national policy was based, in large part, on the International Principles. (See Commonwealth of Australia; Joint Standing Committee on Foreign Affairs and Trade: Human Rights Subcommittee: "Inquiry into Australia's International Efforts to Promote and Protect Human Rights" Canberra, 13 October 1994: Official Hansard Report at p1312. Evidence by the Federal Human Rights Commissioner.)

The author also played an active part in drafting the Convention on the Rights of the Child and the Optional Protocol to the CRC on the sale of children, child prostitution and child pornography. The Optional Protocol is, in fact, an interesting example of the way in which NHRIs can work with the international community and civil society to prepare important new international human rights instruments. In 1991–92, following discussions with the head of the Philippines Human Rights Commission, I prepared a draft Optional Protocol on the subject of the sexual exploitation of children. In 1992 several NHRIs addressed the U.N. Commission on Human Rights – informing the Commission that we regarded this problem as one of the most urgent in the Asia-Pacific region. In 1993 a U.N. sponsored meeting of NHRIs in Tunisia unanimously supported the draft and in the same year over 700 lawyers meeting in Sydney at the World Conference of Family Lawyers also

Finally, the community awareness and political pressure generated by a well publicised national inquiry maximises the likelihood that the NHRI's recommendations to the parliament and/or government will produce practical results. In the world of human rights institutions, integrity and good intentions are important – but credibility in the community comes only with the capacity to demonstrate that the institution is effective – and produces significant results.

The effectiveness of national inquiries has been widely recognised by NGOs as well as NHRIs. This subject was a major focus of the meeting of "NHRIs and NGOs Working in Partnership" already referred to. In its concluding guidelines the Kandy conference recommended that NHRIs and NGOs should:

- Hold joint workshops aimed at promoting awareness of the concept of public inquiries, their objectives and their mechanisms and possible subjects; consult with national institutions and NGOs to ensure that best practice is followed;
- Where consideration is being given to the establishment of a public inquiry, consult in the development of its terms of reference and on a strategic plan for the inquiry;
- Cooperate closely where a national institution is carrying out a public inquiry, particularly in the exchange of information and on-site activities;
- Lobby for legislation to ensure that it is incumbent on legislatures to discuss national human rights institution reports within a specific

---

unanimously supported it. In 2004 the draft supported by NHRIs was one of the main documents placed before the Working Group which had been mandated by CHR to draft the Optional Protocol. (Commonwealth of Australia; Joint Standing Committee on Foreign Affairs and Trade: Human Rights Subcommittee, 13 October 1994: Official Hansard at pp. 1297-1314).

Several NHRIs in the Asia-Pacific region and the APF are currently closely involved in the preparation of a new United Nations Convention to Promote and Protect the Rights of Persons with Disabilities. The author, together with the Swedish Disability Ombudsman, was closely involved in drafting one of the precursor instruments to this Convention – "The Standard Minimum Rules on the Equalisation of Opportunities for People with Disabilities" – and, subsequently, in ensuring that NHRIs would be able to participate in drafting the new Convention (there was initially opposition to this from a number of governments involved in the U.N. Working Group).

time frame and that national human rights institutions are empowered in cases of undue delay to make their reports public;
- Cooperate in facilitating media coverage of public inquiries; cooperate in conveying public inquiry reports to relevant U.N. mechanisms;
- Cooperate in promoting the implementations of any public inquiry's recommendations; and
- Organisations represented also recommended that the Asia-Pacific Forum should organise a regional workshop on public inquiries as part of the Forum's program of annual thematic workshops.[127]

These guidelines, based on the national inquiries which have been carried out by the Australian Human Rights and Equal Opportunity Commission, have subsequently been used in a number of regional training programmes for NHRIs organised by the APF and RWI.

7.4. NATIONAL HUMAN RIGHTS ACTION PLANS:

Another strategy in which NHRIs in various regions are becoming increasingly involved is the development and implementation of national human rights action plans (NHRAPs).[128] The World Conference in 1993 recommended that all countries should develop an NHRAP – in order to establish priorities and benchmarks against which implementation of their international human rights treaty obligations could be measured.[129] This was to take account of the almost universal tendency of governments to ratify international treaties but then do very little about their practical implementation.

[127] Op. cit. footnote 36, Section 5.1–5.7, of the Kandy Declaration.

[128] NHRIs have no specific legislative mandate to do this, but generally rely on those sections of their enabling legislation which empower them to educate, monitor and advise. In those countries where the NHRI has an "incidentals" power this is also obviously relevant (see notes to Table A).

[129] In this context, see also General Comment No. 10 of the Committee on Economic, Social and Cultural Rights, which recommends that NHRIs should be involved in " . . . The identification of national-level benchmarks against which the realization of Covenant obligations can be measured;" (para. 3(d) of the General Comment – see App. III).

While less than 20 countries have developed NHRAPs to date,[130] several countries in the Asia-Pacific region, including Australia, Indonesia, Malaysia, Mongolia, The Philippines and Thailand are among those that have done so. In each case the national institution played a role in developing the plan and in several cases is involved in monitoring its implementation. However, the government is obviously the primary "duty bearer" in respect of international human rights treaty commitments and NHRAPs can only work if there is high level government involvement in their formulation and continuing political will to ensure their implementation. Unfortunately in most countries this has not been the case. (There are, however, signs that this situation is changing – for example in New Zealand.)

Governments must, of course, be prepared to bear the costs of the community consultations which should precede the creation of a NHRAP and the costs of its implementation. If NHRIs are to be given a primary role in developing and monitoring the NHRAP it is essential to recognise that this entails significant costs – and the institution's budget will need to be augmented accordingly. NHRIs should not agree to take on this responsibility if they do not have adequate resources; inadequate monitoring risks bringing them into disrepute.

[130] Those which have plans include: Australia, Bolivia, Brazil, Ecuador, Democratic Republic of the Congo, Indonesia, Latvia, Lithuania, Malawi, Mexico, Moldova, Mongolia, Norway, The Philippines, South Africa, Sweden and Venezuela. (Source: <www.ohchr.org/english/countries/coop/plan_action.htm>).
Several countries, such as Sweden, are currently preparing their second NHRAP.

CHAPTER 8: CONCLUSION

National human rights institutions have come a long way in little more than a decade. Since the United Nations General Assembly adopted the Paris Principles in 1993, the number of NHRIs in the Asia-Pacific region has increased dramatically. Substantial challenges remain in strengthening the legislative mandates of several NHRIs, improving their accessibility and enhancing their effectiveness. Nevertheless, they have become a major force in monitoring governments' compliance with their international treaty obligations, promoting an understanding of human rights and addressing and redressing human rights violations.

However, these institutions are evolving in an international and regional context which is changing rapidly. They will continue to confront numerous and sometimes complex challenges – including several, such as operating in an environment of armed conflict, for which they are not designed. Other "institutions" on which NHRIs' capacity to carry out their mandate heavily depends – including the legislature and the judiciary – are still weak or corrupt in many Asian and Pacific countries. While NHRIs must not intrude on the important "monitoring" functions of these institutions and of other independent agencies, their responsibility for ensuring equal protection of the law and the harmonisation of domestic legislation with international human rights norms means they will continue to have a substantial stake in assisting to improve the performance of these other institutions and co-operating with them in appropriate ways.

The Paris Principles were intended to be, and indeed still are, only minimum normative standards for NHRIs. Other guidelines subsequently developed by practitioners are more detailed, more rigorous and sometimes more relevant to current challenges than the United Nations Principles. The latter have, however, played a critical role in setting basic benchmarks which governments must comply with if they wish to establish an institution which can be effective and command public confidence.

NHRIs are playing an increasingly active and important role in assisting the international Treaty Bodies mandated to monitor the most important human rights instruments – both by providing them with information and by following up their recommendations. They are also assisting the United Nations Special Rapporteurs in a number of important areas and contributing significantly to debates in the U.N. Commission on Human Rights. The role of NHRIs in developing appropriate international norms is increasingly being recognised and they are currently playing a significant part in the development of a new international instrument to protect and promote the rights of people with disabilities.

At the national level NHRIs – from Mongolia to Australia and India to Fiji – have played a very significant role in assisting courts to interpret and appropriately apply international human rights treaties. A number of the cases in which NHRIs have intervened concern civil and political rights. However, NHRIs have also been instrumental in securing landmark decisions relating to the interpretation of international instruments concerning economic, social and cultural rights and the rights of particularly vulnerable groups such as children and those affected by mental illness. In several important cases these decisions by national courts have been followed in other countries – thus contributing to the development of regional and international jurisprudence.

NHRIs have also demonstrated the capacity to develop innovative and effective new strategies for promoting and protecting human rights – most notably the technique of conducting national inquiries. These have not only produced important legislative and policy reforms; they have also demonstrated NHRIs' capacity to educate public opinion on important human rights issues and, in several cases, mobilise hundreds of millions of dollars for programmes to improve the plight of particularly vulnerable groups – such as homeless adolescents, people affected by mental illness and indigenous communities.

The association which NHRIs have established in this region, the Asia-Pacific Forum, is the most effective such association in any region. It is playing an increasingly important role in many areas – including: the identification of "best practice" for NHRIs; facilitating their access to relevant information; assisting, through the Advisory Council of Jurists, in enhancing regional understanding of relevant international norms; and, through staff exchanges and training programmes, enabling NHRIs to strengthen their professional expertise. The APF is also playing a critical "gatekeeper" role in accrediting as members only NHRIs which actually comply with the Paris Principles.

Eighteen countries in the Asia-Pacific region now have NHRIs, twelve of which currently comply with United Nation standards and several more are likely to be recognised as complying in the near future. In addition, four countries which do not yet have NHRIs have prepared legislation to establish them and several more have committed themselves to do so. It is therefore highly likely that in the next few years there will be a significant increase in the number of such institutions. The author is currently working in several of these countries and the challenge of ensuring that new institutions comply with, and preferably exceed, the minimum standards prescribed by the United Nations remains.

APPENDICES

APPENDIX I

PRINCIPLES RELATING TO THE STATUS AND FUNCTIONING OF NATIONAL INSTITUTIONS FOR PROTECTION AND PROMOTION OF HUMAN RIGHTS (THE PARIS PRINCIPLES)

Competence and responsibilities

1. A national institution shall be vested with competence to promote and protect human rights.

2. A national institution shall be given as broad a mandate as possible, which shall be clearly set forth in a constitutional or legislative text, specifying its composition and its sphere of competence.

3. A national institution shall, *inter alia,* have the following responsibilities:

(a) To submit to the Government, Parliament and any other competent body, on an advisory basis either at the request of the authorities concerned or through the exercise of its power to hear a matter without higher referral, opinions, recommendations, proposals and reports on any matters concerning the promotion and protection of human rights; the national institution may decide to publicize them; these opinions, recommendations, proposals and reports, as well as any prerogative of the national institution, shall relate to the following areas:

(i) Any legislative or administrative provisions, as well as provisions relating to judicial organizations, intended to preserve and extend the protection of human rights; in that connection, the national institution shall examine the legislation and administrative provisions in force, as well as bills and proposals, and shall make such recommendations as it deems appropriate in order to ensure that these provisions conform to the fundamental principles of human rights; it shall, if necessary, recommend the adoption of new legislation, the amendment of legislation in force and the adoption or amendment of administrative measures;

(ii) Any situation of violation of human rights which it decides to take up;

(iii) The preparation of reports on the national situation with regard to human rights in general, and on more specific matters;

(iv) Drawing the attention of the Government to situations in any part of the country where human rights are violated and making proposals to it for initiatives to put an end to such situations and, where necessary, expressing an opinion on the positions and reactions of the Government;

(b) To promote and ensure the harmonization of national legislation regulations and practices with the international human rights instruments to which the State is a party, and their effective implementation;

(c) To encourage ratification of the above-mentioned instruments or accession to those instruments, and to ensure their implementation;

(d) To contribute to the reports which States are required to submit to United Nations bodies and committees, and to regional institutions, pursuant to their treaty obligations and, where necessary, to express an opinion on the subject, with due respect for their independence;

(e) To cooperate with the United Nations and any other organization in the United Nations system, the regional institutions and the national institutions of other countries that are competent in the areas of the promotion and protection of human rights;

(f) To assist in the formulation of programmes for the teaching of, and research into, human rights and to take part in their execution in schools, universities and professional circles;

(g) To publicize human rights and efforts to combat all forms of discrimination, in particular racial discrimination, by increasing public awareness, especially through information and education and by making use of all press organs.

Composition and guarantees of independence and pluralism

1. The composition of the national institution and the appointment of its members, whether by means of an election or otherwise, shall be established in accordance with a procedure which affords all necessary guarantees to ensure the pluralist representation of the social forces (of civilian society) involved in the promotion and protection of human rights, particularly by powers which will enable effective cooperation to be established with, or through the presence of, representatives of:

(a) Non-governmental organizations responsible for human rights and efforts to combat racial discrimination, trade unions, concerned social and professional organizations, for example, associations of lawyers, doctors, journalists and eminent scientists;

(b) Trends in philosophical or religious thought;

(c) Universities and qualified experts;

(d) Parliament

(e) Government departments (if these are included, their representatives should participate in the deliberations only in an advisory capacity).

2. The national institution shall have an infrastructure which is suited to the smooth conduct of its activities, in particular adequate funding. The purpose of this funding should be to enable it to have its own staff and premises, in order to be independent of the Government and not be subject to financial control which might affect its independence.

3. In order to ensure a stable mandate for the members of the national institution, without which there can be no real independence, their appointment shall be effected by an official act which shall establish the specific duration of the mandate. This mandate may be renewable, provided that the pluralism of the institution's membership is ensured.

Methods of Operation

Within the framework of its operation, the national institution shall:

(a) Freely consider any questions falling within its competence, whether they are submitted by the Government or taken up by it without referral to a higher authority, on the proposal of its members or of any petitioner;

(b) Hear any person and obtain any information and any documents necessary for assessing situations falling within its competence;

(c) Address public opinion directly or through any press organ, particularly in order to publicize its opinions and recommendations;

(d) Meet on a regular basis and whenever necessary in the presence of all its members after they have been duly convened;

(e) Establish working groups from among its members as necessary, and set up local or regional sections to assist it in discharging its functions;

(f) Maintain consultation with the other bodies, whether jurisdictional or otherwise, responsible for the promotion and protection of human rights (in particular ombudsmen, mediators and similar institutions);

(g) In view of the fundamental role played by the non-governmental organizations in expanding the work of the national institutions, develop relations with the non-governmental organizations devoted to promoting and protecting human rights, to economic and social development, to combating racism, to protecting particularly vulnerable groups (especially children, migrant workers, refugees, physically and mentally disabled persons) or to specialized areas.

Additional principles concerning the status of commissions with quasi-jurisdictional competence

A national institution may be authorized to hear and consider complaints and petitions concerning individual situations. Cases may be brought before it by individuals, their representatives, third parties, non-governmental organizations, associations of trade unions or any other representative organizations. In such circumstances, and without prejudice to the principles stated above concerning the other powers of the commissions, the functions entrusted to them may be based on the following principles:

(a) Seeking an amicable settlement through conciliation or, within the limits prescribed by the law, through binding decisions or, where necessary, on the basis of confidentiality;

(b) Informing the party who filed the petition of his rights, in particular the remedies available to him, and promoting his access to them;

(c) Hearing any complaints or petitions or transmitting them to any other competent authority within the limits prescribed by the law;

(d) Making recommendations to the competent authorities, especially by proposing amendments or reforms of the laws, regulations and administrative practices, especially if they have created the difficulties encountered by the persons filing the petitions in order to assert their rights.

APPENDIX II

AMNESTY INTERNATIONAL'S RECOMMENDATIONS FOR EFFECTIVE PROTECTION AND PROMOTION OF HUMAN RIGHTS INSTITUTIONS

TABLE OF CONTENTS

4.B *Methodologies of investigation*
4.B.1 Independent investigation professionals
4.B.2 Training
4.B.3 Protection of witnesses
4.B.4 Protection of evidence
4.C *Individual complaints*
4.C.1 Who can complain?
4.C.2 Reaching out to victims
4.C.3 Keeping the interests of victims at the centre of the process

4.D *Addressing failed investigations effectively*
4.D.1 Separation of roles of the NHRI and the judiciary
4.D.2 Parallel jurisdiction of NHRI and the judiciary
4.D.3 Role of NHRI in following up the actions of prosecutors and the judiciary in cases where crimes are alleged

5 Recommendations and non-judicial remedies
5.1 Remedies and interim measures
5.2 Remedies but not impunity
5.3 Recommendations should be followed up

6 Human rights education

7 Visits to places of detention
7.1 Modalities of visits

8 Publicity
8.1 Media
8.2 Annual reports
8.3 Confidentiality

9 Accessibility
9.1 Regional offices
9.2 Accessible premises
9.3 Communication with victims

10 Budget

INTRODUCTION: STANDARDS ARE A PRE-REQUISITE FOR EFFECTIVE ACTION

National human rights institutions (NHRIs) include institutions such as ombudspersons for the defense of human rights, and the institutions in Latin America known as "*defensorias del pueblo*" and "*procuradorias de derechos humanos*". Such NHRIs can be distinguished from non-governmental human rights organizations by their very establishment as a quasi-governmental agency occupying a unique place between the judicial and executive functions of the state, and where these exist, the elected representatives of the people. The aim of their establishment should be to promote and protect human rights, through effective investigation of broad human rights concerns and individuals' complaints about human rights violations they have suffered, and through making recommendations accordingly.

Amnesty International has developed the following recommendations, based on the organization's observations of the work of NHRIs and their impact throughout the world. This document includes examples of good and bad practice. Amnesty International believes that these recommendations are essential elements to ensure the independent and effective establishment and functioning of national human rights institutions. They should be considered alongside other guidelines such as the "Principles relating to the status of national institutions" (adopted in the UN Commission on Human Rights Resolution 1992/54, known as "the Paris Principles") as a tool both to assess the effectiveness of existing national human rights institutions, and to ensure that new NHRIs are set up with the requisite ingredients for effective and independent functioning.

The recommendations set out in this document are Amnesty International's assessment of a foundation for effective work to promote and protect human rights. However, implementation of these recommendations on a formal level should not be seen as an end in itself – NHRIs should be judged on their results in effecting inprovement in the human rights situation in their country, and in providing investigations and remedies in individual cases. The results of their investigations should be open to scrutiny by civil society, including human rights defenders. They should work to combat impunity for all those who order, carry out, and cover up human rights violations. NHRIs should be judged on how they implement these goals, not solely on their legal or institutional framework. Amnesty International has received reports of many examples of good practices and good results in these aims, but also many shortcomings, and these recommendations are meant to encourage best practices in all NHRIs. It is Amnesty International's experience that those NHRIs which have been set up according to the principles in these recommendations and are functioning well and enjoy a level of credibility and trust which facilitates their relationship with the executive, the judiciary and most importantly, the victims of human rights violations, and makes their work even more effective.

Some of the recommendations concern the establishment of NHRIs and as such are aimed at governments, but others concern the operation of NHRIs, and are therefore aimed at governments, so that they can do all that is necessary to facilitate the efficient running of NHRIs, but also the NHRIs themselves. They may also be useful to those in civil society who are monitoring their performance.

APPENDIX II

The position of NHRIs as institutions within the state structure and yet independent – and where necessary, critical – is relatively new development in the protection of human rights. It is important to clarify their true role: NHRIs should never be seen as a replacement or alternative to an independent, impartial, properly resourced, accessible judiciary, whose rulings are enforced. NHRIs can however constitute an effective complement to the judiciary and other other institutions within the state in promoting and protecting human rights standards. There can be no alternative to a determined government policy to holding the perpetrators of human rights violations accountable.

AMNESTY INTERNATIONAL'S RECOMMENDATIONS ON EFFECTIVE PROTECTION AND PROMOTION OF HUMAN RIGHTS

1. Establishment of NHRIs to ensure independence and effective action

The following recommendations on the establishment are to ensure that action can be taken by the NHRI in full independence and to ensure its ability to take effective action to address violations. Formal independence without effective action is not sufficient.

1.1 Founding legislation

NHRIs must be independent from the executive functions of government and its founding charter should reflect this. It is essential therefore that NHRIs should be established by law or, preferably, by constitutional amendment. Where NHRIs are established merely by presidential or other kinds of decree, it is easier to abolish them, or to limit powers which are necessary to their effective functioning.

1.2 Consultation with civil society

The consultation process on and about the establishment of NHRIs should include representatives of civil society, such as human rights organizations, human rights defenders, lawyers, journalists, academics, the medical profession, social workers, trade unionists, and non-governmental organizations generally. Members of sectors of the population such as women, children and those representing their interests, religious, ethnic and racial groups, and other groups which are vulnerable to human rights violations (and which may be under-represented amongst civil society bodies) should also be consulted about the kind of assistance they require to promote and protect their human rights. The consultation process should be transparent, adequate, effective and properly resourced to ensure proper consultation.

1.3 Effective jurisdiction in federal states

Amnesty International has frequently noted that NHRIs have difficulties in ensuring that they can address violations throughout the territory of federal states. In some federal countries, NHRIs have been established with mandates that only permit them to consider cases where federal personnel commit human rights violations, or where human rights violations take place during the enforcement of federal law.

Amnesty International recommends therefore that any legislation in federal systems setting up an NHRI is made explicitly applicable to all parts of the federal system so that there are no *de facto* gaps in jurisdiction. Any NHRI, whether in a federal state or otherwise, should be able to examine all human rights violations, as defined by international human rights law, throughout the country's territory and regardless of the identity of the perpetrator.

All citizens with complaints of human rights violations should be able to bring them to an NHRI.

1.4 Cooperation with other institutions

The founding legislation of an NHRI should include provisions whereby the NHRI is empowered, on its own initiative, to submit reports to, and where appropriate, to address in person, legislative bodies, the executive, or other political institutions.

The NHRI should be directed to establish effective cooperation with other human rights institutions, whether domestic or from other countries, non-governmental organizations, including human rights organizations, and UN human rights bodies. In some cases, it may be useful to develop memoranda of understanding between NHRIs and other institutions to facilitate such relationships. NHRIs should use such contacts to exchange first-hand information about reports of human rights violations and also to share expertise and experience of best practices.

The NHRI should consider using the NGO sector=s wider social outreach mechanics, which in many cases is larger than that of the NHRI itself, to publicise its activities and to facilitate receiving complaints from sections of society who are either geographically, politically or socially remote. In all its contacts with NGOs and other organs of civil society an NHRI must take steps to protect its independence and impartiality.

1.5 Referrals

Where complainants raise problems which are outside the mandate of the NHRI, referrals may be appropriate to other organizations. This may be appropriate to help with, for example, medical, housing or social problems or consumer difficulties, particularly where complainants coming to the NHRI for help are having difficulties in obtaining assistance. In one case reported to Amnesty International, the NHRI gives the complainant a short letter on NHRI letterhead to bring to the referral agency outlining the problem and suggesting an appropriate response, which frequently leads to a quicker solution for the complainant and is a much appreciated service.

1.6 Assess priorities, measure goals, follow up

NHRIs frequently have a broad remit and scarce resources. It is therefore important to assess priorities through consultation with those affected, and work on priorities strategically, ensuring that those goals are met before ending work on the issue.

Violations of the right to life and the right to physical and mental integrity frequently involve crimes under international law, such as extrajudicial and other unlawful killings, torture, "disappearance", war crimes and crimes against humanity. In many countries NHRIs will need to prioritize work on such violations in order to be effective and credible in their work to protect and promote human rights.

NHRIs should also be empowered to take action on violations of other rights particularly social, cultural and economic rights.

NHRIs should assess priorities and needs through consultation with victims of human rights violations, and the availability of redress through other institutions within the country.

2. Membership

NHRIs require experienced, trained and skilled staff, and particularly strong, independent and effective leadership. NHRIs workers include those who lead the NHRI and take main responsibility for the work. In many cases they are appointed by the legislative or executive parts of government. Amnesty International refers to them in this document as "members". NHRI workers also include the staff who assist them, either through administrative or substantive investigative and legal work.

2.1 Qualities of members of the NHRI

Members should be selected on the basis of proven expertise, knowledge and experience in the promotion and protection of human rights. They should have practical expertise and abilities.

2.2 Leadership

It is Amnesty International's experience that the leadership of NHRIs is particularly important, indeed vital, for the effective functioning of NHRIs, as frequently the actions of the senior leadership of the organization sets the tone for the activities of the institution as a whole. It is of primary importance that the highest calibre candidates, with proven expertise of practical human rights work, be appointed.

2.3 Selection procedures and consultation

The independent procedures of selection, appointment, removal and terms of tenure of NHRI members and staff should be clearly specified, laid down in its founding legislation, so as to afford the strongest possible guarantees of competence, impartiality and independence.

The selection, appointment, and removal procedures of the members of the NHRI should not be handled exclusively by the executive branch of government.

The method of selection and appointment of the members of the NHRI should be fair and transparent, so as to afford all necessary guarantees of independence. Broad representation is also important, and steps should be taken to guarantee this – for example – by allowing members of civil society to nominate possible candidates for membership of the NHRI.

The selection and appointment process should involve representatives of civil society, especially human rights defenders representing the interests of particularly vulnerable sections of society (and members of those groups also), and may also include NGOs, opposition leaders, trade unionists, social workers, journalists.

Civil society should participate in the selection and appointment process as far as possible.

2.4 Representation of society

The NHRI members and staff should as far as possible include representation of all sections of society, including women, ethnic minorities, and people with disabilities, who may be under-represented in other official bodies and would have particular relevant experience of the needs of those sectors of society. Non-nationals should not be deterred or specifically prohibited from taking up a post at the NHRI.

2.5 Freedom from bias and expectations for further career advancement

The members and staff should consist of men and women known for their integrity and impartiality of judgement who shall decide matters before them on the basis of facts and in accordance with the law, without any restrictions, improper influences, inducements, pressures, threats or interferences from any quarter or for any reason, for example, alliegances to political parties, or strong links with the executive part of government.

In some cases, there may be an expectation that office in an NHRI is a stepping stone leading to ministerial or other political office which limits the independence of NHRI members and staff – as with such expectations, they may be less willing to criticize the executive.

Salaries and working conditions have a positive role to play in recruiting and retaining effective staff, and in ensuring independence. This, along with local factors, such as salary levels for similar positions, whether in the public or private sector, must be taken into account when setting and revising staff terms and conditions.

2.6 Effective support to fulfil tasks

There should be sufficient staffing to fulfil the tasks allotted to the NHRI. The key issue is to ensure effective oversight and action. NHRIs must have a functioning and efficient secretariat to carry out the tasks entrusted to the members.

2.7 Privileges and immunities

Like the judiciary, members of NHRIs should be immune from criminal or civil legal action for all tasks undertaken by them in the proper exercise of their official functions. However, decisions made by them in their official capacity should still be subject to judicial review by the courts.

3. Mandate and powers

The mandate should make the NHRI truly independent in action, to promote and protect human rights in whatever manner is most appropriate. It should not be set up as a purely advisory body to advise the government, rather it should listen to victims of human rights violations, and have their concerns at the heart of its work. It should also work to promote a culture of respect for human rights through education and raising of awareness of human rights issues.

The scope of the NHRI=s concerns should be principally and clearly defined in terms of international human rights law. This should include states' obligations under international law to respect and also to ensure that rights are respected by all, that is, to take steps to ensure that domestic law and practice form a framework where the abuses of human rights by non-state actors are effectively addressed. NHRIs should make recommendations for changes in law and practice where states are not fulfilling their obligation be able to take reasonable steps to protect citizens from abuses of their human rights by other citizens.

3.1 Scope of human rights within an NHRI's jurisdiction

NHRIs should enjoy the broadest possible mandate to address human rights concerns as set out in international human rights law and standards. The mandate should not be defined solely in terms of those rights that are specifically provided for in the country's constitution – particularly as some constitutions do not contain key rights such as the right to life. Rather NHRIs should take as their frame of reference the definitions of human rights as set out in international human rights instruments and standards, whether or not the state has ratified the relevant treaties. The mandate should include the power to protect and promote economic, social and cultural rights, as well as civil and political rights.

This is particularly important to ensure that human rights violations are monitored and acted upon in an accurate way. For example, Amnesty International has received reports that cases of torture are routinely described as "abuses of official position" rather than torture, which leads to a misleading assessment of human rights violations occuring in the country, as well as a failure to take appropriate action.

3.2 Accountability to ensure effective action

NHRIs should report publicly on their activities and be held accountable for their results – either to an independent civil society body, or to a functioning and exacting parliamentary body. This is particularly important as an ineffective NHRI which does not address human rights violations actively can be an instrument of impunity, rather than a tool to promote and protect human rights.

3.3 Asserting human rights for all

The mandate should include the power specifically to promote and protect the rights those sections of society which are particularly at risk of violations of human rights, for example, children, women, people with disabilities, ethnic minorities, refugees, human rights defenders and non-nationals such as asylum-seekers and migrant workers. It should promote the right not to suffer discrimination, as this is often the source and motivation of other human rights violations, such as torture.

Frequently Amnesty International has received information indicating that NHRIs encounter difficulties because they are perceived to be promoting the rights of criminals because of their work on prison conditions, or the torture of criminal suspects. It is therefore important that all NHRIs emphasise the universal applicability of human rights standards to **all** persons.

APPENDIX II

3.4 Participation in international human rights law fora

NHRIs should recommend and facilitate the signature, ratification or accession of its state to new human rights treaties.

The mandate should include the power to monitor government fulfilment of international and regional human rights treaties and human rights obligations under domestic law. This should include the power to monitor and report – independently on its own behalf, not on behalf of its government – on compliance with and implementation of relevant and necessary international human rights standards, essential to the promotion and protection of human rights, including the Universal Declaration of Human Rights, the International Covenant on Cultural and Political Rights (ICCPR), the International Covenant on Economic, Social and Cultural Rights (ICESCR), the UN Declaration and Convention against Torture, the Convention of the Rights of the Child, the Convention on the Elimination of All Forms of Discrimination against Women, the Convention on the Elimination of All Forms of Racial Discrimination, as well as the Declaration on the Right and Responsibility of Individuals, Groups and Organs of Society to Promote and Protect Universally Recognized Human Rights and Fundamental Freedoms, the UN Code of Conduct for Law Enforcement Officials, the UN Body of Principles for the Protection of All Persons under Any Form of Detention or Imprisonment, the UN Rules for the Protection of Juveniles Deprived of their Liberty, the Basic Principles on the Use of Force and Firearms by Law Enforcement Officials and the UN Principles on the Effective Prevention and Investigation of Extra-legal, Arbitrary or Summary Executions. They should also assess compliance with standards relating to the administration of justice, such as the Basic Principles on the Role of Lawyers, the Basic Principles on the Independence of the Judiciary, the Guidelines on the Role of Prosecutors, and the Declaration of Basic Principles of Justice for Victims of Crime and Abuse of Power.

NHRIs should as far as possible attend and participate in international meetings and fora including the treaty monitoring bodies and UN political bodies concerned with human rights. When doing so, they should represent themselves as independent NHRIs, rather than representing their government.

NHRIs should have the power to take note of and ultimately apply international human rights law and standards in their work. It is essential therefore that NHRIs establish effective means to keep abreast of recent developments of international human rights law and standards.

The NHRI should possess the power to follow-up on recommendations and reports made in relation to implementation and compliance with international human rights standards mentioned above. This should include a suitable framework within which the NHRI may compel the relevant authority to explain and report to the NHRI, within a reasonable period of time, as to why, for example, it has not followed and did not apply recommendations made by human rights treaty bodies or thematic mechanisms.

NHRIs should prepare "shadow reports" (reports of their assessment of the human rights situation in their country) to submit to the UN human rights treaty monitoring bodies on their own behalf; they should not write the state's reports to treaty monitoring bodies.

3.5 Advising governments on domestic legislation

The mandate should include the power to review the effectiveness of existing legislation or administrative provisions in protecting human rights and should be able to make recommendations for the amendment of such legislation or the introduction of new legislation as necessary.

This is especially important regarding internal security laws, administrative detention laws, and police detention and interrogaton procedures, which can often facilitate human rights violations, or where enabling legislation implementing international standards does not implement the international obligations effectively.

The NHRI should also examine bills and proposals for new legislation put forward by the government or parliament to assess its conformity with international human rights standards and to ensure the state's compliance with international human rights standards.

3.6 Participation in domestic legal cases

NHRIs should have the power to bring legal cases to protect the rights of individuals or to promote changes in law and practice. Amnesty International has received information about excellent work including the use of legal applications such as judicial review, constitutional applications and challenges, etc.

NHRIs should have the legal power to bring applications on behalf of those who may be unable to bring cases to protect their rights themselves (for example, children, those with mental health problems or otherwise lacking mental capacity, prisoners).

NHRIs should also have the legal power to bring cases (such as judicial review) to challenge the legality of executive action and to obtain judicial orders to remedy the situation, particularly where the executive has ignored the NHRIs recommendations on the subject.

NHRIs must also have the legal power to submit advice to the courts, such as *amicus curiae* briefs or third party interventions, on legal issues within its field of expertise in an independent capacity, without being a party to the case. This is important to ensure that the courts are informed about specialized human rights law concerns and to ensure that human rights standards are actively implemented in court decisions.

3.7 Effective communication with government to bring about change

NHRIs should be mindful of their official position within state structures and communicate their recommendations confidently and with the expectation that the executive part of government, or the prosecuting authorities, should implement them. NHRIs should open strong and effective methods of communication with all agencies of government, the prosecuting authorities and the judiciary in order to promote their recommendations, and should ensure compliance with recommendations, and not accept recommendations being ignored. NHRIs should also make recommendations to parts of the state, for example, the judiciary and the legislative organs.

4. Investigations and Inquiries

4.A General recommendations on investigations

The NHRI should have the powers to conduct wide-ranging national enquiries on human rights concerns; they should have access to government information; they should respond to victims' concerns in their investigations.

4.A.1 Timelimits

Although some reasonable time limits may be used to ensure that complainants come forward speedily with their complaints, NHRIs should undertake any investigation where there is evidence in existence to consider: they should not be inhibited by arbitrary time limits on investigations, and should not be inflexible in rejecting cases for being brought to their attention outside of timelimits.

4.A.2 Power to investigate on its own initiative

NHRIs should have precisely defined powers to investigate on its own initiative situations and cases of reported human rights violations. It should be able to set clear priorities for its work in accordance with the seriousness of the violations reported to it, specifically including alleged violations of the right to life and security of the person, and the right to physical and mental integrity, including the right not to be tortured; as well as to the right not to be arbitrarily arrested or detained.

Many NHRIs lose credibility within their countries by failing to engage with such issues directly, and instead focussing almost exclusively on human rights education or promotion or implementation of those rights which involve less criticism of the government.

NHRIs should accept information from any reliable source, and should cooperate with national and international NGOs.

4.A.3 Investigating individual cases and wider patterns

Pending completion of investigations the NHRI should always identify any systematic pattern of human rights violations, and address the root causes, rather than solely treating each case in isolation. They should not look at individual cases in isolation, nor report abstractly on trends and developments – rather they should focus on the facts of individual cases, and identifying patterns, using well-researched, well-attested and evidenced cases.

4.A.4 Persistent problems and root causes

In their reports, NHRIs should conduct a critical analysis of the factors which have contributed to the persistence of human rights violations within the national territory. This should include an assessment of the failure of existing institutions and legal mechanisms to provide adequate human rights protection, and its links with impunity, the administration of justice, and for example, treatment of foreign nationals, women, and prisoners.
Recommendations for legal and institutional reform to address human rights violations should be proposed on the basis of the findings.

4.A.5 Addressing all perpetrators without fear

Many NHRIs undermine themselves and lose credibility by asking the alleged violators of human rights – such as the armed forces or the police – to investigate allegations of violations of human rights themselves, rather than the NHRI making an investigation itself. On some occasions, NHRIs simply forward the complainant's initial communication of his or her complaint to the alleged perpetrators (including the complainant's name, address, and other details) to ask the alleged perpetrators, or their colleagues, to investigate. This does not constitute an impartial investigation and can put complainants at risk.

Especially, NHRIs should be authorized to investigate the conduct of the police and the security forces throughout the national territory, and should promptly, effectively, independently and impartially carry out such investigations – especially in situations of internal armed conflict, and during states of emergency. This authorization should not just be made explicit in its implementing legislation; it should also be made a practical reality in its work. NHRIs should not be debarred from operating during states of emergency.

NHRIs should also undertake investigations into human rights violations, even if those responsible include politicians or other powerful agents in society. To do this effectively, the NHRI should have adequate facilities to conduct thorough investigations, independent of the security forces, whose conduct it will be called upon to assess. It should also have effective powers to protect its own staff and witnesses engaged in such investigations.

This is an all too frequent failure of NHRIs around the world, and a major cause of frustration and cynicism towards NHRIs from victims and the general population within countries, as well as NGOs, especially when the actions of major violators of human rights have not been addressed in a satisfactory way.

4.A.6 Compelling evidence

State officials should be legally obliged to cooperate with the NHRI's investigations. NHRIs should have full and effective powers to compel the attendance of witnesses and the disclosure and production of documents and other pieces of evidence. Effective sanctions should be in place to use when the NHRI's work is obstructed or otherwise interfered with.

4.A.7 Accurate statistics lead to an accurate picture of human rights violations

NHRIs should collect and publish accurate data on, for example, reports of "disappearances", deaths in custody, rape and other forms of torture. Collection of data should be a by-product of day to day work, rather than an aim in itself. Statistics should detail the nature of the complaints, how and when they were investigated, the findings, and follow-up to recommendations.

4.B. Methodologies of investigation

In carrying out investigations NHRIs should pursue all available sources of information. These may include statements from victims, witnesses and alleged perpetrators; medical reports; police investigation files; court files; media reports; information from NGOs, families of victims and lawyers.

This is particularly important as investigations that, for example, simply constitute an examination of an existing police investigations file, may lead to a repetition of failures in investigation and in such cases, this may promote or contribute to impunity.

Amnesty International has also received information about cases where the onus of proof is on the complainant to prove his case, rather than the NHRI carrying out an investigation. NHRIs should always take steps to investigate information independently.

4.B.1 Independent investigation professionals

NHRIs should have their own investigative machinery and should have access to expert assistance (forensic pathologists, forensic doctors, ballistic experts, specialists on sexual violence etc.) whenever required to investigate alleged violations of human rights, particularly those involving physical injury (including injuries from sexual violence) and death. It is also important to have access to relevant experts to assist with interviews with victims who may be suffering from the psychological effects of torture, including sexual violence, to identify and record the psychological effects, and to ensure that interviews are conducted in a manner which does not lead to further psychological damage.

Sometimes it will be necessary to bring expertise in from outside the country, where no trained expertise is available.

Wherever possible, such forensic expertise should be at hand at short notice so that effective investigations and recording of, for example, injuries caused by torture or sexual violence, or post mortem investigations, can be made efficiently. When such reliable forensic information is available, then it is much more likely that effective action can be taken in prosecutions of perpetrators.

Such experts should be truly independent – frequently Amnesty International has received reports that such experts have strong links with state officials such as the police, as most of their work is for such state officials. Amnesty International has received some reports of investigators for NHRIs who are actually police officers on secondment from the regular police forces – who were unwilling to investigate allegations against fellow police officers.

NHRIs should have adequate facilities to carry out on-the-spot investigations, including transport, to be able to obtain access to any place in the territory where human rights violations take place.

4.B.2 Training

Effective and practical training of staff working on investigations – especially sharing of skills and best practice from colleagues abroad – should be a priority. Frequently investigations undertaken with good will fail because of lack of training in investigative sciences and skills. They should also receive training in international human rights law so that they can identify and understand legal issues regarding their investigations.

4.B.3 Protection of witnesses

NHRIs should have full and effective access to mechanisms to ensure that witnesses, complainants, or others providing evidence to the NHRI are given appropriate protection. Mechanisms should be in place, which can be triggered by the NHRI, that can lead to the suspension or transfer of officials allegedly involved – without prejudice pending completion of investigations – to other duties where they would have no power over witnesses or complainants.

4.B.4 Protection of evidence

Evidence gathered during investigations, such as witness statements, reports (including reports such as post mortem examinations or other expert reports) and physical evidence (such as evidence gathered during exhumations) should be kept securely by the NHRI.

4.C. Individual complaints

4.C.1 Who can complain?

NHRIs should have powers to begin investigations on its own initiative. It should be able to receive communications not only from the complainants themselves but also, if the complainants themselves are unable or prevented from doing so, from lawyers, relatives or others acting on their behalf, including non-governmental groups. Individual complaints procedures should be free of charge.

It is important that all people have the opportunity to be represented in applications to NHRIs, regardless of their status under national law. Children, prisoners, the mentally ill, and foreign nationals, for example, must all have access to the NHRI.

4.C.2 Reaching out to victims

NHRIs should use networks of communication and outreach already existing among NGOs and civil society groups such as medical associations, to ensure that victims of human rights violations are aware of the procedures open to them.

4.C.3 Keeping the interests of victims at the centre of the process

Victims or relatives should have access to all relevant information and documents relating to the investigation into their complaints and be granted all necessary facilities to present evidence. Victims should in particular, be kept informed of the process of the NHRI's investigation, and be given reasons for decisions taken about their case, and consulted where there are choices as to how their case will develop.

NHRIs should be able to provide financial assistance to witnesses enabling them to travel and be accommodated in order to present their evidence before the NHRI.

Where the NHRI is unable to take up a case, for example, because it is outside its mandate, it should inform the complainant as soon as possible and give reasons for its decision.

4.D. Addressing failed investigations effectively

Where the police have made an inconclusive or otherwise unsatisfactory investigation, the NHRI should undertake a prompt, thorough, effective and impartial investigation and not be hampered or otherwise inhibited by following the conclusions of a previous investigation. Investigations should not simply constitute an examination of an existing police investigations file.

An NHRI which fails to investigate individual complaints effectively may be an instrument of impunity – rather than allowing a victim access to a remedy, it closes off opportunities to secure a remedy, deterring the reporting of abuses.

4.D.1 Separation of roles of the NHRI and the judiciary

A clear line should be drawn between appropriate roles for the NHRI and the judiciary. The NHRI should be able to investigate, but should not have judicial powers. The result of the NHRI's investigations should be referred to appropriate judicial bodies without delay so that they can take appropriate action.

Evidence obtained by NHRIs should not be made inadmissible in other proceedings simply by virtue of having been first given to the NHRI.

Amnesty Internation has received reports which indicate that some NHRIs consider that investigations by the police or the security forces *prima facie* are sufficient investigations. It is important that NHRIs make their own assessment of the effectiveness of such investigations and follow up themselves with prompt, effective, thorough and impartial investigations where existing internal police or army investigations, or judicial investigations are not effective.

Where the NHRI finds evidence that certain individuals may have been responsible for committing human rights violations or for ordering, encouraging or permitting them, the facts of the case should be investigated promptly, effectively, thoroughly and impartially by authorities empowered to bring criminal prosecutions, and if appropriate, those responsible should be brought to justice in legal proceedings which respect internationally-recognized rights to a fair trial, and do not lead to punishments involving torture or cruel, inhuman or degrading treatment, including the death penalty.

NHRIs should have powers to recommend that superior officers are brought to justice for acts committed under their authority and should be mandated to closely follow subsequent legal proceedings in the case, by monitoring trials, or if necessary appearing before the court to make legal submissions to press for appropriate legal action to be taken within a reasonable time. If the NHRI, in the course of its work, is able to identify short-comings in the law whereby it is not possible to hold such officers accountable, the NHRI should make recommendations for legal reform that would ensure that domestic law does not facilitate impunity.

The government should ensure that any prosecutions for crimes involving the abuse of human rights are brought by authorities which are distinctly independent from the security forces or other bodies allegedly implicated in human rights violations.

4.D.2 Parallel jurisdiction of NHRI and the judiciary

The fact that a complainant has been charged and a criminal prosecution is under way should not be a pretext for stopping NHRIs from acting on a complaint, or taking any other action within their mandate to address human rights concerns.

Where prosecutions are pending, the NHRI should not consider the substance of the criminal charge, but should be able to look at ancilliary matters relating to the human rights of the accused person, for example, allegations that he or she has been tortured while in custody.

In some jurisdictions, the NHRI is not permitted to receive complaints from a person who has been charged with an offence or who is otherwise under judicial supervision; therefore if the judiciary is not taking appropriate steps to protect the accused person from human rights violations such as torture and ill-treatment in custody, then that person is without recourse to protect their rights.

4.D.3 Role of NHRI in following up the actions of prosecutors and the judiciary in cases of criminal acts

Although it is important to maintain independence of function between the judiciary and the NHRI, the NHRI should monitor whether its recommendations are followed up. Amnesty International frequently receives reports that an NHRI has recommended that, on the basis of their investigations, criminal investigations and prosecutions should be initiated – but the police or prosecuting authorities take no action.

NHRIs should not stand by in silence where recommendations to investigate and bring prosecutions are ignored. In such cases, the NHRI should continue to request that the authorities take up the case, if necessary through domestic and international publicity, or where possible, to bring judicial review action challenging the decision of the prosecuting authorities. NHRIs should not be complicit with impunity.

Where domestic remedies for human rights violations are exhausted or ineffective, NHRIs should raise the matter with the international bodies mandated to assess compliance with human rights standards, such as the human rights treaty monitoring bodies, or the United Nations' thematic mechanisms and special procedures, such as the Special Rapporteurs.

5. Recommendations and non-judicial remedies

5.1 Remedies and interim measures

NHRIs should have powers to ensure effective non-judicial remedies, including interim measures to protect the life and safety of an individual and adequate medical treatment where necessary; it should ensure measures of redress and rehabilitation are taken in appropriate cases.

5.2 Remedies but not impunity

NHRIs should not broker agreements for only reparations, such as compensation, to be paid, where the appropriate response would rather be reparation and prosecution of the perpetrator – for example in cases of torture.

Amnesty International has received reports that some NHRIs order compensation for crimes such as torture, and where the government encourages this or other forms of conciliation rather than bringing cases forward for prosecution. Conclusion of a case through friendly settlement should not prevent or hamper prosecutions for crimes under international law, such as torture, war crimes, or crimes against humanity.

5.3 Recommendations should be followed up

The government should undertake an obligation to respond, within a reasonable time, to the case- specific as well as the more general findings, conclusions and recommendations made by the NHRI. The government's response should be made public.

In cases where the government fails to respond, or refuses to respond or implement recommendations, the NHRI should continue to take all possible measures to press the government, for example, through pressure by the media, through parliament, and through international pressure of opinion and bringing the case to the attention of the international human rights bodies, such as the treaty monitoring bodies and the special mechanisms. Cases should remain open and as far as practically possible, the members and staff who dealt with the case up to the NHRI giving its recommendation should remain actively involved with the case and monitoring the implementation of the recommendation to ensure that the situation has been remedied. Continuity of staff is important to ensure that the initial problem has been addressed effectively.

6. Human rights education

Amnesty International has noted that a population which is educated in their human rights is an asset to assist NHRIs to carry out their task. Educating the population on human rights is a task that NHRIs working even under the most repressive governments are able to attempt, so it is important that it is done effectively.

General human rights education should be undertaken in a practical, illustrative way – if possible using media broadcasts to illustrate or dramatise human rights issues – rather than producing glossy, but abstract, promotional material which simply sets out general principles. It is also vital to ensure that material is disseminated to suitable target audiences.

Human rights training should be targetted at people who may have to consider and apply human rights issues in their work – law-makers, administrative decision-makers, judges, lawyers, the medical profession, teachers, social workers, prison officers and police officers, and the armed forces – and they should be encouraged to promote human rights standards among their colleagues. Again, this professional education should be undertaken in a practical way to illustrate the transformative effect of using human rights standards in daily professional life. NGOs and victims groups should be encouraged to participate in such training to ensure that a variety of viewpoints are expressed within the education process.

7. Visits to places of detention

An important role that NHRIs can fulfil is as independent professional body empowered to visit places of detention, with the aim of making recommendations to change conditions in order to prevent the incidence of torture and other cruel, inhuman and degrading treatment or punishment.

Amnesty International has received reports of a wide range of competence in fulfilling this role among NHRIs around the world. Amnesty International has received information regarding cases where an NHRI has given assurances that a certain individual although reported to have been tortured, was fine and in good health, only for the organization's representatives to visit the same individual shortly afterwards to find him showing signs of torture consistent with earlier reports – giving rise to the possibilities that either the NHRI had not visited, or had misreported their findings, or lacked the necessary expertise to carry out visits. Thorough training is essential.

On the other hand, Amnesty International has received excellent general reports by NHRIs detailing the conditions of detention, and making recommendations which have led to a decrease in the incidence of torture and cruel, inhuman and degrading treatment and punishment. Unfortunately, recommendations are frequently not implemented by governments.

Even in cases where NHRIs undertake effective visits to places of detention, they are not provided with the human and practical resources (such as transport to all places of detention in all regions) so that they can ensure effective coverage and assessment of all places of detention.

7.1 Modalities of visits

The modalities of visits provided for in the Geneva Conventions of 1949 – Article 126 of the Third Geneva Convention, and Article 143 of the Fourth Geneva Convention – should be used by NHRIs in setting out the modalities for visits to places of detention.

These modalities are that:

1. the visiting mechanism shall have access to all places of detention, and have access to all premises in which detainees may be held.

Frequently, NHRIs are denied access to particular categories of places of detention, such as police stations, military prisons, or prisons where detainees are held under security or "anti-terrorist" legislation. These are frequently the very institutions from which many reliably attested complaints of torture are received, so it is vitally important that independent monitors have access to those places to assess conditions and make recommendations for change.

2. the visiting mechanism shall be able to interview detainees without witnesses, either personally or through the mechanism's own interpreter.

3. the visiting mechanism shall have liberty to select the places they wish to visit.

Frequently NHRIs are required to seek permission or give long notice of their visit. NHRIs should be able to visit "any place,at any time" without prior authorization in order to make a true assessment of conditions of detention.

4. the duration and frequency of visits shall not be restricted.

The only reason for denying access to a particular place of detention should be physical danger equal to the provision within the Geneva Conventions regarding compelling military necessity – which in practice means that a place of detention should only be out of bounds for visits if it is under weapon fire, and only during the period of danger. State security should not be an issue which would affect visits. The NHRI itself should assess and take appropriate precautions regarding any other risks, such as risk to health through disease prevalent within a certain institution.

8. Publicity

8.1 Media

NHRIs should ensure that they have access to the media in order to publicise their work to ensure that the population as a whole is aware of the services that the NHRI can provide; that they have human rights that can be protected and enforced; and to ensure a forum for discussion of human rights and publicity (therefore transparency) of the NHRI's activities. It is very important that the NHRI be seen by all to be taking effective action. NHRIs should also publicise their role as an institution independent from the executive part of the government, and its policies regarding confidentiality and security.

The NHRI should use the most effective media available to make contact with as many people as possible – so, for example, in places where illiteracy is high or where newspapers are hard to obtain, radio broadcasts should be used.

8.2 Annual reports

NHRIs should ensure that their reports, particularly their annual reports, are published and circulated widely.
Amnesty International recommends that NHRIs should be empowered to publish their materials at any time. Amnesty International has received reports that some NHRIs must present their reports to parliament or other political bodies before they are empowered to publish their reports, and frequently parliamentary time is not made available for this purpose. Therefore the NHRI is effectively silenced.

Many NHRIs do not produce annual reports – it is very important that they do so in order to be accountable and transparent, and to be seen to be fulfilling its role, evaluating its results, and planning its future activities. Statistics on the numbers and types of cases received, action taken and results achieved by the NHRI in resolving the cases should be included.

8.3 Confidentiality

Although there should be an assumption in favour of transparency, particularly in reports and the findings of investigations, in such publicity, care should be taken that sensitive details which could lead to complainants, their families, witnesses and human rights defenders being put in danger, or which leads to an invasion of their privacy, should not be released. However this need for confidentiality for sensitive information should not be used as an excuse not to publish any information at all, as this could be an excuse to cover up evidence of human rights violations.

9. Accessibility

9.1 Regional offices

Local and regional offices are vitally important to the effective functioning of NHRIs in a large country, or a county with isolated and inaccessible centres of population, or where transportation is difficult. Mechanisms should allow local offices a positive role in following up cases. Unfortunately Amnesty International has received reports of local offices undertaking prompt and effective investigations, but they are are not empowered to follow up with local authorities: instead they have to refer cases to a central office. This can frequently become a "black hole" of bureaucracy, and effectively, cases are not followed up. Where there is a network of local and central offices, effective coordination and communication between all should be ensured. Responsibility for following up on cases must be clearly allocated and periodic evaluations should ensure that follow-up is taking place.

9.2 Accessible premises

NHRI offices must be stationed in appropriate places – unfortunately Amnesty International has received reports of NHRI offices being located near military installations or police stations. In such cases, potential complainants may fear being noticed or monitored by the security forces if they bring their complaints. Amnesty International has received other reports of offices being intimidatingly smart or located in very up-market areas, so that the poor and other disadvantaged groups feel too uncomfortable and conspicuous to be seen going there. Other reports indicate that some offices are located in inaccessible areas where it is difficult for complainants to visit.

Within offices, there should be facilities such as private meeting rooms where complainants can discuss their complaints with NHRI staff in confidence.

9.3 Communication with victims

NHRIs should take steps to ensure effective communications between itself and potential complainants.

Amnesty International has received reports of excellent initiatives to facilitate such contact – such as free-phone (toll-free) telephone lines, email and internet access, and travelling offices (one example was a specially adapted bus) or travelling field officers who can go to very isolated areas. NGO networks can also facilitate contacts with victims and witnesses.

In countries where some complainants are likely only to be able to speak minority or local languages, these should be catered for. When using interpreters, careful consideration should be given to issues of confidentiality and impartiality. Cultural sensitivities should also be taken into account, which may include the gender of the interpreter. Interviewees (including complainants and witnesses) should consent to the use of interpreters.

In countries where there is widespread illiteracy, there should be common use of oral communication techniques, such as radio, and NHRI staff should take care to explain their procedures verbally, rather than relying on explanatory leaflets.

10. Budget

The government must provide the NHRI with adequate funding and resources in order to be able to fully carry out, and without restrictions and limitations, the aims and functions set out within the mandate, and particularly, to address the demands of the caseload that has been brought to its attention. The NHRI should have all necessary human and material resources to examine, thoroughly, effectively, speedily and throughout the country, the evidence and other case material concerning specific allegations of violations reported to it.

NHRIs are mandated by international standards, such as the Paris Principles, and by recommendations of civil society, such as the recommendations in this document, to cover a wide range of human rights issues, and clearly some prioritization of activities by NHRIs is required. Professional training and sharing of working skills so that NHRIs can maximise effective action within the bounds of resource constraints is therefore important.

Amnesty International has received reports that restrictions in NHRI budgets are used as a punitive measure to control an NHRI which is deemed to be too critical of government. AI has received reports of many examples where once set up, NHRIs are underfunded to the extent that they cannot function effectively – leading to reasonable doubts about how serious the government was in the first place about improving the implementation human rights through the NHRI.

The mandate should specifically and explicitly include the power to be able to establish effective and alternative routes to receive funding, either from private donors or international agencies, for whatever human rights activities the NHRI is undertaking. NHRIs should develop guidelines to ensure that any such fundraising does not compromise its independence and impartiality.

Funding should be secured with a longterm perspective to enable the NHRI to plan and develop its activities with confidence about being able to fulfil them.
AI Index: IOR 40/007/2001 1 October 2001

UNITED NATIONS TREATY BODIES' GENERAL COMMENTS

APPENDIX III

CESCR GENERAL COMMENT NO. 10: THE ROLE OF NATIONAL HUMAN RIGHTS INSTITUTIONS IN THE PROTECTION OF ECONOMIC, SOCIAL AND CULTURAL RIGHTS. (14/12/98. E/C.12/1998/25)

The role of national human rights institutions in the protection of economic, social and cultural rights[*]

1. Article 2, paragraph 1, of the Covenant obligates each State party "to take steps ... with a view to achieving progressively the full realization of the [Covenant] rights ... by all appropriate means". The Committee notes that one such means, through which important steps can be taken, is the work of national institutions for the promotion and protection of human rights. In recent years there has been a proliferation of these institutions and the trend has been strongly encouraged by the General Assembly and the Commission on Human Rights. The Office of the United Nations High Commissioner for Human Rights has established a major programme to assist and encourage States in relation to national institutions.

2. These institutions range from national human rights commissions through Ombudsman offices, public interest or other human rights "advocates", to "defensores del pueblo". In many cases, the institution has been established by the Government, enjoys an important degree of autonomy from the executive and the legislature, takes full account of international human rights standards which are applicable to the country concerned, and is mandated to perform various activities designed to promote and protect human rights. Such institutions have been established in States with widely differing legal cultures and regardless of their economic situation.

3. The Committee notes that national institutions have a potentially crucial role to play in promoting and ensuring the indivisibility and interdependence of all human rights. Unfortunately, this role has too often either not been accorded to the institution or has been neglected or given a low priority by it. It is therefore essential that full attention be given to economic, social and cultural rights in all of the relevant activities of these institutions. The following list is indicative of the types of activities that can be, and in some instances already have been, undertaken by national institutions in relation to these rights:

(a) The promotion of educational and information programmes designed to enhance awareness and understanding of economic, social and cultural rights, both within the

---

[*] Adopted at the 51st meeting (nineteenth session), on 1 December 1998.

population at large and among particular groups such as the public service, the judiciary, the private sector and the labour movement;
(b) The scrutinizing of existing laws and administrative acts, as well as draft bills and other proposals, to ensure that they are consistent with the requirements of the International Covenant on Economic, Social and Cultural Rights;
(c) Providing technical advice, or undertaking surveys in relation to economic, social and cultural rights, including at the request of the public authorities or other appropriate agencies;
(d) The identification of national-level benchmarks against which the realization of Covenant obligations can be measured;
(e) Conducting research and inquiries designed to ascertain the extent to which particular economic, social and cultural rights are being realized, either within the State as a whole or in areas or in relation to communities of particular vulnerability;
(f) Monitoring compliance with specific rights recognized under the Covenant and providing reports thereon to the public authorities and civil society; and
(g) Examining complaints alleging infringements of applicable economic, social and cultural rights standards within the State.
4. The Committee calls upon States parties to ensure that the mandates accorded to all national human rights institutions include appropriate attention to economic, social and cultural rights and requests States parties to include details of both the mandates and the principal relevant activities of such institutions in their reports submitted to the Committee.

APPENDIX IV

CERD GENERAL RECOMMENDATION NO. XVII: ESTABLISHMENT OF NATIONAL INSTITUTIONS TO FACILITATE IMPLEMENTATION OF THE CONVENTION. (25/03/93. GEN. REC. NO. 17.)

General Recommendation XVII
Establishment of national institutions to facilitate implementation of the Convention
(Forty-second session, 1993)[*]

The Committee on the Elimination of Racial Discrimination,
Considering the practice of States parties concerning the implementation of the International Convention on the Elimination of All Forms of Racial Discrimination,
Convinced of the necessity to encourage further the establishment of national institutions to facilitate the implementation of the Convention,
Emphasizing the need to strengthen further the implementation of the Convention,
1. *Recommends* that States parties establish national commissions or other appropriate bodies, taking into account, *mutatis mutandis*, the principles relating to the status of national institutions annexed to Commission on Human Rights resolution 1992/54 of 3 March 1992, to serve, *inter alia*, the following purposes:
(a) To promote respect for the enjoyment of human rights without any discrimination, as expressly set out in article 5 of the International Convention on the Elimination of All Forms of Racial Discrimination;
(b) To review government policy towards protection against racial discrimination;
(c) To monitor legislative compliance with the provisions of the Convention;
(d) To educate the public about the obligations of States parties under the Convention;
(e) To assist the Government in the preparation of reports submitted to the Committee on the Elimination of Racial Discrimination;
2. *Also recommends* that, where such commissions have been established, they should be associated with the preparation of reports and possibly included in government delegations in order to intensify the dialogue between the Committee and the State party concerned.

---

[*] Contained in document A/48/18.

APPENDIX V

CRC GENERAL COMMENT NO. 2: THE ROLE OF INDEPENDENT NATIONAL HUMAN RIGHTS INSTITUTIONS IN THE PROTECTION AND PROMOTION OF THE RIGHTS OF THE CHILD. (15/11/2002. CRC/GC/2002/2.)

1. Article 4 of the Convention on the Rights of the Child obliges States parties to "undertake all appropriate legislative, administrative and other measures for the implementation of the rights recognized in the present Convention". Independent national human rights institutions (NHRIs) are an important mechanism to promote and ensure the implementation of the Convention, and the Committee on the Rights of the Child considers the establishment of such bodies to fall within the commitment made by States parties upon ratification to ensure the implementation of the Convention and advance the universal realization of children's rights. In this regard, the Committee has welcomed the establishment of NHRIs and children's ombudspersons/children's commissioners and similar independent bodies for the promotion and monitoring of the implementation of the Convention in a number of States parties.

2. The Committee issues this general comment in order to encourage States parties to establish an independent institution for the promotion and monitoring of implementation of the Convention and to support them in this regard by elaborating the essential elements of such institutions and the activities which should be carried out by them. Where such institutions have already been established, the Committee calls upon States to review their status and effectiveness for promoting and protecting children's rights, as enshrined in the Convention on the Rights of the Child and other relevant international instruments.

3. The World Conference on Human Rights, held in 1993, in the Vienna Declaration and Programme of Action reaffirmed "... the important and constructive role played by national institutions for the promotion and protection of human rights", and encouraged "... the establishment and strengthening of national institutions". The General Assembly and the Commission on Human Rights have repeatedly called for the establishment of national human rights institutions, underlining the important role NHRIs play in promoting and protecting human rights and enhancing public awareness of those rights. In its general guidelines for periodic reports, the Committee requires that States parties furnish information on "any independent body established to promote and protect the rights of the child ...",[6] hence, it consistently addresses this issue during its dialogue with States parties.

---

[6] General guidelines regarding the form and contents of periodic reports to be submitted by States parties under article 44, paragraph 1 (b), of the Convention (CRC/C/58), para. 18.

4. NHRIs should be established in compliance with the Principles relating to the status of national institutions for the promotion and protection of human rights (The "Paris Principles") adopted by the General Assembly in 1993[7] transmitted by the Commission on Human Rights in 1992.[8] These minimum standards provide guidance for the establishment, competence, responsibilities, composition, including pluralism, independence, methods of operation, and quasi-judicial activities of such national bodies.

5. While adults and children alike need independent NHRIs to protect their human rights, additional justifications exist for ensuring that children's human rights are given special attention. These include the facts that children's developmental state makes them particularly vulnerable to human rights violations; their opinions are still rarely taken into account; most children have no vote and cannot play a meaningful role in the political process that determines Governments' response to human rights; children encounter significant problems in using the judicial system to protect their rights or to seek remedies for violations of their rights; and children's access to organizations that may protect their rights is generally limited.

6. Specialist independent human rights institutions for children, ombudspersons or commissioners for children's rights have been established in a growing number of States parties. Where resources are limited, consideration must be given to ensuring that the available resources are used most effectively for the promotion and protection of everyone's human rights, including children's, and in this context development of a broad-based NHRI that includes a specific focus on children is likely to constitute the best approach. A broad-based NHRI should include within its structure either an identifiable commissioner specifically responsible for children's rights, or a specific section or division responsible for children's rights.

7. It is the view of the Committee that every State needs an independent human rights institution with responsibility for promoting and protecting children's rights. The Committee's principal concern is that the institution, whatever its form, should be able, independently and effectively, to monitor, promote and protect children's rights. It is essential that promotion and protection of children's rights is "mainstreamed" and that all human rights institutions existing in a country work closely together to this end.

---

[7] Principles relating to the status of national institutions for the promotion and protection of human rights (The "Paris Principles"), General Assembly resolution 48/134 of 20 December 1993, annex.

[8] Commission on Human Rights resolution 1992/54 of 3 March 1992, annex.

Mandate and powers

8. NHRIs should, if possible, be constitutionally entrenched and must at least be legislatively mandated. It is the view of the Committee that their mandate should include as broad a scope as possible for promoting and protecting human rights, incorporating the Convention on the Rights of the Child, its Optional Protocols and other relevant international human rights instruments – thus effectively covering children's human rights, in particular their civil, political, economic, social and cultural rights. The legislation should include provisions setting out specific functions, powers and duties relating to children linked to the Convention on the Rights of the Child and its Optional Protocols. If the NHRI was established before the existence of the Convention, or without expressly incorporating it, necessary arrangements, including the enactment or amendment of legislation, should be put in place so as to ensure conformity of the institution's mandate with the principles and provisions of the Convention.

9. NHRIs should be accorded such powers as are necessary to enable them to discharge their mandate effectively, including the power to hear any person and obtain any information and document necessary for assessing the situations falling within their competence. These powers should include the promotion and protection of the rights of all children under the jurisdiction of the State party in relation not only to the State but to all relevant public and private entities.

Establishment process

10. The NHRI establishment process should be consultative, inclusive and transparent, initiated and supported at the highest levels of Government and inclusive of all relevant elements of the State, the legislature and civil society. In order to ensure their independence and effective functioning, NHRIs must have adequate infrastructure, funding (including specifically for children's rights, within broad-based institutions), staff, premises, and freedom from forms of financial control that might affect their independence.

Resources

11. While the Committee acknowledges that this is a very sensitive issue and that State parties function with varying levels of economic resources, the Committee believes that it is the duty of States to make reasonable financial provision for the operation of national human rights institutions in light of article 4 of the Convention. The mandate and powers of national institutions may be meaningless, or the exercise of their powers limited, if the national institution does not have the means to operate effectively to discharge its powers.

APPENDIX V

Pluralistic representation

12. NHRIs should ensure that their composition includes pluralistic representation of the various elements of civil society involved in the promotion and protection of human rights. They should seek to involve, among others, the following: human rights, anti-discrimination and children's rights non-governmental organizations (NGOs), including child- and youth-led organizations; trade unions; social and professional organizations (of doctors, lawyers, journalists, scientists, etc.); universities and experts, including children's rights experts. Government departments should be involved in an advisory capacity only. NHRIs should have appropriate and transparent appointment procedures, including an open and competitive selection process.

Providing remedies for breaches of children's rights

13. NHRIs must have the power to consider individual complaints and petitions and carry out investigations, including those submitted on behalf of or directly by children. In order to be able to effectively carry out such investigations, they must have the powers to compel and question witnesses, access relevant documentary evidence and access places of detention. They also have a duty to seek to ensure that children have effective remedies – independent advice, advocacy and complaints procedures – for any breaches of their rights. Where appropriate, NHRIs should undertake mediation and conciliation of complaints.

14. NHRIs should have the power to support children taking cases to court, including the power (a) to take cases concerning children's issues in the name of the NHRI and (b) to intervene in court cases to inform the court about the human rights issues involved in the case.

Accessibility and participation

15. NHRIs should be geographically and physically accessible to all children. In the spirit of article 2 of the Convention, they should proactively reach out to all groups of children, in particular the most vulnerable and disadvantaged, such as (but not limited to) children in care or detention, children from minority and indigenous groups, children with disabilities, children living in poverty, refugee and migrant children, street children and children with special needs in areas such as culture, language, health and education. NHRI legislation should include the right of the institution to have access in conditions of privacy to children in all forms of alternative care and to all institutions that include children.

16. NHRIs have a key role to play in promoting respect for the views of children in all matters affecting them, as articulated in article 12 of the Convention, by Government and throughout society. This general principle should be applied to the

establishment, organization and activities of national human rights institutions. Institutions must ensure that they have direct contact with children and that children are appropriately involved and consulted. Children's councils, for example, could be created as advisory bodies for NHRIs to facilitate the participation of children in matters of concern to them.

17. NHRIs should devise specially tailored consultation programmes and imaginative communication strategies to ensure full compliance with article 12 of the Convention. A range of suitable ways in which children can communicate with the institution should be established.

18. NHRIs must have the right to report directly, independently and separately on the state of children's rights to the public and to parliamentary bodies. In this respect, States parties must ensure that an annual debate is held in Parliament to provide parliamentarians with an opportunity to discuss the work of the NHRI in respect of children's rights and the State's compliance with the Convention.

Recommended activities

19. The following is an indicative, but not exhaustive, list of the types of activities which NHRIs should carry out in relation to the implementation of children's rights in light of the general principles of the Convention. They should:

(a) Undertake investigations into any situation of violation of children's rights, on complaint or on their own initiative, within the scope of their mandate;

(b) Conduct inquiries on matters relating to children's rights;

(c) Prepare and publicize opinions, recommendations and reports, either at the request of national authorities or on their own initiative, on any matter relating to the promotion and protection of children's rights;

(d) Keep under review the adequacy and effectiveness of law and practice relating to the protection of children's rights;

(e) Promote harmonization of national legislation, regulations and practices with the Convention on the Rights of the Child, its Optional Protocols and other international human rights instruments relevant to children's rights and promote their effective implementation, including through the provision of advice to public and private bodies in construing and applying the Convention;

(f) Ensure that national economic policy makers take children's rights into account in setting and evaluating national economic and development plans;

(g) Review and report on the Government's implementation and monitoring of the state of children's rights, seeking to ensure that statistics are appropriately disaggregated and other information collected on a regular basis in order to determine what must be done to realize children's rights;

(h) Encourage ratification of or accession to any relevant international human rights instruments;

(i) In accordance with article 3 of the Convention requiring that the best interests of children should be a primary consideration in all actions concerning them, ensure that the impact of laws and policies on children is carefully considered from development to implementation and beyond;

(j) In light of article 12, ensure that the views of children are expressed and heard on matters concerning their human rights and in defining issues relating to their rights;

(k) Advocate for and facilitate meaningful participation by children's rights NGOs, including organizations comprised of children themselves, in the development of domestic legislation and international instruments on issues affecting children;

(l) Promote public understanding and awareness of the importance of children's rights and, for this purpose, work closely with the media and undertake or sponsor research and educational activities in the field;

(m) In accordance with article 42 of the Convention which obligates State parties to "make the principles and provisions of the Convention widely known, by appropriate and active means, to adults and children alike", sensitize the Government, public agencies and the general public to the provisions of the Convention and monitor ways in which the State is meeting its obligations in this regard;

(n) Assist in the formulation of programmes for the teaching of, research into and integration of children's rights in the curricula of schools and universities and in professional circles;

(o) Undertake human rights education which specifically focuses on children (in addition to promoting general public understanding about the importance of children's rights);

(p) Take legal proceedings to vindicate children's rights in the State or provide legal assistance to children;

(q) Engage in mediation or conciliation processes before taking cases to court, where appropriate;

(r) Provide expertise in children's rights to the courts, in suitable cases as amicus curiae or intervenor;

(s) In accordance with article 3 of the Convention which obliges States parties to "ensure that the institutions, services and facilities responsible for the care or protection of children shall conform with the standards established by competent authorities, particularly in the areas of safety, health, in the number and suitability of their staff, as well as competent supervision", undertake visits to juvenile homes (and all places where children are detained for reform or punishment) and care institutions to report on the situation and to make recommendations for improvement;

(t) Undertake such other activities as are incidental to the above.

Reporting to the Committee on the Rights of the Child and cooperation between NHRIs and United Nations agencies and human rights mechanisms

20. NHRIs should contribute independently to the reporting process under the Convention and other relevant international instruments and monitor the integrity of government reports to international treaty bodies with respect to children's rights, including through dialogue with the Committee on the Rights of the Child at its pre-sessional working group and with other relevant treaty bodies.

21. The Committee requests that States parties include detailed information on the legislative basis and mandate and principal relevant activities of NHRIs in their reports to the Committee. It is appropriate for States parties to consult with independent human rights institutions during the preparation of reports to the Committee. However, States parties must respect the independence of these bodies and their independent role in providing information to the Committee. It is not appropriate to delegate to NHRIs the drafting of reports or to include them in the government delegation when reports are examined by the Committee.

22. NHRIs should also cooperate with the special procedures of the Commission on Human Rights, including country and thematic mechanisms, in particular the Special Rapporteur on the sale of children, child prostitution and child pornography and the Special Representative of the Secretary-General for Children and Armed Conflict.

23. The United Nations has a long-standing programme of assistance for the establishment and strengthening of national human rights institutions. This programme, which is based in the Office of the High Commissioner for Human Rights (OHCHR), provides technical assistance and facilitates regional and global

cooperation and exchanges among national human rights institutions. States parties should avail themselves of this assistance where necessary. The United Nations Children's Fund (UNICEF) also offers expertise and technical cooperation in this area.

24. As articulated in article 45 of the Convention, the Committee may also transmit, as it considers appropriate, to any specialized United Nations agency, OHCHR and any other competent body any reports from States parties that contain a request or indicate a need for technical advice or assistance in the establishment of NHRIs.

NHRIs and States parties

25. The State ratifies the Convention on the Rights of the Child and takes on obligations to implement it fully. The role of NHRIs is to monitor independently the State's compliance and progress towards implementation and to do all it can to ensure full respect for children's rights. While this may require the institution to develop projects to enhance the promotion and protection of children's rights, it should not lead to the Government delegating its monitoring obligations to the national institution. It is essential that institutions remain entirely free to set their own agenda and determine their own activities.

NHRIs and NGOs

26. Non-governmental organizations play a vital role in promoting human rights and children's rights. The role of NHRIs, with their legislative base and specific powers, is complementary. It is essential that institutions work closely with NGOs and that Governments respect the independence of both NHRIs and NGOs.

Regional and international cooperation

27. Regional and international processes and mechanisms can strengthen and consolidate NHRIs through shared experience and skills, as NHRIs share common problems in the promotion and protection of human rights in their respective countries.

28. In this respect, NHRIs should consult and cooperate with relevant national, regional and international bodies and institutions on children's rights issues.

29. Children's human rights issues are not constrained by national borders and it has become increasingly necessary to devise appropriate regional and international responses to a variety of child rights issues (including, but not limited to, the trafficking of women and children, child pornography, child soldiers, child labour, child abuse, refugee and migrant children, etc.). International and regional mechanisms and exchanges are encouraged, as they provide NHRIs with an

opportunity to learn from each other's experience, collectively strengthen each other's positions and contribute to resolving human rights problems affecting both countries and regions.

OTHER RELEVANT DOCUMENTS AND TABLES

APPENDIX VI

THE MILLENNIUM DEVELOPMENT GOALS AND TARGETS

Goal 1. Eradicate extreme poverty and hunger

Target 1.
Halve, between 1990 and 2015, the proportion of people whose income is less than one dollar a day

Target 2.
Halve, between 1990 and 2015, the proportion of people who suffer from hunger

Goal 2. Achieve universal primary education

Target 3.
Ensure that, by 2015, children everywhere, boys and girls alike, will be able to complete a full course of primary schooling

Goal 3. Promote gender equality and empower women

Target 4.
Eliminate gender disparity in primary and secondary education, preferably by 2005, and in all levels of education no later than 2015

Goal 4. Reduce child mortality

Target 5.
Reduce by two thirds, between 1990 and 2015, the under-five mortality rate

Goal 5. Improve maternal health

Target 6.
Reduce by three quarters, between 1990 and 2015, the maternal mortality ratio

Goal 6. Combat HIV/AIDS, malaria and other diseases

Target 7.
Have halted by 2015 and begun to reverse the spread of HIV/AIDS

Target 8.
Have halted by 2015 and begun to reverse the incidence of malaria and other major diseases

APPENDIX VI

Goal 7. Ensure environmental sustainability

Target 9.

Integrate the principles of sustainable development into country policies and programmes and reverse the loss of environmental resources

Target 10.

Halve, by 2015, the proportion of people without sustainable access to safe drinking water and sanitation

Target 11.

By 2020, to have achieved a significant improvement in the lives of at least 100 million slum dwellers

Goal 8. Develop a global partnership for development

Target 12.

Develop further an open, rule-based, predictable, non-discriminatory trading and financial system.

Includes a commitment to good governance, development and poverty reduction – both nationally and internationally

Target 13.

Address the special needs of the least developed countries.

Includes: tariff and quota-free access for least developed countries' exports; enhanced programme of debt relief for heavily indebted poor countries (HIPC) and cancellation of official bilateral debt; and more generous ODA for countries committed to poverty reduction

Target 14.

Address the special needs of landlocked developing countries and small island developing States (through the Programme of Action for the Sustainable Development of Small Island Developing States and the outcome of the twenty-second special session of the General Assembly)

Target 15.

Deal comprehensively with the debt problems of developing countries through national and international measures in order to make debt sustainable in the long term

Target 16.

In cooperation with developing countries, develop and implement strategies for decent and productive work for youth

Target 17.

In cooperation with pharmaceutical companies, provide access to affordable essential drugs in developing countries

Target 18.

In cooperation with the private sector, make available the benefits of new technologies, especially information and communications

APPENDIX VII

THE MAASTRICHT GUIDELINES ON VIOLATIONS OF ECONOMIC, SOCIAL AND CULTURAL RIGHTS

Introduction

On the occasion of the tenth anniversary of the Limburg Principles on the Implementation of the International Covenant on Economic, Social and Cultural Rights (hereinafter "the Limburg Principles"), a group of more than 30 experts met in Maastricht from 22 to 26 January 1997 at the invitation of the International Commission of Jurists (Geneva, Switzerland), the Urban Morgan Institute on Human Rights (Cincinnati, Ohio, United States of America) and the Centre for Human Rights of the Faculty of Law of Maastricht University (the Netherlands). The objective of this meeting was to elaborate on the Limburg Principles as regards the nature and scope of violations of economic, social and cultural rights and appropriate responses and remedies.

The participants unanimously agreed on the following guidelines which they understand to reflect the evolution of international law since 1986. These guidelines are designed to be of use to all who are concerned with understanding and determining violations of economic, social and cultural rights and in providing remedies thereto, in particular monitoring and adjudicating bodies at the national, regional and international levels.

MAASTRICHT GUIDELINES ON VIOLATIONS OF ECONOMIC, SOCIAL AND CULTURAL RIGHTS

I. The significance of economic, social and cultural rights

1. Since the Limburg Principles were adopted in 1986, the economic and social conditions have declined at alarming rates for over 1.6 billion people, while they have advanced also at a dramatic pace for more than a quarter of the world's population. The gap between rich and poor has doubled in the last three decades, with the poorest fifth of the world's population receiving 1.4 per cent of the global income and the richest fifth 85 per cent. The impact of these disparities on the lives of people – especially the poor – is dramatic and renders the enjoyment of economic, social and cultural rights illusory for a significant portion of humanity.

2. Since the end of the Cold War, there has been a trend in all regions of the world to reduce the role of the State and to rely on the market to resolve problems of human welfare, often in response to conditions generated by international and national financial markets and institutions and in an effort to attract investments from the multinational enterprises whose wealth and power exceed that of many States. It is no longer taken for granted that the realization of economic, social and cultural rights depends significantly on action by the State, although, as a matter of international law, the State remains ultimately responsible for guaranteeing the realization of these rights. While the challenge of addressing violations of economic,

social and cultural rights is rendered more complicated by these trends, it is more urgent than ever to take these rights seriously and, therefore, to deal with the accountability of Governments for failure to meet their obligations in this area.

3. There have also been significant legal developments enhancing economic, social and cultural rights since 1986, including the emerging jurisprudence of the Committee on Economic, Social and Cultural Rights and the adoption of instruments, such as the revised European Social Charter of 1996 and the Additional Protocol to the European Charter providing for a System of Collective Complaints, and the San Salvador Protocol to the American Convention on Human Rights in the Area of Economic, Social and Cultural Rights of 1988. Governments have made firm commitments to address more effectively economic, social and cultural rights within the framework of seven United Nations world summit conferences (1992-1996). Moreover, the potential exists for improved accountability for violations of economic, social and cultural rights through the proposed optional protocols to the International Covenant on Economic, Social and Cultural Rights and the Convention on the Elimination of All Forms of Discrimination against Women. Significant developments within national civil society movements and regional and international NGOs in the field of economic, social and cultural rights have taken place.

4. It is now undisputed that all human rights are indivisible, interdependent, interrelated and of equal importance for human dignity. Therefore, States are as responsible for violations of economic, social and cultural rights as they are for violations of civil and political rights.

5. As in the case of civil and political rights, the failure by a State party to comply with a treaty obligation concerning economic, social and cultural rights is, under international law, a violation of that treaty. Building upon the Limburg Principles, the considerations below relate primarily to the International Covenant on Economic, Social and Cultural Rights (hereinafter "the Covenant"). They are equally relevant, however, to the interpretation and application of other norms of international and domestic law in the field of economic, social and cultural rights.

II. The meaning of violations of economic, social and cultural rights
Obligations to respect, protect and fulfil

6. Like civil and political rights, economic, social and cultural rights impose three different types of obligations on States: the obligations to respect, protect and fulfil. Failure to perform any one of these three obligations constitutes a violation of such rights. The obligation to respect requires States to refrain from interfering with the enjoyment of economic, social and cultural rights. Thus, the right to housing is violated if the State engages in arbitrary forced evictions. The obligation to protect requires States to prevent violations of such rights by third parties. Thus, the failure to ensure that private employers comply with basic labour standards may amount to a violation of the right to work or the right to just and favourable conditions of work. The obligation to fulfil requires States to take appropriate legislative, administrative, budgetary, judicial and other measures towards the full realization of such rights.

Thus, the failure of States to provide essential primary health care to those in need may amount to a violation.

Obligations of conduct and of result

7. The obligations to respect, protect and fulfil each contain elements of obligation of conduct and obligation of result. The obligation of conduct requires action reasonably calculated to realize the enjoyment of a particular right. In the case of the right to health, for example, the obligation of conduct could involve the adoption and implementation of a plan of action to reduce maternal mortality. The obligation of result requires States to achieve specific targets to satisfy a detailed substantive standard. With respect to the right to health, for example, the obligation of result requires the reduction of maternal mortality to levels agreed at the 1994 Cairo International Conference on Population and Development and the 1995 Beijing Fourth World Conference on Women.

Margin of discretion

8. As in the case of civil and political rights, States enjoy a margin of discretion in selecting the means for implementing their respective obligations. State practice and the application of legal norms to concrete cases and situations by international treaty monitoring bodies as well as by domestic courts have contributed to the development of universal minimum standards and the common understanding of the scope, nature and limitation of economic, social and cultural rights. The fact that the full realization of most economic, social and cultural rights can only be achieved progressively, which in fact also applies to most civil and political rights, does not alter the nature of the legal obligation of States which requires that certain steps be taken immediately and others as soon as possible. Therefore, the burden is on the State to demonstrate that it is making measurable progress toward the full realization of the rights in question. The State cannot use the "progressive realization" provisions in article 2 of the Covenant as a pretext for non-compliance. Nor can the State justify derogations or limitations of rights recognized in the Covenant because of different social, religious and cultural backgrounds.

Minimum core obligations

9. Violations of the Covenant occur when a State fails to satisfy what the Committee on Economic, Social and Cultural Rights has referred to as "a minimum core obligation to ensure the satisfaction of, at the very least, minimum essential levels of each of the rights ... Thus, for example, a State party in which any significant number of individuals is deprived of essential foodstuffs, of essential primary health care, of basic shelter and housing, or of the most basic forms of education is, prima facie, violating the Covenant". Such minimum core obligations apply irrespective of the availability of resources of the country concerned or any other factors and difficulties.

Availability of resources

10. In many cases, compliance with such obligations may be undertaken by most States with relative ease, and without significant resource implications. In other cases, however, full realization of the rights may depend upon the availability of

adequate financial and material resources. Nonetheless, as established by Limburg Principles 25-28, and confirmed by the developing jurisprudence of the Committee on Economic, Social and Cultural Rights, resource scarcity does not relieve States of certain minimum obligations in respect of the implementation of economic, social and cultural rights.

State policies

11. A violation of economic, social and cultural rights occurs when a State pursues, by action or omission, a policy or practice which deliberately contravenes or ignores obligations of the Covenant, or fails to achieve the required standard of conduct or result. Furthermore, any discrimination on grounds of race, colour, sex, language, religion, political or other opinion, national or social origin, property, birth or other status with the purpose or effect of nullifying or impairing the equal enjoyment or exercise of economic, social and cultural rights constitutes a violation of the Covenant.

Gender discrimination

12. Discrimination against women in relation to the rights recognized in the Covenant, is understood in the light of the standard of equality for women under the Convention on the Elimination of All Forms of Discrimination against Women. That standard requires the elimination of all forms of discrimination against women including gender discrimination arising out of social, cultural and other structural disadvantages.

Inability to comply

13. In determining which actions or omissions amount to a violation of an economic, social or cultural right, it is important to distinguish the inability from the unwillingness of a State to comply with its treaty obligations. A State claiming that it is unable to carry out its obligations for reasons beyond its control has the burden of proving that this is the case. A temporary closure of an educational institution due to an earthquake, for instance, would be a circumstance beyond the control of the State, while the elimination of a social security scheme without an adequate replacement programme could be an example of unwillingness by the State to fulfil its obligations.

Violations through acts of commission

14. Violations of economic, social and cultural rights can occur through the direct action of States or other entities insufficiently regulated by States. Examples of such violations include:

(a) The formal removal or suspension of legislation necessary for the continued enjoyment of an economic, social and cultural right that is currently enjoyed;

(b) The active denial of such rights to particular individuals or groups, whether through legislated or enforced discrimination;

(c) The active support for measures adopted by third parties which are inconsistent with economic, social and cultural rights;

(d) The adoption of legislation or policies which are manifestly incompatible with pre-existing legal obligations relating to these rights, unless it is done with the

purpose and effect of increasing equality and improving the realization of economic, social and cultural rights for the most vulnerable groups;
(e) The adoption of any deliberately retrogressive measure that reduces the extent to which any such right is guaranteed;
(f) The calculated obstruction of, or halt to, the progressive realization of a right protected by the Covenant, unless the State is acting within a limitation permitted by the Covenant or it does so due to a lack of available resources or force majeure;
(g) The reduction or diversion of specific public expenditure, when such reduction or diversion results in the non-enjoyment of such rights and is not accompanied by adequate measures to ensure minimum subsistence rights for everyone.

Violations through acts of omission

15. Violations of economic, social and cultural rights can also occur through the omission or failure of States to take necessary measures stemming from legal obligations. Examples of such violations include:
(a) The failure to take appropriate steps as required under the Covenant;
(b) The failure to reform or repeal legislation which is manifestly inconsistent with an obligation of the Covenant;
(c) The failure to enforce legislation or put into effect policies designed to implement provisions of the Covenant;
(d) The failure to regulate activities of individuals or groups so as to prevent them from violating economic, social and cultural rights;
(e) The failure to utilize the maximum of available resources towards the full realization of the Covenant;
(f) The failure to monitor the realization of economic, social and cultural rights, including the development and application of criteria and indicators for assessing compliance;
(g) The failure to remove promptly obstacles which it is under a duty to remove to permit the immediate fulfilment of a right guaranteed by the Covenant;
(h) The failure to implement without delay a right which it is required by the Covenant to provide immediately;
(i) The failure to meet a generally accepted international minimum standard of achievement, which is within its powers to meet;
(j) The failure of a State to take into account its international legal obligations in the field of economic, social and cultural rights when entering into bilateral or multilateral agreements with other States, international organizations or multinational corporations.

III. Responsibility for violations

State responsibility

16. The violations referred to in section II are in principle imputable to the State within whose jurisdiction they occur. As a consequence, the State responsible must establish mechanisms to correct such violations, including monitoring investigation, prosecution, and remedies for victims.

Alien domination or occupation

17. Under circumstances of alien domination, deprivations of economic, social and cultural rights may be imputable to the conduct of the State exercising effective control over the territory in question. This is true under conditions of colonialism, other forms of alien domination and military occupation. The dominating or occupying power bears responsibility for violations of economic, social and cultural rights. There are also circumstances in which States acting in concert violate economic, social and cultural rights.

Acts by non–State entities

18. The obligation to protect includes the State's responsibility to ensure that private entities or individuals, including transnational corporations over which they exercise jurisdiction, do not deprive individuals of their economic, social and cultural rights. States are responsible for violations of economic, social and cultural rights that result from their failure to exercise due diligence in controlling the behaviour of such non-State actors.

Acts by international organizations

19. The obligations of States to protect economic, social and cultural rights extend also to their participation in international organizations, where they act collectively. It is particularly important for States to use their influence to ensure that violations do not result from the programmes and policies of the organizations of which they are members. It is crucial for the elimination of violations of economic, social and cultural rights for international organizations, including international financial institutions, to correct their policies and practices so that they do not result in deprivation of economic, social and cultural rights. Member States of such organizations, individually or through the governing bodies, as well as the secretariat and non-governmental organizations, should encourage and generalize the trend of several such organizations to revise their policies and programmes to take into account issues of economic, social and cultural rights, especially when these policies and programmes are implemented in countries that lack the resources to resist the pressure brought by international institutions on their decision-making affecting economic, social and cultural rights.

IV. Victims of violations

Individuals and groups

20. As is the case with civil and political rights, both individuals and groups can be victims of violations of economic, social and cultural rights. Certain groups suffer disproportionate harm in this respect, such as lower-income groups, women, indigenous and tribal peoples, occupied populations, asylum seekers, refugees and internally displaced persons, minorities, the elderly, children, landless peasants, persons with disabilities and the homeless.

Criminal sanctions

21. Victims of violations of economic, social and cultural rights should not face criminal sanctions purely because of their status as victims, for example, through

laws criminalizing persons for being homeless. Nor should anyone be penalized for claiming their economic, social and cultural rights.

V. Remedies and other responses to violations

Access to remedies

22. Any person or group who is a victim of a violation of an economic, social or cultural right should have access to effective judicial or other appropriate remedies at both national and international levels.

Adequate reparation

23. All victims of violations of economic, social and cultural rights are entitled to adequate reparation, which may take the form of restitution, compensation, rehabilitation and satisfaction or guarantees of non-repetition.

No official sanctioning of violations

24. National judicial and other organs must ensure that any pronouncements they may make do not result in the official sanctioning of a violation of an international obligation of the State concerned. At a minimum, national judiciaries should consider the relevant provisions of international and regional human rights law as an interpretative aide in formulating any decisions relating to violations of economic, social and cultural rights.

National institutions

25. Promotional and monitoring bodies such as national ombudsman institutions and human rights commissions, should address violations of economic, social and cultural rights as vigorously as they address violations of civil and political rights.

Domestic application of international instruments

26. The direct incorporation or application of international instruments recognizing economic, social and cultural rights within the domestic legal order can significantly enhance the scope and effectiveness of remedial measures and should be encouraged in all cases.

Impunity

27. States should develop effective measures to preclude the possibility of impunity of any violation of economic, social and cultural rights and to ensure that no person who may be responsible for violations of such rights has immunity from liability for their actions.

Role of the legal professions

28. In order to achieve effective judicial and other remedies for victims of violations of economic, social and cultural rights, lawyers, judges, adjudicators, bar associations and the legal community generally should pay far greater attention to these violations in the exercise of their professions, as recommended by the International Commission of Jurists in the Bangalore Declaration and Plan of Action of 1995.

Special rapporteurs

29. In order to further strengthen international mechanisms with respect to preventing, early warning, monitoring and redressing violations of economic, social

and cultural rights, the United Nations Commission on Human Rights should appoint thematic special rapporteurs in this field.

New standards

30. In order to further clarify the contents of States' obligations to respect, protect and fulfil economic, social and cultural rights, States and appropriate international bodies should actively pursue the adoption of new standards on specific economic, social and cultural rights, in particular the right to work, to food, to housing and to health.

Optional protocols

31. The optional protocol providing for individual and group complaints in relation to the rights recognized in the Covenant should be adopted and ratified without delay. The proposed optional protocol to the Convention on the Elimination of All Forms of Discrimination against Women should ensure that equal attention is paid to violations of economic, social and cultural rights. In addition, consideration should be given to the drafting of an optional complaints procedure under the Convention on the Rights of the Child.

Documenting and monitoring

32. Documenting and monitoring violations of economic, social and cultural rights should be carried out by all relevant actors, including NGOs, national Governments and international organizations. It is indispensable that the relevant international organizations provide the support necessary for the implementation of international instruments in this field. The mandate of the United Nations High Commissioner for Human Rights includes the promotion of economic, social and cultural rights and it is essential that effective steps be taken urgently and that adequate staff and financial resources be devoted to this objective. Specialized agencies and other international organizations working in the economic and social spheres should also place appropriate emphasis upon economic, social and cultural rights as rights and, where they do not already do so, should contribute to efforts to respond to violations of these rights.

APPENDIX VIII

THE OPTIONAL PROTOCOL TO THE CONVENTION AGAINST TORTURE (CAT) – PART 4

Adopted on 18 December 2002 at the fifty-seventh session of the General Assembly of the United Nations by resolution A/RES/57/199.

PART IV

National Preventive Mechanisms
Article 17

Each State Party shall maintain, designate or establish at the latest one year after the entry into force of the present Protocol or of its ratification or accession, one or several independent national preventive mechanisms for the prevention of torture at the domestic level. Mechanisms established by decentralised units may be designated as national preventive mechanisms for the purposes of the present Protocol, if they are in conformity with its provisions.

Article 18

1. The States Parties shall guarantee the functional independence of the national preventive mechanisms as well as the independence of their personnel.

2. The States Parties shall take the necessary measures in order for the experts of the national mechanism to have the required capabilities and professional knowledge. They shall strive for a gender balance and the adequate representation of ethnic and minority groups in the country.

3. The States Parties undertake to make available the necessary resources for the functioning of the national preventive mechanisms.

4. When establishing national preventive mechanisms, States Parties shall give due consideration to the Principles relating to the Status and Functioning of National Institutions for Protection and Promotion of Human Rights.

Article 19

The national preventive mechanisms shall be granted at least the powers to:

1. Regularly examine the treatment of the persons deprived of their liberty in places according to article 4, with a view to strengthening, if necessary, their protection from torture, cruel, inhuman or degrading treatment or punishment;

2. Make recommendations to the relevant authorities with the aim of improving the treatment and the conditions of the persons deprived of their liberty and to prevent torture, cruel, inhuman or degrading treatment or punishment, taking into consideration the relevant norms of the United Nations;

3. Submit proposals and observations concerning existing or draft legislation.

Article 20

In order to enable the national preventive mechanisms to fulfill their mandate, the States Parties to the present Protocol undertake to grant them:

1. Access to all information concerning the number of persons deprived of their liberty in places of detention as defined in article 4, as well as the number of places and their location;

2. Access to all information referring to the treatment of these persons as well as their conditions of detention;

3. Access to all places of detention and their installations and facilities;

4. The opportunity to have private interviews with the persons deprived of their liberty without witnesses, either personally or with a translator if deemed necessary, as well as with any other person whom the national preventive mechanism believes may supply relevant information;

5. The liberty to choose the places it wants to visit and the persons it wants to interview;

6. The right to have contacts with the Sub-Committee on Prevention, to send it information and to meet with it.

Article 21

1. No authority or official shall order, apply, permit or tolerate any sanction against any person or organisation for having communicated to the national preventive mechanism any information, whether true or false, and no such person or organisation shall be otherwise prejudiced in any way.

2. Confidential information collected by the national preventive mechanism shall be privileged. No personal data shall be published without the express consent of the person concerned.

Article 22

The competent authorities of the State Party concerned shall examine the recommendations of the national preventive mechanism and enter into a dialogue with it on possible implementation measures.

Article 23

The States Parties to the present Protocol undertake to publish and disseminate the annual reports of the national preventive mechanisms.

APPENDIX IX

SPECIAL RAPPORTEURS OF THE COMMISSION ON HUMAN RIGHTS

Title / Mandate	Mandate established		Mandate extended		Name & country of origin of the mandate-holder(s)
	in	by	in	by	
Special Rapporteur on adequate housing as a component of the right to an adequate standard of living	2000	resolution 2000/9	2003	resolution 2003/27 (for 3 years)	Mr. Miloon KOTHARI (India)
Working Group on people of African descent	2002	resolution 2002/68	2003	resolution 2003/30 (for 3 years)	Chairperson-Rapporteur : Mr. Peter Lesa KASANDA (Zambia) Mr. Joe FRANS (Sweden) Mr. George N. JABBOUR (Syrian Arab Republic) Mr. Roberto B. MARTINS (Brazil) Ms. Irina ZLATESCU (Romania)
Working Group on Arbitrary Detention	1991	resolution 1991/42	2003	resolution 2003/31 (for 3 years)	Chairperson-Rapporteur: Ms. Leila ZERROUGUI (Algeria) Mr. Tamás BÁN (Hungary) Ms. Manuela Carmena CASTRILLO (Spain) Mr. Seyyed Mohammad HASHEMI (Islamic Republic of Iran) Ms. Soledad VILLAGRA DE BIEDERMANN (Paraguay)
Special Rapporteur on the sale of children, child prostitution and child pornography	1990	resolution 1990/68	2004	ECOSOC decision 2004/285 (for 3 years)	Mr. Juan Miguel PETIT (Uruguay)
Special Rapporteur on the right to education	1998	resolution 1998/33	2004	resolution 2004/25 (for 3 years)	Mr. Vernor MUÑOZ VILLALOBOS(Costa Rica)
Working Group on Enforced or Involuntary Disappearances	1980	resolution 20 (XXXVI)	2004	resolution 2004/40 (for 3 years)	Chairperson-Rapporteur: Mr. Stephen J. TOOPE (Canada) Mr. Joel ADEBAYO ADEKANYE (Nigeria)

APPENDIX IX

					Mr. Santiago CORCUERA CABEZUT(Mexico) Mr. Darko GÖTTLICHER (Croatia) Mr. Saeed Rajaee KHORASANI (Islamic Republic of Iran)
Special Rapporteur on extrajudicial, summary or arbitrary executions	1982	resolution 1982/35	2004	resolution 2004/37 (for 3 years)	Mr. Philip ALSTON (Australia)
Independent Expert on the question of human rights and extreme poverty	1998	resolution 1998/25	2004	resolution 2004/23 (for 2 years)	Mr. Arjun SENGUPTA (India)
Special Rapporteur on the right to food	2000	resolution 2000/10	2003	resolution 2003/25 (for 3 years)	Mr. Jean ZIEGLER (Switzerland)
Special Rapporteur on the promotion and protection of the right to freedom of opinion and expression	1993	resolution 1993/45	2005	resolution 2005/38 (for 3 years)	Mr. Ambeyi LIGABO (Kenya)
Special Rapporteur on freedom of religion or belief	1986	resolution 1986/20	2004	resolution 2004/36 (for 3 years)	Ms. Asma JAHANGIR (Pakistan)
Special Rapporteur on the right of everyone to the enjoyment of the highest attainable standard of physical and mental health	2002	resolution 2002/31 (for 3 years)	2005	resolution 2005/24 (for 3 years)	Mr. Paul HUNT (New Zealand)
Special Representative of the Secretary-General on the situation of human rights defenders	2000	resolution 2000/61	2003	resolution 2003/64 (for 3 years)	Ms. Hina JILANI(Pakistan)
Special Rapporteur on the independence of judges and lawyers	1994	resolution 1994/41	2003	resolution 2003/43 (for 3 years)	Mr. Leandro DESPOUY (Argentina)
Special Rapporteur on the situation of human rights and fundamental freedoms of indigenous people	2001	resolution 2001/57	2004	resolution 2004/62 (for 3 years)	Mr. Rodolfo STAVENHAGEN (Mexico)
Representative of the Secretary-General on the human rights of internally displaced persons	2004	resolution 2004/55 (for 2 years)			Mr. Walter Kälin (Switzerland)

Working Group on the use of mercenaries as a means of impeding the exercise of the right of peoples to self-determination	2005	resolution 2005/2 (for 3 years)			Ms. Amada BENAVIDES DE PÉREZ (Colombia) Ms. Najat AL-HAJJAJI (Libyan Arab Jamahiriya) Mr. José Luis GÓMEZ DEL PRADO (Spain) Mr. Alexander Ivanovich NIKITIN (Russian Federation) Ms. Shaista SHAMEEM (Fiji)
Special Rapporteur on the human rights of migrants	1999	resolution 1999/44	2005	resolution 2005/47 (for 3 years)	Mr. Jorge A. BUSTAMANTE (Mexico)
Independent Expert on minority issues	2005	resolution 2005/79 (2 years)			Ms. Gay MCDOUGALL (United Status of America)
Special Rapporteur on contemporary forms of racism, racial discrimination, xenophobia and related intolerance	1993	resolution 1993/20	2005	Resolution 2005/64 (for 3 years)	Mr. Doudou DIÈNE (Senegal)
Independent Expert on human rights and international solidarity	2005	resolution 2005/55 (for 3 years)			Mr. Rudi Muhammad RIZKI (Indonesia)
Independent Expert on the effects of economic reform policies and foreign debt	2000	resolution 2000/82	2003	resolution 2003/21 (for 3 years)	Mr. Bernards Andrew NYAMWAYA MUDHO (Kenya)
Special Rapporteur on the promotion and protection of human rights while countering terrorism	2005	resolution 2005/80 (for 3 years)			Mr. Martin SCHEININ (Finland)
Special Rapporteur on torture and other cruel, inhuman or degrading treatment or punishment	1985	resolution 1985/33	2004	resolution 2004/41 (for 3 years)	Mr. Manfred Nowak (Austria)
Special Rapporteur on the adverse effects of the illicit movement and dumping of toxic and dangerous products and wastes on the enjoyment of human rights	1995	resolution 1995/81	2004	resolution 2004/17 (for 3 years)	Mr. Okechukwu IBEANU (Nigeria)
Special Rapporteur on trafficking in persons,	2004	resolution 2004/110			Ms. Sigma HUDA (Bangladesh)

especially in women and children		(for 3 years)			
Special Representative of the SG on human rights and transnational corporations and other business enterprises	2005	resolution 2005/69 (for 2 years)			Mr. John Ruggie (United States of America)
Special Rapporteur on violence against women, its causes and consequences	1994	resolution 1994/45	2003	resolution 2003/45 (for 3 years)	Ms. Yakin ERTÜRK (Turkey)

EXAMPLES OF NATIONAL INQUIRES CONDUCTED BY THE HUMAN RIGHTS AND EQUAL OPPORTUNITY COMMISSION OF AUSTRALIA:

Appendix X The Homeless Children Inquiry
Appendix XI The Racial Violence Inquiry
Appendix XII Summary of the National Inquiry on Human Rights and Mental Illness

APPENDIX X

THE HOMELESS CHILDREN INQUIRY

The Homeless Children Inquiry was a national inquiry conducted by the Australian Human Rights and Equal Opportunity Commission with reference to the principles of the Declaration on the Rights of the Child[9] (which stipulates that children are entitled, inter alia, to special protection, adequate housing and protection against neglect, cruelty and exploitation). The report of this Inquiry was presented to the federal government and parliament in February 1989 and then made public. The Inquiry did more than just describe the very serious problems affecting 25,000 homeless children – some of whom were dying from abuse or neglect; it identified the inadequacies of government responses, and made recommendations to correct them. Some of these recommendations went into specific detail on the design of social programs. (This level of involvement with the details of policy was found necessary to give definite content to the economic and social rights involved.)

Giving practical effect to rights with significant public resource implications involves political processes. The level of responses to the Homeless Children Inquiry – in public and political discussion, and in program responses (the federal government provided $A100 Million over four years) – resulted, in large part, from the human rights basis of the Inquiry. That is, to have a situation identified as a major breach of fundamental international standards on human rights is not just a legal point – it is, in itself, a major political argument.

The Inquiry heard evidence in every State and Territory from a wide range of individuals and non government organizations. This extensive process of consultation assisted in framing a comprehensive set of recommendations on a wide range of issues dealt with by applicable human rights principles.

A government inquiry conducted without reference to human rights principles might look at homelessness purely as a problem in the supply of housing. Human rights

[9] At this stage we were still negotiating the text of the Convention on the Rights of the Child – which was not finalised until 1989. The Convention, which was one of the most widely and rapidly ratified in history, entered into force on 2 September 1990.

instruments dictate a broader approach. First, the right to housing requires that shelter be accessible to young people – not just physically available. It also requires that a range of appropriate accommodation options be available, particularly for those groups who are the subject of particular disadvantage and/or discrimination (such as Aboriginal young people – and young people with disabilities).

Other relevant rights – including the right to special protection and, specifically, protection against neglect or abuse – led the Inquiry to conclude that accommodation services should be integrated with other support services where these are necessary, (including services to promote family reconciliation whenever possible and appropriate). Increased assistance and support services for families were also emphasised by the Inquiry as a means of preventing homelessness, (taking account of the references in the international human rights instruments to the central role of the family).

Human rights principles also led the Inquiry to reject simplistic solutions, like forcing young people to return home if they are mature enough to make their own decisions not to, or locking homeless children up in institutions.

The Inquiry was also concerned by the vulnerability of homeless young people in their contact with the legal system. It made recommendations for improving the availability, accessibility and quality of advocacy and information services in dealing with the criminal justice system, child welfare systems and social security and accommodation authorities. These recommendations, although directly related to the needs of homeless children, were also relevant to the protection of the rights of all children and young people, both regarding civil and political rights and economic and social rights.

For several years following the Inquiry the Commission continued to actively monitor government responses to the Inquiry's report, including by reconvening the formal hearings of the Inquiry to receive evidence from governments and community organizations on the implementation of its recommendations.

In summary, the Federal government and most State governments implemented a number of major changes to programs and policies in response to the report of this Inquiry. Significant legislative amendments were also made.

APPENDIX XI

THE RACIAL VIOLENCE INQUIRY

This national inquiry was conducted by reference to the Convention on the Elimination of All Forms of Racial Discrimination. It examined racist violence and intimidation as forms of racial discrimination, and assessed their impact on the equal enjoyment of human rights in the civil, political, economic, social and cultural spheres.

The Report of the Inquiry, released in March 1991, analysed the adequacy of government and community responses, in particular by reference to the right to equal protection of the law. It also examined preventive measures. The Inquiry found that racist violence against Aboriginal people was widespread and included officially perpetrated violence. It found that although the number of incidents of racist violence against other groups was relatively low, there was a need for improved policies and procedures.

The Report recommended legislative measures in a number of areas, including that Australia should introduce national legislation against incitement to racial hatred, in order to fulfil its obligations under Article 4(a) of the Convention on the Elimination of All Forms of Racial Discrimination. The Inquiry also made major recommendations in the areas of community education, and human rights training for public officials including police.

Following the release of its report the Commission worked for some time with both State and Federal authorities to ensure that its recommendations were implemented.

APPENDIX XII

SUMMARY OF THE NATIONAL INQUIRY ON HUMAN RIGHTS AND MENTAL ILLNESS

DISCRIMINATION AGAINST PERSONS WITH DISABILITIES AND THE LAW – LESSONS FROM A NATIONAL INQUIRY (Stockholm, 3 December 1996)
Address by Brian Burdekin AO[*]

Distinguished Guests, I am delighted to have the opportunity to contribute to this important conference.

In my present position I have the opportunity to visit and assess the situation relating to human rights in a wide range of countries. Unfortunately, discrimination against people with disabilities is still a widespread phenomenon. Indeed, in many countries, it is as yet unrecognised as a violation of human rights – or even regarded as a problem! Clearly the international community still has a long way to go in addressing the frequently degrading and sometimes humiliating circumstances in which hundreds of millions of our fellow human beings spend their lives.

Nor is this phenomenon confined to poorer countries. It still constitutes one of the major human rights issued in many of the world's wealthiest nations – including the one from which I come, Australia. At this point, however, I believe it is appropriate to record the fact that our host country, Sweden, along with Australia and several other European states, has played a leading role in developing international standards for the protection of individuals with disabilities. In the context of the theme of this conference, these international standards represent an important benchmark for the elaboration of national legislation and regulations designed to promote and protect human rights.

It is, of course, essential to recognise that while legislation is often a necessary, it is never a sufficient, pre-condition for the protection of human rights. This at least was my experience during the eight years that I was Federal Human Rights Commissioner of Australia. I mention this because I frequently find, in countries where I am now working, a tendency on the part of lawyers and legislators to regard law reform as an end in itself. Indeed, there is even a tendency on the part of some human rights advocates to overestimate its significance.

So while legislation proscribing discrimination is important, based on my own experience it is only 10% of the basic human rights equation; the other 90%

[*] Former Federal Human Rights Commissioner of Australia; Special Advisor to the U.N. High Commissioner for Human Rights

includes, most importantly, adequate resources to implement the standards which are (or should be) embodied in the legislation and a proactive programme of community education. The evidence available to me indicates that securing these resources and educating community attitudes requires continuous, and on occasion, aggressive advocacy.

To illustrate this point I would like to take an example from my own country relating to the rights of people affected by a psychiatric disability or mental illness. While the facts are Australian, we know that the incidence of psychiatric disability is very similar in all countries. We also know, unfortunately, that many of the serious violations of human rights I am about to mention are not confined to Australia but are equally serious in many other countries.

After a three year inquiry, which included examining over 1,300 witnesses and submissions and conducting open hearings in twenty cities and towns across Australia, we concluded:

That notwithstanding the existence of anti-discrimination legislation in most jurisdictions, people with a psychiatric disability were routinely discriminated against, in both the public and the private sector.

That legislation relating to Australians affected by a psychiatric disability was generally outdated, and that law reform in this area invariably received a low priority.

That our court system (based on the "Westminster System") was generally inaccessible to individuals affected by psychiatric and other disabilities and that, while our legal system protected their human rights in theory, it was an abysmal failure in reality

That this fundamental failure of law and policy was largely being ignored by our parliaments, policy makers and the legal profession.

That this situation was only possible because of widespread public ignorance concerning the nature and prevalence of psychiatric disability

That this public ignorance generated irrational fear – which was a fundamental cause of discrimination, marginalization and even victimization of those with a psychiatric disability.

That the discrimination was so entrenched in public and official attitudes that it was "systemic" and therefore required sweeping reforms and a major injection of resources.

That it was precisely those who were most vulnerable and disadvantaged – individuals with dual or multiple disabilities – for whom there were no programmes – or for whom existing programmes were grossly inadequate.

That the allocation of such limited resources as were available clearly discriminated against those living in rural and regional areas – and that in these areas our youth suicide rate was 300% higher than in our major cities.

That our doctors were generally very poorly trained in the field of psychiatric disability – and that our health system generally routinely discriminated against people with a psychiatric disability.

That law reform was urgently needed – but that many of the human rights violations occurring were caused not by acts which were unlawful – but by omission and by official neglect – problems which in the longer term required fundamental changes in public attitudes and a major injection of resources.

I believed we learned several important lessons from this inquiry – and it is those which I would particularly like to share with you.

First, we learned that gross violations of human rights, affecting hundreds of thousands of individuals, can still occur in a modern democracy enjoying freely elected parliaments, an independent judiciary, free trade unions and "the rule of law".

Second, we learned that this was possible because our legal system (along with many others) had never really taken seriously the basic right of individuals with a disability to be treated with dignity and enjoy genuine equality.

Third, we learned that most discrimination against those with a psychiatric disability was based on fear – and that fear was almost invariably based or ignorance. (Clearly, changing public attitudes was essential if any law reforms were going to be successful).

Fourth, we learned that our traditional institutions of justice (the courts) were hopelessly inadequate in addressing and redressing human rights violations. Clearly, we needed an independent, accessible, National Institution which could assist those with a psychiatric disability (and indeed other forms of disability) to ensure their human rights were protected.

Fifth, given that the inquiry was based on the "Principles for the Protection of those Affected by Mental Illness and the Improvement of Mental Health Care" (an international instrument designed to supplement the basic international human rights covenants), we demonstrated that international standards are a valuable benchmark – against which the performance of governments can, and should, be measured.

Sixth, the inquiry demonstrated the momentum which can be generated when individuals with a disability and their carers are given the opportunity to inform the public of the discrimination they routinely suffer. As a result of our findings Federal and State governments allocated $A600 million in additional funds for programmes and services for those affected by a psychiatric disability. Uniform national standards were introduced – both for the legal protection of individuals and for health care systems. A number of public education programmes were also established.

Seventh, we learned that public policies supposedly developed to better protect the basic rights and freedoms of particularly vulnerable groups need to be carefully scrutinised and monitored. (Many of the worst abuses in Australia had accompanied the introduction of policies of "deinstitutionalization" – which the public had been told would be more "humane" and consistent with individual rights and freedoms. The policy, as in several other countries, was fine in theory. It became a disaster in practice because governments failed to provide adequate resources for community based services. Many individuals with a major psychiatric disability were reduced to lives of squalor and homelessness – thus reinforcing existing community stereotypes rather than dispelling them).

Eighth, we demonstrated (in the legislation and reforms which were introduced following our report) that it was not only desirable in theory, but possible in practice, to breathe real meaning into international human rights treaties and instruments by, on the one hand, using them as the benchmark for evaluating national conditions and, on the other, using the principles they embody as the basis for preparing new legislation designed to proscribe discrimination and protect human rights.

Ninth, we learned that well publicised public inquiries to which the public and media were regularly invited, can be an extremely powerful tool in generating pressure for political action. At the beginning of the process, media interest in the subject of psychiatric disability was almost exclusively confined to "bad news" stories of psychiatric patients causing damage in the community or injury to others. By the end of the process, hundreds of news stories emanating from evidence presented to the inquiry (frequently informing the public of gross abuse of individuals with a psychiatric disability) had produced significant improvements in public attitudes generally – and a reduction in discriminatory practices. (One interesting indicator of the effectiveness of the process was the media coverage of the release of the inquiry's report. Not only was it responsible and detailed, it was approximately double in quantity to the coverage which occurred when Sydney won its bid to host the Olympics in the year 2000!)

Tenth, we learned that it is sometimes more effective to channel limited energy and resources into a general inquiry into systemic discrimination, than repeatedly attempt to investigate individual cases of abuse or discrimination – important as these may be. This is particularly the case where the discrimination or other human rights violations occurring relate to individuals whose disability may make it less likely, or even unlikely, that they will ever lodge an individual complaint.

The national inquiry to which I have just referred was conducted by the Australian Human Rights and Equal Opportunity Commission – the "National Institution" in Australia, established by legislation, with a broad mandate to protect human rights and prevent discrimination. The Commission has six Commissioners – (one of whom is specifically responsible for disability discrimination) – and a staff of nearly 200.

In 1993, the World Conference on Human Rights, in its concluding Declaration and Programme of Action, called on all nations to accord priority to the establishment and strengthening of independent National Institutions for the promotion and protection of human rights. The High Commissioner has, accordingly, made this one of his highest priorities. As his Special Advisor in this area, I am currently working in 18 countries – all of which have either already passed legislation to establish a National Human Rights Commission or Ombudsman – or are clearly committed to doing so

These independent "National Institutions" take various forms; some are Commissions, some are Ombudsman Institutions – but all have in common the following fundamental characteristics:

Independence from Government
A broad-based charter to protect human rights and prevent discrimination – (including in relation to people with disabilities).
Pluralistic composition (i.e. the membership of the Commission must reflect the composition of civil society).
Adequate resources to perform their tasks.

While we still have a long way to go, I am pleased to be able to report to you that there is a rapidly growing recognition among nation States that the international human rights treaties will ultimately only be effective for many of the most vulnerable and disadvantaged when independent National Institutions have been established at the national level – to complement the essential work done by NGOs and carer organizations and support them in their advocacy role.

This is an abridged version of a paper delivered by Professor Burdekin in Sweden in 1996

HUMAN RIGHTS AND EQUAL OPPORTUNITY COMMISSION ACT 1986*

Act No. 125 of 1986 as amended
This compilation was prepared on 27 March 2006
incorporating amendments up to Act No. 128 of 2005
and SLI 2006 No. 50

The text of any of those amendments not in force on that date is appended in the Notes section

The operation of amendments that have been incorporated may be affected by application provisions that are set out in the Notes section

Prepared by the Office of Legislative Drafting and Publishing, Attorney-General's Department, Canberra

CONTENTS

---

* The following legislation was either taken from the Asia Pacific Forum of National Human Rights Institutions' web site (<www.asiapacificforum.net/>) or from the official web site of the National Institution in question. Wherever possible we have attempted to include the most up to date and consolidated versions. However, we recognize that there may be recent amendments of which we are unaware and we would welcome any advice in this regard.

With respect to the interpretation and commentary we have provided on the New Zealand legislation we are indebted to Mr. Peter Hosking, the former Proceedings Commissioner of New Zealand, for his advice and assistance.

AUSTRALIA

AN ACT TO ESTABLISH THE HUMAN RIGHTS AND EQUAL OPPORTUNITY COMMISSION, TO MAKE PROVISION IN RELATION TO HUMAN RIGHTS AND IN RELATION TO EQUAL OPPORTUNITY IN EMPLOYMENT, AND FOR RELATED PURPOSES

PART I—PRELIMINARY

1 Short title [see Note 1]
This Act may be cited as the Human Rights and Equal Opportunity Commission Act 1986.

2 Commencement [*see* Note 1]
This Act shall come into operation on a day to be fixed by Proclamation.

3 Interpretation
(1) In this Act, unless the contrary intention appears:
Aboriginal person means a person of the Aboriginal race of Australia.
act means an act done:

(a) by or on behalf of the Commonwealth or an authority of the Commonwealth;
(b) under an enactment;
(c) wholly within a Territory; or
(d) partly within a Territory, to the extent to which the act was done within a Territory.

affected person, in relation to a complaint, means a person on whose behalf the complaint was lodged.
alleged unlawful discrimination means:

(a) in relation to a complaint—the acts, omissions or practices that are alleged in the complaint and that would, if proven, constitute unlawful discrimination; and
(b) in relation to an application to the Federal Court or the Federal Magistrates Court under Division 2 of Part IIB—the acts, omissions or practices that are alleged in the application and that would, if proven, constitute unlawful discrimination.

appointed member means the President or the Human Rights Commissioner.
Australia includes the external Territories.
Australian Capital Territory enactment means an enactment of the Australian Capital Territory within the meaning of the *Australian Capital Territory (Self-Government) Act 1988*, or an instrument made under such an enactment.
authority means:

(a) in relation to the Commonwealth:

(i) a body (whether incorporated or unincorporated) established for a purpose of the Commonwealth by or under a Commonwealth enactment;

(ii) an incorporated company over which the Commonwealth is in a position to exercise control;

(iii) a person holding or performing the duties of an office or appointment established or made under a Commonwealth enactment or by the Governor-General or a Minister of the Commonwealth (not being an office or appointment referred to in subparagraph (c)(iii));

(iv) a body, or a person holding or performing the duties of an office or appointment, that is declared by the regulations to be an authority of the Commonwealth for the purposes of this Act;

(b) in relation to a State:

(i) a body (whether incorporated or unincorporated) established for a purpose of the State by or under a law of the State;

(ii) an incorporated company over which the State is in a position to exercise control;

(iii) a person holding or performing the duties of an office or appointment established or made under a law, or by the Governor or a Minister, of the State;

(iv) a local government body in the State; or

(v) a body, or a person holding or performing the duties of an office or appointment, that is declared by the regulations to be an authority of the State for the purposes of this Act; or

(c) in relation to a Territory:

(i) a body (whether incorporated or unincorporated) established for a purpose of the Territory by or under a Commonwealth enactment or a law of the Territory;

(ii) an incorporated company over which the Administration of the Territory is in a position to exercise control;

(iii) a person holding or performing the duties of an office or appointment established or made under a law of the Territory or by the Administrator of a Territory; or

(iv) a body, or a person holding or performing the duties of an office or appointment, that is declared by the regulations to be an authority of the Territory for the purposes of this Act.

class member, in relation to a representative complaint, means any of the persons on whose behalf the complaint was lodged, but does not include a person who has withdrawn under section 46PC.

Commission means the Human Rights and Equal Opportunity Commission established by this Act.

Commonwealth enactment means an Act or an instrument (other than a Territory enactment, an Australian Capital Territory enactment or a Northern Territory enactment) made under an Act, and includes any other legislation applied as a law of the Commonwealth, to the extent that it operates as such a law.

complainant, in relation to a complaint, means a person who lodged the complaint, whether on the person's own behalf or on behalf of another person or persons.

complaint, except in Part IIC, means a complaint lodged under Division 1 of Part IIB.

compulsory conference means a conference under section 46PJ.

Convention means the Discrimination (Employment and Occupation) Convention, 1958 adopted by the General Conference of the International Labour Organization on 25 June 1958, a copy of the English text of which is set out in Schedule 1, as that Convention applies in relation to Australia.

Covenant means the International Covenant on Civil and Political Rights, a copy of the English text of which is set out in Schedule 2, as that International Covenant applies in relation to Australia.

Declarations means:

(a) the Declaration of the Rights of the Child proclaimed by the General Assembly of the United Nations on 20 November 1959, a copy of the English text of which is set out in Schedule 3;
(b) the Declaration on the Rights of Mentally Retarded Persons proclaimed by the General Assembly of the United Nations on 20 December 1971, a copy of the English text of which is set out in Schedule 4; and
(c) the Declaration on the Rights of Disabled Persons proclaimed by the General Assembly of the United Nations on 9 December 1975, a copy of the English text of which is set out in Schedule 5.

Disability Discrimination Commissioner means the Disability Discrimination Commissioner appointed under the Disability Discrimination Act 1992.

discrimination, except in Part IIB, means:

(a) any distinction, exclusion or preference made on the basis of race, colour, sex, religion, political opinion, national extraction or social origin that has the effect of nullifying or impairing equality of opportunity or treatment in employment or occupation; and
(b) any other distinction, exclusion or preference that:
   (i) has the effect of nullifying or impairing equality of opportunity or treatment in employment or occupation; and
   (ii) has been declared by the regulations to constitute discrimination for the purposes of this Act; but does not include any distinction, exclusion or preference:
(c) in respect of a particular job based on the inherent requirements of the job; or
(d) in connection with employment as a member of the staff of an institution that is conducted in accordance with the doctrines, tenets, beliefs or teachings of a particular religion or creed, being a distinction, exclusion or preference made in good faith in order to avoid injury to the religious susceptibilities of adherents of that religion or that creed.

enactment means a Commonwealth enactment or a Territory enactment.

Federal Court means the Federal Court of Australia.

human rights means the rights and freedoms recognised in the Covenant, declared by the Declarations or recognised or declared by any relevant international instrument.

instrument includes a rule, regulation or by-law.

instrumentality, in relation to a State, includes:

- (a) a person holding or performing the duties of an office established by or under a law of that State;
- (b) a person employed in the public service of that State; and
- (c) a person employed by a body established for a purpose of that State by or under a law of that State.

international instrument includes a declaration made by an international organisation.

Judge means:

- (a) a Judge of a court created by the Parliament or of a court of a State; or
- (b) a person who has the same designation and status as a Judge of a court created by the Parliament.

law means a law of the Commonwealth, a law of a Territory or a law of a State.

law of a State means a State enactment or any other law in force in a State, other than a law of the Commonwealth.

law of a Territory means a Territory enactment or any other law in force in a Territory, other than a law of the Commonwealth.

law of the Commonwealth means a Commonwealth enactment or any other law in force throughout Australia.

member means a member of the Commission, and includes the President.

Minister means:

- (a) in relation to a State—a Minister of the Crown of that State; and
- (b) in relation to the Australian Capital Territory or the Northern Territory—a Minister of that Territory.

Northern Territory enactment means an enactment of the Northern Territory within the meaning of the *Northern Territory (Self-Government) Act 1978* or an instrument made under such an enactment.

practice means a practice engaged in:

- (a) by or behalf of the Commonwealth or an authority of the Commonwealth;
- (b) under an enactment;
- (c) wholly within a Territory; or
- (d) partly within a Territory, to the extent to which the practice was or is engaged in within a Territory.

President means President of the Commission.

Privacy Commissioner means the Privacy Commissioner appointed under the *Privacy Act 1988*.

proposed enactment means:

(a) a proposed law introduced into the Parliament of the Commonwealth or the legislature of a Territory;
(b) a proposed law prepared on behalf of:
  (i) the Government of the Commonwealth or the Administration of a Territory;
  (ii) a Minister of State of the Commonwealth; or
  (iii) a body established by law that has the function of recommending proposed laws of the Commonwealth or of a Territory; or
(c) an instrument proposed to be made under a law of the Commonwealth or under a law of a Territory.

Race Discrimination Commissioner means the Race Discrimination Commissioner appointed under the *Racial Discrimination Act 1975*.

relevant international instrument means an international instrument in respect of which a declaration under section 47 is in force.

representative complaint means a complaint lodged on behalf of at least one person who is not a complainant.

respondent, in relation to a complaint, means the person or persons against whom the complaint is made.

Sex Discrimination Commissioner means the Sex Discrimination Commissioner appointed under the *Sex Discrimination Act 1984*.

State includes the Australian Capital Territory and the Northern Territory.

State enactment means a State Act or an instrument made under a State Act and includes an Australian Capital Territory enactment and a Northern Territory enactment.

terminate, in relation to a complaint, means decline to inquire into the complaint, or discontinue an inquiry into the complaint.

Territory does not include the Australian Capital Territory or the Northern Territory.

Territory Act means an Act passed by a legislature of a Territory

Territory enactment means a Territory Act, an Ordinance of a Territory or an instrument made under such an Act or Ordinance, and includes any other legislation applied as a law of the Commonwealth, to the extent that it operates as such a law.

Torres Strait Islander means a descendant of an indigenous inhabitant of the Torres Strait Islands.

trade union means:
(a) an organisation of employees that is:
  (i) a registered organisation within the meaning of Schedule 1 to the *Workplace Relations Act 1996*; or
  (ii) a transitionally registered association within the meaning of Schedule 10 to the *Workplace Relations Act 1996*.
(b) a trade union within the meaning of any State Act or law of a Territory; or
(c) any other similar body.

unlawful discrimination means any acts, omissions or practices that are unlawful under:
(aa) Part 4 of the Age Discrimination Act 2004; or

(a) Part 2 of the Disability Discrimination Act 1992; or
(b) Part II or IIA of the *Racial Discrimination Act 1975*; or
(c) Part II of the *Sex Discrimination Act 1984*;

and includes any conduct that is an offence under:

(ca) Division 2 of Part 5 of the *Age Discrimination Act 2004* (other than section 52); or
(d) Division 4 of Part 2 of the *Disability Discrimination Act 1992*; or
(e) subsection 27(2) of the *Racial Discrimination Act 1975*; or
(f) section 94 of the *Sex Discrimination Act 1984*.

(2) In this Act, a reference to the Governor of a State shall, in relation to the Northern Territory, be construed as a reference to the Administrator of the Northern Territory.

(3) In this Act:

(a) a reference to, or to the doing of, an act includes a reference to a refusal or failure to do an act; and
(b) a reference, in relation to the doing of an act or the engaging in of a practice, to the person who did the act or engaged in the practice shall, in the case of an act done or practice engaged in by an unincorporated body of persons, be read as a reference to that body.

(4) In the definition of ***human rights*** in subsection (1):

(a) the reference to the rights and freedoms recognised in the Covenant shall be read as a reference to the rights and freedoms recognised in the Covenant as it applies to Australia; and
(b) the reference to the rights and freedoms recognised or declared by any relevant international instrument shall:
  (i) in the case of an instrument (not being a declaration referred to in subparagraph (ii)) that applies to Australia—be read as a reference to the rights and freedoms recognised or declared by the instrument as it applies to Australia; or
  (ii) in the case of an instrument being a declaration made by an international organisation that was adopted by Australia—be read as a reference to the rights and freedoms recognised or declared by the declaration as it was adopted by Australia.

(5) A reference in this Act to the making of a declaration by an international organisation shall be read as a reference to the making or adopting of a declaration, proclamation or other statement by such an organisation in any way, whether by the passing of a resolution, the issuing of an instrument or otherwise.

(6) A reference in this Act to the adoption by Australia of an international instrument being a declaration made by an international organisation shall be read as

a reference to the casting by Australia of a vote in favour of the making of the declaration by the organisation at the meeting of the organisation at which the declaration was made or to the giving of some other public notification by Australia expressing its support for the declaration.

(7) A reference in this Act to a person acting on behalf of the Commission is a reference to:

(a) a person, or each of a body of persons, acting pursuant to a delegation under section 19; or

(b) an instrumentality of a State performing a function of the Commission pursuant to an arrangement in force under section 16.

(8) Except so far as the contrary intention appears, an expression that is used both in this Act and in the Convention (whether or not a particular meaning is assigned to it by the Convention) has, in this Act, for the purposes of the operation of this Act in relation to the Convention, the same meaning as it has in the Convention.

(9) A reference in this Act to prejudice to the security, defence or international relations of Australia includes a reference to any such prejudice that might result from the divulging of information or matters communicated in confidence by or on behalf of the government of a foreign country, an authority of a government of a foreign country or an international organisation to the Government of the Commonwealth, to an authority of the Commonwealth or to a person receiving the communication on behalf of the Commonwealth or of an authority of the Commonwealth.

4 Operation of State and Territory laws

(1) This Act is not intended to exclude or limit the operation of a law of a State or Territory that is capable of operating concurrently with this Act.

(2) If:

(a) a law of a State or Territory deals with a matter dealt with by this Act; and

(b) an act or omission by a person that constitutes an offence against that law also constitutes an offence against this Act;

the person may be prosecuted and convicted either under that law of the State or Territory or under this Act, but nothing in this subsection renders a person liable to be punished more than once in respect of the same act or omission.

5 Extension to external Territories

This Act extends to every external Territory.

6 Extent to which Act binds the Crown

(1) This Act binds the Crown in right of the Commonwealth and of Norfolk Island but, except as otherwise expressly provided by this Act, does not bind the Crown in right of a State.

(1A) Part IIB binds the Crown in right of the States.

(2) Nothing in this Act renders the Crown in right of the Commonwealth, of a State or of Norfolk Island liable to be prosecuted for an offence.

6A Application of the *Criminal Code*

Chapter 2 of the *Criminal Code* applies to all offences against this Act.

Note: Chapter 2 of the *Criminal Code* sets out the general principles of criminal responsibility.

PART II—HUMAN RIGHTS AND EQUAL OPPORTUNITY COMMISSION

Division 1—Establishment and Constitution of Commission

7 Human Rights and Equal Opportunity Commission

(1) There is established by this Act a Commission by the name of the Human Rights and Equal Opportunity Commission.

(2) The Commission:

(a) is a body corporate, with perpetual succession;

(b) shall have a common seal;

(c) may acquire, hold and dispose of real and personal property; and

(d) may sue and be sued in its corporate name.

(3) All courts, judges and persons acting judicially shall take judicial notice of the imprint of the common seal of the Commission appearing on a document and shall presume that the document was duly sealed.

8 Constitution of Commission

(1) The Commission shall consist of:

(a) a President; and

(b) a Human Rights Commissioner; and

(c) the Race Discrimination Commissioner; and

(ca) the Aboriginal and Torres Strait Islander Social Justice Commissioner; and

(d) the Sex Discrimination Commissioner; and

(f) the Disability Discrimination Commissioner.

(2) The members must act in a way that promotes the collegiate nature of the Commission.

(6) The functions of the Commission under paragraphs 11(1)(aa), 11(1)(ab), 11(1)(f) and 31(b) and the functions of the Commission under paragraphs 11(1)(p) and 31(k), to the extent that they relate to the performance of the first-mentioned functions, shall be performed by the President, and a reference in this Act to the Commission or to a member of the Commission shall, in relation to the performance of any of those functions, be read as a reference to the President.

(7) The performance of the functions or the exercise of the powers of the Commission is not affected by reason only of a vacancy in the office of President, Human Rights Commissioner, Race Discrimination Commissioner,

Aboriginal and Torres Strait Islander Social Justice Commissioner, Sex Discrimination Commissioner or Disability Discrimination Commissioner.

8A The President

(1) The President is to be appointed by the Governor-General as a full-time member or a part-time member.

(2) The President is the senior member of the Commission.

(3) The President is responsible for managing the administrative affairs of the Commission.

8B The Human Rights Commissioner

(1) The Human Rights Commissioner is to be appointed by the Governor-General as a full-time member.

(2) A person is not qualified to be appointed as the Human Rights Commissioner unless the Governor-General is satisfied that the person has appropriate qualifications, knowledge or experience.

9 Arrangement for appointment of the holder of a judicial office of a State

(1) The Governor-General may, for the purpose of appointing to the Commission a person who is the holder of a judicial office of a State, enter into such arrangement with the Governor of that State as is necessary to secure that person's services.

(2) An arrangement under subsection (1) may provide for the Commonwealth to reimburse a State with respect to the services of the person to whom the arrangement relates.

10 Appointment of Judge as member not to affect tenure etc.

(1) The appointment of the holder of a judicial office as a member, or service by the holder of a judicial office as a member, does not affect the person's tenure of that judicial office or the person's rank, title, status, precedence, salary, annual or other allowances or other rights or privileges as the holder of that judicial office and, for all purposes, the person's service as a member shall be taken to be service as the holder of that judicial office.

(2) In this section, ***judicial office*** means:

(a) an office of Judge of a court created by the Parliament; or

(b) an office the holder of which has, by virtue of holding that office, the same status as a Judge of a court created by the Parliament.

Division 2—Duties, functions and powers of Commission

10A Duties of Commission

(1) It is the duty of the Commission to ensure that the functions of the Commission under this or any other Act are performed:

(a) with regard for:

(i) the indivisibility and universality of human rights; and

(ii) the principle that every person is free and equal in dignity and rights; and

(b) efficiently and with the greatest possible benefit to the people of Australia.

(2) Nothing in this section imposes a duty on the Commission that is enforceable by proceedings in a court.

11 Functions of Commission

(1) The functions of the Commission are:

(a) such functions as are conferred on the Commission by the *Age Discrimination Act 2004*, the *Racial Discrimination Act 1975*, the *Sex Discrimination Act 1984* or any other enactment;

(aa) to inquire into, and attempt to conciliate, complaints of unlawful discrimination;

(ab) to deal with complaints lodged under Part IIC;

(b) such functions as are to be performed by the Commission pursuant to an arrangement in force under section 16;

(c) such functions as are expressed to be conferred on the Commission by any State enactment, being functions in relation to which the Minister has made a declaration under section 18;

(d) the functions conferred on the Commission by section 31;

(e) to examine enactments, and (when requested to do so by the Minister) proposed enactments, for the purpose of ascertaining whether the enactments or proposed enactments, as the case may be, are, or would be, inconsistent with or contrary to any human right, and to report to the Minister the results of any such examination;

(f) to inquire into any act or practice that may be inconsistent with or contrary to any human right, and:

(i) where the Commission considers it appropriate to do so—to endeavour, by conciliation, to effect a settlement of the matters that gave rise to the inquiry; and

(ii) where the Commission is of the opinion that the act or practice is inconsistent with or contrary to any human right, and the Commission has not considered it appropriate to endeavour to effect a settlement of the matters that gave rise to the inquiry or has endeavoured without success to effect such a settlement—to report to the Minister in relation to the inquiry;

(g) to promote an understanding and acceptance, and the public discussion, of human rights in Australia;

(h) to undertake research and educational programs and other programs, on behalf of the Commonwealth, for the purpose of promoting human rights, and to co-ordinate any such programs undertaken by any other persons or authorities on behalf of the Commonwealth;

(j) on its own initiative or when requested by the Minister, to report to the Minister as to the laws that should be made by the Parliament, or action that should be taken by the Commonwealth, on matters relating to human rights;

(k) on its own initiative or when requested by the Minister, to report to the Minister as to the action (if any) that, in the opinion of the Commission, needs to be taken by Australia in order to comply with the provisions of the Covenant, of the Declarations or of any relevant international instrument;

(m) on its own initiative or when requested by the Minister, to examine any relevant international instrument for the purpose of ascertaining whether there are any inconsistencies between that instrument and the Covenant, the Declarations or any other relevant international instrument, and to report to the Minister the results of any such examination;

(n) to prepare, and to publish in such manner as the Commission considers appropriate, guidelines for the avoidance of acts or practices of a kind in respect of which the Commission has a function under paragraph (f);

(o) where the Commission considers it appropriate to do so, with the leave of the court hearing the proceedings and subject to any conditions imposed by the court, to intervene in proceedings that involve human rights issues; and

(p) to do anything incidental or conducive to the performance of any of the preceding functions.

(2) The Commission shall not:

(a) regard an enactment or proposed enactment as being inconsistent with or contrary to any human right for the purposes of paragraph (1)(e) by reason of a provision of the enactment or proposed enactment that is included solely for the purpose of securing adequate advancement of particular persons or groups of persons in order to enable them to enjoy or exercise human rights equally with other persons; or

(b) regard an act or practice as being inconsistent with or contrary to any human right for the purposes of paragraph (1)(f) where the act or practice is done or engaged in solely for the purpose referred to in paragraph (a) of this subsection.

(3) Notwithstanding paragraphs (1)(a), (d) and (f), the functions of the Commission do not include inquiring into an act or practice of an intelligence agency, and, where a complaint is made to the Commission alleging that an act or practice of such an agency is inconsistent with or contrary to any human right, constitutes discrimination, or is unlawful under the *Racial Discrimination Act 1975*, the *Sex Discrimination Act 1984*, the *Disability Discrimination Act 1992*, or the *Age Discrimination Act 2004*, the Commission shall refer the complaint to the Inspector-General of Intelligence and Security.

(4) A reference in subsection (3) to an intelligence agency is a reference to the Australian Secret Intelligence Service, the Australian Security Intelligence Organisation, the Office of National Assessments, that part of the Department of Defence known as the Defence Signals Directorate (including any part of the Defence Force that performs functions on behalf of that part of the Department),

that part of the Department of Defence known as the Defence Imagery and Geospatial Organisation (including any part of the Defence Force that performs functions on behalf of that part of the Department) or that part of the Department of Defence known as the Defence Intelligence Organisation.

13 Powers of Commission

(1) The Commission has power to do all things that are necessary or convenient to be done for or in connection with the performance of its functions.

(2) The Commission may at any time report to the Minister on any matter arising in the course of the performance of its functions and shall report to the Minister on such a matter if requested by the Minister to do so.

14 Form of examinations or inquiries to be at discretion of Commission etc.

(1) For the purpose of the performance of its functions, the Commission may make an examination or hold an inquiry in such manner as it thinks fit and, in informing itself in the course of an examination or inquiry, is not bound by the rules of evidence.

(2) Where the Commission considers that the preservation of the anonymity of a person:

- (a) who has made a complaint to the Commission; or
- (b) who:
  - (i) has furnished or proposes to furnish information;
  - (ii) has produced or proposes to produce a document;
  - (iii) has given or proposes to give evidence; or
  - (iv) has made or proposes to make a submission;

to the Commission or to a person acting on behalf of the Commission; is necessary to protect the security of employment, the privacy or any human right of the person, the Commission may give directions prohibiting the disclosure of the identity of the person.

(3) The Commission may direct that:

- (a) any evidence given before the Commission or any information given to the Commission; or
- (b) the contents of any document produced to the Commission;

shall not be published, or shall not be published except in such manner, and to such persons, as the Commission specifies.

(4) Where the Commission has given a direction under subsection (3) in relation to the publication of any evidence or information or of the contents of a document, the direction does not prevent a person from communicating to another person a matter contained in the evidence, information or document if the first-mentioned person has knowledge of the matter otherwise than by reason of the evidence or information having been given or the document having been produced to the Commission.

(5) In deciding whether or not to give a direction under subsection (3), the Commission shall have regard to the need to prevent such of the following as are relevant to the circumstances:
   (a) prejudice to the security, defence or international relations of Australia;
   (b) prejudice to relations between the Commonwealth Government and the Government of a State or between the Government of a State and the Government of another State;
   (c) the disclosure of deliberations or decisions of the Cabinet, or of a Committee of the Cabinet, of the Commonwealth or of a State;
   (d) the disclosure of deliberations or advice of the Federal Executive Council or the Executive Council of a State;
   (e) the disclosure, or the ascertaining by a person, of the existence or identity of a confidential source of information in relation to the enforcement of the criminal law;
   (f) the endangering of the life or physical safety of any person;
   (g) prejudice to the proper enforcement of the law or the protection of public safety;
   (h) the disclosure of information the disclosure of which is prohibited, absolutely or subject to qualifications, by or under another enactment;
   (j) the unreasonable disclosure of the personal affairs of any person;
   (k) the unreasonable disclosure of confidential commercial information.

(6) In having regard to the matters mentioned in paragraphs (5)(a) to (k), inclusive, the Commission shall try to achieve an appropriate balance between the need to have regard to those matters and the desirability of ensuring that interested persons are sufficiently informed of the results of the Commission's examination or inquiry.

(7) A person shall not contravene a direction given by the Commission under subsection (2) or (3) that is applicable to the person.
   Penalty:
   (a) in the case of a natural person—$1,000; or
   (b) in the case of a body corporate—$5,000.

(7A) Subsection (7) is an offence of strict liability.
   Note: For ***strict liability***, see section 6.1 of the *Criminal Code*.

(8) In subsection (1), ***function*** does not include a function conferred on the Commission by the *Sex Discrimination Act 1984*, the *Disability Discrimination Act 1992*, or the *Age Discrimination Act 2004*.

15 Commission may engage in consultations

For the purposes of the performance of its functions, the Commission may work with and consult appropriate persons, governmental organisations and non-governmental organisations.

16 Inter-governmental arrangements

(1) The Minister may make an arrangement with a Minister of a State for or in relation to:

(a) the performance on a joint basis of any functions of the Commission;

(b) the performance by that State or by an instrumentality of that State on behalf of the Commonwealth of any functions of the Commission; or

(c) the performance by the Commission of functions on behalf of that State relating to human rights or to discrimination in employment or occupation.

(2) An arrangement under this section may contain such incidental or supplementary provisions as the Minister and the Minister of the State with whom the arrangement is made think necessary.

(2A) An act done by or in relation to a State, or an instrumentality of a State, acting (whether on a joint basis or otherwise) under an arrangement made under this section shall be deemed, for the purposes of this Act, the *Racial Discrimination Act 1975*, the *Sex Discrimination Act 1984*, the *Disability Discrimination Act 1992* and the *Age Discrimination Act 2004*, to have been done by, or in relation to, the President.

(3) The Minister may arrange with the Minister of a State with whom an arrangement is in force under this section for the variation or revocation of the arrangement.

(4) An arrangement under this section, or the variation or revocation of such an arrangement, shall be in writing, and a copy of each instrument by which an arrangement under this section is made, varied or revoked shall be published in the *Gazette*.

17 Advisory committees

(1) The Minister shall establish at least one advisory committee, and may, if the Minister considers it desirable, establish 2 or more advisory committees, to perform such of the following functions as the Minister directs:

(a) to advise the Commission in relation to the performance of the Commission's functions;

(b) when requested by the Minister, to report to the Minister as to the action (if any) that needs to be taken by Australia in order to comply with the provisions of the Convention and, in particular, to advise the Minister in respect of national policies relating to equality of opportunity and treatment in employment and occupation.

(2) The Commission may, with the approval of the Minister, establish an advisory committee or advisory committees to advise the Commission in relation to the performance of the Commission's functions.

18 Declarations by Minister

Where the Minister is satisfied that a function expressed to be conferred on the Commission by a State enactment could conveniently be performed by the

Commission, the Minister may, by notice in writing published in the *Gazette*, so declare.

19 Delegation

(1) The Commission may, by writing under its common seal, delegate to a member of the Commission, a member of the staff of the Commission or another person or body of persons all or any of the powers conferred on the Commission under this Act.

(2) A member may, by writing signed by the member, delegate to:

(aa) a member of the Commission; or

(a) a member of the staff of the Commission; or

(b) any other person or body of persons;

approved by the Commission, all or any of the powers exercisable by the member under this Act.

(2A) Subsection (2) does not allow the President to delegate to another member of the Commission any of the President's powers under Part IIB or IIC.

(2B) Subsection (2) does not allow the President to delegate any of the President's powers relating to:

(a) functions of the Commission under paragraphs 11(1)(f) and 11(1)(p) that are to be performed by the President because of subsection 8(6); or

(b) functions of the Commission under paragraphs 31(b) and 31(k) that are to be performed by the President because of subsection 8(6);

to a member of the Commission other than the Human Rights Commissioner.

(2C) The requirement in subsection (2) for approval by the Commission does not apply to a delegation by the President.

(5) Subject to any provision in the instrument of delegation, a person to whom a power of the Commission has been delegated under subsection (1) may, for the purposes of the exercise of that power, exercise any power conferred on a member of the Commission by this Act.

(6) In subsection (1), ***power*** does not include a power conferred on the Commission by the *Racial Discrimination Act 1975*, the *Sex Discrimination Act 1984*, the *Disability Discrimination Act 1992*, or the *Age Discrimination Act 2004*.

(7) In this section, unless the contrary intention appears, ***member*** means a member of the Commission.

Division 3—Functions relating to human rights

19A Division applies to victimisation offences

In this Division, a reference to an act or practice that is inconsistent with or contrary to any human right includes a reference to an act that is an offence under subsection 26(2).

20 Performance of functions relating to human rights

(1) Subject to subsection (2), the Commission shall perform the functions referred to in paragraph 11(1)(f) when:

(a) the Commission is requested to do so by the Minister;

(b) a complaint is made in writing to the Commission alleging that an act or practice is inconsistent with or contrary to any human right; or

(c) it appears to the Commission to be desirable to do so.

(2) The Commission may decide not to inquire into an act or practice, or, if the Commission has commenced to inquire into an act or practice, may decide not to continue to inquire into the act or practice, if:

(a) the Commission is satisfied that the act or practice is not inconsistent with or contrary to any human right;

(b) the Commission is satisfied that the person aggrieved by the act or practice does not desire that the inquiry be held or continued; or

(c) in a case where a complaint has been made to the Commission in relation to the act or practice:

(i) the complaint was made more than 12 months after the act was done or after the last occasion when an act was done pursuant to the practice;

(ii) the Commission is of the opinion that the complaint is frivolous, vexatious, misconceived or lacking in substance;

(iii) where some other remedy has been sought in relation to the subject matter of the complaint—the Commission is of the opinion that the subject matter of the complaint has been adequately dealt with;

(iv) the Commission is of the opinion that some other more appropriate remedy in relation to the subject matter of the complaint is reasonably available to the person aggrieved by the act or practice;

(v) where the subject matter of the complaint has already been dealt with by the Commission or by another statutory authority—the Commission is of the opinion that the subject matter of the complaint has been adequately dealt with; or

(vi) the Commission is of the opinion that the subject matter of the complaint could be more effectively or conveniently dealt with by another statutory authority.

(3) The Commission shall, before the expiration of the period of 2 months commencing when a complaint is made to the Commission in respect of an act or practice, decide whether or not to inquire into the act or practice.

(4) Where the Commission decides not to inquire into, or not to continue to inquire into, an act or practice in respect of which a complaint was made to the Commission, the Commission shall, unless the complaint has been transferred under subsection (4A), forthwith give notice in writing to the complainant of that decision and of the reasons for that decision.

(4A) Where:

(a) a complaint has been made to the Commission in relation to an act or practice; and

(b) because the Commission is of the opinion that the subject-matter of the complaint could be more effectively or conveniently dealt with by the Privacy Commissioner in the performance of the functions referred to in paragraph 27(1)(a) or 28(1)(b) or (c) of the *Privacy Act 1988*, the Commission decides not to inquire, or not to continue to inquire, into that act or practice;

the Commission shall:

(c) transfer the complaint to the Privacy Commissioner;

(d) forthwith give notice in writing to the complainant stating that the complaint has been so transferred; and

(e) give to the Privacy Commissioner any information or documents that relate to the complaint and are in the possession, or under the control, of the Commission.

(4B) A complaint transferred under subsection (4A) shall be taken to be a complaint made to the Privacy Commissioner under Part V of the *Privacy Act 1988*.

(5) Where it appears to the Commission that:

(a) a person wishes to make a complaint to the effect that another person has done an act, or engaged in a practice, that is inconsistent with or contrary to any human right; and

(b) that person requires assistance to formulate the complaint or to reduce it to writing;

it is the duty of the Commission to take reasonable steps to provide appropriate assistance to that person.

(6) A person who is detained in custody (in this subsection and subsection (7) referred to as the ***detainee***) is entitled:

(a) upon making a request to the person (in this subsection and subsection (7) referred to as the ***custodian***) in whose custody the detainee is detained, or to any other person (in this subsection and subsection (7) referred to as a ***custodial officer***) performing duties in connection with the detention:

(i) to be provided with facilities for preparing a complaint in writing under this Division, for giving in writing to the Commission, after the complaint has been made, any other relevant information and for enclosing the complaint or the other information (if any) in a sealed envelope; and

(ii) to have sent to the Commission, without undue delay, a sealed envelope delivered by the detainee to the custodian or to a custodial officer and addressed to the Commission; and

(b) to have delivered to the detainee, without undue delay, any sealed envelope, addressed to the detainee and sent by the Commission, that comes into the possession or under the control of the custodian or of a custodial officer.

(7) Where a sealed envelope addressed to the Commission is delivered by the detainee to the custodian or to a custodial officer for sending to the Commission, or a sealed envelope addressed to the detainee and sent by the

Commission comes into the possession or under the control of the custodian or of a custodial officer, neither the custodian nor any custodial officer is entitled to open the envelope or to inspect any document enclosed in the envelope.

(8) For the purposes of subsections (6) and (7), the Commission may make arrangements with the appropriate authority of a State or Territory for the identification and delivery of sealed envelopes sent by the Commission to persons detained in custody in that State or Territory.

21 Power to obtain information and documents

(1) Where the Commission has reason to believe that a person is capable of giving information or producing documents relevant to a matter under examination or inquiry under this Division, a member may, by notice in writing served on that person, require that person at such place, and within such period or on such date and at such time, as are specified in the notice:

- (a) to give to the Commission, by writing signed by that person or, in the case of a body corporate, on behalf of the body corporate, any such information; or
- (b) to produce to the Commission any such documents.

(2) Where:

- (a) a person is required by a notice under subsection (1) to give information or produce a document to the Commission; and

(b) the information or document originated with, or has been received from, an intelligence agency;

the person shall forthwith notify that agency of the making of the requirement.

(3) A reference in subsection (2) to an intelligence agency is a reference to the Australian Secret Intelligence Service, the Australian Security Intelligence Organisation, the Office of National Assessments, or the Defence Imagery and Geospatial Organisation, the Defence Intelligence Organisation or the Defence Signals Directorate of the Department of Defence.

(4) Where documents are produced to the Commission in accordance with a requirement under subsection (1), the Commission:

- (a) may take possession of, and may make copies of, or take extracts from, the documents;
- (b) may retain possession of the documents for such period as is necessary for the purposes of the examination or inquiry to which the documents relate; and
- (c) during that period shall permit a person who would be entitled to inspect any one or more of the documents if they were not in the possession of the Commission to inspect at all reasonable times such of the documents as that person would be so entitled to inspect.

(5) Where the Commission has reason to believe that a person is capable of giving information relevant to a matter under inquiry under this Division, a member may, by notice in writing served on the person, require the person to attend

before the member, on such date and at such time and place as are specified in the notice, to answer questions relevant to the matter under inquiry.

(6) A person who attends at a place pursuant to a requirement made of the person under subsection (1) or (5) is entitled to be paid by the Commonwealth a reasonable sum for the person's attendance at that place.

22 Power to examine witnesses

(1) A member may administer an oath or affirmation to a person required to attend before the member pursuant to section 21 and may examine the person on oath or affirmation.

(2) The oath or affirmation to be taken or made by a person for the purposes of this section is an oath or affirmation that the evidence the person will give will be true.

23 Failure to comply with requirement

(1) A person shall not refuse or fail:

(a) to be sworn or make an affirmation; or

(b) to give information or produce a document;

when so required under this Act.

Penalty:

(a) in the case of a natural person—$1,000; or

(b) in the case of a body corporate—$5,000.

(2) A person who, after having been served with a notice under subsection 21(5):

(a) refuses or fails to comply with the notice; or

(b) when attending before a member in compliance with the notice, refuses or fails to answer a question that is required by the member to be answered;

is guilty of an offence punishable on conviction by a fine not exceeding:

(c) in the case of a natural person—$1,000; or

(d) in the case of a body corporate—$5,000.

(2A) Subsections (1) and (2) do not apply if the person has a reasonable excuse.

Note: A defendant bears an evidential burden in relation to the matter in subsection (2A) (see subsection 13.3(3) of the *Criminal Code*).

(3) Without limiting the generality of the expression ***reasonable excuse*** in this section, it is hereby declared for the avoidance of doubt that it is a reasonable excuse for a person to refuse or fail to furnish information, produce a document or answer a question when required to do so under this Act, that the information, the production of the document or the answer to a question might tend to incriminate that person.

24 Disclosure of information or contents of documents

(1) Where the Attorney-General furnishes to the Commission a certificate certifying that the giving to the Commission, or to a person acting on behalf of the Commission, of information concerning a specified matter (including the giving of information in answer to a question) or the production to the

Commission, or to a person acting on behalf of the Commission, of a specified document would be contrary to the public interest:

(a) by reason that it would prejudice the security, defence or international relations of Australia;

(b) by reason that it would involve the disclosure of communications between a Minister of the Commonwealth and a Minister of a State, being a disclosure that would prejudice relations between the Commonwealth Government and the Government of a State;

(c) by reason that it would involve the disclosure of deliberations or decisions of the Cabinet or of a Committee of the Cabinet;

(d) by reason that it would involve the disclosure of deliberations or advice of the Executive Council;

(e) by reason that it would prejudice the conduct of an investigation or inquiry into crime or criminal activity that is currently being pursued or would prejudice the fair trial of any person;

(f) by reason that it would disclose, or enable a person to ascertain, the existence or identity of a confidential source of information in relation to the enforcement of the criminal law;

(g) by reason that it would prejudice the effectiveness of the operational methods or investigative practices or techniques of agencies responsible for the enforcement of the criminal law; or

(h) by reason that it would endanger the life or physical safety of any person;

neither the Commission nor any other person is entitled to require a person to give any information concerning the matter or to produce the document.

(1A) In relation to the performance of functions by the Aboriginal and Torres Strait Islander Social Justice Commissioner under Part IIA, subsection (1) (other than paragraphs (1)(a) and (b)) has effect in relation to a certificate given by the Attorney-General of a State or Territory in the same way as it has effect in relation to a certificate given by the Attorney-General of the Commonwealth. For the purposes of this additional effect, references to the Cabinet, a Committee of the Cabinet or the Executive Council are to be treated as references to the corresponding body or committee of the State or Territory concerned.

(2) Without limiting the operation of subsection (1), where the Attorney-General furnishes to the Commission a certificate certifying that the giving to the Commission, or to a person acting on behalf of the Commission, of information as to the existence or non-existence of information concerning a specified matter (including the giving of information in answer to a question) or as to the existence or non-existence of any one or more documents required to be produced to the Commission, or to a person acting on behalf of the Commission, would be contrary to the public interest:

(a) by reason that it would prejudice the security, defence or international relations of Australia; or

(b) by reason that it would prejudice the proper performance of the functions of the Australian Crime Commission;

neither the Commission nor a person acting on behalf of the Commission is entitled, pursuant to this Act, to require a person to give any information as to the existence or non-existence of information concerning that matter or as to the existence or non-existence of that document or those documents.

(3) Notwithstanding the provisions of any law, a person is not excused:

(a) from giving any information, or producing a document, when required to do so pursuant to this Act; or

(b) from answering a question that the person is required to answer by a member before whom the person is attending in compliance with a notice served on the person under subsection 21(5);

on the ground that the giving of the information, the production of the document or the answering of the question:

(c) would disclose legal advice furnished to a Minister, to a person or body that acts on behalf of the Commonwealth, or to an authority of the Commonwealth;

(d) would contravene the provisions of any other Act or would be contrary to the public interest; or

(e) might make the person liable to a penalty.

(4) A person is not liable to any penalty under the provisions of any other law by reason of:

(a) giving information or producing a document when required to do so pursuant to this Act; or

(b) answering a question that the person is required to answer by a member before whom the person is attending in compliance with a notice served on the person under subsection 21(5).

26 Offences relating to administration of Act

(1) A person shall not hinder, obstruct, molest or interfere with:

(a) a member participating in an inquiry or examination under this Act; or

(b) a person acting on behalf of the Commission, while that person is holding an inquiry or carrying out an investigation under this Act.

Penalty:

(a) in the case of a natural person—$1,000; or

(b) in the case of a body corporate—$5,000.

(2) A person who:

(a) refuses to employ another person;

(b) dismisses, or threatens to dismiss, another person from the other person's employment;

(c) prejudices, or threatens to prejudice, another person in the other person's employment; or

(d) intimidates or coerces, imposes any pecuniary or other penalty upon, or takes any other disciplinary action in relation to, another person;

by reason that the other person:

(e) has made, or proposes to make, a complaint to the Commission;

(f) has alleged, or proposes to allege, that a person has done an act or engaged in a practice that is inconsistent with or contrary to any human right;

(g) has furnished, or proposes to furnish, any information or documents to the Commission or to a person acting on behalf of the Commission; or

(h) has given or proposes to give evidence before the Commission or to a person acting on behalf of the Commission;

is guilty of an offence punishable upon conviction:

(j) in the case of a natural person—by a fine not exceeding $2,500 or imprisonment for a period not exceeding 3 months, or both; or

(k) in the case of a body corporate—by a fine not exceeding $10,000.

(3) It is a defence to a prosecution for an offence under subsection (2) constituted by subjecting, or threatening to subject, a person to a detriment specified in paragraph (2)(a), (b), (c) or (d) on the ground that the person has alleged that another person has done an act or engaged in a practice that is inconsistent with or contrary to any human right if it is proved that the allegation was false and was not made in good faith.

Note: Sections 136.1, 137.1 and 137.2 of the *Criminal Code* deal with making false or misleading statements, giving false or misleading information and producing false or misleading documents.

27 Commission to give opportunity for making of submissions

Where it appears to the Commission as a result of an inquiry into an act or practice that the act or practice is inconsistent with or contrary to any human right, the Commission shall not furnish a report to the Minister in relation to the act or practice until it has given a reasonable opportunity to the person who did the act or engaged in the practice, to do, at the option of the person, either or both of the following:

(a) to appear before the Commission, whether in person or by a representative, and make oral submissions in relation to the act or practice;

(b) to make written submissions to the Commission in relation to the act or practice.

28 Nature of settlements

The Commission shall, in endeavouring to effect a settlement of a matter that gave rise to an inquiry, have regard to the need to ensure that any settlement of the matter reflects a recognition of human rights and the need to protect those rights.

29 Reports to contain recommendations

(1) Where, after an examination of an enactment or proposed enactment, the Commission finds that the enactment is, or the proposed enactment would be, inconsistent with or contrary to any human right, the Commission shall include in its report to the Minister relating to the results of the examination any recommendations by the Commission for amendment of the enactment or

proposed enactment to ensure that the enactment is not, or the proposed enactment would not be, inconsistent with or contrary to any human right.

(2) Where, after an inquiry into an act done or practice engaged in by a person, the Commission finds that the act or practice is inconsistent with or contrary to any human right, the Commission:

(a) shall serve notice in writing on the person setting out its findings and the reasons for those findings;

(b) may include in the notice any recommendations by the Commission for preventing a repetition of the act or a continuation of the practice;

(c) may include in the notice any recommendation by the Commission for either or both of the following:

(i) the payment of compensation to, or in respect of, a person who has suffered loss or damage as a result of the act or practice;

(ii) the taking of other action to remedy or reduce loss or damage suffered by a person as a result of the act or practice;

(d) shall include in any report to the Minister relating to the results of the inquiry particulars of any recommendations that it has made pursuant to paragraph (b) or (c);

(e) shall state in that report whether, to the knowledge of the Commission, the person has taken or is taking any action as a result of the findings, and recommendations (if any), of the Commission and, if the person has taken or is taking any such action, the nature of that action; and

(f) shall serve a copy of that report on the person and, if a complaint was made to the Commission in relation to the act or practice:

(i) where the complaint was made by a person affected by the act or practice—shall serve a copy of that report on the complainant; or

(ii) if the complaint was made by another person—may serve a copy of that report on the complainant.

(3) Where:

(a) a complaint is made to the Commission in relation to an act or practice; and

(b) after an inquiry into the act or practice, the Commission finds that:

(i) the existence of the act or practice has not been established; or

(ii) the act or practice is not inconsistent with or contrary to any human right;

the Commission shall give a copy of a report setting out its findings, and the reasons for those findings, to the complainant and:

(c) in a case to which subparagraph (b)(i) applies—to the person alleged to have done the act or engaged in the practice; or

(d) in a case to which subparagraph (b)(ii) applies—to the person who did the act or engaged in the practice.

(4) In setting out findings and reasons in a notice to be served or a report to be given under this section the Commission may exclude any matter if the Commission considers it desirable to do so having regard to any of the matters

mentioned in subsection 14(5) and to the obligations of the Commission under subsection 14(6).

(5) Where, under subsection (4), the Commission excludes any matter from a report, the Commission shall prepare a report setting out the excluded matter and its reasons for excluding the matter and shall furnish the report to the Minister.

Division 4—Functions relating to equal opportunity in employment

30 Interpretation etc.

(1) In this Division:

act includes an act done:

(a) by or on behalf of a State or an authority of a State;
(b) under a law of a State;
(c) wholly within a State; or
(d) partly within a State, to the extent to which the act was done within a State.

practice includes a practice engaged in:

(a) by or on behalf of a State or an authority of a State;
(b) under a law of a State;
(c) wholly within a State; or
(d) partly within a State, to the extent to which the practice was or is engaged in within a State.

(1A) In this Division, a reference to an act or practice that constitutes discrimination includes a reference to an act that is an offence under subsection 26(2).

(2) This Division binds the Crown in right of a State.

31 Functions of Commission relating to equal opportunity

The following functions are hereby conferred on the Commission:

(a) to examine enactments, and (when requested to do so by the Minister) proposed enactments, for the purpose of ascertaining whether the enactments or proposed enactments, as the case may be, have, or would have, the effect of nullifying or impairing equality of opportunity or treatment in employment or occupation, and to report to the Minister the results of any such examination;
(b) to inquire into any act or practice, including any systemic practice, that may constitute discrimination and:
    (i) where the Commission considers it appropriate to do so—to endeavour, by conciliation, to effect a settlement of the matters that gave rise to the inquiry; and
    (ii) where the Commission is of the opinion that the act or practice constitutes discrimination, and the Commission has not considered it appropriate to endeavour to effect a settlement of the matters that gave rise to the inquiry or has endeavoured without success to effect such a settlement—to report to the Minister in relation to the inquiry;

(c) to promote an understanding and acceptance, and the public discussion, of equality of opportunity and treatment in employment and occupation in Australia;
(d) to undertake research and educational programs and other programs, on behalf of the Commonwealth, for the purpose of promoting equality of opportunity and treatment in employment and occupation, and to co-ordinate any such programs undertaken by any other persons or authorities on behalf of the Commonwealth;
(e) on its own initiative or when requested by the Minister, to report to the Minister as to the laws that should be made by the Parliament, or action that should be taken by the Commonwealth, on matters relating to equality of opportunity and treatment in employment and occupation;
(f) when requested by the Minister, to report to the Minister as to the action (if any) that, in the opinion of the Commission, needs to be taken by Australia in order to comply with the provisions of the Convention;
(g) on its own initiative or when requested by the Minister, to examine any relevant international instrument for the purpose of ascertaining whether there are any inconsistencies between that instrument and the Convention, and to report to the Minister the results of any such examination;
(h) to prepare, and to publish in such manner as the Commission considers appropriate, guidelines for the avoidance of acts or practices of a kind in respect of which the Commission has a function under paragraph (b);
(j) where the Commission considers it appropriate to do so, with the leave of the court hearing the proceedings and subject to any conditions imposed by the court, to intervene in proceedings that involve discrimination issues;
(k) to do anything incidental or conducive to the performance of any of the preceding functions.

32 Performance of functions relating to equal opportunity

(1) Subject to subsections (2) and (3), the Commission shall perform the functions referred to in paragraph 31(b) when:
(a) the Commission is requested to do so by the Minister;
(b) a complaint is made in writing to the Commission alleging that an act or practice constitutes discrimination; or
(c) it appears to the Commission to be desirable to do so.

(2) The Commission shall not inquire into an act or practice, or, if the Commission has commenced to inquire into an act or practice, shall not continue to inquire into the act or practice, if the Commission is satisfied that the subject matter of the complaint is dealt with under a prescribed enactment or a prescribed State enactment.

(3) The Commission may decide not to inquire into an act or practice, or, if the Commission has commenced to inquire into an act or practice, may decide not to continue to inquire into the act or practice, if:

(a) the Commission is satisfied that the act or practice does not constitute discrimination;
(b) the Commission is satisfied that the person aggrieved by the act or practice does not desire that the inquiry be held or continued; or
(c) in a case where a complaint has been made to the Commission in relation to the act or practice:
  (i) the complaint was made more than 12 months after the act was done or after the last occasion when an act was done pursuant to the practice;
  (ii) the Commission is of the opinion that the complaint is frivolous, vexatious, misconceived or lacking in substance;
  (iii) where some other remedy has been sought in relation to the subject matter of the complaint—the Commission is of the opinion that the subject matter of the complaint has been adequately dealt with;
  (iv) the Commission is of the opinion that some other more appropriate remedy in relation to the subject matter of the complaint is reasonably available to the complainant;
  (v) where the subject matter of the complaint has already been dealt with by the Commission or by another statutory authority—the Commission is of the opinion that the subject matter of the complaint has been adequately dealt with; or
  (vi) the Commission is of the opinion that the subject matter of the complaint could be more effectively or conveniently dealt with by another statutory authority.

33 Application of certain provisions of Division 3

Subsections 20(3), (4) and (5) and sections 21, 22, 23, 24, 26 and 27 apply in relation to the functions of the Commission set out in section 31, and in relation to the performance of those functions, as if:

(a) references in those provisions to acts or practices were references to acts or practices within the meaning of this Division;
(b) the words "is inconsistent with or contrary to any human right" were omitted from subsection 20(5) and the words "constitutes discrimination" were substituted;
(c) references in section 21 to a matter under examination or inquiry under Division 3 were references to a matter under examination or inquiry under this Division, not being an act mentioned in paragraph (a), (b), (c) or (d) of the definition of ***act*** in subsection 30(1) or a practice mentioned in paragraph (a), (b), (c) or (d) of the definition of ***practice*** in that subsection;
(d) the words "is inconsistent with or contrary to any human right" were omitted from sections 26 and 27 and the words "constitutes discrimination" were substituted; and
(e) a reference in any of those provisions to another of those provisions were a reference to that other provision as applied by this section.

34 Nature of settlements

The Commission shall, in endeavouring to effect a settlement of a matter that gave rise to an inquiry, have regard to the need to ensure that any settlement of the matter reflects a recognition of the right of every person to equality of opportunity and treatment in respect of employment and occupation and the need to protect that right.

35 Reports to contain recommendations

(1) Where, after an examination of an enactment or proposed enactment, the Commission finds that the enactment has, or the proposed enactment would have, the effect of nullifying or impairing equality of opportunity or treatment in employment or occupation, the Commission shall include in its report to the Minister relating to the results of the examination any recommendations by the Commission for amendment of the enactment or proposed enactment to ensure that the enactment does not have, or the proposed enactment would not have, the effect of nullifying or impairing equality of opportunity or treatment in employment or occupation.

(2) Where, after an inquiry into an act done or practice engaged in by a person, the Commission finds that the act or practice constitutes discrimination, the Commission:

- (a) shall serve notice in writing on the person setting out its findings and the reasons for those findings;
- (b) may include in the notice any recommendations by the Commission for preventing a repetition of the act or a continuation of the practice;
- (c) may include in the notice any recommendation by the Commission for either or both of the following:
  - (i) the payment of compensation to, or in respect of, a person who has suffered loss or damage as a result of the act or practice;
  - (ii) the taking of other action to remedy or reduce loss or damage suffered by a person as a result of the act or practice;
- (d) shall include in any report to the Minister relating to the results of the inquiry particulars of any recommendations that it has made pursuant to paragraph (b) or (c);
- (e) shall state in that report whether, to the knowledge of the Commission, the person has taken or is taking any action as a result of the findings, and recommendations (if any), of the Commission and, if the person has taken or is taking any such action, the nature of that action; and
- (f) shall serve a copy of that report on the person and, if a complaint was made to the Commission in relation to the act or practice:
  - (i) where the complaint was made by a person affected by the act or practice—shall serve a copy of that report on the complainant; or
  - (ii) if the complaint was made by another person—may serve a copy of that report on the complainant.

(3) Where:

(a) a complaint is made to the Commission in relation to an act or practice; and
(b) after an inquiry into the act or practice, the Commission finds that:
(i) the existence of the act or practice has not been established; or
(ii) the act or practice does not constitute discrimination;
the Commission shall give a copy of a report setting out its findings, and the reasons for those findings, to the complainant and:
(c) in a case to which subparagraph (b)(i) applies—to the person alleged to have done the act or engaged in the practice; or
(d) in a case to which subparagraph (b)(ii) applies—to the person who did the act or engaged in the practice.

(4) In setting out findings and reasons in a notice to be served or a report to be given under this section the Commission may exclude any matter if the Commission considers it desirable to do so having regard to any of the matters mentioned in subsection 14(5) and to the obligations of the Commission under subsection 14(6).

(5) Where, under subsection (4), the Commission excludes any matter from a report, the Commission shall prepare a report setting out the excluded matter and its reasons for excluding the matter and shall furnish the report to the Minister.

Division 5—Administrative provisions

36 Acting President and Human Rights Commissioner

(2) The Minister may appoint a person to act as President:
(a) during a vacancy in the office of President, whether or not an appointment has previously been made to the office; or
(b) during any period, or during all periods, when the President is absent from duty or from Australia or is, for any other reason, unable to perform the functions of the office of President.

(3) The Minister may appoint a person to act as Human Rights Commissioner:
(a) during a vacancy in the office of Human Rights Commissioner, whether or not an appointment has previously been made to the office; or
(b) during any period, or during all periods, when the Human Rights Commissioner is absent from duty or from Australia, or is, for any other reason, unable to perform the functions of the office of Human Rights Commissioner.

(9) At any time when a person who is not a member of the Commission is acting as President or Human Rights Commissioner, the person shall be deemed to be a member of the Commission for the purposes of sections 21, 22, 23, 24 and 26 (including those sections as applied by section 33) and sections 42, 48 and 49.

(10) The validity of anything done by or in relation to a person purporting to act under subsection (2) or (3) shall not be called in question on the ground that:
(a) the occasion for the person's appointment had not arisen;

(b) there is a defect or irregularity in connection with the person's appointment;
(c) the person's appointment had ceased to have effect; or
(d) the occasion for the person to act had not arisen or had ceased.

37 Terms and conditions of appointment

(1) Subject to subsection (2), an appointed member holds office for such period, not exceeding 7 years, as is specified in the instrument of the member's appointment, but is eligible for re-appointment.
(4) An appointed member, other than a member who is a Judge, holds office on such terms and conditions (if any) in respect of matters not provided for by this Act as are determined by the Governor-General.

38 Remuneration and allowances

(1) Subject to this section, an appointed member shall be paid such remuneration as is determined by the Remuneration Tribunal but, if no determination of that remuneration by the Tribunal is in operation, an appointed member shall be paid such remuneration as is prescribed.
(2) An appointed member shall be paid such allowances as are prescribed.
(3) Subsections (1) and (2) have effect subject to the *Remuneration Tribunal Act 1973*.
(4) If a person who is a Judge is appointed as a member, the person is not, while receiving salary or annual allowance as a Judge, entitled to remuneration under this Act.

39 Leave of absence

(1) A person appointed as a full-time member has such recreation leave entitlements as are determined by the Remuneration Tribunal.
(1A) The Minister may grant a person appointed as a full-time member leave of absence, other than recreation leave, on such terms and conditions as to remuneration or otherwise as the Minister determines.
(2) The Minister may grant to a person appointed as a part-time member leave of absence from a meeting of the Commission.

40 Resignation

An appointed member may resign from the office of member by writing signed by the member and delivered to the Governor-General.

41 Termination of appointment

(1) The Governor-General may terminate the appointment of a member by reason of misbehaviour or physical or mental incapacity.
(2) If:
    (a) a member becomes bankrupt, applies to take the benefit of any law for the relief of bankrupt or insolvent debtors, compounds with creditors or makes an assignment of remuneration for their benefit;

(b) a full-time member engages, except with the approval of the Minister, in paid employment outside the duties of the office of member;
(c) a full-time member is absent from duty, except on leave of absence, for 14 consecutive days, or for 28 days in any period of 12 months;
(d) a part-time member is absent, except on leave granted by the Minister in accordance with subsection 39(2), from 3 consecutive meetings of the Commission; or
(e) a member fails, without reasonable excuse, to comply with section 42;
the Governor-General shall terminate the appointment of that member.

(3) In subsections (1) and (2), ***member*** means an appointed member but does not include a member who is a Judge.

(4) If an appointed member who is a Judge ceases to be a Judge, the Governor-General may terminate the appointment of the member.

42 Disclosure of interests

(1) A member who has a direct or indirect pecuniary interest in a matter being considered or about to be considered by the Commission shall, as soon as possible after the relevant facts have come to the member's knowledge, disclose the nature of the interest at a meeting of the Commission.

(2) A disclosure under subsection (1) shall be recorded in the minutes of the meeting of the Commission and the member shall not:
(a) be present during any deliberation of the Commission with respect to that matter; or
(b) take part in any decision of the Commission with respect to that matter.

43 Staff

(1) The staff necessary to assist the Commission shall be persons engaged under the Public Service Act 1999.

(2) For the purposes of the Public Service Act 1999:
(a) the President and the APS employees assisting the President together constitute a Statutory Agency; and
(b) the President is the Head of that Statutory Agency.

43A Commission may make administrative services available to the Privacy Commissioner

The Commission may make administrative services available to the Privacy Commissioner for the purpose of assisting the Privacy Commissioner in the performance of his or her functions under the *Privacy Act 1988* or any other Act.

44 Meetings of the Commission

(1) The Minister or the President may, at any time, convene a meeting of the Commission.

(2) The President shall convene such meetings of the Commission as, in the President's opinion, are necessary for the efficient performance of its functions.

(3) At a meeting of the Commission a quorum is constituted by a number of members that is not less than one-half of the number of members for the time being holding office under section 8.
(4) The President shall preside at all meetings of the Commission at which the President is present.
(5) If the President is not present at a meeting of the Commission, the members present are to elect one of their number to preside at the meeting.
(6) Questions arising at a meeting of the Commission shall be determined by a majority of the votes of the members present and voting.
(7) The person presiding at a meeting of the Commission has a deliberative vote, and, in the event of an equality of votes, also has a casting vote.
(8) The Commission may regulate the conduct of proceedings at its meetings as it thinks fit and shall cause minutes of those proceedings to be kept.

45 Annual report

(1) The Commission shall, as soon as practicable after each 30 June, prepare and furnish to the Minister a report of its operations during the year that ended on that 30 June, being operations under this Act and operations under any other enactment or any State enactment.
(2) The first report of the Commission shall include a report of the operations of the Human Rights Commission under the *Human Rights Commission Act 1981* for the period that commenced immediately after the end of the year to which the last report furnished by the Human Rights Commission under that Act related and ended immediately before the commencement of this Act.

46 Reports to be tabled in Parliament

The Minister shall cause a copy of every report furnished to the Minister by the Commission under this Part other than subsection 29(5) to be laid before each House of the Parliament within 15 sitting days of that House after the report is received by the Minister.

Division 6—Corporate plan

46AA Corporate plan

(1) The Commission must prepare corporate plans.
(2) The first corporate plan:
    (a) is to be for a period of 3 years; and
    (b) must be given to the Minister within 12 months after the commencement of this section.
(3) Each subsequent corporate plan is to be for a period of 3 years beginning immediately after the period of the previous corporate plan.
(4) The Commission may review and revise a corporate plan at any time.
(5) In performing its duties and functions, the Commission must take account of the corporate plan then in force.

46AB Matters to be included in corporate plan

Each corporate plan must:

(a) set out the general policies and strategies that the Commission intends to adopt in order to perform its duties and functions; and

(b) include such performance indicators and targets as the Commission considers appropriate.

46AC Corporate plans to be given to Minister

As soon as practicable after the Commission prepares or revises a corporate plan, it must give a copy of the plan to the Minister.

PART IIA—ABORIGINAL AND TORRES STRAIT ISLANDER SOCIAL JUSTICE COMMISSIONER

Division 1—Establishment and functions

46A Interpretation

In this Part:

Commissioner means the Aboriginal and Torres Strait Islander Social Justice Commissioner.

human rights means:

(a) the rights and freedoms recognised by the International Convention on the Elimination of All Forms of Racial Discrimination, a copy of which is set out in the Schedule to the *Racial Discrimination Act 1975*; and

(b) the rights and freedoms recognised by the Covenant; and

(c) the rights and freedoms declared by the Declarations or recognised or declared by any relevant international instrument.

46B Aboriginal and Torres Strait Islander Social Justice Commissioner

(1) There is to be an Aboriginal and Torres Strait Islander Social Justice Commissioner, who is to be appointed by the Governor-General.

(2) A person is not qualified to be appointed unless the Governor-General is satisfied that the person has significant experience in community life of Aboriginal persons or Torres Strait Islanders.

46C Functions of the Commission that are to be performed by the Commissioner

(1) The following functions are conferred on the Commission:

(a) to submit a report to the Minister, as soon as practicable after 30 June in each year, regarding the enjoyment and exercise of human rights by Aboriginal persons and Torres Strait Islanders, and including recommendations as to the action that should be taken to ensure the enjoyment and exercise of human rights by those persons;

(b) to promote discussion and awareness of human rights in relation to Aboriginal persons and Torres Strait Islanders;

(c) to undertake research and educational programs, and other programs, for the purpose of promoting respect for the human rights of Aboriginal persons and Torres Strait Islanders and promoting the enjoyment and exercise of human rights by Aboriginal persons and Torres Strait Islanders;

(d) to examine enactments, and proposed enactments, for the purpose of ascertaining whether they recognise and protect the human rights of Aboriginal persons and Torres Strait Islanders, and to report to the Minister the results of any such examination.

(2) The functions of the Commission under subsection (1) are to be performed by the Commissioner on behalf of the Commission.

(3) In the performance of functions under this section, the Commissioner may consult any of the following:

(a) organisations established by Aboriginal or Torres Strait Islander communities;

(b) organisations of indigenous peoples in other countries;

(c) international organisations and agencies;

(d) such other organisations, agencies or persons as the Commissioner considers appropriate.

(4) In the performance of functions under this section, the Commissioner must, as appropriate, have regard to:

(a) the Universal Declaration of Human Rights, the International Covenant on Civil and Political Rights, the International Covenant on Economic, Social and Cultural Rights, the Convention on the Elimination of All Forms of Racial Discrimination and the Convention on the Rights of the Child; and

(b) such other instruments relating to human rights as the Commissioner considers relevant; and

(c) the object of the *Council for Aboriginal Reconciliation Act 1991*.

Division 2—Administrative provisions

46D Terms and conditions of appointment

(1) Subject to this Division, the Commissioner holds office for such period, not exceeding 7 years, as is specified in the instrument of appointment, but is eligible for re-appointment.

(2) The Commissioner holds office on such terms and conditions (if any) in respect of matters not provided for by this Act as are determined by the Governor-General.

46E Remuneration

(1) The Commissioner is to be paid such remuneration as is determined by the Remuneration Tribunal, but if no determination of that remuneration by the Remuneration Tribunal is in operation, the Commissioner is to be paid such remuneration as is prescribed.

(2) The Commissioner is to be paid such allowances as are prescribed.

(3) This section has effect subject to the *Remuneration Tribunal Act 1973*.

46F Leave of absence

(1) The Commissioner has such recreation leave entitlements as are determined by the Remuneration Tribunal.

(2) The Minister may grant the Commissioner leave of absence other than recreation leave, on such terms and conditions as to remuneration or otherwise as the Minister determines.

46G Outside employment

The Commissioner must not, except with the approval of the Minister, engage in paid employment outside the duties of the office of Commissioner.

46H Resignation

The Commissioner may resign from the office of Commissioner by writing given to the Governor-General.

46I Termination of appointment

(1) The Governor-General may terminate the appointment of the Commissioner because of:
   (a) misbehaviour; or
   (b) a disability that makes the Commissioner incapable of performing the inherent requirements of the office.

(2) The Governor-General must terminate the appointment of the Commissioner if the Commissioner:
   (a) becomes bankrupt, applies to take the benefit of any law for the relief of bankrupt or insolvent debtors, compounds with creditors or makes an assignment of remuneration for their benefit; or
   (b) is absent from duty, except on leave of absence, for 14 consecutive days or for 28 days in any period of 12 months; or
   (c) engages in paid employment outside the duties of the office of Commissioner otherwise than with the approval of the Minister.

46J Acting Commissioner

(1) The Minister may appoint a person to act as Commissioner:
   (a) during a vacancy in the office of Commissioner, whether or not an appointment has previously been made to the office; or
   (b) during any period, or during all periods, when the Commissioner is absent from duty or from Australia, or is, for any other reason, unable to perform the functions of the office of Commissioner.

(2) The validity of anything done by a person purporting to act under an appointment made under subsection (1) is not to be called in question on the ground that:
   (a) the occasion for the person's appointment had not arisen; or
   (b) there is a defect or irregularity in or in connection with the appointment; or
   (c) the appointment had ceased to have effect; or
   (d) the occasion for the person to act had not arisen or had ceased.

Division 3—Miscellaneous

46K Commissioner may obtain information from government agencies

(1) If the Commissioner has reason to believe that a government agency has information or a document relevant to the performance by the Commissioner of functions under this Part, the Commissioner may give a written notice to the agency requiring the agency:

(a) to give the information to the Commissioner in writing signed by or on behalf of the agency; or

(b) to produce the document to the Commissioner.

(2) The notice must state:

(a) the place at which the information or document is to be given or produced to the Commissioner; and

(b) the time at which, or period within which, the information or document is to be given or produced.

(3) A government agency must not, in response to a requirement under this section:

(a) give information in a manner that would reveal the identity of a particular individual; or

(b) produce a document that reveals the identity of a particular individual;

unless the individual has consented to the giving of the information or the production of the document.

(4) If:

(a) subsection (3) would prevent a government agency from complying with a requirement under this section to produce a document; and

(b) the agency is able to provide a copy of the document that has had deleted from it the information that would reveal the identity of the individual concerned;

the agency must comply with the requirement by producing a copy with that information deleted.

(5) In this section:

government agency means:

(a) an authority of the Commonwealth, or of a State or Territory; or

(b) a person who performs the functions of, or performs functions within, an authority of the Commonwealth, or of a State or Territory.

46L Commissioner must give information to the Commission

The Commissioner must give to the Commission such information as the Commission from time to time requires relating to the operations of the Commissioner under this Part.

46M Minister must table etc. report of Commissioner

The Minister must cause a copy of each report received by the Minister under paragraph 46C(1)(a):

(a) to be laid before each House of the Parliament within 15 sitting days of that House after the report is received by the Minister; and

(b) to be sent to the Attorney-General of each State and Territory within 7 days after the report is first laid before either House of the Parliament under paragraph (a).

PART IIB—REDRESS FOR UNLAWFUL DISCRIMINATION

Division 1—Conciliation by the President

46P Lodging a complaint

(1) A written complaint may be lodged with the Commission, alleging unlawful discrimination.

(2) The complaint may be lodged:

(a) by a person aggrieved by the alleged unlawful discrimination:

(i) on that person's own behalf; or

(ii) on behalf of that person and one or more other persons who are also aggrieved by the alleged unlawful discrimination; or

(b) by 2 or more persons aggrieved by the alleged unlawful discrimination:

(i) on their own behalf; or

(ii) on behalf of themselves and one or more other persons who are also aggrieved by the alleged unlawful discrimination; or

(c) by a person or trade union on behalf of one or more other persons aggrieved by the alleged unlawful discrimination.

(3) A person who is a class member for a representative complaint is not entitled to lodge a separate complaint in respect of the same subject matter.

(4) If it appears to the Commission that:

(a) a person wishes to make a complaint under subsection (1); and

(b) the person requires assistance to formulate the complaint or to reduce it to writing;

the Commission must take reasonable steps to provide appropriate assistance to the person.

46PA Amendment of complaint

(1) Any complainant may at any time amend the complaint, with the leave of the President.

(2) Subsection (1) does not, by implication, limit any other power to amend the complaint.

46PB Conditions for lodging a representative complaint

(1) A representative complaint may be lodged under section 46P only if:

(a) the class members have complaints against the same person; and

(b) all the complaints are in respect of, or arise out of, the same, similar or related circumstances; and

(c) all the complaints give rise to a substantial common issue of law or fact.

(2) A representative complaint under section 46P must:

(a) describe or otherwise identify the class members; and

(b) specify the nature of the complaints made on behalf of the class members; and

(c) specify the nature of the relief sought.

(3) In describing or otherwise identifying the class members, it is not necessary to name them or specify how many there are.

(4) A representative complaint may be lodged without the consent of class members.

46PC Additional rules applying to representative complaints

(1) A class member may, by notice in writing to the Commission, withdraw from a representative complaint at any time before the President terminates the complaint under section 46PH.

(2) The President may, on application in writing by any affected person, replace any complainant with another person as complainant.

(3) The President may at any stage direct that notice of any matter be given to a class member or class members.

46PD Referral of complaint to President

If a complaint is made to the Commission under section 46P, the Commission must refer the complaint to the President.

46PE Complaints against the President, Commission or a Commissioner

(1) This section applies to a complaint if any of the respondents to the complaint is:

(a) the President; or

(b) the Commission; or

(c) a Commissioner.

(2) If any complainant makes a written request to the President for termination of the complaint, the President must terminate the complaint, if the President is satisfied that all the affected persons agree to the termination.

(3) If the President terminates the complaint under subsection (2), the President must comply with the notification requirements of subsections 46PH(2) and (3).

(4) The President cannot delegate any of his or her powers in relation to the complaint except under paragraph 19(2)(b).

46PF Inquiry by President

(1) If a complaint is referred to the President under section 46PD, the President must inquire into the complaint and attempt to conciliate the complaint.

(2) If the President thinks that 2 or more complaints arise out of the same or substantially the same circumstances or subject, the President may hold a single inquiry, or conduct a single conciliation, in relation to those complaints.

(3) With the leave of the President, any complainant or respondent may amend the complaint to add, as a respondent, a person who is alleged to have done the alleged unlawful discrimination.

Note: In some cases, a person is regarded as having done unlawful discrimination by being treated as responsible for the acts and omissions of another person. See sections 56 and 57 of the *Age Discrimination Act 2004*, sections 122 and 123 of the *Disability Discrimination Act 1992*, sections 18A and 18E of the *Racial Discrimination Act 1975* and sections 105, 106 and 107 of the *Sex Discrimination Act 1984*.

(4) A complaint cannot be amended after it is terminated by the President under section 46PH.

46PG Withdrawal of complaint

(1) Any complainant to a complaint may withdraw the complaint, with the leave of the President.

(2) The President must grant leave if the President is satisfied that all the affected persons agree to withdrawal of the complaint. The President cannot grant leave unless the President is satisfied that they all agree.

46PH Termination of complaint

(1) The President may terminate a complaint on any of the following grounds:

(a) the President is satisfied that the alleged unlawful discrimination is not unlawful discrimination;

(b) the complaint was lodged more than 12 months after the alleged unlawful discrimination took place;

(c) the President is satisfied that the complaint was trivial, vexatious, misconceived or lacking in substance;

(d) in a case where some other remedy has been sought in relation to the subject matter of the complaint—the President is satisfied that the subject matter of the complaint has been adequately dealt with;

(e) the President is satisfied that some other more appropriate remedy in relation to the subject matter of the complaint is reasonably available to each affected person;

(f) in a case where the subject matter of the complaint has already been dealt with by the Commission or by another statutory authority—the President is satisfied that the subject matter of the complaint has been adequately dealt with;

(g) the President is satisfied that the subject matter of the complaint could be more effectively or conveniently dealt with by another statutory authority;

(h) the President is satisfied that the subject matter of the complaint involves an issue of public importance that should be considered by the Federal Court or the Federal Magistrates Court;

(i) the President is satisfied that there is no reasonable prospect of the matter being settled by conciliation.

(2) If the President decides to terminate a complaint, the President must notify the complainants in writing of that decision and of the reasons for that decision.

(3) On request by an affected person who is not a complainant, the President must give the affected person a copy of the notice that was given to the complainants under subsection (2).

(4) The President may revoke the termination of a complaint, but not after an application is made to the Federal Court or the Federal Magistrates Court under section 46PO in relation to the complaint.

46PI President's power to obtain information

(1) This section applies if the President has reason to believe that a person is capable of providing information (***relevant information***) or producing documents (***relevant documents***) relevant to an inquiry under this Division.

(2) The President may serve a written notice on the person, requiring the person to do either or both of the following within a reasonable period specified in the notice, or on a reasonable date and at a reasonable time specified in the notice:
   (a) give the President a signed document containing relevant information required by the notice;
   (b) produce to the President such relevant documents as are specified in the notice.

(3) If the notice is served on a body corporate, the document referred to in paragraph (2)(a) must be signed by an officer of the body corporate.

(4) If a document is produced to the President in accordance with a requirement under this section, the President:
   (a) may take possession of the document; and
   (b) may make copies of the document or take extracts from the document; and
   (c) may retain possession of the document for as long as is necessary for the purposes of the inquiry to which the document relates.

(5) While the President retains any document under this section, the President must allow the document to be inspected, at all reasonable times, by any person who would be entitled to inspect the document if it were not in the possession of the President.

46PJ Directions to attend compulsory conference

(1) For the purpose of dealing with a complaint in accordance with section 46PF, the President may decide to hold a conference, to be presided over by the President or by a suitable person (other than a member) appointed by the President.

(2) The conference must be at a reasonable time and at a reasonable place.

(3) If the President decides to hold a conference, the President must, by notice in writing, direct each complainant and each respondent to attend the conference.

(4) The President may also, by notice in writing, direct any of the following persons to attend the conference:
   (a) any person who, in the opinion of the President, is likely to be able to provide information relevant to the inquiry;
   (b) any person whose presence at the conference is, in the opinion of the President, likely to be conducive to the settlement of the matter to which the alleged unlawful discrimination relates.

(5) A person who is directed under this section to attend a conference is entitled to be paid by the Commonwealth a reasonable sum for the person's attendance at the conference.

(6) In a notice to a person under this section, the President may require the person to produce such documents at the conference as are specified in the notice.

46PK Proceedings at compulsory conference

(1) The person presiding at a compulsory conference may require a person attending the conference to produce a document.

(2) A compulsory conference is to be held in private and, subject to this Act, is to be conducted in such manner as the person presiding at the conference thinks fit.

(3) The person presiding at the conference must ensure that the conduct of the conference does not disadvantage either the complainant or the respondent.

(4) Subject to subsection (5), a body of persons, whether corporate or unincorporate, that is directed under section 46PJ to attend a conference is taken to attend if an officer or employee of that body attends on behalf of that body.

(5) Unless the person presiding at a compulsory conference consents:

(a) an individual is not entitled to be represented at the conference by another person; and

(b) a body of persons, whether corporate or unincorporate, is not entitled to be represented at the conference by a person other than an officer or employee of that body.

(6) Despite paragraph (5)(a), an individual who is unable to attend a compulsory conference because the individual has a disability is entitled to nominate another person to attend instead on his or her behalf.

(7) If, in the opinion of the person presiding at the conference, an individual is unable to participate fully in the conference because the individual has a disability, the individual is entitled to nominate another person to assist him or her at the conference.

(8) If a person attends a compulsory conference on behalf of a body of persons, whether corporate or unincorporate, any conduct by the person in attending or appearing is taken, for the purposes of this Act, to be conduct of the body.

(9) In this section, ***disability*** has the same meaning as in the *Disability Discrimination Act 1992*.

46PL Failure to attend compulsory conference

(1) A person who has been given a direction under section 46PJ to attend a conference must not:

(a) fail to attend as required by the direction; or

(b) fail to attend and report from day to day unless excused, or released from further attendance, by the person presiding at the conference.

Penalty: 10 penalty units.

(2) Subsection (1) does not apply if the person has a reasonable excuse.

Note: A defendant bears an evidential burden in relation to the matter in subsection (2) (see subsection 13.3(3) of the *Criminal Code*).

(3) Subsection (1) is an offence of strict liability.

Note: For ***strict liability***, see section 6.1 of the *Criminal Code*.

46PM Failure to give information or produce documents

(1) A person must not refuse or fail:

(a) to give information; or

(b) to produce a document;

when so required under section 46PI, 46PJ or 46PK.

Penalty: 10 penalty units.

(1A) Subsection (1) does not apply if the person has a reasonable excuse.

Note: A defendant bears an evidential burden in relation to the matter in subsection (1A) (see subsection 13.3(3) of the *Criminal Code*).

(2) Subsection 4K(2) of the *Crimes Act 1914* does not apply to this section.

(3) It is a reasonable excuse for the purposes of this section for an individual to refuse or fail to answer a question or produce a document on the ground that the answer or the production of the document might tend to incriminate the individual or to expose the individual to a penalty. This subsection does not limit what is a reasonable excuse for the purposes of this section.

46PN False or misleading information

A person must not give information or make a statement to the Commission, to the President or to any other person exercising powers or performing functions under this Act, knowing that the information or statement is false or misleading in a material particular.

Penalty: Imprisonment for 6 months.

Division 2—Proceedings in the Federal Court and the Federal Magistrates Court

46PO Application to court if complaint is terminated

(1) If:

(a) a complaint has been terminated by the President under section 46PE or 46PH; and

(b) the President has given a notice to any person under subsection 46PH(2) in relation to the termination;

any person who was an affected person in relation to the complaint may make an application to the Federal Court or the Federal Magistrates Court, alleging unlawful discrimination by one or more of the respondents to the terminated complaint.

Note: Part IVA of the *Federal Court of Australia Act 1976* allows representative proceedings to be commenced in the Federal Court in certain circumstances.

(2) The application must be made within 28 days after the date of issue of the notice under subsection 46PH(2), or within such further time as the court concerned allows.

(3) The unlawful discrimination alleged in the application:

(a) must be the same as (or the same in substance as) the unlawful discrimination that was the subject of the terminated complaint; or

(b) must arise out of the same (or substantially the same) acts, omissions or practices that were the subject of the terminated complaint.

(4) If the court concerned is satisfied that there has been unlawful discrimination by any respondent, the court may make such orders (including a declaration of right) as it thinks fit, including any of the following orders or any order to a similar effect:

(a) an order declaring that the respondent has committed unlawful discrimination and directing the respondent not to repeat or continue such unlawful discrimination;

(b) an order requiring a respondent to perform any reasonable act or course of conduct to redress any loss or damage suffered by an applicant;

(c) an order requiring a respondent to employ or re-employ an applicant;

(d) an order requiring a respondent to pay to an applicant damages by way of compensation for any loss or damage suffered because of the conduct of the respondent;

(e) an order requiring a respondent to vary the termination of a contract or agreement to redress any loss or damage suffered by an applicant;

(f) an order declaring that it would be inappropriate for any further action to be taken in the matter.

(5) In the case of a representative proceeding under Part IVA of the *Federal Court of Australia Act 1976*, subsection (4) of this section applies as if a reference to an applicant included a reference to each person who is a group member (within the meaning of Part IVA of the *Federal Court of Australia Act 1976*).

(6) The court concerned may, if it thinks fit, grant an interim injunction pending the determination of the proceedings.

(7) The court concerned may discharge or vary any order made under this section (including an injunction granted under subsection (6)).

(8) The court concerned cannot, as a condition of granting an interim injunction, require a person to give an undertaking as to damages.

46PP Interim injunction to maintain status quo etc.

(1) At any time after a complaint is lodged with the Commission, the Federal Court or the Federal Magistrates Court may grant an interim injunction to maintain:

(a) the status quo, as it existed immediately before the complaint was lodged; or

(b) the rights of any complainant, respondent or affected person.

(2) The application for the injunction may be made by the Commission, a complainant, a respondent or an affected person.

(3) The injunction cannot be granted after the complaint has been withdrawn under section 46PG or terminated under section 46PE or 46PH.

(4) The court concerned may discharge or vary an injunction granted under this section.

(5) The court concerned cannot, as a condition of granting the interim injunction, require a person to give an undertaking as to damages.

46PQ Right of representation

(1) A party in proceedings under this Division:
   (a) may appear in person; or
   (b) may be represented by a barrister or a solicitor; or
   (c) may be represented by another person who is not a barrister or solicitor, unless the court is of the opinion that it is inappropriate in the circumstances for the other person to appear.

(2) A person, other than a barrister or solicitor, is not entitled to demand or receive any fee or reward, or any payment for expenses, for representing a party in proceedings under this Division.

46PR Court not bound by technicalities

In proceedings under this Division, the Federal Court and the Federal Magistrates Court are not bound by technicalities or legal forms. This section has effect subject to Chapter III of the Constitution.

46PS Report by President to court

(1) The President may provide the Federal Court or the Federal Magistrates Court with a written report on a complaint that has been terminated under section 46PH.

(2) The report must not set out or describe anything said or done in the course of conciliation proceedings under this Part (including anything said or done at a conference held under this Part).

(3) The President may give a copy of the report to the applicant and the respondent, and to any relevant member of the Commission.

46PT Assistance by Commission

The Commission may help a person to prepare the forms required for the person to make an application under this Division.

46PU Assistance in proceedings before the court

(1) A person who:
   (a) has commenced or proposes to commence proceedings in the Federal Court or the Federal Magistrates Court under this Division; or
   (b) is a respondent in proceedings in the Federal Court or the Federal Magistrates Court under this Division;

may apply to the Attorney-General for the provision of assistance under this section in respect of the proceedings.

(2) If a person makes an application for assistance and the Attorney-General is satisfied that:
   (a) it will involve hardship to that person to refuse the application; and
   (b) in all the circumstances, it is reasonable to grant the application;

the Attorney-General may authorise the provision by the Commonwealth to that person, on such conditions (if any) as the Attorney-General determines, of such legal or financial assistance in respect of the proceedings as the Attorney-General determines.

46PV *Amicus curiae* function of Commission members

(1) A special-purpose Commissioner has the function of assisting the Federal Court and the Federal Magistrates Court, as *amicus curiae*, in the following proceedings under this Division:
   (a) proceedings in which the special-purpose Commissioner thinks that the orders sought, or likely to be sought, may affect to a significant extent the human rights of persons who are not parties to the proceedings;
   (b) proceedings that, in the opinion of the special-purpose Commissioner, have significant implications for the administration of the relevant Act or Acts;
   (c) proceedings that involve special circumstances that satisfy the special-purpose Commissioner that it would be in the public interest for the special-purpose Commissioner to assist the court concerned as *amicus curiae*.
(2) The function may only be exercised with the leave of the court concerned.
(3) In this section, ***special-purpose Commissioner*** means:
   (a) the Aboriginal and Torres Strait Islander Social Justice Commissioner; and
   (b) the Disability Discrimination Commissioner; and
   (c) the Human Rights Commissioner; and
   (d) the Race Discrimination Commissioner; and
   (e) the Sex Discrimination Commissioner.

PART IIC—REFERRAL OF DISCRIMINATORY AWARDS AND DETERMINATIONS TO OTHER BODIES

46PW Referral of discriminatory industrial instruments to the Australian Industrial Relations Commission

(1) A complaint in writing alleging that a person has done a discriminatory act under an industrial instrument may be lodged with the Commission by:
   (a) a person aggrieved by the act, on that person's own behalf or on behalf of that person and one or more other persons aggrieved by the act; or
   (b) 2 or more persons aggrieved by the act, on their own behalf or on behalf of themselves and one or more other persons aggrieved by the act; or
   (c) a person or persons who are in a class of persons aggrieved by the act, on behalf of all the persons in the class; or
   (d) a trade union, on behalf of one or more of its members aggrieved by the act or on behalf of a class of its members aggrieved by the act.
(2) If the Commission receives a complaint under this section, the Commission must notify the President accordingly.
(3) If it appears to the President that the act is a discriminatory act, the President must refer the industrial instrument to the Australian Industrial Relations

Commission. However, the President need not refer the industrial instrument if the President is of the opinion that the complaint is frivolous, vexatious, misconceived or lacking in substance.

(4) If the President decides not to refer the industrial instrument, the President must give notice in writing of that decision to the complainant or each of the complainants, together with notice of the reasons for the decision.

(5) If the President refers the industrial instrument to the Australian Industrial Relations Commission, the President must give notice in writing of the outcome of the referral to the complainant or each of the complainants.

(6) The President may obtain documents or information under section 46PI for the purposes of this section.

(7) In this section:

discriminatory act under an industrial instrument means an act that would be unlawful under Part II of the *Sex Discrimination Act 1984* except for the fact that the act was done in direct compliance with an industrial instrument.

industrial instrument includes any of the following instruments within the meaning given by the *Workplace Relations Act 1996*:

(a) a collective agreement;
(b) an award or a variation or order affecting an award;
(c) a transitional award or a variation or order affecting a transitional award;
(d) a pre-reform certified agreement;
(e) a Preserved State Agreement;
(f) a notional agreement preserving State awards.

(8) For the purposes of the definition of ***discriminatory act under an industrial instrument*** in subsection (7), the fact that an act is done in direct compliance with the industrial instrument does not of itself mean that the act is reasonable.

46PX Referral of discriminatory determinations to the Remuneration Tribunal

(1) A complaint in writing alleging that a person has done a discriminatory act under a determination may be lodged with the Commission by:

(a) a person aggrieved by the act, on that person's own behalf or on behalf of that person and one or more other persons aggrieved by the act; or
(b) 2 or more persons aggrieved by the act, on their own behalf or on behalf of themselves and one or more other persons aggrieved by the act; or
(c) a person or persons who are in a class of persons aggrieved by the act, on behalf of all the persons in the class.

(2) If the Commission receives a complaint under this section, the Commission must notify the President accordingly.

(3) If it appears to the President that the act is a discriminatory act, the President must refer the determination to the Remuneration Tribunal. However, the President need not refer the determination if the President is of the opinion that the complaint is frivolous, vexatious, misconceived or lacking in substance.

(4) If the President decides not to refer the determination, the President must give notice in writing of that decision to the complainant or each of the complainants, together with notice of the reasons for the decision.
(5) If the President refers the determination to the Remuneration Tribunal, the President must give notice in writing of the outcome of the referral to the complainant or each of the complainants.
(6) The President may obtain documents or information under section 46PI for the purposes of this section.
(7) In this section:

determination means:
  (a) a determination made on or after 19 January 1994 by the Remuneration Tribunal under the *Remuneration Tribunal Act 1973*; or
  (b) a variation made on or after 19 January 1994 by that Tribunal to a determination made by it under that Act before 19 January 1994.

discriminatory act under a determination means an act that would be unlawful under Part II of the *Sex Discrimination Act 1984* except for the fact that the act was done in direct compliance with a determination.

(8) For the purposes of the definition of ***discriminatory act under a determination*** in subsection (7), the fact that an act is done in direct compliance with the determination does not of itself mean that the act is reasonable.

46PY Referral of discriminatory determinations to the Defence Force Remuneration Tribunal

(1) A complaint in writing alleging that a person has done a discriminatory act under a determination may be lodged with the Commission by:
  (a) a person aggrieved by the act, on that person's own behalf or on behalf of that person and one or more other persons aggrieved by the act; or
  (b) 2 or more persons aggrieved by the act, on their own behalf or on behalf of themselves and one or more other persons aggrieved by the act; or
  (c) a person or persons who are in a class of persons aggrieved by the act, on behalf of all the persons in the class.
(2) If the Commission receives a complaint under this section, the Commission must notify the President accordingly.
(3) If it appears to the President that the act is a discriminatory act, the President must refer the determination to the Defence Force Remuneration Tribunal. However, the President need not refer the determination if the President is of the opinion that the complaint is frivolous, vexatious, misconceived or lacking in substance.
(4) If the President decides not to refer the determination, the President must give notice in writing of that decision to the complainant or each of the complainants, together with notice of the reasons for the decision.
(5) If the President refers the determination to the Defence Force Remuneration Tribunal, the President must give notice in writing of the outcome of the referral to the complainant or each of the complainants.

(6) The President may obtain documents or information under section 46PI for the purposes of this section.

(7) In this section:

determination means:

(a) a determination made on or after 15 January 1996 by the Defence Force Remuneration Tribunal under section 58H of the *Defence Act 1903*; or

(b) a variation made on or after 15 January 1996 by that Tribunal to a determination made by it under that section before 15 January 1996.

discriminatory act under a determination means an act that would be unlawful under Part II of the *Sex Discrimination Act 1984* except for the fact that the act was done in direct compliance with a determination.

(8) For the purposes of the definition of ***discriminatory act under a determination*** in subsection (7), the fact that an act is done in direct compliance with the determination does not of itself mean that the act is reasonable.

PART III—MISCELLANEOUS

47 Declaration of international instruments

(1) The Minister may, after consulting the appropriate Minister of each State, by writing, declare an international instrument, being:

(a) an instrument ratified or acceded to by Australia; or

(b) a declaration that has been adopted by Australia;

to be an international instrument relating to human rights and freedoms for the purposes of this Act.

(2) Where the Minister makes a declaration under subsection (1):

(a) there shall be published in the *Gazette*:

(i) a copy of the international instrument;

(ii) a copy of Australia's instrument of ratification of or accession to the international instrument or of the terms of any explanation given by Australia of its vote in respect of the international instrument; and

(iii) a copy of the instrument of declaration under subsection (1); and

(b) subject to subsection (3), the declaration under subsection (1) has effect on and from the date on which the copies referred to in paragraph (a) were published in the *Gazette* or, if those copies were published in the *Gazette* on different dates, on the later or latest of those dates.

(3) The provisions of section 48 (except paragraphs (1)(a) and (b) and subsection (2)) and sections 48A, 48B and 49 of the *Acts Interpretation Act 1901* apply, by force of this section, to a declaration made under subsection (1) of this section in like manner as those provisions apply to regulations.

(4) Nothing in the provisions applied by subsection (3) affects the operation of a declaration made under subsection (1) at any time before it becomes void, or is disallowed, in accordance with those provisions.

48 Protection from civil actions

(1) The Commission, a member or a person acting on behalf of the Commission is not liable to an action or other proceeding for damages for or in relation to an act done or omitted to be done in good faith in performance or purported performance of any function, or in exercise or purported exercise of any power, conferred on the Commission.

(3) Where:

(a) a complaint has been made to the Commission; or

(b) a submission has been made, a document or information has been furnished, or evidence has been given, to the Commission or to a person acting on behalf of the Commission;

a person is not liable to an action, suit or proceeding in respect of loss, damage or injury of any kind suffered by another person by reason only that the complaint or submission was made, the document or information was furnished or the evidence was given.

49 Non-disclosure of private information

(1) A person who is, or has at any time been, a member of the Commission or a member of the staff referred to in section 43 or is acting, or has at any time acted, on behalf of the Commission shall not, either directly or indirectly:

(a) make a record of, or divulge or communicate to any person, any information relating to the affairs of another person acquired by the first-mentioned person by reason of that person's office or employment under or for the purposes of this Act or by reason of that person acting, or having acted, on behalf of the Commission;

(b) make use of any such information as is mentioned in paragraph (a); or

(c) produce to any person a document relating to the affairs of another person furnished for the purposes of this Act.

Penalty: $5,000 or imprisonment for 1 year, or both.

(2) A person who is, or has at any time been, a member of the Commission or a member of the staff referred to in section 43 or is acting, or has at any time acted, on behalf of the Commission shall not be required:

(a) to divulge or communicate to a court any information relating to the affairs of another person acquired by the first-mentioned person by reason of that person's office or employment under or for the purposes of this Act or by reason of that person acting, or having acted, on behalf of the Commission; or

(b) to produce in a court a document relating to the affairs of another person of which the first-mentioned person has custody, or to which that person has access, by reason of that person's office or employment under or for the purposes of this Act or by reason of that person acting, or having acted, on behalf of the Commission;

except where it is necessary to do so for the purposes of this Act.

(3) Nothing in this section prohibits a person from:

(a) making a record of information that is, or is included in a class of information that is, required or permitted by an Act to be recorded, if the record is made for the purposes of or pursuant to that Act;
(b) divulging or communicating information, or producing a document, to an instrumentality of a State in accordance with an arrangement in force under section 16; or
(c) divulging or communicating information, or producing a document, that is, or is included in a class of information that is or class of documents that are, required or permitted by an Act to be divulged, communicated or produced, as the case may be, if the information is divulged or communicated, or the document is produced, for the purposes of or pursuant to that Act.

Note: A defendant bears an evidential burden in relation to a matter in subsection (3) (see subsection 13.3(3) of the *Criminal Code*).

(4) Nothing in subsection (2) prevents a person being required, for the purposes of or pursuant to an Act, to divulge or communicate information, or to produce a document, that is, or is included in a class of information that is or class of documents that are, required or permitted by that Act to be divulged, communicated or produced.

(4A) Subsection (1) does not prevent the Commission, or a person acting on behalf of the Commission, from giving information or documents in accordance with paragraph 20(4A)(e).

Note: A defendant bears an evidential burden in relation to a matter in subsection (4A) (see subsection 13.3(3) of the *Criminal Code*).

(4B) Subsection (1) does not prevent a person from making a record of, divulging, communicating or making use of information, or producing a document, if the person does so:
(a) in the performance of a duty under or in connection with this Act; or
(b) in the course of acting for or on behalf of the Commission.

Note: A defendant bears an evidential burden in relation to the matter in subsection (4B) (see subsection 13.3(3) of the *Criminal Code*).

(5) In this section:

court includes any tribunal, authority or person having power to require the production of documents or the answering of questions.

produce includes permit access to.

49A Information stored otherwise than in written form

If information is recorded or stored by means of a mechanical, electronic or other device, any duty imposed by this Act to produce the document recording that information is to be construed as a duty to provide a document containing a clear reproduction in writing of the information.

49B Jurisdiction of Federal Court and Federal Magistrates Court

The Federal Court and the Federal Magistrates Court have concurrent jurisdiction with respect to civil matters arising under Part IIB or IIC.

49C Compensation for acquisition of property

(1) If the application of any of the provisions of this Act would result in an acquisition of property from any person having been made otherwise than on just terms, the person is entitled to such compensation from the Commonwealth as is necessary to ensure that the acquisition is made on just terms.

(2) The Federal Court and the Federal Magistrates Court have concurrent jurisdiction with respect to matters arising under subsection (1) and that jurisdiction is exclusive of the jurisdiction of all other courts, other than jurisdiction of the High Court under section 75 of the Constitution.

50 Regulations

The Governor-General may make regulations, not inconsistent with this Act, prescribing matters:

(a) required or permitted by this Act to be prescribed; or

(b) necessary or convenient to be prescribed for carrying out or giving effect to this Act.

SCHEDULE 1—CONVENTION CONCERNING DISCRIMINATION IN RESPECT OF EMPLOYMENT AND OCCUPATION

Section 3

The General Conference of the International Labour Organisation,

Having been convened at Geneva by the Governing Body of the International Labour Office, and having met in its Forty-second Session on 4 June 1958, and

Having decided upon the adoption of certain proposals with regard to discrimination in the field of employment and occupation, which is the fourth item on the agenda of the session, and

Having determined that these proposals shall take the form of an international Convention, and

Considering that the Declaration of Philadelphia affirms that all human beings, irrespective of race, creed or sex, have the right to pursue both their material well-being and their spiritual development in conditions of freedom and dignity, of economic security and equal opportunity, and

Considering further that discrimination constitutes a violation of rights enunciated by the Universal Declaration of Human Rights,

adopts this twenty-fifth day of June of the year one thousand nine hundred and fifty-eight the following Convention, which may be cited as the Discrimination (Employment and Occupation) Convention, 1958:

Article 1

1. For the purpose of this Convention the term "discrimination" includes—

(*a*) any distinction, exclusion or preference made on the basis of race, colour, sex, religion, political opinion, national extraction or social origin, which has the effect of nullifying or impairing equality of opportunity or treatment in employment or occupation;

(*b*) such other distinction, exclusion or preference which has the effect of nullifying or impairing equality of opportunity or treatment in employment or occupation as may be determined by the Member concerned after consultation with representative employer's and worker's organisations, where such exist, and with other appropriate bodies.

2. Any distinction, exclusion or preference in respect of a particular job based on the inherent requirements thereof shall not be deemed to be discrimination.

3. For the purpose of this Convention the terms "employment" and "occupation" include access to vocational training, access to employment and to particular occupations, and terms and conditions of employment.

Article 2

Each Member for which this Convention is in force undertakes to declare and pursue a national policy designed to promote, by methods appropriate to national conditions and practice, equality of opportunity and treatment in respect of employment and occupation, with a view to eliminating any discrimination in respect thereof.

Article 3

Each Member for which this Convention is in force undertakes, by methods appropriate to national conditions and practice—

(*a*) to seek the co-operation of employers' and workers' organisations and other appropriate bodies in promoting the acceptance and observance of this policy;

(*b*) to enact such legislation and to promote such educational programmes as may be calculated to secure the acceptance and observance of the policy;

(*c*) to repeal any statutory provisions and modify any administrative instructions or practices which are inconsistent with the policy;

(*d*) to pursue the policy in respect of employment under the direct control of a national authority;

(*e*) to ensure observance of the policy in the activities of vocational guidance, vocational training and placement services under the direction of a national authority;

(*f*) to indicate in its annual reports on the application of the Convention the action taken in pursuance of the policy and the results secured by such action.

Article 4

Any measures affecting an individual who is justifiably suspected of, or engaged in, activities prejudicial to the security of the State shall not be deemed to be discrimination, provided that the individual concerned shall have the right to appeal to a competent body established in accordance with national practice.

Article 5

1. Special measures of protection or assistance provided for in other Conventions or Recommendations adopted by the International Labour Conference shall not be deemed to be discrimination.

2. Any Member may, after consultation with representative employers' and workers' organisations, where such exist, determine that other special measures designed to meet the particular requirements of persons who, for reasons such as sex, age, disablement, family responsibilities or social or cultural status, are generally recognised to require special protection or assistance, shall not be deemed to be discrimination.

Article 6

Each Member which ratifies this Convention undertakes to apply it to non-metropolitan territories in accordance with the provisions of the Constitution of the International Labour Organisation.

Article 7

The formal ratifications of this Convention shall be communicated to the Director-General of the International Labour Office for registration.

Article 8

1. This Convention shall be binding only upon those Members of the International Labour Organisation whose ratifications have been registered with the Director-General.

2. It shall come into force twelve months after the date on which the ratifications of two Members have been registered with the Director-General.

3. Thereafter, this Convention shall come into force for any Member twelve months after the date on which its ratification has been registered.

Article 9

1. A Member which has ratified this Convention may denounce it after the expiration of ten years from the date on which the Convention first comes into force, by an act communicated to the Director-General of the International Labour Office for registration.
Such denunciation shall not take effect until one year after the date on which it is registered.

2. Each Member which has ratified this Convention and which does not, within the year following the expiration of the period of ten years mentioned in the preceding paragraph, exercise the right of denunciation provided for in this Article, will be bound for another period of ten years and, thereafter, may denounce this Convention at the expiration of each period of ten years under the terms provided for in this Article.

Article 10

1. The Director-General of the International Labour Office shall notify all Members of the International Labour Organisation of the registration of all

ratifications and denunciations communicated to him by the Members of the Organisation.

2. When notifying the members of the Organisation of the registration of the second ratification communicated to him, the Director-General shall draw the attention of the Members of the Organisation to the date upon which the Convention will come into force.

Article 11

The Director-General of the International Labour Office shall communicate to the Secretary-General of the United Nations for registration in accordance with Article 102 of the Charter of the United Nations full particulars of all ratifications and acts of denunciation registered by him in accordance with the provisions of the preceding Articles.

Article 12

At such times as it may consider necessary the Governing Body of the International Labour Office shall present to the General Conference a report on the working of this Convention and shall examine the desirability of placing on the agenda of the Conference the question of its revision in whole or in part.

Article 13

1. Should the Conference adopt a new Convention revising this Convention in whole or in part, then, unless the new Convention otherwise provides—

(*a*) the ratification by a Member of the new revising Convention shall *ipso jure* involve the immediate denunciation of this Convention, notwithstanding the provisions of Article 9 above, if and when the new revising Convention shall have come into force;

(*b*) as from the date when the new revising Convention comes into force this Convention shall cease to be open to ratification by the Members.

2. This Convention shall in any case remain in force in its actual form and content for those Members which have ratified it but have not ratified the revising Convention.

Article 14

The English and French versions of the text of this Convention are equally authoritative.

SCHEDULE 2—INTERNATIONAL COVENANT ON CIVIL AND POLITICAL RIGHTS

Section 3

The States Parties to the present Covenant,

Considering that, in accordance with the principles proclaimed in the Charter of the United Nations, recognition of the inherent dignity and of the equal and inalienable rights of all members of the human family is the foundation of freedom, justice and peace in the world,

Recognizing that these rights derive from the inherent dignity of the human person,

Recognizing that, in accordance with the Universal Declaration of Human Rights, the ideal of free human beings enjoying civil and political freedom from fear and want can only be achieved if conditions are created whereby everyone may enjoy his civil and political rights, as well as his economic, social and cultural rights,

Considering the obligation of States under the Charter of the United Nations to promote universal respect for, and observance of, human rights and freedoms,

Realizing that the individual, having duties to other individuals and to the community to which he belongs, is under a responsibility to strive for the promotion and observance of the rights recognized in the present Covenant,

Agree upon the following articles:

PART I

Article 1

1. All peoples have the right of self-determination. By virtue of that right they freely determine their political status and freely pursue their economic, social and cultural development.

2. All peoples may, for their own ends, freely dispose of their natural wealth and resources without prejudice to any obligations arising out of international economic co-operation, based upon the principle of mutual benefit, and international law. In no case may a people be deprived of its own means of subsistence.

3. The States Parties to the present Covenant, including those having responsibility for the administration of Non-Self-Governing and Trust Territories, shall promote the realization of the right of self-determination, and shall respect that right, in conformity with the provisions of the Charter of the United Nations.

PART II

Article 2

1. Each State Party to the present Covenant undertakes to respect and to ensure to all individuals within its territory and subject to its jurisdiction the rights recognized in the present Covenant, without distinction of any kind, such as race, colour, sex, language, religion, political or other opinion, national or social origin, property, birth or other status.

2. Where not already provided for by existing legislative or other measures, each State Party to the present Covenant undertakes to take the necessary steps, in accordance with its constitutional processes and with the provisions of the present Covenant, to adopt such legislative or other measures as may be necessary to give effect to the rights recognized in the present Covenant.

3. Each State Party to the present Covenant undertakes:

(*a*) To ensure that any person whose rights or freedoms as herein recognized are violated shall have an effective remedy, notwithstanding that the violation has been committed by persons acting in an official capacity;

(*b*) To ensure that any person claiming such a remedy shall have his right thereto determined by competent judicial, administrative or legislative authorities, or by any other competent authority provided for by the legal system of the State, and to develop the possibilities of judicial remedy;

(*c*) To ensure that the competent authorities shall enforce such remedies when granted.

Article 3

The States Parties to the present Covenant undertake to ensure the equal right of men and women to the enjoyment of all civil and political rights set forth in the present Covenant.

Article 4

1. In time of public emergency which threatens the life of the nation and the existence of which is officially proclaimed, the States Parties to the present Covenant may take measures derogating from their obligations under the present Covenant to the extent strictly required by the exigencies of the situation, provided that such measures are not inconsistent with their other obligations under international law and do not involve discrimination solely on the ground of race, colour, sex, language, religion or social origin.

2. No derogation from articles 6, 7, 8 (paragraphs 1 and 2), 11, 15, 16 and 18 may be made under this provision.

3. Any State Party to the present Covenant availing itself of the right of derogation shall immediately inform the other States Parties to the present Covenant, through the intermediary of the Secretary-General of the United Nations, of the provisions from which it has derogated and of the reasons by which it was actuated. A further communication shall be made, through the same intermediary, on the date on which it terminates such derogation.

Article 5

1. Nothing in the present Covenant may be interpreted as implying for any State, group or person any right to engage in any activity or perform any act aimed at the destruction of any of the rights and freedoms recognized herein or at their limitation to a greater extent than is provided for in the present Covenant.

2. There shall be no restriction upon or derogation from any of the fundamental human rights recognized or existing in any State Party to the present Covenant pursuant to law, conventions, regulations or custom on the pretext that the present Covenant does not recognize such rights or that it recognizes them to a lesser extent.

PART III

Article 6

1. Every human being has the inherent right to life. This right shall be protected by law. No one shall be arbitrarily deprived of his life.

2. In countries which have not abolished the death penalty, sentence of death may be imposed only for the most serious crimes in accordance with the law in force at the time of the commission of the crime and not contrary to the provisions of the present Covenant and to the Convention on the Prevention and Punishment of the Crime of Genocide. This penalty can only be carried out pursuant to a final judgment rendered by a competent court.

3. When deprivation of life constitutes the crime of genocide, it is understood that nothing in this article shall authorize any State Party to the present Covenant to derogate in any way from any obligation assumed under the provisions of the Convention on the Prevention and Punishment of the Crime of Genocide.

4. Anyone sentenced to death shall have the right to seek pardon or commutation of the sentence. Amnesty, pardon or commutation of the sentence of death may be granted in all cases.

5. Sentence of death shall not be imposed for crimes committed by persons below eighteen years of age and shall not be carried out on pregnant women.

6. Nothing in this article shall be invoked to delay or to prevent the abolition of capital punishment by any State Party to the present Covenant.

Article 7

No one shall be subjected to torture or to cruel, inhuman or degrading treatment or punishment. In particular, no one shall be subjected without his free consent to medical or scientific experimentation.

Article 8

1. No one shall be held in slavery; slavery and the slave-trade in all their forms shall be prohibited.

2. No one shall be held in servitude.

3. (*a*) No one shall be required to perform forced or compulsory labour;

(*b*) Paragraph 3(*a*) shall not be held to preclude, in countries where imprisonment with hard labour may be imposed as a punishment for a crime, the performance of hard labour in pursuance of a sentence to such punishment by a competent court;

(*c*) For the purpose of this paragraph the term "forced or compulsory labour" shall not include:

(i) Any work or service, not referred to in sub-paragraph (*b*), normally required of a person who is under detention in consequence of a lawful order of a court, or of a person during conditional release from such detention;

(ii) Any service of a military character and, in countries where conscientious objection is recognized, any national service required by law of conscientious objectors;

(iii) Any service exacted in cases of emergency or calamity threatening the life or well-being of the community;

(iv) Any work or service which forms part of normal civil obligations.

Article 9

1. Everyone has the right to liberty and security of person. No one shall be subjected to arbitrary arrest or detention. No one shall be deprived of his liberty except on such grounds and in accordance with such procedure as are established by law.

2. Anyone who is arrested shall be informed, at the time of arrest, of the reasons for his arrest and shall be promptly informed of any charges against him.

3. Anyone arrested or detained on a criminal charge shall be brought promptly before a judge or other officer authorized by law to exercise judicial power and shall be entitled to trial within a reasonable time or to release. It shall not be the general rule that persons awaiting trial shall be detained in custody, but release may be subject to guarantees to appear for trial, at any other stage of the judicial proceedings, and, should occasion arise, for execution of the judgment.

4. Anyone who is deprived of his liberty by arrest or detention shall be entitled to take proceedings before a court, in order that that court may decide without delay on the lawfulness of his detention and order his release if the detention is not lawful.

5. Anyone who has been the victim of unlawful arrest or detention shall have an enforceable right to compensation.

Article 10

1. All persons deprived of their liberty shall be treated with humanity and with respect for the inherent dignity of the human person.

2. (*a*) Accused persons shall, save in exceptional circumstances, be segregated from convicted persons and shall be subject to separate treatment appropriate to their status as unconvicted persons;

(*b*) Accused juvenile persons shall be separated from adults and brought as speedily as possible for adjudication.

3. The penitentiary system shall comprise treatment of prisoners the essential aim of which shall be their reformation and social rehabilitation. Juvenile offenders shall be segregated from adults and be accorded treatment appropriate to their age and legal status.

Article 11

No one shall be imprisoned merely on the ground of inability to fulfil a contractual obligation.

Article 12

1. Everyone lawfully within the territory of a State shall, within that territory, have the right to liberty of movement and freedom to choose his residence.

2. Everyone shall be free to leave any country, including his own.

3. The above-mentioned rights shall not be subject to any restrictions except those which are provided by law, are necessary to protect national security, public order (*ordre public*), public health or morals or the rights and freedoms of others, and are consistent with the other rights recognized in the present Covenant.

4. No one shall be arbitrarily deprived of the right to enter his own country.

Article 13

An alien lawfully in the territory of a State Party to the present Covenant may be expelled therefrom only in pursuance of a decision reached in accordance with law and shall, except where compelling reasons of national security otherwise require, be allowed to submit the reasons against his expulsion and to have his case reviewed by, and be represented for the purpose before, the competent authority or a person or persons especially designated by the competent authority.

Article 14

1. All persons shall be equal before the courts and tribunals. In the determination of any criminal charge against him, or of his rights and obligations in a suit at law, everyone shall be entitled to a fair and public hearing by a competent, independent and impartial tribunal established by law. The Press and the public may be excluded from all or part of a trial for reasons of morals, public order (*ordre public*) or national security in a democratic society, or when the interest of the private lives of the parties so requires, or to the extent strictly necessary in the opinion of the court in special circumstances where publicity would prejudice the interests of justice; but any judgment rendered in a criminal case or in a suit at law shall be made public except where the interest of juvenile persons otherwise requires or the proceedings concern matrimonial disputes or the guardianship of children.

2. Everyone charged with a criminal offence shall have the right to be presumed innocent until proved guilty according to law.

3. In the determination of any criminal charge against him, everyone shall be entitled to the following minimum guarantees, in full equality;

(*a*) To be informed promptly and in detail in a language which he understands of the nature and cause of the charge against him;

(*b*) To have adequate time and facilities for the preparation of his defence and to communicate with counsel of his own choosing;

(*c*) To be tried without undue delay;

(*d*) To be tried in his presence, and to defend himself in person or through legal assistance of his own choosing; to be informed, if he does not have legal assistance, of this right; and to have legal assistance assigned to him, in any case where the interests of justice so require, and without payment by him in any such case if he does not have sufficient means to pay for it;

(*e*) To examine, or have examined, the witnesses against him and to obtain the attendance and examination of witnesses on his behalf under the same conditions as witnesses against him;

(*f*) To have the free assistance of an interpreter if he cannot understand or speak the language used in court;

(*g*) Not to be compelled to testify against himself or to confess guilt.

4. In the case of juvenile persons, the procedure shall be such as will take account of their age and the desirability of promoting their rehabilitation.

5. Everyone convicted of a crime shall have the right to his conviction and sentence being reviewed by a higher tribunal according to law.

6. When a person has by a final decision been convicted of a criminal offence and when subsequently his conviction has been reversed or he has been pardoned on the ground that a new or newly discovered fact shows conclusively that there has been a miscarriage of justice, the person who has suffered punishment as a result of such conviction shall be compensated according to law, unless it is proved that the non-disclosure of the unknown fact in time is wholly or partly attributable to him.

7. No one shall be liable to be tried or punished again for an offence for which he has already been finally convicted or acquitted in accordance with the law and penal procedure of each country.

Article 15

1. No one shall be held guilty of any criminal offence on account of any act or omission which did not constitute a criminal offence, under national or international law, at the time when it was committed. Nor shall a heavier penalty be imposed than the one that was applicable at the time when the criminal offence was committed. If, subsequent to the commission of the offence, provision is made by law for the imposition of a lighter penalty, the offender shall benefit thereby.

2. Nothing in this article shall prejudice the trial and punishment of any person for any act or omission which, at the time when it was committed, was criminal according to the general principles of law recognized by the community of nations.

Article 16

Everyone shall have the right to recognition everywhere as a person before the law.

Article 17

1. No one shall be subjected to arbitrary or unlawful interference with his privacy, family, home or correspondence, nor to unlawful attacks on his honour and reputation.

2. Everyone has the right to the protection of the law against such interference or attacks.

Article 18

1. Everyone shall have the right to freedom of thought, conscience and religion. This right shall include freedom to have or to adopt a religion or belief of his choice, and freedom, either individually or in community with others and in public or private, to manifest his religion or belief in worship, observance, practice and teaching.

2. No one shall be subject to coercion which would impair his freedom to have or to adopt a religion or belief of his choice.

3. Freedom to manifest one's religion or beliefs may be subject only to such limitations as are prescribed by law and are necessary to protect public safety, order, health or morals or the fundamental rights and freedoms of others.

4. The States Parties to the present Covenant undertake to have respect for the liberty of parents and, when applicable, legal guardians to ensure the religious and moral education of their children in conformity with their own convictions.

Article 19

1. Everyone shall have the right to hold opinions without interference.

2. Everyone shall have the right to freedom of expression; this right shall include freedom to seek, receive and impart information and ideas of all kinds, regardless of frontiers, either orally, in writing or in print, in the form of art, or through any other media of his choice.

3. The exercise of the rights provided for in paragraph 2 of this article carries with it special duties and responsibilities. It may therefore be subject to certain restrictions, but these shall only be such as are provided by law and are necessary:

(*a*) For respect of the rights or reputations of others;

(*b*) For the protection of national security or of public order (*ordre public*), or of public health or morals.

Article 20

1. Any propaganda for war shall be prohibited by law.

2. Any advocacy of national, racial or religious hatred that constitutes incitement to discrimination, hostility or violence shall be prohibited by law.

Article 21

The right of peaceful assembly shall be recognized. No restrictions may be placed on the exercise of this right other than those imposed in comformity with the law and which are necessary in a democratic society in the interests of national security or public safety, public order (*ordre public*), the protection of public health or morals or the protection of the rights and freedoms of others.

Article 22

1. Everyone shall have the right to freedom of association with others, including the right to form and join trade unions for the protection of his interests.

2. No restrictions may be placed on the exercise of this right other than those which are prescribed by law and which are necessary in a democratic society in the interests of national security or public safety, public order (*ordre public*), the protection of public health or morals or the protection of the rights and freedoms of others. This article shall not prevent the imposition of lawful restrictions on members of the armed forces and of the police in their exercise of this right.

3. Nothing in this article shall authorize States Parties to the International Labour Organisation Convention of 1948 concerning Freedom of Association and Protection of the Right to Organize to take legislative measures which would prejudice, or to apply the law in such a manner as to prejudice, the guarantees provided for in that Convention.

Article 23

1. The family is the natural and fundamental group unit of society and is entitled to protection by society and the State.

2. The right of men and women of marriageable age to marry and to found a family shall be recognized.

3. No marriage shall be entered into without the free and full consent of the intending spouses.

4. States Parties to the present Covenant shall take appropriate steps to ensure equality of rights and responsibilities of spouses as to marriage, during marriage and at its dissolution. In the case of dissolution, provision shall be made for the necessary protection of any children.

Article 24

1. Every child shall have, without any discrimination as to race, colour, sex, language, religion, national or social origin, property or birth, the right to such measures of protection as are required by his status as a minor, on the part of his family, society and the State.

2. Every child shall be registered immediately after birth and shall have a name.

3. Every child has the right to acquire a nationality.

Article 25

Every citizen shall have the right and the opportunity, without any of the distinctions mentioned in article 2 and without unreasonable restrictions:

(*a*) To take part in the conduct of public affairs, directly or through freely chosen representatives;

(*b*) To vote and to be elected at genuine periodic elections which shall be by universal and equal suffrage and shall be held by secret ballot, guaranteeing the free expression of the will of the electors;

(*c*) To have access, on general terms of equality, to public service in his country.

Article 26

All persons are equal before the law and are entitled without any discrimination to the equal protection of the law. In this respect, the law shall prohibit any discrimination and guarantee to all persons equal and effective protection against discrimination on any ground such as race, colour, sex, language, religion, political or other opinion, national or social origin, property, birth or other status.

Article 27

In those States in which ethnic, religious or linguistic minorities exist, persons belonging to such minorities shall not be denied the right, in community with the other members of their group, to enjoy their own culture, to profess and practise their own religion, or to use their own language.

PART IV

Article 28

1. There shall be established a Human Rights Committee (hereafter referred to in the present Covenant as the Committee). It shall consist of eighteen members and shall carry out the functions hereinafter provided.

2. The Committee shall be composed of nationals of the States parties to the present Covenant who shall be persons of high moral character and recognized competence in the field of human rights, consideration being given to the usefulness of the participation of some persons having legal experience.

3. The members of the Committee shall be elected and shall serve in their personal capacity.

Article 29

1. The members of the Committee shall be elected by secret ballot from a list of persons possessing the qualifications prescribed in article 28 and nominated for the purpose by the States Parties to the present Covenant.

2. Each State Party to the present Covenant may nominate not more than two persons. These persons shall be nationals of the nominating State.

3. A person shall be eligible for renomination.

Article 30

1. The initial election shall be held no later than six months after the date of the entry into force of the present Covenant.

2. At least four months before the date of each election to the Committee, other than an election to fill a vacancy declared in accordance with article 34, the Secretary-General of the United Nations shall address a written invitation to the States Parties to the present Covenant to submit their nominations for membership of the Committee within three months.

3. The Secretary-General of the United Nations shall prepare a list in alphabetical order of all the persons thus nominated, with an indication of the States Parties which have nominated them, and shall submit it to the States Parties to the present Covenant no later than one month before the date of each election.

4. Elections of the members of the Committee shall be held at a meeting of the States Parties to the present Covenant convened by the Secretary-General of the United Nations at the Headquarters of the United Nations. At that meeting, for which two thirds of the States Parties to the present covenant shall constitute a quorum, the persons elected to the Committee shall be those nominees who obtain the largest number of votes and an absolute majority of the votes of the representatives of States Parties present and voting.

Article 31

1. The Committee may not include more than one national of the same State.

2. In the election of the Committee, consideration shall be given to equitable geographical distribution of membership and to the representation of the different forms of civilization and of the principal legal systems.

Article 32

1. The members of the Committee shall be elected for a term of four years. They shall be eligible for re-election if renominated. However, the terms of nine of the members elected at the first election shall expire at the end of two years; immediately after the first election, the names of these nine members shall be chosen by lot by the Chairman of the meeting referred to in article 30, paragraph 4.

2. Elections at the expiry of office shall be held in accordance with the preceding articles of this part of the present Covenant.

Article 33

1. If, in the unanimous opinion of the other members, a member of the Committee has ceased to carry out his functions for any cause other than absence of a temporary character, the Chairman of the Committee shall notify the Secretary-General of the United Nations, who shall then declare the seat of that member to be vacant.

2. In the event of the death or the resignation of a member of the Committee, the Chairman shall immediately notify the Secretary-General of the United Nations,

who shall declare the seat vacant from the date of death or the date on which the resignation takes effect.

Article 34

1. When a vacancy is declared in accordance with article 33 and if the term of office of the member to be replaced does not expire within six months of the declaration of the vacancy, the Secretary-General of the United Nations shall notify each of the States Parties to the present Covenant, which may within two months submit nominations in accordance with article 29 for the purpose of filling the vacancy.

2. The Secretary-General of the United Nations shall prepare a list in alphabetical order of the persons thus nominated and shall submit it to the States Parties to the present Covenant. The election to fill the vacancy shall then take place in accordance with the relevant provisions of this part of the present Covenant.

3. A member of the Committee elected to fill a vacancy declared in accordance with article 33 shall hold office for the remainder of the term of the member who vacated the seat on the Committee under the provisions of that article.

Article 35

The members of the Committee shall, with the approval of the General Assembly of the United Nations, receive emoluments from United Nations resources on such terms and conditions as the General Assembly may decide, having regard to the importance of the Committee's responsibilities.

Article 36

The Secretary-General of the United Nations shall provide the necessary staff and facilities for the effective performance of the functions of the Committee under the present Covenant.

Article 37

1. The Secretary-General of the United Nations shall convene the initial meeting of the Committee at the Headquarters of the United Nations.

2. After its initial meeting, the Committee shall meet at such times as shall be provided in its rules of procedure.

3. The Committee shall normally meet at the Headquarters of the United Nations or at the United Nations Office at Geneva.

Article 38

Every member of the Committee shall, before taking up his duties, make a solemn declaration in open committee that he will perform his functions impartially and conscientiously.

Article 39

1. The Committee shall elect its officers for a term of two years. They may be re-elected.

2. The Committee shall establish its own rules of procedure, but these rules shall provide, *inter alia*, that:

(*a*) Twelve members shall constitute a quorum;

(*b*) Decisions of the Committee shall be made by a majority vote of the members present.

Article 40

1. The States Parties to the present Covenant undertake to submit reports on the measures they have adopted which give effect to the rights recognized herein and on the progress made in the enjoyment of those rights:

(*a*) Within one year of the entry into force of the present Covenant for the States Parties concerned;

(*b*) Thereafter whenever the Committee so requests.

2. All reports shall be submitted to the Secretary-General of the United Nations, who shall transmit them to the Committee for consideration. Reports shall indicate the factors and difficulties, if any, affecting the implementation of the present Covenant.

3. The Secretary-General of the United Nations may, after consultation with the Committee, transmit to the specialized agencies concerned copies of such parts of the reports as may fall within their field of competence.

4. The Committee shall study the reports submitted by the States Parties to the present Covenant. It shall transmit its reports, and such general comments as it may consider appropriate, to the States Parties. The Committee may also transmit to the Economic and Social Council these comments along with the copies of the reports it has received from States Parties to the present Covenant.

5. The States Parties to the present Covenant may submit to the Committee observations on any comments that may be made in accordance with paragraph 4 of this article.

Article 41

1. A State Party to the present Covenant may at any time declare under this article that it recognizes the competence of the Committee to receive and consider communications to the effect that a State Party claims that another State Party is not fulfilling its obligations under the present Covenant. Communications under this article may be received and considered only if submitted by a State Party which has made a declaration recognizing in regard to itself the competence of the Committee. No communications shall be received by the Committee if it concerns a State Party which has not made such a declaration. Communications received under this article shall be dealt with in accordance with the following procedure:

(*a*) If a State Party to the present Covenant considers that another State Party is not giving effect to the provisions of the present Covenant, it may, by written communication, bring the matter to the attention of that State Party. Within three months after the receipt of the communication, the receiving State shall afford the State which sent the communication an explanation or any other statement in writing clarifying the matter which should include, to the extent possible and pertinent, reference to domestic procedures and remedies taken, pending, or available in the matter.

(*b*) If the matter is not adjusted to the satisfaction of both States Parties concerned within six months after the receipt by the receiving State of the initial communication, either State shall have the right to refer the matter to the Committee, by notice given to the Committee and to the other State.

(*c*) The Committee shall deal with a matter referred to it only after it has ascertained that all available domestic remedies have been invoked and exhausted in the matter, in conformity with the generally recognized principles of international law. This shall not be the rule where the application of the remedies is unreasonably prolonged.

(*d*) The Committee shall hold closed meetings when examining communications under this article.

(*e*) Subject to the provisions of sub-paragraph (*c*), the Committee shall make available its good offices to the States Parties concerned with a view to a friendly solution of the matter on the basis of respect for human rights and fundamental freedoms as recognized in the present Covenant.

(*f*) In any matter referred to it, the Committee may call upon the States Parties concerned, referred to in sub-paragraph (*b*), to supply any relevant information.

(*g*) The States Parties concerned, referred to in sub-paragraph (*b*), shall have the right to be represented when the matter is being considered in the Committee and to make submissions orally and/or in writing.

(*h*) The Committee shall, within twelve months after the date of receipt of notice under sub-paragraph (*b*), submit a report:

(i) If a solution within the terms of sub-paragraph (*e*) is reached, the Committee shall confine its report to a brief statement of the facts and of the solution reached;

(ii) If a solution within the terms of sub-paragraph (*e*) is not reached, the Committee shall confine its report to a brief statement of the facts; the written submissions and record of the oral submissions made by the States Parties concerned shall be attached to the report.

In every matter, the report shall be communicated to the States Parties concerned.

2. The provisions of this article shall come into force when ten States Parties to the present Covenant have made declarations under paragraph 1 of this article.

Such declarations shall be deposited by the States Parties with the Secretary-General of the United Nations, who shall transmit copies thereof to the other States Parties. A declaration may be withdrawn at any time by notification to the Secretary-General. Such a withdrawal shall not prejudice the consideration of any matter which is the subject of a communication already transmitted under this article; no further communication by any State Party shall be received after the notification of withdrawal of the declaration has been received by the Secretary-General, unless the State Party concerned has made a new declaration.

Article 42

1. (*a*) If a matter referred to the Committee in accordance with article 41 is not resolved to the satisfaction of the States Parties concerned, the Committee may, with the prior consent of the States Parties concerned, appoint an *ad hoc* Conciliation Commission (hereinafter referred to as the Commission). The good offices of the Commission shall be made available to the States Parties concerned

with a view to an amicable solution of the matter on the basis of respect for the present Covenant;

(*b*) The Commission shall consist of five persons acceptable to the States Parties concerned. If the States Parties concerned fail to reach agreement within three months on all or part of the composition of the Commission the members of the Commission concerning whom no agreement has been reached shall be elected by secret ballot by a two-thirds majority vote of the Committee from among its members.

2. The members of the Commission shall serve in their personal capacity. They shall not be nationals of the States Parties concerned, or of a State not party to the present Covenant, or of a State Party which has not made a declaration under article 41.

3. The Commission shall elect its own Chairman and adopt its own rules of procedure.

4. The meetings of the Commission shall normally be held at the Headquarters of the United Nations or at the United Nations Office at Geneva. However, they may be held at such other convenient places as the Commission may determine in consultation with the Secretary-General of the United Nations and the States Parties concerned.

5. The secretariat provided in accordance with article 36 shall also service the commissions appointed under this article.

6. The information received and collated by the Committee shall be made available to the Commission and the Commission may call upon the States Parties concerned to supply any other relevant information.

7. When the Commission has fully considered the matter, but in any event not later than twelve months after having been seized of the matter, it shall submit to the Chairman of the Committee a report for communication to the States Parties concerned.

(*a*) If the Commission is unable to complete its consideration of the matter within twelve months, it shall confine its report to a brief statement of the status of its consideration of the matter;

(*b*) If an amicable solution to the matter on the basis of respect for human rights as recognized in the present Covenant is reached, the Commission shall confine its report to a brief statement of the facts and of the solution reached.

(*c*) If a solution within the terms of sub-paragraph (*b*) is not reached, the Commission's report shall embody its findings on all questions of fact relevant to the issues between the States Parties concerned, and its views on the possibilities of an amicable solution of the matter. This report shall also contain the written submissions and a record of the oral submissions made by the States Parties concerned.

(*d*) If the Commission's report is submitted under sub-paragraph (*c*), the States Parties concerned shall, within three months of the receipt of the report, notify the Chairman of the Committee whether or not they accept the contents of the report of the Commission.

8. The provisions of this article are without prejudice to the responsibilities of the Committee under article 41.

9. The States Parties concerned shall share equally all the expenses of the members of the Commission in accordance with estimates to be provided by the Secretary-General of the United Nations.

10. The Secretary-General of the United Nations shall be empowered to pay the expenses of the members of the Commission, if necessary, before reimbursement by the States Parties concerned, in accordance with paragraph 9 of this article.

Article 43

The members of the Committee, and of the *ad hoc* conciliation commissions which may be appointed under article 42, shall be entitled to the facilities, privileges and immunities of experts on mission for the United Nations as laid down in the relevant sections of the Convention on the Privileges and Immunities of the United Nations.

Article 44

The provisions for the implementation of the present Covenant shall apply without prejudice to the procedures prescribed in the field of human rights by or under the constituent instruments and the conventions of the United Nations and of the specialized agencies and shall not prevent the States Parties to the present Covenant from having recourse to other procedures for settling a dispute in accordance with general or special international agreements in force between them.

Article 45

The Committee shall submit to the General Assembly of the United Nations through the Economic and Social Council, an annual report on its activities.

PART V

Article 46

Nothing in the present Covenant shall be interpreted as impairing the provisions of the Charter of the United Nations and of the constitutions of the specialized agencies which define the respective responsibilities of the various organs of the United Nations and of the specialized agencies in regard to the matters dealt with in the present Covenant.

Article 47

Nothing in the present Covenant shall be interpreted as impairing the inherent right of all peoples to enjoy and utilize fully and freely their natural wealth and resources.

PART VI

Article 48

1. The present Covenant is open for signature by any State Member of the United Nations or member of any of its specialized agencies, by any State Party to the Statute of the International Court of Justice, and by any other State which has been invited by the General Assembly of the United Nations to become a party to the present Covenant.

2. The present Covenant is subject to ratification. Instruments of ratification shall be deposited with the Secretary-General of the United Nations.

3. The present Covenant shall be open to accession by any State referred to in paragraph 1 of this article.

4. Accession shall be effected by the deposit of an instrument of accession with the Secretary-General of the United Nations.

5. The Secretary-General of the United Nations shall inform all States which have signed this Covenant or acceded to it of the deposit of each instrument of ratification or accession.

Article 49

1. The present Covenant shall enter into force three months after the date of the deposit with the Secretary-General of the United Nations of the thirty-fifth instrument of ratification or instrument of accession.

2. For each State ratifying the present Covenant or acceding to it after the deposit of the thirty-fifth instrument of ratification or instrument of accession, the present Covenant shall enter into force three months after the date of the deposit of its own instrument of ratification or instrument of accession.

Article 50

The provisions of the present Covenant shall extend to all parts of federal States without any limitations or exceptions.

Article 51

1. Any State Party to the present Covenant may propose an amendment and file it with the Secretary-General of the United Nations. The Secretary-General of the United Nations shall thereupon communicate any proposed amendments to the States Parties to the present Covenant with a request that they notify him whether they favour a conference of States Parties for the purpose of considering and voting upon the proposals. In the event that at least one third of the States Parties favours such a conference, the Secretary-General shall convene the conference under the auspices of the United Nations. Any amendment adopted by a majority of the States Parties present and voting at the conference shall be submitted to the General Assembly of the United Nations for approval.

2. Amendments shall come into force when they have been approved by the General Assembly of the United Nations and accepted by a two-thirds majority of the States Parties to the present Covenant in accordance with their respective constitutional processes.

3. When amendments come into force, they shall be binding on those States Parties which have accepted them, other States Parties still being bound by the provisions of the present Covenant and any earlier amendment which they have accepted.

Article 52

Irrespective of the notifications made under article 48, paragraph 5, the Secretary-General of the United Nations shall inform all States referred to in paragraph 1 of the same article of the following particulars:

(*a*) Signatures, ratifications and accessions under article 48;

(*b*) The date of the entry into force of the present Covenant under article 49 and the date of the entry into force of any amendments under article 51.

Article 53

1. The present Covenant, of which the Chinese, English, French, Russian and Spanish texts are equally authentic, shall be deposited in the archives of the United Nations.

2. The Secretary-General of the United Nations shall transmit certified copies of the present Covenant to all States referred to in article 48.

IN FAITH WHEREOF the undersigned, being duly authorized thereto by their respective Governments, have signed the present Covenant, opened for signature at New York, on the nineteenth day of December, one thousand nine hundred and sixty-six.

SCHEDULE 3—DECLARATION OF THE RIGHTS OF THE CHILD

Section 3

Whereas the peoples of the United Nations have, in the Charter, reaffirmed their faith in fundamental human rights and in the dignity and worth of the human person, and have determined to promote social progress and better standards of life in larger freedom,

Whereas the United Nations has, in the Universal Declaration of Human Rights, proclaimed that everyone is entitled to all the rights and freedoms set forth therein, without distinction of any kind, such as race, colour, sex, language, religion, political or other opinion, national or social origin, property, birth or other status,

Whereas the child, by reason of his physical and mental immaturity, needs special safeguards and care, including appropriate legal protection, before as well as after birth,

Whereas the need for such special safeguards has been stated in the Geneva Declaration of the Rights of the Child of 1924, and recognized in the Universal Declaration of Human Rights and in the statutes of specialized agencies and international organizations concerned with the welfare of children,

Whereas mankind owes to the child the best it has to give,

Now therefore,

The General Assembly

Proclaims this Declaration of the Rights of the Child to the end that he may have a happy childhood and enjoy for his own good and for the good of society the rights and freedoms herein set forth, and calls upon parents, upon men and women as individuals, and upon voluntary organizations, local authorities and national Governments to recognize these rights and strive for their observance by legislative and other measures progressively taken in accordance with the following principles:

Principle 1

The child shall enjoy all the rights set forth in this Declaration. Every child, without any exception whatsoever, shall be entitled to these rights, without distinction or discrimination on account of race, colour, sex, language, religion, political or other opinion, national or social origin, property, birth or other status, whether of himself or of his family.

Principle 2

The child shall enjoy special protection, and shall be given opportunities and facilities, by law and by other means, to enable him to develop physically, mentally, morally spiritually and socially in a healthy and normal manner and in conditions of freedom and dignity. In the enactment of laws for this purpose, the best interests of the child shall be the paramount consideration.

Principle 3

The child shall be entitled from his birth to a name and a nationality.

Principle 4

The child shall enjoy the benefits of social security. He shall be entitled to grow and develop in health; to this end, special care and protection shall be provided both to him and to his mother, including adequate pre-natal and post-natal care. The child shall have the right to adequate nutrition, housing, recreation and medical services.

Principle 5

The child who is physically, mentally or socially handicapped shall be given the special treatment, education and care required by his particular condition.

Principle 6

The child, for the full and harmonious development of his personality, needs love and understanding. He shall, wherever possible, grow up in the care and under the responsibility of his parents, and, in any case, in an atmosphere of affection and of moral and material security; a child of tender years shall not, save in exceptional circumstances, be separated from his mother. Society and the public authorities shall have the duty to extend particular care to children without a family and to those without adequate means of support. Payment of State and other assistance towards the maintenance of children of large families is desirable.

Principle 7

The child is entitled to receive education, which shall be free and compulsory, at least in the elementary stages. He shall be given an education which will promote his general culture and enable him, on a basis of equal opportunity, to develop his abilities, his individual judgment, and his sense of moral and social responsibility, and to become a useful member of society.

The best interests of the child shall be the guiding principle of those responsible for his education and guidance; that responsibility lies in the first place with his parents.

The child shall have full opportunity for play and recreation, which should be directed to the same purposes as education; society and the public authorities shall endeavour to promote the enjoyment of this right.

Principle 8

The child shall in all circumstances be among the first to receive protection and relief.

Principle 9

The child shall be protected against all forms of neglect, cruelty and exploitation. He shall not be the subject of traffic, in any form.

The child shall not be admitted to employment before an appropriate minimum age; he shall in no case be caused or permitted to engage in any occupation or employment which would prejudice his health or education, or interfere with his physical, mental or moral development.

Principle 10

The child shall be protected from practices which may foster racial, religious and any other form of discrimination. He shall be brought up in a spirit of understanding, tolerance, friendship among peoples, peace and universal brotherhood, and in full consciousness that his energy and talents should be devoted to the service of his fellow men.

SCHEDULE 4—DECLARATION ON THE RIGHTS OF MENTALLY RETARDED PERSONS

Section 3

The General Assembly,

Mindful of the pledge of the States Members of the United Nations under the Charter to take joint and separate action in co-operation with the Organization to promote higher standards of living, full employment and conditions of economic and social progress and development,

Reaffirming faith in human rights and fundamental freedoms and in the principles of peace, of the dignity and worth of the human person and of social justice proclaimed in the Charter,

Recalling the principles of the Universal Declaration of Human Rights, the International Covenants on Human Rights, the Declaration of the Rights of the Child and the standards already set for social progress in the constitutions, conventions, recommendations and resolutions of the International Labour Organisation, the United Nations Educational, Scientific and Cultural Organization, the World Health Organization, the United Nations Children's Fund and other organizations concerned,

Emphasizing that the Declaration on Social Progress and Development has proclaimed the necessity of protecting the rights and assuring the welfare and rehabilitation of the physically and mentally disadvantaged,

Bearing in mind the necessity of assisting mentally retarded persons to develop their abilities in various fields of activities and of promoting their integration as far as possible in normal life,

Aware that certain countries, at their present stage of development, can devote only limited efforts to this end,

Proclaims this Declaration on the Rights of Mentally Retarded Persons and calls for national and international action to ensure that it will be used as a common basis and frame of reference for the protection of these rights:

1. The mentally retarded person has, to the maximum degree of feasibility, the same rights as other human beings.

2. The mentally retarded person has a right to proper medical care and physical therapy and to such education, training, rehabilitation and guidance as will enable him to develop his ability and maximum potential.

3. The mentally retarded person has a right to economic security and to a decent standard of living. He has a right to perform productive work or to engage in any other meaningful occupation to the fullest possible extent of his capabilities.

4. Whenever possible, the mentally retarded person should live with his own family or with foster parents and participate in different forms of community life. The family with which he lives should receive assistance. If care in an institution becomes necessary, it should be provided in surroundings and other circumstances as close as possible to those of normal life.

5. The mentally retarded person has a right to a qualified guardian when this is required to protect his personal well-being and interests.

6. The mentally retarded person has a right to protection from exploitation, abuse and degrading treatment. If prosecuted for any offence, he shall have a right to due process of law with full recognition being given to his degree of mental responsibility.

7. Whenever mentally retarded persons are unable, because of the severity of their handicap, to exercise all their rights in a meaningful way or it should become necessary to restrict or deny some or all of these rights, the procedure used for that restriction or denial of rights must contain proper legal safeguards against every form of abuse. This procedure must be based on an evaluation of the social capability of the mentally retarded person by qualified experts and must be subject to periodic review and to the right of appeal to higher authorities.

SCHEDULE 5—DECLARATION ON THE RIGHTS OF DISABLED PERSONS

Section 3

The General Assembly,

Mindful of the pledge made by Member States, under the Charter of the United Nations; to take joint and separate action in co-operation with the Organization to promote higher standards of living, full employment and conditions of economic and social progress and development,

Reaffirming its faith in human rights and fundamental freedoms and in the principles of peace, of the dignity and worth of the human person and of social justice proclaimed in the Charter,

AUSTRALIA

Recalling the principles of the Universal Declaration of Human Rights, the International Covenants on Human Rights, the Declaration of the Rights of the Child and the Declaration on the Rights of Mentally Retarded Persons, as well as the standards already set for social progress in the constitutions, conventions, recommendations and resolutions of the International Labour Organisation, the United Nations Educational, Scientific and Cultural Organization, the World Health Organization, the United Nations Children's Fund and other organizations concerned,

Recalling also Economic and Social Council resolution 1921 (LVIII) of 6 May 1975 on the prevention of disability and the rehabilitation of disabled persons,

Emphasizing that the Declaration on Social Progress and Development has proclaimed the necessity of protecting the rights and assuring the welfare and rehabilitation of the physically and mentally disadvantaged,

Bearing in mind the necessity of preventing physical and mental disabilities and of assisting disabled persons to develop their abilities in the most varied fields of activities and of promoting their integration as far as possible in normal life,

Aware that certain countries, at their present stage of development, can devote only limited efforts to this end,

Proclaims this Declaration on the Rights of Disabled Persons and calls for national and international action to ensure that it will be used as a common basis and frame of reference for the protection of these rights:

1. The term "disabled person" means any person unable to ensure by himself or herself, wholly or partly, the necessities of a normal individual and/or social life, as a result of deficiency, either congenital or not, in his or her physical or mental capabilities.

2. Disabled persons shall enjoy all the rights set forth in this Declaration. These rights shall be granted to all disabled persons without any exception whatsoever and without distinction or discrimination on the basis of race, colour, sex, language, religion, political or other opinions, national or social origin, state of wealth, birth or any other situation applying either to the disabled person himself or herself or to his or her family.

3. Disabled persons have the inherent right to respect for their human dignity. Disabled persons, whatever the origin, nature and seriousness of their handicaps and disabilities, have the same fundamental rights as their fellow-citizens of the same age, which implies first and foremost the right to enjoy a decent life, as normal and full as possible.

4. Disabled persons have the same civil and political rights as other human beings; paragraph 7 of the Declaration on the Rights of Mentally Retarded Persons applies to any possible limitation or suppression of those rights for mentally disabled persons.

5. Disabled persons are entitled to the measures designed to enable them to become as self-reliant as possible.

6. Disabled persons have the right to medical, psychological and functional treatment, including prosthetic and orthetic appliances, to medical and social

rehabilitation, education, vocational training and rehabilitation, aid, counselling, placement services and other services which will enable them to develop their capabilities and skills to the maximum and will hasten the process of their social integration or reintegration.

7. Disabled persons have the right to economic and social security and to a decent level of living. They have the right, according to their capabilities, to secure and retain employment or to engage in a useful, productive and remunerative occupation and to join trade unions.

8. Disabled persons are entitled to have their special needs taken into consideration at all stages of economic and social planning.

9. Disabled persons have the right to live with their families or with foster parents and to participate in all social, creative or recreational activities. No disabled person shall be subjected, as far as his or her residence is concerned, to differential treatment other than that required by his or her condition or by the improvement which he or she may derive therefrom. If the stay of a disabled person in a specialized establishment is indispensable, the environment and living conditions therein shall be as close as possible to those of the normal life of a person of his or her age.

10. Disabled persons shall be protected against all exploitation, all regulations and all treatment of a discriminatory, abusive or degrading nature.

11. Disabled persons shall be able to avail themselves of qualified legal aid when such aid proves indispensable for the protection of their persons and property. If judicial proceedings are instituted against them, the legal procedure applied shall take their physical and mental condition fully into account.

12. Organizations of disabled persons may be usefully consulted in all matters regarding the rights of disabled persons.

13. Disabled persons, their families and communities shall be fully informed, by all appropriate means, of the rights contained in this Declaration.

Notes to the *Human Rights and Equal Opportunity Commission Act 1986*

Note 1

The *Human Rights and Equal Opportunity Commission Act 1986* as shown in this compilation comprises Act No. 125, 1986 amended as indicated in the Tables below. The *Human Rights and Equal Opportunity Commission Act 1986* was amended by the *Workplace Relations Amendment (Work Choices) (Consequential Amendments) Regulations 2006 (No. 1)* (SLI 2006 No. 50). The amendments are incorporated in this compilation.

All relevant information pertaining to application, saving or transitional provisions prior to 13 October 1999 is not included in this compilation. For subsequent information *see* Table A.

Table of Acts

Act	Number and year	Date of Assent	Date of commencement	Application, saving or transitional provisions
Human Rights and Equal Opportunity Commission Act 1986	125, 1986	6 Dec 1986	10 Dec 1986 (*see Gazette* 1986, No. S631)	
Statute Law (Miscellaneous Provisions) Act 1987	141, 1987	18 Dec 1987	S. 3: 1 Feb 1987 *(a)*	S. 5(1)
Statute Law (Miscellaneous Provisions) Act 1988	38, 1988	3 June 1988	S. 3: Royal Assent *(b)*	S. 5(1)
Statutory Instruments (Tabling and Disallowance) Legislation Amendment Act 1988	99, 1988	2 Dec 1988	2 Dec 1988	—
Privacy Act 1988	119, 1988	14 Dec 1988	1 Jan 1989 (*see Gazette* 1988, No. S399)	—
Defence Legislation Amendment Act 1990	75, 1990	22 Oct 1990	S. 5: Royal Assent *(c)*	—
Law and Justice Legislation Amendment Act 1990	115, 1990	21 Dec 1990	Part 1 (ss. 1, 2), Parts 3 and 4 (ss. 40–49): 21 Dec 1990 Ss. 3, 5, 6, 8, 9, 16, 17, 20–23, 28, 30, 32, 33, 38 and 39: 4 Feb 1991 (*see Gazette* 1991, GN3, p. 278) Remainder: 21 June 1991	—
Industrial Relations Legislation Amendment Act 1991	122, 1991	27 June 1991	Ss. 4(1), 10(b) and 15–20: 1 Dec 1988 Ss. 28(b)–(e), 30 and 31: 10 Dec 1991 (*see Gazette* 1991, No. S332) Remainder: Royal Assent	S. 31(2)
Human Rights and Equal Opportunity Legislation Amendment	132, 1992	30 Oct 1992	26 Nov 1992 (*see* s. 2 and *Gazette* 1992, No. S346)	—

Act	Number and year	Date of Assent	Date of commencement	Application, saving or transitional provisions
Act 1992				
as amended by				
Human Rights Legislation Amendment Act 1995	59, 1995	28 June1995	(*see* 59, 1995 below)	—
Sex Discrimination and other Legislation Amendment Act 1992	179, 1992	16 Dec 1992	13 Jan 1993	Ss. 2(2) and 4
Human Rights and Equal Opportunity Legislation Amendment Act (No. 2) 1992	180, 1992	16 Dec 1992	13 Jan 1993	—
Qantas Sale Act 1992	196, 1992	21 Dec 1992	Schedule (Parts 3, 6): *(d)*	S. 2(6) (am. by 60, 1993, s. 4; 168, 1994, s. 3)
as amended by				
Qantas Sale Amendment Act 1993	60, 1993	3 Nov 1993	10 Mar 1993	—
Qantas Sale Amendment Act 1994	168, 1994	16 Dec 1994	Schedule (item 17): Royal Assent *(e)*	—
Human Rights Legislation Amendment Act 1995	59, 1995	28 June 1995	Schedule (item 25): 30 Oct 1992 Remainder: Royal Assent	Ss. 4 and 5
Human Rights Legislation Amendment Act (No. 1) 1999	133, 1999	13 Oct 1999	Ss. 1–3 and 21: Royal Assent S. 22 and Schedule 1 (items 53, 60): 10 Dec 1999 (*see Gazette* 1999, No. S598) Remainder: 13 Apr 2000	Ss. 4–22 [*see* Table A]
Public Employment (Consequential and Transitional) Amendment Act 1999	146, 1999	11 Nov 1999	Schedule 1 (items 520–523): 5 Dec 1999 (*see Gazette* 1999, No. S584) *(f)*	—
Australian Security Intelligence Organisation Legislation Amendment	161, 1999	10 Dec 1999	Schedule 3 (items 1, 29): *(g)*	—

Act	Number and year	Date of Assent	Date of commencement	Application, saving or transitional provisions
Act 1999				
Federal Magistrates (Consequential Amendments) Act 1999	194, 1999	23 Dec 1999	Schedule 16: *(h)*	—
Privacy Amendment (Office of the Privacy Commissioner) Act 2000	2, 2000	29 Feb 2000	1 July 2000 (*see Gazette* 2000, No. S229)	—
Criminal Code Amendment (Theft, Fraud, Bribery and Related Offences) Act 2000	137, 2000	24 Nov 2000	Ss. 1–3 and Schedule 1 (items 1, 4, 6, 7, 9–11, 32): Royal Assent Remainder: 24 May 2001	Sch. 2 (items 418, 419) [*see* Table A]
Law and Justice Legislation Amendment (Application of Criminal Code) Act 2001	24, 2001	6 Apr 2001	S. 4(1), (2) and Schedule 32: *(i)*	S. 4(1), (2) [*see* Table A]
Human Rights and Equal Opportunity Commission Amendment Act 2002	22, 2002	4 Apr 2002	13 Apr 2000	—
Statute Law Revision Act 2002	63, 2002	3 July 2002	Schedule 1 (item 21): *(j)*	—
Workplace Relations Legislation Amendment (Registration and Accountability of Organisations) (Consequential Provisions) Act 2002	105, 2002	14 Nov 2002	Schedule 3 (item 50): 12 May 2003 (*see* s. 2 and *Gazette* 2002, No. GN49)	—
Australian Crime Commission Establishment Act 2002	125, 2002	10 Dec 2002	Schedule 2 (item 77): 1 Jan 2003	—
Age Discrimination (Consequential Provisions) Act 2004	40, 2004	21 Apr 2004	Schedule 1 (items 1–8): 23 June 2004 (*see* s. 2) Schedule 2 (items 22–25): [*see (k)* and Note 2]	—
Law and Justice	62, 2004	26 May 2004	Schedule 1 (item	—

Act	Number and year	Date of Assent	Date of commencement	Application, saving or transitional provisions
Legislation Amendment Act 2004			38): 27 May 2004	
Aboriginal and Torres Strait Islander Commission Amendment Act 2005	32, 2005	22 Mar 2005	Schedule 4 (item 24): 24 Mar 2005	—
Statute Law Revision Act 2005	100, 2005	6 July 2005	Schedule 1 (item 26): Royal Assent	—
Intelligence Services Legislation Amendment Act 2005	128, 2005	4 Nov 2005	Schedules 1–8: 2 Dec 2005 Remainder: Royal Assent	—

(a) The *Human Rights and Equal Opportunity Commission Act 1986* was amended by section 3 only of the *Statute Law (Miscellaneous Provisions) Act 1987*, subsection 2(17) of which provides as follows:

(17) The amendment of the *Human Rights and Equal Opportunity Commission Act 1986* made by this Act shall be deemed to have come into operation on the commencement of the *Inspector-General of Intelligence and Security Act 1986*.

(b) The *Human Rights and Equal Opportunity Commission Act 1986* was amended by section 3 only of the *Statute Law (Miscellaneous Provisions) Act 1988*, subsection 2(1) of which provides as follows:

(1) Subject to this section, this Act commences on the day on which it receives the Royal Assent.

(c) The *Human Rights and Equal Opportunity Commission Act 1986* was amended by section 5 only of the *Defence Legislation Amendment Act 1990*, subsection 2(1) of which provides as follows:

(1) Subject to this section, this Act commences on the day on which it receives the Royal Assent.

(d) The *Human Rights and Equal Opportunity Commission Act 1986* was amended by the *Qantas Sale Act 1992*, subsections 2(2), (5) and (6) of which provide as follows:

(2) Subject to subsection (3), the remaining provisions of this Act commence on a day or days to be fixed by Proclamation.

(5) If, on the 100% sale day, Part 3 of the Schedule has not commenced, then, on the day on which Part 7 of the Schedule commences, Parts 3 and 6 of the Schedule are taken to have been repealed.

(6) If a provision of this Act has not commenced before 31 August 1995, the provision is taken to have been repealed on that day.

The Schedule (Parts 3 and 6) are taken to have been repealed on 31 August 1995.

(e) The *Qantas Sale Act 1992* was amended by the Schedule (item 17) only of the *Qantas Sale Amendment Act 1994*, subsection 2(1) of which provides as follows:

(1) Subject to this section, this Act commences on the day on which it receives the Royal Assent.

(f) The *Human Rights and Equal Opportunity Commission Act 1986* was amended by Schedule 1 (items 520–523) only of the *Public Employment (Consequential and Transitional) Amendment Act 1999*, subsections 2(1) and (2) of which provide as follows:

(1) In this Act, ***commencing time*** means the time when the *Public Service Act 1999* commences.

(2) Subject to this section, this Act commences at the commencing time.

(g) The *Human Rights and Equal Opportunity Commission Act 1986* was amended by Schedule 3 (item 29) only of the *Australian Security Intelligence Organisation Legislation Amendment Act 1999*, subsection 2(2) of which provides as follows:

(2) Subject to subsections (3) to (6), Schedule 3 commences immediately after the commencement of the other Schedules to this Act.

The other Schedules to this Act commenced on Royal Assent.

(h) The *Human Rights and Equal Opportunity Commission Act 1986* was amended by Schedule 16 only of the *Federal Magistrates (Consequential Amendments) Act 1999*, subsection 2(3) of which provides as follows:

(3) If Schedule 1 to the *Human Rights Legislation Amendment Act (No. 1) 1999* commences after the commencement of section 1 of this Act, Schedule 16 to this Act commences immediately after the commencement of Schedule 1 to the *Human Rights Legislation Amendment Act (No. 1) 1999.*

Schedule 1 to the *Human Rights Legislation Amendment Act (No. 1) 1999* commenced on 13 April 2000.

(i) The *Human Rights and Equal Opportunity Commission Act 1986* was amended by Schedule 32 only of the *Law and Justice Legislation Amendment (Application of Criminal Code) Act 2001*, subsection 2(1)(a) of which provides as follows:

(1) Subject to this section, this Act commences at the later of the following times:

(a) immediately after the commencement of item 15 of Schedule 1 to the *Criminal Code Amendment (Theft, Fraud, Bribery and Related Offences) Act 2000*;

Item 15 commenced on 24 May 2001.

(j) The *Human Rights and Equal Opportunity Commission Act 1986* was amended by Schedule 1 (item 21) only of the *Statute Law Revision Act 2002*, subsection 2(1) (item 16) of which provides as follows:

(1) Each provision of this Act specified in column 1 of the table commences, or is taken to have commenced, on the day or at the time specified in column 2 of the table.

Commencement information		
Column 1	**Column 2**	**Column 3**
Provision(s)	**Commencement**	**Date/Details**
16. Schedule 1, item 21	Immediately after item 15 of Schedule 16 to the *Federal Magistrates (Consequential Amendments) Act 1999* commenced	13 April 2000

(k) Subsection 2(1) [items 6 and 7] and (4) of the *Age Discrimination (Consequential Provisions) Act 2004* provides as follows:

(1) Each provision of this Act specified in column 1 of the table commences, or is taken to have commenced, on the day or at the time specified in column 2 of the table.

Provision(s)	**Commencement**	**Date/Details**
6. Schedule 2, item 22	Immediately after the commencement of Schedule 1 to the *Australian Human Rights Commission Legislation Act 2004*, subject to subsection (4)	[*see* Note 2]
7. Schedule 2, items 23 to 28	The later of: (a) immediately after the commencement of the *Age Discrimination Act 2004*; and (b) immediately after the commencement of Schedule 1 to the *Australian Human Rights Commission Legislation Act 2004*	[*see* Note 2] (paragraph (b) applies)

(4) If the *Age Discrimination Act 2004* does not commence before the commencement of item 21 of Schedule 1 to the *Australian Human Rights Commission Legislation Act 2004*, item 22 of Schedule 2 to this Act does not commence at all.

Table of Amendments

ad. = added or inserted am. = amended rep. = repealed rs. = repealed and substituted

Provision affected	How affected
Part I	
S. 3	am. No. 119, 1988; No. 115, 1990; Nos. 132 and 180, 1992; Nos. 133 and 194, 1999; No. 105, 2002; No. 40, 2004; SLI 2006 No. 50
S. 4	rs. No. 133, 1999
S. 6	am. No. 22, 2002

ad. = added or inserted am. = amended rep. = repealed rs. = repealed and substituted

Provision affected	How affected
S. 6A	ad. No. 24, 2001
Part II	
Division 1	
S. 8	am. No. 119, 1988; Nos. 132 and 180, 1992; No. 59, 1995; No. 133, 1999; No. 2, 2000
S. 8A	ad. No. 59, 1995
	am. No. 133, 1999
S. 8B	ad. No. 59, 1995
Division 2	
Heading to Div. 2 of Part II	rs. No. 59, 1995
S. 10A	ad. No. 59, 1995
S. 11	am. No. 141, 1987; No. 75, 1990; No. 132, 1992; Nos. 133 and 161, 1999; No. 40, 2004; No. 128, 2005
S. 12	rep. No. 59, 1995
Heading to s. 13	am. No. 59, 1995
S. 14	am. No. 132, 1992; No. 24, 2001; No. 40, 2004
S. 16	am. No. 38, 1988; No. 132, 1992; No. 133, 1999; No. 40, 2004
S. 19	am. No. 132, 1992 (as am. by No. 59, 1995); No. 180, 1992; No. 59, 1995; No. 133, 1999; No. 40, 2004
Division 3	
S. 19A	ad. No. 179, 1992
S. 20	am. No. 119, 1988
S. 21	am. No. 75, 1990; No. 128, 2005
S. 23	am. No. 24, 2001
S. 24	am. No. 180, 1992; No. 125, 2002
S. 25	rep. No. 137, 2000
Note to s. 26	ad. No. 137, 2000
Division 4	
S. 30	am. No. 179, 1992
S. 31	am. No. 133, 1999; No. 100, 2005
S. 33	am. No. 137, 2000
Division 5	
S. 36	am. No. 132, 1992; No. 59, 1995; No. 62, 2004
S. 37	am. No. 133, 1999
S. 38	am. No. 59, 1995
S. 39	am. No. 122, 1991; No. 146, 1999
S. 41	am. No. 122, 1991
S. 43	am. No. 59, 1995; Nos. 133 and 146, 1999

ad. = added or inserted am. = amended rep. = repealed rs. = repealed and substituted

Provision affected	How affected
Heading to s. 43A	am. No. 2, 2000
S. 43A	ad. No. 59, 1995
	am. No. 2, 2000
S. 44	am. No. 59, 1995
Division 6	
Div. 6 of Part II	ad. No. 59, 1995
Ss. 46AA–46AC	ad. No. 59, 1995
Part IIA	
Part IIA	ad. No. 180, 1992
Division 1	
Ss. 46A, 46B	ad. No. 180, 1992
S. 46C	ad. No. 180, 1992
	am. No. 32, 2005
Division 2	
Ss. 46D, 46E	ad. No. 180, 1992
S. 46F	ad. No. 180, 1992
	am. No. 146, 1999
Ss. 46G–46J	ad. No. 180, 1992
Division 3	
Ss. 46K–46M	ad. No. 180, 1992
Part IIB	
Part IIB	ad. No. 133, 1999
Division 1	
Ss. 46P, 46PA–46PE	ad. No. 133, 1999
S. 46PF	ad. No. 133, 1999
Note to s. 49PF(3)	am. No. 40, 2004
S. 46PG	ad. No. 133, 1999
S. 46PH	ad. No. 133, 1999
	am. No. 194, 1999
Ss. 46PI–46PK	ad. No. 133, 1999
Ss. 46PL, 46PM	ad. No. 133, 1999
	am. No. 24, 2001
S. 46PN	ad. No. 133, 1999
Division 2	
Heading to Div. 2 of Part IIB	rs. No. 194, 1999
Heading to s. 46PO	am. No. 194, 1999
S. 46PO	ad. No. 133, 1999
	am. No. 194, 1999
Note to s. 46PO(1)	am. No. 194, 1999

ad. = added or inserted am. = amended rep. = repealed rs. = repealed and substituted

Provision affected	How affected
S. 46PP	ad. No. 133, 1999
	am. No. 194, 1999
S. 46PQ..............................	ad. No. 133, 1999
	am. No. 194, 1999
S. 46PR..............................	ad. No. 133, 1999
	am. No. 194, 1999; No. 63, 2002
Heading to s. 46PS	am. No. 194, 1999
S. 46PS	ad. No. 133, 1999
	am. No. 194, 1999
S. 46PT	ad. No. 133, 1999
Heading to s. 46PU............	am. No. 194, 1999
S. 46PU..............................	ad. No. 133, 1999
	am. No. 194, 1999
S. 46PV..............................	ad. No. 133, 1999
	am. No. 194, 1999
Part IIC	
Part IIC	ad. No. 133, 1999
S. 46PW.............................	ad. No. 133, 1999
	rs. SLI 2006 No. 50
Ss. 46PX, 46PY	ad. No. 133, 1999
Part III	
S. 47....................................	am. No. 99, 1988
S. 48....................................	am. No. 38, 1988
S. 49....................................	am. No. 119, 1988; No. 24, 2001
Note to s. 49(3)..................	ad. No. 24, 2001
Note to s. 49(4A)...............	ad. No. 24, 2001
S. 49A................................	ad. No. 133, 1999
Heading to s. 49B	am. No. 194, 1999
S. 49B	ad. No. 133, 1999
	am. No. 194, 1999
S. 49C	ad. No. 133, 1999
	am. No. 194, 1999

Note 2
Age Discrimination (Consequential Provisions) Act 2004 (No. 40, 2004)
The following amendments commence immediately after the commencement of Schedule 1 to the *Australian Human Rights Commission Legislation Act 2004*:
Schedule 2
Australian Human Rights Commission Act 1986
22 Paragraph 11(1)(a)

Omit "by the *Disability Discrimination Act 1992*, the *Age Discrimination Act 2004*", substitute "by the *Age Discrimination Act 2004*, the *Disability Discrimination Act 1992*".

Note: If the *Age Discrimination Act 2004* does not commence before the commencement of item 21 of Schedule 1 to the *Australian Human Rights Commission Legislation Act 2004*, this item does not commence at all. See subsection 2(4).

23 Paragraph 11(5)(c)

Repeal the paragraph, substitute:

(c) whether, in the Attorney-General's opinion, the proceedings have significant implications for the administration of any of the following Acts:

(i) this Act;
(ii) the *Age Discrimination Act 2004*;
(iii) the *Disability Discrimination Act 1992*;
(iv) the *Racial Discrimination Act 1975*;
(v) the *Sex Discrimination Act 1984*;

24 Paragraph 31(2)(c)

Repeal the paragraph, substitute:

(c) whether, in the Attorney-General's opinion, the proceedings have significant implications for the administration of any of the following Acts:

(i) this Act;
(ii) the *Age Discrimination Act 2004*;
(iii) the *Disability Discrimination Act 1992*;
(iv) the *Racial Discrimination Act 1975*;
(v) the *Sex Discrimination Act 1984*;

25 After subparagraph 46PV(1)(b)(i)

Insert:

(ia) the *Age Discrimination Act 2004*;

As at 27 March 2006 the amendments are not incorporated in this compilation.

Table A

Application, saving or transitional provisions

Human Rights Legislation Amendment Act (No. 1) 1999 (No. 133, 1999)

Division 1—Interpretation

4 Interpretation

In this Part:

appropriate Commissioner means:

(a) in relation to a complaint lodged under the old DDA—the Disability Discrimination Commissioner; and

(b) in relation to a complaint lodged under the old RDA—the Race Discrimination Commissioner; and

(c) in relation to a complaint lodged under the old SDA—the Sex Discrimination Commissioner.

Court means the Federal Court of Australia.

holding of an inquiry means a holding of an inquiry referred to in a notice given under:

(a) section 83 of the old DDA; or
(b) section 25E of the old RDA; or
(c) section 63 of the old SDA.

new HREOCA means the *Human Rights and Equal Opportunity Commission Act 1986* as amended by Schedule 1 to this Act.

old DDA means the *Disability Discrimination Act 1992* before being amended by Schedule 1 to this Act.

old RDA means the *Racial Discrimination Act 1975* before being amended by Schedule 1 to this Act.

old SDA means the *Sex Discrimination Act 1984* before being amended by Schedule 1 to this Act.

purported complaint means a document purporting to be a complaint.

starting day means the day on which this Part commences.

Division 2—Treatment of complaints lodged before starting day

Subdivision A—Treatment of complaint depends on the stage it has reached

5 Purported complaint lodged but no decision as to whether it is a complaint

(1) A purported complaint is treated in the way set out in subsection (2) if, before the starting day:

(a) it was lodged with the Commission; and
(b) the Commission had not decided whether it was a complaint within the meaning of the old DDA, old RDA or old SDA.

(2) On the starting day:

(a) the purported complaint is taken to have been lodged under section 46P of the new HREOCA; and
(b) the Commission must then decide whether it is a complaint within the meaning of the new HREOCA.

6 Administrative appeal on Commission's decision as to whether complaint

(1) A purported complaint is treated in the way set out in subsection (2) if:

(a) before the starting day, the Commission decided that it was, or was not, a complaint within the meaning of the old DDA, old RDA or old SDA; and
(b) on or after the starting day, the Court makes an order under the *Administrative Decisions (Judicial Review) Act 1977* to refer the matter to which the decision relates to the Commission for further consideration.

(2) On the day on which the order is made:

(a) the purported complaint is taken to have been lodged under section 46P of the new HREOCA; and

(b) the Commission must then decide whether it is a complaint within the meaning of the new HREOCA.

7 Complaint lodged but Commissioner not notified of it

(1) A purported complaint is treated in the way set out in subsection (2) if, before the starting day:

(a) it was lodged with the Commission; and

(b) the Commission decided that it was a complaint within the meaning of the old DDA, old RDA or old SDA; and

(c) the Commission had not notified the appropriate Commissioner of it.

(2) On the starting day:

(a) the purported complaint is taken to have been lodged under section 46P of the new HREOCA; and

(b) the Commission is taken to have decided that it is a complaint within the meaning of the new HREOCA.

8 Commissioner notified of complaint but had not decided to dismiss or refer it

(1) A complaint is treated in the way set out in subsection (2) if, before the starting day:

(a) the Commission had notified the appropriate Commissioner of the complaint; and

(b) the appropriate Commissioner had not made a decision not to inquire, or not to continue to inquire, into the complaint; and

(c) the appropriate Commissioner had not referred the complaint to the Commission.

(2) On the starting day, the complaint is taken to have been referred to the President under section 46PD of the new HREOCA.

9 Commissioner decided to dismiss complaint

(1) A complaint is treated in the way set out in subsection (2) if:

(a) before the starting day, the appropriate Commissioner decided not to inquire, or not to continue to inquire, into the complaint; and

(b) on the starting day, the complainant could have required the appropriate Commissioner to:

(i) refer the complaint to the President under section 71 of the old DDA if that section had not been repealed by this Act; or

(ii) refer the Commissioner's decision to the President, or refer the complaint to the Commission, under section 24 of the old RDA if that section had not been repealed by this Act; or

(iii) refer the Commissioner's decision to the President, or refer the complaint to the Commission, under section 52 of the old SDA if that section had not been repealed by this Act.

(2) On the starting day, the President is taken to have terminated the complaint under section 46PH of the new HREOCA.

Note: The President is required to give a notice of termination of the complaint under section 14 of this Act.

10 Presidential review of Commissioner's decision to dismiss complaint

(1) A complaint is treated in the way set out in subsection (2) if, before the starting day:

(a) the appropriate Commissioner decided not to inquire, or not to continue to inquire, into the complaint; and

(b) the complainant required the appropriate Commissioner to refer the complaint, or the Commissioner's decision, to the President; and

(c) the President had not made a decision under whichever of the following sections is applicable:

(i) section 101 of the old DDA;

(ii) section 24AA of the old RDA;

(iii) section 52A of the old SDA.

(2) On the starting day, the President is taken to have terminated the complaint under section 46PH of the new HREOCA.

Note: The President is required to give a notice of termination of the complaint under section 14 of this Act.

11 Administrative review of President's decision

(1) A complaint is treated in the way set out in subsection (2) if:

(a) before the starting day, the President made a decision in relation to the complaint under:

(i) section 101 of the old DDA; or

(ii) section 24AA of the old RDA; or

(iii) section 52A of the old SDA; and

(b) on or after the starting day, the Court makes an order under the *Administrative Decisions (Judicial Review) Act 1977* to refer the matter to which the decision relates to the Commission for further consideration.

(2) On the day the order is made, the President is taken to have terminated the complaint under section 46PH of the new HREOCA.

Note: The President is required to give a notice of termination of the complaint under section 14 of this Act.

12 Complaint referred to Commission but inquiry not started

(1) A complaint is treated in the way set out in subsection (2) if, before the starting day:

(a) the appropriate Commissioner referred the complaint to the Commission; and

(b) a holding of an inquiry into the complaint had not started under the old DDA, old RDA or old SDA; and

(c) the complaint had not been withdrawn under whichever of the following sections is applicable:

(i) section 79 of the old DDA;

(ii) section 25A of the old RDA;

(iii) section 59 of the old SDA.

(2) On the starting day, the President is taken to have terminated the complaint under section 46PH of the new HREOCA.

Note: The President is required to give a notice of termination of the complaint under section 14 of this Act.

13 Inquiry started

(1) A complaint is treated in the way set out in subsection (2) if, before the starting day:

(a) a holding of an inquiry into the complaint had started under the old DDA, old RDA or old SDA; and

(b) the complaint had not been withdrawn under whichever of the following sections is applicable:

(i) section 79 of the old DDA;

(ii) section 25A of the old RDA;

(iii) section 59 of the old SDA.

(2) The amendments made by Schedule 1 to this Act do not apply in relation to the complaint.

Subdivision B—Other rules about complaints lodged before starting day

14 Notice of termination

(1) If the President is taken to have terminated a complaint under section 9, 10, 11 or 12, then the President must notify the complainants in writing of the termination and the reasons for the termination.

(2) Subsection (1) does not apply if all the complainants requested the appropriate Commissioner not to inquire into the complaint.

(3) The President must give a person a copy of the notice that was given to the complainants under subsection (1) if:

(a) the person was a person on whose behalf the complaint was lodged; and

(b) the person requested the President for a copy of the notice.

(4) The President is not required to notify any person under section 46PH of the new HREOCA.

15 Work done by Commissioner is taken to have been done by President

Any thing done, or information obtained, by the appropriate Commissioner in relation to a complaint that is referred to the President under section 8 is taken to have been done or obtained by the President.

16 Special rules apply to proceedings to enforce a determination

Sections 46PQ, 46PR and 46PT of the new HREOCA apply for the purposes of proceedings in the Court:

(a) for an order to enforce a determination in relation to a complaint; or
(b) for an order directing a Commonwealth agency (or the principal executive of a Commonwealth agency) to comply;

if the proceedings started on or after the starting day under:

(c) section 105A or 106F of the old DDA; or
(d) section 25ZC or 25ZI of the old RDA; or
(e) section 83A or 84F of the old SDA.

Division 3—Other transitional and application provisions

17 Protection from civil actions

The amendments made by items 30, 31, 83, 84, 119 and 120 of Schedule 1 do not apply to a complaint lodged before the starting day under the old DDA, old RDA or old SDA.

18 Referrals under the old SDA

The amendments made by items 1, 2, 85, 86, 97, 100, 122, 123, 124 and 125 of Schedule 1 do not apply to a complaint lodged before the starting day under section 50A, 50C or 50E of the old SDA.

19 Inquiries started by Human Rights Commissioner

The amendment made by item 52 of Schedule 1 does not apply in relation to an inquiry that the Human Rights Commissioner started before the starting day.

20 When a person cannot lodge a complaint under the new HREOCA

A person cannot lodge a complaint under section 46P of the new HREOCA if:

(a) the person is a class member for a representative complaint in respect of the same subject matter; and
(b) a holding of an inquiry into the representative complaint had started under the old DDA, old RDA or old SDA.

21 Regulations

(1) The Governor-General may make regulations prescribing matters:

(a) required or permitted by this Act to be prescribed; or
(b) necessary or convenient to be prescribed for carrying out or giving effect to this Act.

(2) In particular, regulations may be made in relation to matters of a transitional or saving nature arising out of the enactment of this Act.

22 Transitional—powers of a Secretary

A thing done by the Commission before the commencement of this section in exercising powers referred to in subsection 43(2) of the *Human Rights and Equal Opportunity Commission Act 1986* has effect, for the purpose of the exercise by the President after the commencement of this section of powers referred to in that subsection, as if the thing had been done by the President.

Criminal Code Amendment (Theft, Fraud, Bribery and Related Offences) Act 2000 (No. 137, 2000)

Schedule 2

418 Transitional—pre-commencement offences

(1) Despite the amendment or repeal of a provision by this Schedule, that provision continues to apply, after the commencement of this item, in relation to:

(a) an offence committed before the commencement of this item; or

(b) proceedings for an offence alleged to have been committed before the commencement of this item; or

(c) any matter connected with, or arising out of, such proceedings;

as if the amendment or repeal had not been made.

(2) Subitem (1) does not limit the operation of section 8 of the *Acts Interpretation Act 1901*.

419 Transitional—pre-commencement notices

If:

(a) a provision in force immediately before the commencement of this item required that a notice set out the effect of one or more other provisions; and

(b) any or all of those other provisions are repealed by this Schedule; and

(c) the first-mentioned provision is amended by this Schedule;

the amendment of the first-mentioned provision by this Schedule does not affect the validity of such a notice that was given before the commencement of this item.

Law and Justice Legislation Amendment (Application of Criminal Code) Act 2001 (No. 24, 2001)

4 Application of amendments

(1) Subject to subsection (3), each amendment made by this Act applies to acts and omissions that take place after the amendment commences.

(2) For the purposes of this section, if an act or omission is alleged to have taken place between 2 dates, one before and one on or after the day on which a particular amendment commences, the act or omission is alleged to have taken place before the amendment commences.

FIJI

HUMAN RIGHTS COMMISSION ACT 1999

ARRANGEMENT OF SECTIONS

SECTION

PART 1 – PRELIMINARY

PART II – HUMAN RIGHTS COMMISSION

PART III – UNFAIR DISCRIMINATION

PART IV – COMPLAINTS AND INVESTIGATIONS

PART V – MISCELLANEOUS

FIJI

ACT NO. 10 OF 1999

AN ACT

TO CONFER FUNCTIONS ON THE HUMAN RIGHTS COMMISSION IN ADDITION TO THOSE IN THE CONSTITUTION, TO REGULATE ITS PROCEDURE, AND FOR RELATED MATTERS

ENACTED by the Parliament of the Fiji Islands –

PART 1 – PRELIMINARY

Short title and commencement

(1) This Act may be cited as the Human Rights Commission Act 1999.

(2.) This Act commences on a date or dates to be appointed by the Minister by notice in the Gazette.

(3) The Minister may appoint a different date for the commencement of different provisions.

Interpretation

1. In this Act, unless the context otherwise requires –

"Bill of Rights" means the Bill of Rights contained in Chapter 4 of the Constitution;

"Commission" means the Human Rights Commission which was established by section 42(1) of the Constitution and which has the additional functions conferred by this Act;

"Commissioner" means any member of the Human Rights Commission, except that in Part II it does not include the Chairperson;

"Constitution" means the Constitution Amendment Act 1997;

"department" means a department in the public service;

"employment" includes –

(a) the employing of an independent contractor;

(b) the relationship between a person for whom work is done by a contract worker pursuant to a contract and the person who supplies that worker;
(c) employment in the public service, including the Fiji Police Force, the Fiji Prisons Service and the Republic of the Fiji Military Forces;
(d) unpaid work;

"functions of the Commission" means the functions conferred on the Commission by section 42(2) of the Constitution, by or under this Act, or by or under any other written law.

"human rights" means the rights embodied in the United Nations Covenants and Conventions on Human Rights and includes the rights and freedoms set out in the Bill of Rights;

"Minister" means the Minister responsible for human rights matters;

"Proceedings Commissioner" means the person designated as such under section 11;

"prohibited ground of discrimination" means a ground set out in section 38(2) of the Constitution.

Act to bind State

3. This Act binds the State.

Application of Act

4. This Act applies both within and outside the Fiji Islands.

PART II – HUMAN RIGHTS COMMISSION

Incorporation of the Commission

5. – (1) The Commission is a body corporate with perpetual succession and a common seal, may enter into contracts, may sue and be sued in its corporate name, has the power to acquire, hold and dispose of property both real and personal and generally may do all such acts and things as are necessary for and incidental to the performance of its functions by or under the Constitution, this Act or any other written law.

(2) Without limiting any other provision of this Act, the Commission has the rights, powers and privileges of a natural person of full age and capacity.

Functions of the Commission

6. – (1) In order to ensure that it complies with the Principles Relating to the Status and Functions of National Institutions for the Promotion and Protection of Human Rights (the " Paris Principles") the Commission has, in addition to the functions conferred on it by section 42(2) of the Constitution –

a) the function of promoting and protecting the human rights of all persons in the Fiji Islands; and

b) any other function conferred on it by or under this Act or by or under any other written law.

(2) For the purpose of performing its functions the Commission has the powers and duties conferred by this Act.

Powers and duties of the Commission

7. – (1) The Commission has the following powers and duties—

(a) to increase general awareness of human rights, including by making public statements and educating public opinion and public officials, co-ordinating human rights programmes and acting as a source of human rights information;
(b) to invite and receive representations from members of the public on any matter affecting human rights;
(c) to consult and co-operate with other persons and bodies concerned with the promotion and protection of human rights;
(d) to enquire generally into any matter, including any enactment or law, or any procedure or practice whether governmental or non-government, if it appears to the Commission that human rights are, or may be , infringed thereby;
(e) to make recommendations to the Government on the desirability of legislative, administrative or other action so as to give better protection to human rights;
(f) to promote better compliance in the Fiji Islands with standards laid down in international instruments on human rights;
(g) to encourage the ratification of international instruments by the State and, where appropriate, to recommend the withdrawal of reservations entered into those instruments;
(h) to advise the Government on its reporting obligations under international human rights instruments and, without derogating from the primacy of the Government's responsibility for preparing those reports, to advise on the content of the reports;

(i) to make recommendations on the implications of any proposed Act or regulations or any proposed policy of the Government that may affect human rights;
(j) to investigate allegations of contraventions of human rights and allegations of unfair discriminations, of its own motion or on complaint by individuals, groups or institutions on their own behalf or on behalf or on behalf of others;
(k) to resolve complaints by conciliation and to refer unresolved complaints to the courts for decision;
(l) to advise on any human rights matter referred to it by the Government, having regard to the available resources and priorities of the Commission;
(m) to publish guidelines for the avoidance of acts or practices that may be may be inconsistent with or contrary to human rights;
(n) to take part in international meetings and other activities on human rights and to co-operate with other national, regional and international human rights bodies.

(2) The Commission may, from time to time, in the public interest or in the interests of any person or department, publish in any manner it thinks fit reports relating generally to the exercise of its functions or to any particular case or cases investigated under this Act.

(3) The Commission must not investigate (but may comment on) any decision by a court of law.

Membership of the Commission

8. In advising the President as to the persons to be appointed as members of the Commission pursuant to section 42 of the Constitution, the Prime Minister must have regard not only to their personal attributes but also to –

(a) their knowledge or experience of the different aspects of matters likely to come before the Commission; and
(b) the desirability of having as members of the Commission persons with a diversity of the personal characteristics referred to in subsection 38(2) of the Constitution.

Disqualification from office

9. A person is not qualified to be Commissioner if he or she is, and is deemed to have vacated office if he or she becomes, –

(a) a member of the House of Representatives or of the Senate;
(b) a member of a local authority;
(c) an office-holder of a political party;
(d) an undischarged bankrupt or insolvent; or

(e) a person who has been removed from public office under subsection 172(2) of the Constitution.

Conditions of appointment

10. – (1) A Commissioner must not –

(a) actively engage in politics;
(b) subject to subsection (2), engage either directly or indirectly in the management or control of a body corporate, or of any other body carrying on business for profit.

(2) Nothing in subsection (1)(b) prevents a Commissioner from –

(a) holding office in a professional body in relation to which his or her qualifications are relevant; or
(b) engaging in the direct or indirect management or control of a body corporate, or of any other body carrying on business for profit, if leave for such engagement is granted by the Minister.

(3) The salary of a Commissioner is as prescribed by the Prescription of Salaries Act (Cap.2)

Functions of Chairperson

11. The functions of the Chairperson are –

(a) to chair meetings of the Commission;
(b) to be responsible for matters of administration in relation to the Commission;
(c) to allocate spheres of responsibility among Commissioners;
(d) any other functions conferred or imposed on the Chairperson by the Constitution, this Act or any other written law.

Proceedings Commissioner

12. – (1) The Chairperson may from time to time in writing designate a Commissioner, or the Chairperson himself or herself, to act as Proceedings Commissioner for the purposes of this Act.

(2) A designation under subsection (1) may operate for a specified period of time and may either be general or specify a particular case or cases or class of cases.

(3) Until a designation under subsection (1) is revoked, it continues in force according to its terms.

(4) A designation under this section is revocable at will and no such designation prevents the exercise of any function by the Commission as a whole.

Meetings of the Commission

13. – (1) Meetings of the Commission are to be held at such times and places as the Commission or the Chairperson from time to time appoints.

(2) At a meeting of the Commission, the quorum necessary for the transaction of business is the Chairperson and one Commissioner.

Funds of the Commission

14. – (1) The funds of the Commission consist of –

(a) any moneys appropriated by Parliament for the purposes of the Commission and paid to the Commission;
(b) all other moneys lawfully received by the Commission for its purposes; and
(c) all accumulations of income derived from any such money.

(2) The accounts of the Commission must be audited by the Auditor General.

Adequacy of funding

15. – The Minister must use his or her best endeavors to ensure that moneys appropriated by the Parliament for the Commission under section 14(1)(a) are adequate –

(a) for the performance of the functions of the Commission; and
(b) to maintain the Commission's independence and impartiality.

Staff of the Commission

16.- (1) The Commission must appoint –

(a) a Director of the Commission; and
(b) any other employees, including casual and contract employees, needed for the efficient performance of the functions of the Commission.

(2) The Director and other employees of the Commission are subject to the control and direction of the Commission.

(3) The Director and other employees of the Commission hold office on terms and conditions determined by the Commission after consultation with the Public Service Commission.

(4) The Director of the Commission is entitled to such remuneration determined from time to time by the Higher Salaries Commission.

PART III – UNFAIR DISCRIMINATION

Areas where unfair discrimination prohibited

17. – (1) It is unfair discrimination for a person, while involved in any of the areas set out in subsection (3), directly or indirectly to differentiate adversely against or harass any other person by reason of a prohibited ground of discrimination.

(2) Without limiting subsection (1), sexual harassment, for the purposes of this section, constitutes harassment by reason of a prohibited ground of discrimination.

(3) The areas to which subsection (1) applies are-

- (a) the making of an application for employment, or procuring employees for an employer, or procuring employment for other persons;
- (b) employment;
- (c) participation in, or the making of an application for participation in, a partnership;
- (d) the provision of an approval, authorization or qualification that is needed for any trade, calling or profession;
- (e) the provision of training, or facilities or opportunities for training, to help fit a person for any employment;
- (f) subject to subsection (4), membership, or the making of an application for membership, of an employers' organization, an employees' organization or an organization that exists for members of a particular trade, calling or profession;
- (g) the provision of goods, services or facilities, including facilities by way of banking or insurance or for grants, loans, credit or finance;
- (h) access by the public to any place, vehicle, vessel, aircraft or hovercraft which members of the public are entitled or allowed to enter or use;
- (i) the provision of land, housing or other accommodation;
- (j) access to, and participation in, education.

(4) Subsection (3)(f) does not apply to access to membership of a private club or to the provision of services or facilities to member of a private club.

Genuine occupational qualification

18. – (1) It is not unfair discrimination in relation to any of the areas referred to in paragraphs (a) to (e) of section 17(3) if the prohibited ground of discrimination is a genuine occupational qualification.

(2) For the avoidance of doubt, adverse differentiation by reason of a prohibited ground of discrimination is a genuine occupational qualification where a position is for the purposes of an organized religion and the differentiation complies with the doctrines, rules or established customs of the religion.

Genuine justification

19. Adverse differentiation by reason of a prohibited ground of discrimination in relation to any of the areas referred to in paragraphs (f) to (j) of section 17(3) is not unfair discrimination if there is genuine justification for the differentiation.

Guidelines on genuine occupational qualification and genuine justification

20. Without limiting the Commission's power to issue guidelines on any other matter within its jurisdiction on the Commission may, for the avoidance of acts and practices which might amount to unfair discrimination, from time to time issue non-binding guidelines on genuine occupational qualifications and genuine justification.

Social justice and affirmative action

21. A programme, whether provided by the Government or by the private sector, designed to achieve for any groups or categories of persons who are disadvantaged effective equality of access to the areas set out in section 17(3) is not unfair discrimination, provided it complies in other respects with the Bill of Rights.

Victimization

22. It is unfair discrimination for a person while involved in any of the areas set out in section 17(3) to victimize any other person on the ground that that person, or a relative or associate of that person –

(a) intends to make use of his or her rights under this Act or the Bill of Rights;
(b) has made use of his or her rights, or promoted the rights of some other person, under this Act or the Bill of Rights;
(c) has given information or evidence in relation to any complaint, investigation or proceeding under this Act or the Bill of the Rights;
(d) has declined to do any act which would contravene this Act or the Bill of the Rights; or

(e) has otherwise done anything under or by reference to this Act or the Bill of Rights.

Employment applications and advertisements

23. – (1) It is unfair discrimination –

(a) to use or circulate any form of application, or to make any of enquiry or about any person seeking employment, which indicates, or could reasonably be understood as indicating, an intention directly or indirectly to differentiate adversely by reason of a prohibited ground of discrimination; or

(b) to publish or display, or cause or allow to be published or displayed, any advertisement or notice which indicates, or could reasonably be understood as indicating, an intention to differentiate adversely by reason of a prohibited ground of discrimination.

(2) Subsection (1) does not affect the operation of sections 18, 19 and 21.

Liability of employers and principals

24. – (1) Subject to subsection (3), anything done or omitted by a person as an employee of another person is, for the purposes of this Act, to be treated as done or omitted by the other person as well as by the first – mentioned person, whether or not it was done with that other person's knowledge or approval.

(2) Anything done or omitted by a person as the agent of another person is, for the purposes of this Act, to be treated as done or omitted by that other person as well as by the first-mentioned person, unless it was done or omitted without that other person's express or implied authority, previous or subsequent.

(3) In proceedings under this Act against any person in respect of an act alleged to have been done or omitted by an employee of that person, it is a defence for that person to prove that he or she took all steps reasonably practicable to prevent the employee from doing or omitting the act, or from doing or omitting as an employee of that person acts or omissions of that description.

PART IV – COMPLAINTS AND INVESTIGATIONS

Complaints about contravention of human rights

25. Any person may make a complaint to the Commission, including a representative complaint on behalf of other persons with a similar cause of complaint, about a contravention or alleged contravention of human rights.

Complaints about unlawful discrimination

26. Any person may make a complaint to the Commission, including a representative complaint on behalf of other persons with a similar cause of complaint, about unfair discrimination.

Discretion whether to investigate

27. – (1) The Commission must investigate any complaint received by it, unless, before commencing or during the investigation it decides not to do so because –

(a) the complaint is not within the jurisdiction of the Commission;
(b) the complaint is trivial, frivolous, vexatious or not made in good faith;
(c) the complainant, or a person acting on his or her behalf, has brought proceedings relating to the same matter in a court or tribunal;
(d) the complainant has available another remedy or channel of complaint that the complainant could reasonably be expected to use;
(e) the complainant has not a sufficient interest in the complaint;
(f) the person alleged to be aggrieved does not desire that the complaint be investigated;
(g) the complaint has been delayed too long to justify an investigation;
(h) the Commission has before it matters more worthy of its attention; or
(i) the resources of the Commission are insufficient for adequate investigation,

and may defer or discontinue an investigation for any of these reasons.

(2) No decision by the Commission to decline, defer or discontinue an investigation into a complaint affects the Commission's power to inquire generally into a matter of its own initiative.

Investigation of Commission's own motion

28. The Commission may investigate of its own motion any act, omission, practice, requirement or condition which is or appears to be unfair discrimination or a contravention of human rights or which has been referred to it by the High Court.

Letters from prisoners or patients

29. Notwithstanding any written law to the contrary (other than the Constitution), a letter written by –

(a) a person in custody; or
(b) a patient in a hospital,

and addressed to the Commission must be forwarded immediately, unopened and unaltered, to the Commission by the person in charge of the place or institution where the writer of the letter is detained or in which he or she is a patient.

Investigation procedure

30. – (1) Before investigating any matter within its jurisdiction, the Commission must inform –

(a) the complainant (if any);
(b) the person alleged to be aggrieved, if not the complainant;
(c) the person to whom the investigation relates; and
(d) in relation to an investigation relating to a department the person holding or performing the duties of the office of Secretary of the department, of the Commission's intention to make the investigation.

(2) An investigation under this Act must be conducted in private.

(3) The Commission may hear or obtain information from any person whom the Commission considers can assist in the investigation and may make whatever enquiries it thinks fit.

(4) Nothing in this Act requires the Commission to hold any hearing and no person is entitled as of right to be heard by the Commission.

(5) The Commission must not in any report make any comment that is adverse to or derogatory of any person to whom a complaint relates without –

(a) providing the person with a reasonable opportunity of being heard; and
(b) fairly setting out in the report the person's defence (if any).

(6) In conducting an investigation, the Commission is not bound by the strict rules of evidence or procedure, but must act fairly at all times.

Conciliation

31. – (1) The Commission may, before commencing an investigation, or during or after an investigation, call a conciliation conference of the parties to the conciliation by formally requesting, by post, telephone, facsimile, electronic mail or otherwise, the attendance of each party at a time and place specified.

(2) If a person fails to comply with a request made under subsection (1) the Commission may issue a summons requiring the person to attend a conciliation conference at a time and place specified in the summons.

(3) The objectives of a conciliation conference are to identify the matters at issue between the parties and to use the best endeavors of the Commission to secure a settlement between the parties on the matters at issue.

Power to require information to be provided

32. – (1) Subject to this section and to section 33, for the purposes of an investigation a Commissioner may, by notice in writing, require any person to furnish any information, or to produce any document, record or thing in the possession or under the control of that person that is in the opinion of the Commissioner relevant to the investigation.

(2) If a Commissioner has reason to believe that a person is able to give information relevant to an investigation, the Commissioner may, by notice in writing, require the person to attend before him or her, on a date and at the time and place specified in the notice, to answer questions relevant to the investigation.

(3) For the purposes of an investigation the Commission and the Commissioner have the same powers as a judge of the High Court in respect of the attendance and examination of witnesses and the production of documents.

(4) Notwithstanding anything in any other written law (other than the Constitution), a person is not excused from giving information, producing a document, record or thing or answering a question when required to do so pursuant to this Act, if the only ground for refusal is that the giving of the information, the production of the document, record or thing or the answer to the question-

(a) would contravene a provision of a written law, would be contrary to the public interest, or might tend to incriminate the person or make him or her liable to a penalty; or
(b) would disclose legal advice furnished to a Minister or a department,

but the information, document, record, thing or answer is not admissible in evidence against the person in proceedings other than proceedings for an offence against section 47.

(5) Subject to section 33,a person is not excused from giving information, producing a document, record or thing or answering a question when required to do so pursuant to this Act on the ground that –

(a) a claim of State privilege could be made in relation to the material concerned; or
(b) the material is commercially sensitive.

(6) Except on the trial of any person for perjury in respect of his or her sworn or affirmed testimony, or proceedings for an offence against section 47, no statement made or answer given by that or any other person in the course of any inquiry by or proceedings before the Commission or a Commissioner is admissible in evidence against any person in any court or at any inquiry or other proceedings, and no evidence in respect of proceedings before the Commission or a Commissioner must be given against any person.

Disclosure of certain matters not to be required

33. – (1) If the Attorney General certifies that the disclosure of information concerning a specified matter (including the furnishing of information in answer to a question or the disclosure to the Commission or a Commissioner of the contents of a specified document or record or the production of a specified thing) would be contrary to the public interest because it would –

(a) seriously harm the commercial interests of any person or body;
(b) prejudice the security, defence or international relations of the State; or
(c) involve the disclosure of deliberations or decisions of the Cabinet or of a committee of the Cabinet,

the Commission or a Commissioner cannot require a person to give information concerning the matter, to answer the questions concerning the matter or to produce the document, record or thing.

(2) The Commission must withhold publication of any written material which comes into its possession in the course of an investigation and which is the subject of a certificate by the Attorney General under subsection (1).

Procedure after investigation

34. – (1) After completing an investigation, the Commission must inform the parties of the result of the investigation and whether, in its opinion-

(a) the complaint does not have substance, or cannot be established to have substance or, in relation to an investigation of the Commission's own motion, that the matter ought not to be proceeded with; or
(b) the complaint has substance or, in relation to an investigation of the Commission's own motion, that the matter ought to be proceeded with.

(2) If the Commission is of the opinion that a complaint does not have substance, or cannot be established to have substance, but considers nonetheless that it may be possible to reach a settlement between any of the parties concerned, the Commission

may act as a conciliator and use its best endeavors to reach a settlement of the complaint.

(3) If the Commission is of the opinion that a complaint does not have substance, or cannot be established to have substance, or if the Commission pursuant to section 27(1) decides not to investigate, or investigate further, a complaint, it must inform the complainant of the complainant's right to bring civil proceedings before the High Court-

(a) in relation to a complaint of unfair discrimination – pursuant to section 36 of this Act;
(b) in relation to a complaint of contravention of the Bill of Rights – pursuant to section 41 of the Constitution.

(4) If the Commission has investigated a complaint and is of the opinion that the complaint has substance, it must act as conciliator in relation to the complaint and use its best endeavors to effect a settlement in relation to the complaint.

(5) For the purposes of this section, "settlement" includes a satisfactory assurance by the person to whom a complaint or investigation relates against repetition of the conduct that was the subject – matter of the complaint or the investigation or against conduct of a similar kind.

(6) Whether or not it takes any of the actions referred to in subsection (2), (3) and (4), the Commission may –

(a) advise the parties of their respective rights, including, in relation to a complaint of contravention of the Bill of Rights, the complainant's right to bring proceedings in the High Court under section 41 of the Constitution;
(b) refer to the complaint and, if it considers appropriate, the result of the investigation to another competent authority;
(c) make recommendations to the competent authority, proposing amendments to or reform of any laws, regulations or administrative provisions or practices which have created the difficulties or hardship encountered by the complainant or the aggrieved person;
(d) recommend to the relevant authority, in respect of a person who in the opinion of the Commission has contravened human rights, either prosecution of the person or the taking of other action, and the authority must consider

Functions of Proceedings Commissioner

35. – (1) The functions of the Proceedings Commissioner include –

(a) in relation to a complaint or an investigation of the Commission's own motion – deciding whether an application should be made for an order under section 40 and, if so, making the application;
(b) in relation to a complaint resulting from a failure by a party to observe the terms of a settlement on a previous occasion – deciding whether to institute proceedings against the party and, if so, instituting the proceedings;
(c) in a relation to a complaint or an investigation of the Commission's own motion, if it appears to the Proceedings Commissioner that a settlement has not been reached and that no action or further action by the Commission is likely to facilitate a settlement – deciding whether to institute proceedings against the person against whom the complaint was made or to whom the investigation related, and if so, instituting the proceedings.

(2) The Proceedings Commissioner must not institute proceedings against a person referred to in paragraph (b) or (c) of subsection (1) unless the Commissioner has given the person an opportunity to be heard.

Proceedings

36. – (1) Civil proceedings in the High Court lie at the suit of the Proceedings Commissioner against a person referred to in paragraph (b) or (c) of section 35 (1) for unfair discrimination or a contravention of the Bill of Rights.

(2) The Proceedings Commissioner may, under subsection (1), bring proceedings on behalf of a class of persons if the Commissioner considers that a person referred to in paragraph (b) or (c) of section 35 (1) has engaged in unfair discrimination which affects that class or has contravened the Bill of Rights in relation to that class.

(3) If proceedings are commenced by the Proceedings Commissioner under subsection (1), neither the complainant (if any) nor the aggrieved person (if not the complainant) may be an original party to the proceedings, or, unless the High Court so orders, join or be joined in the proceedings.

(4) Notwithstanding subsection (1), the complainant (if any) or the aggrieved person (if not the complainant) may bring proceedings before the High Court if –

(a) the Commission is of the opinion that the complaint does not have substance or cannot be established to have substance or that the matter ought not to be proceeded with;
(b) the Commission pursuant to section 27(1) decides not to investigate, or to investigate further, a complaint; or
(c) the Proceedings Commissioner would be entitled to bring proceedings, but –

(i) agrees to the complainant, in the case of a complaint, or an aggrieved person, in relation to an investigation of the Commission's own motion, bringing proceedings; or
(ii) decides not to take proceedings.

(5) Nothing in this section limits the right of any person to apply to the High Court for redress for a contravention of the Bill of Rights under section 41 of the Constitution.

Right of Proceedings Commissioner to appear in High Court

37. – (1) The Proceedings Commissioner may appear and be heard in the High Court, the Court of Appeal or the Supreme Court in relation to any proceedings under section 36, whether or not the Proceedings Commissioner is or was a party to the proceedings.

(2) With leave of the court, tribunal or arbitrator, the Proceedings Commissioner may appear and be heard in relation to any proceedings before a court, tribunal or arbitrator in which human rights are in issue.

(3) If the Proceedings Commissioner appears before any court, tribunal or arbitrator, he or she may, unless the rules of procedure of the court, tribunal or arbitrator otherwise provide –

(a) appear in person or by a legal practitioner;
(b) adduce evidence and cross-examine witnesses, unless the proceedings are by way of appeal,

Remedies

38. – (1) In any proceedings before the High Court brought under section 36 by the Proceedings Commissioner, a complainant or an aggrieved person, the plaintiff may seek any or all of the remedies described in subsection (2) of this section.

(2) If in any proceedings as mentioned in subsection (1) the High Court is satisfied on the balance of probabilities that the defendant has engaged in unfair discrimination or has contravened the Bill of Rights, it may grant one or more of the following remedies-

a) a declaration that the defendant has engaged in unfair discrimination or contravened the Bill of Rights;
b) an order restraining the defendant from continuing or repeating the conduct complained of or causing or permitting others to engage in conduct of the same kind or of any similar kind specified in the order;
c) damages

d) an order that the defendant perform any act specified in the order with a view to redressing any loss or damage suffered by the complainant or the aggrieved person or to preventing conduct of a similar kind in the future;
e) a declaration that a contract requiring performance of anything that constitutes unfair discrimination or contravenes the Bill of Rights is void and unenforceable;
f) such other relief as the High Court thinks fit.

(3) It is not a defence to proceedings under this section that the unfair discrimination or contravention of the Bill of Rights was unintentional or without negligence on the part of the defendant, but the High Court must take the conduct of the defendant into account in deciding what remedy, if any, to grant.

(4) In any proceedings under section 36, the High Court may make such award as to costs as it thinks fit, whether or not it grants any other remedy.

(5) If the Proceedings Commissioner is a party to proceedings, any costs in the proceedings awarded against the Commissioner under subsection (4) must be paid by the Commission and the Commission is not entitled to be indemnified by the complainant or, as the case may be, the aggrieved person for such costs.

Damages

39. – (1) In proceedings under section 36 for unfair discrimination or a contravention of the Bill of Rights, the High Court may award damages against the defendant in respect of any one or more of the following –

(a) pecuniary loss suffered or expense incurred by the complainant or the aggrieved person as a result of the conduct complained of;
(b) expenses reasonably incurred by the complainant or the aggrieved person in seeking redress for the conduct complained of;
(c) loss of any benefit, whether or not of a monetary kind, which the complainant or the aggrieved person might reasonably have been expected to obtain but for the conduct complained of;
(d) humiliation, loss of dignity and injury to feelings of the complainant or the aggrieved person.

(2) Subject to subsection (3), the Commission must pay any damages recovered by the Proceedings Commissioner under this section to the complainant or the aggrieved person on whose behalf the proceedings were brought.

(3) If the complainant or the aggrieved person is an unmarried minor or a person of unsound mind the Proceedings Commissioner may, in his or her discretion, pay the

damages to the Public Trustee or to any person or trustee corporation acting as the trustee of the property of that person.

Power to make interim order

40. – (1) In respect of any matter which is the subject of an investigation by the Commission and in which the High Court has or may have jurisdiction, a judge may make an interim order if he or she is satisfied that it is necessary in the interests of justice to make the order to preserve the position of the parties pending the result of the investigation and the final determination of any proceedings resulting from the investigation.

(2) An application for an interim order under subsection (1) may be made by the Proceedings Commissioner or, in a case to which section 36(4) applies, the complainant or the aggrieved person.

(3) A copy of an application under subsection (3) must be served on the defendant, who must be given an opportunity to be heard before a decision on the application is made.

(4) If an interim order has been made, the defendant may appeal to the Court of Appeal to rescind or vary the order, unless the order was made with the defendant's consent.

Substantial merits, evidence and hearings

41. In any proceedings under this Act before the High Court, the court –

(a) must act according to equity, good conscience and the substantial merits of the case, without regard to technicalities;
(b) may receive as evidence any statement, document, information or matter that will or might in the court's opinion assist it to deal effectively with the matters before it, whether or not it would be admissible but for this section;
(c) may, if it considers it desirable to do so –

   (i) order that any hearing held by it be heard in private, either in whole or part;
   (ii) make an order prohibiting the publication of any report or account of the evidence or other proceedings before it (whether heard in public or in private) either in whole or in part;
   (iii) make an order prohibiting the publication of any book or document produced at the hearing.

PART V – MISCELLANEOUS

Annual Report

42. – (1) Without limiting the right of the Commission to report at any other time, the Commission must, within 3 months after the end of each financial year, furnish to the President a report on the exercise of its functions under the Constitution and this Act during the year, and must submit a copy to each House of the Parliament for laying before that House and for consideration by the relevant committee (if any) of that House.

(2) Following the tabling of the Annual Report in both Houses of the Parliament, the Commission must hold a public meeting at a time and place it fixes to discuss the contents of the Annual Report and the carrying out of its functions during the year.

Delegation of functions by Commission or Commissioner

43. – (1) The Commission may from time to time by writing under the hand of the Chairperson, delegate to a Commissioner any of the functions or powers of the Commission under the Constitution or this Act, except the functions set out in section 42(2) of the Constitution and section 6 of this Act, this power of delegation, and the power to make any report under this Act.

(2) With the prior written approval of the Minister, any Commissioner may from time to time, by writing under his or her hand, delegate to any employee of the Commission any of the Commissioner's powers under this Act, except this power of delegation and the power to make any report under this Act.

Nature of delegation

44. – (1) The following provisions apply to a delegation under section 43 –

(a) it may made to a specified person or to the holder for the time being of a specified office or to the holders of offices of a specified class.
(b) It may be made subject to such restrictions and conditions as the Commissioner or Commissioner thinks fit, and may be made either generally or in relation to any particular case or class of cases;
(c) It is revocable at will and no such delegation prevents the exercise of any function by the Commission or Commissioner, as the case may be;
(d) Until revoked, it continues in force according to its terms and if, in the case of a delegation by a Commissioner, the Commissioner by whom it was made ceases to hold office, it continues to have effect as if made by his or her successor.

(2) A person purporting to exercise any power of the Commission or of a Commissioner by virtue of a delegation under section 43 must, when required to do so, produce evidence of his or her authority to exercise the power.

Commissioners and employees to maintain secrecy

45. – (1) Subject to this section, a Commissioner or any employee of the Commission who, either directly or indirectly and either while remaining or after ceasing to be a Commissioner or employee, makes a record of, or divulges or communicates to any person, any information acquired in the performance of his or her duties under this Act, commits an offence and is liable on conviction to a fine of $1000.

(2) Subsection (1) does not prevent a Commissioner or an employee of the Commission from making a record of, or divulging or communicating to any person, information acquired by the Commissioner or the employee in the performance of his or her duties for purposes connected with the performance of the functions of the Commission under the Constitution or this Act.

(3) Subsection (1) does not prevent the Commission from disclosing in a report made under this Act any matter which in the Commission's opinion ought to be disclosed in the course of setting out the grounds for the conclusions and recommendations contained in the report.

(4) Subsection (1) does not prevent the Commission from disclosing information or making a statement to the public or a section of the public with respect to the performance of the functions of the Commission.

(5) The Commission must not, in disclosing information or making a statement under subsection (4), disclose the name of a complainant or aggrieved person or any other information that would enable the complainant or aggrieved person to be identified unless it is fair and reasonable in all the circumstances to do so.

Protection from suit

46. Neither the Commission, a Commissioner nor an employee of the Commission is liable to an action, suit or proceeding for or in relation to an act done or omitted to be done in good faith in exercise or purported exercise of a power or authority conferred by the Constitution or this Act.

Offences

47. – (1) A person who refuses or fails, without reasonable excuse –

(a) to attend before the Commission or a Commissioner;

(b) to be sworn or make an affirmation;
(c) to furnish information;
(d) to produce a document, record or thing; or
(e) to answer a question,

when required to do so pursuant to this Act, commits an offence and is liable on conviction to a fine of $1,000 and to imprisonment for 6 months.

(2) A person who –

(a) without reasonable excuse, willfully obstructs, hinders or resists the Commission, a Commissioner or an employee of the Commission in the performance of their functions; or
(b) furnishes information or makes a statement to the Commission, a Commissioner or an employee of the Commission knowing that it is false or misleading in a material manner,

commits an offence and is liable on conviction to a fine of $1,000 and to imprisonment for 12 months.

Expenses and allowances

48. The Commission may, in its discretion, pay to –

(a) any person by whom a complaint has been made; or
(b) any person who attends or who furnishes information for the purposes of an investigation,

such amounts in respect of expenses properly incurred or by way of allowances or compensation for loss of time, as are payable under the Criminal Procedure Code to a witness attending at a trial or an inquiry at the High Court.

Regulations

49. The Minister may make regulations, not inconsistent with this Act, prescribing all matters that are required or permitted by this Act to be prescribed or that are convenient to be prescribed for carrying out or giving effect to this Act.

Passed by the House of Representatives this 3rd day of February 1999.

Passed by the Senate this 9th day of March 1999.

INDIA

THE PROTECTION OF HUMAN RIGHTS ACT, 1993
NO 10 OF 1994

An Act to provide for the constitution of a National Human Rights Commission. State Human Rights Commission in States and Human Rights Courts for better protection of Human Rights and for matters connected therewith or incidental thereto.

Be it enacted by the parliament in the forty-fourth year of the Republic of India as follows–

CHAPTER I

PRELIMINARY

1. Short title, extent and commencement

(1) This Act may be called the Protection of Human Rights Act, 1993.
(2) It extends to the whole of India. Provided that it shall apply to the State of Jammu and Kashmir only in so far as it pertains to the matters relatable to any of the entries enumerated in List I or List III in the Seventh Schedule to the Constitution as applicable to that State.
(3) It shall be deemed to have come into force on the 28th day of September, 1993.

2. Definitions

(1) In this Act, unless the context otherwise requires-
(a) "armed forces" means the naval, military and air forces and includes any other armed forces of the Union;
(b) "Chairperson" means the Chairperson of the Commission or of the State Commission, as the case may be;
(c) "Commission" means the National Human Rights Commission under section 3;
(d) "human rights" means the rights relating to life, liberty, equality and dignity of the individual guaranteed by the Constitution or embodied in the International Covenants and enforceable by courts in India.
(e) "Human Rights Court" means the Human Rights Court specified under section 30;
(f) "International Covenants" means the International Covenant on Civil and Political Rights and the International Covenant on Economic, Social and Cultural Rights adopted by the General Assembly of the United Nations on the 16th December, 1966;
(g) "Member" means a Member of the Commission or of the State Commission, as the case may be, and includes the Chairperson;

(h) "National Commission for Minorities" means the National Commission for Minorities constituted under section 3 of the National Commission for Minorities Act, 1992;
(i) "National Commission for the Scheduled Castes and Scheduled Tribes" means the National Commission for the Scheduled Castes and Scheduled Tribes referred to in article 338 of the Constitution;
(j) "National Commission for Women" means the National Commission for Women constituted under section 3 of the National Commission for Women Act, 1990;
(k) "Notification" means a notification published in the official Gazette;
(l) "Prescribed" means prescribed by rules made under this Act;
(m) "Public servant" shall have the meaning assigned to it in section 21 of the Indian Penal Code;
(n) "State Commission" means a State Human Rights Commission constituted under section 21.
(2) Any reference in this Act to a law, which is not in force in the State of Jammu and Kashmir, shall, in relation to that State, be construed as a reference to a corresponding law, if any, in force in that State. Chapter II

THE NATIONAL HUMAN RIGHTS COMMISSION

3. Constitution of a National Human Rights Commission

(1) The Central Government shall constitute a body to be known as the National Human Rights Commission to exercise the powers conferred upon, and to perform the functions assigned to it, under this Act.
(2) The Commission shall consist of
(a) A Chairperson who has been a Chief Justice of the Supreme Court;
(b) One Member who is or has been, a Judge of the Supreme Court;
(c) One Member who is, or has been, the Chief Justice of a High Court;
(d) Two Members to be appointed from amongst persons having knowledge of, or practical experience in, matters relating to human rights.
(3) The Chairpersons of the National Commission for Minorities, the National Commission for the Scheduled Castes and Scheduled Tribes and the National Commission for Women shall be deemed to be Members of the Commission for the discharge of functions specified in clauses (b) to (j) of section 12.
(4) There shall be a Secretary-General who shall be the Chief Executive Officer of the Commission and shall exercise such powers and discharge such functions of the Commission as it may delegate to him.
(5) The headquarters of the Commission shall be at Delhi and the Commission may, with the previous approval of the Central Government, establish offices at other places in India.

4. Appointment of Chairperson and other Members

(1) The Chairperson and other Members shall be appointed by the President by warrant under his hand and seal. Provided that every appointment under this sub-section shall be made after obtaining the recommendations of a Committee consisting of
(a) The Prime Minister – Chairperson
(b) Speaker of the House of the People – Member
(c) Minister in-charge of the Ministry of Home Affairs in the Government of India – Member
(d) Leader of the Opposition in the House of the People – Member
(e) Leader of the Opposition in the Council of States – Member
(f) Deputy Chairman of the Council of States – Member
Provided further that no sitting Judge of the Supreme Court or sitting Chief Justice of a High Court shall be appointed except after consultation with the Chief Justice of India.
(2) No appointment of a Chairperson or a Member shall be invalid merely by reason of any vacancy in the Committee.

5. Removal of a Member of the Commission

(1) Subject to the provisions of sub-section (2), the Chairperson or any other Member of the Commission shall only be removed from his office by order of the President on the ground of proved misdermour or incapacity after the Supreme Court, on reference being made to it by the President, has, on inquiry held in accordance with the procedure prescribed in that behalf by the Supreme Court, reported that the Chairperson or such other Member, as the case may be, ought on any such ground to be removed.
(2) Notwithstanding anything in sub-section (1), the President may by order remove from office the Chairperson or any other Member if the Chairperson or such other Member, as the case may be
(a) is adjudged an insolvent; or
(b) engages during his term of office in any paid employment out side the duties of his office: or
(c) is unfit to continue in office by reason of infirmity of mind or body; or
(d) is of unsound mind and stands so declared by a competent court; or
(e) is convicted and sentenced to imprisonment for an offence which in the opinion of the President involves moral turpitude.

6. Term of office of Members

(1) A person appointed as Chairperson shall hold office for a term of five years from the date on which he enters upon his office or until he attains the age of seventy years, whichever is earlier.

(2) A person appointed as a Member shall hold office for a term of five years from the date on which he enters upon his office and shall be eligible for re-appointment for another term of five years. Provided that no Member shall hold office after he has attained the age of seventy years.
(3) On ceasing to hold office, a Chairperson or a Member shall be ineligible for further employment under the Government of India or under the Government of any State.

7. Member to act as Chairperson or to discharge his functions in certain circumstances

(1) In the event of the occurrence of any vacancy in the office of the Chairperson by reason of his death, resignation or otherwise, the President may, by notification, authorise one of the Members to act as the Chairperson until the appointment of a new Chairperson to fill such vacancy.
(2) When the Chairperson is unable to discharge his functions owing to absence on leave or otherwise, such one of the Members as the President may, by notification, authorise in this behalf, shall discharge the functions of the Chairperson until the date on which the Chairperson resumes his duties.

8. Terms and conditions of service of Members

The salaries and allowances payable to, and other terms and conditions of service of, the Members shall be such as may be prescribed. Provided that neither the salary and allowances nor the other terms and conditions of service of a Member shall be varied to his disadvantage after his appointment.

9. Vacancies, etc., not to invalidate the proceedings of the Commission.

No act or proceedings of the Commission shall be questioned or shall be invalidated merely on the ground of existence of any vacancy or defect in the constitution of the Commission.

10. Procedure to be regulated by the Commission

(1) The Commission shall meet at such time and place as the Chair son may think fit.
(2) The Commission shall regulate its own procedure.
(3) All orders and decisions of the Commission shall be audited by the Secretary-General or any other officer of the Commission duly authorised by the Chairperson in this behalf.

11. Officers and other staff of the Commission

(1) The Central Government shall make available to the Commission :

(a) an officer of the rank of the Secretary to the Government of India who shall be the Secretary-General of the Commission; and
(b) such police and investigative staff under an officer not below the rank of a Director General of Police and such other officers and staff as may be necessary for the efficient performance of the functions of the Commission.
(2) Subject to such rules as may be made by the Central Government in this behalf, the Commission may appoint such other administrative, technical and scientific staff as it may consider necessary.
(3) The salaries, allowances and conditions of service of the officers and other staff appointed under sub-section (2) shall be such as may be prescribed.

CHAPTER III

FUNCTIONS AND POWERS OF THE COMMISSION

12. Functions of the Commission

The Commission shall perform all or any of the following functions, namely:
(a) inquire, suo motu or on a petition presented to it by a victim or any person on his behalf, into complaint of
(i) violation of human rights or abetment thereof or
(ii) negligence in the prevention of such violation,
by a public servant;
(b) intervene in any proceeding involving any allegation of violation of human rights pending before a court with the approval of such court;
(c) visit, under intimation to the State Government, any jail or any other institution under the control of the State Government, where persons are detained or lodged for purposes of treatment, reformation or protection to study the living conditions of the inmates and make recommendations thereon;
(d) review the safeguards provided by or under the Constitution or any law for the time being in force for the protection of human rights and recommend measures for their effective implementation;
(e) review the factors, including acts of terrorism that inhibit the enjoyment of human rights and recommend appropriate remedial measures;
(f) study treaties and other international instruments on human rights and make recommendations for their effective implementation;
(g) undertake and promote research in the field of human rights;
(h) spread human rights literacy among various sections of society and promote awareness of the safeguards available for the protection of these rights through publications, the media, seminars and other available means;
(i) encourage the efforts of non-governmental organisations and institutions working in the field of human rights;
(j) such other functions as it may consider necessary for the protection of human rights.

13. Powers relating to inquiries

(1) The Commission shall, while inquiring into complaints under this Act, have all the powers of a civil court trying a suit under the Code of Civil Procedure, 1908, and in particular in respect of the following matters, namely:
(a) summoning and enforcing the attendance of witnesses and examine them on oath;
(b) discovery and production of any document;
(c) receiving evidence on affidavits;
(d) requisitioning any public record or copy thereof from any court or office;
(e) issuing commissions for the examination of witnesses or documents;
(f) any other matter which may be prescribed.
(2) The Commission shall have power to require any person, subject to any privilege which may be claimed by that person under any law for the time being in force, to furnish information on such points or matters as, in the opinion of the Commission, may be useful for, or relevant to, the subject matter of the inquiry and any person so required shall be deemed to be legally bound to furnish such information within the meaning of section 176 and section 177 of the Indian Penal Code.
(3) The Commission or any other officer, not below the rank of a Gazetted Officer, specially authorised in this behalf by the Commission may enter any building or place where the Commission has reason to believe that any document relating to the subject matter of the inquiry may be found, and may seize any such document or take extracts or copies therefrom subject to the provisions of section 100 of the Code of Criminal Procedure, 1973, in so far as it may be applicable.
(4) The Commission shall be deemed to be a civil court and when any offence as is described in section 175, section 178, section 179, section 180 or section 228 of the Indian Penal Code is committed in the view or presence of the Commission, the Commission may, after recording the facts constituting the offence and the statement of the accused as provided for in the Code of Criminal Procedure, 1973, forward the case to a Magistrate having jurisdiction to try the same and the Magistrate to whom any such case is forwarded shall proceed to hear the complaint against the accused as if the case has been forwarded to him under section 346 of the Code of Criminal Procedure, 1973.
(5) Every proceeding before the Commission shall be deemed to be a judicial proceeding within the meaning of sections 193 and 228, and for the purposes of section 196, of the Indian Penal Code, and the Commission shall be deemed to be a civil court for all the purposes of section 195 and Chapter XXVI of the Code of Criminal Procedure, 1973.

14. Investigation

(1) The Commission may, for the purpose of conducting any investigation pertaining to the inquiry, utilise the services of any officer or investigation agency of the Central Government or any State Government with the concurrence of the Central Government or the State Government, as the case may be.

(2) For the purpose of investigating into any matter pertaining to the inquiry, any officer or agency whose services are utilised under sub-section (1) may, subject to the direction and control of the Commission.
(a) summon and enforce the attendance of any person and examine him;
(b) require the discovery and production of any document; and
(c) requisition any public record or copy thereof from any office.
(3) The provisions of section 15 shall apply in relation to any statement made by a person before any officer or agency whose services are utilised under sub-section (1) as they apply in relation to any statement made by a person in the course of giving evidence before the Commission.
(4) The officer or agency whose services are utilised under sub-section (1) shall investigate into any matter pertaining to the inquiry and submit a report thereon to the Commission within such period as may be specified by the Commission in this behalf.
(5) The Commission shall satisfy itself about the correctness of the facts stated and the conclusion, if any, arrived at in the report subbed to it under sub-section (4) and for this purpose the Commission may make such inquiry (including the examination of the person or persons who conducted or assisted in the investigation) as it thinks fit.

15. Statement made by persons to the Commission

No statement made by a person in the course of giving evidence before the Commission shall subject him to, or be used against him in, any civil or criminal proceeding except a prosecution for giving false evidence by such statement:
Provided that the statement —
(a) is made in reply to the question which he is required by the Commission to answer; or
(b) is relevant to the subject matter of the inquiry.

16. Persons likely to be prejudicially affected to be heard

If, at any stage of the inquiry, the Commission –
(a) considers it necessary to inquire into the conduct of any person; or
(b) is of the opinion that the reputation of any person is likely to be prejudicially affected by the inquiry;
it shall give to that person a reasonable opportunity of being heard in the inquiry and to produce evidence in his defence:
Provided that nothing in this section shall apply where the credit of a witness is being impeached.

CHAPTER IV

PROCEDURE

17. Inquiry into complaints

The Commission while inquiring into the complaints of violations of human rights may –
(i) call for information or report from the Central Government or any State Government or any other authority or organisation subordinate thereto within such time as may be specified by it;
Provided that –
(a) if the information or report is not received within the time stipulated by the Commission, it may proceed to inquire re into the complaint on its own;
(b) if, on receipt of information or report, the Commission is satisfied either that no further inquiry is required or that the required action has been initiated or taken by the concerned Government or authority, it may not proceed with the complaint and inform the complainant accordingly;
(ii) without prejudice to anything contained in clause (i), if it confers necessary, having regard to the nature of the complaint, initiate an inquiry.

18. Steps after inquiry

The Commission may take any of the following steps upon the completion of an inquiry held under this Act namely:
(1) where the inquiry discloses, the commission of violation of human rights or negligence in the prevention of violation of human rights by a public servant, it may recommend to the concerned Government or authority the initiation of proceedings for prosecution or such other action as the Commission may deem fit against the concerned person or persons;
(2) approach the Supreme Court or the High Court concerned for such directions, orders or writs as that Court may deem necessary;
(3) recommend to the concerned Government or authority for the grant of such immediate interim relief to the victim or the members of his family as the Commission may consider necessary;
(4) subject to the provisions of clause (5), provide a copy of the inquiry report to the petitioner or his representative;
(5) the Commission shall send a copy of its inquiry report together with its recommendations to the concerned Government or authority and the concerned Government or authority shall, within a period of one month, or such further time as the Commission may allow, forward its comments on the report, including the action taken or proposed to be taken thereon, to the Commission;
(6) the Commission shall publish its inquiry report together with the comments of the concerned Government or authority, if any, and the action taken or proposed to

be taken by the concerned Government or authority on the recommendations of the Commission.

19. Procedure with respect to armed forces

(1) Notwithstanding anything contained in this Act, while dealing with complaints of violation of human rights by members of the armed forces, the Commission shall adopt the following procedure, namely:
(a) it may, either on its own motion or on receipt of a petition, seek a report from the Central Government;
(b) after the receipt of the report, it may, either not proceed with the complaint or, as the case may be, make its recommendations to that Government.
(2) The Central Government shall inform the Commission of the action taken on the recommendations within three months or such further time as the Commission may allow.
(3) The Commission shall publish its report together with its recommendations made to the Central Government and the action taken by that Government on such recommendations.
(4) The Commission shall provide a copy of the report published under sub-section (3) to the petitioner or his representative.

20. Annual and special reports of the Commission

(1) The Commission shall submit an annual report to the Central Government and to the State Government concerned and may at any time submit special reports on any matter which, in its opinion, is of such urgency or importance that it should not be deferred till submission of the annual report.
(2) The Central Government and the State Government, as the case may be, shall cause the annual and special reports of the Commission to be laid before each House of Parliament or the State Legislature respectively, as the case may be, along with a memorandum of action taken or proposed to be taken on the recommendations of the Commission and the reasons for non-acceptance of the recommendations, if any.

CHAPTER V

STATE HUMAN RIGHTS COMMISSIONS

21. Constitution of State Human Rights Commissions

(1) A State Government may constitute a body to be known as the .... (name of the State) Human Rights Commission to exercise the powers conferred upon, and to perform the functions assigned to, a State Commission under this chapter.
(2) The State Commission shall consist of
(a) a Chairperson who has been a Chief Justice of a High Court;

(b) one Member who is, or has been, a Judge of a High Court;
(c) one Member who is, or has been, a district judge in that State;
(d) two Members to be appointed from amongst persons having knowledge of, or practical experience in, matters relating to human rights.
(3) There shall be a Secretary who shall be the Chief Executive Officer of the State Commission and shall exercise such powers and discharge such functions of the State Commission as it may delegate to him.
(4) The headquarters of the State Commission shall be at such place as the State Government may, by notification, specify.
(5) A State Commission may inquire into violation of human rights only in respect of matters relatable to any of the entries enumerated in List II and List lll in the Seventh Schedule to the Constitution:
Provided that if any such matter is already being inquired into by the Commission or any other Commission duly constituted under any law for the time being in force, the State Commission shall not inquire into the said matter:
Provided further that in relation to the Jammu and Kashmir Human Rights Commission, this sub-section shall have effect as if for the words and figures "List II and List III in the Seventh Schedule to the Constitution", the words and figures "List III in the Seventh Schedule to the Constitution as applicable to the State of Jammu and Kashmir and in respect of matters in relation to which the Legislature of that State has power to make laws" had been substituted.

22. Appointment of Chairperson and other Members of State Commission

(1) The Chairperson and other Members shall be appointed by the Governor by warrant under his hand and seal:
Provided that every appointment under this sub-section shall be made after obtaining the recommendation of a Committee consisting of
(a) the Chief Minister – Chairperson
(b) Speaker of the Legislative – Member Assembly
(c) Minister in-charge of the Department – Member of Home, in that State
(d) Leader of the Opposition in the – Member Legislative Assembly
Provided further that where there is a Legislative Council in a State, the Chairman of that Council and the Leader of the Opposition in that Council shall also be members of the Committee.
Provided also that no sitting Judge of a High Court or a sitting District Judge shall be appointed except after consultation with the Chief Justice of the High Court of the concerned State.
(2) No appointment of a Chairperson or a Member of the State Commission shall be invalid merely by reason of any vacancy in the Committee.

23. Removal of a Member of the State Commission

(1) Subject to the provisions of sub-section (2), the Chairperson or any other member of the State Commission shall only be removed from his office by order of

the President on the ground of proved misbehaviour or incapacity after the Supreme Court, on a reference being made to it by the President, has, on inquiry held in accordance with the procedure prescribed in that behalf by the Supreme Court, reported that the Chairperson or such other Member, as the case may be, ought on any such ground to be removed.

(2) Notwithstanding anything in sub-section (1), the President may by order remove from office the Chairperson or any other Member if the Chairperson or such other Member, as the case may be –

(a) is adjudged an insolvent; OR

(b) engages during his term of office in any paid employment outside the duties of his office; OR

(c) is unfit to continue in office by reason of infirmity of mind or body; OR

(d) is of unsound mind and stands so declared by a competent court; OR

(e) is convicted and sentenced to imprisonment for an offence which in the opinion of the President involves moral turpitude.

24. Term of office of Members of the State Commission

(1) A person appointed as Chairperson shall hold office for a term of five years from the date on which he enters upon his office or until he attains the age of seventy years, whichever is earlier;

(2) A person appointed as a Member shall hold office for a term of five years from the date on which he enters upon his office and shall be eligible for re-appointment for another term of five years;

Provided that no Member shall hold office after he has attained the age of seventy years.

(3) On ceasing to hold office, a Chairperson or a Member shall be ineligible for further employment under the Government of a State or under the Government of India.

25. Member to act as Chairperson or to discharge his functions in certain circumstances

(1) In the event of the occurrence of any vacancy in the office of the Chairperson by reason of his death, resignation or otherwise, the Governor may, by notification, authorise one of the Members to act as the Chairperson until the appointment of a new Chairperson to fill such vacancy.

(2) When the Chairperson is unable to discharge his functions owing to absence on leave or otherwise, such one of the Members as the Governor may, by notification, authorise in this behalf, shall discharge the functions of the Chairperson until the date on which the Chairperson resumes his duties.

26. Terms and conditions of service of Members of the State Commission

The salaries and allowances payable to, and other terms and conditions of service of, the Members shall be such as may be prescribed by the State Government.
Provided that neither the salary and allowances nor the other terms and conditions of service of a Member shall be varied to his disadvantage after his appointment.

27. Officers and other staff of the State Commission

(1) The State Government shall make available to the Commission
(a) an officer not below the rank of a Secretary to the State Government who shall be the Secretary of the State Commission; and
(b) such police and investigative staff under an officer not below the rank of an Inspector General of Police and such other officers and staff as may be necessary for the efficient performance of the functions of the State Commission.
(2) subject to such rules as may be made by the State Government in this behalf, the State Commission may appoint such other administrative, technical and scientific staff as it may consider necessary.
(3) The salaries, allowances and conditions of service of the officers and other staff appointed under sub-section (2) shall be such as may be prescribed by the State Government.

28. Annual and special reports of State Commission

(1) The State Commission shall submit an annual report to the State Government and may at any time submit special reports on any matter which, in its opinion, is of such urgency or importance that it should not be deferred till submission of the annual report.
(2) The State Government shall cause the annual and special reports of the State Commission to be laid before each House of State Legislature where it consists of two Houses, or where such Legislature consists of one House, before that House along with a memorandum of action taken or proposed to be taken on the recommendations of the State Commission and the reasons for non-acceptance of the reactions, if any.

29. Application of certain provisions relating to National Human Rights Commission to State Commissions

The provisions of sections 9, 10, 12, 13, 14, 15, 16, 17 and 18 shall apply to a State Commission and shall have effect, subject to the following modifications, namely:-
(a) references to "Commission" shall be construed as references to "State Commission";
(b) in section 10, in sub-section (3), for the word "Secretary General", the word "Secretary" shall be substituted;
(c) in section 12, clause (f) shall be omitted;

(d) in section 17, in clause (i), the words "Central Government or any" shall be omitted;

CHAPTER VI

HUMAN RIGHTS COURTS

30. For the purpose of providing speedy trial of offences arising out of violation of human rights, the State

Government may, with the concurrence of the Chief Justice of the High Court, by notification, specify for each district a Court of Session to be a Human Rights Court to try the said offences.
Provided that nothing in this section shall apply if
(a) a Court of Session is already specified as a special court; or
(b) a special court is already constituted, for such offences under any other law for the time being in force.

31. Special Public Prosecutor

For every Human Rights Court, the State Government shall, by notification, specify a Public Prosecutor or appoint an advocate who has been in practice as an advocate for not less than seven years, as a Special Public Prosecutor for the purpose of conducting cases in that Court.

CHAPTER VII

FINANCE, ACCOUNTS AND AUDIT

32. Grants by the Central Government

(1) The Central Government shall after due appropriation made by Parliament by law in this behalf, pay to the Commission by way of grants such sums of money as the Central Government may think fit for being utilised for the purposes of this Act.
(2) The Commission may spend such sums as it thinks fit for performing the functions under this Act, and such sums shall be treated as expenditure payable out of the grants referred to in sub-section (1).

33. Grants by the State Government

(1) The State Government shall, after due appropriation made by Legislature by law in this behalf, pay to the State Commission by way of grants such sums of money as the State Government may think fit for being utilised for the purposes of this Act.
(2) The State Commission may spend such sums as it thinks fit for performing the functions under Chapter V, and such sums shall be treated as expenditure payable out of the grants referred to in sub-section (1).

34. Accounts and Audit

(1) The Commission shall maintain proper accounts and other relevant records and prepare an annual statement of accounts in such form as may be prescribed by the Central Government in consultation with the Comptroller and Auditor-General of India.
(2) The Accounts of the Commission shall be audited by the Comptroller and Auditor-General at such intervals as may be specified by him and any expenditure incurred in connection with such audit shall be payable by the Commission to the Comptroller and Auditor-General.
(3) The Comptroller and Auditor-General or any person appointed by him in connection with the audit of the accounts of the Commission under this Act shall have the same rights and privileges and the authority in connection with such audit as the Comptroller and Auditor-General generally has in connection with the audit of Government accounts and, in particular, shall have the right to demand the production of books, accounts, connected vouchers and other documents and papers and to inspect any of the offices of the Commission.
(4) The accounts of the Commission as certified by the Comptroller and Auditor-General or any other person appointed by him in this behalf, together with the audit report thereon shall be forwarded only to the Central Government by the Commission and the Central Government shall cause the audit report to be laid as soon as may be after it is received before each House of Parliament.

35. Accounts and Audit of State Commission

(1) The State Commission shall maintain proper accounts and other relevant records and prepare an annual statement of accounts in such form as may be prescribed by the State Government in consultation with the Comptroller and Auditor-General of India.
(2) The accounts of the State Commission shall be audited by the Comptroller and Auditor-General at such intervals as may be specified by him and any expenditure incurred in connection with such audit shall be payable by the State Commission to the Comptroller and Auditor-General.
(3) The Comptroller and Auditor-General or any person appointed by him in connection with the audit of the accounts of the State Commission under this Act shall have the same rights and privileges and the authority in connection with such audit as the Comptroller and Auditor-General generally has in connection with the audit of Government accounts and, in particular, shall have the right to demand the production of books, accounts, connected vouchers and other documents and papers and to inspect any of the offices of the State Commission.
(4) The accounts of the State Commission, as certified by the Comptroller and Auditor-General or any other person appointed by him in this behalf, together with the audit report thereon, shall be forwarded annually to the State Government by the State Commission and the State Government shall cause the audit report to be laid, as soon as may be after it is received, before the State Legislature.

CHAPTER VIII

MISCELLANEOUS

36. Matters not subject to jurisdiction of the Commission

(1) The Commission shall not inquire into any matter which is pending before a State Commission or any other Commission duly constituted under any law for the time being in force.
(2) The Commission or the State Commission shall not inquire into any matter after the expiry of one year from the date on which the act constituting violation of human rights is alleged to have been committed.

37. Constitution of special investigation teams

Notwithstanding anything contained in any other law for the time being in force, where the Government considers it necessary so to do, it may constitute one or more special investigation teams, consisting of such police officers as it thinks necessary for purposes of investigation and prosecution of offences arising out of violations of human rights.

38. Protection of action taken in good faith

No suit or other legal proceeding shall lie against the Central Government, State Government, Commission, the State Commission or any Member thereof or any person acting under the direction either of the Central Government, State Government, Commission or the State Commission in respect of anything which is in good faith done or intended to be done in pursuance of this Act or of any rules or any order made thereunder or in respect of the publication by or under the authority of the Central Government, State Government, Commission or the State Commission of any report paper or proceedings.

39. Members and officers to be public servants

Every Member of the Commission, State Commission and every officer appointed or authorised by the Commission or the State Commission to exercise functions under this Act shall be deemed to be a public servant within the meaning of section 21 of the Indian Penal Code.

40. Power of Central Government to make rules

(1) The Central Government may, by notification, make rules to carry out the provisions of this Act.
(2) In particular and without prejudice to the generality of the foregoing power, such rules may provide for all or any of the following matters namely:

(a) the salaries and allowances and other terms and conditions of service of the Members under section 8;
(b) the conditions subject to which other administrative, technical and scientific staff may be appointed by the Commission and the salaries and allowances of officers and other staff under sub-section (3) of section 11;
(c) any other power of a civil court required to be prescribed under clause (f) of sub-section (1) of section 13;
(d) the form in which the annual statement of accounts is to be pre pared by the Commission under sub-section (1) of section 34; and
(e) any other matter which has to be, or may be, prescribed.
(3) Every rule made under this Act shall be laid, as soon as may be after it is made, before each House of Parliament, while it is in session, for a total period of thirty days which may be comprised in one session or in two or more successive sessions, and if, before the expiry of the session immediately following the session or the successive sessions aforesaid, both Houses agree in making any modification in the rule or both Houses agree that the rule should not be made, the rule shall thereafter have effect only in such modified form or be of no effect, as the case may be; so however, that any such modification or annulment shall be without prejudice to the validity of anything previously done under that rule.

41. Power of State Government to make rules

(1) The State Government may, by notification, make rules to carry out the provisions of this Act.
(2) In particular and without prejudice to the generality of the foregoing power, such rules may provide for all or any of the following matters, namely:
(a) the salaries and allowances and other terms and conditions of service of the members under section 26;
(b) the conditions subject to which other administrative, technical and scientific staff may be appointed by the State Commission and the salaries and allowances of officers and other staff under sub-section (3) of section 27;
(c) the form in which the annual statement of accounts is to be prepared under sub-section (1) of section 35.
(3) Every rule made by the State Government under this section shall be laid, as soon as may be after it is made, before each House of the State Legislature where it consists of two Houses, or where such Legislature consists of one House, before that House.

42. Power to remove difficulties

(1) If any difficulty arises in giving effect to the provisions of this Act, the Central Government, may by order published in the Official Gazette, make such provisions, not inconsistent with the provisions of this Act as appear to it to be necessary or expedient for removing the difficulty.

Provided that no such order shall be made after the expiry of the period of two years from the date of commencement of this Act.
(2) Every order made under this section shall, as soon as may be after it is made, be laid before each house of Parliament.

43. Repeal and Savings

(1) The Protection of Human Rights Ordinance, 1993 is hereby repealed.
(2) Notwithstanding such repeal, anything done or any action taken under the said Ordinance, shall be deemed to have been done or taken under the corresponding provisions of this Act.

THE HOUSE OF REPRESENTATIVES OF THE REPUBLIC OF INDONESIA

REPUBLIC OF INDONESIA

LEGISLATION

NUMBER 39 OF 1999

CONCERNING

HUMAN RIGHTS

WITH THE MERCY OF GOD ALMIGHTY

THE PRESIDENT OF THE REPUBLIC OF INDONESIA,

Considering:

a. whereas human beings, as creations of God Almighty charged with the task of managing and protecting the universe, with total devotion to and responsibility for the welfare of humanity, being His creation are bestowed with basic rights to guarantee their human dignity and worth, and harmony with their environment;

b. whereas human rights are basic rights bestowed by God on human beings, are universal and eternal in nature, and for this reason must be protected, respected and upheld, and may not be disregarded, diminished, or appropriated by anyone whosoever;

c. whereas besides basic rights, humans also have basic obligations to one another and to society as a whole, with regard to society, nation and state;

d. whereas as a member of the United Nations, the nation of Indonesia has a moral and legal responsibility to respect, execute, and uphold the Universal Declaration on Human Rights promulgated by the United Nations, and several other international instruments concerning human rights ratified by the Republic of Indonesia;

e. now, therefore, upon consideration of paragraphs a, b, and c, and to implement Decree of the People's Legislative Assembly of the Republic of Indonesia Number XVII/MPR/1998 concerning Human Rights, it is considered necessary to enact provisions in an Act concerning Human Rights;

In view of:

1. Article 5 clause (1), Article 20 clause (1), Article 27 clause (1) and clause (2), Article 28, Article 29 clause (1) and clause (2), Article 30, and Article 31, Article 32, Article 333 clause (1) and clause (3), and Article 34 of the 1945 Constitution;
2. Decree of the People's Legislative Assembly of the Republic of Indonesia No. XVII/MPR/1998 concerning Human Rights;

with approval of

THE HOUSE OF REPRESENTATIVES OF THE REPULIC OF INDONESIA

DECREES

To enact: **ACT CONCERNING HUMAN RIGHTS**

CHAPTER 1
GENERAL PROVISIONS

Article 1

The terms used in this Act have the following meanings:

1. Human rights mean a set of rights bestowed by God Almighty in the essence and being of humans as creations of God which must be respected, held in the highest esteem and protected by the state, law, Government, and all people in order to protect human dignity and worth.

2. Human obligations mean a set of obligations which, if not undertaken, would make it impossible for human rights to be executed and upheld.

3. Discrimination means all limitations, affronts or ostracism, both direct and indirect, on grounds of differences in religion, ethnicity, race, group, faction, social status, economic status, sex, language, or political belief, that results in the degradation, aberration, or eradication of recognition, execution, or application of human rights and basic freedoms in political, economic, legal, social, cultural, or any other aspects of life.

4. Torture means all deliberate acts that cause deep pain and suffering, both physical or emotional, inflicted on an individual person to obtain information or knowledge from that person or from a third party, by punishing an individual for an act carried out or suspected to have been carried out by an individual or third party, or by threatening or coercing an individual or third party, or for

reasons based on discriminative considerations, should this pain or suffering arise as a result of provocation by, with the approval of, or with the knowledge of any person or public official whosoever.

5. Children mean all unmarried persons under the age of 18, including, should this be in their interest, all unborn children.

6. Human rights violations mean all actions by individuals or groups of individuals, including the state apparatus, both intentional and unintentional, that unlawfully diminish, oppress, limit and/or revoke the human rights of an individual or group of individuals guaranteed by the provisions set forth in this Act, and who do not or may not obtain fair and total legal restitution under the prevailing legal mechanism.

CHAPTER II
BASIC RIGHTS

Article 2

The Republic of Indonesia acknowledges and holds in high esteem the rights and freedoms of humans as rights which are bestowed by God and which are an integral part of humans, which must be protected, respected, and upheld in the interests of promoting human dignity, prosperity, contentment, intellectual capacity and justice.

Article 3

(1) Everyone is born equal in dignity and human rights, and is bestowed with the intellect and reason to live with others in a spirit of brotherhood.

(2) Everyone has the right to be recognized, guaranteed, protected, and treated fairly before the law and is entitled to equal legal certitude and treatment before the law.

(3) Everyone has the right without any discrimination, to protection of human rights and obligations.

Article 4

The right to life, the right to not to be tortured, the right to freedom of the individual, to freedom of thought and conscience, the right not to be enslaved, the right to be acknowledged as an individual before the law, and the right not to be prosecuted retroactively under the law are human rights that cannot be diminished under any circumstances whatsoever.

Article 5

(1) Everyone is recognized as an individual who has the right to demand and obtain equal treatment and protection before the law as befits his or her human dignity.

(2) Everyone has the right to truly just support and protection from an objective, impartial judiciary.

(3) All members of disadvantaged groups in society, such as children, the poor, and the disabled, are entitled to greater protection of human rights.

Article 6

(1) In the interests of upholding human rights, the differences and needs of indigenous peoples must be taken into consideration and protected by the law, the public and the Government.

(2) The cultural identity of indigenous peoples, including indigenous land rights, must be upheld, in accordance with the development of the times.

Article 7

(1) Everyone has the right to use all effective national legal means and international forums against all violations of human rights guaranteed under Indonesian law, and under international law concerning human rights which has been ratified by Indonesia.

(2) Provisions set forth in international law concerning human rights ratified by the Republic of Indonesia, are recognized under this Act as legally binding in Indonesia.

Article 8

The principal responsibility for protecting, promoting, upholding, and fulfilling human rights lies with the Government.

INDONESIA

CHAPTER 3
HUMAN RIGHTS AND FREEDOMS

Section One

Right to Life

Article 9

(1) Everyone has the right to life, to sustain life, and to improve his or her standard of living.

(2) Everyone has the right to peace, happiness, and well-being.

(3) Everyone has the right to an adequate and healthy environment.

Section Two
Right to Marry and Bear Children

Article 10

(1) Everyone has the right to marry legally, to found a family, and to bear children.

(2) Marriage shall be entered into only with the free and full consent of the intending spouses, in accordance with prevailing legislation.

Section Three
Right to Self Development

Article 11

Everyone has the right to grow and develop in a way that he feels fit.

Article 12

Everyone has the right to protection of his self-development, to obtain an education, to educate himself, and to improve the quality of his life to become responsible, content, and prosperous people, in accordance with his human rights.

Article 13

Everyone has the right to develop and benefit from scientific knowledge and technology, arts and culture as befits human dignity, in the interests of his own welfare, and the welfare of the nation and humanity.

Article 14

(1) Everyone has the right to communicate and obtain information they need to develop themselves as individuals and to develop their social environment.

(2) Everyone has the right to seek, obtain, own, store, process, and impart information using all available facilities.

Article 15

Everyone has the right to develop himself by individually and collectively protecting his rights, in the interests of developing his society, nation, and state.

Article 16

Everyone has the right to undertake social and charitable works, to found organizations for this purpose, including organizing private schooling and education, and to raise funds for these purposes, in line with prevailing legislation.

Section Four

Right to Justice

Article 17

Everyone without discrimination, has the right to justice by submitting applications, grievances, and charges, of a criminal, civil, and administrative nature, and to a hearing by an independent and impartial tribunal, according to legal procedure that guarantees a hearing by a just and fair judge allowing an objective and impartial verdict to be reached.

Article 18

(1) Everyone arrested, detained, or charged for a penal offence has the right to be presumed innocent until proven guilty according to law in a trial at which he has had all the guarantees necessary for his defense, according to prevailing law.

(2) No one shall be charged or held guilty of a penal offence for any act or omission which did not constitute a penal offence under prevailing law, at the time when it was committed.

(3) Should any changes be made to law, the provisions most advantageous to the person held guilty shall apply.

(4) Everyone brought before a tribunal has the right to legal aid from the start of the hearing until a legally binding decision is made by the tribunal.

(5) No one shall be charged more than once for an action or omission concerning which a tribunal has previously made a legally binding decision.

Article 19

(1) No offender or criminal shall be threatened with punishment in the form of seizure of part or whole of assets he legally owns.

(2) No person found guilty by a tribunal shall be imprisoned or incarcerated for being unable to fulfill the obligations of a loan agreement.

Section Five
Right to Freedom of the Individual

Article 20

(1) No one shall be held in slavery or servitude.

(2) Slavery, the slave trade and servitude shall be prohibited in all their forms.

Article 21

Everyone has the right to integrity of the individual, both spiritual and physical, and as such shall not become the object of any research without his approval.

Article 22

(1) Everyone has the right to freedom to choose his religion and to worship according to the teachings of his religion and beliefs.

(2) The state guarantees everyone the freedom to choose and practice his religion and to worship according to his religion and beliefs.

Article 23

(1) Everyone has the freedom to choose and hold his political beliefs.

(2) Everyone has the freedom to hold, impart and widely disseminate his beliefs, orally or in writing through printed or electronic media, taking into consideration religious values, morals, law and order, the public interest and national unity.

Article 24

(1) Everyone has the right to peaceful assembly and association.

(2) Every citizen or group has the right to found a political party, non-government organization, or other organization in order to take part in the government or administration of the state and nation for the purpose of protecting and promoting human rights, according to prevailing law.

Article 25

Every citizen has the right to express his opinion in public, and this includes the right to strike, according to prevailing law.

Article 26

(1) Everyone has the right to have, obtain, change and maintain his nationality.

(2) Everyone has the freedom to choose his nationality, and without discrimination has the right to enjoy his rights as a citizen and is required to undertake his obligations as a citizen in accordance with the law.

Article 27

(1) All Indonesian citizens have the right to freedom of movement and residence within the borders of Indonesia.

(2) All Indonesian citizens have the right to leave and return to the Republic of Indonesia, according to prevailing law.

Section Six
The Right to Security

Article 28

(1) Everyone has the right to seek and receive political asylum from another country.

(2) The right as referred to in clause (1) does not apply perpetrators of non-political crimes or of acts that contravene the objectives and principles of the United Nations.

Article 29

(1) Everyone has the right to protection of the individual, his family, opinion, honor, dignity, and rights.

(2) Everyone has the right to recognition everywhere as a person before the law'

Article 30

Everyone has the right to security and protection against the threat of fear from any act or omission.

Article 31

(1) No one shall be subject to arbitrary interference with his home.

(2) No one shall set foot in or enter the enclosure of a house or enter a house without the permission of the person who lives there, except for reasons provided for under prevailing legislation.

Article 32

No one shall be subject to arbitrary interference with his correspondence, including electronic communications, except upon the order of a court or other legitimate authority according to prevailing legislation.

Article 33

(1) Everyone has the right to freedom from torture, or cruel, inhuman and degrading punishment or treatment.

(2) Everyone has the right to freedom from abduction and assassination.

Article 34

No one shall be subject to arbitrary arrest, detention, torture or exile.

Article 35

Everyone has the right to live in a peaceful, safe and secure society and nation which fully respects, protects and executes human rights and obligations as set forth in the provisions in this Act.

Section Seven
Right to Welfare

Article 36

(1) Everyone has the right to own property, both alone and in association with others, for the development of himself, his family, nation, and society through lawful means.

(2) No one shall be subjected to arbitrary or unlawful seizure of his property.

(3) The right to ownership has a social function.

Article 37

(1) The right to ownership of a property in the public interest shall not be revoked, except with the restoration of fair, proper and adequate compensation, based on prevailing legislation.

(2) In the event that in the public interest a property must be destroyed or abandoned, either permanently or temporarily, compensation shall be paid in accordance with prevailing legislation, unless otherwise decreed.

Article 38

(1) All citizens have the right to work as befits a human being, in line with his or her ability and capacity.

(2) Everyone has the right to free choice of employment and the right to just conditions of work.

(3) Everyone, both men and women, who works has the right to equal pay for equal work, and the right to equal work conditions.

(4) Everyone, both men and women, who works has the right to fair and adequate remuneration, ensuring for himself and his family an existence worthy of human dignity.

Article 39

Everyone has the right to form and join trade unions for the protection and promotion of his interests, in accordance with prevailing law.

Article 40

Everyone has the right to a place to live and the right to an adequate standard of living.

Article 41

(1) Everyone has the right to the social security necessary for an adequate existence and for the development of his well-being.

(2) The disabled, elderly, pregnant women and children have a right to special facilities and treatment.

Article 42

In the event of old age, physical and/or mental disability, every citizen has the right to special care, education, training and assistance at the expense of the state, ensuring an existence worthy of human dignity, and building his self confidence and capacity to participate in the life of nation, state, and society.

Section Eight
Right to Participate in Government

Article 43

(1) Every citizen has the right to vote and be voted for in general elections and has equal rights to a direct, free, secret, fair and just vote, in accordance with prevailing law.

(2) Every citizen has the right to participate in government either directly or through his freely elected representative, in ways laid down by provisions set forth in legislation.

(3) Every citizen has the right to be appointed to any position in the government.

Article 44

Every citizen, both individually and collectively, has the right to submit orally or in writing requests, complaints and/or proposals to the government for the implementation of a clean, effective and efficient government, in line with prevailing legislation.

Section Nine
Women's Rights

Article 45

Under this Act, women's rights are human rights.

Article 46

The general election system, political party system, system of electing members of people's representative organizations, and the system of appointing executives, judges and civil servants must ensure that women are adequately represented.

Article 47

The nationality of a woman married to a foreign citizen shall not automatically change to that of her husband; rather, she has the right to maintain, change, or re-gain her nationality.

Article 48

Women and men have equal rights to adequate access to and conditions of schooling and education.

Article 49

(1) Women have the right to select, be selected and appointed to an adequate job, position or a profession, in line with prevailing law.

(2) Women have the right to special protection in the undertaking of work or a profession that could put her safety and/or her reproductive health.

(3) The special rights to which women are entitled arising from their reproductive function are guaranteed and protected by law.

Article 50

Women of full age and/or who are married have the authority to take both criminal and civil legal action as individuals, unless determined otherwise under religious law.

Article 51

(1) During marriage, a wife and husband have equal rights and responsibilities with regard to all aspects of marriage, contact with their children, and rights to joint control of assets.

(2) Following dissolution of marriage, a wife and her former husband have equal rights and responsibilities with regard to all matters concerning their children, taking into account the best interests of the child.

(3) Following dissolution of marriage, a wife and her former husband have equal rights with regard to all matters concerning joint assets while not undermining children's rights, in accordance with prevailing law.

Section Ten
Children's Rights

Article 52

(1) All children have the right to protection by parents, family, society, and state.

(2) Children's rights are human rights which in the children's interest are recognized and protected before the law at the time of conception.

Article 53

(1) From conception, every child has the right to life, to maintain life and to improve his standard of living.

(2) From birth, every child has the right to a name and nationality.

Article 54

In the event of physical and/or mental disability, every child has the right to special care, education, training and assistance at the expense of the state, ensuring an existence worthy of human dignity, and building his self confidence and capacity to participate in the life of nation, state, and society.

Article 55

Every child has the right to practice his religion, and to think and express himself as befits his intellectual capacity and age under the guidance of a parent or guardian.

Article 56

(1) Every child has the right to know who his parents are and to be brought up and cared for by his own parents.

(2) Should the parents of a child not be able to bring up and care for their child adequately and in accordance with the provision set forth in this Act, the child concerned may be fostered and/or adopted by another person, based on and in accordance with procedures laid down in prevailing legislation.

Article 57

(1) Every child has the right to be raised, cared for, educated and guided through life by his parents or guardian until he is of full age, in accordance with prevailing legislation.

(2) Should both the parents of a child die before he is of full age, or should both parents be unable for a valid reason to fulfill their obligations as parents, the courts shall appoint the child a guardian or foster parent.

(3) Foster parent or guardians as referred to in clause (2) are responsible for properly fulfilling all the obligations of a parent.

Article 58

(1) Every child has the right to protection before the law against all forms of physical and mental violence, neglect, mistreatment and sexual assault while under the care of his parents, guardian, or any other party responsible for his care.

(2) Should a child's parent, guardian, or benefactor commit any form of physical or mental abuse; neglect; mistreatment; sexual assault, including rape; or murder of a child under his protection, he shall be subject to maximum legal sanctions.

Article 59

(1) Every child has the right not to be separated from his parents against his wishes, except for valid legal reasons and procedures indicating that this separation is in the best interests of the child.

(2) Under the circumstances referred to in clause (1), the child's right to regular direct meetings and individual contact with his parents is guaranteed and protected by the provisions set forth in this Act.

Article 60

(1) Every child has the right to access to education and schooling as befits his interests, talents, and intellectual capacity.

(2) Every child has the right to seek, receive, and impart information as befits his intellectual capacity and age in the interests of his own development, insofar as this meets moral requirements.

Article 61

Every child has the right to rest and mix with children of his own age, and to play and create as befits his intellectual capacity in the interests of his own development.

Article 62

Every child has the right to access to adequate health services and social security as befits his physical, emotional and spiritual needs.

Article 63

Every child has the right not to be involved in war, armed conflict, social unrest, and other incidents involving violence.

Article 64

Every child has the right to protection from financial exploitation, and from doing any work which is dangerous and/or which could interfere with his education or his physical, mental, or spiritual health.

Article 65

Every child has the right to protection from sexual exploitation and abuse, abduction and child trading, and from the misuse of narcotics, psychotropics, and other addictive substances.

Article 66

(1) Every child has the right not to be the object of oppression, torture, or inhuman legal punishment.

(2) Sentence of death or life imprisonment shall not be handed down child offenders.

(3) Every child has the right not to have his freedom unlawfully taken from him.

(4) Children may be arrested, detained, or jailed only in accordance with prevailing legislation and only as a measure of last resort.

(5) Every child whose freedom is taken from him has the right to humane treatment, as befits the personal development needs of his age, and shall not be separated from his parents unless this is in his own interest.

(6) Every child whose freedom is taken from him has the right to access effective legal or other aid at every stage of ongoing legal proceedings.

(7) Every child whose freedom is taken from him has the right to defend himself and to access to a private hearing before an objective and impartial Child Tribunal.

CHAPTER IV
HUMAN OBLIGATIONS

Article 67

Everyone within the territory of the Republic of Indonesia is required to comply with Indonesian legislation and Indonesian Law, including unwritten law and international law concerning human rights ratified by Indonesia.

Article 68

Every citizen is required to participate in measures to defend the state in accordance with prevailing legislation.

Article 69

(1) Everyone is required to respect the human rights of others, and social, national, and state morals, ethics and order.

(2) Every human right gives rise to the basic obligation and responsibility to uphold the human rights of others, and it is the duty of government to respect, protect uphold and promote these rights and obligations.

Article 70

In executing his rights and obligations, everyone shall observe the limitations set forth in the provisions in this Act, in order to ensure that the rights and freedoms of others are respected, and in the interests of justice, taking into account the moral, security, and public order considerations of a democratic society.

CHAPTER V

GOVERNMENT DUTIES AND OBLIGATIONS

Article 71

The government shall respect, protect, uphold and promote human rights as laid down in this Act, other legislation, and international law concerning human rights ratified by the Republic of Indonesia.

Article 72

The duties and responsibilities of the government as referred to in Article 71, include measures towards effective implementation in law, politics, economics, social and cultural aspects, state security, and other areas.

CHAPTER VI

LIMITATIONS AND PROHIBITIONS

Article 73

The rights and freedoms governed by the provisions set forth in this Act may be limited only by and based on law, solely for the purposes of guaranteeing recognition and respect for the basic rights and freedoms of another person, fulfilling moral requirements, or in the public interest.

Article 74

No provisions set forth in this Act shall be interpreted to mean that the government, or any political parties, factions, or any party whosoever is permitted to degrade, impair or eradicate the basic rights and freedoms governed by this Act.

CHAPTER VII

THE NATIONAL COMMISSION ON HUMAN RIGHTS

Article 75

The National Commission on Human Rights aims to:

a. develop conditions conducive to the execution of human rights in accordance with Pancasila, the 1945 Constitution, the United Nations Charter, and the Universal Declaration of Human Rights; and,
b. improve the protection and upholding of human rights in the interests of the personal development of Indonesian people as a whole and their ability to participate in several aspects of life.

Article 76

(1) To achieve these aims, the National Commission on Human Rights functions to study, research, disseminate, monitor and mediate human rights issues.

(2) Members of the National Commission on Human Rights are drawn from public figures who are professional, dedicated, have a high level of integrity, who fully who fully comprehend the aspirations of a democratic and welfare state based on justice, and who respect human rights and obligations.

(3) The National Commission on Human Rights is domiciled in the capital city of the Republic of Indonesia.

(4) Representative offices of the National Commission on Human Rights may be established in the regions.

Article 77

The National Commission on Human Rights is based on the principles of Pancasila.

Article 78

(1) The National Commission on Human Rights comprises:
  a. Plenary Council; and
  b. Sub-commissions.

(2) The National Commission on Human Rights has a Secretary General for the provision of services.

Article 79

(1) The Plenary Council is holder of the highest authority in the National Commission on Human Rights

(2) The Plenary Council consists of all members of the National Commission on Human Rights.

(3) The Plenary Council determines the Rules and Regulations, Work Program and Work Mechanism of the National Commission on Human Rights.

Article 80

(1) The activities of the National Commission on Human Rights are implemented by Sub-commissions.

(2) Provisions governing these Sub-commissions are set forth in the Rules and Regulations of the National Commission on Human Rights.

Article 81

(1) The Secretariat General provides administrative services for the implementation of the operations of the National Commission on Human Rights.

(2) The Secretariat General is headed by a Secretary General who is assisted by work units in the form of bureaus;

(3) The position of Secretary General is held by a Civil Servant who is not a Member of the National Commission on Human Rights.

(4) The Secretary General is appointed by the Plenary Council and this appointment shall be ratified in a Presidential Decree.

(5) The position, duties, responsibilities and organizational structure of the Secretariat General shall be set forth in a Presidential Decree.

Article 82

Provisions concerning the Plenary Council and Sub-commissions are set forth in greater detail in the Rules and Regulations of the National Commission on Human Rights.

Article 83

(1) The National Commission on Human Rights comprises 35 (thirty five) members selected by the House of Representatives of the Republic of Indonesia based on the recommendation of the National Commission on Human Rights, and validated by the President as Head of State.

(2) The National Commission on Human Rights is headed by a Chair and two Vice-Chairs.

(3) The Chair and the Vice-Chairs are elected by and from among the Members.

(4) The Chair, Vice-Chairs, and Members serve for a period of five years, and may be re-appointed for a further five-year period.

Article 84

Those eligible for appointment as members of the National Commission on Human Rights are Indonesian citizens who:

a. have experience in the promotion and protection of individuals or groups whose human rights have been violated;
b. are experienced as lawyers, judges, police, attorneys, or other members of the legal profession;
c. are experienced in legislative and executive affairs and in the affairs of high level state institutions; or
d. are religious figures, public figures, members of NGOs, or from higher education establishments.

Article 85

(1) Discharge of a Member of the National Commission on Human Rights is based on the resolution of the Plenary Council and shall be made known to the House of Representatives and ratified by a Presidential Decree.

(2) A Member may be discharged:

a. in the event of his/her death;
b. upon the request of the Member him/herself;
c. in the event that prolonged psychological or spiritual ill-health prevents the member from carrying out his duties consecutively for a period of one year;
d. in the event that he perpetrates a gross criminal act; or
e. in the event that he/she perpetrates a reprehensible act or other act which the Plenary Council deems to besmirch the dignity and reputation, and/or diminish the independence and credibility of the National Commission on Human Rights.

Article 86

Provisions concerning the election, appointment, and discharge of Members and leadership of the National Commission on Human Rights are set forth in the Rules and Regulations of the National Commission on Human Rights.

Article 87

(1) All Members of the National Commission on Human Rights are required to:

a. study prevailing legislation and decrees of the National Commission on Human Rights;
b. participate actively and sincerely towards attaining the objectives of the National Commission on Human Rights;
c. maintain confidentiality of information that by nature is a secret of the National Commission on Human Rights obtained based on his position as a member.

(2) All Members of the National Commission on Human Rights have the right to:
a. submit proposals and ideas to the Plenary Council and Sub-commissions;
b. provide input into the decision making of the Plenary Council and Sub-commissions;
c. propose nominees for and elect the Chair and Vice-Chairs on the Plenary Council;
d. nominate prospective Members of the National Commission on Human Rights for interim and regular replacement.

Article 88

Provisions concerning the rights and obligations of members of the National Commission on Human Rights are set forth in greater detail in the Rules and Regulations of the National Commission on Human Rights.

Article 89

(1) To carry out the functions of the National Commission on Human Rights with realize aims as referred to in Article 76, the National Commission on Human Rights has the authority to:
a. study and examine international human rights instruments with the aim of providing recommendations concerning their possible accession and ratification;
b. study and examine legislation in order to provide recommendations concerning drawing up, amending and revoking of legislation concerning human rights;
c. publish study and examination reports;
d. carry out literature studies, field studies, and comparative studies with other countries;
e. discuss issues related to protecting, upholding and promoting human rights; and,
f. conduct cooperative research and examination into human rights with organizations, institutions or other parties, at regional, national and international levels.

(2) To carry out its function as disseminator as referred to in Article 76 , the National Commission on Human Rights is charged with and authorized to:

a. disseminate information concerning human rights to the Indonesian public;
b. take steps to raise public awareness about human rights through formal and non-formal education institutes and other bodies;
c. cooperate with organizations, institutions or other parties at national, regional and international level with regard human rights;

(3) To carry out its supervisory function as referred to in Article 76, the National Commission on Human Rights is charged with and authorized to:
a. monitor the execution of human rights and compile reports of the output of this monitoring;
b. investigate and examine incidents occurring in society which either by their nature or scope likely constitute violations of human rights;
c. call on complainants, victims and accused to request and hear their statements;
d. call on witnesses to request and hear their witness statements, and in the case of prosecution witness to request submission of necessary evidence;
e. survey incident locations and other locations as deemed necessary;
f. call on related parties to give written statements or to submit necessary authenticated documents as required upon approval of the Head of Court;
g. examine houses, yards, buildings, and other places that certain parties reside in or own, upon approval of the Head of Court;
h. on approval of the Head of Court, provide input into particular cases currently undergoing judicial process if the case involves violation of human rights of public issue and court investigation, and the input of the National Commission on Human Rights shall be made known to the parties by the judge;

(4) To carry out its function as mediator as referred to in Article 76, the National Commission on Human Rights is charged with and authorized to:
a. arbitrate between the two parties;
b. resolve cases through consultation, negotiation, mediation, conciliation and expert evaluation;
c. give recommendations to the parties for resolving conflict through the courts;
d. submit recommendations concerning cases of human rights violations to the Government in order that their resolution may be followed up on;
e. submit recommendations concerning cases of human rights violations to the House of Representatives of the Republic of Indonesia for their follow up.

Article 90

(4) All people and groups of people who have strong grounds that their human rights have been violated may submit an oral or written complaint to the National Commission on Human Rights.

(5) Complaints will be dealt with only if the true identity of the complainant is made known, and if adequate and clear evidence/statement of the subject matter of the complaint is provided.

(6) In the case in which a complaint is made by a third party, the complaint must have the approval of the party whose rights have been violated as victim, with the exception of certain human rights violations as based on the consideration of the National Commission on Human Rights.

(7) Violation of human rights as referred to in clause (3) also covers complaints made by proxy concerning violation of human rights experienced by the public

Article 91

(1) Investigation shall not be undertaken, or shall be suspended if already underway, in the event that:
  a. there is insufficient evidence;
  b. the subject matter of the complaint is not a violation of human rights;
  c. the complaint is not presented in good faith, or if the complainant is not in earnest;
  d. more effective legal measures are available to resolve the complaint;
  e. resolution through available legal means, in accordance with the law.

(2) The mechanism for executing the authority not to undertake or to suspend investigation as referred to in clause (1) is set forth in the Rules and Regulations of the National Commission on Human Rights.

Article 92

(2) In certain cases and if deemed necessary to protect the interests and rights of those involved, or to realize the resolution of an issue, the National Commission on Human Rights may decide to keep confidential the identity of the complainant, those providing statements or other evidence, and parties related to the subject matter of the complaint or monitoring.

(3) The National Commission on Human Rights may decide to keep confidential or restrict dissemination of a statement or other evidence obtained by the National Commission on Human Rights which is related to the subject matter of the complaint or monitoring.

(4) Decision as referred to in clause (2) is based on the consideration that dissemination of the statement or other evidence could:
  a. endanger state security and safety;

b. endanger public safety and order;
c. endanger the safety of an individual;
d. besmirch the good name of an individual;
e. divulge state secrets or other matters which must be kept confidential in the government decision-making process;
f. divulge matters which must be kept confidential in the process of investigating, litigating, and trying a criminal case;
g. hamper the resolution of an existing issue;
h. divulge matters of trade secret.

Article 93

Investigation of human rights violations is to be closed, unless deemed otherwise by the National Commission on Human Rights.

Article 94

(1) Complainants, victims, witnesses and other related parties as referred to in Article 89 clause (3) letters c and d, are required to meet the request of the National Commission on Human Rights.

(2) Should the requirement referred to in clause (1) not be met, the party in question shall be subject to the provisions set forth in Article 95.

Article 95

Should a person called on fail to appear or refuse to give a statement, the National Commission on Human Rights may seek the assistance of the Head of Court to enforce its request, in accordance with prevailing law.

Article 96

(1) Resolution as referred to in Article 89 clause (4) letters a and b, shall be carried out by a Member of the National Commission on Human Rights appointed as mediator;

(2) Resolution reached as referred to in clause (1) shall be in the form of a written agreement signed by both parties and validated by the mediator;

(3) Written agreement as referred to in clause (2) constitutes a mediation settlement which is legally binding and officially valid;

(4) In the event that a mediation settlement is not executed by one of the parties within the period of time set forth in the settlement, the other party may entreat

the local District Court to declare that this settlement be executed, by appending the words, “For the Justice of God Almighty”.

(5) A Court may not refuse the request referred to in clause (4).

Article 97

The National Commission on Human Rights is required to submit annual reports on concerning the execution of its functions, tasks and authority, and on the condition of human rights and on cases handled to the House of Representatives and the President, and submit carbon copies to the Supreme Court.

Article 98

The budget for the National Commission on Human Rights shall come from the National Budget.

Article 99

Provisions and regulations concerning the functions, tasks and authority of the National Commission on Human Rights are set forth in the Rules and Regulations of the National Commission on Human Rights.

CHAPTER VIII
PUBLIC PARTICIPATION

Article 100

All people, groups, political organizations, community organizations, and self-reliant organizations and other non-government organizations, have the right to participate in protecting, upholding and promoting human rights.

Article 101

All people, groups, political organizations, community organizations, and self-reliant organizations and other non-government organizations, have the right to submit reports of human rights violations to the National Commission on Human Rights or other competent agency, in the interests of protecting, upholding and promoting human rights.

Article 102

All people, groups, political organizations, community organizations, and self-reliant organizations and other non-government organizations, have the right to submit proposals to concerning matters and policy related to human rights to the National Commission on Human Rights or other agency.

Article 103

All people, groups, political organizations, community organizations, and self-reliant organizations, higher educational institutes, study agencies or other non-government organization, both individually and in cooperation with the National Commission on Human Rights, have the right to study, educate and disseminate information about human rights.

CHAPTER IX
HUMAN RIGHTS TRIBUNAL

Article 104

(1) To hear gross violations of human rights, a Human Rights Tribunal shall be set up in the domain of the District Court;

(2) Tribunal as referred to in clause (1) shall be established under law within a period of 4 (four) years.

(3) Prior to the establishment of the Human Rights Tribunal referred to in clause (2), cases of human rights violations as referred to in clause (1) shall be heard by an authorized tribunal.

CHAPTER X
TRANSITIONAL PROVISIONS

Article 105

(1) All provisions concerning human rights set forth in other legislation shall remain valid insofar as these are governed by this Act.

(2) At the time this Act comes into force:

a. the National Commission of Human Rights established based on Presidential Decree No. 50 of 1993 concerning the National Commission on Human Rights shall be deemed the National Commission on Human Rights according to this Act;
b. the Chair, Vice-Chairs, and Members of the National Commission on Human Rights shall continue to carry out their functions, tasks and authority according to this Act until such time new members of the National Commission on Human Rights are appointed;

c. all issues currently being handled by the National Commission on Human Rights shall continue to be resolved according to the provisions set forth in this Act.

(3) Within 2 (two) years of this Act coming into force, the organizational structure, membership, tasks and authority, and regulations of the National Commission on Human Rights must be brought into accordance with this Act.

CHAPTER XI
CONCLUDING PROVISIONS

Article 106

This Act comes into force on the date of its enactment.

For the public to be informed, it is ordered that this Act be promulgated in the State Gazette of the Republic of Indonesia.

Ratified in Jakarta,
23 September 1999

PRESIDENT OF THE REPUBLIC OF INDONESIA

BAHARUDDIN JUSUF HAIBIBIE

Enacted in Jakarta
23 September 1999

SECRETARY FOR STATE

MULADI

STATE GAZETTE OF THE REPUBLIC OF INDONESIA NUMBER 165 OF 1999

REPUBLIC OF KOREA

NATIONAL HUMAN RIGHTS COMMISSION ACT
ACT NO. 6481, MAY 24, 2001

CHAPTER 1 GENERAL PROVISIONS

Article 1 (Purpose)
The purpose of this Act is to contribute to the embodiment of human dignity and worth as well as to the safeguard of the basic order of democracy, by establishing the National Human Rights Commission to ensure that inviolable, fundamental human rights of all individuals are protected and the standards of human rights are improved.

Article 2 (Definitions)
The definitions of terms used in this Act shall be as follows:
1. The term "human rights" means any of human dignity, worth, liberties and rights which are guaranteed by the Constitution and Acts of the Republic of Korea or recognized by international human rights treaties entered into and ratified by the Republic of Korea and international customary law;
2. The term "detention or protective facility" means a facility falling under any of the following items:
  (a) Prison, prison for the youth, detention center and its branch, facility for probation, institute of forensic psychiatry, juvenile reformatory, and juvenile classification review board;
  (b) Police station cell, and facility where a judicial police officer investigates, detains and impounds persons in order to perform his/her duties;
  (c) Military prison (including its branch, detention house for the unconvicted, and military police guardhouse);
  (d) House for protecting foreigners; and
  (e) Protective facility for many persons; and
3. The term "protective facility for many persons" means a facility for detaining and caring for many persons□which is prescribed by the Presidential Decree.

Article 3 (Establishment and Independence of National Human Rights Commission)
(1) The National Human Rights Commission (hereinafter referred to the "Commission") shall be established to deal with affairs for the protection and promotion of human rights under this Act.
(2) The Commission independently deals with the matters which fall under its jurisdiction.

Article 4 (Scope of Application)
This Act shall apply to all citizens of the Republic of Korea and all foreigners residing therein.

CHAPTER 2 ORGANIZATION AND OPERATION OF COMMISSION

Article 5 (Organization of Commission)
(1) The Commission shall be comprised of eleven commissioners for human rights (hereinafter referred to as a "commissioner") including one president and three full-time commissioners.
(2) Four persons selected by the National Assembly (including two full-time commissioners), four persons nominated by the President of the Republic of Korea, and three persons nominated by the Chief Justice of the Supreme Court, from among those persons who have professional knowledge and experience on the matters of human rights and are recognized to be capable of performing duties of human rights protection and promotion fairly and independently, shall be appointed by the President of the Republic of Korea to be commissioners.
(3) The president of the Commission shall be appointed by the President of the Republic of Korea from among the commissioners.
(4) The president and full-time commissioners of the Commission shall be appointed as public officials in political service.
(5) Four or more of the commissioners shall be women.
(6) In case the term of office of a commissioner expires, he/she shall continuously perform his/her duties until his/her successor is appointed.

Article 6 (Duties of President of Commission)
(1) The president of the Commission shall represent the Commission and exercise the overall control of the affairs thereof.
(2) In case the president of the Commission is unable to perform his/her duties for any inevitable reason, a full-time commissioner, whom the president designates in advance, shall act on behalf of the president.
(3) The president of the Commission may attend the National Assembly and state opinions on affairs falling under the jurisdiction of the Commission, and shall, if required by the National Assembly, attend thereat and make a report or reply.
(4) The president of the Commission may attend the State Council, present his/her opinion and recommend the Prime Minister to submit any bill related to affairs under the jurisdiction of the Commission (including the draft of the Presidential Decree concerning the enforcement of this Act).
(5) When the president of the Commission performs duties related to the budget of the Commission, he/she shall be deemed to be the head of a central government office under the provision of Article 14 of the Budget and Accounts Act.

Article 7 (Term of Office of President and Commissioners)
(1) The term of office of the president and commissioners of the Commission shall be three years, but the consecutive appointment may be extended for one extra term only.
(2) In case the term of office of a commissioner expires or there occurs a vacancy, the President of the Republic of Korea shall appoint a successor within 30 days after the date of such expiration or vacancy.
(3) The term of office of the commissioner who is appointed as successor of a vacancy shall start anew. (The date of enforcement is November 25, 2001.)

Article 8 (Status Guarantee of Commissioner)
A commissioner shall not be removed from his/her office against his/her will unless he/she is sentenced to imprisonment without labor or a heavier punishment: *Provided*, That in case it is very difficult or impossible for him/her to perform his/her duties due to any physical or mental handicap, he/she may retire from his/her office by the resolution of consent of 2/3 or more of all commissioners.

Article 9 (Disqualifications for Commissioner)
(1) A person who falls under any of the following subparagraphs shall be disqualified for a commissioner:
1. A person other than a citizen of the Republic of Korea;
2. A person who falls under any subparagraph of Article 33 of the State Public Officials Act;
3. A member of a political party;
4. A person who is registered as a candidate in any such election as held under the Act on the Election of Public Officials and the Prevention of Election Malpractices.
(2) In case a commissioner comes to fall under any subparagraph of paragraph (1) above, he/she shall, *ipso facto*, retire from his/her office.

Article 10 (Prohibition of Concurrent Offices of Commissioner)
(1) A commissioner shall neither concurrently take the office falling under any of the following subparagraphs nor perform the duties thereof during his/her office:
1. A member of the National Assembly or any local council;
2. A public official of any other state organ or a local government (excluding a public official for education); and
3. Other positions or affairs as determined by the rule of the Commission.
(2) The commissioners shall neither join a political party nor participate in political activities.

Article 11 (Restriction on Retired Human Rights Commissioner's Taking Public Office)
For two years after a commissioner retires from his/her office, he/she shall neither be appointed to be a public official other than a public official for education nor run

for a candidate in any election under the Act on the Election of Public Officials and the Prevention of Election Malpractices.

Article 12 (Subcommittees)
(1) The Commission may establish subcommittees in order to have them perform parts of the affairs of the Commission.
(2) A subcommittee shall be composed of three commissioners, and necessary matters concerning its affairs and operation shall be prescribed by the rule of the Commission.

Article 13 (Meeting Proceedings and Resolution Quorum)
(1) The president of the Commission shall preside over the meeting of the Commission and the resolution thereof shall, except as otherwise provided by this Act, require the consent of a majority of all the incumbent commissioners.
(2) The resolution of the meeting of a subcommittee shall require the attendance and consent of all the members thereof.

Article 14 (Publication of Proceedings)
The proceedings of the Commission shall be made public: *Provided*, That they may not be made public if deemed necessary by the Commission or a subcommittee.

Article 15 (Advisory Organ)
(1) The Commission may establish an advisory organ in order to ask advice on matters which are necessary for the performance of its duties.
(2) Necessary matters concerning the organization and operation of the advisory organ shall be prescribed by the rule of the Commission.

Article 16 (Secretariat)
(1) A Secretariat shall be established to deal with general affairs of the Commission.
(2) There shall be one Secretary General and necessary staff members in the Secretariat and the Secretary General shall be appointed by the President of the Republic of Korea on the recommendation of the president of the Commission with the deliberation of the Commission.
(3) Public officials in Grade or higher from among the staff belonging to the Secretariat shall be appointed by the President of the Republic of Korea on the recommendation of the president of the Commission and those in Grade □ or lower shall be appointed by the president of the Commission.
(4) The Secretary General shall, under the direction of the president of the Commission, exercise the overall control of the affairs of the Secretariat and command and supervise the staff belonging thereto.

Article 17 (Establishment of Disciplinary Committee)
(1) Under the Commission, there shall be established a disciplinary committee to resolve on a disciplinary action against the staff belonging to the Commission.

(2) The composition, authority and deliberation procedure of the disciplinary committee, kinds and effects of disciplinary actions and other necessary matters therefore shall be prescribed by the rule of the Commission.

Article 18 (Organization and Operation of Commission)
Except as provided by this Act, matters necessary for the organization of the Commission shall be prescribed by the Presidential Decree and those necessary for its operation shall be prescribed by the rule of the Commission.

CHAPTER 3 DUTIES AND AUTHORITIES OF COMMISSION

Article 19 (Duties)
The Commission shall perform duties falling under the following subparagraphs:

1. Investigation and research with respect to statutes(including bills submitted to the National Assembly), legal systems, policies and practices related to human rights, and recommendation for their improvement or presentation of opinions thereon;
2. Investigation and remedy with respect to human rights violations;
3. Investigation and remedy with respect to discriminatory acts;
4. Survey on human rights conditions;
5. Education and public awareness on human rights;
6. Presentation and recommendation of guidelines for categories of human rights violations, standards for their identification and preventive measures therefor;
7. Research and recommendation or presentation of opinions with respect to the accession of any international treaty on human rights and the implementation of the treaty;
8. Cooperation with organizations and individuals engaged in any activity to protect and promote human rights;
9. Exchange and cooperation with international organizations related to human rights and human rights institutions of other countries; and
10. Other matters deemed necessary to protect and improve human rights.

Article 20 (Consultation with State Organs)
(1) If the head of a related state administrative organ or local government intends to enact or amend any statute which includes contents likely to affect the protection and promotion of human rights, he/she shall notify the Commission in advance.
(2) The Commission may, if deemed necessary for the performance of its duties, request state organs, local governments and other public or private organizations (hereinafter referred to as "related entities") to consult with it.
(3) Those related entities which receive a request under paragraph (2) shall faithfully comply therewith unless there exists any justifiable reason.

Article 21 (Hearing of Commission's Opinion in Preparing Governmental Report)
If a related state organ prepares a governmental report under the provisions of any international treaty on human rights, it shall hear opinions of the Commission.

Article 22 (Submission of Materials and Reference for Information)
(1) The Commission may, if deemed necessary for the performance of its duties, require the related entities to submit necessary materials to it or refer to the said entities for information.
(2) The Commission may require any person who is deemed to know the facts necessary for the performance of its duties or to have professional knowledge or experience to present himself/herself in order to hear his/her statement.
(3) Those entities which are so required or referred to under paragraph (1) shall, without delay, comply with such requirement or reference.

Article 23 (Hearing)
(1) The Commission may, if deemed necessary for the performance of its duties, require the representative of the related entity, the interested persons or other persons who have much knowledge and experience on relevant matters to present themselves and hear the statements of the relevant facts and opinions from them.
(2) The procedures and methods of hearings held by the Commission under paragraph (1) above shall be prescribed by the rule of the Commission.

Article 24 (Visit and Investigation of Facilities)
(1) The Commission(including a subcommittee) may, if deemed necessary, visit detention or protective facilities to conduct an investigation by its resolution.
(2) A commissioner, who visits and investigates under paragraph (1), may be accompanied by members of the staff of the Commission and experts, who are deemed necessary to perform their duties, and may delegate the investigation on any matter to them by specifying its scope. In this case, the experts as so delegated shall, if investigating the said matter, be accompanied by members of the staff of the Commission.
(3) The commissioner, member of the staff of the Commission or expert, who visits and investigates under paragraph (2)(hereinafter referred to as the "commissioner, etc." in this Article), shall show the interested persons an identification verifying his/her authority to do so, and the head or administrator of a detention or protective facility visited and investigated by the commissioner, etc. shall immediately provide conveniences necessary for such visit and investigation.
(4) The commissioner, etc., who visits and investigates under paragraph (2), may hold an interview with staff members concerned or detainees of the relevant detention or protective facility (hereinafter referred to as a "facility detainee") and also may have them present oral or written statements or opinions.
(5) Staff members concerned of the relevant detention or protective facility may be present at an interview with detainees held by the commissioner, etc.: *Provided*, That it shall be prohibited to record the contents of the said interview.

(6) Other necessary matters for the procedures and methods of visit and investigation of detention or protective facilities shall be prescribed by the Presidential Decree.

Article 25 (Recommendation of Improvement or Rectification of Policies and Practices)
(1) The Commission may, if deemed necessary to protect and promote human rights, recommend related entities to improve or rectify specific policies and practices, or may present opinions thereon.
(2) The heads of related entities receiving any recommendation under paragraph (1) shall respect and endeavor to implement the said recommendation.
(3) In case the heads of related entities receiving any recommendation under paragraph (1) fail to implement the said recommendation, they shall clarify the reasons for such failure to the Commission in writing.
(4) The Commission may, if deemed necessary, publish its recommendation and presented opinions under paragraph (1) and the reasons clarified by the heads of related entities under paragraph (3).

Article 26 (Education and Public Awareness on Human Rights)
(1) The Commission shall conduct the education and raise public awareness necessary to awaken and enhance everyone's consciousness of human rights.
(2) The Commission may consult with the Minister of Education and Human Resources Development to include contents concerning human rights in the curriculum of schools under the provision of Article 23 of the Elementary and Secondary Education Act.
(3) The Commission may consult with the heads of schools established under the provision of Article 2 of the Higher Education Act on necessary matters for the development of human rights education and research.
(4) The Commission may consult with the heads of related state organs or local governments to include subject-matters of human rights in employment or promotion examinations and training or education courses for public officials.
(5) The Commission may, in consultation with the heads of research institutions or study associations established under the Act on the Establishment, Operation and Fosterage of Government-Invested Research Institutions, etc., make a request for researches on human rights to them or carry out such researches jointly with them.
(6) The Commission may recommend the organizations or facilities for social education under the Social Education Act to include subject-matters of human rights in their education programs.

Article 27 (Center for Human Rights Materials)
(1) The Commission may establish a center for human rights materials.
(2) The center for human rights materials shall collect, arrange and preserve domestic and foreign information and data concerning human rights, and may provide them to the public.

(3) The center for human rights materials shall be deemed to be a library under the Libraries and Reading Promotion Act.
(4) Necessary matters for the establishment and operation of the center for human rights materials shall be prescribed by the rule of the Commission.

Article 28 (Presentation of Opinions to Courts and Constitutional Court)
(1) In case a trial, which significantly affects the protection and promotion of human rights, is pending, the Commission may, if requested by a court or the Constitutional Court or if deemed necessary by the Commission, present its opinions on *de jure* matters to the competent division of the court or the Constitutional Court.
(2) In case a trial with respect to matters investigated or dealt with by the Commission under the provisions of Chapter □ is pending, it may, if requested by a court or the Constitutional Court or if deemed necessary by the Commission, present the opinions on *de facto* and *de jure* matters to the competent division of the court or the Constitutional Court.

Article 29 (Preparation, etc. of Report)
(1) The Commission shall prepare an annual report on its activities for the preceding year, human rights situation and improvement measures and report thereon to the President of the Republic of Korea and the National Assembly.
(2) Except for the report under paragraph (1), the Commission may, if deemed necessary, make any other special report to the President of the Republic of Korea and the National Assembly.
(3) The related entities, etc. may present to the Commission their opinions on the report under paragraphs (1) and (2) as well as the results of the measures which they have already taken or plans of measures to be taken.
(4) The Commission shall open the report under paragraphs (1) and (2) to the public: *Provided*, That any matter which requires confidentiality on the ground of national security or protection of reputation or privacy of an individual, or the release of which is restrained by any other Act, may not be made public.

CHAPTER 4 INVESTIGATION OF VIOLATIONS OF HUMAN RIGHTS AND REMEDY

Article 30 (Matters Subject to Investigation of Commission)
(1) In any case falling under the following subparagraphs, the person whose human rights are violated (hereinafter referred to as a "victim") or any other person or organization, that comes to know the violation of human rights, may file a petition to the Commission:

1. In case such human rights as guaranteed in Articles 10 through 22 of the Constitution are violated by the performance of duties (excluding the legislation of the National Assembly and the trial of a court or the Constitutional Court) of state organs, local governments or detention or protective facilities; or

2. In case there exists a discriminatory act of any violation of the right of equality by a juristic person, organization or private individual.

(2) The term "discriminatory act of violating the right of equality" means any of the following acts of unreasonable discrimination on the ground of gender, religion, disability, age, social status, regional, national or ethnic origin, physical condition such as features marital status, pregnancy or delivery, family status, race, skin color, thought or political opinion, criminal record of which effective term of the punishment has expired, sexual orientation, or history of diseases: *Provided*, That if the favorable treatment for particular persons (including groups of particular persons; hereinafter the same shall apply) is excluded from the scope of discriminatory acts by any other Act, such favorable treatment shall not be deemed to be a discriminatory act:

1. Any act of favorably treating, excluding, differentiating or unfavorably treating a particular person in employment (including recruitment, appointment, training, assignment of tasks, promotion, payment of wages and payment of commodities other than wages□financing, age limit, retirement, and dismissal, etc.);
2. Any act of favorably treating, excluding, differentiating or unfavorably treating a particular person in the supply or use of goods, services, transportation, commercial facilities, land and residential facilities; and
3. Any act of favorably treating, excluding, differentiating or unfavorably treating a particular person in the use of educational facilities or vocational training institutions.

(3) Even if any petition under paragraph (1) is not filed, the Commission may, *ex officio*, initiate an investigation when it deems that there exists a reasonable ground for believing that human rights have been violated and that such violation is serious.

(4) Necessary matters concerning the procedures and methods of a petition under paragraph (1) shall be prescribed by the rule of the Commission.

Article 31 (Guarantee of Petition Right of Detainee of Detention or Protective Facility)

(1) If a detainee of any relevant detention or protective facility intends to file a petition to the Commission, the public official or staff belonging to the said facility (hereinafter referred to as the "public official concerned, etc.") shall immediately afford such detainee time, a place, and conveniences necessary to prepare the written petition.

(2) If any detainee desires to file a petition in the presence of a commissioner or the staff member of the Commission (hereinafter referred to as a "commissioner, etc."), the public official concerned, etc. shall immediately notify the Commission.

(3) The public official concerned, etc. shall immediately send the written petition which is prepared by a detainee under paragraph (1) to the Commission and deliver the voucher of the document receipt which is issued by the Commission to the said detainee. In case of the notice under paragraph (2), a document verifying such notice

and a document of fixed interview date which are issued by the Commission shall be delivered immediately to the same detainee.
(4) If the Commission is informed under paragraph (2) or deems that there exists any reasonable ground that a detainee truly desires to file a petition, it shall have a commissioner, etc. visit the relevant detention or protective facility to receive an oral or written petition from the said detainee. In this case, the commissioner, etc. who receives the petition shall immediately prepare a document verifying such receipt and deliver that document to the same detainee.
(5) With respect to the visit to the relevant detention or protective facility and receipt of any petition by a commissioner, etc. under paragraph (4) of this Article, Article 24 (3) and (4) of this Act shall apply *mutatis mutandis*.
(6) The staff of the relevant detention or protective facility shall not participate in an interview which a commissioner, etc. holds with detainees who have filed petitions (including those who intend to do so), or shall not hear or record the contents of such interview: *Provided*, That the said staff may watch them at a distance of visibility.
(7) The public official concerned, etc. shall not peruse a written petition or document prepared by a detainee for the purpose of the presentation thereof to the Commission.
(8) Measures which detention or protective facilities shall take to guarantee the free preparation and presentation of a written petition by a detainee and other necessary procedures and methods, shall be prescribed by the Presidential Decree.

Article 32 (Rejection of Petition, etc.)
(1) The Commission shall reject a petition which falls under any of the following subparagraphs:

1. In case the contents of a petition do not fall under the scope of the matters subject to the investigation of the Commission;
2. In case the contents of a petition are deemed manifestly false or ill-founded;
3. In case a petition is filed by any person other than a victim, but it is manifest that the victim does not desire the investigation thereof;
4. In case a petition is filed after one or more years have elapsed since the facts causing the petition happened: *Provided*, That this shall not apply to the case that the statutory limitation for public or civil prosecution with respect to such facts is not completed and that the Commission determines to investigate;
5. In case at the time when a petition is filed to the Commission, with respect to the facts causing the petition, a trial at a court or the Constitutional Court, a criminal investigation by an investigation agency or a procedure for the relief of rights under any other Act is in progress or terminated: *Provided*, That this shall not apply if the Commission receives a petition against cases identical with those falling under crimes of Articles 123 through 125 of the Criminal Act which are being investigated by the investigation agency;
6. In case a petition is filed under any pseudonym or anonym;
7. In case the Commission deems it improper to investigate a petition;

8. In case a petition is withdrawn by the detainee who files it;
9. In case a petition, with the facts identical with any other petition which has already been dismissed by the Commission, is filed;
10. In case the purport of a petition is contrary to the final judgment of a court or decision of the Constitutional Court on the facts causing the petition.

(2) In case the Commission rejects a petition under paragraph (1), it may, if deemed necessary, deliver the petition to related entities. In this case, those related entities to which the petition is delivered shall, if requested by the Commission, inform the Commission of the results of treatment thereof without delay.
(3) The Commission may, even after initiating the investigation on a petition, reject it in any case falling under any subparagraph of paragraph (1).
(4) In case the Commission rejects or delivers a petition, it shall immediately inform the petitioner, by specifying the reason. In this case, the Commission may, if deemed necessary, advise the relevant victim or petitioner on the procedures and measures for the relief of his/her rights.

Article 33 (Other Remedies and Transfer)
(1) In case the Commission deems that the contents of a petition show a clear purport to file a petition to any relevant state organ with authority, according to the procedure for remedies as prescribed by any other Act, it shall transfer, without delay, such petition to such state organ.
(2) In case, after the Commission initiates an investigation on a petition under Article 30 (1), a criminal investigation on the petition with the same facts causing the petition is initiated by another petition or accusations of relevant victims, the said petition shall be delivered to the competent investigation agency.
(3) In case the Commission delivers a petition under paragraphs (1) and (2), it shall, without delay, inform the petitioner and those related entities to which the petition is delivered shall, if requested by the Commission, inform the Commission of the results of disposition thereof.

Article 34 (Cooperation between Investigation Agency and Commission)
(1) If there exists any reasonable ground that the facts causing a petition fall under criminal acts and it is deemed that there exists a necessity either for preventing the suspect thereof from escaping or destroying evidence or for obtaining evidence, the Commission may request the Prosecutor General or the head of the competent investigation agency to initiate an investigation as well as to take necessary measures
(2) The Prosecutor General or the head of the competent investigation agency who receives a request under paragraph (1) shall, without delay, inform the Commission of the results of the measures taken by him/her.

Article 35 (Purpose of Investigation)
(1) The Commission shall endeavor not to impede the performance of functions of state organs in the course of its investigation.

(2) The Commission shall not conduct investigation for the purpose of infringing on the privacy of any individual or unduly participating either in any pending judicial proceedings or in an indictment of any case under investigation.

Article 36 (Methods of Investigation)
(1) The Commission may investigate petitions by such methods as prescribed in the following subparagraphs:

1. To require a petitioner, a victim or the respondent (hereinafter referred to as the "party concerned") or an interested person to be present and submit a written statement, or to hear his/her statement;
2. To require the party concerned, an interested person or the related entity to submit such materials as deemed related to matters subject to investigation;
3. To conduct an on-site inspection or evaluation of any such place, facility or material as deemed related to matters subject to investigation and
4. To refer to the party concerned, an interested person or the related entity, etc. for such fact or information as deemed related to matters subject to investigation.

(2) The Commission may, if deemed necessary for the investigation, have a commissioner, etc. visit any relevant place or facility to conduct an on-site inspection or evaluation of any place, facility or material. In this case, a commissioner, etc. may require any party concerned or related person to present himself/herself and hear his/her statement at such place or facility.
(3) Any person who is required to submit a written statement under paragraph (1) 1 shall submit it within 14 days.
(4) The presence of the respondent under paragraphs (1) and (2) of this Article may be required only if it is difficult to judge any relevant case by the very written statement of the person who commits a violation of human rights or discriminatory act and if there exists any reasonable ground that a violation of human rights and a discriminatory act under the provision of Article 30 (1) are deemed to occur.
(5) A commissioner, etc. who conducts investigation under paragraph (2) may require the head or a staff member managing the relevant place or facility (hereafter referred to as a "related person" in this Article) to submit the necessary materials or articles.
(6) A commissioner, etc. who conducts investigation under paragraph (5) shall carry an identification card indicating his/her authorities and show the card to the related persons.
(7) If the Commission requests the head of any related state organ to submit relevant materials or articles or intends to conduct an on-site inspection or evaluation of the said materials or articles or relevant facilities, the head may reject such submission, inspection or evaluation by clearly explaining to the Commission that those materials, articles or facilities fall under any of the following subparagraphs. In this case, the Commission may request the head to identify any necessary matters and the head shall faithfully comply with such request:

1. In case of the state's classified information having a substantial effect on national security or diplomatic relations; or
2. Any case as deemed to be liable to cause a serious obstacle to any criminal investigation or trial in pending.

Article 37 (Authority to Interrogate or Inspect)
(1) If the Commission intends to know the location of materials or the concerned person necessary for the investigation under the provision of Article 36, it may interrogate such person that the Commission has any reasonable ground to believe that the person knows the contents thereof or may inspect the documents and other articles which the Commission has any reasonable ground to believe that they include such contents.
(2) The provisions of Article 36 (5) through (7) shall apply *mutatis mutandis* to the provision of paragraph (1).

Article 38 (Recusal, etc. of Commissioner)
(1) A commissioner and a conciliation member under the provision of Article 41 (hereinafter referred to as the "commissioner" in this Article) shall, if falling under any of the following subparagraphs, be excluded from the participation in the deliberation and resolution on the relevant petition:
1. In case the commissioner or any person who is or was his/her spouse is the party concerned of the relevant petition or holds any rights or obligations jointly with the party concerned;
2. In case the commissioner is or was a blood relative of the party concerned of the relevant petition;
3. In case the commissioner has testified or made an evaluation concerning the relevant petition;
4. In case the commissioner participates or participated in the relevant petition as an agent of the party concerned; or
5. In case the commissioner has involved in any criminal investigation, trial, or relief procedures under any other Act with respect to the relevant petition.
(2) The party concerned may, if there exists any ground for which it would be difficult to expect the impartial deliberation and resolution of the commissioner, make a request for recusal to the president of the Commission, who shall, in turn, make a decision thereon without referring the request to the Commission for resolution: *Provided*, That if it is inadequate that the president of the Commission makes the decision, the said request shall be referred to the Commission for the resolution.
(3) Any commissioner may voluntarily refrain from the deliberation and resolution on the relevant petition, if he/she falls under either any of subparagraphs of paragraph (1) or paragraph (2).

Article 39 (Dismissal of Petition)
(1) The Commission shall dismiss a petition if the contents thereof fall under any of the following subparagraphs as a result of investigation:

1. In case the contents are false;
2. In case the contents are not related to any act of violating human rights subject to the investigation; and
3. In case it is deemed that any further remedy is not required because the injury related to the petition has already been relieved.

(2) The Commission shall, if dismissing a petition, inform the party concerned of the result and grounds.

Article 40 (Recommendation of Compromise)
With respect to any petition the investigation of which is in progress or completed, the Commission may propose to both parties concerned a remedy necessary for the fair resolution of the case concerning the petition and recommend a compromise.

Article 41 (Establishment and Composition of Conciliation Committee)
(1) A conciliation committee, which is comprised of three conciliation members, shall be established under the Commission to ensure the speedy and fair settlement of conciliation.
(2) The conciliation committee shall deliberate and resolve on the case of petition which is referred by the Commission.
(3) Two of the conciliation members shall be commissioned by the Commission from among the commissioners and the other member from among the persons who fall under any of the following subparagraphs: The latter shall be commissioned to work part-time and one of three conciliation members shall be qualified as an attorney-at-law:

1. Persons who have professional knowledge and experience on human rights affairs and whose term of service related to human rights in a state organ or non-governmental organization is ten years or more;
2. Persons whose term of service as judge, public prosecutor, military judge advocate or attorney-in-law is ten years or more; or
3. Persons whose term of service as assistant professor (or corresponding position thereto) or higher either at college or at an authorized research institute is ten years or more.

(4) Necessary matters concerning the commission and term of office of the conciliation members, the operation of the conciliation committee and the procedures of conciliation, etc. shall be prescribed by the rule of the Commission.
(5) With respect to matters concerning the procedures for conciliation which are not prescribed both by this Act and by the rule of the Commission, the Judicial Conciliation of Civil Disputes Act shall apply *mutatis mutandis* .

Article 42 (Conciliation)
(1) If with respect to the relevant petition, the Commission decides that there was an act of violating human rights, but the compromise under the provision of Article 40 is not reached, it may, at the request of the party concerned or *ex officio*, refer the petition to the conciliation committee for the relevant procedure.

(2) The conciliation shall be completed at the time when, after the procedures are initiated, both parties concerned enter the compromised matters in the document of conciliation by fixing their signature and seal and the conciliation committee, in turn, identifies it.
(3) If both parties concerned fail to reach a compromise in the course of the procedures for conciliation, the conciliation committee may make a decision in lieu of the conciliation in order to fairly settle the case.
(4) The decision in lieu of conciliation may include any of the following:

1. Stoppage of an act of violating human rights subject to the investigation;
2. Restitution, compensation for damage or other necessary remedies; or
3. Measures necessary for the prevention of recurrence of the same or similar act of violating human rights.

(5) If the conciliation committee makes a decision in lieu of conciliation, it shall serve both parties concerned with the written decision without delay.
(6) If any party concerned fails to raise an objection within 2 weeks after he/she has been served with the written decision under paragraph (5), he/she shall be deemed to accept the conciliation.

Article 43 (Effect of Conciliation)
The conciliation under the provision of Article 42 (2) and the decision in lieu of conciliation in case of no objections under the provision of Article 42 (6) shall have the same effect as a settlement at court.

Article 44 (Recommendation of Remedies, etc.)
(1) If the Commission deems that there occurred any violation of human rights as a result of the investigation of any petition, it may recommend the respondent or the head of the organ or organization to which he/she belongs or the supervisory institution thereof (hereinafter referred to as the "institution, etc. to which the respondent belongs") any of the following subparagraphs:

1. Implementation of remedial measures under subparagraphs of Article 42 (4); and
2. Rectification or improvement of any relevant statute, legal system, policy or practice.

(2) The provisions of Article 25 (2) through (4) shall apply *mutatis mutandis* to the head of the institution, etc. to which the respondent belongs, who has received recommendation under paragraph (1) of this Article.

Article 45 (Accusation and Recommendation of Disciplinary Action)
(1) If as a result of the investigation of any petition, the Commission deems that the contents of the petition correspond to an act of crime against which a criminal punishment is required, it may file an accusation to the Prosecutor General: *Provided*, That in case the accused is the military personnel or civilian personnel in the military service, the accusation may be filed to the Chief of General Staff of the armed force to which the said accused belongs or the Minister of National Defense.

(2) If the Commission finds any violation of human rights after investigation of any petition, it may recommend a disciplinary action against the respondent or any other person responsible for the same violation to the head of the institution, etc. to which he/she belongs.
(3) The Prosecutor General, the Chief of General Staff of the armed force, or the Minister of National Defense, who has received an accusation under paragraph (1), shall complete the criminal investigation within 3 months after being so received and notify the Commission of the results thereof: *Provided*, That he/she shall, if failing to do so within 3 months, submit the reason therefor.
(4) The head of the institution, etc. to which the respondent belongs, who has received a recommendation from the Commission under paragraph (2), shall respect the said recommendation and notify the Commission of the results of disposition thereof.

Article 46 (Provision of Opportunity to State Opinion)
(1) The Commission shall provide the respondent with an opportunity to state his/her opinion before either making a recommendation or taking a measure under the provisions of Article 44 or 45.
(2) In any such case as referred to in paragraph (1), any party concerned or interested person may state his/her oral or written opinion or present necessary materials to the Commission.

Article 47 (Request for Legal Aid for Victim)
(1) The Commission may, if deemed necessary to investigate petitions, obtain evidence or relieve victims, request the Korea Legal Aid Corporation or any other institution to render legal aid to the said victims.
(2) Legal aid under paragraph (1) shall not be requested against the explicit will of the relevant victim.
(3) Necessary matters concerning the procedures, contents and methods of legal aid under paragraph (1) shall be prescribed by the rule of the Commission.

Article 48 (Recommendation of Urgent Relief Measures)
(1) The Commission may, in case after receiving any petition it deems that it is considerably probable any violation of human rights subject to the investigation is in progress and that it is likely to cause any irrecoverable damage if left as violated, recommend the respondent or the head of the institution, etc. to which he/she belongs to take a measure which falls under any of the following subparagraphs at the request of the petitioner or victim or *ex officio* before making a decision on the petition:

1. Provision of medical service, meal or clothing;
2. Participation in the on-site inspection and evaluation of any relevant place, facility or materials or the verification and evaluation which is conducted by any other organ;
3. Change of detention or accommodation places of detainees;
4. Stoppage of violations of human rights;

5. Displacement of any public official who is deemed to effect violations of human rights from his/her present assigned position; and
6. Other necessary matters for protecting the life or security of person of the victim.

(2) The Commission may, if deemed necessary, take any necessary measure for protecting the life, security of person and reputation of any party concerned or interested person, obtaining evidence or preventing the destruction thereof, or recommend the interested person and the head of the institution, etc. to which he/she belongs to take such a measure.

Article 49 (Non-Release of Investigation and Conciliation)
The investigation of any petition and the conciliation and deliberation conducted by the Commission shall be confidential: *Provided*, That they may be released if the Commission makes a resolution in favor thereof.

Article 50 (Release of Results of Settlement)
The Commission may release the contents and results of any investigation and conciliation, the recommendation to the related entities and the measures taken by such entities under this Chapter: *Provided*, That this shall not apply to any case in which such a release is restrained by any other Act or it is likely to infringe on the privacy of any individual.

CHAPTER 5 SUPPLEMENTARY PROVISIONS

Article 51 (Prohibition of False Impersonation)
Any person shall not exercise the authority of the Commission by falsely pretending to be a commissioner or its staff.

Article 52 (Prohibition of Disclosure of Secret)
A person, who was or is a commissioner, advisory member or staff member of the Commission, and any other person, who performed or performs affairs of the Commission after having been dispatched or entrusted by the Commission, shall not disclose any secret which comes to their knowledge or is acquired by them in the course of performing their duties.

Article 53 (Prohibition of Use of Similar Name)
No person other than the Commission shall use the name of the National Human Rights Commission or any other name similar thereto.

Article 54 (Dispatch of Public Official, etc.)
(1) The Commission may, if deemed necessary for the performance of its duties, request the head of any related entity, etc. to dispatch a public official or staff member under his/her control to the Commission.

(2) The head of the related entity, etc. who is requested to dispatch a public official or staff member under his/her control to the Commission under paragraph (1) may do so in consultation with the Commission.
(3) The public official or staff member who is dispatched to the Commission under paragraph (2) shall perform affairs of the Commission, separated from the entity to which he/she belongs.
(4) The head of the related entity, etc. who has dispatched a public official or staff member under his/her control to the Commission under paragraph (2) shall not take unfavorable measures against the said public official or staff in terms of personnel matters and treatment.

Article 55 (Prohibition of Unfavorable Treatment, and Supports)
(1) Any person shall not be subject to any removal from his/her office, transfer to another position, disciplinary action and unjust treatment as well as other unfavorable measures in status or treatment on account of his/her petition, statement, witness, presentation of materials or reply under this Act.
(2) The Commission may give any necessary support or reward to a person who either reveals the fact of any violation of human rights or finds and presents evidence or materials.
(3) The contents and procedures of support or reward under paragraph (2) and other necessary matters shall be prescribed by the rule of the Commission.

CHAPTER 6 PENAL PROVISIONS

Article 56 (Obstruction of Performance of Human Rights Protection Duties)
(1) A person who falls under any of the following subparagraphs shall be punished by imprisonment for not more than 5 years or by a fine not exceeding 30 million won:

1. A person who assaults or intimidates a commissioner or staff member of the Commission who performs affairs thereof;
2. A person who assaults or intimidates a commissioner or staff member of the Commission for the purpose of coercing or hindering any act in relation to the performance of duties of the said commissioner or staff or compelling him/her to resign his/her office;
3. A person who obstructs the performance of duties of a commissioner or staff member of the Commission by any deceitful plan; and
4. A person who destroys, falsifies or alters any evidence related to the case of the violation of any other person's human rights subject to the investigation by the Commission under Chapter □ of this Act, or uses any such evidence as so falsified or altered.

(2) If blood relatives or the head of house of any person, or family members living with him/her commit a crime under paragraph (1) 4 for him/her, they shall not be punished.

Article 57 (Obstruction of Preparation of Written Petition)
A person who fails to permit or obstructs any petition in violation of the provision of Article 31 shall be punished by imprisonment for not more than 3 years or by a fine not exceeding 10 million won. (The date of enforcement is November 25, 2001.)

Article 58 (False Impersonation)
A person who exercises the authority of the Commission by falsely pretending to be a commissioner or its staff in violation of the provision of Article 51 shall be punished by imprisonment for not more than 2 years or by a fine not exceeding 7 million won.

Article 59 (Disclosure of Secret)
A person who discloses any such secret as coming to his/her knowledge acquired by him/her in the course of performing his/her duties in violation of the provision of Article 52 shall be punished by imprisonment with or without labor for not more than 2 years or by qualification suspension for not more than 5 years.

Article 60 (Obstruction of Urgent Relief Measures)
A person who obstructs the measures taken by the Commission under the provision of Article 48 (1) or (2) shall be punished by imprisonment for not more than one year or by a fine not exceeding 5 million won.

Article 61 (Violation of Guarantee of Petition Right of Detainee)
A person who violates the provisions of Article 31 (6) or (7) shall be punished by a fine not exceeding 10 million won.

Article 62 (Legal Fiction as Public Official in Application of Penal Provisions)
Any person other than a public official from among the commissioners of the Commission shall be deemed to be a public official in the application of penal provisions under the Criminal Act or any other Act.

Article 63 (Fine for Negligence)
(1) A person who falls under any of the following subparagraphs shall be punished by a fine for negligence not exceeding 10 million won:

1. A person who refuses, obstructs or evades either a visit and investigation under the provision of Article 24 (1) or an on-site inspection under the provision of Article 36 without any justifiable reason;
2. A person who fails to comply with the request for submitting a written statement or presenting himself/herself by the Commission under the provision of Article 36 (1) 1 or (2) without any justifiable reason; and
3. A person who fails to comply with the request for submission of materials and the reference for any fact under the provisions of Article 36 (1) 2 and 4 or (5) without any justifiable reason, or submits false materials.

(2) A person who violates the provisions of Article 53, shall be punished by a fine for negligence not exceeding 3 million won.

(3) A fine for negligence as prescribed in paragraphs (1) and (2) shall be imposed by the president of the Commission in accordance with the Presidential Decree.
(4) A person who is dissatisfied with any disposition of fine for negligence as prescribed in paragraph (3) may raise an objection to the president of the Commission within 30 days after being notified of such disposition.
(5) If a person who is subject to a disposition of fine for negligence under paragraph (3) raises an objection under paragraph (4), the imposition authority shall, without delay, notify the competent court, which, in turn, shall proceed to a trial on a fine for negligence pursuant to the Non-Contentious Case Litigation Procedure Act.
(6) If an objection is not raised within the period as prescribed in paragraph (4) and a fine for negligence is not paid, the fine for negligence shall be collected by referring to the practices of dispositions on default of national taxes.

ADDENDA <ACT NO. 6481, MAY 24, 2001>

(1) (Enforcement Date) This Act shall enter into force 6 months after the date of its promulgation: *Provided*, That the appointment of the commissioners and staff of the Commission, the enactment and promulgation of its rule concerning the enforcement of this Act, and the preparation for its establishment may be conducted even before this Act enters into force.
(2) (Application Example concerning Commencement of Term of Office of Commissioners) The term of office of those commissioners who are initially appointed under this Act shall be deemed to commence on the date when this Act enters into force.
(3) (Enactment of Presidential Decree) The president of the Commission may recommend the Prime Minister to submit the draft of the Presidential Decree concerning the enforcement of this Act.

Disclaimer

In case there is any divergence in interpreting the National Human Rights Commission Act between the Korean and English versions, the Korean version shall prevail.

LAWS OF MALAYSIA

ACT 597

HUMAN RIGHTS COMMISSION OF MALAYSIA ACT 1999

Date of Royal Assent 27 August 1999

Date of publication in the
Gazette 09 September 1999
Arrangement of Sections

Part I
PRELIMINARY
Section

Part II
ESTABLISHMENT OF THE HUMAN RIGHTS COMMISSION OF MALAYSIA
Section

Part III
POWERS OF INQUIRY OF THE COMMISSION
Section

Part IV
STAFF OF THE COMMISSION
Section

An Act to provide for the establishment of the Human Rights Commission of Malaysia; to set out the powers and functions of such commission for the protection and promotion of human rights in Malaysia; and to provide for matters connected therewith or incidental thereto.

ENACTED by the Parliament of Malaysia as follows:
Part I
Part II
Part III
Part IV
Part V

PART I

PRELIMINARY

Short title and commencement

1. (1) This Act may be cited as the Human Rights Commission of Malaysia Act 1999.

(2) This Act shall come into operation on a date to be appointed by the Minister by notification published in the *Gazette*.

Interpretation

2. In this Act, unless the context otherwise requires-

"Government" means the Government of Malaysia;

"human rights" refers to fundamental liberties as enshrined in Part II of the Federal Constitution;

"Minister" means the Minister charged with the responsibility for human rights.

PART II

ESTABLISHMENT OF THE HUMAN RIGHTS COMMISSION OF MALAYSIA

Establishment of the Commission

3. (1) There is hereby established a Commission which shall be known as the Human Rights Commission of Malaysia (the "Commission").

(2) The Commission shall be a body corporate having perpetual succession and a common seal, which may sue and be sued in its name and, subject to and for the purpose of this Act, may enter into contracts and may acquire, purchase, take, hold and enjoy movable and immovable property of every description and may convey, assign, surrender, yield up, charge, mortgage, demise, reassign, transfer or otherwise dispose of, or deal with, any movable or immovable property or any interest therein vested in the Commission upon such terms as it deems fit.

(3) The Commission shall have a common seal which shall bear such device as the Commission shall approve and such seal may be broken, changed, altered or made anew as the Commission thinks fit.

(4) The common seal shall be kept in the custody of the Secretary to the Commission or such other person as may be authorized by the Commission and shall be authenticated by the Secretary or such authorized person or by any officer authorized by the Secretary or such authorized person in writing.

(5) All deeds, documents and other instruments purporting to be sealed with the common seal, authenticated as specified in subsection (4) shall until the contrary is proved, be deemed to have been validly executed.

(6) The common seal of the Commission shall be officially and judicially noticed.

Functions and powers of the Commission

4. (1) In furtherance of the protection and promotion of human rights in Malaysia, the functions of the Commission shall be –

(a) to promote awareness of the provide education in relation to human rights;
(b) to advise and assist the Government in formulating legislation and administrative directives and procedures and recommend the necessary measures to be taken;
(c) to recommend to the Government with regard to the subscription or accession of treaties and other international instruments in the field of human rights; and
(d) to inquire into complaints regarding infringements of human rights referred to in section 12.

(2) For the purpose of discharging its functions, the Commission may exercise any or all of the following powers:
(a) to promote awareness of human rights and to undertaken research by conducting programmes, seminars and workshops and to disseminate and distribute the results of such research;

(b) to advise the Government and/or the relevant authorities of complaints against such authorities and recommend to the Government and/or such authorities appropriate measures to be taken;
(c) to study and verify any infringement of human rights in accordance with the provisions of this Act;
(d) to visit places of detention in accordance with procedures as prescribed by the lays relating to the places of detention and to make necessary recommendations;
(e) to issue public statement on human rights as and when necessary; and
(f) to undertake any other appropriate activities as are necessary in accordance with the written laws in force, if any, in relation to such activities.

(3) The visit by the Commission to any place of detention under paragraph (2)(d) shall not be refused by the person in charge of such place of detention if the procedures provided in the laws regulating such places of detention are complied with.

(4) For the purpose of this Act, regard shall be had to the Universal Declaration of Human Rights 1948 to the extent that it is not inconsistent with the Federal Constitution.

Members of the Commission and term of office

5. (1) The Commission shall consist of not more than twenty members.

(2) Members of the Commission shall be appointed by the Yang di-Pertuan Agong, on the recommendation of the Prime Minister.

(3) Members of the Commission shall be appointed from amongst prominent personalities including those from various religious and racial backgrounds.

(4) Every member shall hold office for a period of two years and is eligible for reappointment.

Chairman and Vice-Chairman

6. (1) The Yang di-Pertuan Agong shall designate one of the members appointed under section 5 to be the Chairman of the Commission.

(2) The Chairman's term of office shall be his period of membership on the Commission.

(3) A Vice-Chairman shall be elected by the members of the Commission from amongst themselves.

(4) Where the Chairman of the Commission is for any reason unable to perform the function of the Chairman, or during any period of vacancy in the office of the Chairman, the Vice-Chairman shall perform the function of the Chairman.

Meeting of the Commission

7. (1) The Chairman of the Commission shall preside at all meetings of the Commission.

(2) If the Chairman is absent from any meeting, the Vice-Chairman of the Commission shall preside at such meeting.

(3) The quorum at all meeting shall be two thirds of the number of the members of the Commission.

(4) The members of the Commission shall use their best endeavours to arrive at all decisions of the meeting by consensus failing which the decision by a two-thirds majority of the members present shall be required.

(5) The Commission shall determine the conduct of its own proceedings.

Remuneration

8. (1) The Chairman of the Commission shall be paid such remuneration and allowances as the Yang di-Pertuan Agong may determine.

(2) Every member of the Commission shall be paid allowances at such rates as the Yang di-Pertuan Agong may determine.

Vacation of office

9. The office of a member of the Commission shall become vacant –

(a) upon the death of the member;

(b) upon the member resigning from such office by the letter addressed to the Yang di-Pertuan Agong;

(c) upon the expiration of his term of office; or

(d) upon the member being removed from office on any of the grounds specified in section 10.

Disqualification

10. A member of the Commission may be removed from office by the Yang di-Pertuan Agong if –

(a) the member is adjudged insolvent by a court of competent jurisdiction;

(b) the Yang di-Pertuan Agong, after consulting a medical officer or a registered medical practitioner, is of the opinion that the member is physically or mentally incapable of continuing his office;

(c) the member absents himself from three consecutive meeting of the Commission without obtaining leave of the Commission or, in the case of the Chairman, without leave of the Minister;
(d) the Yang di-Pertuan Agong, on the recommendation of the Prime Minister, is of the opinion that the member-
(i) has engaged in any paid office or employment which conflicts with his duties as a member of the Commission;
(ii) has misbehaved or has conducted himself in such a manner as to bring disrepute to the Commission; or
(iii) has acted in contravention of this Act and in conflict with his duties as a member of the Commission.

Resignation
11. A member of the Commission may at any time resign his office by a letter addressed to the Yang di-Pertuan Agong.

PART III

POWERS OF INQUIRY OF THE COMMISSION

Commission may inquire on own motion or on complaint
12. (1) The Commission may, on its own motion or on a complaint made to it by an aggrieved person or group of persons or a person acting on behalf of an aggrieved person or a group of persons, inquire into allegation of the infringement of the human rights of such person or group of persons.

(2) The Commission shall not inquire into any complaint relating to any allegation of the infringement of human rights which-
(a) is the subject matter of any proceedings pending in any court, including any appeals; or
(b) has been finally determined by any court.

(3) If the Commission inquires into an allegation under subsection 12(1) and during the pendency of such inquiry the allegation becomes the subject matter of any proceedings in any court, the Commission shall immediately cease to do the inquiry.

Procedure where infringement is not disclosed or is disclosed
13. (1) Where an inquiry conducted by the Commission under section 12 does not disclose the infringement of human rights, the Commission shall record that finding and shall forthwith inform the person making the complaint.
(2) Where an inquiry conducted by the Commission under section 12 discloses the infringement of human rights, the Commission shall have the power to refer the matter, where appropriate, to the relevant authority or person with the necessary recommendations.

Powers relating to inquiries

14. (1) The Commission shall, for the purposes of an inquiry under this Act, have the power-

(a) to procure and receive all such evidence, written or oral, and to examine all such persons as witnesses, as the Commission thinks necessary or desirable to procure or examine;

(b) to require that the evidence, whether written or oral, of any witness be given on oath or affirmation, such oath or affirmation being that which could be required of the witness if he were giving evidence in a court of law, and to administer or cause to be administered by an officer authorized in that behalf by the Commission an oath or affirmation to every such witness;

(c) to summon any person residing in Malaysia to attend any meeting of the Commission to give evidence or produce any document or other thing in his possession, and to examine him as a witness or require him to produce any document or other thing in his possession;

(d) to admit notwithstanding any of the provisions of the Evidence Act 1950 [*Act 56*}, any evidence, whether written or oral, which may be inadmissible in civil or criminal proceedings; and

(e) to admit or exclude the public from such inquiry or any part thereof.

(2) Notwithstanding paragraph (1)(*c*), where a person summoned is a person under detention under any other written law, such summons shall be issued in accordance with the laws applicable in relation to the place of detention.

Evidence before the Commission

15. (1) A person who gives evidence before the Commission shall, in respect of such evidence, be entitled to all the privileges to which a witness giving evidence before a court of law is entitled in respect of evidence given by him before such court.

(2) No person shall, in respect of any evidence written or oral given by that person to or before the Commission, be liable to any action or proceeding, civil or criminal in any court except when the person is charged with giving or fabricating false evidence.

PART IV

STAFF OF THE COMMISSION

Appointment of Secretary and the staff

16. (1) The Commission shall appoint a Secretary to the Commission.

(2) The Commission may appoint such other officers and servants as may be necessary to assist the Commission in the discharge of its functions under this Act.

Delegation of powers

17. The Commission may delegate to any officer referred to in subsection 16(2) any of its powers, and the officer to whom such powers are delegated may exercise those powers subject o the direction of the Commission.

Protection of members, officers and servants of the Commission

18. (1) No action, suit, prosecution or proceeding shall be instituted in any court against the Commission or against any member, officer, or servant of the Commission in respect of any act, neglect or default done or committed by him in such capacity provided that he at the time had carried out his functions in good faith.

(2) Any member, officer or servant of the Commission shall be required to produce in any court, any document received by, or to disclose to any court, any matter or thing coming to the notice of the Commission in the course of any inquiry conducted by the Commission under this act.

(3) No action or proceeding, civil or criminal shall be instituted in any court against any member of the Commission in respect of any report made by the Commission under this Act or against any other person in respect of the publication by such person of a substantially true account of such report.

(4) Chapters IX and X of the Penal Code [*Act 574*] shall apply to members, officers and servants of the Commission as if references to "public servant" had been replaced with "member, officer or servant of the Commission".

PART V

GENERAL

Funds

19. (1) The Government shall provide the Commission with adequate funds annually to enable the Commission to discharge its function under this Act.

(2) The Commission shall not receive any foreign fund.

(3) Notwithstanding subsection (2), the Commission may receive funds without any conditions from any individual or organization only for the purpose of promoting awareness of and providing education in relation to human rights as many be approved by the Commission.

(4) The Commission shall cause proper audited accounts to be kept of its income and expenditure, and assets and liabilities.

(5) The financial year of the Commission shall be the calendar year.

(6) Any expenses incurred by the Commission in any action or proceeding, civil or criminal, brought by or against the Commission before any court shall be paid out of the funds of the Commission and any costs paid to, or recovered by, the Commission in any such action or proceeding, civil or criminal, shall be credited to the funds of the Commission.

(7) Any expenses incurred by any member, officer or servant of the Commission, in any civil action or proceeding, brought against him in any court in respect of any act which is done or purported to be done by him under this Act or on the direction of the Commission shall be paid out of the funds of the Commission unless such expenses are recovered by him in such civil action or proceeding.

Application of Act 240

20. The Statutory Bodies (Accounts and Annual Reports) Act 1980 [*Act 240*] shall apply to the Commission.

Annual Report

21. (1) The Commission shall not later than the first meeting of Parliament of the following year, submit an annual report to Parliament of all its activities during the year to which the report relates.

(2) The report shall contain a list of all matters referred to it, and the action taken in respect of them together with the recommendations of the Commission in respect of each matter.

(3) The Commission may, whenever it considers it necessary to do so, submit special reports to Parliament in respect of any particular matter or matters refereed to it, and the action taken in respect thereof.

Regulations

22. The Minister may make regulations for the purpose of carrying out or giving effect to the provisions of this Act, including for prescribing the procedure to be followed in the conduct of inquiries under this Act.

Power to make disciplinary regulations

23. (1) The Commission may, with the approval of the Minister, make such regulations as it thinks necessary or expedient to provide for the discipline of the officers and servants of the Commission.

(2) Where any disciplinary regulations are made under this section, the Commission shall cause notice of the effect of those regulations to be given in such manner as it thinks necessary for bringing it to the notice of all officers and servants of the Commission who are affected by those regulations and those regulations shall, notwithstanding sections 19 and 20 of the Interpretation Acts 1948 and 1967 [*Act 388*], have effect as soon as the notice has been given without publications in *Gazette*.

LAW OF MONGOLIA

7 December 2000, Ulaanbaatar city

THE NATIONAL HUMAN RIGHTS
COMMISSION OF MONGOLIA ACT

CHAPTER ONE GENERAL PROVISIONS

Article 1. Purpose of the Law

1.1. The purpose of this Law shall be to determine legal basis and operational principles of, and to regulate the relations arising out of the exercise of powers by the National Human Rights Commission of Mongolia (hereinafter referred to as 'the Commission').

Article 2. Legislation on the Commission

2.1. Legislation on the Commission shall consist of the Constitution of Mongolia[6], this Law and other legislative acts enacted in conformity with them.

2.2. If an international treaty to which Mongolia is a State Party (the international treaties of Mongolia) provides otherwise than this Law, the provisions of that international treaty shall prevail.

Article 3. The Commission and its Operational Principles

3.1. The Commission is an institution mandated with the promotion and protection of human rights and charged with monitoring over the implementation of the provisions on human rights and freedoms, provided in the Constitution of Mongolia, laws and international treaties of Mongolia.

3.2. The Commission shall consist of 3 (three) members (Commissioners).

3.3. The Commission shall adhere in its operations to the principles of the rule of law, independence, protection of human rights, freedoms and legitimate interests, justice and transparency.

3.4. It shall be prohibited for any business entity, organisation, official or individual person to influence and/or interfere with the activities of the Commission and its Members.

---

[6] The Constitution of Mongolia was published in the issue # 1of 1992 of the 'State Gazette'.

CHAPTER TWO APPOINTMENT AND RELEASE OF COMMISSIONERS, SUSPENSION OF THEIR POWERS AND DISMISSAL

Article 4. Candidates for Commissioners
4.1. A candidate for Commissioners shall be a Mongolian citizen of high legal and political qualification, with appropriate knowledge and experience in human rights, with a clean criminal record and who has reached the age of 35 (thirty-five).

Article 5. Nomination of Candidates for and Appointment of Commissioners
5.1. The Speaker of the State Great Hural (Parliament) shall nominate names for candidates for Commissioners to the State Great Hural on the basis of respective proposals by the President, the Parliamentary Standing Committee on Legal Affairs and the Supreme Court.

5.2. If the State Great Hural declines to appoint a candidate as a Commissioner, then the Speaker of the State Great Hural shall submit the name of another person within 14 (fourteen) days in accordance with procedure provided in Art 5.1.

5.3. A name of the same person shall not be nominated again.

5.4. The State Great Hural shall consider and decide on this issue within 30 (thirty) days from the date of submission of the names for candidates.

5.5. In case any of Commissioners has been released, resigned from his/her official position or deceased before the expiry of the term of his/her office, the Great State Hural shall appoint replacement for that Commissioner within 60 (sixty) days from that date in accordance with this Law.

5.6. A Chief Commissioner shall be appointed for a term of 3 (three) years from among Commissioners by the State Great Hural, based on the proposal by the Speaker of the State Great Hural.

5.7. Commissioners shall not hold any job or office concurrently other than that mandated by this Law, except that of engaging in training and research. If any of Commissioners has been holding another job or office before his/her appointment, then he/she shall be released from that job or office from the day on which he/she has taken an oath of office.

Article 6. Term of Office of Commissioners
6.1. A single term of office for Commissioners shall be 6 (six) years.

6.2. Powers of Commissioners shall start by taking an oath of office to the Constitution of Mongolia, and shall end by the swearing in of the newly appointed Commissioners.

6.3. Commissioners may be re-appointed only once.

Article 7. Swearing in of the Members of Commission

7.1. Commissioners shall take an oath of office to the Constitution of Mongolia within 30 (thirty) days from the date of appointment by swearing in: 'I do swear to observe faithfully the Constitution of Mongolia, and to fulfil dutifully my obligations to promote and protect the human rights and freedoms, which are guaranteed in the laws and international treaties of Mongolia.'

7.2. The Speaker of the State Great Hural shall approve the procedure for ceremony of taking an oath by Commissioners.

Article 8. Release and Suspension from the Office, and Dismissal of Commissioners

8.1. The State Great Hural shall release a Commissioner from his/her office in the following cases:

8.1.1. A Commissioner has been nominated as a candidate for the President of Mongolia, or for the Member of the State Great Hural;

8.1.2. A Commissioner has been appointed or elected to another official position;

8.1.3. A Commissioner has requested on his/her own because he/she becomes unable to exercise his/her powers due to health conditions or for any other excusable reasons.

8.2. The State Great Hural shall discuss and make a decision within 14 (fourteen) days from the date of receipt of a proposal and decision from the competent authority on whether to suspend his/her powers, if a Commissioner has been implicated in the crime, as well as has been arrested as provided in Art 23.1. of this Law.

8.3. The State Great Hural shall restore his/her powers and adopt a resolution to that effect, on the basis of a decision by the competent authority or official, which has established that a Commissioner has not been implicated in the crime or not guilty of committing it.

8.4. The State Great Hural shall dismiss him/her from the office and adopt a resolution to that effect, if a crime, which has been proved to be committed by a Commissioner, and a final binding judgement to that effect by the Court has come into force.

CHAPTER THREE COMPLAINTS LODGING TO THE COMMISSION

Article 9. Right to Lodge Complaints

9.1. Citizens of Mongolia, either individually or in a group, shall have the right to lodge complaints to the Commission in accordance with this Law, in case of violations of human rights and freedoms, guaranteed in the Constitution of Mongolia, laws and international treaties of Mongolia, by business entities, organisations, officials or individual persons.

9.2. Unless otherwise provided in laws and international treaties of Mongolia, foreign citizens and/or stateless persons who are residing in the territory of Mongolia, shall exercise the same right to lodge complaints to the Commission on equal footing as the citizens of Mongolia.

9.3. Complaints may be lodged in by representation of lawful representatives-parents, care-takers and/or guardians for the persons, who do not have full civil law capacity or have some limited or partial capacity, as well as by representatives provided under the law for the persons, who are considered missing or declared as deceased.

9.4. Non-governmental organisations and trade union organisations shall exercise equally the right provided in Art 9.1. and lodge complaints through their representatives.

9.5. Representatives provided in Art 9.3 and Art 9.4 shall have a document of proof for their own representation powers.

Article 10. Form of Lodging Complaints

10.1. Complaints shall be lodged in writing in Mongolian language or verbally in person. Persons, who do not know Mongolian language, may lodge complaints in their mother tongue and their complaints must be translated into Mongolian language and duly certified in accordance with procedure provided for it.

Article 11. Requirements for Complaints

11.1. Complaints shall reflect the following items:

11.1.1. A Complainant must have had his/her complaint decided through an administrative process;

11.1.2. A Complainant must indicate, which rights and freedoms guaranteed in the Constitution of Mongolia, laws and international treaties of Mongolia, have been violated;

11.1.3. The Complainant must write his/her own name, residential or postal address, and has signed it;

11.1.4. The Complainant must attach the name, address, phone-number and other related documents of the business entity, organisation, official or individual person who is implicated in the complaint;

11.2. Commissioners shall not receive complaints about criminal and civil cases and/or disputes, which are at the stage of registration/inquiry of cases, investigation and/or on trial or have been already decided.

Article 12. Period for Receiving and Replying to Complaints
12.1. A Complainant shall lodge a complaint within 1 (one) year from the date on which his/her rights and freedoms were violated or from the date on which he/she came to know about such violation.

12.2. The Commission shall not accept any complaint without a name or address on it.

12.3. The Commission shall give a reply within 30 (thirty) days from the date of receipt of a complaint, and if there is need for additional research and inquiry required, the Chief Commissioner may extend it up to 60 (sixty) days.

CHAPTER FOUR POWERS OF THE COMMISSION AND ITS MEMBERS

Article 13. Powers of the Commission
13.1. The Commission shall exercise the following powers:

13.1.1. To put forward proposals on any human rights-related issues;

13.1.2. To put forward recommendations and/or proposals on whether laws or administrative decisions are in conformity with the key human rights principles;

13.1.3. To put forward proposals on the implementation of international human rights treaties and/or drafting of Government reports thereon;

13.2. The Commission shall carry out the following activities within its powers:

13.2.1. To conduct research on human rights issues and provide necessary information;

13.2.2. To collaborate with the international, regional and other national human rights institutions;

13.2.3. To produce reports on the human rights situation in Mongolia;

13.2.4. To increase public awareness about the laws and/or international treaties relating to human rights;

13.2.5. To promote human rights education activities;

13.2.6. To encourage ratification of and/or accession to the international human rights treaties.

Article 14. Powers of the Chairperson of the Commission
14.1. A Chief Commissioner shall exercise the following powers.

14.1.1. To represent the Commission in domestic and/or foreign relations;

14.1.2. To appoint and/or release the Director of the Staff;

14.1.3. To deal with internal organisational matters of the Commission;

Article 15. Powers of Commissioners with respect to the acceptance of Complaints
15.1. Commissioners shall exercise the following powers with respect to the acceptance of complaints:

15.1.1. To accept and examine complaints;

15.1.2. To refuse to accept the complaints which do not meet the requirements provided in Art 11 of this Law;

15.1.3. To transfer complaints with respect to criminal and/ or civil cases and disputes to relevant authorities or officials according to their jurisdiction;

15.1.4. To explain to the Complainant what rights and duties he/she has with regard to the restoration of violated rights.

Article 16. Powers of Commissioners with respect to Inquiry of Complaints
16.1. Commissioners shall exercise the following powers during the course of inquiry into complaints:

16.1.1. To take explanations in writing from the Complainant and relevant business entities, organisations, officials or individual persons and take explanations orally and take notes thereon if the Complainant is illiterate;

16.1.2. To summon the Complainant and relevant persons;

16.1.3. To have unrestricted access to any business entity or organisation and to participate in their meetings and conferences, and to meet in person with the relevant officials;

16.1.4. To obtain without any charge the necessary evidence, official documents and information from organisations and/or officials, and to get acquainted with them on the spot;

16.1.5. To appoint experts from the appropriate organisations in a case of necessity for the specialised knowledge, and to get their expert-opinions;

16.1.6. To transfer a complaint to the relevant authorities or officials according to their jurisdiction, if it is considered that this complaint has a nature of criminal or civil case during the course of examination;

16.1.7. To conduct alone an inquiry into the activities of business entities, organisations or officials, or jointly on the basis of a proposal by the competent State authority and their officials;

16.1.8. To access the confidential data/secrets of the State, organisation or individual person in accordance with procedure established by the relevant law, if Commissioners considers it necessary during the course of exercise of his/her powers;

16.2. Commissioners shall keep in good faith the confidential data/secrets of the State, organisation or individual person, which he/she came to know about during the course of conducting the official business or which has been informed to him/her in trust.

Article 17. Powers of Commissioners in respect of Decision-making on Complaints

17.1. Commissioners shall exercise the following powers with respect to making a decision on complaints:

17.1.1. To submit claims to the Courts with regard to issues of violations of human rights and freedoms by business entities, organisations, officials or individual persons to participate in person or through a representative in judicial proceedings in accordance with procedure established by the law;

17.1.2. To put forward requests to the competent authorities or officials with regard to imposing administrative sanctions on officials who, as he/she considers, have violated human rights and freedoms;

17.1.3. To demand organisations or officials to stop activities which violate human rights and freedoms, or which create conditions for such violations;

17.1.4. To decide the issues by way of conciliation of the parties.

17.1.5. To return a complaint to the Complainant if he/she considers it to be without grounds.

17.2. Claims lodged under Art 17.1.1 shall be exempted from court expenses.

17.3. Commissioners shall have an obligation to inform the Complainant with regard to results of his/her complaint examination activities.

Article 18. Other Powers of Commissioners with respect to Fulfilling of Human Rights and Freedoms

18.1. Commissioners may participate in the advisory capacity in sessions of the State Great Hural or in meetings of the Government Cabinet at the request of the Speaker of the State Great Hural or the Prime Minister.

18.2. Commissioners may conduct inquiries at his/her own initiative on the basis of information with regard to violations of human rights and freedoms or at the request of business entities, organisations or officials.

18.3. Commissioners shall get acquainted with the decisions concerning civil and criminal cases as well as have access to the documents which rejected instituting a case or the cases which have been dropped, with a view to conducting human rights research.

18.4. Commissioners shall refer to the officials or authorities with law-initiating competence his/her proposals with regard to improving the legislation connected with fulfilling human rights and freedoms.

18.5. Commissioners shall provide advice on human rights issues at the request of State authorities.

Article 19. Demands and Recommendations of Commissioners

19.1. Commissioners shall issue demands and/or make recommendations during the course of exercise of his/her powers.

19.2. Commissioners shall write and deliver demands to relevant organisations in order to restore human rights and freedoms and eliminate the violations if he/she has considered that business entity, organisation or official has violated human rights and freedoms.

19.3. Commissioners shall make recommendations within his/her own competence and deliver them to relevant business entities, organisations or officials in order to eliminate reasons and conditions in case there is possibility for violations of human rights and freedoms.

19.4. Business entities, organisations or officials shall inform in writing with regard to measures undertaken within 1 (one) week if they have received demands, and within 30 (thirty) days if they have received recommendations from Commissioners.

19.5. Commissioners may approach the Court, according to the procedure established by law, with regard to the business entities, organisations or officials which have refused to undertake relevant measures as provided under his/her demands and/or recommendations.

19.6. Commissioners shall have a right to publish and report his/her issued demands or recommendations through the mass media.

Article 20. Report of the Commission
20.1. The Commission shall submit to the State Great Hural a report on the human rights situation in Mongolia within the 1st (first) quarter of every year.

20.2. Report of the Commission shall be published in the 'State Gazette'.

CHAPTER FIVE GUARANTEES FOR THE POWERS OF COMMISSIONERS

Article 21. Political Guarantees
21.1. It shall be prohibited for the Commission and its Secretariat to conduct political activities. Commissioners shall suspend his/her political party membership during the period of his/her term of office.

21.2. Commissioners shall treat respectfully his/her official position in exercising his/her freedom of thought, opinion and expression, of speech and press, of conscience and religious belief.

Article 22. Economic and Social Guarantees
22.1. Expenses for the activities of Commissioners shall be financed from the State Consolidated Budget, and the State shall provide economic guarantees for carrying out his/her activities.

22.2. The State Great Hural shall approve and reflect specifically the budget of the Commission in the State Consolidated Budget on the basis of a latter's proposal, and this budget shall fulfil the requirements for the independent conduct of its activities.

22.3. Commissioners shall receive a salary equal to that of the Member of the Government Cabinet.

22.4. In case the term of office of Commissioners has expired, or he/she has been relieved from the office because of the health condition or for any other excusable reasons, Commissioners shall be provided with the allowance for period of up to 6 (six) months, which is not less than the salary level when he/she was Commissioners, until he/she gets transferred to another job or official position in line with his/her profession or expertise, or get employed in different job without scaling down the salary, and if he/she is employed in job with lesser salary, then he/she shall be provided with the difference of that salary during the same period.

Article 23. Legal Guarantees

23.1. If Commissioners has been arrested in a criminal act or on the site of crime with all implicating evidence, it shall be reported by the relevant official to the Chairperson of the State Great Hural within the following 24 (twenty four) hours. In all other cases it shall be prohibited to detain, imprison or impose administrative sanctions by way of a judicial process on Commissioners, and to conduct the search of his/her home, office room and body.

23.2. Unless otherwise provided by the law, it shall be prohibited to release and/or dismiss Commissioners as well as to transfer him/her to another job or official position without his/her consent.

23.3. It shall be prohibited to divulge the confidentiality of correspondence related to the exercise of powers by Commissioners.

23.4. Business entities, organisations and their officials and citizens shall have obligations to render all kinds of assistance to Commissioners in exercise of his/her powers.

CHAPTER SIX MISCELLANEOUS

Article 24. Work Organisation of the Commission

24.1. The Commission shall have a Secretariat. The Commission shall approve the by-laws of its Secretariat, and shall establish the posts and salary fund within the budget limits approved by the State Great Hural.

24.2. Staff of the Commission shall be civil administrative servants.

24.3. The Commission may establish ex-officio boards, which consist of the representatives of advocates' association, confederation of trade unions and/or human rights non-governmental organisations, to be assisted in conducting its activities.

24.4. The Commission may have research conducted by research organisations or non-governmental organisations on the issues, which are considered as required.

Article 25. Seal, Stamp and Official Blank Paper of the Commission
25.1. The Commission shall use a seal, stamp and official blank paper with the State Coat of Arms, made according to the regulation established.

Article 26. Liability for Violation of the Law on the Commission
26.1. The Court shall impose the following administrative sanctions on the persons who has violated this Law:

26.1.1. A citizen who has violated Art 3.4 of this Law shall be liable to a fine of Tg 5,000-40,000, an official to Tg 10,000-50,000, and a business entity or organisation to Tg 50,000-150,000 (Tugrug is national currency);

26.1.2. A citizen who has violated Art 19.4 and Art 23.4 of this Law shall be liable to a fine to Tg 10,000-50,000, an official to Tg 20,000-60,000 and a business entity or organisation to Tg 30,000-250,000.

SPEAKER OF THE STATE GREAT HURAL L. ENEBISH

KINGDOM OF NEPAL

THE HUMAN RIGHTS COMMISSION ACT, 2053 (1997)

Preamble:

Whereas, it is expedient to establish an independent and autonomous National Human Rights Commission in regard to have effective enforcement as well as protection and promotion of tile Human Rights conferred by the Constitution and her prevailing laws;

Be it enacted by Parliament in the twenty-fifth year of the reign of his Majesty the King Birendra Bir Bikram Shah Dev.

CHAPTER - 1
PRELIMINARY

1. Short Title and Commencement:

    (1) This Act may be called "The Human Rights Commission Act, 2053 1997."

    (2) This Act shall come into force forthwith.

2. Definitions: In This Act, unless the subject or context otherwise requires:-

    (a) "Commission" means the National Human Rights Commission constituted under Section 3.

    (b) "Constitution" means the Constitution of the Kingdom of Nepal, 2047 (1990).

    (c) "Chairman" means the Chairman of the Commission and this term also includes the Member of the Commission who acts as an Acting Chairman pursuant to Section 20.

    (d) "Member" means the Member of the Commission and this term also includes the Chairman.

    (e) "Secretary" means the Secretary of the Commission.

    (f) "Human Rights" means the rights relating to lire, liberty, equality and dignity of the individual guaranteed by the Constitution and other prevailing laws and the rights embodied in the international treaties relating to human rights to which Nepal is a party

(g) "Prescribed" or "As Prescribed" means prescribed or as prescribed in the Rules framed under this Act.

CHAPTER - 2
PROVISIONS RELATING TO CONSTITUTION OF THE COMMISSION, TERMS OF SERVICE OF MEMBERS

3. Establishment and Constitution of the Commission:

(1) The National Human Rights Commission comprising the Chairman and Members as follows shall be established and constituted:

(a) One person from amongst the retired Chief Just ice or Judges of the Supreme Court – Chair

(b) Three persons from amongst the persons having rendered outstanding contribution in the field of law, human rights, social work or communications and journalism; ensuring having regard to representation from all the fields to the extent possible – Member

(c) One person from amongst the persons who have served in any office of constitutional bodies or who served in office of special class of His Majesty's Government and got retirement – Member

(2) In addition to the qualifications referred to in sub-section (1), in order to become eligible to be appointed as the Chairman or Member, any person shall have to possess the following qualifications:

(a) To be a citizen of Nepal.

(b) To have attained forty years of age.

(c) Not to have been convicted by, a court in a criminal offense involving moral turpitude

(3) A person once appointed to the office of Member of the Commission shall not be eligible for appointment to an office in any other government service.

(4) The Chairman or Member of the Commission shall not be entitled to carry on professional business elsewhere until he holds office in the Commission.

(5) The Commission shall be a body with perpetual succession.

(6) The Commission shall have a separate seal of its own.

(7) The Commission may, like an individual, acquire, use, sell, dispose of or otherwise deal with movable, immovable property.

(8) The Commission may, like an individual, sue by its own name and it may also be sued.

4. Appointment of Chairman and Member:

(1) His Majesty shall, upon the recommendation of the Recommendation Committee constituted pursuant to sub-section (2), appoint the Chairman and Members of the Commission.

(2) There shall be a Recommendation Committee as follows to make recommendation for appointment of Members of the Commission:

(a) The Prime Minister – Chair

(b) The Chief Justice – Member

(c) The leader of the Opposition in the House of Representatives – Member

(3) The Committee constituted pursuant to sub-section (2) may regulate its working procedures on its own

(4) It shall be the responsibility of the Chief Secretary of His Majesty's Government to make necessary arrangements vis-à-vis the meetings of the committee constituted pursuant to sub-section (2).

5. Term of office of Members:

The term of office of the Members shall be five years from the date of appointment. They shall be eligible for reappointment.

6. Vacation of Office:

The office of the Member shall be vacant in the following circumstances:

(a) If he dies,

(b) If his resignation is accepted by His Majesty,

(c) If the term of office is completed under section 5.

(d) If the Human Rights Committee of the House of Representatives, by a two-thirds majority of the meeting attended by at least two-third members of its total members, adopts a resolution that any Member of the Commission is not to hold the appropriate office by reasons of incompetence or misbehaviour, and the resolution so adopted is approved by the meeting of the House of Representatives. Provided that a Member accused of such charge shall be given a reasonable opportunity to defend himself in the Human Rights Committee of the House of Representatives.

7. Conditions of Service of Members:

The remuneration facilities and other conditions of service of the Chairman and Members of the Commission shall be is prescribed. Provided that such remuneration and facilities shall not be less than the remuneration and facilities to which the Judges of the Supreme Court are entitled.

8. Meeting of tile Commission:

(1) The meetings of the Commission shall be held on such date and in such place as the Chairman appoints.

(2) The Commission shall ordinarily meet twice 1 month.

(3) If three Members are present ill a meeting of tile Commission, it shall be deemed to constitute a quorum for the meeting.

(4) The meetings of the Commission shall be chaired by the and ill the event of absence of the Chairman, the meeting shall be chaired by the senior Member.

(5) The decisions of the Commission shall be made by the majority of the Members Ill the event of a tie, the Chairman shall exercise tile casting vote.

(6) No act or proceedings of the Commission shall be invalidated merely oil the ground of existence of vacancy of the office of any Member.

(7) The Commission may itself regulate other procedures relating to its meetings.

CHAPTER - 3
PROVISIONS RELATING TO FUNCTIONS AND PROCEDURES OF THE COMMISSION

9. Functions and Duties of the Commission:

(1) It shall be the principal duty of the Commission to protect and promote the human rights.

(2) In order to perform the duty referred to in sub-section (1), the Commission way carry out the following functions:

(a) To conduct inquiries into and investigations of ally following matters, upon a petition or complaint presented to the commission by a victim himself or ally person oil his behalf or upon the information received by it from ally source, or on its own initiative:-

(1) Violation of human rights and abetment thereof,

(2) Recklessness or negligence in the prevention of violations of the human rights by any concerned person, organization or body.

(b) Inquiries into and investigations of the matters referred to in clause (a) may be conducted by the Commission itself or through a body or employee of His Majesty's Government or any person; and such a body" employee or person shall conduct inquiries and investigations ill accordance with the directions of the Commission and submit a report to the Commission;

(c) If the Commission deems that the received petition, complaint or information has no basis in fact or is of the nature that it can't be enforced by the courts of Nepal it may keep such petition or complaint pending, with setting out the reasons therefore,

(d) In respect of the proceedings consisting of a claim 011 violations of human lights which is sub Judice in a court, to inquire into the matter with the permission of the court,

(e) To visit, inspect and observe any, body, jail or any organization under His Majesty's Government and to make necessary recommendations to His Majesty's Government on reformations to be made oil the functions and procedures physical facilities etc. of such all organization for the protection of human rights,

(f) To review the provisions oil safeguards provided by the Constitution and other prevailing law for the enforcement of human rights and make necessary recommendations for effective implementation of such provisions,

(g) To study international treaties and instruments on human lights and make necessary and appropriate recommendations to His Majesty's Government for effective implementation of the related provisions,

(h) To undertake or cause to be undertaken research works in the field of human rights,

(i) To publicize and propagate human lights education among various, symposiums, conferences, and vigilant as to the existing legal guarantees oil the protection of human rights;

(j) To encourage the functions and efforts of institutions working ill the non-governmental sector.

(k) To review the existing human rights situation of the country,

(l) To make necessary recommendations to His Majesty's Government on reports to be furnished by Nepal tinder the provisions set forth ill international treaties oil human rights, and

(m) To carry out such other functions as it may deem necessary and appropriate for the enforcement, promotion and protection of human rights.

(3) On the matter of Nepal's obligation to furnish reports under international treaties on human rights, His Majesty's Government shall furnish reports upon receiving opinion of the Commission thereon.

10. Matters Not Subject to Jurisdiction of the Commission:

The Commission shall have no powers to inquire into or institute ally other proceedings oil any of the following matters pursuant to this Act:

(a) A matter under the jurisdiction of the Military Act, provided that nothing will prevent the Commission from carrying out the functions referred to in this Act on a matter with respect of the court may hear a case pursuant to the Constitution and the prevailing law.

(b) A matter certified by, the Chief Secretary of His Majesty's Government that it may have adverse effect oil the treaty concluded between His

Majesty's Government and any foreign government or international or inter-governmental organization, or oil the security of the Kingdom of Nepal,

(c) A matter certified by the Attorney General that it may have adverse effect oil an inquiry into and investigation of any crime pursuant to the law or on finding out the crime or the criminal.

11. Powers of the Commission Relating to Inquiries:

(1) The Commission shall, while inquiring into petitions or complaints or reports made under its jurisdiction, have the same powers as the court has under the prevailing law of Nepal in respect of the following matters:

(a) Requiring ally person to appear in the Commission, and taking and recording his statement or information

(b) Summoning the attendance of witnesses and examining them,

(c) Ordering the production of any document,

(d) Requesting ally document or copy thereof from any governmental or public office or court,

(e) Examining evidences,

(f) Doing or causing to be done in-site inspection, ordering the production of any physical proof

(2) The Commission way prescribe such limitation of time as it may think fit for enforcing the attendance of lily person, producing ally document or procuring ally evidence pursuant to sub-section (I).

(3) In case the Commission has the reasonable grounds to believe that any thing or document relating to subject matter of its inquiry or investigation is ill possession of ally, person or is in any place, it may, pursuant to the existing law of Nepal, search or cause to be searched such person or place and seize or cause to be seized any such goods or take or cause to be liken extracts or copies or duplicates of such document.

(4) The Commission may, if it thinks it necessary, conduct public hearing on an inquiry of any event.

(5) The Commission way make a reference, along with its special stricture to His Majesty's Government or authorized body or authority to take action against a person who does not send the documents or necessary evidences required by the Commission ill connection all inquiry or who does not cooperate it or a person who has asked to appear ill the Commission and does not appear ill the Commission by being self-willed.

(6) The Commission may, as per necessity, constitute committees or sub-committees in regard to any function required to be performed by it under this Act. and the functions, duties and powers of such committees or sub-committees and allowances and facilities to be received by the members of such committees or sub-committees shall be as prescribed by the Commission.

(7) The Commission may, as per necessity, avail itself of tile service or experts of the concerned subject or specialized agencies. The service, term and facilities of the experts rendering such a service shall be as prescribed by the Commission.

12. Complaint and Proceeding Relating to Violation of Human Rights:

The procedures on filing complaints on violations of human rights and proceedings relating thereto shall be as prescribed.

13. Process of Implementation of Decisions of the Commission:

(1) If, while taking proceedings by the Commission on the complaints and petitions filed under its jurisdiction pursuant to Section 11, the accused is found guilty, it shall write to the concerned body, or authority to take necessary action against the guilty.

(2) While writing pursuant to sub-section (1), if the Commission thinks it necessary to provide the victims with necessary compensation, it shall also write therefore.

(3) The bases and procedures to be followed while providing compensation pursuant to sub-section (2) shall be as prescribed.

(4) Upon receiving a writing for actions pursuant to sub-sections (1) and (2), the concerned body or authority shall take action as written by the Commission, or if such action cannot be taken, setting out the reasons thereof, the concerned body or authority shall send the report of the action taken accordingly to the Commission within three months of the date of receipt of the writing from the Commission.

14. To Submit Reports:

(1) The Commission shall each year prepare annual report on the acts and actions carried out by it and submit it to His Majesty, and His Majesty will cause such a report to be laid before Parliament.

(2) The Commission shall each year publish details of acts and actions carried out by it for information of the general public. Provided that if the Commission deems it necessary, it may publish the details of its functions at any time.

15. Financial Management

(1) The Commission may obtain such means and resources from different bodies by, way of grants as are required for the performance of its functions.

(2) The Commission may obtain financial assistance with a view to helping the performance of the functions referred red in Section 9.

(3) The sums of financial assistance obtained pursuant to sub-sections (2) shall be expended in accordance with the terms agreed into between the donor and the Commission.

(4) The Commission shall have to maintain accounts of its incomes and expenditures and other relevant records pursuant to the prevailing law.

(5) The accounts of the Commission shall be audited by the Auditor General.

(6) Other provisions on financial management of the Commission shall be as prescribed.

CHAPTER - 4
MISCELLANEOUS

16. Office of the Commission: The headquarters of the Commission shall be located in Kathmandu Valley. The Commission may as pet- necessity set up branch offices in different areas in the Kingdom of Nepal.

17. Secretary:

(1) There shall be Secretary in the Commission.

(2) The Secretary shall be appointed by His Majesty on the recommendation of the Commission. The term of office, service, terms and other facilities of the Secretary shall be equivalent to that of the Secretary of His Majesty's Government.

18. Staff of the Commission:

(1) The Commission may appoint such staff as are required for its functions, and the service, terms and facilities of the staff so appointed shall be as prescribed.

(2) Notwithstanding anything contained in sub-section (1), the Commission may ask His Majesty's Government to provide the staff required for the Commission. It shall be the duty of His Majesty's Government to provide the staff so asked.

(3) In case the Commission asks any governmental office for assistance in the performance of its functions, such an office shall have to provide assistance.

19. Delegation of Powers:

The Commission may delegate any of the powers conferred on it under this Act to the Chairman or Member or staff of the Commission or to an officer employee of His Majesty's Government or the committee or sub-committee to be constituted under this Act or to any person.

20. To Act as Chairman:

In the event of the occurrence of any vacancy in the office of the Chairman, His Majesty may authorize the senior Member to act as Acting Chairman until the appointment of a new Chairman.

21. Oath:

Before assuming the office, the Chairman shall take all oath before His Majesty and the members, before the Chairman as specified ill the Schedule.

22. Contact with His Majesty's Government:

While making liaison with His Majesty's Government, the Commission shall do so through the Secretariat of the Council of Ministers.

23. To Frame Rules:

The Commission may, in order to carry out the objectives of this Act, frame necessary rules. While making such rules the Commission may consult His Majesty's Government. Provided that ill making rules relating to remuneration and facilities, His Majesty's Government shall be required to he consulted.

24. Saving: No suit or legal proceedings shall be instituted against the Commission or Chairman or Member or staff or ally person designated by the Commission in respect of any act or action which is in good faith done or intended to be done pursuant to this Act or rules framed under this Act.

Schedule
(Relating to Section 21)
Oath

I……………………so swear ill the name of god/solemnly affirm that I will bear loyalty to the Constitution of the Kingdom of Nepal, 1990 and faithfully discharge the responsibility and duty of the office of Chairman/Member assumed by me, without fear, favour, affection, ill-will or greed and that I will not communicate or divulge any matter which becomes known to we ill the course of discharges of my duties in any circumstance where I shall be holding. office or not, except ill pursuance of the prevailing law.

Date of Royal Seal – 2053-9-24-4 (8 Jan. 1997)

NEW ZEALAND

HUMAN RIGHTS ACT

1993 No 82

AMENDMENTS
1994 No 138
1994 No 151
1999 No 100
2001 No 96

An Act to consolidate and amend the Race Relations Act 1971 and the Human Rights Commission Act 1977 and to provide better protection of human rights in New Zealand in general accordance with United Nations Covenants or Conventions on Human Rights

1. Short Title and commencement–
(1) This Act may be cited as the Human Rights Act 1993

(2) This Act shall come into force on the 1st day of February 1994

[2. Interpretation–
1) In this Act, unless the context otherwise requires
"act" includes an activity, condition, enactment, policy, practice, or requirement

"Chief Commissioner" means the Commissioner appointed as the Chief Human Rights Commissioner under section 8(1)(a)

"Commission" means the Human Rights Commission continued by section 4

"Commissioner" means a member of the Commission

"Director of Human Rights Proceedings" or **"Director"** means the Director of Human Rights Proceedings or alternate Director of Human Rights Proceedings appointed under section 20A

"dispose", in sections 53 and 54, includes sell, assign, lease, let, sublease, sublet, license, or mortgage, and agree to dispose

"dispute resolution meeting" means a meeting of the kind referred to in section 77(2)(c)

"dispute resolution services" includes the provision of answers to questions by members of the public about discrimination and compliance with this Act

"employer", in Part 2, includes—
(a) the employer of an independent contractor; and
(b) the person for whom work is done by contract workers under a contract between that person and the person who supplies those contract workers; and
(c) the person for whom work is done by an unpaid worker

"employment agreement" has the meaning given to that term by section 5 of the Employment
Relations Act 2000

"employment contract" has the meaning given to that term by section 2 of the Employment Contracts Act 1991

"Equal Employment Opportunities Commissioner" means the Commissioner appointed as the Equal Employment Opportunities Commissioner under section 8(1)(c)

"General manager" means the General manager of the Commission appointed by the Chief
Commissioner under section 18; and includes any acting general manager of the Commission

"Human Rights Review Tribunal or Tribunal" means the Tribunal continued by section 93
"Minister" means the Minister of Justice

"Office of Human Rights Proceedings or Office" means the office referred to in section 20

"prohibited ground of discrimination" has the meaning given to it by section 21

"Race Relations Commissioner" means the Commissioner appointed as the Race Relations
Commissioner under section 8(1)(b)

"relative", in relation to any person, means any other person who—
(a) is related to the person by blood, marriage, affinity, or adoption; or
(b) is wholly or mainly dependent on the person; or
(c) is a member of the person's household

"residential accommodation", in sections 53 and 54, includes accommodation in a dwelling house, flat, hotel, motel, boarding house, or camping ground

"superannuation scheme" means any superannuation scheme, fund, or plan, or any provident fund, setup to confer, on its members or other persons, retirement or other benefits, such as accident, disability, sickness, or death benefits

"trustees", in relation to a superannuation scheme, includes the person or persons appointed to administer a superannuation scheme constituted under an Act of Parliament of New Zealand.

(2) Unless the context otherwise requires, every reference in this Act to a complaint alleging a breach of 1 or more Parts of this Act includes a complaint that appears to allege or concern such a breach (whether or not it refers to the relevant Part in question).

(3) Unless the context otherwise requires, every reference in this Act to a person against whom a complaint is made includes a body of any kind against whom a complaint is made.

3. Act to bind the Crown—
This Act shall bind the Crown.

Cf 1971 No 150 s 2; 1977 No 49 s 3

PART 1 - HUMAN RIGHTS COMMISSION

4. Continuation of Human Rights Commission—
(1) There shall continue to be a Human Rights Commission, which shall be the same body as the Human Rights Commission established under section 4 of the Human Rights Commission Act 1977.

(2) The Commission shall be a body corporate with perpetual succession and a common seal, and shall be capable of acquiring, holding, and disposing of real and personal property, and of suing and being sued.

(3) Without limiting any other provision of this Act, the Commission shall have the rights, powers, and privileges of a natural person.

[(4) The capacities, rights, and powers referred to in subsections (2) and (3) may be exercised only—

(a) by persons authorised by or under this Act to perform functions of the Commission, for the purposes of performing those functions; or

(b) by the Director of Human Rights Proceedings, his or her alternate, or the staff of the Office of Human Rights Proceedings (acting in accordance with directions issued by the Director or his or her alternate), for the purposes of exercising or performing a function, power, or duty of the Director under this Act.]

Cf 1977 No 49 s 4

[FUNCTIONS AND POWERS OF COMMISSION]

[5. Functions and powers of Commission—
(1) The primary functions of the Commission are—

(a) to advocate and promote respect for, and an understanding and appreciation of, human rights in New Zealand society; and

(b) to encourage the maintenance and development of harmonious relations between individuals and among the diverse groups in New Zealand society

(2) The Commission has, in order to carry out its primary functions under subsection (1), the following functions:

(a) to be an advocate for human rights and to promote and protect, by education and publicity, respect for, and observance of, human rights:

(b) to encourage and co-ordinate programmes and activities in the field of human rights:

(c) to make public statements in relation to any matter affecting human rights, including statements promoting an understanding of, and compliance with, this Act or the New Zealand Bill of Rights Act 1990 (for example, statements promoting understanding of measures to ensure equality, of indirect discrimination, or of institutions and procedures under this Act for dealing with complaints of unlawful discrimination):

(d) to promote by research, education, and discussion a better understanding of the human rights dimensions of the Treaty of Waitangi and their relationship with domestic and international human rights law:

(e) to prepare and publish, as the Commission considers appropriate, guidelines and voluntary codes of practice for the avoidance of acts or practices that may be inconsistent with, or contrary to, this Act:

(f) to receive and invite representations from members of the public on any matter affecting human rights:

(g) to consult and co-operate with other persons and bodies concerned with the protection of human rights:

(h) to inquire generally into any matter, including any enactment or law, or any practice, or any procedure, whether governmental or non-governmental, if it appears to the Commission that the matter involves, or may involve, the infringement of human rights:

(i) to appear in or bring proceedings, in accordance with section 6 or section 92B or section 92E or section 92H or section 97:

(j) to apply to a court or tribunal, under rules of court or regulations specifying the tribunal's procedure, to be appointed as intervener or as counsel assisting the court or tribunal, or to take part in proceedings before the court or tribunal in another way permitted by those rules or regulations, if, in the Commission's opinion, taking part in the proceedings in that way will facilitate the performance of its
functions stated in paragraph (a) of this subsection:

(k) to report to the Prime Minister on—

> (i) any matter affecting human rights, including the desirability of legislative, administrative, or other action to give better protection to human rights and to ensure better compliance with standards laid down in international instruments on human rights:
>
> (ii) the desirability of New Zealand becoming bound by any international instrument on human rights:
>
> (iii) the implications of any proposed legislation (including subordinate legislation) or proposed policy of the Government that the Commission considers may affect human rights:

(l) to make public statements in relation to any group of persons in, or who may be coming to, New Zealand who are or may be subject to hostility, or who have been or may be brought into contempt, on the basis that that group consists of persons against whom discrimination is unlawful under this Act:

(m) to develop a national plan of action, in consultation with interested parties, for the promotion and protection of human rights in New Zealand:

(n) to do anything incidental or conducive to the performance of any of the functions set out in paragraphs (a) to (m):

(o) to exercise or perform any other functions, powers, and duties conferred or imposed on it by or under this Act or any other enactment.

(3) The Commission may, in the public interest or in the interests of a person, department, or organisation, publish reports relating generally to the exercise of its functions under this Act or to a particular inquiry by it under this Act, whether or not the matters to be dealt with in a report of that kind have been the subject of a report to the Minister or the Prime Minister.]

Cf 1977 No 49 ss 5(1), (3), (5), 6(1), (2), 28A, 78(1); 1977 No 49 ss 78(1), 86

[6. Powers relating to declaratory judgments—
(1) If at any time the Commission considers that it may be desirable to obtain a declaratory judgment or order of the High Court in accordance with the Declaratory Judgments Act 1908, the Commission may, despite anything to the contrary in that Act or any other enactment or rule of law, institute proceedings under that Act.

(2) The Commission may exercise the right in subsection (1) only if it considers that the exercise of the right will facilitate the performance of its functions stated in section 5(2)(a).

(3) Subsection (1) does not limit the ability of the Commission to appear in or bring proceedings under section 92B or section 92E or section 92H or section 97.]

Cf 1977 No 49 s 5A; 1983 No 56 s 3

[ACTIVITIES IN PERFORMANCE OF COMMISSION'S FUNCTIONS]

[7. Commission determines general nature of activities—
(1) The members of the Commission acting together determine the strategic direction and the general nature of activities undertaken in the performance of the Commission's functions.

(2) The Chief Commissioner is responsible to the Commission for ensuring that activities undertaken in the performance of the Commission's functions are not inconsistent with determinations of the Commission.]

[MEMBERSHIP OF COMMISSION]

[8. Membership of Commission—

(1) The Commission consists of the following Human Rights Commissioners:

(a) a Commissioner appointed as the Chief Commissioner, whose office is a full-time one:

(b) a Commissioner appointed as the Race Relations Commissioner, whose office is also a full-time one:

[[(c) a Commissioner appointed as the Equal Employment Opportunities Commissioner, whose office is also a full-time one:]]

(d) No more than 5 other Commissioners, whose offices are each part-time ones.

(2) Every Commissioner is appointed by the Governor-General on the recommendation of the Minister.

(3) The powers and functions of the Commission are not affected by a vacancy in its membership.]

Cf 1977 No 49 s 7(1)(a)(c), (ca), (d), (2); 1983 No 56 s 4(1), (2); 1991 No 132 s 3(1); 1993 No 35 s 2

[9. Alternate Commissioners—

(1) The Governor-General may, on the recommendation of the Minister, appoint as alternate

Commissioners persons who may be designated as the alternate of a Commissioner by either the Minister under subsection (2) or the Chief Commissioner under subsection (3).

(2) The Minister may designate a Commissioner or an alternate Commissioner to act as the Chief Commissioner—

(a) during the period following the resignation of the Chief Commissioner and ending when the Chief Commissioner's successor comes into office; or

(b) during the Chief Commissioner's incapacity or in respect of a particular function or activity of the Commission, as the case may be, if—

(i) the Minister is satisfied that the Chief Commissioner is incapacitated by illness, absence, or other sufficient cause from performing the duties of his or her office; or

(ii) the Chief Commissioner considers it is not proper or desirable that he or she should participate in the function or activity.

(3) The Chief Commissioner may designate an alternate Commissioner to act as a Commissioner during the period the Chief Commissioner is acting as Chief Commissioner, or during the period of the Commissioner's incapacity, or in respect of a particular function or activity of the Commission, as the case may be, if—

(a) the Chief Commissioner is a Commissioner acting as the Chief Commissioner under a designation under subsection (2); or

(b) the Chief Commissioner is satisfied that any other Commissioner is incapacitated by illness, absence, or other sufficient cause from performing the duties of his or her office; or

(c) a Judge who is for the time being holding office as a Commissioner declines to participate in, or withdraws from participation in, the particular function or activity of the Commission under section 20C (2); or

(d) any other Commissioner considers it is not proper or desirable that he or she should participate in the function or activity of the Commission.

(4) An alternate Commissioner designated under subsection (2) or subsection (3) must, while the
alternate Commissioner acts as Chief Commissioner or as a Commissioner, be taken to be the Chief Commissioner or the Commissioner in whose place the alternate Commissioner acts.

(5) No designation of an alternate Commissioner, and no act done by an alternate Commissioner, and no act done by the Commission while any alternate Commissioner is acting, may in any proceedings be questioned on the ground that the occasion for the alternate Commissioner's designation had not arisen or had ceased.]

Cf 1977 No 49 s 7B; 1985 No 23 s 2

[10. Meetings of Commission—
(1) Meetings of the Commission are held at such times and places as the Commission or the Chief Commissioner may appoint.

(2) The Chairperson, the Race Relations Commissioner, or any 4 Commissioners, may, at any time, call a special meeting of the Commission.

(3) At a meeting of the Commission, the quorum necessary for the transaction of business is 4
Commissioners.

(4) The Chief Commissioner must preside at all meetings of the Commission at which he or she is present, unless the members present, with the consent of the Chief Commissioner, appoint another member to preside at that meeting.

(5) In the absence of the Chief Commissioner from a meeting, the Commissioners present must appoint 1 of their number to be the Chairperson for the purposes of that meeting.

(6) At a meeting of the Commission, the presiding member has a deliberative vote and, in the case of an equality of votes, also has a casting vote.

(7) A question arising at a meeting of the Commission must be decided by a majority of the valid votes recorded on the question.

(8) Except as provided by or under this Act, the Commission may regulate its procedure in any manner it thinks fit.]

Cf 1977 No 49 s 10

CRITERIA FOR APPOINTMENT

[11. Criteria for appointment—
(1) In recommending persons for appointment as Commissioners or alternate Commissioners, the Minister must have regard to the need for Commissioners and alternate Commissioners appointed to have among them—

(a) knowledge of, or experience in,—

(i) different aspects of matters likely to come before the Commission:

(ii) New Zealand law, or the law of another country, or international law, on human rights:

(iii) the Treaty of Waitangi and rights of indigenous peoples:

(iv) current economic, employment, or social issues:

(v) cultural issues and the needs and aspirations (including life experiences) of different communities of interest and population groups in New Zealand society:

(b) skills in, or experience in,—
(i) advocacy or public education:

(ii) business, commerce, economics, industry, or financial or personnel management:

(iii) community affairs:

(iv) public administration, or the law relating to public administration:

(2) Nothing in this section limits section 12 or section 13.]

Cf 1977 No 49 s 7(3); 1985 No 23 s 3(1)

[12. Further criteria for appointment of Chief Commissioner—
In recommending a person for appointment as Chief Commissioner, the Minister must have regard not only to the criteria stated in section 11 but also to the person's—

(a) ability to provide leadership in relation to the performance of the functions of the Commission (for example, being an advocate for, and promoting, by education and publicity, respect for and observance of human rights):

(b) ability to represent the Commission, and to create and maintain effective relationships between it and other persons or bodies:

(c) knowledge of New Zealand law, the law of other countries, and international law, on human rights, and of New Zealand's obligations under international instruments on human rights:

(d) appreciation of issues or trends in human rights arising in other countries or internationally, and of the relevance of those issues or trends for New Zealand:

(e) ability to perform the functions stated in section 15.]

[13. Further criteria for appointment of Race Relations Commissioner—
In recommending a person for appointment as Race Relations Commissioner, the Minister must have regard not only to the criteria stated in section 11 but also to the person's—

(a) understanding of current race relations in New Zealand, and of the origins and development of those relations:

(b) appreciation of issues or trends in race relations arising in other countries or internationally, and of the relevance of those issues or trends for New Zealand:

(c) ability to perform the functions stated in section 16.]

[14. Further criteria for appointment of Equal Employment Opportunities Commissioner—
In recommending a person for appointment as the Equal Employment Opportunities Commissioner, the Minister must have regard not only to the criteria stated in section 11 but also to the person's—

(a) understanding of principles relating to equal employment opportunities:

(b) appreciation of issues, trends, and developments in the promotion of equal employment opportunities in other countries and internationally, and the relevance of those issues, trends, or developments in New Zealand:

(c) ability to perform the functions stated in section 17.]

FUNCTIONS OF COMMISSIONERS

[15. Functions of Chief Commissioner—
(1) The Chief Commissioner has the following functions:

(a) to chair the Commission, and lead discussions of the Commission (except when the Commission has discussions on matters of race relations):

(b) to ensure that activities undertaken in the performance of the Commission's functions are consistent with the strategic direction and other determinations of the Commission under section 7:

(c) to allocate spheres of responsibility among the Commissioners, and to determine the extent to which Commissioners engage in activities undertaken in the performance of the Commission's functions (except for those stated in section 76), but in each case only after consultation with the Minister:

(d) to act jointly with the Race Relations Commissioner on matters of race relations arising in the course of activities undertaken in the performance of the Commission's functions and to carry out the functions conferred on the Chief Commissioner by section 16(c) and (d):

[[(e) to act jointly with the Equal Employment Opportunities Commissioner on matters concerning equal employment opportunities arising in the course of activities undertaken in the performance of the Commission's functions, and to carry out the functions conferred on the Chief Commissioner by section 17(g):**]]**

(f) to supervise and liaise with the General manager on matters of administration in relation to the Commission and on the activities undertaken in the performance of the Commission's functions:

(g) any other functions, powers, or duties conferred or imposed on him or her by or under this Act or any other enactment.

(2) Subsection (1)(d) and (e) is subject to section 7(2).**]**

Cf 1977 No 49 s 7(1)(a), (5)

[16. Functions of Race Relations Commissioner—
The Race Relations Commissioner has the following functions:

(a) to lead discussions of the Commission in relation to matters of race relations:

(b) to provide advice and leadership on matters of race relations arising in the course of activities undertaken in the performance of the Commission's functions, both when engaging in those activities and otherwise when consulted:

(c) to ensure, acting jointly with the Chief Commissioner, that activities undertaken in the
performance of the Commission's functions in matters of race relations are consistent with the strategic direction and other determinations of the Commission under section 7:

(d) to supervise and liaise with the General manager, acting jointly with the Chief Commissioner, on the activities undertaken in the performance of the Commission's functions in matters of race relations:

(e) any other functions, powers, or duties conferred or imposed on him or her by or under this Act or any other enactment.]

Cf 1971 No 150 s 13; 1977 No 49 s 86

[17. Functions of Equal Employment Opportunities Commissioner—
The Equal Employment Opportunities Commissioner has the following functions:

(a) to lead discussions of the Commission about equal employment opportunities (including pay equity):

(b) to provide advice and leadership on equal employment opportunities arising in the course of activities undertaken in the performance of the Commission's functions, both when engaging in those activities and otherwise when consulted:

(c) to evaluate, through the use of benchmarks developed by the Commissioner, the role that legislation, guidelines, and voluntary codes of practice play in facilitating and promoting best practice in equal employment opportunities:

(d) to lead development of guidelines and voluntary codes of practice to facilitate and promote best practice in equal employment opportunities (including codes that identify related rights and obligations in legislation), in accordance with section 5(2)(e):

(e) to monitor and analyse progress in improving equal employment opportunities in New Zealand, and to report to the Minister on the results of that monitoring and analysis:

(f) to liaise with, and complement the work of, any trust or body that has as 1 of its purposes the promotion of equal employment opportunities (including pay equity):

(g) to ensure, acting jointly with the Chief Commissioner, that activities undertaken in the performance of the Commission's functions in matters of equal employment opportunities are consistent with the strategic direction and other determinations of the Commission under section 7:

(h) any other functions, powers, or duties conferred or imposed on him or her by or under this Act or any other enactment.]

[GENERAL MANAGER AND STAFF OF COMMISSION]

[18. General manager and staff of Commission—

(1) The General manager and staff of the Commission undertake activities required to perform the functions of the Commission in accordance with the strategic direction and other determinations of the Commission under section 7.

(2) The General manager—

(a) is responsible to the Chief Commissioner and reports to him or her; and

(b) is appointed by the Chief Commissioner, in accordance with clause 1 of Schedule 1.

(3) Employees of the Commission are responsible to the General manager and report to him or her.]

[COMMISSIONERS TO ACT INDEPENDENTLY]

[19. Duty to act independently—

Members of the Commission must act independently in the exercise or performance of functions of the Commission.]

[OFFICE OF HUMAN RIGHTS PROCEEDINGS]

[20. Office of Human Rights Proceedings—

(1) The Office of Human Rights Proceedings is part of the Commission and is headed by the Director of Human Rights Proceedings or his or her alternate.

(2) The staff of the Office report to the Director or his or her alternate, and help him or her to exercise or perform the functions, powers, and duties of the Director under this Act.

(3) In exercising or performing the functions, powers, and duties of the Director, the Director or his or her alternate and the staff of the Office must act independently from the Commission and Ministers of the Crown.

(4) However, the Director or his or her alternate is responsible to the Chief Commissioner for the efficient, effective, and economical administration of the activities of the Office.]

[DIRECTOR OF HUMAN RIGHTS PROCEEDINGS]

[20A. Director of Human Rights Proceedings—
(1) The Director of Human Rights Proceedings is appointed by the Governor-General on the recommendation of the Minister.

(2) The Governor-General may, on the recommendation of the Minister, appoint as alternate Director of Human Rights Proceedings a person designated for appointment as alternate Director by the Minister.

(3) The Minister must not designate a person for appointment as alternate Director of Human Rights Proceedings unless—

(a) the Minister is satisfied that the Director is incapacitated by illness, absence, or other sufficient cause from performing the duties of his or her office; or

(b) the Director considers it is not proper or desirable that the Director should perform any particular duty of his or her office.**]**

Cf 1977 No 49 s 7B; 1985 No 23 s 2

[20B. Criteria and requirement for appointment—
(1) In recommending a person for appointment as Director of Human Rights Proceedings or as his or her alternate, the Minister must have regard not only to the person's attributes but also to the person's—

(a) knowledge of, or experience in,—

(i) the different aspects of matters likely to come before the Human Rights Review Tribunal:

(ii) New Zealand law, or the law of another country, or international law, on human rights:

(iii) current economic, employment, or other social issues:

(b) skills in, or experience in, the practice of public law (including the conduct of litigation), and financial and personnel management:

(c) ability to exercise or perform, and to ensure the Office of Human Rights Proceedings helps the person to exercise or perform, efficiently and effectively, the functions, powers, and duties of the Director under this Act.

(2) Every person appointed as Director of Human Rights Proceedings or as his or her alternate must be a barrister or solicitor of the High Court of not less than 5 years' legal experience.]

Cf 1977 No 49 s 7(3); 1985 No 23 s 3(1)

[APPOINTMENT OF JUDGE AS HUMAN RIGHTS COMMISSIONER]

[20C. Appointment of Judge as Human Rights Commissioner—
(1) The appointment of a Judge as a Commissioner or alternate Commissioner or service by a Judge as a Commissioner or alternate Commissioner does not affect his or her tenure of judicial office or his or her rank, title, status, precedence, salary, annual or other allowances, or other rights or privileges as a Judge (including those in relation to superannuation), and, for all purposes, his or her service as a Commissioner or alternate Commissioner must be taken to be service as a Judge.

(2) A Judge who is for the time being holding office as a Commissioner may, at any time, decline to participate in, or withdraw from participation in, any particular function or activity of the Commission if the Judge considers it incompatible with his or her judicial office.]

Cf 1977 No 49 ss 7(5A), 7A; 1983 No 56 ss 4(3), 5; 1985 No 23 s 3(1)

[PROVISIONS RELATING TO OFFICE HOLDERS]

[20D. Office holders to whom sections 20E to 20G apply—
(1) Sections 20E to 20G each applies to a person (the "office holder") who holds 1 of the following offices (the "office"):

(a) Commissioner:

(b) alternate Commissioner:

(c) Director of Human Rights Proceedings:

(d) alternate Director of Human Rights Proceedings.

(2) However, section 20G(c) or (d) do not apply to a Commissioner or alternate Commissioner who is a Judge.

(3) Nothing in subsection (2) limits the application of section 20G(c) or (d) to a Commissioner or alternate Commissioner who ceases to be a Judge during his or her term of office as a Commissioner or alternate Commissioner.]

Cf 1983 No 56 s 6; 1985 No 23 s 3(1)

[20E. Service in office—
The office holder must not be treated as being employed in the service of Her Majesty for the purposes of the State Sector Act 1988 or the Government Superannuation Fund Act 1956 just because he or she is appointed to the office.]

Cf 1971 No 150 s 34; 1977 No 49 s 7(4); 1985 No 23 s 3(1)

[20F. Term of office—
The office holder—

(a) holds the office for the term (not longer than 5 years) the Governor-General, on the recommendation of the Minister, specifies in the person's appointment; and

(b) may, from time to time, be reappointed; and

(c) unless he or she sooner vacates or no longer holds or is removed from the office under section 20G, continues in it until his or her successor comes into it, even though the term for which he or she was appointed has expired.]

Cf 1971 No 150 s 12(1), (2); 1977 No 49 s 8; 1985 No 23 s 3(1)

[20G. Vacation of office—
The office holder—

(a) may resign from the office by delivering to the Minister a notice in writing to that effect and stating when the resignation takes effect:

(b) ceases to hold office if he or she dies:

(c) ceases to hold office if he or she is, under the Insolvency Act 1967, adjudged bankrupt:

(d) may, at any time, be removed from the office by the Governor-General for incapacity affecting performance of duty, neglect of duty, or misconduct, proved to the satisfaction of the Governor-General.]

Cf 1971 No 150 s 12(3); 1977 No 49 s 9; 1985 No 23 s 3(1)

[ADMINISTRATIVE PROVISIONS RELATING TO HUMAN RIGHTS COMMISSION AND OFFICE OF HUMAN RIGHTS PROCEEDINGS]

[20H. Administrative provisions set out in Schedules 1 and 2—
(1) Schedule 1 applies in respect of the Commission.

(2) Schedule 2 applies in respect of the Office.]

PART 1A – DISCRIMINATION BY GOVERNMENT, RELATED PERSONS AND BODIES, OR PERSONS OR BODIES ACTING WITH LEGAL AUTHORITY

[20I. Purpose of this Part—

The purpose of this Part is to provide that, in general, an act or omission that is inconsistent with the right to freedom from discrimination affirmed by section 19 of the New Zealand Bill of Rights Act 1990 is in breach of this Part if the act or omission is that of a person or body referred to in section 3 of the New Zealand Bill of Rights Act 1990.]

[20J. Acts or omissions in relation to which this Part applies—

(1) This Part applies only in relation to an act or omission of a person or body referred to in section 3 of the New Zealand Bill of Rights Act 1990, namely—

(a) the legislative, executive, or judicial branch of the Government of New Zealand; or

(b) a person or body in the performance of any public function, power, or duty conferred or imposed on that person or body by or pursuant to law.

(2) Despite subsection (1), this Part does not apply in relation to an act or omission that is unlawful under any of sections 22, 23, 61 to 63, and 66.

(3) If this Part applies in relation to an act or omission, Part 2 does not apply to that act or omission.

(4) Nothing in this Part affects the New Zealand Bill of Rights Act 1990.]

[20K. Purposes for which section 20L applies—

Section 20L applies only for the purposes of—

(a) any inquiry undertaken by the Commission under section 5(2)(h):

(b) the assessment, consideration, mediation, or determination of a complaint under Part 3:

(c) any determination made by the Director under Part 3 concerning the provision of representation in proceedings before the Human Rights Review Tribunal:

(d) any determination made in proceedings before the Human Rights Review Tribunal or in any proceedings in any court on an appeal from a decision of that Tribunal:

(e) any determination made by any court or tribunal in proceedings brought under this Act by the Commission:

(f) any other process or proceedings commenced or conducted under Part 3:

(g) any related matter.]

[20L. Acts or omissions in breach of this Part—
(1) An act or omission in relation to which this Part applies (including an enactment) is in breach of this Part if it is inconsistent with section 19 of the New Zealand Bill of Rights Act 1990.

(2) For the purposes of subsection (1), an act or omission is inconsistent with section 19 of the New Zealand Bill of Rights Act 1990 if the act or omission—

(a) limits the right to freedom from discrimination affirmed by that section; and

(b) is not, under section 5 of the New Zealand Bill of Rights Act 1990, a justified limitation on that right.

(3) To avoid doubt, subsections (1) and (2) apply in relation to an act or omission even if it is authorized or required by an enactment.]

PART 2 – UNLAWFUL DISCRIMINATION

[Application of Part to persons and bodies referred to in section 3 of New Zealand Bill of Rights Act 1990

[21A. Application of this Part limited if section 3 of New Zealand Bill of Rights Act 1990 applies—
(1) The only provisions of this Part that apply to an act or omission of a person or body described in subsection (2) are—

(a) sections 21 to 35 (which relate to discrimination in employment matters), 61 to 64 (which relate to racial disharmony, and social and racial harassment) and 66 (which relates to victimisation); and

(b) sections 65 and 67 to 74, but only to the extent that those sections relate to conduct that is unlawful under any of the provisions referred to in paragraph (a).

(2) The persons and bodies referred to in subsection (1) are the ones referred to in section 3 of the New Zealand Bill of Rights Act 1990, namely—

(a) the legislative, executive, and judicial branches of the Government of New Zealand; and

(b) every person or body in the performance of any public function, power, or duty conferred or imposed on that person or body by or pursuant to law.]

[ACTS OR OMISSIONS AUTHORISED OR REQUIRED BY LAW

[21B. Relationship between this Part and other law—
(1) To avoid doubt, an act or omission of any person or body is not unlawful under this Part if that act or omission is authorised or required by an enactment or otherwise by law.

(2) Nothing in this Part affects the New Zealand Bill of Rights Act 1990.]

[PROHIBITED GROUNDS OF DISCRIMINATION

[21. Prohibited grounds of discrimination—
(1) For the purposes of this Act, the prohibited grounds of discrimination are—

(a) Sex, which includes pregnancy and childbirth:

(b) Marital status, which means the status of being—

(i) Single; or

(ii) Married; or

(iii) Married but separated; or

(iv) A party to a marriage now dissolved; or

(v) Widowed; or

(vi) Living in a relationship in the nature of a marriage:

(c) Religious belief:

(d) Ethical belief, which means the lack of a religious belief, whether in respect of a particular religion or religions or all religions:

(e) Colour:

(f) Race:

(g) Ethnic or national origins, which includes nationality or citizenship:

(h) Disability, which means—

(i) Physical disability or impairment:

(ii) Physical illness:

(iii) Psychiatric illness:

(iv) Intellectual or psychological disability or impairment:

(v) Any other loss or abnormality of psychological, physiological, or anatomical structure or function:

(vi) Reliance on a guide dog, wheelchair, or other remedial means:

(vii) The presence in the body of organisms capable of causing illness:

(i) Age, which means,—

(i) For the purposes of sections 22 to 41 and section 70 of this Act and in relation to any different treatment based on age that occurs in the period beginning with the 1st day of February 1994 and ending with the close of the 31st day of January 1999, any age commencing with the age of 16 years and ending with the date on which persons of the age of the person whose age is in issue qualify for national superannuation **[[**under section 7 of the New Zealand Superannuation Act 2001**]]** (irrespective of whether or not the particular person qualifies for national superannuation at that age or any other age):

(ii) For the purposes of sections 22 to 41 and section 70 of this Act and in relation to any different treatment based on age that occurs on or after the 1st day of February 1999, any age commencing with the age of 16 years:

(iii) For the purposes of any other provision of Part 2 of this Act, any age commencing with the age of 16 years:

(j) Political opinion, which includes the lack of a particular political opinion or any political opinion:

(k) Employment status, which means—

(i) Being unemployed; or

[[(ii) Being a recipient of a benefit under the Social Security Act 1964 or an entitlement under [the Injury Prevention, Rehabilitation, and Compensation Act 2001]:]]

(l) Family status, which means—

(i) Having the responsibility for part-time care or full-time care of children or other dependants; or

(ii) Having no responsibility for the care of children or other dependants; or

(iii) Being married to, or being in a relationship in the nature of a marriage with, a particular person; or

(iv) Being a relative of a particular person:

(m) Sexual orientation, which means a heterosexual, homosexual, lesbian, or bisexual orientation.

(2) Each of the grounds specified in subsection (1) of this section is a prohibited ground of discrimination, for the purposes of this Act, if—

(a) It pertains to a person or to a relative or associate of a person; and

(b) It either—

(i) Currently exists or has in the past existed; or

(ii) Is suspected or assumed or believed to exist or to have existed by the person alleged to have discriminated.]

DISCRIMINATION IN EMPLOYMENT MATTERS

22. Employment—
(1) Where an applicant for employment or an employee is qualified for work of any description, it shall be unlawful for an employer, or any person acting or purporting to act on behalf of an employer,—

(a) To refuse or omit to employ the applicant on work of that description which is available; or

(b) To offer or afford the applicant or the employee less favourable terms of employment, conditions of work, superannuation or other fringe benefits, and opportunities for training, promotion, and transfer than are made available to applicants or employees of the same or substantially similar capabilities employed in the same or substantially similar circumstances on work of that description; or

(c) To terminate the employment of the employee, or subject the employee to any detriment, in circumstances in which the employment of other employees employed on work of that description would not be terminated, or in which other employees employed on work of that description would not be subjected to such detriment; or

(d) To retire the employee, or to require or cause the employee to retire or resign,— by reason of any of the prohibited grounds of discrimination.

(2) It shall be unlawful for any person concerned with procuring employment for other persons or procuring employees for any employer to treat any person seeking employment differently from other persons in the same or substantially similar circumstances by reason of any of the prohibited grounds of discrimination.

Cf 1977 No 49 s 15(1), (2); 1992 No 16 s 3

23. Particulars of applicants for employment—
It shall be unlawful for any person to use or circulate any form of application for employment or to make any inquiry of or about any applicant for employment which indicates, or could reasonably be understood as indicating, an intention to commit a breach of section 22 of this Act.

Cf 1977 No 49 s 18; 1992 No 16 s 7

EXCEPTIONS IN RELATION TO EMPLOYMENT MATTERS

24. Exception in relation to crews of ships and aircraft—
Nothing in section 22 of this Act shall apply to the employment or an application for employment of a person on a ship or aircraft, not being a New Zealand ship or aircraft, if the person employed or seeking employment was engaged or applied for it outside New Zealand.

Cf 1977 No 49 s 15(8)

25. Exception in relation to work involving national security—
(1) Nothing in section 22 of this Act shall apply to any restrictions on the employment of any person on work involving the national security of New Zealand—

(a) By reference to his or her—

(i) Religious or ethical belief; or

(ii) Political opinion; or

(iii) Disability, within the meaning of section 21(1)(h)(iii) or section 21(1)(h)(iv) of this Act; or

(iv) Family status, within the meaning of section 21(1)(l)(iii) or section 21(1)(l)(iv) of this Act; or

(v) National origin; or

(b) By reference to the national origin of any relative of that person.

(2) It shall not be a breach of section 22 of this Act to decline to employ a person under the age of 20 years on work involving the national security of New Zealand where that work requires a secret or top secret security clearance.

Cf 1977 No 49 s 15(10)

26. Exception in relation to work performed outside New Zealand—
Nothing in section 22 of this Act shall prevent different treatment based on sex, religious or ethical belief, or age if the duties of the position in respect of which that treatment is accorded—

(a) Are to be performed wholly or mainly outside New Zealand; and

(b) Are such that, because of the laws, customs, or practices of the country in which those duties are to be performed, they are ordinarily carried out only by a person who is of a particular sex or religious or ethical belief, or who is in a particular age group.

Cf 1977 No 49 ss 15(9), 15A(1)(b); 1992 No 16 s 4

27. Exceptions in relation to authenticity and privacy—
(1) Nothing in section 22 of this Act shall prevent different treatment based on sex or age where, for reasons of authenticity, being of a particular sex or age is a genuine occupational qualification for the position or employment.

(2) Nothing in section 22 of this Act shall prevent different treatment based on sex, religious or ethical belief, disability, age, political opinion, or sexual orientation where the position is one of domestic employment in a private household.

(3) Nothing in section 22 of this Act shall prevent different treatment based on sex where—

(a) The position needs to be held by one sex to preserve reasonable standards of privacy; or

(b) The nature or location of the employment makes it impracticable for the employee to live elsewhere than in premises provided by the employer, and—

(i) The only premises available (being premises in which more than one employee is required to sleep) are not equipped with separate sleeping accommodation for each sex; and

(ii) It is not reasonable to expect the employer to equip those premises with separate accommodation, or to provide separate premises, for each sex.

(4) Nothing in section 22 of this Act shall prevent different treatment based on sex, race, ethnic or national origins, or sexual orientation where the position is that of a counsellor on highly personal matters such as sexual matters or the prevention of violence.

(5) Where, as a term or condition of employment, a position ordinarily obliges or qualifies the holder of that position to live in premises provided by the employer, the employer does not commit a breach of section 22 of this Act by omitting to apply that term or condition in respect of employees of a particular sex or marital status if in all the circumstances it is not reasonably practicable for the employer to do so.

Cf 1977 No 49 ss 15(3), 15A(1)(a); 1992 No 16 s 4

28. Exceptions for purposes of religion—
(1) Nothing in section 22 of this Act shall prevent different treatment based on sex where the position is for the purposes of an organised religion and is limited to one sex so as to comply with the doctrines or rules or established customs of the religion.

(2) Nothing in section 22 of this Act shall prevent different treatment based on religious or ethical belief where—

(a) That treatment is accorded under section 65 of the Private Schools Conditional Integration Act 1975; or

(b) The sole or principal duties of the position (not being a position to which section 65 of the Private Schools Conditional Integration Act 1975 applies)—

(i) Are, or are substantially the same as, those of a clergyman, priest, pastor, official, or teacher among adherents of that belief or otherwise involve the propagation of that belief; or

(ii) Are those of a teacher in a private school; or

(iii) Consist of acting as a social worker on behalf of an organisation whose members comprise solely or principally adherents of that belief.

(3) Where a religious or ethical belief requires its adherents to follow a particular practice, an employer must accommodate the practice so long as any adjustment of the employer's activities required to accommodate the practice does not unreasonably disrupt the employer's activities.

Cf 1977 No 49 s 15(6), (7)

29. Further exceptions in relation to disability—
(1) Nothing in section 22 of this Act shall prevent different treatment based on disability where—

(a) The position is such that the person could perform the duties of the position satisfactorily only with the aid of special services or facilities and it is not reasonable to expect the employer to provide those services or facilities; or

(b) The environment in which the duties of the position are to be performed or the nature of those duties, or of some of them, is such that the person could perform those duties only with a risk of harm to that person or to others, including the risk of infecting others with an illness, and it is not reasonable to take that risk.

(2) Nothing in subsection (1)(b) of this section shall apply if the employer could, without unreasonable disruption, take reasonable measures to reduce the risk to a normal level.

(3) Nothing in section 22 of this Act shall apply to terms of employment or conditions of work that are set or varied after taking into account—

(a) Any special limitations that the disability of a person imposes on his or her capacity to carry out the work; and

(b) Any special services or facilities that are provided to enable or facilitate the carrying out of the work.

30. Further exceptions in relation to age—
(1) Nothing in section 22(1)(a) or section 22(1)(d) of this Act shall apply in relation to any position or employment where being of a particular age or in a particular age group is a genuine occupational qualification for that position or employment, whether for reasons of safety or for any other reason.

(2) Nothing in section 22(1)(b) of this Act shall prevent payment of a person at a lower rate than another person employed in the same or substantially similar circumstances where the lower rate is paid on the basis that the first-mentioned person has not attained a particular age, not exceeding 20 years of age.

(3) Nothing in section 22(1)(a) of this Act shall prevent preferential treatment based on age accorded to persons who are to be paid in accordance with subsection (2) of this section.

Cf 1977 No 49 s 15A(2)-(4); 1992 No 16 s 4

[30A. Exception in relation to employment-related retirement benefits—
(1) Nothing in section 22(1)(b) prevents different treatment based on age with respect to, or in any way related to, the payment of a benefit to an employee on retirement if—

(a) The employee's entitlement to that benefit ("the retirement benefit"), or the calculation of that retirement benefit, is determined in whole or in part (and whether directly or indirectly) by the employee's age; and

(b) The retirement benefit is a term of a written employment contract that was in force on or before 1 February 1999; and

(c) The employee was, on or before 1 February 1999, a party to that employment contract.

(2) If a retirement benefit was a term of an employee's written employment contract on 1 February 1999, subsection (1) continues to apply in relation to the payment of that retirement benefit even if either or both of the following things occur after that date:

(a) The employee and the employer enter into a new written employment contract **[[**or employment agreement**]]** under which the employee remains entitled to that retirement benefit:

(b) A different person becomes the employee's employer as a result of a merger, takeover, restructuring, or reorganisation, but the employee remains entitled to that retirement benefit by virtue of any enactment or agreement.

(3) This section does not limit section 149.**]**

31. Exception in relation to employment of a political nature—
Nothing in section 22 of this Act shall prevent different treatment based on political opinion where the position is one as—

(a) A political adviser or secretary to a member of Parliament; or

(b) A political adviser to a member of a local authority; or

(c) A political adviser to a candidate seeking election to the House of Representatives or to a local authority within the meaning of the **[**Local Electoral Act 2001**]**; or

(d) A member of the staff of a political party.

32. Exception in relation to family status—
Nothing in section 22 of this Act shall prevent restrictions imposed by an employer—

(a) On the employment of any person who is married to, or living in a relationship in the nature of marriage with, or who is a relative of, another employee if—

(i) There would be a reporting relationship between them; or

(ii) There is a risk of collusion between them to the detriment of the employer; or

(b) On the employment of any person who is married to, or living in a relationship in the nature of marriage with, or who is a relative of, an employee of another employer if there is a risk of collusion between them to the detriment of that person's employer.

33. Armed Forces—
Nothing in section 22 of this Act shall prevent preferential treatment based on sex being given within the Armed Forces to any member of those forces who has the duty of serving in an active combat role in those forces.

Cf 1977 No 49 s 16(2)(b)

34. Regular forces and Police—
(1) Nothing in section 22(1)(c) or section 22(1)(d) of this Act shall prevent the Chief of Defence Force from instituting, under section 57A of the Defence Act 1990, the discharge or release of a member of the regular forces.

(2) Nothing in section 22(1)(c) or section 22(1)(d) of this Act shall prevent the Commissioner of Police from instituting, under section 5A of the Police Act 1958, the removal of a member of the Police.

35. General qualification on exceptions—
No employer shall be entitled, by virtue of any of the exceptions in this Part of this Act, to accord to any person in respect of any position different treatment based on a prohibited ground of discrimination even though some of the duties of that position would fall within any of those exceptions if, with some adjustment of the activities of the employer (not being an adjustment involving unreasonable disruption of the activities of the employer), some other employee could carry out those particular duties.

Cf 1977 No 49 s 15(4)

DISCRIMINATION IN PARTNERSHIPS

36. Partnerships—
(1) It shall be unlawful for a firm, or for persons jointly promoting the formation of a firm,—

(a) To refuse or to omit to offer a person admission to the firm as a partner; or

(b) To offer or afford a person less favourable terms and conditions as a partner than are made available to other members or prospective members of the firm,— by reason of any of the prohibited grounds of discrimination.

(2) It shall be unlawful for a firm—

(a) To deny any partner increased status in the firm or an increased share in the capital or profits of the firm; or

(b) To expel any partner from the firm or to subject any partner to any other detriment,— by reason of any of the prohibited grounds of discrimination.

(3) Nothing in subsection (1) or subsection (2) of this section shall prevent the fixing of reasonable terms and conditions in relation to a partner or prospective partner who, by reason of disability or age,—

(a) Has a restricted capacity to participate or to continue to participate in the partnership; or

(b) Requires special conditions if he or she is to participate or to continue to participate in the partnership.

Cf 1977 No 49 s 19; 1992 No 16 s 8

DISCRIMINATION BY INDUSTRIAL AND PROFESSIONAL ASSOCIATIONS, QUALIFYING BODIES, AND VOCATIONAL TRAINING BODIES

37. Organisations of employees or employers and professional and trade associations—

(1) It shall be unlawful for an organisation to which this section applies, or for any person acting or purporting to act on behalf of any such organisation,—

(a) To refuse or omit to accept any person for membership; or

(b) To offer any person less favourable terms of membership and less favourable access to any benefits, facilities, or services, including the right to stand for election and hold office in the organisation, than would otherwise be made available; or

(c) To deprive a person of membership, or suspend him or her, in circumstances in which other persons would not be deprived of membership or suspended,— by reason of any of the prohibited grounds of discrimination.

(2) Nothing in this section shall prevent an organisation to which this section applies from charging different fees to persons in different age groups.

(3) This section applies to an organisation of employees, an organisation of employers, or any other organisation that exists for the purposes of members who carry on a particular profession, trade, or calling.

Cf 1977 No 49 s 20; 1992 No 16 s 9

38. Qualifying bodies—
(1) It shall be unlawful for an authority or body empowered to confer an approval, authorisation, or qualification that is needed for, or facilitates, engagement in a profession, trade, or calling, or any person acting or purporting to act on behalf of any such authority or body,—

(a) To refuse or omit to confer that approval, authorisation, or qualification on a person; or

(b) To confer that approval, authorisation, or qualification on less favourable terms and conditions than would otherwise be made available; or

(c) To withdraw that approval, authorisation, or qualification or vary the terms on which it is held, in circumstances in which it would not otherwise be withdrawn or varied,— by reason of any of the prohibited grounds of discrimination.

(2) For the purposes of this section "confer" includes renew or extend.

Cf 1977 No 49 s 21(1), (3); 1992 No 16 s 10(1)

39. Exceptions in relation to qualifying bodies—
(1) Nothing in section 38 of this Act shall apply where the authorisation or qualification is needed for, or facilitates engagement in, a profession or calling for the purposes of an organised religion and is limited to one sex or to persons of that religious belief so as to comply with the doctrines or rules or established customs of that religion.

(2) Nothing in section 38 of this Act shall prevent different treatment based on disability where—

(a) The person seeking or holding the approval, authorisation, or qualification is not, by reason of that person's disability, able to perform the duties required of a person who holds the approval, authorisation, or qualification; or

(b) The environment in which the duties required of a person who holds the approval, authorisation, or qualification are to be performed or the nature of those duties, or of some of them, are such that, if that approval, authorisation, or qualification were granted to or retained by the person with a disability, there would be a risk of harm to that person or others, including the risk of infecting others with an illness, and it is not reasonable to take that risk; or

(c) Conditions placed on the granting of the approval, authorisation, or qualification to any person or on the retention of the approval, authorisation, or qualification by any person are reasonably related to the disability of that person.

(3) Nothing in section 38 of this Act shall apply where—

(a) The authority or body imposes a reasonable and appropriate minimum age under which the approval, authorisation, or qualification will not be conferred; or

(b) The authority or body imposes reasonable and appropriate terms and conditions on the grant or retention of the approval, authorisation, or qualification by reason of the age of the person seeking or holding it.

Cf 1977 No 49 s 21(2), (2A); 1992 No 16 s 10(2)

40. Vocational training bodies—
It shall be unlawful for any organisation or association which has as its function or one of its principal functions the provision of training, or facilities or opportunities for training (including facilities or opportunities by way of financial grants), that would help to fit a person for any employment, or for any person acting or purporting to act on behalf of any such organisation or association,—

(a) To refuse or omit to provide training, or facilities or opportunities for training; or

(b) To provide training, or facilities or opportunities for training, on less favourable terms and conditions than would otherwise be made available; or

(c) To terminate training, or facilities or opportunities for training,—
by reason of any of the prohibited grounds of discrimination.

Cf 1977 No 49 s 22(1); 1992 No 16 s 11(1)

41. Exceptions in relation to vocational training bodies—
(1) Nothing in section 40 of this Act shall prevent an organisation or association from affording persons preferential access to facilities for training that would help to fit them for employment where it appears to that organisation or association that those persons are in special need of training by reason of the period for which they have not been engaged in regular full-time employment.

(2) Subject to subsection (3) of this section, nothing in section 40 of this Act shall apply where a person's disability is such that there would be a risk of harm to that person or to others, including the risk of infecting others with an illness, if that person were to be provided with training, or facilities or opportunities for training, and it is not reasonable to take that risk.

(3) Nothing in subsection (2) of this section shall apply if the organisation or association providing training, or facilities or opportunities for training, could, without unreasonable disruption, take reasonable measures to reduce the risk to a normal level.

(4) Nothing in section 40 of this Act shall prevent an organisation or association from providing training, or facilities or opportunities for training (including facilities or opportunities by way of financial grants), only for persons above a particular age or in a particular age group.

(5) Nothing in section 40 of this Act shall prevent the making of financial grants by an organisation or association only to persons above a particular age or in a particular age group.

(6) Nothing in section 40 of this Act shall prevent an organisation or association from charging different fees to persons in different age groups.

Cf 1977 No 49 s 22(3), (4), (5), (6); 1992 No 16 s 11(3)

DISCRIMINATION IN ACCESS TO PLACES, VEHICLES, AND FACILITIES

42. Access by the public to places, vehicles, and facilities—
(1) It shall be unlawful for any person—

(a) To refuse to allow any other person access to or use of any place or vehicle which members of the public are entitled or allowed to enter or use; or

(b) To refuse any other person the use of any facilities in that place or vehicle which are available to members of the public; or

(c) To require any other person to leave or cease to use that place or vehicle or those facilities,—

by reason of any of the prohibited grounds of discrimination.

(2) In this section the term "vehicle" includes a vessel, an aircraft, or a hovercraft.

Cf 1977 No 49 s 23(1), (3)

43. Exceptions in relation to access by the public to places, vehicles, and facilities—
(1) Section 42 of this Act shall not prevent the maintenance of separate facilities for each sex on the ground of public decency or public safety.

(2) Nothing in section 42 of this Act requires any person to provide for any person, by reason of the disability of that person, special services or special facilities to enable any such person to gain access to or use any place or vehicle when it would not be reasonable to require the provision of such special services or facilities.

[(3) Nothing in subsection (2) limits section 47A of the Building Act 1991.]

(4) Subject to subsection (5) of this section, nothing in section 42 of this Act shall apply where the disability of a person is such that there would be a risk of harm to that person or to others, including the risk of infecting others with an illness, if that person were to have access to or use of any place or vehicle and it is not reasonable to take that risk.

(5) Subsection (4) of this section shall not apply if the person in charge of the place, vehicle, or facility could, without unreasonable disruption, take reasonable measures to reduce the risk to a normal level.

Cf 1977 No 49 s 23(2)

DISCRIMINATION IN PROVISION OF GOODS AND SERVICES

44. Provision of goods and services—
(1) It shall be unlawful for any person who supplies goods, facilities, or services to the public or to any section of the public—

(a) To refuse or fail on demand to provide any other person with those goods, facilities, or services; or

(b) To treat any other person less favourably in connection with the provision of those goods, facilities, or services than would otherwise be the case,—

by reason of any of the prohibited grounds of discrimination.

(2) For the purposes of subsection (1) of this section, but without limiting the meaning of the terms "goods", "facilities", and "services" in that subsection, the term "facilities" includes facilities by way of banking or insurance or for grants, loans, credit, or finance.

(3) Where any club, or any branch or affiliate of any club, that grants privileges to members of any other club, branch, or affiliate refuses or fails on demand to provide those privileges to any of those members, or treats any of those members less favourably in connection with the provision of those privileges than would otherwise be the case, by reason of any of the prohibited grounds of discrimination, that club, branch, or affiliate shall be deemed to have committed a breach of this section.

(4) Subject to subsection (3) of this section, nothing in this section shall apply to access to membership of a club or to the provision of services or facilities to members of a club.

Cf 1977 No 49 s 24(1)-(3)

45. Exception in relation to courses and counselling—
Nothing in section 44 of this Act shall prevent the holding of courses, or the provision of counselling, restricted to persons of a particular sex, race, ethnic or national origin, or sexual orientation where highly personal matters, such as sexual matters or the prevention of violence, are involved.

46. Exception in relation to public decency or safety—
Section 44 of this Act shall not apply to the maintenance or provision of separate facilities or services for each sex on the ground of public decency or public safety.

Cf 1977 No 49 s 24(4)

47. Exception in relation to skill—
Where the nature of a skill varies according to whether it is exercised in relation to men or women, a person does not commit a breach of section 44 of this Act by exercising the skill in relation to one sex only, in accordance with that person's normal practice.

Cf 1977 No 49 s 24(5)

48. Exception in relation to insurance—
(1) It shall not be a breach of section 44 of this Act to offer or provide annuities, life insurance policies, accident insurance policies, or other policies of insurance, whether for individual persons or groups of persons, on different terms or conditions for each sex or for persons with a disability or for persons of different ages if the different treatment—

(a) Is based on—

(i) Actuarial or statistical data, upon which it is reasonable to rely, relating to life-expectancy, accidents, or sickness; or

(ii) Where no such data is available in respect of persons with a disability, reputable medical or actuarial advice or opinion, upon which it is reasonable to rely, whether or not contained in an underwriting manual; and

(b) Is reasonable having regard to the applicability of the data or advice or opinion, and of any other relevant factors, to the particular circumstances.

(2) In assessing, for the purposes of this section, whether it is reasonable to rely on any data or advice or opinion, and whether different treatment is reasonable, the Commission or the Complaints Division may—

(a) Require justification to be provided for reliance on the data or advice or opinion and for the different treatment; and

(b) Request the views of the Government Actuary on the justification for the reliance and for the different treatment.

Cf 1977 No 49 s 24(6)

49. Exception in relation to sport—
(1) Subject to subsection (2) of this section, nothing in section 44 of this Act shall prevent the exclusion of persons of one sex from participation in any competitive sporting activity in which the strength, stamina, or physique of competitors is relevant.

(2) Subsection (1) of this section does not apply in relation to the exclusion of persons from participation in—

(a) The coaching of persons engaged in any sporting activity; or

(b) The umpiring or refereeing of any sporting activity; or

(c) The administration of any sporting activity; or

(d) Sporting activities by persons who have not attained the age of 12 years.

(3) It shall not be a breach of section 44 of this Act to exclude any person from any competitive sporting event or activity if that person's disability is such that there would be a risk of harm to that person or to others, including the risk of infecting others with an illness, if that person were to take part in that competitive sporting event or activity and it is not reasonable to take that risk.

(4) It shall not be a breach of section 44 of this Act to conduct competitive sporting events or activities in which only persons with a particular disability or age qualification may take part.

50. Exception in relation to travel services—
It shall not be a breach of section 44 of this Act to provide group travel services which are expressed to be solely for the benefit of persons in a particular age group.

51. Exception in relation to reduced charges—
It shall not be a breach of section 44 of this Act to provide goods, services, or facilities at a reduced fee, charge, or rate on the ground of age, disability, or employment status, whether or not there are conditions applicable to the reduced fee, charge, or rate.

52. Exception in relation to disability—
It shall not be a breach of section 44 of this Act for a person who supplies facilities or services—

(a) To refuse to provide those facilities or services to any person if—

(i) That person's disability requires those facilities or services to be provided in a special manner; and

(ii) The person who supplies the facilities or services cannot reasonably be expected to provide them in that special manner; or

(b) To provide those facilities or services to any person on terms that are more onerous than those on which they are made available to other persons, if—

(i) That person's disability requires those facilities or services to be provided in a special manner; and

(ii) The person who supplies the facilities or services cannot reasonably be expected to provide them without requiring more onerous terms.

Cf Equal Opportunity Act 1984, s 29(2) (Victoria)

DISCRIMINATION IN PROVISION OF LAND, HOUSING, AND OTHER ACCOMMODATION

53. Land, housing, and other accommodation—
(1) It shall be unlawful for any person, on his or her own behalf or on behalf or purported behalf of any principal,—

(a) To refuse or fail to dispose of any estate or interest in land or any residential or business accommodation to any other person; or

(b) To dispose of such an estate or interest or such accommodation to any person on less favourable terms and conditions than are or would be offered to other persons; or

(c) To treat any person who is seeking to acquire or has acquired such an estate or interest or such accommodation differently from other persons in the same circumstances; or

(d) To deny any person, directly or indirectly, the right to occupy any land or any residential or business accommodation; or

(e) To terminate any estate or interest in land or the right of any person to occupy any land or any residential or business accommodation,—
by reason of any of the prohibited grounds of discrimination.

(2) It shall be unlawful for any person, on his or her own behalf or on behalf or purported behalf of any principal, to impose or seek to impose on any other person

any term or condition which limits, by reference to any of the prohibited grounds of discrimination, the persons or class of persons who may be the licensees or invitees of the occupier of any land or any residential or business accommodation.

Cf 1977 No 49 s 25(1), (2)

54. Exception in relation to shared residential accommodation—
Nothing in section 53 of this Act shall apply to residential accommodation which is to be shared with the person disposing of the accommodation, or on whose behalf it is disposed of.

Cf 1977 No 49 s 25(4)

55. Exception in relation to hostels, institutions, etc—
Nothing in section 53 of this Act shall apply to accommodation in any hostel or in any establishment (such as a hospital, club, school, university, religious institution, or retirement village), or in any part of a hostel or any such establishment, where accommodation is provided only for persons of the same sex, marital status, or religious or ethical belief, or for persons with a particular disability, or for persons in a particular age group.

Cf 1977 No 49 s 25(3)

56. Further exception in relation to disability—
(1) Subject to subsection (2) of this section, nothing in section 53 of this Act shall apply, in relation to any accommodation, if the disability of the person is such that there would be a risk of harm to that person or others, including the risk of infecting others with an illness, if that person were to live in that accommodation and it is not reasonable to take that risk.

(2) Subsection (1) of this section shall not apply if the person in charge of the accommodation could, without unreasonable disruption, take reasonable measures to reduce the risk to a normal level.

DISCRIMINATION IN ACCESS TO EDUCATIONAL ESTABLISHMENTS

57. Educational establishments—
(1) It shall be unlawful for an educational establishment, or the authority responsible for the control of an educational establishment, or any person concerned in the management of an educational establishment or in teaching at an educational establishment,—

(a) To refuse or fail to admit a person as a pupil or student; or

(b) To admit a person as a pupil or a student on less favourable terms and conditions than would otherwise be made available; or

(c) To deny or restrict access to any benefits or services provided by the establishment; or

(d) To exclude a person as a pupil or a student or subject him or her to any other detriment,—

by reason of any of the prohibited grounds of discrimination.

(2) In this section "educational establishment" includes an establishment offering any form of training or instruction and an educational establishment under the control of an organisation or association referred to in section 40 of this Act.

Cf 1977 No 49 s 26(1), (3)

58. Exceptions in relation to establishments for particular groups—
(1) An educational establishment maintained wholly or principally for students of one sex, race, or religious belief, or for students with a particular disability, or for students in a particular age group, or the authority responsible for the control of any such establishment, does not commit a breach of section 57 of this Act by refusing to admit students of a different sex, race, or religious belief, or students not having that disability or not being in that age group.

(2) Nothing in section 57 of this Act shall prevent an organisation or association from affording persons preferential access to facilities for training that would help to fit them for employment where it appears to that organisation or association that those persons are in special need of training by reason of the period for which they have not been engaged in regular full-time employment.

(3) Nothing in section 57 of this Act shall prevent an organisation or association from providing training, or facilities or opportunities for training (including facilities or opportunities by way of financial grants), only for persons above a particular age or in a particular age group.

(4) Nothing in section 57 of this Act shall prevent the making of financial grants by an organisation or association only to persons above a particular age or in a particular age group.

(5) Nothing in section 57 of this Act shall prevent an organisation or association from charging different fees to persons in different age groups.

Cf 1977 No 49 s 26(2)

59. Exception in relation to courses and counselling—
Nothing in section 57 of this Act shall prevent the holding or provision, at any educational establishment, of courses or counselling restricted to persons of a particular sex, race, ethnic or national origin, or sexual orientation, where highly personal matters, such as sexual matters or the prevention of violence, are involved.

60. Further exceptions in relation to disability—
(1) Nothing in section 57 of this Act makes it unlawful to refuse admission to an educational establishment to a person whose disability is such that that person requires special services or facilities that in the circumstances cannot reasonably be made available (being services or facilities that are required to enable the person to participate in the educational programme of that establishment or to enable the person to derive substantial benefits from that programme).

(2) Subject to subsection (3) of this section, nothing in section 57 of this Act shall apply where the person's disability is such that there would be a risk of harm to that person or to others, including the risk of infecting others with an illness, if that person were to be admitted to an educational establishment and it is not reasonable to take that risk.

(3) Nothing in subsection (2) of this section shall apply if the person in charge of the educational establishment could, without unreasonable disruption, take reasonable measures to reduce the risk to a normal level.

Cf Equal Opportunity Act 1984, s 28(5) (Victoria)

OTHER FORMS OF DISCRIMINATION

61. Racial disharmony—
(1) It shall be unlawful for any person—

(a) To publish or distribute written matter which is threatening, abusive, or insulting, or to broadcast by means of radio or television words which are threatening, abusive, or insulting; or

(b) To use in any public place as defined in section 2(1) of the Summary Offences Act 1981, or within the hearing of persons in any such public place, or at any meeting to which the public are invited or have access, words which are threatening, abusive, or insulting; or

(c) To use in any place words which are threatening, abusive, or insulting if the person using the words knew or ought to have known that the words were reasonably likely to be published in a newspaper, magazine, or periodical or broadcast by means of radio or television,—

being matter or words likely to excite hostility against or bring into contempt any group of persons in or who may be coming to New Zealand on the ground of the colour, race, or ethnic or national origins of that group of persons.

(2) It shall not be a breach of subsection (1) of this section to publish in a newspaper, magazine, or periodical or broadcast by means of radio or television a report relating to the publication or distribution of matter by any person or the broadcast or use of words by any person, if the report of the matter or words accurately conveys the intention of the person who published or distributed the matter or broadcast or used the words.

(3) For the purposes of this section,—
"Newspaper" means a paper containing public news or observations on public news, or consisting wholly or mainly of advertisements, being a newspaper that is published periodically at intervals not exceeding 3 months:

"Publishes" or **"distributes"** means publishes or distributes to the public at large or to any member or members of the public:

"Written matter" includes any writing, sign, visible representation, or sound recording.

Cf 1971 No 150 s 9A; 1977 No 49 s 86; 1989 No 127 s 2

62. Sexual harassment—
(1) It shall be unlawful for any person (in the course of that person's involvement in any of the areas to which this subsection is applied by subsection (3) of this section) to make a request of any other person for sexual intercourse, sexual contact, or other form of sexual activity which contains an implied or overt promise of preferential treatment or an implied or overt threat of detrimental treatment.

(2) It shall be unlawful for any person (in the course of that person's involvement in any of the areas to which this subsection is applied by subsection (3) of this section) by the use of language (whether written or spoken) of a sexual nature, or of visual material of a sexual nature, or by physical behaviour of a sexual nature, to subject any other person to behaviour that—

(a) Is unwelcome or offensive to that person (whether or not that is conveyed to the first-mentioned person); and

(b) Is either repeated, or of such a significant nature, that it has a detrimental effect on that person in respect of any of the areas to which this subsection is applied by subsection (3) of this section.

(3) The areas to which subsections (1) and (2) of this section apply are—

(a) The making of an application for employment:

(b) Employment, which term includes unpaid work:

(c) Participation in, or the making of an application for participation in, a partnership:

(d) Membership, or the making of an application for membership, of an industrial union or professional or trade association:

(e) Access to any approval, authorisation, or qualification:

(f) Vocational training, or the making of an application for vocational training:

(g) Access to places, vehicles, and facilities:

(h) Access to goods and services:

(i) Access to land, housing, or other accommodation:

(j) Education.

(4) Where a person complains of sexual harassment, no account shall be taken of any evidence of the person's sexual experience or reputation.

63. Racial harassment—
(1) It shall be unlawful for any person to use language (whether written or spoken), or visual material, or physical behaviour that—

(a) Expresses hostility against, or brings into contempt or ridicule, any other person on the ground of the colour, race, or ethnic or national origins of that person; and

(b) Is hurtful or offensive to that other person (whether or not that is conveyed to the first-mentioned person); and

(c) Is either repeated, or of such a significant nature, that it has a detrimental effect on that other person in respect of any of the areas to which this subsection is applied by subsection (2) of this section.

(2) The areas to which subsection (1) of this section applies are—

(a) The making of an application for employment:

(b) Employment, which term includes unpaid work:

(c) Participation in, or the making of an application for participation in, a partnership:

(d) Membership, or the making of an application for membership, of an industrial union or professional or trade association:

(e) Access to any approval, authorisation, or qualification:

(f) Vocational training, or the making of an application for vocational training:

(g) Access to places, vehicles, and facilities:

(h) Access to goods and services:

(i) Access to land, housing, or other accommodation:

(j) Education.

64. Choice of procedures—
Where the circumstances giving rise to a complaint of "sexual harassment" or "racial harassment" under this Act are such that an employee would also be entitled to bring personal grievance proceedings under the [Employment Relations Act 2000], the employee may take one but not both of the following steps:

(a) The employee may make, in relation to those circumstances, a complaint under this Act; or

(b) The employee may invoke, in relation to those circumstances, the procedures applicable under the [Employment Relations Act 2000] in relation to personal grievances under the relevant [employment agreement].

65. Indirect discrimination—
Where any conduct, practice, requirement, or condition that is not apparently in contravention of any provision of this Part of this Act has the effect of treating a person or group of persons differently on one of the prohibited grounds of discrimination in a situation where such treatment would be unlawful under any provision of this Part of this Act other than this section, that conduct, practice,

condition, or requirement shall be unlawful under that provision unless the person whose conduct or practice is in issue, or who imposes the condition or requirement, establishes good reason for it.

Cf 1977 No 49 s 27; 1992 No 16 s 12

66. Victimisation—

(1) It shall be unlawful for any person to treat or to threaten to treat any other person less favourably than he or she would treat other persons in the same or substantially similar circumstances—

[(a) on the ground that that person, or any relative or associate of that person,—

(i) intends to make use of his or her rights under this Act or to make a disclosure under the Protected Disclosures Act 2000; or

(ii) has made use of his or her rights, or promoted the rights of some other person, under this Act, or has made a disclosure, or has encouraged disclosure by some other person, under the Protected Disclosures Act 2000; or

(iii) has given information or evidence in relation to any complaint, investigation, or proceeding under this Act or arising out of a disclosure under the Protected Disclosures Act 2000; or

(iv) has declined to do an act that would contravene this Act; or

(v) has otherwise done anything under or by reference to this Act; or]

(b) On the ground that he or she knows that that person, or any relative or associate of that person, intends to do any of the things mentioned in subparagraphs (i) to (v) of paragraph

(a) of this subsection or that he or she suspects that that person, or any relative or associate of that person, has done, or intends to do, any of those things.

(2) Subsection (1) of this section shall not apply where a person is treated less favourably because he or she has knowingly made a false allegation or otherwise acted in bad faith.

Cf 1977 No 49 s 31

67. Advertisements—
(1) It shall be unlawful for any person to publish or display, or to cause or allow to be published or displayed, any advertisement or notice which indicates, or could reasonably be understood as indicating, an intention to commit a breach of any of the provisions of this Part of this Act.

(2) For the purposes of subsection (1) of this section, use of a job description with a gender connotation (such as "postman" or "stewardess") shall be taken to indicate an intention to discriminate, unless the advertisement contains an indication to the contrary.

Cf 1971 No 150 s 7; 1977 No 49 s 32

68. Liability of employer and principals—
(1) Subject to subsection (3) of this section, anything done or omitted by a person as the employee of another person shall, for the purposes of this Part of this Act, be treated as done or omitted by that other person as well as by the first-mentioned person, whether or not it was done with that other person's knowledge or approval.

(2) Anything done or omitted by a person as the agent of another person shall, for the purposes of this Part of this Act, be treated as done or omitted by that other person as well as by the first-mentioned person, unless it is done or omitted without that other person's express or implied authority, precedent or subsequent.

(3) In proceedings under this Act against any person in respect of an act alleged to have been done by an employee of that person, it shall be a defence for that person to prove that he or she took such steps as were reasonably practicable to prevent the employee from doing that act, or from doing as an employee of that person acts of that description.

Cf 1977 No 49 s 33

69. Further provision in relation to sexual or racial harassment in employment—
(1) Where—

(a) A request of the kind described in section 62(1) of this Act is made to an employee; or

(b) An employee is subjected to behaviour of the kind described in section 62(2) or section 63 of this Act—

by a person who is a customer or a client of the employee's employer, the employee may make a complaint in writing about that request or behaviour to the employee's employer.

(2) The employer, on receiving a complaint under subsection (1) of this section,—

(a) Shall inquire into the facts; and

(b) If satisfied that such a request was made or that such behaviour took place,—

shall take whatever steps are practicable to prevent any repetition of such a request or of such behaviour.

(3) Where any person, being a person in relation to whom an employee has made a complaint under subsection (1) of this section,—

(a) Either—

(i) Makes to that employee after the complaint a request of the kind described in section 62(1) of this Act; or

(ii) Subjects that employee after the complaint to behaviour of the kind described in section 62(2) or section 63 of this Act; and

(b) The employer of that employee has not taken whatever steps are practicable to prevent the repetition of such a request or such behaviour,—

that employer shall be deemed to have committed a breach of this Act and the provisions of this Act shall apply accordingly.

SPECIAL PROVISIONS RELATING TO SUPERANNUATION SCHEMES

70. Superannuation schemes—
(1) Subject to subsection (3) of this section, nothing in section 22 or section 44 of this Act relating to different treatment on the ground of age or disability shall apply to any condition in, or requirement of, a superannuation scheme in existence at the commencement of this Act in relation to a person who was a member of the scheme at the commencement of this Act or who becomes a member of the scheme before the [1st day of January 1996].

(2) It shall continue to be lawful for the provisions of a superannuation scheme to provide—

(a) Different benefits for members of each sex on the basis of the same contributions; or

(b) The same benefits for members of each sex on the basis of different contributions,— if the different treatment—

(c) Is based on actuarial or statistical data, upon which it is reasonable to rely, relating to life expectancy, accidents, or sickness; and

(d) Is reasonable having regard to the applicability of the data, and of any other relevant factors, to the particular circumstances.

(3) It shall continue to be unlawful to require an applicant for membership of a superannuation scheme to have attained a minimum age.

(4) Nothing in section 22 or section 44 of this Act shall prevent the provisions of a superannuation scheme from—

(a) Providing or requiring different contributions for members; or

(b) Providing benefits for members that differ in nature or amount,— by reason of the disability or age of those members, if the different treatment—

(c) Is based on—

(i) Actuarial or statistical data, upon which it is reasonable to rely, relating to life-expectancy, accidents, or sickness; or

(ii) Where no such data is available in respect of persons with a disability, reputable medical or actuarial advice or opinion, upon which it is reasonable to rely, whether or not contained in an underwriting manual; and

(d) Is reasonable having regard to the applicability of the data or advice or opinion, and of any other relevant factors, to the particular circumstances.

(5) Nothing in section 22 or section 44 of this Act shall prevent the provisions of a superannuation scheme, or the trustees of the scheme, from—

(a) Requiring an applicant for membership of the scheme to be under a specified maximum age; or

(b) Permitting a member of the scheme to elect to make increased or reduced contributions to the scheme either temporarily or indefinitely; or

(c) Specifying an age of eligibility for each type of benefit provided for members of the scheme; or

(d) Subject to section 9C of the Superannuation Schemes Act 1989, requiring persons who become members of the scheme on or after the 1st day of January 1995 to leave the scheme on reaching the age at which persons of that age ordinarily qualify for national superannuation [under section 7 of the New Zealand Superannuation Act 2001]; or

(e) Providing benefits on the death or disability of members of the scheme that decrease in value as the age of members increases; or

(f) Providing benefits for members of the scheme that differ in nature and amount according to the member's period of membership (including any period deemed by the trustees of the scheme to be membership) of the scheme and of any scheme replaced by that scheme, and, in the case of a superannuation scheme provided by an employer, of any scheme to which the employer has paid contributions on behalf of the employee.

(6) In assessing for the purposes of this section whether it is reasonable to rely on any data or advice or opinion and whether different treatment is reasonable, the Commission or the Complaints Division may—

(a) Require justification to be provided for reliance on the data or advice or opinion and for the different treatment; and

(b) Request the views of the Government Actuary on the justification for the reliance and for the different treatment.

71. Reports on superannuation schemes—
The Commission shall from time to time, after consultation with the Government Actuary, report to the Minister on whether discrimination on the prohibited grounds has been eliminated from superannuation schemes.

Cf 1977 No 49 s 89

[72. Power to vary trust deeds—
(1) Notwithstanding any Act or rule of law or the provisions of the instrument or conditions governing any superannuation scheme, the trustees of the scheme may make such amendments to that instrument or those conditions as are necessary or desirable to give effect to the provisions of sections 22, 44, and 70 of this Act.

(2) Every amendment to the provisions of an instrument or conditions governing any superannuation scheme made under subsection (1) of this section on or after the commencement of the Human Rights Amendment Act 1994 must be made by deed.]

Cf 1977 No 49 s 90

OTHER MATTERS

73. Measures to ensure equality—
(1) Anything done or omitted which would otherwise constitute a breach of any of the provisions of this Part of this Act shall not constitute such a breach if—

(a) It is done or omitted in good faith for the purpose of assisting or advancing persons or groups of persons, being in each case persons against whom discrimination is unlawful by virtue of this Part of this Act; and

(b) Those persons or groups need or may reasonably be supposed to need assistance or advancement in order to achieve an equal place with other members of the community.

(2) Nothing in this Part of this Act—

(a) Limits the power of the Crown to establish or arrange work or training schemes or employment assistance measures, eligibility for which may, in whole or in part, be determined by a person's age, employment status, or family status; or

(b) Makes it unlawful for any person to recruit or refer any other person who is of a particular age or of a particular employment status or of a particular family status for any work or training scheme or employment assistance measure that is established or arranged by the Crown, the eligibility for which may, in whole or in part, be determined by a person's age, employment status, or family status.

Cf 1977 No 49 s 29; 1992 No 16 s 13(1)

74. Measures relating to pregnancy, childbirth, or family responsibilities—
For the avoidance of doubt it is hereby declared that preferential treatment granted by reason of—

(a) A woman's pregnancy or childbirth; or

(b) A person's responsibility for part-time care or full-time care of children or other dependants—

shall not constitute a breach of this Part of this Act.

Cf 1977 No 49 s 30

[PART 3 - RESOLUTION OF DISPUTES ABOUT COMPLIANCE WITH PART 1A AND PART 2

[75. Object of this Part—
The object of this Part is to establish procedures that—

(a) facilitate the provision of information to members of the public who have questions about discrimination; and

(b) recognise that disputes about compliance with Part 1A or Part 2 are more likely to be successfully resolved if those disputes can be resolved promptly by the parties themselves; and

(c) recognise that, if disputes about compliance with Part 1A or Part 2 are to be resolved promptly, expert problem-solving support, information, and assistance needs to be available to the parties to those disputes; and

(d) recognise that the procedures for dispute resolution under this Part need to be flexible; and

(e) recognise that judicial intervention at the lowest level needs to be that of a specialist decision making body that is not inhibited by strict procedural requirements; and

(f) recognise that difficult issues of law may need to be determined by higher courts.]

[76. Functions of Commission under this Part—
(1) The primary functions of the Commission under this Part are—

(a) to provide information to members of the public who have questions about discrimination; and

(b) to facilitate the resolution of disputes about compliance with Part 1A or Part 2, by the parties concerned, in the most efficient, informal, and cost-effective manner possible.

(2) The Commission has, in order to carry out its function under subsection (1)(b), the following functions:

(a) to receive and assess a complaint alleging that there has been a breach of Part 1A or Part 2, or both:

(b) to gather information in relation to a complaint of that kind (including one referred back to it by the Director under section 90(1)(b), or the Tribunal under section 92D) for the purposes of paragraphs (c) and (d):

(c) to offer services designed to facilitate resolution of the complaint, including information, expert problem-solving support, mediation, and other assistance:

(d) to take action or further action under this Part in relation to the complaint, if the complainant or aggrieved person wishes to proceed with it, unless section 80(2) or (3) applies:

(e) to provide information gathered in relation to a complaint to the parties concerned.]

[77. Dispute resolution services—
(1) The Commission must provide dispute resolution services for the purposes of carrying out its functions under section 76.

(2) Services provided under this section may include—

(a) the provision of general information about discrimination and legal obligations in relation to discrimination:

(b) the provision of information about what services are available for persons who have disputes about compliance with Part 1A or Part 2:

(c) the provision of a venue for, and a mediator at, any dispute resolution meeting that—

(i) is designed to enable each party to discuss and seek to resolve any complaint, without prejudice to his or her position; and

(ii) is convened at the request, or with the agreement of, the parties or, if section 84(4) applies, by the Commission:

(d) other services (of a type that can address a variety of circumstances) that assist persons to resolve, promptly and effectively, their disputes about compliance with Part 1A or Part 2.]

[78. Method of providing services—
Services provided under section 77 may be provided in any manner, including—

(a) by a telephone, facsimile, internet, or email service (whether as a means of explaining where information can be found or as a means of actually providing the information or of otherwise seeking to resolve the problem); or

(b) by publishing pamphlets, brochures, booklets, or codes; or

(c) by specialists who—

(i) respond to requests or themselves identify how, where, and when their services can best support the object of this Part; or

(ii) provide their services in the manner, and at the time and place that is, most likely to resolve the problem or dispute in question; or

(iii) provide their services in all of the ways described in this paragraph.]

[79. How complaints received to be treated—
(1) This section applies if the Commission receives, under section 76(2)(a), a complaint alleging that there has been a breach of Part 1A or Part 2 or both Parts.

(2) If the complaint or part of it concerns an enactment, or an act or omission that is authorised or required by an enactment, the complaint or relevant part of it must be treated only as a complaint that the enactment is in breach of Part 1A.

(3) Despite every other provision of this section, if the complaint or part of it concerns a judgment or other order of a court, or an act or omission of a court affecting the conduct of any proceedings, the Commission must take no further action in relation to the complaint or relevant part of it.

(4) If the complaint or part of it concerns an act or omission by a person or body referred to in section 3 of the New Zealand Bill of Rights Act 1990, and neither subsection (2) nor subsection (3) applies, the complaint or relevant part of it—

(a) must be treated only as a complaint that there is a breach of Part 1A, unless the act or omission complained of involves conduct that—

(i) is unlawful under any of sections 22, 23, 61 to 63, and 66; or

(ii) is unlawful under any of sections 65 and 67 to 74, but only to the extent that those sections relate to conduct that is unlawful under any provision referred to in subparagraph (i):

(b) must be treated only as a complaint that there has been a breach of the relevant provision or provisions of Part 2 if the act or omission complained of involves conduct that is unlawful under any of sections 22, 23, 61 to 63, and 66.

(5) If the complaint or relevant part of it concerns a breach of Part 2, and none of subsections (2) to (4) applies to the complaint or relevant part of it, the complaint or relevant part of it must be treated only as a complaint that there has been a breach of the relevant provision or provisions of Part 2.

(6) Nothing in this section prevents the Commission from involving any person that it considers appropriate in information gathering and the resolution of disputes.]

[80. Taking action or further action in relation to complaint—
(1) The Commission may only take action or further action under this Part in relation to a complaint if the complainant or person alleged to be aggrieved (if not the complainant) informs the Commission that he or she wishes to proceed with the complaint.

(2) The Commission may decline to take action or further action under this Part in relation to a complaint if the complaint relates to a matter of which the complainant or the person alleged to be aggrieved (if not the complainant) has had knowledge for more than 12 months before the complaint is received by the Commission.

(3) The Commission may also decline to take action or further action under this Part in relation to a complaint if, in the Commission's opinion,—

(a) the subject matter of the complaint is trivial; or

(b) the complaint is frivolous or vexatious or is not made in good faith; or

(c) having regard to all the circumstances of the case, it is unnecessary to take further action in relation to the complaint; or

(d) there is in all the circumstances an adequate remedy or right of appeal, other than the right to petition Parliament or to make a complaint to the Ombudsman, that it would be reasonable for the complainant or the person alleged to be aggrieved (if not the complainant) to exercise.

(b) includes a satisfactory assurance by the person to whom the complaint relates against the repetition of the conduct that was the subject matter of the complaint or against further conduct of a similar kind.]

[84. Reference of complaint to Director or from Director or Tribunal—
(1) The complainant, aggrieved person, or party seeking to enforce a settlement may refer a complaint to the Director so that he or she may decide, under section 90(1)(a) or (c), whether to represent that person in proceedings before the Human Rights Tribunal.

(2) The Commission must promptly inform all parties concerned of every reference of a complaint back to the Commission, whether the reference back is one by the Director, under section 90(1)(b), or one by the Tribunal, under section 92D.

(3) A requirement under this section to inform a person is satisfied if all reasonable efforts have been made to inform the person.

(4) If a complaint is referred back to the Commission by the Director, under section 90(1)(b), or by the Tribunal, under section 92D, the Commission may, without limiting its other powers, require the parties to attend a dispute resolution meeting or other form of mediation designed to facilitate resolution of the complaint.]

[85. Confidentiality of information disclosed at dispute resolution meeting—
(1) Except with the consent of the parties or the relevant party, persons referred to in subsection (2) must keep confidential—

(a) a statement, admission, or document created or made for the purposes of a dispute resolution meeting; and

(b) information that is disclosed orally for the purposes of, and in the course of, a dispute resolution meeting.

(2) Subsection (1) applies to every person who—

(a) is a mediator for a dispute resolution meeting; or

(b) attends a dispute resolution meeting; or

(c) is a person employed or engaged by the Commission; or

(d) is a person who assists either a mediator at a dispute resolution meeting or a person who attends a dispute resolution meeting.]

[86. Evidence as to dispute resolution meeting—

(1) No mediator at a dispute resolution meeting may give evidence in any proceedings, whether under this Act or any other Act, about—

(a) the meeting; or

(b) anything related to the meeting that comes to his or her knowledge for the purposes of, or in the course of, the meeting.

(2) No evidence is admissible in any court, or before any person acting judicially, of any statement, admission, document, or information that, under section 85(1), is required to be kept confidential.]

[87. Certain information not to be made available—

Any statement, admission, document, or information disclosed or made to the mediator at a dispute resolution meeting for the purposes of the dispute resolution meeting must not be made available under the Official Information Act 1982 or the Local Government Official Information and Meetings Act 1987 by a person to whom section 85(1) applies, except with the consent of the parties or the relevant party.]

Cf 1977 No 49 s 38(7); 1983 No 56 s 12(4)

[88. Limits on effect of section 80(1) or sections 85 to 87—

Nothing in section 80(1) or sections 85 to 87—

(a) prevents the discovery or affects the admissibility of any evidence (being evidence that is otherwise discoverable or admissible and that existed independently of the mediation process) just because the evidence was presented for the purposes of, or in the course of, a dispute resolution meeting; or

(b) prevents the gathering of information by the Commission for research or educational purposes so long as the parties and the specific matters in issue between them are not identifiable; or

(c) prevents the disclosure by any person employed or engaged by the Commission to any other person employed or engaged by the Commission of matters that need to be disclosed for the purposes of giving effect to this Act; or

(d) prevents the disclosure of information by any person, if that person has reasonable grounds to believe that disclosure is necessary to prevent, or minimise the danger of, injury to any person or damage to any property.]

[89. Enforcement of terms of settlement agreed by parties—
A settlement between parties to a complaint may be enforced by proceedings before the Tribunal brought under section 92B(4)—

(a) by the complainant (if any) or the aggrieved person (if not the complainant); or

(b) by the person against whom the complaint was made.]

[90. Functions of Director of Human Rights Proceedings under this Part—
(1) The Director's functions under this Part include, in relation to a complaint,—

(a) deciding, in accordance with sections 91(1) and 92, whether, and to what extent, to provide representation for a party who requests the Director to provide representation in proceedings before the Tribunal or in related proceedings seeking to enforce a settlement reached on a previous occasion (including a settlement secured at a dispute resolution meeting), and providing representation for the party accordingly:

(b) deciding, in accordance with section 91(2), whether to refer the complaint back to the Commission:

(c) deciding, in accordance with sections 91(3) and 92, whether, and to what extent, to provide representation for a complainant, aggrieved person (if not the complainant), or group of persons who requests, or who request, the Director to provide representation in proceedings before the Tribunal or in related proceedings against the person against whom the complaint was made or the Attorney-General, and providing representation for the complainant, aggrieved person, or group of persons, accordingly.

(2) The Director's functions under this Part include, in relation to a request from the Commission to provide representation in proceedings brought under section 92B, section 92E, or section 97 or in proceedings in which the Commission is entitled to appear and be heard under section 92H, deciding, in accordance with sections 91(3) and 92, whether, and to what extent, to provide representation for the Commission in proceedings before the Tribunal or in related proceedings.

[[(3) In this section and sections 92 and 92C, "related proceedings", in relation to proceedings before the Tribunal, means proceedings of any of the following descriptions:

(a) an appeal to the High Court against a decision of the Tribunal:

(b) proceedings in the High Court arising out of—

(i) the statement of a case under section 122; or

(ii) the removal of proceedings or a matter at issue in them under section 122A:

(c) an appeal to the Court of Appeal against a decision of the High Court made in proceedings described in paragraph (a) or paragraph (b):

(d) an appeal to the Supreme Court against—

(i) a decision of the High Court made in proceedings described in paragraph (a) or paragraph (b); or

(ii) a decision of the Court of Appeal made in proceedings described in paragraph (c).**]]]**

[91. Requirements for Director's decisions under section 90—
(1) The Director may make a decision under section 90(1)(a) if it appears to him or her that a party has failed to observe the terms of a settlement reached on a previous occasion.

(2) The Director may make a decision under section 90(1)(b) if—

(a) it appears to the Director that the complaint may yet be able to be resolved by the parties and the Commission (for example, by mediation); or

(b) it is unclear to the Director, from information available to him or her, in relation to the complaint, whether a party has failed to observe the terms of a settlement reached on a previous occasion.

(3) The Director may make a decision under section 90(1)(c) or (2) if it appears to him or her that a settlement has not been reached and that no action or further action by the Commission is likely to facilitate a settlement.**]**

[92. Matters Director to have regard to in deciding whether to provide representation in proceedings before Tribunal or in related proceedings—
(1) In deciding under section 90(1)(a) or (c) or section 90(2) whether, and to what extent, to provide representation for a complainant, aggrieved person, group of persons, party to a settlement of a complaint, or the Commission, the Director—

(a) must have regard to the matters stated in subsection (2):

(b) may have regard to any other matter that the Director considers relevant.

(2) The matters referred to in subsection (1)(a) are—

(a) whether the complaint raises a significant question of law:

(b) whether resolution of the complaint would affect a large number of people (for example, because the proceedings would be brought by or affect a large group of persons):

(c) the level of harm involved in the matters that are the subject of the complaint:

(d) whether the proceedings in question are likely to be successful:

(e) whether the remedies available through proceedings of that kind are likely to suit the particular case:

(f) whether there is likely to be any conflict of interest in the provision by the Director of representation to any person described in subsection (1):

(g) whether the provision of representation is an effective use of resources:

(h) whether or not it would be in the public interest to provide representation.]

[92A. Director to notify and report on decisions on representation—
(1) Promptly after making a decision under section 90(1)(a) or (c), the Director must notify the complainant, aggrieved person, group of persons, or party seeking to enforce a settlement reached on a previous occasion—

(a) of the terms of the decision; and

(b) if the Director has decided not to provide representation for the complainant, aggrieved person, class of persons, or party seeking to enforce a settlement, of the reasons for the decision.

(2) Promptly after making a decision under section 90(2), the Director must notify the Commission—

(a) of the terms of the decision; and

(b) of the reasons for the decision.

(3) If the Director decides to provide representation to the Commission in proceedings in which the Commission is entitled to be heard under section 92H, but subsequently concludes that there is, or may be, a conflict of interest in the provision, or continued provision, of legal representation by the Director to both the complainant and the Commission, the Director must—

(a) cease to provide representation to the Commission; and

(b) promptly advise the Commission of the Director's decision.

(4) The Director must report to the Minister, at least once each year and without referring to identifiable individuals concerned, on the Director's decisions under section 90(1)(a) and (c), and, as soon as practicable, the Minister must present a copy of the report to the House of Representatives.]

[PROCEEDINGS

[92B. Civil proceedings arising from complaints—
(1) If a complaint referred to in section 76(2)(a) has been made, the complainant, the person aggrieved (if not the complainant), or the Commission may bring civil proceedings before the Human Rights Review Tribunal—

(a) for a breach of Part 1A (other than a breach of Part 1A that is an enactment, or an act or omission authorised or required by an enactment or otherwise by law), against the person or persons alleged to be responsible for the breach:

(b) for a breach of Part 1A that is an enactment, or an act or omission authorised or required by an enactment or otherwise by law, against the Attorney-General, or against a person or body referred to in section 3(b) of the New Zealand Bill of Rights Act 1990 alleged to be responsible for the breach:

(c) for a breach of Part 2, against the person or persons alleged to be responsible for the breach.

(2) If a complaint under section 76(2)(a) relates to a discriminatory practice alleged to be in breach of Part 1A or Part 2 and to affect a class of persons, proceedings under subsection (1) may be brought by the Commission on behalf of the class of persons affected.

(3) A person against whom a complaint referred to in section 76(2)(a) has been made may bring civil proceedings before the Tribunal in relation to the complaint if

no proceedings in relation to the complaint have been brought under subsection (1) by, or on behalf of, the complainant or person aggrieved or a class of persons.

(4) If parties to a complaint under section 76(2)(a) have reached a settlement of the complaint (whether through mediation or otherwise) but one of them is failing to observe a term of the settlement, another of them may bring proceedings before the Tribunal to enforce the settlement.

(5) The rights given by subsections (1), (3), and (4) are not limited or affected just because the
Commission or a mediator at a dispute resolution meeting or the Director is taking any action in relation to the complaint concerned.

(6) Despite subsection (2), the Commission may bring proceedings under subsection (1) only if—

(a) the complainant or person aggrieved (if not the complainant) has not brought proceedings; and

(b) the Commission has obtained the agreement of that person before bringing the proceedings; and

(c) it considers that bringing the proceedings will facilitate the performance of its functions stated in section 5(2)(a).

(7) Despite subsections (1) to (6), no proceedings may be brought under this section in respect of a complaint or relevant part of a complaint to which section 79(3) applies.]

[92C. Representation in civil proceedings arising from complaints—
(1) A party to proceedings before the Tribunal or related proceedings may appear and be heard—

(a) in person, or by a barrister or solicitor provided by the person; or

(b) by a barrister or solicitor provided by the Director if, and to the extent that, the Director has decided, under section 90(1)(a) or (c) or (2), to provide representation for the party in the proceedings.

(2) The Tribunal may, on an application for the purpose by any person, give directions as to the representation, in proceedings before it, of a plaintiff of a kind referred to in section 92N(1) to (3) or of any other party to the proceedings who may be able to bring, take part in, or defend the proceedings, only through a representative.

(3) The Office of Human Rights Proceedings must pay all costs of representation provided—

(a) by the Director for a complainant, aggrieved person, group of persons, or party to a settlement of a complaint; and

(b) in accordance with a decision of the Director under section 90(1)(a) or (c).

(4) The Office of Human Rights Proceedings must pay any award of costs made against a person in proceedings for which representation is provided for that person by the Director.

(5) Any award of costs made in favour of a person in proceedings for which representation is provided for that person by the Director must be paid to the Office of Human Rights Proceedings.

(6) Nothing in this Act limits or affects the entitlement to legal aid (if any) of a party in respect of proceedings or intended proceedings (whether or not representation for the party in the proceedings may, or is to be, is being, or has been, provided in accordance with a decision of the Director under section 90(1)(a) or (c)).]

[92D. Tribunal may refer complaint back to Commission, or adjourn proceedings to seek resolution by settlement—
(1) When proceedings under section 92B are brought, the Tribunal—

(a) must (whether through a member or officer) first consider whether an attempt has been made to resolve the complaint (whether through mediation or otherwise); and

(b) must refer the complaint under section 76(2)(a) to which the proceedings relate back to the Commission unless the Tribunal is satisfied that attempts at resolution, or further attempts at resolution, of the complaint by the parties and the Commission—

(i) will not contribute constructively to resolving the complaint; or

(ii) will not, in the circumstances, be in the public interest; or

(iii) will undermine the urgent or interim nature of the proceedings.

(2) The Tribunal may, at any time before, during, or after the hearing of proceedings, refer a complaint under section 76(2)(a) back to the Commission if it appears to the Tribunal, from what is known to it about the complaint, that the complaint may yet be able to be resolved by the parties and the Commission (for example, by mediation).

(3) The Tribunal may, instead of exercising the power conferred by subsection (2), adjourn any proceedings relating to a complaint under section 76(2)(a) for a specified period if it appears to the Tribunal, from what is known about the complaint, that the complaint may yet be able to be resolved by the parties.]

[92E. Civil proceedings arising from inquiry by Commission—
(1) If the Commission considers that an inquiry by it under section 5(2)(h) has disclosed or may have disclosed a breach of a kind referred to in any of paragraphs (a) to (c), it may bring civil proceedings before the Tribunal,—

> (a) for a breach of Part 1A (other than a breach of Part 1A that is an enactment, or an act or omission authorised or required by an enactment or otherwise by law), against the person or persons alleged to be responsible for the breach:
>
> (b) for a breach of Part 1A that is an enactment, or an act or omission authorised or required by an enactment or otherwise by law, against the Attorney-General, or against a person or body referred to in section 3(b) of the New Zealand Bill of Rights Act 1990 alleged to be responsible for the breach:
>
> (c) for a breach of Part 2, against the person or persons alleged to be responsible for the breach.

(2) The Commission may exercise the right in subsection (1) only if it considers that the exercise of the right will facilitate the performance of its functions stated in section 5(2)(a).

(3) This section does not limit section 6 or section 92H or section 97.]

[92F. Proof of justified limits and exceptions—
(1) The onus of proving, in any proceedings under this Part, that an act or omission is, under section 5 of the New Zealand Bill of Rights Act 1990, a justified limit on the right to freedom from discrimination affirmed by section 19 of the New Zealand Bill of Rights Act 1990 lies on the defendant.

(2) The onus of proving, in any proceedings under this Part, that conduct is, under any provision of Part 2, excepted from conduct that is unlawful under any provision of Part 2 lies on the defendant.]

Cf 1977 No 49 s 39

[92G. Right of Attorney-General to appear in civil proceedings—
(1) The Attorney-General may appear and be heard, in person or by a barrister or solicitor,—

(a) in proceedings before the Human Rights Review Tribunal alleging a breach of Part 1A, or alleging a breach of Part 2 by a person or body referred to in section 3 of the New Zealand Bill of Rights Act 1990:

(b) in proceedings in any of the following courts in relation to proceedings of a kind referred to in paragraph (a) that are or have been before the Human Rights Review Tribunal:

(i) a District Court:

(ii) the High Court:

(iii) the Court of Appeal:

[[(iv) the Supreme Court.]]

(2) The right to appear and be heard given by subsection (1) may be exercised whether or not the Attorney-General is or was a party to the proceedings before the Human Rights Review Tribunal.

(3) If, under subsection (1), the Attorney-General appears in any proceedings of a kind described in that subsection, he or she has, unless those proceedings are by way of appeal, the right to adduce evidence and the right to cross-examine witnesses.]

Cf 1977 No 49 s 38A; 1983 No 56 s 13; 1993 No 35 s 3(5)

[92H. Right of Commission to appear in civil proceedings—
(1) The Commission may appear and be heard, in person or by a barrister or solicitor,—

(a) in proceedings before the Human Rights Review Tribunal; and

(b) in proceedings in any of the following courts in relation to proceedings that are or have been before the Human Rights Review Tribunal:

(i) a District Court:

(ii) the High Court:

(iii) the Court of Appeal:

[[(iv) the Supreme Court.]]

(2) The right to appear and be heard given by subsection (1) may be exercised—

(a) whether or not the Commission is or was a party to the proceedings before the Human Rights Review Tribunal; but

(b) only if the Commission considers that the exercise of the right will facilitate the performance of its functions stated in section 5(2)(a).

(3) If, under subsection (1), the Commission appears in any proceedings of a kind described in that subsection, it has, unless those proceedings are by way of appeal, the right to adduce evidence and the right to cross-examine witnesses.

(4) This section is not limited by section 92B or section 92E or section 97.]

Cf 1977 No 49 s 38A; 1983 No 56 s 13; 1993 No 35 s 3(5)

[REMEDIES

[92I. Remedies—
(1) This section is subject to sections 92J and 92K (which relate to the only remedy that may be granted by the Tribunal if it finds that an enactment is in breach of Part 1A).

(2) In proceedings before the Human Rights Review Tribunal brought under section 92B(1) or (4) or section 92E, the plaintiff may seek any of the remedies described in subsection (3) that the plaintiff thinks fit.

(3) If, in proceedings referred to in subsection (2), the Tribunal is satisfied on the balance of probabilities that the defendant has committed a breach of Part 1A or Part 2 or the terms of a settlement of a complaint, the Tribunal may grant 1 or more of the following remedies:

(a) a declaration that the defendant has committed a breach of Part 1A or Part 2 or the terms of a settlement of a complaint:

(b) an order restraining the defendant from continuing or repeating the breach, or from engaging in, or causing or permitting others to engage in, conduct of the same kind as that constituting the breach, or conduct of any similar kind specified in the order:

(c) damages in accordance with sections 92M to 92O:

(d) an order that the defendant perform any acts specified in the order with a view to redressing any loss or damage suffered by the complainant or, as the case may be, the aggrieved person as a result of the breach:

(e) a declaration that any contract entered into or performed in contravention of any provision of Part 1A or Part 2 is an illegal contract:

(f) an order that the defendant undertake any specified training or any other programme, or implement any specified policy or programme, in order to assist or enable the defendant to comply with the provisions of this Act:

(g) relief in accordance with the Illegal Contracts Act 1970 in respect of any such contract to which the defendant and the complainant or, as the case may be, the aggrieved person are parties:

(h) any other relief the Tribunal thinks fit.

(4) It is no defence to proceedings referred to in subsection (2) or subsection (5) that the breach was unintentional or without negligence on the part of the party against whom the complaint was made, but, subject to section 92P, the Tribunal must take the conduct of the parties into account in deciding what, if any, remedy to grant.

(5) In proceedings before the Human Rights Review Tribunal brought, under section 92B(3), by the person against whom a complaint was made, that person may seek a declaration that he or she has not committed a breach of Part 1A or Part 2.]

Cf 1977 No 49 s 38(5), (6), (8); 1983 No 56 s 12(3)

[92J. Remedy for enactments in breach of Part 1A—
(1) If, in proceedings before the Human Rights Review Tribunal, the Tribunal finds that an enactment is in breach of Part 1A, the only remedy that the Tribunal may grant is the declaration referred to in subsection (2).

(2) The declaration that may be granted by the Tribunal, if subsection (1) applies, is a declaration that the enactment that is the subject of the finding is inconsistent with the right to freedom from discrimination affirmed by section 19 of the New Zealand Bill of Rights Act 1990.

(3) The Tribunal may not grant a declaration under subsection (2) unless that decision has the support of all or a majority of the members of the Tribunal.

(4) Nothing in this section affects the New Zealand Bill of Rights Act 1990.]

[92K. Effect of declaration—

(1) A declaration under section 92J does not—

> (a) affect the validity, application, or enforcement of the enactment in respect of which it is given; or
>
> (b) prevent the continuation of the act, omission, policy, or activity that was the subject of the complaint.

(2) If a declaration is made under section 92J and that declaration is not overturned on appeal or the time for lodging an appeal expires, the Minister for the time being responsible for the administration of the enactment must present to the House of Representatives—

> (a) a report bringing the declaration to the attention of the House of Representatives; and
>
> (b) a report containing advice on the Government's response to the declaration.

(3) The Minister referred to in subsection (2) must carry out the duties imposed on the Minister by that subsection within 120 days of the date of disposal of all appeals against the granting of the declaration or, if no appeal is lodged, the date when the time for lodging an appeal expires.]

[92L. Costs—

(1) In any proceedings under section 92B or section 92E or section 97, the Tribunal may make any award as to costs that it thinks fit, whether or not it grants any other remedy.

(2) Without limiting the matters that the Tribunal may consider in determining whether to make an award of costs under this section, the Tribunal may take into account whether, and to what extent, any party to the proceedings—

> (a) has participated in good faith in the process of information gathering by the Commission:
>
> (b) has facilitated or obstructed that information-gathering process:

(c) has acted in a manner that facilitated the resolution of the issues that were the subject of the proceedings.]

Cf 1977 No 49 s 38(7); 1983 No 56 s 12(4)

[92M. Damages—
(1) In any proceedings under section 92B(1) or (4) or section 92E, the Tribunal may award damages against the defendant for a breach of Part 1A or Part 2 or the terms of a settlement of a complaint in respect of any 1 or more of the following:

(a) pecuniary loss suffered as a result of, and expenses reasonably incurred by the complainant or, as the case may be, the aggrieved person for the purpose of, the transaction or activity out of which the breach arose:

(b) loss of any benefit, whether or not of a monetary kind, that the complainant or, as the case may be, the aggrieved person might reasonably have been expected to obtain but for the breach:

(c) humiliation, loss of dignity, and injury to the feelings of the complainant or, as the case may be, the aggrieved person.

(2) This section applies subject to sections 92J, 92N, and 92O.]

Cf 1977 No 49 s 40(1)

[92N. Directions as to payment of damages in certain cases—
(1) If the plaintiff is an unmarried minor, the Tribunal may, in its discretion, direct the defendant to pay damages awarded under section 92M to [[Public Trust]] or to a person or trustee corporation acting as the manager of any property of the plaintiff.

(2) If the plaintiff is a mentally disordered person within the meaning of section 2(1) of the Mental Health (Compulsory Assessment and Treatment) Act 1992 whose property is not being managed under the Protection of Personal and Property Rights Act 1988, but who lacks, in the opinion of the Tribunal, the mental capacity to manage his or her own affairs in relation to his or her own property, the Tribunal may, in its discretion, direct the defendant to pay damages awarded under section 92M to [[Public Trust]].

(3) If the plaintiff is a person whose property is being managed under the Protection of Personal and Property Rights Act 1988, the Tribunal must ascertain whether the terms of the property order cover management of money received as damages and,—

(a) if damages fall within the terms of the property order, the Tribunal must direct the defendant to pay damages awarded under section 92M to the person or trustee corporation acting as the property manager; or

(b) if damages do not fall within the terms of the property order, the Tribunal may, in its discretion, direct the defendant to pay damages awarded under section 92M to **[[**Public Trust**]]**.

(4) If money is paid to **[[**Public Trust**]]** under any of subsections (1) to (3),—

(a) section 12 of the Minors' Contracts Act 1969 applies in the case of an unmarried minor; and

[[(b) sections 108D, 108F, and 108G of the Protection of Personal and Property Rights Act 1988 apply, with any necessary modifications, in the case of a person referred to in subsection (2) or subsection (3)(b) of this section; and**]]**

[[(c) section 108E of the Protection of Personal and Property Rights Act 1988 applies, with any necessary modifications, in the case of a person referred to in subsection (3)(a) of this section.**]]]**

Cf 1977 No 49 s 40; 1983 No 56 s 14(2)

[92O. Tribunal may defer or modify remedies for breach of Part 1A or Part 2 or terms of settlement—

(1) If, in any proceedings under this Part, the Tribunal determines that an act or omission is in breach of Part 1A or Part 2 or the terms of a settlement of a complaint, it may, on the application of any party to the proceedings, take 1 or more of the actions stated in subsection (2).

(2) The actions are,—

(a) instead of, or as well as, awarding damages or granting any other remedy,—

(i) to specify a period during which the defendant must remedy the breach; and

(ii) to adjourn the proceedings to a specified date to enable further consideration of the remedies or further remedies (if any) to be granted:

(b) to refuse to grant any remedy that has retrospective effect:

(c) to refuse to grant any remedy in respect of an act or omission that occurred before the bringing of proceedings or the date of the determination of the Tribunal or any other date specified by the Tribunal:

(d) to provide that any remedy granted has effect only prospectively or only from a date specified by the Tribunal:

(e) to provide that the retrospective effect of any remedy is limited in a way specified by the Tribunal.]

[92P. Matters to be taken into account in exercising powers given by section 92O—

(1) In determining whether to take 1 or more of the actions referred to in section 92O, the Tribunal must take account of the following matters:

(a) whether or not the defendant in the proceedings has acted in good faith:

(b) whether or not the interests of any person or body not represented in the proceedings would be adversely affected if 1 or more of the actions referred to in section 92O is, or is not, taken:

(c) whether or not the proceedings involve a significant issue that has not previously been considered by the Tribunal:

(d) the social and financial implications of granting any remedy sought by the plaintiff:

(e) the significance of the loss or harm suffered by any person as a result of the breach of Part 1A or Part 2 or the terms of a settlement of a complaint:

(f) the public interest generally:

(g) any other matter that the Tribunal considers relevant.

(2) If the Tribunal finds that an act or omission is in breach of Part 1A or that an act or omission by a person or body referred to in section 3 of the New Zealand Bill of Rights Act 1990 is in breach of Part 2, in determining whether to take 1 or more of the actions referred to in section 92O, the Tribunal must, in addition to the matters specified in subsection (1), take account of—

(a) the requirements of fair public administration; and

(b) the obligation of the Government to balance competing demands for the expenditure of public money.]

[MONETARY LIMITS ON REMEDIES TRIBUNAL MAY GRANT

[92Q. Monetary limits on remedies Tribunal may grant—
(1) Proceedings under section 92B or section 92E may be brought before the Human Rights Review Tribunal irrespective of the amount of damages claimed or the value of the property in respect of which any remedy is sought.

(2) However, except as provided in sections 92R to 92V, the Tribunal must not award any damages or grant any remedy in any proceedings of that kind if the making of that award or the granting of that remedy would, because of the monetary limits contained in sections 29 to 34 of the District Courts Act 1947, be beyond the jurisdiction of a District Court.

(3) For the purposes of subsection (2), if civil proceedings under section 92B are brought on behalf of more than 1 complainant or, as the case may be, more than 1 aggrieved person, those proceedings must, for the purpose of applying any monetary limit under subsection (2), be treated as if each complainant or, as the case may be, each aggrieved person on whose behalf those proceedings are brought, were the plaintiff in a separate action against the defendant.]

Cf 1977 No 49 s 41; 1983 No 56 s 15; 1993 No 5 s 3(6)

[GRANTING OF REMEDIES BY HIGH COURT ON REFERENCE FROM TRIBUNAL

[92R. Tribunal to refer granting of remedies to High Court—
The Human Rights Review Tribunal must refer the granting of a remedy in any proceedings under section 92B or section 92E to the High Court if the Tribunal is satisfied on the balance of probabilities that a defendant in the proceedings has committed a breach of Part 1A or Part 2 or the terms of a settlement of a complaint, but that—

(a) the granting of the appropriate remedy under section 92I would be outside the limits imposed by section 92Q; or

(b) that the granting of a remedy in those proceedings would be better dealt with by the High Court.]

Cf 1977 No 49 s 42(1)

[92S. Further provisions on reference to High Court—
(1) A reference under section 92R is made by sending, to the Registrar of the High Court nearest to where the proceedings were commenced, a report on the proceedings that—

(a) sets out the Tribunal's finding with regard to the breach of Part 1A or Part 2 or the terms of a settlement of a complaint; and

(b) includes, or is accompanied by, a statement of the considerations to which the Tribunal has had regard in making the reference to that Court.

(2) A copy of the report must be given or sent promptly to every party to the proceedings.

(3) Except as provided in this Act, the procedure for a reference under section 92R is the same as the procedure prescribed by rules of court in respect of appeals, and those rules apply with all necessary modifications.]

Cf 1977 No 49 s 42(4)-(6), (8)

[92T. High Court decides remedies on reference from Tribunal—
(1) This section applies where the granting of a remedy in any proceedings under section 92B or section 92E is referred to the High Court under section 92R.

(2) The High Court may direct the Tribunal to amplify any report made under section 92S(1).

(3) Every person who, under section 92S(2), is given or sent a copy of a report under section 92S(1) is entitled to be heard and to tender in the High Court evidence as to the remedy (if any) to be granted on the basis of the Tribunal's finding that the defendant has committed a breach of Part 1A or Part 2 or the terms of a settlement of a complaint.

(4) However, no person referred to in subsection (3) may, on the reference under section 92R, challenge the finding of the Tribunal referred to in subsection (3).

(5) The High Court must decide, on the basis of the Tribunal's finding that the defendant has committed a breach of Part 1A or Part 2, whether 1 or more of the remedies set out in section 92I or the remedy set out in section 92J is to be granted.]

Cf 1977 No 49 s 42(2), (5), (6)

[92U. High Court's decision on remedies to be included in, and given effect to as part of, Tribunal's determination—
(1) Every decision of the High Court under section 92T(5)—

(a) must be remitted to the Tribunal for inclusion in its determination with regard to the proceedings; and

(b) has effect as part of that determination despite the limits imposed by section 92Q.

(2) Nothing in subsection (1)—

(a) limits sections 123 to 125; or

(b) prevents the making of an appeal in accordance with section 123 in respect of a determination of the Tribunal in which a decision of the High Court is included in accordance with subsection (1)(a).]

Cf 1977 No 49 s 42(3), (9)

[ABANDONMENT OR AGREEMENT TO BRING CLAIM WITHIN TRIBUNAL'S JURISDICTION

[92V. Abandonment to enable Tribunal to make award of damages—
(1) This section applies where the Tribunal would have jurisdiction in any proceedings under section 92B or section 92E to make an award of damages in accordance with section 92M if the amount of the award were within the limit for the time being fixed by section 29(1) of the District Courts Act 1947 (as applied by section 92Q(2)).

(2) The Tribunal may make an award within that limit if the plaintiff abandons the excess.

(3) An award of damages in those proceedings in accordance with section 92M operates to discharge from liability in respect of the amount abandoned in that way any person against whom the proceedings are brought and the subsequent award is made.

(4) This section overrides sections 92Q to 92U.]

Cf 1977 No 49 s 43

[92W. Extension of jurisdiction by agreement between parties—
(1) If, in any proceedings under section 92B or section 92E, only section 92Q prevents the Tribunal from granting any 1 or more of the remedies stated in section

92I, and the parties to the proceedings, by memorandum signed by them or their respective solicitors or agents, agree that the Tribunal is to have jurisdiction to grant any 1 or more of those remedies irrespective of section 92Q, the Tribunal has jurisdiction to grant 1 or more of those remedies accordingly.

(2) This section overrides sections 92Q to 92U.]]

Cf 1977 No 49 s 44(1)

PART 4 – [HUMAN RIGHTS REVIEW TRIBUNAL]

93. [Human Rights] Review Tribunal—
The Tribunal constituted by section 45 of the Human Rights Commission Act 1977 and[, immediately before 1 January 2002 (being the date of the commencement of the Human Rights Amendment Act 2001),] known as the Complaints Review Tribunal shall continue in being[, and, on and after 1 January 2002, is called the Human Rights Review Tribunal].

Cf 1977 No 49 s 45; 1993 No 35 s 3(1)

FUNCTIONS AND POWERS OF TRIBUNAL

94. Functions of Tribunal—
The functions of the Tribunal shall be—

(a) To consider and adjudicate upon proceedings brought pursuant to [sections 92B, 92E, 95, and 97]:

(b) To exercise and perform such other functions, powers, and duties as are conferred or imposed on it by or under this Act or any other enactment.

Cf 1977 No 49 s 46; 1993 No 35 s 4(2)

95. Power to make interim order—
(1) In respect of any matter in which the Tribunal has jurisdiction under this Act to make any final determination, the Chairperson of the Tribunal shall have power to make an interim order if he or she is satisfied that it is necessary in the interests of justice to make the order to preserve the position of the parties pending a final determination of the proceedings.

[(2) An application for an interim order may be made,—

(a) in the case of proceedings under section 92B(1), 92B(2), 92B(3), or 92B(4), by the person or body bringing the proceedings; and

(b) in the case of proceedings under section 92E, by the Commission.]

(3) A copy of the application shall be served on the defendant who shall be entitled to be heard before a decision on the application is made.

Cf 1977 No 49 s 46A; 1993 No 35 s 4(1)

96. Review of interim orders—
Where an interim order has been made, the defendant may, with the leave of the Tribunal and instead of appealing against the order, apply to the High Court to vary or rescind the order unless that order was made with the defendant's consent.

Cf 1977 No 49 s 46B; 1993 No 35 s 4(1)

[97. Power in respect of exception for genuine occupational qualification or genuine justification—
(1) The Tribunal may exercise the power referred to in subsection (2), but only—

(a) in respect of a matter in which it has jurisdiction under this Act to make a final determination; and

(b) on an application by the Commission, a person or persons against whom a complaint under section 76(2)(a) has been made, or a person who is the subject of an inquiry under section 5(2)(h).

(2) The power is to declare that an act, omission, practice, requirement, or condition that would otherwise be unlawful under Part 2 is not unlawful because it constitutes either or both—

(a) a genuine occupational qualification, in respect of sections 22 to 41:

(b) a genuine justification, in respect of sections 42 to 60.]

CONSTITUTION OF TRIBUNAL

98. Membership of Tribunal—
The Tribunal shall consist of—

(a) A Chairperson; and

(b) Two other persons appointed by the Chairperson for the purposes of each hearing from a panel maintained by the Minister under section 101 of this Act.

Cf 1977 No 49 s 47; 1993 No 35 s 5(1)

99. Chairpersons of Tribunal—
(1) Every Chairperson of the Tribunal shall be appointed by the Governor-General on the recommendation of the Minister.

(2) Where the Governor-General on the recommendation of the Minister considers it necessary, the Governor-General may appoint 2 persons to the office of Chairperson of the Tribunal.

(3) Where there are 2 Chairpersons of the Tribunal, each Chairperson shall exercise principally those parts of the Tribunal's jurisdiction that are specified from time to time in his or her warrant of appointment but nothing shall prevent each Chairperson from exercising any other part of the Tribunal's jurisdiction.

(4) Where a second Chairperson of the Tribunal is appointed, a new warrant of appointment may be issued to the existing Chairperson specifying the parts of the Tribunal's jurisdiction that the existing Chairperson is principally to exercise.

(5) In this Part of this Act, a reference to "the Chairperson" or "the Chairperson of the Tribunal" shall be read as a reference to either Chairperson where there are 2 Chairpersons of the Tribunal.

Cf 1977 No 49 s 47A; 1993 No 35 s 5(1)

[99A. Criteria and requirement for appointment of Chairpersons—
(1) In recommending a person for appointment as a Chairperson of the Tribunal, the Minister must have regard not only to the matters stated in section 101(2) but also to the person's—

(a) experience in dispute resolution:

(b) experience as a Chairperson and in other leadership roles:

(c) ability to perform the functions of a Chairperson of the Tribunal.

(2) Every person appointed as a Chairperson of the Tribunal must be a barrister or solicitor of the High Court of not less than 5 years' practice.]

100. Appointment and term of office—
(1) Repealed.

(2) Except as otherwise provided in section 103 of this Act, every person appointed as a Chairperson of the Tribunal shall hold office for such term, not exceeding 5 years, as the Governor-General on the recommendation of the Minister shall specify in the instrument appointing that Chairperson.

(3) Any person appointed as a Chairperson may hold that office concurrently with any other office held by him or her and may from time to time be reappointed.

(4) Where the term for which a Chairperson has been appointed expires, that Chairperson, unless sooner vacating or removed from office under section 103 of this Act, shall continue to hold office, by virtue of the appointment for the term that has expired, until—

(a) That Chairperson is reappointed; or

(b) A successor to that Chairperson is appointed; or

(c) That Chairperson is informed in writing by the Minister that that Chairperson is not to be reappointed and that a successor to that Chairperson is not to be appointed.

Cf 1977 No 49 s 47B; 1993 No 35 s 5(1)

101. Panel—
(1) The Minister shall maintain a panel of not more than 20 persons who may be appointed pursuant to section 98 of this Act.

[(2) In considering the suitability of persons for inclusion on the Panel, the Minister must have regard to the need for persons included on the Panel to have between them knowledge of, or experience in,—

(a) different aspects of matters likely to come before the Tribunal:

(b) New Zealand law, or the law of another country, or international law, on human rights:

(c) public administration, or the law relating to public administration:

(d) current economic, employment, or social issues:

(e) cultural issues and the needs and aspirations (including life experiences) of different communities of interest and population groups in New Zealand society.]

[(2A) At least 3 members of the panel must be barristers or solicitors of the High Court of not less than 5 years' practice.]

(3) The name of a person shall be removed from the panel if—

(a) The person dies or is, under the Insolvency Act 1967, adjudged bankrupt; or

(b) The Minister directs that the name of the person be removed from the panel for disability affecting performance of duty, neglect of duty, or misconduct, proved to the satisfaction of the Minister; or

(c) A period of 5 years has elapsed since the date on which the Minister last approved the entry of the person's name; or

(d) The person requests by writing addressed to the Minister that his or her name be removed.

(4) Where subsection (3)(c) or subsection (3)(d) of this section applies, the name of the person shall not be removed from the panel until any hearings in respect of which that person was appointed to the Tribunal have concluded.

Cf 1977 No 49 s 47C; 1993 No 35 s 5(1)

102. Deputy Chairperson—
(1) In any case in which a Chairperson of the Tribunal becomes incapable of acting by reason of illness, absence, or other sufficient cause, or if a Chairperson deems it not proper or desirable that he or she should adjudicate on any specified matter, the Governor-General, on the recommendation of the Minister, may appoint a suitable person to be the deputy of that Chairperson to act for that Chairperson for the period or purpose stated in the appointment.

(2) No person shall be appointed as a Deputy Chairperson unless he or she is eligible for appointment as a Chairperson.

(3) Every Deputy Chairperson appointed under this section shall, while acting for a Chairperson, be deemed to be a Chairperson of the Tribunal.

(4) No appointment of a Deputy Chairperson, and no act done by a Deputy Chairperson as such, and no act done by the Tribunal while he or she is acting as such, shall in any proceedings be questioned on the ground that the occasion for the appointment had not arisen or had ceased.

Cf 1977 No 49 s 48; 1993 No 35 s 5(1)

103. Vacation of office by Chairperson and Deputy Chairperson—
(1) A Chairperson and any Deputy Chairperson of the Tribunal may at any time resign his or her office by delivering a notice in writing to that effect to the Minister.

(2) A Chairperson and any Deputy Chairperson of the Tribunal shall be deemed to have vacated his or her office if he or she dies or is, under the Insolvency Act 1967, adjudged bankrupt.

(3) A Chairperson and any Deputy Chairperson of the Tribunal may at any time be removed from office by the Governor-General for disability affecting performance of duty, neglect of duty, or misconduct, proved to the satisfaction of the Governor-General.

Cf 1977 No 49 s 49; 1993 No 35 s 5(1)

PROCEDURE OF TRIBUNAL

104. Sittings of Tribunal—

(1) Sittings of the Tribunal shall be held at such times and places as the Tribunal or Chairperson from time to time appoints.

(2) Any sitting may be adjourned from time to time and from place to place by the Tribunal or a Chairperson or by the Secretary to the Tribunal.

(3) No sitting of the Tribunal shall take place unless all the members are present, but the decision of a majority of the members shall be the decision of the Tribunal.

(4) A Chairperson shall preside at all sittings of the Tribunal.

(5) Subject to the provisions of this Act and of any regulations made under this Act, the Tribunal may regulate its procedure in such manner as the Tribunal thinks fit and may prescribe or approve forms for the purposes of this Act.

Cf 1977 No 49 s 50; 1993 No 35 s 5(2)

[105. Substantial merits—

(1) The Tribunal must act according to the substantial merits of the case, without regard to technicalities.

(2) In exercising its powers and functions, the Tribunal must act—

(a) in accordance with the principles of natural justice; and

(b) in a manner that is fair and reasonable; and

(c) according to equity and good conscience.]

106. Evidence in proceedings before Tribunal—
[(1) The Tribunal may—

(a) call for evidence and information from the parties or any other person:

(b) request or require the parties or any other person to attend the proceedings to give evidence:

(c) fully examine any witness:

(d) receive as evidence any statement, document, information, or matter that may, in its opinion, assist to deal effectively with the matter before it, whether or not it would be admissible in a court of law.]

(2) The Tribunal may take evidence on oath, and for that purpose any member or officer of the Tribunal may administer an oath.

(3) The Tribunal may permit a person appearing as a witness before it to give evidence by tendering a written statement and, if the Tribunal thinks fit, verifying it by oath.

(4) Subject to subsections (1) to (3) of this section, the Evidence Act 1908 shall apply to the Tribunal in the same manner as if the Tribunal were a Court within the meaning of that Act.

Cf 1977 No 49 s 52

107. Sittings to be held in public except in special circumstances—
(1) Except as provided by subsections (2) and (3) of this section, every hearing of the Tribunal shall be held in public.

(2) The Tribunal may deliberate in private as to its decision in any matter or as to any question arising in the course of any proceedings before it.

(3) Where the Tribunal is satisfied that it is desirable to do so, the Tribunal may, of its own motion or on the application of any party to the proceedings,—

(a) Order that any hearing held by it be heard in private, either as to the whole or any portion thereof:

(b) Make an order prohibiting the publication of any report or account of the evidence or other proceedings in any proceedings before it (whether heard in public or in private) either as to the whole or any portion thereof:

(c) Make an order prohibiting the publication of the whole or part of any books or documents produced at any hearing of the Tribunal.

(4) Every person commits an offence and is liable on summary conviction to a fine not exceeding $3,000 who acts in contravention of any order made by the Tribunal under subsection (3)(b) or subsection (3)(c) of this section.

Cf 1977 No 49 s 54

108. Persons entitled to be heard—
(1) Any person who is a party to the proceedings before the Tribunal, and any person who satisfies the Tribunal that he or she has an interest in the proceedings greater than the public generally, may appear and may call evidence on any matter that should be taken into account in determining the proceedings.

[(2) If any person who is not a party to the proceedings before the Tribunal wishes to appear, the person must give notice to the Tribunal and to every party before appearing.]

(3) A person who has a right to appear or is allowed to appear before the Tribunal may appear in person or be represented by his or her counsel or agent.

[108A. Tribunal to give notice of proceedings—
The Tribunal must notify the Attorney-General promptly of the bringing of proceedings before the Tribunal alleging a breach of Part 1A, or alleging a breach of Part 2 by a person or body referred to in section 3 of the New Zealand Bill of Rights Act 1990, if the Attorney-General is not a party to the proceedings.]

[108B. Submissions in relation to remedies—
(1) Before the Tribunal grants any remedy under Part 3, it must give the parties to the proceedings and, if the remedy under consideration is a declaration under section 92J, the Attorney-General, an opportunity to make submissions on—

(a) the implications of granting that remedy; and

(b) the appropriateness of that remedy.

(2) Subsection (1) does not limit any provision in Part 3 or section 108.]

109. Witness summons—
(1) The Tribunal may[, if it considers it necessary,] of its own motion, or on the application of any party to the proceedings, issue a witness summons to any person requiring that person to attend before the Tribunal to give evidence at the hearing of the proceedings.

(2) The witness summons shall state—

(a) The place where the person is to attend; and

(b) The date and time when the person is to attend; and

(c) The papers, documents, records, or things which that person is required to bring and produce to the Tribunal; and

(d) The entitlement to be tendered or paid a sum in respect of allowances and travelling expenses; and

(e) The penalty for failing to attend.

(3) The power to issue a witness summons may be exercised by the Tribunal or a Chairperson, or by any officer of the Tribunal purporting to act by the direction or with the authority of the Tribunal or a Chairperson.

110. Service of summons—
(1) A witness summons may be served—

(a) By delivering it personally to the person summoned; or

(b) By posting it by registered letter addressed to the person summoned at that person's usual place of residence.

(2) The summons shall,—

(a) Where it is served under subsection (1)(a) of this section, be served at least 24 hours before the attendance of the witness is required; or

(b) Where it is served under subsection (1)(b) of this section, be served at least 10 days before the date on which the attendance of the witness is required.

(3) If the summons is posted by registered letter, it shall be deemed for the purposes of subsection (2)(b) of this section to have been served at the time when the letter would be delivered in the ordinary course of post.

111. Witnesses' allowances—
(1) Every witness attending before the Tribunal to give evidence pursuant to a summons shall be entitled to be paid witnesses' fees, allowances, and travelling expenses according to the scales for the time being prescribed by regulations made

under the Summary Proceedings Act 1957, and those regulations shall apply accordingly.

(2) On each occasion on which the Tribunal issues a summons under section 109(1) of this Act, the Tribunal, or the person exercising the power of the Tribunal under subsection (3) of that section, shall fix an amount which, on the service of the summons, or at some other reasonable time before the date on which the witness is required to attend, shall be paid or tendered to the witness.

(3) The amount fixed under subsection (2) of this section shall be the estimated amount of the allowances and travelling expenses to which, in the opinion of the Tribunal or person, the witness will be entitled according to the prescribed scales if the witness attends at the time and place specified in the summons.

(4) Where a party to the proceedings has requested the issue of the witness summons, the fees,
allowances, and travelling expenses payable to the witness shall be paid by that party.

(5) Where the Tribunal has of its own motion issued the witness summons, the Tribunal may direct that the amount of those fees, allowances, and travelling expenses—

(a) Form part of the costs of the proceedings; or

(b) Be paid from money appropriated by Parliament for the purpose.

112. Privileges and immunities—
Witnesses and counsel appearing before the Tribunal shall have the same privileges and immunities as witnesses and counsel have in proceedings in a District Court.

113. Non-attendance or refusal to co-operate—
(1) Every person commits an offence who, after being summoned to attend to give evidence before the Tribunal or to produce to the Tribunal any papers, documents, records, or things, without sufficient cause,—

(a) Fails to attend in accordance with the summons; or

(b) Refuses to be sworn or to give evidence, or, having been sworn, refuses to answer any question that the person is lawfully required by the Tribunal or any member of it to answer concerning the proceedings; or

(c) Fails to produce any such paper, document, record, or thing.

(2) Every person who commits an offence against subsection (1) of this section is liable on summary conviction to a fine not exceeding $1,500.

(3) No person summoned to attend before a Tribunal shall be convicted of an offence against subsection (1) of this section unless there was tendered or paid to that person travelling expenses in accordance with section 111 of this Act.

114. Power to commit for contempt—
(1) If any person—

> (a) Assaults, threatens, or intimidates, or intentionally insults, the Tribunal or any member of it or any special adviser to or officer of the Tribunal, during a sitting of the Tribunal, or in going to, or returning from, any sitting; or
>
> (b) Intentionally interrupts the proceedings of the Tribunal or otherwise misbehaves while the Tribunal is sitting; or
>
> (c) Intentionally and without lawful excuse disobeys an order or direction of a member of the Tribunal in the course of any proceedings before the Tribunal,—

any officer of the Tribunal, with or without the assistance of any member of the Police or other person, may, in accordance with any order given by a member of the Tribunal, take the person into custody and detain him or her for a period expiring not later than 1 hour following the rising of the Tribunal, and the Chairperson may, if he or she thinks fit, by warrant under his or her hand, commit the person to prison for any period not exceeding 10 days or impose a fine not exceeding $1,500.

(2) A warrant under subsection (1) of this section may be filed in any District Court and shall then be enforceable as an order made by that Court.

115. Tribunal may dismiss trivial, etc, proceedings—
The Tribunal may at any time dismiss any proceedings brought under [section 92B or section 92E] of this Act if it is satisfied that they are trivial, frivolous, or vexatious or are not brought in good faith.

Cf 1977 No 49 s 55

[116. Reasons to be given—
(1) This section applies to the following decisions of the Tribunal:

> (a) a decision to grant 1 or more of the remedies described in section 92I or the remedy described in section 92J or an order under section 95:

(b) a decision to make a declaration under section 97:

(c) a decision to dismiss proceedings brought under section 92B or section 92E or section 95 or section 97.

(2) Every decision to which this section applies must be in writing and must show the Tribunal's reasons for the decision, including—

(a) relevant findings of fact; and

(b) explanations and findings on relevant issues of law; and

(c) conclusions on matters or issues it considers require determination in order to dispose of the matter.

(3) The Tribunal must notify the parties, the Attorney-General, and the Human Rights Commission of every decision of the Tribunal.]

117. Seal of Tribunal—
The Tribunal shall have a seal, which shall be judicially noticed in all Courts and for all purposes.

Cf 1977 No 49 s 57

118. Members of Tribunal not personally liable—
No member of the Tribunal shall be personally liable for any act done or omitted to be done by the Tribunal or any member thereof in good faith in pursuance or intended pursuance of the functions, duties, powers, or authorities of the Tribunal.

Cf 1977 No 49 s 58

119. Remuneration and travelling allowances—
(1) The Tribunal is hereby declared to be a statutory Board within the meaning of the Fees and Travelling Allowances Act 1951.

(2) There shall be paid to the members of the Tribunal, out of money appropriated by Parliament for the purpose, remuneration by way of fees, salary, or allowances and travelling allowances and expenses in accordance with the Fees and Travelling Allowances Act 1951, and the provisions of that Act shall apply accordingly.

Cf 1977 No 49 s 59

120. Services for Tribunal—
(1) The [Department for Courts] shall furnish such secretarial, recording, and clerical services as may be necessary to enable the Tribunal to discharge its functions.

(2) The cost of any services provided by the [Department for Courts] pursuant to this section shall be paid from public money appropriated by Parliament for the purpose.

Cf 1977 No 49 s 60

121. Enforcement—
[(1) The following orders made by the Tribunal may, on registration of a certified copy in the District Court, be enforced in all respects as if they were an order of that Court:

(a) an order for the award of costs under section 92L; and

(b) an order for the award of damages under section 92M; and

(c) an interim order under section 95.]

(2) Every person commits an offence and is liable on summary conviction to a fine not exceeding $5,000 who contravenes or refuses to comply with any other order of the Tribunal made under [section 92I or an interim order of the Tribunal made under section 95].

Cf 1977 No 49 s 61

122. Stating case for High Court—
(1) The Tribunal may, at any time, before or during the hearing or before delivering its decision, on the application of any party to the proceedings or of its own motion, state a case for the opinion of the High Court on any question of law arising in any proceedings before the Tribunal.

[(1A) If, in any proceedings before the Tribunal, the validity of any regulation is questioned, the Tribunal must, unless it considers that there is no arguable case in support of the contention that the regulation is invalid, either—

(a) state a case for the opinion of the High Court on the relevant question or questions of law; or

(b) if the leave of the High Court is obtained, order, under section 122A(1), that the proceedings before it or the relevant matter or matters at issue be removed to the High Court for determination.]

(2) The Tribunal shall give notice to the parties to the proceedings of the Tribunal's intention to state a case under this section, specifying the registry of the High Court in which the case is to be filed.

(3) Except where the Tribunal intends to state the case of its own motion, the question shall be in the form of a special case drawn up by the parties to the proceedings, and, if the parties do not agree, to be settled by the Tribunal.

(4) Where the Tribunal intends to state the case of its own motion, it shall itself state and sign a case setting forth the facts and questions of law arising for the determination of the High Court.

(5) The High Court shall hear and determine any question submitted to it under this section, and shall remit the case with its opinion to the Tribunal.

Cf 1977 No 49 s 62

[122A. Removal to High Court of proceedings or issue—
(1) The Tribunal may, with the leave of the High Court, order that proceedings before it under this Act, or a matter at issue in them, be removed to the High Court for determination.

(2) The Tribunal may make an order under this section, with the leave of the High Court, before or during the hearing, and either on the application of a party to the proceedings or on its own initiative, but only if—

> (a) an important question of law is likely to arise in the proceedings or matter other than incidentally; or
>
> (b) the validity of any regulation is questioned in proceedings before the Tribunal (whether on the ground that it authorises or requires unjustifiable discrimination in circumstances where the statutory provision purportedly empowering the making of the regulation does not authorise the making of a regulation authorising or requiring unjustified discrimination, or otherwise); or
>
> (c) the nature and the urgency of the proceedings or matter mean that it is in the public interest that they or it be removed immediately to the High Court; or
>
> (d) the High Court already has before it other proceedings, or other matters, that are between the same parties and involve issues that are the same as, or similar or related to,

those raised by the proceedings or matter; or

(e) the Tribunal is of the opinion that, in all the circumstances, the High Court should determine the proceedings or matter.

(3) Despite subsection (2), if the validity of any regulation is questioned in proceedings before the Tribunal and the leave of the High Court is obtained for the making of an order under this section, the Tribunal must make an order under this section.

(4) If the Tribunal declines to remove proceedings, or a matter at issue in them, to the High Court (whether as a result of the refusal of the High Court to grant leave or otherwise), the party applying for the removal may seek the special leave of the High Court for an order of the High Court that the proceedings or matter be removed to the High Court and, in determining whether to grant an order of that kind, the High Court must apply the criteria stated in subsection (2)(a) to (d).

(5) An order for removal to the High Court under this section may be made subject to any conditions the Tribunal or the High Court, as the case may be, thinks fit.

(6) Nothing in this section limits section 122.]

[122B. Proceedings or issue removed to High Court—
(1) If the Tribunal, acting under section 122A, orders the removal of proceedings, or a matter at issue in them, to the High Court, unless section 122A(2)(b) applies the High Court may, if it considers that the proceedings or matter ought instead to be determined by the Tribunal, order that the Tribunal determine the matter.

(2) If the Tribunal, under section 122A, orders that proceedings, or a matter at issue in them, be removed to the High Court, and the High Court makes no order under subsection (1),—

(a) the High Court must determine the proceedings or matter and may exercise any power that the Tribunal could have exercised in, or in relation to, the proceedings or matter; and

(b) a party to the proceedings may, under section 124, appeal to the Court of Appeal against the determination of the High Court on a question of law arising in the proceedings.]

123. Appeals to High Court—
(1) Where any party is dissatisfied with any interim order made by the Chairperson under section 95 of this Act, that party may appeal to the High Court against the whole or part of that order.

[(2) A party to a proceeding under section 92B or section 92E may appeal to the High Court against all or any part of a decision of the Tribunal—

(a) dismissing the proceeding; or

(b) granting one or more of the remedies described in section 92I; or

(c) granting the remedy described in section 92J; or

(d) refusing to grant the remedy described in section 92J; or

(e) constituting a final determination of the Tribunal in the proceeding.]

[(2A) For the purposes of subsection (2)(d), the Tribunal does not in a proceeding refuse to grant the remedy described in section 92J unless—

(a) a party to the proceeding expressly applies to the Tribunal for the remedy in relation to a particular enactment; and

(b) the Tribunal does not grant the remedy in relation to that enactment.]

(3) Where any party is dissatisfied with any decision of the Tribunal making a declaration under section 97 of this Act, that party may appeal to the High Court against the whole or any part of that decision.

(4) Every appeal under this section shall be made by giving notice of appeal within 30 days after the date of the giving by the Tribunal in writing of the decision to which the appeal relates.

(5) In determining any appeal under this section the High Court shall have the powers conferred on the Tribunal by sections 105 and 106 of this Act, and those sections shall apply accordingly with such modifications as are necessary.

(6) In its determination of any appeal, the Court may—

(a) Confirm, modify, or reverse the order or decision appealed against, or any part of that order or decision:

(b) Exercise any of the powers that could have been exercised by the Tribunal in the proceedings to which the appeal relates.

(7) Notwithstanding anything in subsection (6) of this section, the Court may in any case, instead of determining any appeal, refer to the Tribunal, in accordance with the

rules of Court, for further consideration by the Tribunal, the whole or any part of the matter to which the appeal relates.

(8) Subject to the provisions of this Act, the procedure in respect of any such appeal shall be in
accordance with the rules of Court.

(9) Notice of appeal shall not operate as a stay of proceedings in respect of the decision to which the appeal relates unless the Tribunal or the High Court so orders.

Cf 1977 No 49 s 63

124. Appeal to Court of Appeal on a question of law—
(1) Any party to any proceedings before the High Court under this Act may, with the leave of the High Court, appeal to the Court of Appeal against any determination of the High Court on a question of law arising in those proceedings: Provided that, if the High Court refuses to grant leave to appeal to the Court of Appeal, the Court of Appeal may grant special leave to appeal.

(2) A party desiring to appeal to the Court of Appeal under this section shall, within 21 days after the determination of the High Court, or within such further time as that Court may allow, give notice of his or her application for leave to appeal in such manner as may be directed by the rules of that Court, and the High Court may grant leave accordingly if in the opinion of that Court the question of law involved in the appeal is one which, by reason of its general or public importance or for any other reason, ought to be submitted to the Court of Appeal for decision.

(3) Where the High Court refuses leave to any party to appeal to the Court of Appeal under this section, that party may, within 21 days after the refusal of the High Court or within such further time as the Court of Appeal may allow, apply to the Court of Appeal, in such manner as may be directed by the rules of that Court, for special leave to appeal to that Court, and the Court of Appeal may grant leave accordingly if, in the opinion of that Court, the question of law involved in the appeal is one which, by reason of its general or public importance or for any other reason, ought to be submitted to the Court of Appeal for decision.

(4) On any appeal to the Court of Appeal under this section, the Court of Appeal shall have the same power to adjudicate on the proceedings as the High Court had.

[(5) The same judgment must be entered in the High Court, and the same execution and other
consequences and proceedings must follow on it, as if the decision of the Court of Appeal on an appeal under this section had been given in the High Court.**]**

(6) The decision of the Court of Appeal on any application to that Court for leave to appeal shall be final.

Cf 1977 No 49 s 64

125. Costs of appeal—
The High Court shall have power to make such order as to the whole or any part of the costs of an appeal under section 123 of this Act as may seem just but every order for costs shall follow the outcome of the appeal unless the Court otherwise orders.

Cf 1977 No 49 s 65

126. Additional members of High Court for purposes of Act—
(1) For the purpose of the exercise by the High Court of its jurisdiction and powers—

(a) Under [section 92T]; or

(b) Under [section 123] in respect of any appeal under section 123(2) or section 123(3) of this Act in which a question of fact is involved,—

there shall be 2 additional members of the Court who shall be persons appointed by a Judge of the Court for the purposes of the hearing or appeal from the panel maintained by the Minister under section 101 of this Act.

(2) Before entering upon the exercise of the duties of their office, the additional members shall take an oath before a Judge of the High Court that they will faithfully and impartially perform the duties of their office.

(3) The presence of a Judge of the High Court and of at least one additional member shall be necessary to constitute a sitting of the Court.

(4) The decision of a majority (including the Judge, or, where more than one Judge sits, including a majority of the Judges) of the members present at a sitting of the Court shall be the decision of the Court. If the members present are equally divided in opinion, the decision of the Judge, or of a majority of the Judges, shall be the decision of the Court.

(5) If any question before the Court cannot be decided in accordance with subsection (4) of this section, the question shall be referred to the Court of Appeal for decision in accordance with the practice and procedure of that Court, which for the purpose shall have all the powers of the Court under this Act. The decision of the Court of Appeal in any proceedings under this subsection shall be final and shall take effect and be entered as if it were a decision of the Court under this Act.

(6) There shall be paid to the additional members, out of money appropriated by Parliament for the purpose, remuneration by way of fees, salary, or allowances and travelling allowances and expenses in accordance with the Fees and Travelling Allowances Act 1951, and the provisions of that Act shall apply accordingly as if the Court were a statutory Board within the meaning of that Act.

Cf 1977 No 49 s 66; 1991 No 60 s 3(4)

PART 5 – POWERS IN RELATION TO [INQUIRIES]

[126A. Evidence order—
(1) Any District Court Judge who is satisfied, on an application made by the Commission in accordance with subsection (3), that any person can provide information, documents, or things, or give evidence, that will or may be relevant to a specified inquiry, may make an order—

(a) requiring that person to produce to the Commission any information, or documents, or things specified in the order; or

(b) requiring that person to give evidence to the Commission about matters that, in the opinion of the District Court Judge, are relevant to the inquiry.

(2) If an order is made under subsection (1)(a), the District Court Judge may, as a condition of the order, require the Commission to reimburse the person who is the subject of the order for the actual and reasonable expenses incurred by that person in complying with the order or in producing any specified class of information, documents, or things.

(3) An application by the Commission for an order under subsection (1) must be in writing and must—

(a) set out the reasons why the order is sought; and

(b) if an order is sought under subsection (1)(a), set out the information, documents, or things in respect of which the order is sought; and

(c) explain why the information, documents, things, or evidence in question will or may be relevant to the inquiry.

(4) In this section, "specified inquiry" means an inquiry by the Commission under section 5(2)(h) into the contravention or possible contravention by any person of New Zealand law relating to human rights.]

127. Evidence—
[(1) The Commission may, by notice in writing, require any person who is the subject of an order under section 126A(1)(a) to provide any information, and to produce any documents or things in the possession of or under the control of that person, that are specified in the order.]

[(2) The Commission may summon before it, and examine on oath, any person who is subject to an order under section 126A(1)(b), in accordance with the terms of the order, and a Commissioner may for that purpose administer an oath to the person summoned.]

(3) Every such examination by a [Commission] shall be deemed to be a judicial proceeding within the meaning of section 108 of the Crimes Act 1961 (which relates to perjury).

Cf 1977 No 49 s 73(1) (2)

128. Protection and privileges of witnesses, etc—
(1) Every person shall have the same privileges in relation to the giving of information to, the answering of questions put by, and the production of documents and things to, a [Commission] as witnesses have in any Court.

(2) No person shall be required to supply any information to or to answer any question put by a
[Commission] in relation to any matter, or to produce to a [Commission] any document or paper or thing relating to any matter, in any case where compliance with that requirement would be in breach of an obligation of secrecy or non-disclosure imposed on that person by the provisions of any Act or regulations, other than the Official Information Act 1982.

(3) No person shall be liable to prosecution for an offence against any enactment, other than section 143 of this Act, by reason of that person's compliance with any requirement of a [Commission] under section 127 of this Act.

(4) Where the attendance of any person is required by a [Commission] under section 127 of this Act, the person shall be entitled to the same fees, allowances, and expenses as if the person were a witness in a Court and, for the purpose,—

(a) The provisions of any regulations in that behalf under the Summary Proceedings Act 1957 shall apply accordingly; and

(b) The [Commission] shall have the powers of a Court under any such regulations to fix or disallow, in whole or in part, or to increase, any amounts payable under the regulations.

Cf 1977 No 49 s 73(3), (4), (6), (7)

129. Disclosure of certain matters not to be required—
(1) Where—

(a) The Prime Minister certifies that the giving of any information or the answering of any question or the production of any document or thing might prejudice the security, defence, or international relations of New Zealand (including New Zealand's relations with the Government of any other country or with any international organisation); or

(b) The Attorney-General certifies that the giving of any information or the answering of any question or the production of any document or thing—

(i) Might prejudice the prevention, investigation, or detection of offences; or

(ii) Might involve the disclosure of proceedings of Cabinet, or any committee of Cabinet, relating to matters of a secret or confidential nature, and such disclosure would be injurious to the public interest,—

the [Commission] shall not require the information to be given, or, as the case may be, the document or thing to be produced.

(2) Subject to the provisions of subsection (1) of this section, the rule of law which authorises or requires the withholding of any document, or the refusal to answer any question, on the ground that the disclosure of the document or the answering of the question would be injurious to the public interest shall not apply in respect of any investigation by a [Commission].

Cf 1977 No 49 s 74

130. Proceedings privileged—
(1) This section applies to every Commissioner and every person engaged or employed in connection with the work of the Commission [and the Director of Human Rights Proceedings].

(2) Subject to subsection (3) of this section,—

(a) No proceedings, civil or criminal, shall lie against any person to whom this section applies for anything he or she may do or report or say in the course of the exercise or intended exercise of his or her duties under this Act, unless it is shown that he or she acted in bad faith:

(b) No person to whom this section applies shall be required to give evidence in any Court, or in any proceedings of a judicial nature, in respect of anything coming to his or her knowledge in the exercise of his or her functions.

(3) Nothing in subsection (2) of this section applies in respect of proceedings for—

(a) An offence against section 78 or section 78A(1) or section 105 or section 105A or section 105B of the Crimes Act 1961; or

(b) The offence of attempting or conspiring to commit an offence against section 78 or section 78A (1) or section 105 or section 105A or section 105B of the Crimes Act 1961.

(4) Anything said or any information supplied or any document or thing produced by any person in the course of any inquiry . . . by, or proceedings before, the Commission or a Commissioner under this Act shall be privileged in the same manner as if the inquiry . . . or proceedings were proceedings in a Court.

(5) For the purposes of clause 3 of Part 2 of Schedule 1 to the Defamation Act 1992, any report made by the Commission or a Commissioner under this Act shall be deemed to be an official report made by a person holding an inquiry under the authority of the Parliament of New Zealand.

Cf 1971 No 150 s 20; 1977 No 49 s 76; 1982 No 156 s 50; 1991 No 126 s 29; 1993 No 35 s 6

PART 6 – INCITING RACIAL DISHARMONY

131. Inciting racial disharmony—
(1) Every person commits an offence and is liable on summary conviction to imprisonment for a term not exceeding 3 months or to a fine not exceeding $7,000 who, with intent to excite hostility or ill-will against, or bring into contempt or ridicule, any group of persons in New Zealand on the ground of the colour, race, or ethnic or national origins of that group of persons,—

(a) Publishes or distributes written matter which is threatening, abusive, or insulting, or broadcasts by means of radio or television words which are threatening, abusive, or insulting; or

(b) Uses in any public place (as defined in section 2(1) of the Summary Offences Act 1981), or within the hearing of persons in any such public place, or at any meeting to which the public are invited or have access, words which are threatening, abusive, or insulting,—

being matter or words likely to excite hostility or ill-will against, or bring into contempt or ridicule, any such group of persons in New Zealand on the ground of the colour, race, or ethnic or national origins of that group of persons.

(2) For the purposes of this section, "publishes" or "distributes" and "written matter" have the meaning given to them in section 61 of this Act.

Cf 1971 No 150 s 25; 1977 No 49 s 86

132. No prosecution without Attorney-General's consent—
No prosecution for an offence against section 131 of this Act shall be instituted without the consent of the Attorney-General.

Cf 1971 No 150 s 26

PART 7 – MISCELLANEOUS PROVISIONS

133. Licences and registration—
(1) Where any person is licensed or registered under any enactment to carry on any occupation or activity or where any premises or vehicle are registered or licensed for any purpose under any enactment, and where the person or other authority authorised to renew, revoke, cancel, or review any such licence or registration is satisfied—

(a) That in the carrying on of the occupation or activity; or

(b) That in the use of the premises or vehicle,—

there has been a breach of any of the provisions of Part 2 of this Act, the person or authority, in addition to any other powers which that person or authority has, but subject to subsection (2) of this section, may refuse to renew or may revoke or cancel any such licence or registration, as the case may require, or may impose any other penalty authorised by the enactment, whether by way of censure, fine, or otherwise.

(2) Any procedural requirements of the enactment, including any whereby a complaint is a prerequisite to the exercise by the person or authority of its powers under the enactment, shall be observed.

(3) In any case in which any of the powers conferred by subsection (1) of this section are exercised,—

(a) The person or authority shall in giving its decision state that the decision is being made pursuant to subsection (1) of this section; and

(b) Any person who would have been entitled to appeal against that decision if it had been made on other grounds shall be entitled to appeal against the decision made pursuant to subsection (1) of this section.

(4) In this section the term "enactment" means any provision of any Act, regulations, or bylaws.

Cf 1971 No 150 s 23

134. Access by the public to places, vehicles, and facilities—
(1) Every person commits an offence who—

(a) Refuses to allow any other person access to or use of any place or vehicle which members of the public are entitled or allowed to enter or use; or

(b) Refuses any other person the use of any facilities in that place or vehicle which are available to members of the public; or

(c) Requires any other person to leave or to cease to use that place or vehicle or those facilities,—

when that refusal or requirement is in breach of any of the provisions of Part 2 of this Act.

(2) Every person who commits an offence against this section is liable on summary conviction to a fine not exceeding $3,000.

(3) In this section the term "vehicle" includes a vessel, an aircraft, or a hovercraft.

Cf 1971 No 150 s 24; 1977 No 49 s 86

135. No prosecution without Attorney-General's consent—
No prosecution for an offence against section 134 of this Act shall be instituted without the consent of the Attorney-General.

Cf 1971 No 150 s 26

136. Condition in restraint of marriage—
A condition, whether oral or contained in a deed, will, or other instrument, which restrains or has the effect of restraining marriage shall be void if the person or class of person whom the person subject to the condition may or may not marry is identified or defined, expressly or by implication, by reference to the colour, race, or ethnic or national origins of the person or class of person.

Cf 1971 No 150 s 27(1)

137. Commissioners and staff deemed to be officials—
Every Commissioner and every person engaged or employed in connection with the work of the Commission shall, for the purposes of sections 105, 105A, and 105B of the Crimes Act 1961, be deemed to be officials.

Cf 1977 No 49 s 77; 1987 No 8 s 25(1)

138. No adverse statement—
[The Commission must not], in any report or statement made pursuant to this Act, make any comment that is adverse to any person unless that person has been given an opportunity to be heard.

Cf 1977 No 49 s 78(2); 1991 No 126 s 32

[139. Delegation of functions or powers by Commission—
(1) After consulting with the Minister, the Commission may, by writing signed by the Chief Commissioner, delegate to a Commissioner any function or power of the Commission under this Act, except those stated in sections 7 and 76 and this power of delegation.

(2) Delegations under this section are revocable at will and, until revoked, continue in force according to their tenor.

(3) The delegation of a function or power under this section does not prevent the Commission from performing or exercising the function or power.

(4) If a function or power is delegated under this section, the performance or exercise of the function or power must not be inconsistent with determinations of the Commission under section 7.]

Cf 1977 No 49 s 79

[140. Delegation of powers by certain Commissioners—
(1) The Chief Human Rights Commissioner or the Race Relations Commissioner may, in writing signed by him or her, delegate to an officer or employee of the

Commission any of the Commissioner's functions or powers under this Act, except this power of delegation and the power to make a report under this Act.

(2) A delegation under this section—

(a) may be made to a specified person or to the holder for the time being of a specified office or to the holders of offices of a specified class; and

(b) may be made subject to any restrictions or conditions the Commissioner thinks fit; and

(c) may be made either generally or in relation to any particular case or class of cases; and

(d) is revocable at will and, until revoked, continues in force according to its tenor.

(3) If a function or power is delegated under this section, the performance or exercise of the function or power must not be inconsistent with determinations of the Commission under section 7.

(4) If a function or power is delegated under this section and the Commissioner by whom it was made ceases to hold office, the delegation continues to have effect as if it were made by his or her successor.

(5) A person purporting to exercise a function or power of a Commissioner by virtue of a delegation under this section must, when required to do so, produce evidence of the person's authority to exercise the power.]

Cf 1977 No 49 s 80

141. Annual report—
(1) Without limiting the right of the Commission to report at any other time, the Commission shall, within 3 months after the expiration of each financial year, furnish to the Minister a report on the exercise of its functions under this Act during that year.

(2) The Minister shall lay a copy of the report before the House of Representatives in accordance with section 44A of the Public Finance Act 1989.

Cf 1971 No 150 s 28; 1977 No 49 s 81

[141A. Certain acts not to be questioned—
(1) No action of the Chief Commissioner or the Race Relations Commissioner that is required by this Act to be undertaken jointly with the other may be questioned in any proceedings on the ground that it was not undertaken jointly.

(2) No action of the Chief Commissioner or the Equal Employment Opportunities Commissioner that is required by this Act to be undertaken jointly with the other may be questioned in any proceedings on the ground that it was not undertaken jointly.]

142. Money to be appropriated by Parliament for purposes of this Act—
All fees, salaries, allowances, and other expenditure payable or incurred under or in the administration of this Act shall be payable out of money to be appropriated by Parliament for the purpose.

Cf 1971 No 150 s 32; 1977 No 49 s 82

143. Offences—
Every person commits an offence against this Act and is liable on summary conviction to a fine not exceeding $3,000 who—

(a) Without lawful justification or excuse, wilfully obstructs, hinders, or resists the Commission or a Commissioner or any other person in the exercise of its or his or her powers under this Act:

(b) Without lawful justification or excuse, refuses or wilfully fails to comply with any lawful requirement of the Commission or a Commissioner or any other person under this Act:

(c) Makes any false statement knowing it to be false or intentionally misleads or attempts to mislead the Commission or a Commissioner or any other person in the exercise of its or his or her powers under this Act.

Cf 1971 No 150 s 29; 1977 No 49 s 84

144. Regulations—
(1) The Governor-General may from time to time, by Order in Council, make regulations for all or any of the following purposes:

(a) Prescribing the procedure to be followed under this Act in respect of complaints to and proceedings before the Commission . . . or in respect of proceedings before the Tribunal:

(b) Prescribing forms for the purposes of this Act, and requiring the use of such forms:

(c) Providing for such matters as are contemplated by or necessary for giving full effect to this Act and for its due administration.

[(2) For the avoidance of doubt, it is hereby declared that the power conferred by subsection (1) of this section to make regulations in respect of proceedings before the Tribunal includes power to make regulations in respect of proceedings in connection with the exercise or performance of any function, power, or duty conferred or imposed on the Tribunal by or under any other enactment.]

Cf 1977 No 49 s 85

145. Related amendments to other enactments (Repealed)—

146. Repeals (Repealed)—

147. Revocation (Repealed)—

[TRANSITIONAL PROVISIONS]

[148. Former office of Commissioner abolished—
(1) The office of Commissioner under section 7(1) of the principal Act (as it read immediately before the commencement of this section) is abolished.

(2) No person is entitled to compensation for loss of office as a Commissioner under subsection (1).]

[148A. Certain former Commissioners to be transitional members of Commission—
(1) The person who, immediately before the commencement of this section, held office as Chief Commissioner under section 7(1)(a) (as it read immediately before the commencement of this section) is taken to have been appointed to the office of Chief Commissioner under section 8(1)(a) (as substituted by section 5 of the Human Rights Amendment Act 2001).

(2) The person who, immediately before the commencement of this section, held office as the Race Relations Conciliator is taken to have been appointed to the office of Race Relations Commissioner under section 8(1)(b) (as substituted by section 5 of the Human Rights Amendment Act 2001).

(3) Every person who, immediately before the commencement of this section, held office as Commissioner under section 7(1)(e) (as it read immediately before the commencement of this section) is taken to have been appointed to the office of Commissioner under section 8(1)(d) (as substituted by section 5 of the Human Rights Amendment Act 2001).

(4) The Privacy Commissioner appointed under the Privacy Act 1993 and the Commissioner appointed to be Proceedings Commissioner under section 7(1)(d) (as it read before the commencement of the Human Rights Amendment Act 2001) cease to be Human Rights Commissioners on the commencement of this section.

(5) Every person who is taken to have been appointed to the office of Commissioner under this section is appointed on the same terms and conditions and for the remainder of the term for which the person was appointed under section 7(1) (as it read immediately before the commencement of this section).]

[RACE RELATIONS CONCILIATOR]

[148B. Assets and liabilities vest in Commission—
On the commencement of this section, the assets and liabilities of the Race Relations Conciliator vest in the Commission.]

[148C. References to Race Relations Conciliator—
(1) From the commencement of this section, unless the context otherwise requires, every reference to the Race Relations Conciliator in any instrument, document, or notice is to be read as a reference to the Race Relations Commissioner.

(2) Despite subsection (1), every reference to the Race Relations Conciliator in any contract or other instrument, document, or notice that creates, or is evidence of, an asset or liability, must be read as a reference to the Commission.]

[148D. Proceedings—
Any proceedings to which the Race Relations Conciliator was a party or that he or she was considering bringing, before the commencement of this section, may be brought, continued, completed, and enforced by or against the Commission.]

[148E. Commission to arrange final audited accounts—
The Commission must perform the duties that the Race Relations Conciliator would have had to perform under section 41 of the Public Finance Act 1989 if the Human Rights Amendment Act 2001 had not been enacted, for the period beginning on 1 July 2001 and ending with the close of 31 December 2001.]

[148F. All employees transferred to Commission—
(1) Every person employed by the Race Relations Conciliator immediately before the commencement of this section is, on and from that date, an employee of the Commission on the same terms and conditions that applied to the employee immediately before that date.

(2) For the purposes of every enactment, law, contract, and agreement relating to the employment of the employee,—

(a) the contract of employment of that employee is taken to be unbroken; and

(b) the employee's period of service with the Race Relations Conciliator and every other period of service of that employee that is recognised by the Race Relations Conciliator as continuous service is taken to have been a period of service with the Commission.

(3) A person to whom subsection (1) applies is not entitled to any compensation just because the person has ceased to be an employee of the Race Relations Conciliator.]

[PROCEEDINGS COMMISSIONER]

[148G. Proceedings Commissioner—
(1) The person who, immediately before the commencement of this section, held office as the Proceedings Commissioner under section 7(1)(d) (as it read immediately before the commencement of this section) is taken to have been appointed to the office of Director of Human Rights Proceedings under section 20A (as substituted by section 5 of the Human Rights Amendment Act 2001).

(2) The Director of Human Rights Proceedings is appointed on the same terms and conditions and for the remainder of the term for which he or she was appointed Proceedings Commissioner.]

[148H. References to Proceedings Commissioner—
From the commencement of this section, unless the context otherwise requires, every reference to the Proceedings Commissioner in any instrument, document, or notice is to be read as a reference to the Director.]

148I. Proceedings to which Proceedings Commissioner party—
(1) Proceedings to which the Proceedings Commissioner was a party or that he or she was considering bringing, before the commencement of this section—

(a) must be brought, continued, completed, and enforced by the Director; and

(b) may be brought, continued, completed, and enforced against the Director.

(2) Sections 86 to 92, 95, and 97 (as they read immediately before the commencement of this section) apply (with any necessary modifications) to any proceedings to which the Proceedings Commissioner was a party before the commencement of this section as if—

(a) the Director were the Proceedings Commissioner; and

(b) the Office of Human Rights Proceedings were the Commission; and

(c) the Human Rights Review Tribunal were the Complaints Review Tribunal.

[148J. Complaints referred to Proceedings Commissioner for decision as to proceedings—
(1) Subsection (2) applies—

(a) if a complaint is referred to the Proceedings Commissioner under section 75(g) (as it read immediately before the commencement of this section), but no proceedings have been instituted by the Proceedings Commissioner; or

(b) if the Proceedings Commissioner was required to decide whether to institute proceedings against a party to a settlement under section 82(1)(c) (as it read immediately before the commencement of this section), but no proceedings were instituted by the Proceedings Commissioner before the commencement of this section.

(2) If this subsection applies,—

(a) if the Commissioner has not made a decision on whether to institute proceedings, the Director must decide, under section 90(1)(c), whether to provide representation in relation to the complaint:

(b) if the Commissioner has made a decision to institute proceedings, the Director must provide representation for the complainant or aggrieved party (as the case may be) in the proceedings:

(c) if the Commissioner has made a decision not to institute proceedings, that decision is deemed to have been made by the Director.]

[148K. Transfer of employees from Commission to Office—
(1) The Commission and the Office of Human Rights Proceedings may, after consulting the employee concerned, agree to the transfer of an employee from the Commission to the Office of Human Rights Proceedings on the same terms and conditions that applied to the employee immediately before the date of transfer.

(2) For the purposes of every enactment, law, contract, and agreement relating to the employment of the employee,—

(a) the contract of employment of that employee is taken to have been unbroken; and

(b) the employee's period of service with the Commission, and every other period of service of that employee that is recognised by the Commission as continuous service, is taken to have been a period of service with the Office of Human Rights Proceedings.

(3) An employee of the Commission who is transferred to the Office of Human Rights Proceedings under subsection (1) is not entitled to any compensation just because—

(a) the position held by the employee with the Commission has ceased to exist; or

(b) the person has ceased (as a result of the transfer) to be an employee of the Commission.]

[COMPLAINTS DIVISION]

[148L. Complaints Division abolished—
The Complaints Division of the Commission is abolished.]

[148M. Outstanding complaints to be dealt with by Commission under new procedure—
(1) A complaint lodged with the Complaints Division before the commencement of this Act must be dealt with by the Commission under Part 3 (as substituted by section 9 of the Human Rights Amendment Act 2001) as if the complaint were made to the Commission under section 76(2)(a).

(2) For the purposes of subsection (1),—

(a) if the Complaints Division has called a conciliation conference under section 80(1) (as it read immediately before the commencement of this section) but the conference has not taken place, the Commission must instead offer to convene a dispute resolution meeting; and

(b) if section 79(2) applies to the complaint, the Commission must inform the Attorney-General of the details of the complaint as soon as practicable.

(3) Despite subsection (1), if, in relation to a complaint, the Complaints Division has decided not to investigate the complaint further under section 76(1) or section 77(1)(a) (as they read immediately before the commencement of this section), the Commission must take no action or further action in relation to the complaint.]

148N. Breaches of Part 1A—
No act or omission that occurred before 1 January 2002 is capable of being in breach of Part 1A unless—

(a) the act or omission continues on or after 1 January 2002; or

(b) in the case of an enactment, the enactment is in force on or after 1 January 2002.]

[148O. Complaints about breaches of Part 1A—
(1) Despite section 76, the Commission is not under a duty to receive or assess any complaint alleging a breach of Part 1A that is made to the Commission before 1 April 2002.

(2) The Commission is not under a duty to receive or assess any complaint alleging that an act or omission that occurred before 1 January 2002 and that ceased to continue or to be in force before 1 January 2002 is in breach of Part 1A.]

SAVINGS

149. Special provisions in relation to written employment contracts in force on 1 April 1992—
(1) This section applies to every employment contract (whether a collective employment contract or an individual employment contract) that—

(a) Is in writing; and

(b) Was in force on the 1st day of April 1992; and

(c) Specifies an age at which an employee is required to retire.

(2) Where the parties to an employment contract to which this section applies agree in writing, at any time on or after the 1st day of April 1992, to confirm or vary the age specified in the employment contract, the age, as so confirmed or varied, shall have effect notwithstanding section 22 of this Act.

(3) Where the parties to an employment contract to which this section applies have not agreed in writing to confirm or vary the age specified in the employment contract, section 22 of this Act shall apply in relation to that employment contract.

(4) Where, as at the 1st day of April 1992, the age at which an employer is required to retire, under a term of that employee's employment contract, was specified only in a document that sets out the employer's policy on the retirement ages of the employer's employees or any of them, this section shall not apply in relation to that employee's employment contract.

Cf 1977 No 49 s 15C; 1992 No 16 s 4

150. Charitable instruments—
(1) Nothing in this Act shall apply—

(a) To any provision in an existing or future will, deed, or other instrument where that provision confers charitable benefits, or enables charitable benefits to be conferred, on persons against whom discrimination is unlawful by virtue of Part 2 of this Act; or

(b) To any act done in order to comply with any provision described in paragraph (a) of this subsection.

(2) For the purposes of this section, "charitable benefits" means benefits for purposes that are charitable in accordance with the law of New Zealand.

Cf 1971 No 150 s 36(1); 1977 No 49 s 91(1); 1983 No 56 s 18(1)

151. Other enactments and actions not affected (Repealed)—

152. Expiry of section 151 (Repealed)—

153. Savings—
(1) Nothing in this Act [affects] the right to bring any proceedings, whether civil or criminal, [that may be brought other than under this Act], but, in assessing any damages to be awarded to or on behalf of any person under this Act or otherwise, a Court [must] take account of any damages already awarded to or on behalf of that person in respect of the same cause of action.

(2) Subject to the Illegal Contracts Act 1970, no proceedings, Civil or criminal, shall lie against any person, except as provided by this Act, in respect of any act or omission which is unlawful by virtue only of any of the provisions of Part 2 of this Act.

(3) Nothing in this Act shall affect any enactment or rule of law, or any policy or administrative practice of the Government of New Zealand, that—

(a) Repealed.

(b) Distinguishes between New Zealand citizens and other persons, or between British subjects or Commonwealth citizens and aliens.

(4) Repealed.

Cf 1971 No 150 s 37; 1977 No 49 s 86, 93

PHILIPPINES

EXECUTIVE ORDER NO. 163

DECLARING THE EFFECTIVITY OF THE CREATION OF THE COMMISSION ON HUMAN RIGHTS AS PROVIDED FOR IN THE 1987 CONSTITUTION, PROVIDING GUIDELINES FOR THE OPERATION THEREOF, AND FOR OTHER PURPOSES.

WHEREAS, the 1987 Constitution has been ratified by the people;

WHEREAS, the 1987 Constitution has created an Independent office called the Commission on Human Rights; and

WHEREAS, there is an urgent necessity to constitute the Commission on Human Rights to give effect to the State policy that "the State values the dignity of every human person and guarantees full respect for human rights"

NOW, THEREFORE, I, CORAZON C. AQUINO, President of the Philippines, by virtue of the powers vested in me by the Constitution, do hereby order:

Section 1

The Commission on Human Rights as provided for under Article XIII of the 1987 Constitution is hereby declared to be now in existence. [*see text of Art. XIII immediately following this decree*]

Section 2

(a) The Commission on Human Rights shall be composed of a Chairman and four Members who must be natural-born citizens of the Philippines and, at the time of their appointment, at least thirty five years of age, and must not have been candidates for any elective position in the elections immediately preceding their appointment. However, a majority thereof shall be members of the Philippine Bar.

(b) The Chairman and the Members of the Commission on Human Rights shall not, during their tenure, hold any other office or employment. Neither shall they engage in the practice of any profession or in the active management or control of any business which in any way be affected by the functions of their office, nor shall they be financially interested, directly or indirectly, in any contract with, or in any franchise or privilege granted by the government, any of its subdivisions, agencies, or instrumentalities, including government-owned or controlled corporations or their subsidiaries.

(c) The Chairman and the Members of the Commission on Human Rights shall be appointed by the President for a term of seven years without reappointment. Appointment to any vacancy shall be only for the expired term of the predecessor.

(d) The Chairman and the Members of the Commission on Human Rights shall receive the same salary as the Chairman and Members, respectively, of the

Constitutional Commissions, which shall not be decreased during their term of office

Section 3
The Commission of Human Rights shall have the following powers and functions:

(01) Investigate, on its own or on complaint by any party, all forms of human rights violations involving civil and political rights;

(02) Adopt its operational guidelines and rules of procedure, and cite for contempt for violations thereof in accordance with the Rules of Court.

(03) Provide appropriate legal measures for the protection of human rights of all persons within the Philippines, as well as Filipinos residing abroad, and provide for preventive measures and legal aid services to the under-privileged whose human rights have been violated or need protection;

(04) Exercise visitorial powers over jails, prisons, or detentions facilities;

(05) Establish a continuing program of research, education, and information to enhance respect for the privacy of human rights;

(06) Recommend to the Congress effective measures to promote human rights and to provide for compensation to victims of violations of human rights, or their families;

(07) Monitor the Philippine Government's compliance with international treaty obligations on human rights;

(08) Grant immunity from prosecution to any person whose testimony or whose possession of documents or other evidence is necessary or convenient to determine the truth in any investigation conducted by it or under its authority;

(09) Request the assistance of any department, bureau, office, or agency in the performance of its functions;

(10) Appoint its officers and employees in accordance with law; and

(11) Perform such other duties and functions as may be provided by law.

Section 4
The Presidential Committee on Human Rights, created under Executive Order No. 8 dated March 18, 1986, as modified, is hereby abolished. The Commission on Human Rights shall exercise such functions and powers of the Presidential Committee on

Human Rights under Executive Order No. 8, as modified, which are not inconsistent with the provisions of the 1987 Constitution.

The unexpended appropriations of the Presidential Committee on Human Rights are hereby transferred to the Commission on Human Rights. All properties, records, equipment, buildings, facilities and other assets of the Presidential Committee on Human Rights shall be transferred to the Commission on Human Rights.

The Commission on Human Rights may retain such personnel of the Presidential Committee on Human Rights as may be necessary in the fulfillment of its powers and functions. Any public officer or employee separated from service as a result of the abolition of the Presidential Committee on Human Rights effected under this Executive Order shall receive the benefits to which they may be entitled under existing laws, rules and regulations.

Section 5
The approved annual appropriations of the Commission on Human Rights shall be automatically and regularly released.

Section 6
All laws, orders, issuances, rules and regulations or parts thereof inconsistent with this Executive Order are hereby repealed or modified accordingly.

Section 7
This Executive Order shall take effect immediately.

Done in the City of Manila, this 5th day of May, in the year of Our Lord, nineteen hundred and eighty-seven.

(Signed)

CORAZON C. AQUINO

President of the Philippines

CONSTITUTION OF THE PHILIPPINES (1987)

ARTICLE XIII HUMAN RIGHTS

Section 17.
(1) There is hereby created an independent office called the Commission on Human Rights.

(2) The Commission shall be composed of a Chairman and four Members who must be natural-born citizens of the Philippines and a majority of whom shall be members of the Bar. The term of office and other qualifications and disabilities of the Members of the Commission shall be provided by law.

(3) Until this Commission is constituted, the existing Presidential Committee on Human Rights shall continue to exercise its present functions and powers.

(4) The approved annual appropriations of the Commission shall be automatically and regularly released.

Section 18.
The Commission on Human Rights shall have the following powers and functions:

(1) Investigate, on its own or on complaint by any party, all forms of human rights violations involving civil and political rights;

(2) Adopt its operational guidelines and rules of procedure, and cite for contempt for violations thereof in accordance with the Rules of Court;

(3) Provide appropriate legal measures for the protection of human rights of all persons within the Philippines, as well as Filipinos residing abroad, and provide for preventive measures and legal aid services to the under-privileged whose human rights have been violated or need protection;

(4) Exercise visitorial powers over jails, prisons, or detention facilities;

(5) Establish a continuing program of research, education, and information to enhance respect for the primacy of human rights;

(6) Recommend to Congress effective measures to promote human rights and to provide for compensation to victims of violations of human rights, or their families;

(7) Monitor the Philippine Government's compliance with international treaty obligations on human rights;

(8) Grant immunity from prosecution to any person whose testimony or whose possession of documents or other evidence is necessary or convenient to determine the truth in any investigation conducted by it or under its authority;

(9) Request the assistance of any department, bureau, office, or agency in the performance of its functions;

(10) Appoint its officers and employees in accordance with law; and

(11) Perform such other duties and functions as may be provided by law.

Section 19.
The Congress may provide for other cases of violations of human rights that should fall within the authority of the Commission, taking into account its recommendations.

HUMAN RIGHTS COMMISSION OF SRI LANKA

ACT, NO. 21 OF 1996

An Act to provide for the establishment of the Human Rights Commission of Sri Lanka; to set out the powers and functions of such Commission; and to provide for matters connected therewith or incidental thereto.

1. This Act may be cited as the Human Rights Commission of Sri Lanka Act, No. 21 of 1996 and shall come into operation on such date as the Minister may appoint by Order published in the Gazette (hereinafter referred to as the "appointed date").

PART I : ESTABLISHMENT OF THE HUMAN RIGHTS COMMISSION OF SRI LANKA

1. (1) There shall be established a Commission which shall be called and known as the Human Rights Commission of Sri Lanka (hereinafter in this Act referred to as "the Commission".

   (2) The Commission shall be a body corporate having perpetual succession and a common seal and may sue and be sued in its corporate name.

   (3) The seal of the Commission shall be in the custody of the Secretary of the Commission and may be altered in such manner as may be determined by the Commission.

2. (1) The Commission shall consist of five members, chosen from among persons having knowledge of, or practical experience in, matters relating to human rights.

   (2) The members of the Commission shall be appointed by the President, on the recommendation of the Constitutional Council:

   Provided however, that during the period commencing on the appointed date and ending on the date when the Constitutional Council is established, members of the Commission shall be appointed by the President on the recommendation of the Prime Minister in consultation with the Speaker and the Leader of the Opposition.

   (3) In making recommendations, under subsection (2), the Constitutional Council and the Prime Minister shall have regard to the necessity of the minorities being represented of the Commission.

   (4) One of the members so appointed shall be nominated by the President to the Chairman of the Commission.

   (5) Every member of the Commission shall hold office for a period of three years.

   (6) The office of a member shall become vacant

   (a) upon the death of such member;

(b) upon such member resigning such office by writing addressed to the President;
(c) upon such member being removed from office on any ground specified in section 4; or
(d) on the expiration of his term of office.

3. (1) A member of the Commission may be removed from office
   (a) by the President, if he
      (i) is adjudged an insolvent by a court of competent jurisdiction;
      (ii) engages in any paid employment outside the duties of his office, which in the opinion of the President, formed on the recommendation of the Prime Minister in consultation with the Speaker and the Leader of the Opposition, conflicts with his duties as a member of the Commission;
      (iii) is unfit to continue in office by reason of infirmity of mind or body;
      (iv) is declared to be of unsound mind by a court of competent jurisdiction;
      (v) is convicted of an offence involving moral turpitude; or
      (vi) absents himself from three consecutive meetings without obtaining leave of the Commission; or
   (b) by an order of the President made after an address of Parliament, supported by a majority of the total number of members of Parliament (including those not present) has been presented to the President for such removal on the ground of proved misbehavior or incapacity:
   Provided however that no resolution for the representation of such an address shall be entertained by the Speaker or placed on the Order Paper of Parliament, unless notice of such resolution is signed by not less than one-third of the total number of members of Parliament and sets out full particulars of the alleged misbehavior or incapacity.

(2) The procedure for the presentation and passing on an address of Parliament for the removal of a Judge of the Supreme Court or the Court of Appeal, shall apply in all respects to the presentation and passing of an address or Parliament for the removal of a member of the Commission.

4. Any member who vacates his office, otherwise than by removal under section 4, shall be eligible for re-appointment.

5. (1) The chairman may resign from the office of Chairman by letter addressed to the President.

(2) Subject to the provision of subsection (1), the term of office of the Chairman shall be his period of membership of the Commission.

(3) If the Chairman of the Commission becomes, by reason of illness or infirmity, or absence from Sri Lanka, temporarily unable to perform the duties

of his office, the President may appoint any other member of the Commission to act in his place.

6. No act or proceeding of the Commission shall be deemed to be invalid by reason only of the existence of any vacancy among its members, or defect in the appointment of any member thereof.

7. The salaries of the members of the Commission shall be determined by Parliament and shall be charged on the Consolidated Fund and shall not be diminished during their terms of office.

8. (1) The Chairman of the Commission shall be the Chief Executive officer and shall preside at all meetings of the Commission. In the event of his absence from any meeting, the members of the Commission present at such meeting shall elect one from amongst themselves to preside at such meeting.
(2) The Chairman of any meeting of the Commissioner shall, in addition to his own vote, have a casting vote.
(3) Subject to the other provisions of this Act, the Commission may regulate the procedure in regard to the conduct of meetings of the Commission, and the transaction of business at such meetings.

9. The functions of the Commission shall be:
   (a) to inquire into, and investigate, complaints regarding procedures, with a view to ensuring compliance with the provisions of the Constitution relating to fundamental rights and to promoting respect for and observance of, fundamental rights;
   (b) to inquire into and investigate complaints regarding infringements or imminent infringements of fundamental rights, and to provide for resolution thereof by conciliation and mediation in accordance with the provisions hereinafter provided;
   (c) to advise and assist the government in formulating legislation and administrative directives and procedures, in furtherance of, the promotion and protection of fundamental rights;
   (d) to make recommendations to the Government regarding measures which should be taken to ensure that national laws and administrative practices are in accordance with international human rights norms and standards;
   (e) to make recommendations to the Government on the need to subscribe or accede to treaties and other international instruments in the field of human rights; and
   (f) to promote awareness of, and provide education in relation to, human rights.

10. For the purpose of discharging its functions the Commission may exercise any or all of the following powers: -

(a) investigate any infringement or imminent infringement of fundamental rights in accordance with the succeeding provisions of this Act;

(b) appoint such number of sub-committees at Provincial level, as it considers improving their conditions of detention;

(e) take such steps as it may be directed to take by the Supreme Court, in respect of any matter referred to it by the Supreme Court;

(f) undertake research into, and promote awareness of human rights, by conducting programmes, seminars and workshops and to disseminate and distribute the results of such research;

(g) award in its absolute discretion to an aggrieved person or a person acting on behalf of an aggrieved person, such sum of money as is sufficient to meet the expenses that may have been reasonably incurred by him in making a complaint to the Commission under section 14.

(h) do all such other things as are necessary or conducive to the discharge of its functions.

11. For the purpose of discharging its functions the Commission may exercise any or all of the following powers:-

(a) investigate any infringement or imminent infringement of fundamental rights in accordance with the succeeding provisions of this Act;

(b) appoint such number of sub-committees at Provincial level, as it considers necessary to exercise such powers of the Commission as may be delegated to them, by the Commission, under this Act;

(c) intervene in any proceedings relating to the infringement or imminent infringement of fundamental rights, pending before an court, with the permission of such court;

(d) monitor the welfare of persons detained either by a judicial order or otherwise, by regular inspection of their places of detention, and to make such recommendations as may be necessary for improving their conditions of detention;

(e) take such steps as it may be directed to take by the Supreme Court in respect of any matter referred to it by the Supreme Court;

(f) undertake research into, and promote awareness of, human rights, by conducting programmes, seminars and workshops and to disseminate and distribute the results of such research;

(g) award in its absolute discretion to an aggrieved person or an person acting on behalf of an aggrieved person, such sum money as is sufficient to meet the expenses that may have been reasonably incurred by him in making a complaint to the Commission under section 14;

(h) do all such other things as are necessary or conducive to the discharge of its functions.

PART II : POWERS OF INVESTIGATION OF THE COMMISSION

12. (1) the Supreme Court may refer any matter arising in the course of a hearing of an application made to the Supreme Court under Article 126 of the Constitution to the Commission for inquiry and report.
(2) The Commission shall inquire and report to the Supreme Court on the matters referred to it under subsection (1), within the period, if any, specified in such reference.

13. (1) Where a complaint is made by an aggrieved party in terms of section 14, to the Commission, within one month of the alleged infringement or imminent infringement of a fundamental right by executive or administrative action, the period within which the inquiry into such complaint is pending before the Commission, shall not be taken into account in computing the period of one month within which an application may be made to the Supreme Court by such person in terms of Article 126 (2) of the Constitution.
(2) Where the Supreme Court makes a reference in terms of section 12 (1) to the Commission for inquiry or report, the period commencing from the date of such reference and ending on the date of the report of the Commission, shall not be taken into account in computing the period of two months referred to in Article 126 (5) of the Constitution.

14. The Commission may, on its own motion or on a complaint made to it by an aggrieved person or group of persons or a person acting on behalf of an aggrieved person or a group of persons, investigate an allegation of the infringement or imminent infringement of a fundamental right of such person or group of persons caused –
(a) by executive or administrative action; or
(b) as a result of an act which constitutes an offence under the Prevention of Terrorism Act No. 48 of 1979, committed by any person.

15. (1) Where an investigation conducted by the Commission under section 14 does not disclose the infringement or imminent infringement of a fundamental right by executive or administrative action or by any person referred to in paragraph (b) of section 14, the Commission shall, record that fact, and shall accordingly inform the person making the complaint within thirty days.
(2) Where an investigation conducted by the Commission under section 14 discloses the infringement or imminent infringement of a fundamental right by executive or administrative action, or by any person referred to in paragraph (b) of section 14, the Commission shall have the power to refer the matter, where appropriate, for conciliation or mediation.
(3) Where an investigation conducted by the Commission under section 14 discloses the infringement or imminent infringement of a fundamental right by executive or administrative action, or by any person referred to in paragraph (b)

of section 14, the Commission may, where it appears to the Commission that it is not appropriate to refer such matter for conciliation or mediation, or where it appears to the Commission that it is appropriate to refer the matter for conciliation or mediation, but all or any of the parties object or objects to conciliation or mediation, or where the attempt at conciliation or mediation is not successful-

(a) recommend to the appropriate authorities, that prosecution or other proceedings be instituted against the person or persons infringing such fundamental right;

(b) refer the matter to any court having jurisdiction to hear and determine such matter in accordance with such rules of court as may be prescribed therefor, and within such time as is provided for invoking the jurisdiction of such court, by any person;

(c) make such recommendations as it may think fit, to the appropriate authority or person or persons concerned, with a view to preventing or remedying such infringement, or the continuation of such infringement.

(4) Without prejudice to the generality of the recommendations that may be made under paragraph (c) of subsection (3), the Commission may-

(a) recommend that the act or omission giving rise to the infringement or imminent infringement of a fundamental right be reconsidered or rectified;

(b) recommend that the decision giving rise to the infringement or imminent infringement of a fundamental right be reconsidered or rectified;

(c) recommend that the practice on which the decision, recommendation, act or omission giving rise to the infringement or imminent infringement of a fundamental right was based, be altered; and

(d) recommend that reasons be given for the decision, recommendation, act or omission giving rise to the infringement or imminent infringement of a fundamental right.

(5) No recommendation shall be made by the Commission under the preceding provisions of this section in respect of the infringement or imminent infringement of a fundamental right except after affording an opportunity of being heard to the person alleged to be about to infringe or to have infringed such fundamental right.

(6) A copy of a recommendation made by the Commission under the preceding provisions of this section in respect of the infringement or imminent infringement of a fundamental right shall be sent by the Commission to the person aggrieved, the head of the institution concerned, and the Minister to whom the institution concerned has been assigned.

(7) The Commission shall require any authority or person or persons to whom a recommendation under the preceding provisions of this section is addressed to report to the Commission, within such period as may be specified in such recommendation, the action which such authority or person has taken, or proposes to take, to give effect to such recommendation and it shall be the duty of every such person to report to the Commission accordingly.

(8) Where any authority or person or persons to whom a recommendation under the preceding provisions of this section is addressed, fails to report to the Commission within the period specified in such recommendation or where such person reports to the Commission and the action taken, or proposed to be taken by him to give effect to the recommendations of the Commission, is in view of the Commission, inadequate, the Commission shall make a full report of the facts to the President who shall, cause a copy of such report to be placed before Parliament.

16. (1) Where the Commission refers a matter for conciliation or mediation under section 15 it shall appoint one or more persons to conciliate or mediate between the parties.
(2) The manner of appointment and the powers and functions of conciliators or mediators shall be as prescribed.
(3) The Commission may direct the parties to appear before the conciliators or mediators for the purpose of conciliation or mediation. Sittings of the conciliators or mediators may be held in camera.
(4) In the event of the conciliation or mediation not being successful, or where one party objects to conciliation or mediation, the conciliator or mediator shall report to the Commission accordingly.
(5) Where the conciliators or mediators are successful in resolving the matter by conciliation or mediation they shall inform the Commission of the settlement arrived at.
(6) Where a matter is referred to for conciliation or mediation under this section and a settlement is arrived at, the Commission shall make such directions (including direction as to the payment of compensation) as may be necessary to give effect to such settlement.

17. Where in the course of an inquiry or investigation conducted by the Commission a question arises as to the scope or ambit of a fundamental right, the Commission may refer such question to the Supreme Court under Article 125 of the Constitution, for the determination of the Supreme Court.

18. (1) The Commission shall, for the purposes of an inquiry or investigations under this Act, have the power-
(a) to procure and receive all such evidence, written or oral, and to examine all such persons as witnesses, as the Commission may think it necessary or desirable to procure or examine;
(b) to require the evidence (whether written or oral) of any witness, to be given on oath or affirmation, such oath or affirmation to be that which could be required of the witness if he were giving evidence in a court of law, and to administer and cause to be administered by an officer authorized in that behalf by the Commission an oath or affirmation to every such witness;

(c) to summon any person residing in Sri Lanka, to attend any meeting of the Commission to give evidence or produce any document or other thing in his possession, and to examine him as a witness or require him to produce any document or other thing in his possession;

(d) to admit notwithstanding any of the provisions of the Evidence Ordinance, any evidence, whether written or oral, which might be inadmissible in civil or criminal proceedings.

(e) to admit or exclude the public from such inquiry or investigation or any part thereof.

19. (1) A person who gives evidence before the Commission shall in respect of such evidence, be entitled to all the privileges to which a witness giving evidence before a court of law is entitled in respect of evidence given by him before such court.

(2) No person shall in respect of any evidence written or oral, given by that person to, or before the Commission be liable to any action, prosecution or other proceeding, civil or criminal in any court.

(3) Subject as hereinafter provided, no evidence of any statement made or given by any person to, or before, the Commission, shall be admissible against that person in any action, prosecution or other proceeding, civil or criminal in any court:

Provided that, nothing in the preceding provisions of this subsection shall-

(a) affect, or be deemed or construed to affect, any prosecution or penalty for any offence under Chapter XI of the Penal Code read with section 23 of this Act;

(b) prohibit, or be deemed or construed to prohibit the publication or disclosure of the name, or of the evidence or any part of the evidence of any witness who gives evidence before the Commission for the purposes of the prosecution of that witness for any offence under Chapter XI of the Penal Code.

20. (1) Every summons shall be under the hand of the Chairman of the Commission.

(2) Any summons may be served by delivering it to the person named therein, or where that is not practicable, by leaving it at the last known place of abode of that person, or by registered post.

(3) Every person to whom a summons is served shall attend before the Commission at the time and place mentioned therein, and shall answer the questions put to him by the Commission or produce such documents or other things as are required of him and are in his possession or power, according to the tenor of the summons.

21. (1) Every offence of contempt committed against, or in disrespect of, the authority of the Commission shall be punishable by the Supreme Court as

though it were an offence of contempt committed against, or in disrespect of, the authority of that Court, and the Supreme Court is hereby vested with jurisdiction to try every such offence.

(2) An act done or omitted to be done in relation to the Commission, whether in the presence of the Commission or otherwise, shall constitute an offence of contempt against, or in disrespect of, the authority of the Commission, if such act would, if done or omitted to be done in relation to the Supreme Court, have constituted an offence of contempt against, or in disrespect of, the authority of the such Court.

(3) If any person-

(a) fails without cause, which in the opinion of the Commission is reasonable, to appear before the Commission at the time and place mentioned in the summons served under this Act; or

(b) refuses to be sworn or affirmed, or having being duly sworn or affirmed refuses or fails without cause, which in the opinion of the Commission is reasonable, to answer any question put to him touching the matters being inquired into, or investigated by, the Commission; or

(c) refuses or fails without cause which in the opinion of the Commission is reasonable, to comply with the requirements of a notice or written order or direction issued or made to him, by the Commission; or

(d) upon whom a summons is served under this Act, refuses or fails without cause, which in the opinion of the Commission is reasonable, to produce and show to the Commission any document or other thing, which is in his possession or control and which is in the opinion of the Commission necessary for arriving at the truth of the matters being inquired into, or investigated, such person shall be guilty of the offence of contempt against, or in disrespect of, the authority of the Commission.

(4) Where the Commission determines that a person is guilty of an offence of contempt under subsection (2) or subsection (3), against, or in disrespect of, its authority the Commission may transmit to the Supreme Court, a Certificate setting out such determination; every such Certificate shall be signed by the Chairman of the Commission.

(5) In any proceedings for the punishment of an offence of contempt which the Supreme Court may think fit to take cognizance of, as provided in this section, any document purporting to be a Certificate signed and transmitted to the Court under subsection (4) shall-

(a) be received in evidence, and be deemed to be such a certificate without further, unless the contrary is proved, and

(b) be evidence that the determination set out in the certificate was made by the Commission and of the facts stated in the determination.

(6) In any proceeding taken as provided in this section for the punishment of any alleged offence of contempt against, or in disrespect of, the authority of the Commission, no member of the Commission shall, except with his own consent,

and notwithstanding anything to the contrary in this Act, be summoned or examined as a witness

PART III: STAFF OF THE COMMISSION

22. (1) There shall be appointed a Secretary to the Commission.
(2) There may be appointed such officers and servants as may be necessary to assist the Commission in the discharge of its functions under this Act.

23. The members of the Commission and the officers and servants appointed to assist the Commission shall be deemed to be public servants within the meaning of the Penal Code and every inquiry or investigation conducted under this Act, shall be deemed to be a judicial proceeding within the meaning of that Code.

24. The Commission may delegate to any officer appointed to assist the Commission any of its powers, and the person to whom such powers are so delegated may exercise those powers subject to the direction of the Commission.

25. (1) At the request of the Commission, any officer in the public service may, with the consent of that officer and of the Secretary to the Ministry of the Minister in charge of the subject of Public Administration, be temporarily appointed to the staff of the Commission, with like consent, or with like consent be permanently appointed to such staff.
(2) Where any officer in the Public is temporarily appointed to the staff of the Commission, the provisions of subsection (2) of section 14 of the National Transport Commission Act, No. 37 of 1991 shall, *mutatis mutandis*, apply to, and in relation to, such officer.
(3) Where any officer in the public service is permanently appointed to the staff of the Commission, the provisions of subsection (3) of section 14 of the National Transport Commission Act, No. 37 of 1991 shall, *mutatis mutandis*, apply to, and in relation to, such officer.
(4) Where the Commission employs a person who has agreed to serve to the Government for a specified period, any period of service to the Commission, shall be regarded as service to the Government for the purpose of discharging the obligations of that person under such agreement.

26. (1) No proceedings, civil or criminal, shall be instituted against any member of the Commission or any officer or servant appointed to assist the Commission, other than for contempt, or against any other person assisting the Commission in any other way, for any act which in good faith is done or omitted to be done, by him, as such member or officer or servant or other person.
(2) A member of the Commission or an officer or servant appointed to assist the Commission shall not be required to produce in any court, any document

received by, or to disclose to any court, any matter or thing coming to the notice of, the Commission in the course of any inquiry or investigation conducted by the Commission under this Act, except as may be necessary for the purposes of proceedings for contempt or for an offence under this Act.

(3) No proceedings civil or criminal, shall be instituted in any court against any member of the Commission in respect of any report made by the Commission under this Act or against any person in respect of the publication by such person of substantially true account of such report.

(4) Any expenses incurred by the Commission in any suit or prosecution brought by, or against, the Commission before any court, shall be paid out of the funds of the Commission and any costs paid to, or recovered by, the Commission in any such suit or prosecution, shall be credited to the fund of the Commission.

(5) Any expense incurred by any member of the Commission or any officer or servant thereof or any person appointed to assist the Commission, in any suit or prosecution brought against him in any court in respect of any act which is done, or purported to be done, by him under this Act or on the direction of the Commission shall, if the court holds that the act was done in good faith, be paid out of the funds of the Commission, unless such expense is recovered by him in such suit or prosecution.

27. The Commission shall be deemed to be a scheduled institution within the meaning of the Bribery Act, and the provisions of that Act shall be construed accordingly

PART IV: GENERAL

28. (1) Where a person is arrested or detained under the Prevention of Terrorism (Temporary Provisions) Act, No. 48 of 1979 or a regulation made under the Public Security Ordinance, (Chapter 40) it shall be the duty of the person making such arrest or order of detention, as the case may be, to forthwith and in any case, not later than forty-eight hours from the time of such arrest or detention, inform the Commission of such arrest or detention as the case may be and the place at which the person so arrested or detained is being held in custody or detention. Where a person so held in custody or detention is released or transferred to another place of detention, it shall be the duty of the person making the order for such release or transfer, as the case may be, to inform the Commission of such release or transfer, as the case may be, and in case of a transfer, to inform the Commission of the location of the new place of detention.

(2) Any person authorized by the Commission in writing may enter at any time, any place of detention, police station, prison or any other place in which any person is detained by a judicial order or otherwise, and make such examinations therein or make such inquiries from any person found therein, as

may be necessary to ascertain the conditions of detention of the persons detained therein.

(3) Any person on whom a duty is imposed by subsection (1), and who willfully omits to inform the Commission as required by subsection (1), or who resists or obstructs an officer authorized under subsection (1) in the exercise by that officer of the powers conferred on him by that subsection, shall be guilty of an offence and shall, on conviction after summary trial by a Magistrate, be liable to imprisonment for a period not exceeding one year or to a fine not exceeding five thousand rupees, or to both such fine and imprisonment.

29. (1) The State shall provide the Commission with adequate funds to enable the Commission to discharge the functions assigned to it by this Act.

(2) The Commission shall cause proper accounts to be kept of its income and expenditure, and assets and liabilities.

(3) The financial year of the Commission shall be the calendar year.

(4) Article 154 of the Constitution shall apply to the audit and accounts of the Commission.

30. The Commission shall submit an annual report to Parliament of all its activities during the year to which the report relates. Such report shall contain a list of all matters referred to it, and the action taken in respect of them along with the recommendations of the Commission in respect of each matter. The Commission may, whenever it considers it necessary to do so, submit periodic or special reports to Parliament in respect of any particular matter or matters referred to it, and the action taken in respect thereof.

31. (1) The Minister may make regulations for the purpose of carrying out or giving effect to the principles and provisions of this Act, or in respect of any matter which is required by this Act to be prescribed, or in respect of which regulations are required to be made.

(2) Without prejudice to the generality of the powers conferred by subsection (1), the Minister may make regulations prescribing the procedure to be followed in the conduct of investigation under this Act.

(3) Every regulation made by the Minister shall be published in the Gazette, and shall come into operation on the date of such publication, or on such later date as may be specified in the regulation.

(4) Every regulation made by the Minister shall as soon as convenient after its publication in the Gazette be brought before Parliament for approval. Any regulation which is not so approved shall be deemed to be rescinded as from the date of such disapproval, but without prejudice to anything previously done thereunder.

(5) Notification of the date of which any regulation is so deemed to be rescinded shall be published in the Gazette.

32. In the event of any inconsistency between the Sinhala and Tamil texts of this Act, the Sinhala text shall prevail.

33. In this Act, unless the context otherwise requires –

"fundamental right" means a fundamental right declared and recognized by the Constitution;

"head of the institution" in relation to –

(a) a public officer serving in a Government department, means the head of that department, or where such public officer is the head of that department means the Secretary to the Ministry to which that department has been assigned;

(b) a public officer who is serving in a Ministry means the Secretary to the Ministry, or where such public officer is the Secretary means the Minister in charge of that Ministry;

(c) a scheduled public officer, means the Judicial Service Commission, appointed under Article 112 of the Constitution;

(d) any other public officer, means the principal executive officer under whose general direction and control that public officer is serving;

(e) an officer of a public corporation, local authority or other like institution, means the principal executive officer of that public corporation, local authority or other like institution or where such officer is the principal executive officer of that public corporation, local authority or institution, means the Secretary to the Ministry under which such public corporation, local authority or institution functions;

"human right" means a right declared and recognized by the International Covenant on Civil and Political Rights and the International Covenant on Economic Social and Cultural Rights;

"institution" includes a Government department, public corporation statutory board or commission, local authority, Government-owned business undertaking and a company, the majority of the shares of which are held by the Government;

"local authority" means any Municipal Council, Urban Council or Pradeshiya Sabha and includes any authority created or established by or under any law, to exercise, perform and discharge powers, duties and functions corresponding or similar to, the powers, duties and functions exercised, performed and discharged by any such Council or Sabha;

"public corporation" means any corporation, board or other body which was, or is established by or under any written law other than that Companies Act, No. 17 of 1982, with funds or capital wholly or partly provided by the Government, by way of grant, loan or otherwise.

THAILAND

NATIONAL HUMAN RIGHTS COMMISSION ACT, B.E. 2542 (1999)

BHUMIBOL ADULYADEJ, REX.
Given on the 25th Day of November, B.E. 2542;
Being the 54th Year of the Present Reign.

His Majesty King Bhumibol Adulyadej is graciously pleased to proclaim that:
Whereas it is expedient to have a law on the National Human Rights Commission;
This Act contains provisions relating to the restriction of rights and liberties of the people which section 29 together with section 35 and section 48 of the Constitution of the Kingdom of Thailand allow to be done by virtue of provisions of law;
Be it, therefore, enacted by the King, by and with the advice and
Consent of the National Assembly as follows;

Section 1. This Act is called the "National Human Rights Commission Act, B.E. 2542".

Section 2. This Act shall come into force as from the day following the date of its publication in the Government Gazette.*

Section 3. In this Act:
"human rights" means human dignity, right, liberty and equality of people which are guaranteed or protected under the Constitution of the Kingdom of Thailand or under Thai laws or under treaties which Thailand has obligations to comply;
"Commission" means the National Human Rights Commission;
"President" means the President of the National Human Rights Commission;
"member" means a member of the National Human Rights Commission.

Section 4. The President of the National Human Rights Commission shall have charge and control of the execution of this Act and shall have the powers to issue Regulations or Notifications with the approval of the National Human Rights Commission for the execution of this Act.

Regulations and Notifications under paragraph one that are of general applicability shall come into force after their publication in the Government Gazette.

CHAPTER I

The National Human Rights Commission

Section 5. There shall be the National Human Rights Commission consisting of a President and ten other members appointed, by the King with the advice of the Senate, from the persons having apparent knowledge or experiences in the protection of rights and liberties of the people, having regard also to the participation of men and women and representatives from private organisations in the field of human rights.

The President of the Senate shall countersign the Royal Command appointing the President and members.

Section 6. The President and members shall have the qualifications and shall not be under any prohibition as follows:

(1) being of Thai nationality by birth;
(2) being not less than thirty five years of age;
(3) not being a member of the House of Representatives or the Senate, a political official, a member of a local assembly or a local administrator;
(4) not being a holder of any position of a political party;
(5) not being of unsound mind or of mental infirmity;
(6) not being addicted to drugs;
(7) not being a bankrupt;
(8) not being a person sentenced by a judgment to imprisonment and being detained by a warrant of the Court;
(9) not being a person having been discharged for a period of less than five years on the nomination day after being sentenced by a judgment to imprisonment for a term of two years or more except for an offence committed through negligence;
(10) not having been expelled, dismissed or removed from the official service, a state agency or a State enterprise or from a private agency on the ground of dishonest performance of duties, gross misconduct or corruption;
(11) not having been ordered by a judgment or an order of the Court that is or her assets shall dissolve on the State on the ground of unusual wealth or an unusual increase of his or her assets;
(12) not being an Election Commissioner, an Ombudsman, a member of the National Counter Corruption Commission, a member of the State Audit Commission or a member of the National Economic and Social Council;
(13) not having been removed from office by a resolution of the Senate.

Section 7. A person elected as a member shall:

(1) not be a Government official holding a permanent position or receiving salary;

(2) not be an official or employee of a State agency, State enterprise or local government organisation or not be a director or advisor of a State enterprise or State agency;

(3) not hold any position in a partnership, a company or an organisation carrying out businesses for sharing profits or incomes, or be an employee of any person.

In the case where the Senate has elected a person in (1), (2) or (3) with the consent of that person, the elected person can commence the performance of duties only when he or she has resigned from the position in (1), (2) or (3). This shall be done within fifteen days as from the date of election. If that person has not resigned within the pecified time, it shall be deemed that that person has never been elected to be a member and a new member shall be selected and elected.

Section 8. The selection and election of members shall be proceeded as follows:

(1) There shall be a Selective Committee consisting of the President of the Supreme Court, the President of the Supreme Administrative Court, the Prosecutor-General, the Chairman of the Law Council, Rectors or representatives of higher education institutions which are juristic persons; provided that each institution shall have one representative and all such representatives shall elect among themselves to be five in number, representatives of private organisations in the field of human rights under section 24; provided that each organisation shall have one representative and all such representatives shall elect among themselves to be ten in number, representatives of political parties having a member who is a member of the House of Representatives; provided that each party shall have one representative and all such representatives shall elect among themselves to be five in number, representatives of public media in the businesses of newspaper, radio broadcasting and television broadcasting, being elected from each business to be three in number and the Secretary-General of the National Human Rights Commission as secretary. The Selective Committee shall have the duties to select and prepare a list of names of twenty two persons who are suitable to be members under section 5; provided that regard must be given to the participation of women and men, and submit such list to the President of the Senate. The nomination must be made with consent of the nominated persons including documents or evidence showing that the nominated persons are suitable to be members and have the qualifications and are under no prohibitions under section 6 within sixty days as from the date when a ground for the

selection of persons to be in such office occurs. The resolution making such nomination must be passed by votes of not less than three-fourths of the number of all existing members of the Selective Committee;

(2) The President of the Senate shall convoke the Senate for passing, by secret ballot, a resolution selecting the nominated persons under (1). For this purpose, persons who receive the highest votes which are more than one-half of the total number of the existing senators shall be elected as members in consecutive order, but if no persons are elected or if less than eleven persons are elected, the name-list of those not elected on the first occasion shall be submitted to the senators for voting on another occasion. In such case, the persons who receive the highest votes which are more than one-half of the total number of the existing senators shall be deemed to be elected as members. In the case where there are persons receiving equal votes in any order resulting in having more than eleven elected persons, the President of the Senate shall draw lots to determine who are elected persons. In the case where no person is elected or where less than eleven persons are elected, the Selective Committee shall proceed with the selection and preparation for a list of persons under (1) to be submitted to the Senate for passing a resolution for reelection.

The elected persons under (2) shall meet and elect among themselves the President and notify the President of the Senate of the result. The President of the Senate shall tender the matter to the King for further appointment.

Section 9. Members shall perform their duties with independence and impartiality and shall have regard to the interests of the country and the public. Members shall be a State official under the organic law on counter corruption.

Section 10. Members shall hold office for a term of six years as from the date of their appointment by the King and shall serve for only one term.

Members who vacate office upon the termination of the term shall remain in office to continue to perform their duties until the newly appointed members take office.

In order to have the newly appointed members to perform their duties upon the termination of the term of the outgoing members, the proceeding of selection and election for the new members shall be proceeded sixty days prior to the expiration of the term of office of the outgoing members.

Section 11. Members of the House of Representatives or senators of not less than one-fourth of the total number of the existing members of each house have the right to lodge with the President of the Senate a complaint in order to request the Senate to pass a resolution removing a member from office on the grounds that such member has performed his or her duties without giving regard to the interests of the country and the public or with partiality or misconduct or immoral conduct that may seriously affect or damage the performance of his or her duties or the promotion or protection of human rights, or of having any interest in any activity or business which has directly affected or caused the same damage therein, or having or having had a conduct in violation of human rights or being seriously defective in performing his or her duties.

The resolution of the Senate under paragraph one shall be passed by votes of not less than three-fifths of the total number of the existing members of the Senate.

Section 12. In addition to the vacation of office upon the termination of the term, a member vacates office upon:

(1) death;
(2) resignation;
(3) being disqualified or being under any of the prohibitions under section 6;
(4) acting in contravention of section 7;
(5) being removed from office by a resolution of the Senate under section 11;
(6) being removed from office by a resolution of the Senate under the organic law on counter corruption.

When a case under paragraph one occurs, the remaining members may continue the performance of duties and it shall be deemed that the Commission consists of the remaining members, except where the remaining thereof are less than seven.

Section 13. In the case where members vacate office under section 12, the proceedings under section 8 shall be commenced within thirty days as from the date the members vacate their office. In this case, the Selective Committee shall prepare a list of persons twice the number of those vacating office and submit such list to the President of the Senate.

In the case where members vacate office when the National Assembly is not in session, the proceedings under section 8 shall be proceeded within thirty days as from the date the National Assembly commences its session.

Section 14. At a meeting, the presence of not less than one-half of the total number of existing members shall constitute a quorum.

The President shall preside over the meeting. If the President does not attend the meeting or is unable to perform his or her duties, the members present shall elect one among themselves to preside over the meeting.

The decision of the meeting shall be made by majority of votes; in case of an equality of votes, the person presiding over the meeting shall have an additional vote as casting vote.

In a meeting, if there is a consideration of a matter in which a member has a private interest, that member has no right to attend such meeting.

Section 15. The Commission has the powers and duties as follows:

(1) to promote the respect for and the practice in compliance with human rights principles at domestic and international levels;

(2) to examine and report the commission or omission of acts which violate human rights or which do not comply with obligations under international treaties relating to human rights to which Thailand is a party, and propose appropriate remedial measures to the person or agency committing or omitting such acts for taking action. In the case where it appears that no action has been taken as proposed, the Commission shall report to the National Assembly for further proceeding;

(3) to propose to the National Assembly and the Council of Ministers policies and recommendations with regard to the revision of laws, rules or regulations for the purpose of promoting and protecting human rights;

(4) to promote education, researches and the dissemination of knowledge on human rights;

(5) to promote co-operation and co-ordination among Government agencies, private organisations, and other organisations in the field of human rights; to prepare an annual report for the appraisal of situation in the sphere of human rights in the country and submit it to the National Assembly and the Council of Ministers and disclose to the public;

(6) to assess and prepare an annual report of the performance of the Commission and submit it to the National Assembly;

(7) to propose opinions to the Council of Ministers and the National Assembly in the case where Thailand is to be a party to a treaty concerning the promotion and protection of human rights;

(8) to appoint a sub-committee to perform the tasks as entrusted by the Commission;

(9) to perform other acts under the provisions of this Act or as the law prescribed to be the powers and duties of the Commission.

Section 16. The President and the members shall work regularly on a full-time basis and shall receive monthly remuneration and travel allowance in accordance with the rules and rates as prescribed by a Royal Decree.

The sub-committee shall receive meeting and travel allowances in accordance with the rules and rates as prescribed by a Royal Decree.

CHAPTER II

The Office of the National Human Rights Commission

Section 17. There shall be the Office of the National Human Rights Commission having the status of a Government agency attached to the National Assembly under the law on the organisation of the National Assembly and shall be under the supervision of the President.

Section 18. The Office of the National Human Rights Commission has the responsibility in the general affairs of the Commission and shall have the powers and duties as follows:

(1) to be responsible for the administrative works of the Commission;
(2) to receive petition of human rights violation and submit it to the Commission and to investigate or examine matters which are petitioned as entrusted by the Commission;
(3) to conduct study on and promote education and the dissemination of knowledge in the field of human rights;
(4) to co-operate with Government agencies, private organisations or any other organisations in the field of human rights for the purpose of protecting human rights;
(5) to carry out any other performance as entrusted by the Commission.

Section 19. Officials of the Office of the National Human Rights Commission shall be ordinary officials of the National Assembly under the law on parliamentary official service.

The powers and duties of the Parliamentary Official Service Commission shall be the powers and duties of the Commission and the President shall be in charge of the administration of the affairs and personnel administration of officials of the Office of the National Human Rights commission under the law on the organisation of the National Assembly and the law on parliamentary official service.

Section 20. The Office of the National Human Rights Commission shall have the Secretary-General of the National Human Rights Commission who is responsible for the performance of duties of the Office of the National Human Rights Commission, directly answerable to the President and who is the superior of officials and employees of the Office of the National Human Rights Commission. There shall also be Deputy Secretary-General of the National Human Rights Commission to assist the Secretary-General in the performance of duties.

Section 21. The Office of the National Human Rights Commission shall, with the consent of the Commission, submit an estimated annual budget to the Council of Ministers via the President of the National Assembly for its consideration of appropriation budgets, adequate for the independent administration of the Commission, in an annual appropriations bill or supplementary appropriations bill, as the case may be. In this matter, the Council of Ministers, the House of Representatives, the Senate or the Standing Committees may, if requested by the President, allow the President or the persons entrusted by the President to give explanations.

CHAPTER III

Examination of Human Rights Violations

Section 22. The Commission shall have the duties to examine and propose remedial measures under this Act for the commission or omission of acts which violate human rights and which is not a matter being litigated in the Court or that upon which the Court has already given final order or judgement.

Section 23. Any person whose human rights are violated has the right to lodge a petition in writing which shall contain details as follows:

(1) name and address of the petitioner or his or her representative
(2) facts and circumstances which are causes of the commission or omission of acts which violate human rights;
(3) signature of the petitioner or representative appointed in writing by the petitioner.

Petition may be made verbally in accordance with a Regulation issued by the Commission.

The petition shall be submitted at the Office of the National Human Rights Commission or by registered post with return receipt or to any member or via a private organisation in the field of human rights to be referred to the Office of the National Human Rights Commission or by any other mean as prescribed by the Commission.

Upon receiving the petition under paragraph one, the Office of the National Human Rights Commission shall, without delay, notify the petitioner or the representative; provided that notification shall be made no later than three days as from the date the petition is received.

Section 24. In the case where a petition from a person whose human rights are violated is lodged with a private organisation in the field of human rights or where there appears to the said organisation of such committed or omitted act thereof, if that organisation considers the case to be *prima facie* it may propose the matter to the Commission for further proceeding.

A private organisation in the field of human rights under paragraph one shall be a juristic person under Thai law which carries out business directly related to the promotion and protection of human rights as prescribed by the Commission and which does not have political objectives or seeks profits from carrying out such business.

Section 25. In the case where the Commission deems it appropriate to examine any case of a human rights violation or where the Commission has received a petition of human rights violation under section 23 or has received a petition from a private organisation in the field of human rights under section 24 and is of the opinion that it is a prima facie case which is under its powers and duties, the Commission shall notify a person or agency alleged to be a human rights violator or a person or agency whom the Commission considers to be involved in human rights violation to give a responded statements of facts within the period specified by the Commission. In the said notification, the Commission shall summarise details of facts sufficiently for a correct and complete response.

In the case where the Commission deems the received matter is not within its powers and duties or has rejected to consider such matter, the Commission shall, without delay, notify the petitioner or the private organisation in the field of human rights of which the petition is submitted, and, for the interest of protecting human rights, may refer the matter to a person or agency involved with the matter as it deems appropriate.

In the case where the Commission deems the matter should be appropriately considered by another responsible agency, it may refer the matter to such agency regardless of the stage of proceeding of the matter. In this case, the Commission may make a written inquiry of the progress to the agency. If it appears that that agency has not proceeded or has rejected to consider the matter, the Commission may bring the matter back to its consideration; provided that such matter is within its powers and duties.

In making a referral to another agency or bringing back the matter for consideration under paragraph three, the Commission shall, without delay, notify the petitioner or the private organisation that has made a submission.

Section 26. When the period for responding statements of facts under paragraph one of section 25 has lapsed, the Commission shall proceed its examination of human rights violation by giving the petitioner and those involved an opportunity to provide details and present appropriate evidence to prove facts concerning the act alleged to be a human rights violation.

In conducting the examination of the human rights violation under paragraph one, if the parties are required to be present before the Commission, the parties have the right to bring lawyers or their counsel to the examination proceedings in accordance with the rules prescribed by the Commission.

In conducting the examination of a human rights violation, the Commission may appoint one or more sub-committee to carry out investigation and making factual inquiry, hearing responding statements of facts and evidence and preparing a report in accordance with the regulation prescribed by the Commission and submit it to the Commission. In this case, the sub-committee shall have the same powers and duties as the Commission, except as provided otherwise by the Commission.

In carrying out the examination of human rights violation, the Commission may appoint an official to assist in the performance thereof.

Section 27. In conducting the examination of human rights violation, the Commission shall, if it deems mediation is possible, mediate between persons or agencies involved to reach an agreement for compromise and solution of the problem of human rights violation. If the parties agree to compromise and solve the problem and the Commission considers the agreement is within the scope of human rights protection, the Commission shall prepare a written agreement for the parties and settle the matter.

If it appears tothe Commission thereafter that there is non-compliance with the written agreement under paragraph one, the Commission shall further proceed with the examination under its powers and duties.

Section 28. If the Commission is, subject to section 27 and when the examination is completed, of the opinion that there is a commission or omission of acts which violate human rights, the Commission shall prepare a report of the examination which shall specify details of the circumstances of human rights violation, reasons for such opinion and remedial measures for solving human rights violation which shall clearly set forth the legal duties and methods of performance of a person or agency, including the period for implementation of such measures.

In setting forth the remedial measures under paragraph one, the Commission may require a person or agency to perform his or its duties by appropriate methods to prevent a recurrence of similar human rights violation.

In the case the Commission is of the opinion that the said commission or omission of acts does not violate human rights but there is an unjust practice from which the aggrieved person deserves a remedy, the Commission may set forth remedial guidelines and notify a person or agency to appropriately perform within the scope of powers and duties of such person or agency.

The Commission shall promptly notify the examination report to the person or agency having duties to perform and to the petitioner in case a petition has been lodged with the Commission.

Section 29. The person or agency shall, upon receiving the examination report under section 28, implement the remedial measures for solving the problem of human rights violation within the period specified by the Commission and shall notify the results of the implementation to the Commission.

In the case where the implementation of the remedial measures for solving the problem of human rights violation cannot be completed within the specified period, the person or agency shall, before the expiration of the previous period, request the Commission for an extension of the implementation period together with reasons and the length of period sought for extension; provided that no request shall be made for an extension of the implementation period more than two times.

Section 30. When the period under section 29 is lapsed, if the person or agency has not implemented the remedial measures for solving the human rights violation or has not completed the implementation without justifiable reasons, the Commission shall report to the Prime Minister to order an implementation of the remedial measures within sixty days as from the date the report is received. In this case, the Commission shall specify, to the Prime Minister, details for the exercise of the legal power in the issuance thereof, except the implementation of such remedial measures is not within the power of the Prime Minister, the Commission shall proceed in accordance with section 28.

Section 31. In the case where no proceeding or order for the implementation of remedial measures for solving the human rights violation under section 30 has been taken, the Commission shall report to the National Assembly for further proceeding. In reporting to the National Assembly, if the Commission deems it beneficial to the public, the Commission may disseminate to the public the case in which no implementation of remedial measures for solving the human rights violation has been taken.

Section 32. In the performance of duties, the Commission shall have the powers as follows:

(1) to summon a Government agency, State agency or State enterprise to give written statements of facts or opinions concerning the performance of official duty or other duties or to deliver objects, documents or other related evidence or to send a representative to give statements;

(2) to summon a person, juristic person or private agency concerned to give statements or to deliver objects, documents or other related evidence at the date, time and place as specified.

(3) The delivery of a summons shall be made by a registered post with return receipt to the domicile or office of the receiver. In the case where the delivery by the said mean cannot be made or no action was taken in accordance with the summons within reasonable period, the Commission shall redeliver the summons by the said means or by other means as the Commission deems appropriate;

(4) to request the Court of proper jurisdiction to issue a warrant for entering into a dwelling or any place for the benefits of examining facts or gathering related evidence which shall be proceeded as necessary and without delay. Before commencing an examination or gathering of evidence, a member or an official entrusted shall manifestly show no concealment on his personal identity and shall, as far as possible, conduct the examination and gathering thereof in the presence of the occupier or the caretaker of the place or relevant person. If such persons cannot be found, the examination and gathering shall be conducted in the presence of at least two persons invited to be witnesses. In this case, the occupier or the caretaker of the place or relevant person shall facilitate the performance of duties of the member or the delegated official;

(5) to issue Regulations concerning rules and methods of paying living expense and travel allowance for the witness or the official appointed by the Commission to examine human rights violation.

Section 33. In the performance of duties under this Act, members, members of the sub-committee or official appointed by the Commission to examine human rights violation shall be official under the Penal Code.

CHAPTER IV

Penalties

Section 34. Any person, who fails to give statement, deliver objects, documents or evidence as summoned under section 32 (2) shall be liable to imprisonment for a term not exceeding six months or to a fine not exceeding ten thousand Baht, or to both.

Section 35. Any person, who resists or obstructs the performance of duties under section 32(3) shall be liable to imprisonment for a term not exceeding one year or to a fine not exceeding twenty thousand Baht, or to both.

Transitory Provisions

Section 36. The Selective Committee shall commence the selection proceeding for the election of members under section 8 within sixty days as from the date this Act comes into force.

Section 37. In the case where there is a selection of members when there is no President of the Supreme Administrative Court, Secretary-General of the National Human Rights Commission and private organisations under section 24, the Selective Committee under section 8 shall consist of the President of the Supreme Court, the Prosecutor-General, the Chairman of the Law Council, Rectors or representatives of higher education institutions which are juristic persons, provided that each institution shall have one representative and all such representatives shall elect among themselves to be five in number, representatives of private organisations in the field of human rights that have registered with the Secretariat of the Senate within thirty days as from the date this Act comes into force, provided that each organisation shall have one representative and all such representatives shall elect among themselves to be ten in number, representatives of political parties having a member who is a member of the House of Representatives, provided that each party shall have one representative and all such representatives shall elect among themselves to be five in number, representatives of public media in the businesses of newspaper, radio broadcasting and television broadcasting, being elected from each business to be three in number and the Secretary-General of the Senate as secretary.

The rules and procedures for the registration of private organisations under paragraph one shall be as specified by the President of the Senate.

Countersigned by:
Chuan Leekpai
Prime Minister
Certified correct translation

(Dr. Ackaratorn Chularat)
Secretary-General of the Council of State
Office of the Council of State

The Raoul Wallenberg Institute Human Rights Library

1. Göran Melander (ed.): The Raoul Wallenberg Institute Compilation of Human Rights Instruments
ISBN 0 79233 646 1
2. U. Oji Umozurike: The African Charter on Human and Peoples' Rights
ISBN 90-411-0291-4
3. Bertrand G. Ramcharan (ed.): The Principle of Legality in International Human Rights Institutions; Selected Legal Opinions
ISBN 90 411 0299 X
4. Zelim Skurbaty: As If Peoples Mattered; Critical Appraisal of 'Peoples' and `Minorities' from the International Human Rights Perspective and Beyond
ISBN 90 411 1342 8
5. Gudmundur Alfredsson and Rolf Ring (eds.): The Inspection Panel of the World Bank; A Different Complaints Procedure
ISBN 90 411 1390 8
6. Gregor Noll (ed.): Negotiating Asylum; The EU Acquis, Extraterritorial Protection and the Common Market of Deflection
ISBN 90 411 1431 9
7. Gudmundur Alfredsson, Jonas Grimheden, Bertrand G. Ramcharan and Alfred de Zayas (eds.): International Human Rights Monitoring Mechanisms; Essays in Honour of Jakob Th. Möller
ISBN 90 411 1445 9
8. Gudmundur Alfredsson and Peter Macalister-Smith (eds.): The Land Beyond; Collected Essays on Refugee Law and Policy
ISBN 90 411 1493 9
9. Hans-Otto Sano, Gudmundur Alfredsson and Robin Clapp (eds.): Human Rights and Good Governance; Building Bridges
ISBN 90 411 1776 8
10. Gudmundur Alfredsson and Maria Stavropoulou (eds.): Justice Pending: Indigenous Peoples and Other Good Causes; Essays in Honour of Erica-Irene A. Daes
ISBN 90 411 1876 4
11. Göran Bexell and Dan-Erik Andersson (eds.): Universal Ethics; Perspectives and Proposals from Scandinavian Scholars
ISBN 90 411 1933 7
12. Hans Göran Franck, Revised and edited by William Schabas: The Barbaric Punishment; Abolishing the Death Penalty
ISBN 90 411 2151 X
13. Radu Mares (ed.): Business and Human Rights; A Compilation of Documents
ISBN 90 04 13656 8
14. Manfred Nowak: Introduction to the International Human Rights Regime
ISBN 90 04 13658 4 (Hb)
ISBN 90 04 13672 X (Pb)
15. Göran Melander, Gudmundur Alfredsson and Leif Holmström (eds.): The Raoul Wallenberg Institute Compilation of Human Rights Instruments; Second Revised Edition
ISBN 90 04 13857 9
16. Gregor Noll (ed.): Proof, Evidentiary Assessment and Credibility in Asylum Procedures
ISBN 90 04 14065 4
17. Ineta Ziemele (ed.): Reservations to Human Rights Treaties and the Vienna Convention Regime; Conflict, Harmony or Reconciliation
ISBN 90 04 14064 6
18. Nisuke Ando (ed.), on behalf of the Committee: Towards Implementing Universal Human Rights; Festschrift for the Twenty-Fifth Anniversary of the Human Rights Committee
ISBN 90 04 14078 6

19. Zelim A. Skurbaty (ed.): Beyond a One-Dimensional State: An Emerging Right to Autonomy?
ISBN 90 04 14204 5
20. Joshua Castellino and Niamh Walsh (eds.): International Law and Indigenous Peoples
ISBN 90 04 14336 X
21. Herdís Thorgeirsdóttir: Journalism worthy of the Name Freedom within the Press under Article 10 of the European Convention on Human Rights
ISBN 90 04 14528 1
22. Bertrand G. Ramcharan (ed.): Judicial Protection of Economic, Social and Cultural Rights: Cases and Materials
ISBN 90 04 14562 1
23. Gro Nystuen: Achieving Peace or Protecting Human Rights? Conflicts between Norms Regarding Ethnic Discrimination in the Dayton Peace Agreement
ISBN 90 04 14652 0
24. Maria Deanna Santos: Human Rights And Migrant Domestic Work – A Comparative Analysis of The Socio-Legal Status of Filipina Migrant Domestic Workers in Canada and Hong Kong
ISBN 90 04 14527 3
25. Ragnhildur Helgadóttir: The Influence of American Theories of Judicial Review on Nordic Constitutional Law
ISBN 90 04 15002 1
26. Jonas Grimheden and Rolf Ring (eds.): Human Rights Law: From Dissemination to Application Essays in Honour of Göran Melander
ISBN 90 04 15181 8